FEARLESS AND BOLD

FEARLESS AND BOLD

A HISTORY OF McDANIEL COLLEGE, 1866–2002

James E. Lightner

McDaniel College, 2 College Hill, Westminster, Maryland 21157
Fearless and Bold © 2007 by McDaniel College
All rights reserved. Published 2007

Printed in the United States of America
12 11 10 09 08 07   1 2 3 4 5 6

ISBN: 13: 978-0-615-15998-0

Library of Congress (LCCN): 2007935716

This book was underwritten by McDaniel College and generous gifts from
Donald '61 and Judith Ellis '60 Rembert
Charles '71 and Carol Hoerichs '70 Moore Jr.
William '71 and Laura Westervelt Jr.
George and Patricia Rodgers Benson

It is dedicated to all those distinguished forebears
who were fearless and bold in establishing, preserving,
and advancing the college over these many decades, and to
the readers, whose understanding of the college's heritage
will empower its future.

CONTENTS

Preface

This book had its genesis many years ago when, as a student, I became interested in the history of the college and the people who shaped its destiny. Upon my retirement from the mathematics classroom in 1998, I embarked on a journey to write a complete history of the institution, encouraged by presidents Ralph John and Robert Chambers, because they both saw a need for such a resource. After about two years of general reading and poring over documents in the college archives, I took a more organized approach, researching each decade thoroughly and then writing about that decade before moving forward. This process took about seven years.

I have tried to make the book both informative and interesting. Some sections of each chapter are factual and full of data, while others include accounts of student life (some from personal memoirs or interviews) that are quite humorous and revealing. Along the way, I also tried to debunk a few myths about the college and its development. In the section "Faculty and Administration," I have endeavored to include anyone who was connected with the institution for at least one student generation (four or five years). Attached to each name in brackets are the dates of college service. Where appropriate, birth and death dates are included in parentheses. The goal throughout the process was to create a history that would be simultaneously a ready reference of names, dates, and facts (enrollments, financial data, etc.), as well as a story of the development of the institution, including the many changes in the campus, curriculum, and student life. Each decade's section on student life concludes with a summary of the athletic records and outstanding athletes. Every chapter's narrative concludes with the major college events over the decade.

To provide some context for what occurred within the college, I have included a short timeline of world and national events for the decade at the end of each chapter, as well as an opening paragraph that describes what was going on in the larger world that surrounded the small college in Westminster.

A quick perusal of the bibliography and endnotes will suggest that I relied on many documents in the archives, as well as on the several earlier written histories. I also incorporated comments from many interviews with delightful alumni who willingly shared memories of bygone years. Others had written memoirs including stories from their student days that provided additional insight into the college of an earlier era.

The index is primarily an organized list of the people, buildings, and organizations of the college and is not intended to be comprehensive. We hope it will prove helpful to readers and future researchers alike.

I must acknowledge with great appreciation the special assistance of a number of people who helped with the project: Barbara O'Brien, the college archivist, who tracked down anything I needed to read or see; the staff of the President's Office, Mary Ann Friday, Susan Cullison, and Diane Timmons, who often searched their files for information; Jan Fazzari, former institutional research analyst, and Thomas Steback and Neitzy Feustel of Human Resources, who provided many elusive dates and names; Becky Myers in the Alumni Office, who searched old files for dates and information and assisted with some interviews; the staff of the Communications and Marketing Office, Joyce Muller, Peggy Fosdick, and Edie Buchanan, who guided the publication process and assisted with preparation of the text; and Philip L. Meredith '66, a good friend and former student, who volunteered to read the manuscript chapter by chapter and provided an initial edit as well as many helpful suggestions for improvements in the text. My sincere thanks to all these fine people for their significant help and to the WMC Heritage Society for its support.

The book has taken a lot of time and energy, but it has been a fascinating project, one from which I learned a great deal. It gave me a new appreciation for the institution, its vitality, and its strengths. My hope is that the reader will feel likewise.

—JEL

INTRODUCTION

When we began to consider a title for this book, the words from one of the old college songs, "Dear Western Maryland," kept popping up: *fearless and bold*. The words seemed to capture the history of the institution like few others. Western Maryland College was founded by individuals who did not really know what a college was, nor did they have any money to found a college. But they plunged ahead boldly, though perhaps with a little trepidation. Even after the founder, Fayette R. Buell, went bankrupt, the other early leaders, including J. T. Ward, John Smith, and Joshua Hering, would not let the venture die, and subsequently a board of trustees was formed to purchase the college from him. They envisioned the institution as coeducational, providing collegiate studies for both men and women, in an age when few women went to college or were encouraged to do so. At times, the leaders were criticized for this, but they went fearlessly forward, never doubting their decision (although one can assume that it was seriously debated by those early trustees).

For the first 20 years of the college's existence it was plagued with debt (about $25,000, a considerable sum for the time, given that the annual budget was only about $5,000). But on they went, borrowing funds when they needed to (often from individuals sympathetic to the cause), trying various fund-raising schemes, and always keeping the college afloat, sometimes on a wing and a prayer. There are no records of discussions about closing the college because of financial exigency. Those pioneers were fearless and bold!

Having achieved a certain level of stability and recognition by the 20th century, the college grew and expanded. But it soon faced the pressures caused by World War I and later the economic depression of the 1930s. When many colleges in the country were folding, Western Maryland College went on, doing what it had always done, although with serious financial constraints on everyone. World War II created more enrollment deficiencies, but careful management kept the college on an even keel until a postwar boom moved it forward measurably.

Never a wealthy institution, always tuition driven, and with only a small endowment, the college embarked on its first major fund-raising campaign in 1950 and oversubscribed its $1.5 million goal. In 1960 the first full-time development officer was hired. And for the first time, after many promises but few commitments, the Methodist Church took its "sponsoring" relationship seriously and contributed significant funds to the building of a new library.

Faced with economic pressures and deficit budgets, as well as two costly court cases regarding state aid to church-related institutions, the trustees took another bold step when they dissolved the relationship with the Methodist Church in the 1970s, making the college totally independent. It was a significant (albeit controversial) and wise move, as the college moved forward in stature and financial stability. Twenty years later, during another economic depression, retrenchment was again necessary, but by mid-decade the college was embarking on a campaign to raise $40 million, which was also oversubscribed.

In 2002, after carefully considering 40 years of debate, research, and business analysis, the trustees made the bold but controversial decision to change the name of the college, to remove the misperceptions and confusion as to the nature of the institution and its location. It was renamed for William Roberts McDaniel, a memorable individual who played a significant role in the college's long and colorful history.

Fearless and Bold is an interpretation of that history.

Sketch of the original college building (1867)

C H A P T E R

THE BEGINNINGS

◄ 1866–1870 ►

The year was 1866. The American Civil War was finally over. Four years of bitter fighting, which had found its way as far north as Pennsylvania, had ended with the reestablishment of the Union and almost simultaneously the assassination of the president who could have brought the sides back together in a thoughtful "reconstruction." Westminster, Maryland, itself the site of several skirmishes during the war, was a sleepy little town only 45 miles from Antietam (Sharpsburg), the site of the bloodiest battle in history, and 20 miles from Gettysburg, the setting for the South's northernmost advance and Lee's most disappointing defeat, where President Lincoln delivered a dedicatory address in the national cemetery on November 19, 1863. During the three-day battle, Westminster had heard the thunder of the cannons and the thousands of marching feet heading toward Gettysburg; the recently completed Western Maryland Railroad depot in the center of town was the repository of Union military supplies being shipped from Baltimore and Washington. Yet only a year later, the local citizens were going about their daily lives, and some of them were thinking about their children's education and future. Schools, perhaps even a college, could be a sign of hope for the future after the trauma many Westminster citizens had experienced so close at hand.

THE BEGINNINGS

Western Maryland College evolved in the years immediately following the Civil War from the visions of several individuals and, to a lesser degree, the Methodist Protestant Church. Fayette R. Buell, an educator who had established an academy in Westminster, optimistically envisioned expanding it into a college. James Thomas Ward, a Methodist Protestant minister who had retired to Westminster, realistically envisioned the establishment of a college as a positive move for the town and the church. The Methodist Protestant Church, experiencing difficulties in establishing colleges in various parts of the country for the training of clergy, perhaps reluctantly envisioned such an institution as fulfilling its goals.

The Methodist Protestant Church grew out of the Methodist Episcopal Church, founded by John Wesley in England in 1744 and extended to the American Colonies in 1760. In 1766 Robert Strawbridge began establishing the Methodist Church in Maryland only a few miles from Westminster. The congregation in Westminster was organized in 1767, meeting in private homes and later in the Union Church, built in the mid-18th century on a knoll on North Church Street (now the center of the Westminster Cemetery; the church was demolished in 1891).[1] At the famous Christmas Conference held in 1784 at the Lovely Lane Church in Baltimore, the American Methodist Episcopal Church under the leadership of Francis Asbury formally adopted rules (The Discipline) that ignored lay members' rights, emphasized a hierarchical (episcopal) structure, and incorporated few of the ideas of American democracy. By 1820 a reform movement had grown, among both clergy and laity, fanned by several lay periodicals, to make the church more democratic and responsive to the membership. Several Union Societies of dissidents were formed, and, inevitably, expulsions from the more conservative church resulted.[2] In Baltimore in November 1830, the Union Societies (representing 85 ministers and 5,000 members) held their first national conference, at which the Methodist Protestant Church was formally established.[3]

The Methodist Protestants immediately established a course of independent study for their clergy through significant reading and subsequent examinations by church leaders. But they also saw the need for more formal education for their ministers, and by 1835 the first movement in the Maryland Conference was made toward the establishment of a college.[4] Nothing, however, came of it. In 1863–64, the Maryland Annual Conference was moved to obtain a charter from the State of Maryland that empowered them to found a Conference College,[5] but again none appeared. In areas of the country where the church was stronger, efforts were also made with mixed results. The most

Fayette Rufus Buell, founder

successful were Yadkin College, a two-year coeducational normal school in North Carolina, established in 1856 (but closed in 1895), and Adrian College in Michigan, which was established in 1854 but came under the control of the Methodist Protestant Church in 1867.[6] In his *History of Methodist Reform and the Methodist Protestant Church*, Edward Drinkhouse notes more than a dozen schools that were planned but did not succeed. It is not surprising that church leaders were reluctant to sink funds into yet another proposed college when Buell approached them for support.

Fayette Rufus Buell (1833–1913) was born in Lebanon, New York, on April 27, 1833. He was educated at the Cazenovia Seminary (now part of Cornell University) and at a school in Hamilton, New York, from which he came to Maryland in 1854 to take charge of a school in Carroll County at the request of some county residents. He opened a school on the property of Abner Baile, near New Windsor (the building is now the fellowship hall, Baile Hall, for the Sam's Creek Church of the Brethren), married Baile's daughter Ellen (1837–1932) in 1856, and fathered nine children, three of whom died in infancy. Soon after their marriage the Buells moved to a farm near Peoria, Illinois, but in the summer of 1858, a group from Westminster prevailed upon them to return and again open a school.[7] He subsequently operated an academy fairly successfully in his home (the Old Stone House) at 203 Pennsylvania Avenue. There had been private schools in Carroll County since 1762, especially in the 19th century. Some were established by communities and were even incorporated, and some received state funding.[8] Buell's Westminster Male and Female School opened on April 16, 1860, and operated year-round, with terms

James Thomas Ward,
founder and first college president

beginning in April, July, October, and January. The tuition was $3 to $7 per quarter; females could board. In 1863 Buell changed the name of the school to Westminster Seminary.[9] Then, in 1865, perhaps because of his school's success (or perhaps because he saw that the recently established public schools were improving and private academies might be less attractive), "the wild idea of founding a college took possession of him. He had no money, he knew nothing about colleges, but he was full of energy, fired with zeal, and he had made influential friends."[10] As a member of the local Methodist Protestant Church, he enthusiastically called together a number of church members and friends in February 1866 to consider his proposition. The group heartily approved of his vision but felt they could assume no financial obligation. However, with their help and influence, Buell took his proposal to the Maryland Annual Conference of the Methodist Protestant Church in March 1866. That body declined to become financially responsible in any way but adopted resolutions heartily commending Mr. Buell and his proposed institution to the patronage and consideration of the church and its members.[11] Unfortunately, Buell had too trusting a nature and too little experience at raising money to anticipate the broad gap between the encouraging talk (indeed, even promises from the conference) and actual performance.[12]

James Thomas Ward (1820–97) was born in Georgetown, D.C., on August 21, 1820, of English and Scottish stock, the son of a Methodist Protestant preacher, Rev. Ulysses Ward, and Susan Beall Ward. He was educated by tutors in Washington; at the Columbian Academy (1835–36); and for two years at the Brookville Classical Academy, where he graduated in 1838 with the classical prize. Although he never enrolled in a college, he continued his studious ways, devoting himself to preparing to preach the Gospel under the direction and counsel of Dr. A. A. Lipscomb and Dr. Augustus Webster, after which he was received into the Maryland Annual Conference of the Methodist Protestant Church, in 1841. He led the life of a busy pastor, becoming well known for his preaching and revivals. He served the Pipe Creek circuit in Carroll County for a year (1841–42) as assistant to Dr. John S. Reese. This was followed by the Williamsport, Maryland, circuit (1842–45), Cumberland, Maryland (1845–46), Philadelphia (1847–57), a second term at the Pipe Creek circuit (1857–60), Alexandria, Virginia (1860–61), Libertytown, Maryland (1862–63), and Washington, D.C. (1864–66).[13] With his father he also coedited *Columbian Fountain*, a temperance journal. His diaries suggest that by 1866 his health, which had never been good, was failing, and he could no longer carry out all the duties of a full-time pastor. They also imply that he may have been having difficulty receiving a pastoral appointment because of his political views: During the Civil War he had spoken out against the southern rebellion and strongly supported the Union. He retired from the active ministry and in 1866 decided to settle in Westminster on Littlestown Pike (now 188 Pennsylvania Avenue) on the outskirts of town. He notes in his diary on February 17, 1866: "I thank God for affording me a prospect of deliverance in putting into the heart of my dear father to purchase for me the little place in Westminster. There I hope to find improved health and gain for myself and family a livelihood." He was appointed as a "supernumerary assistant" to Rev. R. Scott Norris of the Pipe Creek circuit. From the moment of his retirement, Ward had no steady income. His supernumerary status was without remuneration. In his diary he often expressed worry over his debts and concern over whether he would be able to make a living from fees for occasional preaching, weddings, and funerals. On April 3, Ward, his wife, Catherine Ann Light Ward (1823–99), whom he had married on May 21, 1845, and his only daughter, Mary Miranda (1852–1934) (another daughter, Clara Virginia, had died at age five in 1854), moved into the farmhouse on the ten acres of his "little farm." Rev. Norris soon brought Ward and Buell, one of the church's members, together, and they often talked about the proposed college. Meanwhile, Buell needed a teacher in his academy and Ward needed some remunerative employment, so an agreement between them was soon reached.[14]

In *A Brief History of My Connection with the College Enterprize at Westminster*, Ward noted that the first he heard about the proposed college was in a letter from Rev. Norris in January 1866. Norris told him that Buell had been apprised of his coming to Westminster and said that Ward's friends suggested that he (Ward) should be associated in some way with that project. Ward replied, "Of the College enterprize . . . it is possible I might be of some service to it. I have a very valuable library, of at least 1,200 volumes, which might be made very serviceable to the College, and I might take charge of some one or two branches of instruction, that would not make my labors too arduous."[15] Ward had been cataloging his many books with an eye to setting up a lending library in Westminster. He continued his cataloging after getting settled in his new home, which he named Rose Hill. In the days following his arrival, he had several discussions with Buell. On April 9, Buell gave him a detailed account of the project, which Ward recorded in his diary: "Had a long interview with Br. Buell concerning the College Enterprize. He is sanguine of success and puts wonderful confidence in my advice and influence. He has bought a most elligible [sic] site for the College buildings and spent in all more than two thousand dollars already. I urge him to 'make haste slowly,' and cautiously, and by doing so I think he may succeed."

With his customary zeal and buoyed by recent encouragement, Buell quickly gathered a group of gentlemen whom he designated the board of directors, which met on April 17, 1866, at the M.P. Church. At this meeting he made known his financial and educational plans for the fledgling college to accommodate 150 students. The board approved of what they heard and urged him to move forward as quickly as possible, *provided he could obtain the necessary funds*. It directed him, together with Ward and A. Reese Durbin (mayor of Westminster 1867–68), to prepare a prospectus for circulation. Before this was completed, Ward met frequently with Buell, who urged him to take a more active part in the project because he believed God had sent Ward to Westminster to make the enterprise a success. Ward told Buell that he was overrating his abilities and influence but that he would do what he could to help. He "hoped Buell would be careful not to build until he saw his way clear to pay for the work when done," and said that progress should depend upon the response to the circular. He also told Buell that "the project is excellent in itself, but it cannot be carried out unless monied men will take hold of it in earnest."[16]

The prospectus, or circular, published on April 24, said:

It is proposed to establish, at Westminster, the county seat of Carroll County, Md., a college of the Highest Order, in two distinct departments, one for Male and the other for Female students; the Institution to be devoted to General Education, American Protestant Christianity, and particularly to the interests of the Methodist Protestant Church. A site of the most commanding and eligible character has already been selected, and a Plan for the College Buildings prepared by a skillful architect, and approved by a number of gentlemen well qualified to judge in such a matter, who have also consented to act as an Advisory Board of Directors for the College.[17]

The prospectus also stated that Buell had made preparations to begin the erection of the buildings at his own expense. Not having sufficient funds of his own to complete the work, however, he was appealing to friends in the community and particularly the members of the Methodist Protestant Church, to raise the sum of $30,000 from donations, the principle to be invested in a permanent fund and only the interest used. Certificates of indebtedness were to be issued to the subscribers and fully redeemed at the end of five years, as a guaranty of which Buell would give a deed of trust on the entire property. The officers of the college were also listed: Rev. Rhesa Scott Norris (1820–97), president of the board of directors; Jesse Reifsnider, Esq. (1810–82), vice president; Rev. J. T. Ward, secretary of the board and principal of the faculty; Prof. F. R. Buell, president and proprietor of the college.[18]

On May 1, Buell purchased about eight acres of land on Parr's Ridge, on the top of what is now called College Hill, from Edward and Margaret Lynch and William and Matilda Miller for the sum of $4,580, of which only $1,000 was paid before the deed was signed. The balance was to be paid in notes on or before specified dates. In a communication in the *Methodist Protestant* newspaper dated May 15, Buell wrote that a cornerstone laying ceremony would probably be held near the end of June or early July because the subscriptions were almost sufficient to proceed at once with the building. This was not really true, for although words of encouragement had been many, monetary responses had been few. Ward again urged Buell not to move forward with a building that would involve large amounts of money he did not have. Buell, however, was still optimistic. Noting that he would need to keep his seminary open one more year until the college would replace it, he proposed that Ward become the principal teacher and take charge of the school. Ward agreed and, noting that sufficient funds for the college did not seem to be forthcoming, suggested that Buell abandon the college project and endeavor to obtain a loan of $4,000 to erect a more suitable building for the academy. If, later, the college developed, the seminary building could be converted to a regular dwelling and sold. Buell agreed, and Ward arranged for a loan from his friend, John Smith of Wakefield, on July 28.[19] Fortuitously, Ward, through his previous pastoral connection at Big Pipe Creek, enjoyed the confidence and friendship of John Smith and Isaac C. Baile, both Methodist Protestant laymen. Buell changed his mind, however, and decided to pursue the college project forthwith, asking for a much larger loan. These two gentlemen, to the astonishment of everyone, including Ward, indicated a willingness to venture some of their considerable wealth in an enterprise that would probably help their former pastor and friend. They agreed to loan Buell $10,000 (Smith $8,000 and Baile $2,000) with which to erect a suitable building and begin operation of the college. They did so on the condition that Rev. Ward would become the head of the college.[20] The $10,000 was secured by a mortgage on the college property dated October 8, 1866, made by Buell and his wife.[21]

Without the long-term generous support of John Smith, the college enterprise would have failed at several junctures. After his sudden death on March 13, 1892, in his 86th year, Ward wrote in a memorial article in the *Western Maryland College Monthly*: "John Smith of Wakefield deserves to be remembered as one of the principal benefactors of Western Maryland College." Wakefield was the Smith family farm, located in the part of Frederick County that became Carroll County in 1837. Smith was born there on November 27, 1806. He received a good basic education and during his early manhood taught school for some time. He was later employed as a store clerk in the city of Baltimore for a few years, but then returned to the farm in Wakefield and prepared for surveying and auctioneering while occupying himself as a farmer. He took over the Wakefield farm after the death of his father, Joshua Smith, in December 1841. He was married in 1848 to Caroline Cookson, and they had 11 children, 9 of whom lived to maturity. In 1852, he became especially interested in the formation of the Carroll and Frederick Rail Road Company (renamed the Western Maryland Railroad Company in 1853), and he was one of the first commissioners and stockholders. He helped survey part of the route that was extended to Westminster in July 1861 and to Union Bridge in 1862, was a prominent purchaser of stock, and was a member of the board of directors for ten years. In 1862, at the urging of friends, he accepted the presidency of the company. In 1859, he and his wife were converted to Methodist Protestantism, his parents' denomination, during a religious revival led by the pastor J. T. Ward at the Pipe Creek Chapel. In 1866, he and his family moved to Westminster, to a large brick home on Main Street (now called Rosser's Choice), and, through Ward, became interested in Buell's enterprise. Seven of his eleven children became students of the college or its preparatory school, and five received the AB degree.[22]

Isaac C. Baile was born in March 1819; he became a surveyor and served Carroll County as a judge of its orphan's court. He and his wife also became Methodist Protestants during the 1859 revival at the Pipe Creek Church led by J.T. Ward. His and his family's benefactions at times of financial stress were critical to the establishment and viability of the college; he aided the college in many ways during his lifetime, including providing wise advice to Ward when

John Smith of Wakefield,
first board of trustees president

needed. He served as assistant treasurer of the board of trustees from 1875 to 1885 (working with Joshua Hering), and treasurer from 1885 until his death in 1892.[23] Baile's son Nathan married John Smith's daughter Mary in 1874.

Once the loan agreement between Smith and Baile and Buell was final, work was begun, and on August 11, 1866, the board of directors met to make plans for the cornerstone laying ceremony. At the meeting, Smith, now president of the Western Maryland Railroad, proposed that the name of the college be changed from Buell College, as it was becoming known locally, to Western Maryland College, presumably because of his connection with the railroad. (As a successful businessman, Smith may also have wanted to position it with a more recognizable and established name so as to increase its financial viability.) The first stone of the foundation was laid on August 27, and the cornerstone was laid in the presence of a large gathering on September 6, 1866. Smith offered free rail passage to all persons wishing to attend the event from the Baltimore and surrounding area. They were met at the train station at 2:30 P.M. by Ward, and everyone marched in procession with the members of the local Masonic Lodge to College Hill, where Rev. James W. Reese (1838–1917), master of the Door to Virtue Lodge, formally laid the stone. Ward reported that at least a thousand people attended the event and that the exercises "were conducted in a most perfect and creditable manner."[24] Included in the lengthy ceremony were four hymns, three prayers, a scriptural reading, four addresses, and miscellaneous remarks by Ward.[25] Reese further described the event as follows: "The crowd of citizens who were present had come together not merely to witness a novel ceremony and to listen to speeches but to testify, by their presence, the interest felt in the inauguration of a great and beneficent enterprise. The hopes of the participants and spectators already high were lifted higher still by the breath of oratory."[26]

He went on to describe College Hill:

Certainly the site chosen for the new college was one of unsurpassed loveliness. Itself one of the "everlasting hills," lifted high above a surrounding country of rare beauty and fertility, with little Westminster nestling at its feet, while the majestic Blue Ridge loomed on the western horizon and freely gave its invigorating breezes; a spot retired yet accessible, it seemed the ideal location for a school. Then, too, the ground . . . possessed associations which seemed almost prophetic of the uses to which it was henceforth destined. The "old common" at the west-end, the playground of the village children, the favorite resort of young men and maidens in search of the picturesque,—what more appropriate place could be selected as a scholastic home for youth? But the "old common" had been more than a playground. Here political meetings were wont to be held and the great questions of free-trade, protective tariff, internal improvements to be discussed for the enlightenment or confusion of citizens eager to learn their duties and their rights; here, annually, on "Independence Day," the grove was vocal with patriotic oratory and music, while the struggles of the Republic were recounted and its future painted in glowing colors—surely an educational work all this, even if intermittent and largely futile. Did not the ceremony of this sunny September day . . . seem to dedicate the hill, most fittingly, to the continuance, in a settled, solid way, of the work of training young people of both sexes, in college walls, for the duties of citizenship which lay before them?[27]

Professor George S. Wills, in *History of Western Maryland College* (vol. 1), also commented on the nature of the site: "A better site for the college . . . could not have been chosen. Besides all the attractions of the hill itself, its elevation of about 800 feet above sea-level makes it possible to see in every direction a landscape whose beauty and variety never fail to appeal to the aesthetic sense. It was near enough to the town to give the teachers and the students the advantages of the town; and it was remote enough to remove them from its distractions."[28] Dr. Joshua W. Hering (1833–1913) gave a speech at a dinner in his honor in 1908 in which he mentioned the significant historical associations that he witnessed as a young Westminster physician: "During the [Civil] war, this hill was the scene of a cavalry encampment. . . . And during the Battle of Gettysburg it bristled with the heavy artillery of the Federal army protecting their large trains that were in this locality. Westminster was at that time the base of supplies for the army of the Potomac, and their wagon trains were here by the thousand; and Meade's guns were stationed on what is now College Hill in order that their trains might be protected."[29]

While the first college building was now under way (in a group of several buildings envisaged by Buell), Ward, though certainly doing everything in his power to help the college succeed, privately noted far less optimism in his diary. He wrote on August 4, 1866:

Br. Buell is very sanguine of the success of the entire enterprise. . . . When I think of the enormous interest he will have to pay, and of the vast expense he will necessarily be at in the building, employing teachers, boarding the pupils, &c., I confess that I fear a disastrous failure. Br. Buell seems to think that the influence of my name . . . will be sufficient to secure so large a number of scholars additional to what he has had hitherto, or could have hereafter without it, that the sums paid by them for board and tuition will enable him to carry out his whole plan, besides supporting himself and family. . . . I have striven to make him cautious, but he has the college on his brain, and will not be content until he sees it, in some form to suit his idea, on the hill.

The cornerstone had been laid, and the building, which would eventually become known as Old Main, was under construction. But at least half of the money needed to complete it was nowhere on the horizon. Buell continued to operate his seminary, with Ward as his principal assistant. Ward assumed responsibility for the day-to-day management of the school, while Buell spent most of his time carefully following the construction on the hill, trying to raise funds, and fending off creditors. Ward commented in his diary (June 26, 1867) of this period:

The care of Br. Buell's School during the past year, and especially during the closing term, was thrown almost entirely upon me, while he reaps nearly all the pecuniary benefit. Were I independent as to money, I would not feel concerning this, as I confess I now feel, suffering as I am for want of means to meet my obligations and knowing not how I am to get means. Br. Buell however has more than once intimated that he considers even what he has paid me as being more than he should have paid. This is the "unkindest cut" of all, and yet I will try to bear it, because I know Br. B. has a heavy burden upon him owing to his college building enterprize which I would do anything in reason that I could do to help forward.

Buell came up with another fund-raising scheme, of selling scholarships for cash, which would entitle the purchaser to reduced college tuition. He felt that having money in hand and the guaranteed enrollment of a scholarship student justified the lowered tuition fee. Buell asked Ward to give up his teaching and spend his time selling scholarships, but Ward declined because he didn't want to be held responsible for scholarships in a yet-to-be-opened college, and he felt that Buell should simply "borrow the money to erect the building, and get as many scholars as he can board and teach, and devote his profits to liquidating the loan."[30] As long as Buell remained the proprietor of the college, Ward felt that he could not obtain much financial help for the place except from donations from his friends. Perhaps an urgent appeal to the Maryland Annual Conference of the Methodist Protestant Church, which would meet the following spring, would help solve some of the problems.[31]

In March 1867, the Maryland Annual Conference received a communication from Buell in which he outlined his proposal for uniting his college with the conference. The minutes of that meeting reported: "He tenders to the Maryland Annual Conference a general supervisory control of the institution, by the annual appointment on their part of a board of directors to assist him in securing suitable instructors, and in the proper management of the institution."[32] The offer was looked upon favorably "inasmuch as he does not ask the assumption of any pecuniary responsibility on the part of the Church." This comment is especially interesting, since Buell had indeed asked

The Buell house, site of the school that grew into the college

the conference for financial help; it had been approved and then reconsidered, with the request finally being referred to the *next* Annual Conference. Ward wrote in his diary on March 22:

Br. Buell's expectation of aid now, when he most needs it, is entirely blasted, so far as the Md. An. Conf. is concerned. I am sure this will wound him deeply, and I fear it will totally destroy the confidence he had in the disposition of the Conference to aid him, and cause him to abandon his purpose of allowing the Conference to have any control of the college. . . . It would have been far more honorable had the Conference declined Br. Buell's tender, than to accept it and promise him aid, while he was present, and then in his absence revoke the promise of aid without relinquishing the preferred control of the Institution. I confess that I feel ashamed of the Conference in this matter.

The conference did appoint the following to the advisory board: Reverends J. J. Murray (president of the Maryland Annual Conference), R. S. Norris, Peter Light Wilson, Daniel Bowers, and J. T. Ward; J. W. Hering, M.D.; and Messrs. John Smith, Michael Baughman, Alfred Zollickoffer, John S. Repp, and Samuel McKinstry. This board met with Buell at the Methodist Protestant Church in Westminster on March 30, 1867, and elected John Smith as chairman and Ward as secretary. It heard from Buell a brief history of the college enterprise and a pledge to take no further steps in management of the college without the board's advice. He also sought their counsel on the course he should pursue to raise funds for the completion of the college building. After each member present had in turn given his views, the following resolution was unanimously adopted:

Whereas, The board of directors appointed by the Maryland Annual Conference at its recent session as an advisory Board to Prof. F. R. Buell, in the management of the Western Maryland College, deem it highly important to the success of the enterprise, that Bro. Buell be enabled to raise the sum of $10,000. Therefore: Resolved, That we do most earnestly recommend and advise Bro. Buell to proceed at once with an effort to raise the sum needed; first, by disposing of at least forty scholarships; and secondly, by securing at least fifty donations of $100 each, toward constituting an endowment fund for the church, the interest of which shall be expended under the direction of the Maryland Annual Conference, in the education of young men proposing to enter the ministry of the M.P. Church, in the Western Maryland College.[33]

Ward reported that after the meeting Buell did make some effort to accomplish what the board had advised but soon abandoned the plan and tried various other means for raising additional funds, without success.

Buell, by this time, had exhausted all the original borrowed funds, and Ward encouraged him to delay completion of the building. But Buell was not to be deterred and was able to get agreement by the builders to complete the building sufficiently for him to open the college in September. He also called the board together on July 16 to consider the applications of potential faculty members (an action Ward again warned against: "You will do wrong to employ teachers unless you see your way clear to pay them"). The board met, patiently heard the precarious financial status of the enterprise, and hoping that Buell understood his situation, gave approval for issuing the *First Annual Circular* of the college, which was to be written by Buell and

First Annual Circular

Ward.[34] This circular of 1867–68 should not be confused with the *First Annual Catalogue,* which was published in March 1868 for the academic year 1868–69 (and includes a list of the 22 women and 48 men enrolled during 1867–68).

Opposite the title page of the circular is a lithograph of the college building with its cupola and separate entrances for men and women, the property surrounded by fences, outside of which sit two horse-drawn vehicles. On the title page Fayette R. Buell's name appears as proprietor. The circular includes the names of the board of directors, a list of the faculty members and the subjects they will teach, a description of the location of the college, the "Accommodations," and a set of "Regulations." Of particular interest are two descriptive paragraphs, one relating to an experiment that was being tried: the education of both sexes in the same institution, leading to the unverified claim that Western Maryland College was the first coeducational institution below the Mason-Dixon Line: "The building, and grounds embracing eight acres, are so arranged that the males are entirely separate from the females; and, although the students of both sexes will be under the same government and instruction, they will at no time be allowed to associate except in the presence of their teachers."[35] This peculiar type of coeducation will be discussed further as the college develops, but Wills points out that separation of the sexes in schools and colleges was not at all unusual in the nineteenth century; Western Maryland College was taking a courageous step by advertising itself as college for both men and women, even if carefully separated into distinct departments.[36]

The second paragraph of interest relates to "Patronage and Direction": "The college has been placed under the special patronage and direction of the Maryland Annual Conference of the Methodist Protestant Church; but nothing will be introduced either into the course of study or discipline and management of the Institution which can be in any way objectionable to students of other religious persuasions." One wonders, in retrospect, why there continued to be such zeal to place the college under the control of the conference, given its reluctance to get involved financially. Probably Ward's hope for forthcoming financial support from the church remained strong.

A column in the *Methodist Protestant*, dated August 13, 1867, reported that the college building was of brick with very spacious dimensions, finished in the "best style" and presenting a splendid appearance; its interior was well arranged, and it compared "very favorably with the best college buildings in the State." The paper went on to say that the college would provide general educational advantages and a thorough course of instruction so as to rank it as a first-class college.

An advertisement in a local paper of August 7, 1867, stated:

The New and Spacious Building [80 by 60 feet and four stories high] for the use of this Institution of Learning being now nearly completed, the First Scholastic Year will commence on Wednesday, September the 4th. Price of board, Washing, &c per year, $180. Tuition alone, from $25 to 60 per year, according to the Class entered. The corps of Teachers has been selected with great care, and consists of competent Professors in each Department of Study. Besides all branches of English, the Latin, Greek, French, German and other Languages will be taught; also, Music (Vocal and Instrumental), Drawing, Painting, Embroidery, Wax Work, &c. The Institution is provided with a Library of 2500 volumes, and valuable Chemical and Philosophical Apparatus. The Proprietor and the Teachers will earnestly aim to make the Institution one of the best in the land, and they respectfully solicit such a share of the public patronage as will sustain and encourage them in their labors.[37]

Buell's anxiety over finances in late summer was temporarily eased when two men were prevailed upon to lend him $6,000 of the $10,000 he needed to complete the building if he could raise the other $4,000. But before the end of August, they reneged. Ward commented sadly, "It seems impossible to move the rich men of either the Church or community to lend him the aid he needs."[38] Ward could not understand the indifference in the Westminster community, since a successful college would be worth much more to the community than to the proprietor.[39] Sanguine of his success as ever, Buell commented to Ward, "I have felt from the first and still feel that God put it into my heart to commence this work, and I have risked and am willing to risk all my property and energies and even life, if need be, in it; nevertheless, whether it succeed or not, I shall be satisfied: God will make good to come of it in some way, and all my desire is that 'His will be done.'"[40]

15

On September 4, 1867, the formal opening exercises of the first academic year of Western Maryland College (WMC) were held in the Study Room for the Female Department, since the Chapel Room had not yet been completed. Present were Buell, Ward, five teachers, the governess and her two assistants, and about 30 students. The program consisted of an address and Bible reading from Proverbs by Buell; the singing of the hymn "A Charge to Keep I Have"; a prayer and address by Ward; and addresses by J. M. Newson (professor of English language and literature), William H. Zimmerman (professor of natural sciences, German, and French), and Daniel W. Hering (principal of the preparatory school). The names of the students were recorded, and Buell announced some of the rules of the institution. Ward's diary chronicles the event, as well as the next two weeks, during which the faculty met to decide what textbooks to use and how to procure them, and plans for the first classes were made. He noted, "Everything at the college is moving on well, and if Br. Buell could only get relief from the present money pressure, I have no doubt great success would attend the institution." On Tuesday, September 17, Ward conducted religious exercises and, his textbooks having arrived from Baltimore, heard the first recitation of his Latin class. Buell must have been disappointed that only 30 students arrived for the first classes, since he had expressed confidence that enough pupils would enroll to enable him to operate the college *and* pay his debts to erect the building. By the end of the year 70 students were enrolled; most were from Carroll County, and several were relatives of Ward or Buell. Wills suggests that, given these demographics, a large number of the enrollees would probably have been students in the Westminster Seminary, had it been continued.[41]

THE FIRST FACULTY

Buell's training for teaching was limited to his studies in New York, which did not include any college work. It is known that he was fairly proficient in music and taught music in local churches from time to time, as well as in his school. He is listed in the first-year circular as professor of mathematics and vocal music. Ward, in uncharacteristically blunt terms, noted of him in 1868 (after working with him in both the seminary and the college): "When I first became acquainted with Br. Buell . . . I supposed him to be eminently qualified for the position he had been occupying; but I am now compelled to say that I have abundant reason to regard him as incompetent. . . . Although professing sufficient ability to conduct an ordinary school, he is not qualified for any professorship in a college."[42] Buell taught only during the first year of the college's existence. Wills gives some insight into the other individuals

A gathering of early faculty;
President Ward is seated on the platform.

and their qualifications.[43] Ward carried the titles of principal, and professor of biblical literature, Greek and Latin languages, although as noted, he was not a college graduate. He did, however, have a fine mind and was widely read. And his 25 years in the ministry had prepared him to teach biblical literature. Although he had taken the classical prize upon his graduation from the Brookville Classical Academy for his work in Latin and Greek, he was 29 years removed from that study, and he regarded himself as quite unprepared to teach the languages. He had worked hard to keep ahead of his classes at the Westminster Seminary in 1866–67 (his only teaching experience), and he did the same with his college classes. He admits in his diary (July 22, 1867): "As to the Greek, I shall have to study it before I can teach it, and even in Latin I shall have much to learn before I can teach the full course named in the circular."

William H. Zimmerman (1838–1921) was 29 years old and was the only member of the original faculty to hold a college degree. He had received his bachelor of arts from Dickinson College in 1861 and also held the master of arts degree from Dickinson (1864) (although this was probably awarded upon payment of a fee, possibly submission of an essay, and evidence of some success in the "learned professions" after graduation, a common custom at the time, which would be followed by Western Maryland College until 1906). Zimmerman had taught and been principal of high schools in Coatesville (1862–63), Elkton (1864–66), and Frederick, Maryland (1866–67) before coming to the Western Maryland faculty.[44] He was remembered by Daniel W.

Hering (in his remarks upon the college's 50th anniversary) as being "nervous, energetic, ingenious, enthusiastic, irrepressible in spirits, ambitious . . . [one who] made a strong impression upon the students." Ward would lean heavily upon him for advice on matters relating to collegiate customs and procedures during his tenure. Zimmerman was married to Jennie Reed in 1863, and she joined him as assistant governess and later stewardess at the college. Although in the first year he was professor of natural sciences, German, and French, the following year his title changed to professor of natural sciences and ancient and modern languages and also vice principal. He resigned in 1871 to take a position as vice president at Washington College but returned to WMC in 1882.

The Newson family arrived in Westminster in 1866. J. M. Newson (1807–84), taught at WMC for less than a year, resigning in April 1868, to become secretary, examiner, treasurer, and superintendent of the Carroll County Board of Education, positions he held until 1883. His forte was English grammar, especially "parsing," and "though of a kindly nature, he was somewhat irascible." The author of this description, again D. W. Hering, goes on to say that Newson "and Professor Zimmerman reacted upon each other about like fire and gunpowder; whenever they came together there was pretty likely to be an explosion. . . . I think the only point on which I ever knew them to agree was that each was ready to acknowledge that the other was utterly unreasonable!"[45] Clara P. Newson, teacher of instrumental music, and Maggie J. Newson, teacher of drawing, painting, and other ornamental branches, were J. M. Newson's daughters. Maggie had taught at the seminary with Ward and Buell. Both taught at WMC for only one year, but their names reappear in the catalogs for 1874–78 as teachers or preceptresses.

Daniel W. Hering (1850–1938), a cousin of Dr. Joshua W. Hering (who would soon have a major role to play in the college's history), was 17 and a member of the freshman class of the college while also serving as principal of the Preparatory Department, in which at least a third to half of the entering students were enrolled. The second year he was listed as professor of English language and mathematics. In the fall of 1869 he left Western Maryland to enter the Sheffield Scientific School at Yale University, where he received his PhB in 1872. He commented in 1917: "To have enjoyed the distinction and the honor of being a student-teacher during the first two years of Western Maryland College, and less than ten years afterwards to have had a similar part as one of the list of fellows in the first two years of the Johns Hopkins University [founded in 1876] . . . [is] an honor indeed, rare, I think, if not unique."[46] He would return to the Western Maryland faculty from 1880 to 1884 as professor of mathematics.

Mrs. F. R. Buell served as governess of the young ladies, assisted by Mrs. J. M. Newson and Mrs. William H. Zimmerman.

CURRICULUM

From its beginning, the institution maintained two separate departments, a Preparatory and a Collegiate Department (in the early academic records, the students were classified as "Preparatorians" or "Collegians"). The *First Annual Circular* notes: "In the Preparatory Department, to which the strictest attention will be paid, all the elements will be thoroughly taught, embracing, among others, English Grammar, Composition, Geography, History, Arithmetic, Penmanship, &c."

In the freshman class of the Collegiate Department the following courses were offered:

English—Grammar and Composition, Geography and History
Natural Sciences—Natural Philosophy and Elements of Chemistry
Mathematics—Arithmetic and Elements of Algebra
Classics—Latin Grammar and Greek Grammar
Modern Languages—German Grammar and French Grammar

The term *English* (or sometimes *Belles Lettres*) seems to have been a catchall for classes deemed appropriate for study that did not fit into any other department. In the sophomore year listing, it included Rhetoric and Political Economy; in the junior year, Moral Science and Elocution; and in the senior year, Mental Philosophy, Logic, and Constitution of the United States. In later catalogs such classes as Ancient and Modern History, Domestic and Political Economy, Physiology, Natural History, and Botany fell into this category.

In mathematics, freshman students studied arithmetic and the elements of algebra. During the second year, algebra was completed and the elements of geometry begun, to be completed in the third year, together with trigonometry and surveying. During the senior year, students studied civil engineering and analytical mechanics.

As to ancient languages, Wills noted that the collegiate program offered in Latin in 1867 (and subsequent years) was not much more than that taught in a good modern preparatory school of the mid-twentieth century; authors read included Caesar, Virgil, Sallust, Cicero, and Tacitus. In Greek, students read Anabasis, Plato, the New Testament, and mythology. Wills concluded that, upon its completion, a diligent student of this program would know the essentials of grammar and be able to read Greek and Latin of moderate difficulty without too much effort. In Modern Languages, students of German were expected to be able to read Schiller's *Tell* and Goethe's *Faust* by the completion of their studies, and French students would have completed Télémaque, Charles XIIth, and Racine.[47] Freshman year must have been a particular delight for the students: English grammar, Latin grammar, Greek grammar, German grammar, and French grammar!

Students of natural science were given a broad overview of many areas of science in an era prior to 20th-century scientific specialization. Chemistry was begun in the first year and continued in the second, along with geology. As juniors they would encounter hydrostatics, pneumatics, acoustics, electricity, magnetism, electromagnetism, optics, and thermotics. As seniors, they would study astronomy, botany, mineralogy, and more chemistry. This incredible array of scientific areas would have been taught in easy language for a general knowledge of the world and the scientific principles necessary for educated people to know. Laboratory work was rare, and only demonstrations requiring simple equipment such as a Leyden jar, a pendulum, an electric spark generator would have been performed. This early curriculum formed the foundation for the college's curricula for the coming years. The faculty would change regularly, but the offerings remained fairly static for decades.

One additional program was added to the curriculum in 1869, a theological course, and one new ministerial student, J. B. Butler, enrolled that September to make himself more competent in his chosen profession. The following year, Dr. Augustus Webster (with whom Ward had studied 30 years before) was added to the faculty as professor of theology, but he really served as an advisor as to the plan of study that would be required of the students over and above the regular collegiate work.

A literary society, called The Irving Society for Washington Irving, which had actually been formed in the seminary by Ward a year earlier, was reorganized and improved by suggestions from Professor Zimmerman and became a part of the college program. Its purpose was to enhance the intellectual life of the college while providing opportunities for social and cultural entertainment.[48] It was composed of the more advanced students of the college, members of the faculty, and other interested persons. During the first year, on February 26, 1868, the society sponsored a lecture by James Frame, Esq., in the Westminster Methodist Protestant Church. The advisory board met at the college during the afternoon and attended the evening lecture. It was reported in the press that, even though the weather was inclement, a large number of citizens of Westminster and some from distant parts of Carroll County attended. Frame's lecture was "The Benefits of Literary Societies as Auxiliaries to the Improvement of Students in College." It was noted that "every sentence he uttered was in language chaste and elegant, and every sentiment advanced was such as met the hearty approval of thoughtful men and women."[49] He approved of the society being coeducational, as it was connected with a college and functioned under the direction of and in concert with the faculty.

At the meeting of the advisory board that afternoon, Buell made a full and candid statement of the financial status of the college, especially the large debt he had undertaken. All the borrowed money had been spent, none of the interest on the loans had been paid, the workmen who had finished enough of the building in time to open the school in September had filed liens against the property for $6,470.81, and a sheriff's sale was not far off.[50] Buell again asked for advice, but most of the gentlemen seemed to be in shock at what he reported. Ward noted that they finally seemed to understand that Buell had "gone into the enterprize without properly counting the cost" and had deceived them "as to his financial abilities as well as in other respects."[51] The board met again the following day in several long sessions and came to the conclusion that for the college to continue to exist, it would have to be managed differently and better than it had been thus far. It was determined that 30 men should be sought who would agree to cover the liens and not demand payment against the college for at least a year. A board of trustees should be formed to procure a charter from the legislature, which would enable the board to hold property. It was also decided that the Maryland Annual Conference should be asked to appoint a suitable agent to visit the churches and congregations throughout the conference to obtain donations for the purchase of the college from Buell by paying the debts he had contracted.

At the conference session on March 17, the situation was reported, and although it was not directly responsible for the disaster, the conference determined to prevent a failure if possible. Resolutions were adopted that approved the requested actions, and Ward was appointed the college agent. John Smith went immediately to Annapolis to begin the work of getting the charter. Ward was successful in finding the money with which to lift the liens, which divided the debt into smaller sums and made it easier to manage. (The 30 subscribers who agreed to transfer the liens were Isaac C. Baile, John Smith, J. W. Hering, Michael Baughman, George Webster, Joshua Smith, Joshua Yingling, John Roop, William A. Norris, Abner Baile, Samuel McKinstry, James W. Beacham, Laurence Zepp, John Babylon, Alfred Zollickoffer, John L. Reifsnider, W. A. Cunningham, J. T. Ward, John Zimmerman, P. Light Wilson, John H. Bowers, Henry Baile, Andrew R. Durbin, John Biggs, Elizabeth Cassell, Edward Lynch, George Shaeffer, David Reese, David Englar, and Peter Baile.) The legislature adopted the charter, which was signed by Governor Thomas Swann on March 30, 1868.

The charter itself has a rather curious history. The directors appointed by the conference requested James Frame, a Baltimore lawyer, to draw it up, but Frame, instead of drawing up a new one, adopted one already existent. In 1864, the Maryland Annual Conference had instructed H. P. Jordan to secure a charter for a Maryland Conference College, which he did, but, as has been noted, no such institution ever was founded. Knowing of this charter, Frame simply changed the name and adapted it for Western Maryland College. Both charters include two interesting and significant provisions, one by omission, the other by formal statement. The omission is of any opportunity for the church to directly elect trustees, explained by the fact that Jordan's charter was copied from a charter granted in 1784 for the University of Maryland (which had no religious affiliation). Indeed, no such provision had been included in any charter for a Maryland college up to that point. Had the conference instructed Jordan to include such a provision, he no doubt would have, but having no such instruction, he merely followed precedent. This also explains why both charters included a provision prohibiting any religious test of either students or teachers, or any pressure on them to attend a specific house of worship. This inclusion in the charter for the Maryland Conference College is particularly incongruous, since the college was to be organized for the specific purpose of instructing and examining candidates for the ministry in the Maryland Conference of the Methodist Protestant Church. Presumably, it never occurred to Jordan, as he prepared the Conference College charter, to eliminate the clause from the older, university charter, which was granted at a time when religious freedom and tolerance were critical issues. Thus, the Western Maryland College charter also included this provision.[52] Samuel B. Schofield and Marjorie C. Crain, authors of *The Formative Years, 1866–1947*, noted that lack of time probably forced Frame to use the old charter, since it may have been as late as March 1 before he received instructions from the (soon to be chartered) board of directors, and, if the plans were to be effected, it was necessary to get the charter through the legislature before it adjourned its 90-day session in early April. Frame was successful in creating a charter on time for the appropriate legislative action and gubernatorial approval by March 30.[53]

The board of trustees was established as an autonomous, self-perpetuating board, replacements to be elected by the board itself as needed. The only provision was that the same proportionate number of trustees would always be chosen from among the members of the Maryland Annual Conference of the Methodist Protestant Church, from Carroll County, and from the State of Maryland at large. This was eventually interpreted as a requirement that one more than one-third of the board would be Methodist Protestant ministers. (The charter has been amended a number of times, and this requirement was removed in April 1968.)[54]

The first board of trustees, as named in the charter, was soon formed. They met in Westminster on June 25 and selected their officers:

John Smith, Esq., president
Rev. J. T. Ward, secretary
J. W. Hering, M.D., treasurer

From the Maryland Annual Conference of the Methodist Protestant Church:

Rev. Silas B. Southerland   Rev. John J. Murray
Rev. James K. Nichols   Rev. Rhesa Scott Norris
Rev. Daniel Bowers   Rev. Lawrence W. Bates
Rev. Edward J. Drinkhouse, M.D.   Rev. Daniel Evans Reese
Rev. Peter Light Wilson   Rev. Daniel W. Bates
Rev. David Wilson, M.D.

From Carroll County:

Rev. James Thomas Ward   John K. Longwell, Esq.
John Smith, Esq.   Joshua Yingling, Esq.
Isaac C. Baile, Esq.   Richard B. Norment, Esq.
Michael Baughman, Esq.   Henry Baile, Esq.
David H. Shriver, Esq.   Fayette R. Buell, Esq.
Joshua W. Hering, M.D.   Alfred Zollickoffer, Esq.

From the state at large:

Hon. George Vickers   John B. Ward, Esq.
Hon. Eli J. Henkle   John G. Clarke, Esq.
Hon. Ormand Hammond   Rev. William H. Todd
John Frame, Esq.   John S. Repp, Esq.
William King, Esq.   Samuel McKinstry, Esq.
James W. Thomson, Esq.

It should be noted that the charter lists Walter J. Turpin, M.D., as a trustee representing the state at large, but his name does not appear on any subsequent list. The names of Rev. William H. Todd and James W. Thomson were added to the list representing the state at large after the charter was adopted.[55] The officers were designated as an executive or "local" committee for the management of all the finances of the college and were responsible to the general board.

At this organizational meeting, the board also adopted the following resolutions:

I. That we deem it expedient to establish a college such as is contemplated by the Act of Incorporation which constitutes the Board of Trustees of Western Maryland College.

II. That we deem it indispensable to the attainment of this object to procure suitable buildings in which to operate, and to do this as soon as practicable.

III. That the buildings and grounds already known as "The Western Maryland College," owned and occupied by Fayette R. Buell, Esq., are

in our judgement, suitable for the purposes contemplated.
IV. That the Rev. J. T. Ward be and he is authorized to act as the Agent
for This Board, to go forth immediately and obtain subscriptions for the
purchase of the property aforesaid . . .[56]

It was also resolved that Rev. David Wilson represent the interests of the college through the columns of the *Methodist Protestant.* This he did quite ably, and the agent, Ward, also made earnest appeals in the newspaper, as well as through a circular that he issued soon thereafter. The board met on July 28 but took no action because some members were not able to attend due to severe storms and flooding that washed away several critical railroad bridges. It convened again on August 6–7, at which time Ward reported on his success and the board resolved to purchase the property. On August 12, 1868, negotiations began whereby the local board of the board of trustees would purchase the college property owned by Buell for $20,000 ($18,875 in cash and the remainder in notes from Henry Baile and others). By the terms of the purchase, all the mortgages against the college were assumed by the board, but the building still had to be finished at least sufficiently for accommodation of an increased number of boarding students, and furnished as well, which involved a heavy outlay of money and much effort. Buell submitted an accounting that the value of the property, including the interest owed on borrowed money, amounted to $23,000, and that he would sell the college for that amount. The local board held firm to its $20,000 offer since Buell had not been able to show that he had even that much tied up in the college, and Buell, due to his precarious, indeed bankrupt, position, was forced to accept that amount. The deed transferring the title to the board of trustees was signed on September 11, the day after Buell and his family moved out of the college building. All was ultimately accomplished for the opening of the now chartered college under the direct management of the board of trustees on September 14, 1868, to begin a continuing struggle with debt and financial worries.[57]

The faculty for this new year, as elected by the trustees, were:[58]
Rev. J. T. Ward, principal, Biblical Literature and Moral Science
William H. Zimmerman, A.M., vice principal, Natural Sciences, Ancient and Modern Languages
Daniel W. Hering, English and Mathematics (Collegiate student, as well)
William H. Ogg, principal of the Primary Department (Collegiate student, as well)
Susie H. Joyce, Vocal and Instrumental Music
Anna S. Hance, preceptress of the Ladies' Department
Mrs. William H. Zimmerman, governess (and manager of the "domestic" side of the college)

The board of trustees met again on September 29 and adopted a series of fourteen "Fundamental Ordinances," which were the by-laws of the board. It also confirmed the action of the local board concerning the purchase of the college property.

Much had transpired between that February 29th meeting of the advisory board and the June 25th meeting of the newly formed board of trustees. In those four months Western Maryland College had evolved from a proprietary institution owned by Fayette R. Buell to a private, chartered (incorporated) college owned by a board of trustees. It was still under the "patronage" of the Methodist Protestant Church, but it was financially independent of the church. Prior to the June meeting, Ward wrote his observations of what had occurred:

> What the Board will do when it meets I cannot tell, but I think it will be to Br. Buell's own interest to let them do what they please with the College property, no matter if he loses all he has put in it; for that will be the case if he refuses it to the board and lets the creditors sell him out. If he had made haste slowly and cautiously, he would at least have kept his own credit, but having plunged ahead against the advice of the very man he voluntarily chose for his advisor, he can only blame himself for what he has suffered and may yet suffer in this connection. I am deeply concerned for his welfare as ever I was (and I claim to have been and to be still his faithful friend), but I am still more concerned for the welfare of the Church and the success of the College as an institution of solid useful and religious instruction. . . . I have found too that he has a habit of over-rating his own abilities and of representing his enterprizes to be succeeding when in fact the case is just the opposite. . . . While I can hardly think that Br. Buell intended to misrepresent in stating that the "institution has flattering prospects of success" [in an article in the Methodist Protestant, May 1868], the fact is exactly the opposite, and unless most important changes can be effected, and that speedily, the Institution must cease to exist, or at any rate pass not only out of his hands but out of the reach of Methodist Protestant control in any way.[59]

In a letter to the Carroll County commissioners regarding a debt owed (probably for back taxes), Buell gives some insight into his feelings about the "forced" sale of the college two months earlier:

Westminster, MD, Oct. 15, 1868

To the honorable, The members of the board of County Commissioners for Carroll County State of Maryland

Gentlemen

You are probably aware that the Western Maryland Coll. has passed from my hands into the hands of the Board of Trustees of said Coll. They *have obtained it at such a price that they have left me heavily in debt for materials and labor for the Coll. which there is not sufficient funds in the purchase price to cancel. They arranged the terms themselves and the result is that I have lost all the labor I performed upon said College, all the money I invested of my own, which was not less than $3000.00, and left me still in debt for materials as stated before. I shall have to labor for years yet to pay for materials to the Western Md. Coll. for which I am still responsible, and in view of these facts and that I am at this time without any income, not longer having the Coll. to make the money with, it having been taken from me on terms against which I strongly protested; and in view of the fact further, that it is a public institution for a public benefit and that Carroll Co., and especially Westminster, must necessarily be largely interested and benefit by the success of this Institution, and that I am only one individual member of this community, and cut off from all personal benefits arising from said Institution except that which is common to all, may I not then take the liberty of asking you to forgive me the debt which Carroll Co. holds against me. I hope this application will be rec'd with favor, and the request granted, that I may be, to some degree at least, released from present embarrassments, and my mind set somewhat at ease. I shall be under great obligations to you if I am only released from this debt. Any further information you may desire will be cheerfully and readily given. Please let me hear from you at your earliest convenience.*

It is obvious that Buell felt quite wronged by what had happened. One observer of the events commented that perhaps he had gotten the impression that the new board would purchase the property at a price of his determination that would clear all his debts and that he would also remain head of the enterprise. The local board felt that $20,000 was a firm and fair price that would pay all the debts and release the mortgages; unfortunately, it did not match Buell's demand. (Further, Henry Baile later denied having promised to pay $700 of the $1,225 in notes additional to the cash payment of $18,875 from the college.[60]) Buell never seems to have become reconciled to the purchase price he agreed to, to the money he actually received, or to not being retained as a central figure in the new organization.[61] He had hoped that the new board would work with him, and when it did not and, he believed, forced him to sell because he was in a "tight place" and could not hold out for his asking price, he felt keenly wronged.[62] For a while, he complained of his mistreatment, by the board and especially by Ward, to anyone who would listen to him, but gradually he realized that such carping would only do harm to the college he had so labored to establish.

However, as late as January 1870, the board was still dealing with Buell's

The Fayette Buell family, c. 1870

unhappiness over his perceived injustice in the sale of the college. A study committee of the board reported that he did not have a valid claim either legally or morally against the board for any portion of the additional amount of money he alleged was due to him (about $3,000). It had been pointed out to him a year earlier that he and his wife had signed a final contract of their own free will.[63] Buell nevertheless continued to serve as a trustee until 1872, when he resigned and was replaced by Dr. Charles Billingslea, representing Carroll County. But his work in the daily life of the institution was over after the first year, and he withdrew his daughters from the college after that year, as well. He later opened another academy in his new residence at the corner of Main and Bond streets in Westminster and taught in Rev. Van Meter's Collegiate Institute for a year or so. Because of his musical talent, which was shared by his large family, he and three of his daughters—Gertrude, Fannie, and Flora—toured the country entertaining as the Buell Family Concert to make money to pay off his debts. In 1881, he moved to Philadelphia.[64]

In 1882, Buell sent a letter to the *American Sentinel*, a local paper, seeking to refute a portion of J. Thomas Scharf's *History of Western Maryland* (1882), which dealt with the history of the college; in his letter he again upbraided Mr. Smith and Dr. Ward for "defrauding" him.[65] In 1911, he wrote to the *American Sentinel* again to "correct" some inaccuracies he perceived in an article about the college's founding. However, some of his "facts" at that time seem to have been confused by the passage of more than 40 years, for he refers to having sold the college to the Methodist Protestant Church, when in fact he sold it to the board of trustees (the church was not involved with the sale at all).[66] Regardless of what had happened to his personal dream, he seems to have retained his affection for Westminster, and he, his wife, and four of his children are buried in the Westminster Cemetery. On the tombstone is recorded "Fayette R. Buell, Born April 1833, Died January 1913, Founder of The Western Maryland College." In spite of his bankruptcy and the subsequent takeover by the new board of trustees (which indeed had to happen to save the college from extinction), Fayette Buell should not be forgotten. His efforts, his vision, and his hopes brought the college into existence. He put everything he had into the college venture, for he saw that a college could succeed in Westminster with the appropriate patronage and community support. He did not bring it to fruition himself because he was too naive in financial matters and too trusting of those who, by their hollow words of encouragement, led him to believe he would obtain the support of the local community and the Methodist Protestant Church when he needed it.[67]

If the charter trustees had acquainted themselves with the history of the many attempts of the Methodist Protestant Church to establish a college, they probably would never have assumed their new roles. Ward often noted in his diary the relative indifference of the church and its leaders to the plight of the colleges (including Western Maryland). Wills pointed out that few of the ministers were college trained themselves, and many had only a limited education; thus, unlike J. T. Ward, they were indifferent to advanced education.[68] Furthermore, establishing a quality institution of higher learning required significant resources, which a relatively poor church and clergy could not sacrifice. Even after the Maryland Annual Conference assumed its more formal sponsorship of the college, its name might have been added to the list of Methodist Protestant collegiate failures had it not been for the untiring work (often interrupted by chronic illness) of James T. Ward. Ward did all he could to help Buell succeed with his proprietary college, while constantly advising him to move slowly and get his finances in order, and when the college was purchased by the newly created board of trustees, Ward immediately transferred his efforts to making the "new" institution a success.

The ministers on the board of trustees seem to have been chosen (the only time the Annual Conference selected them) for their standing in the conference rather than their qualifications to play a pivotal role in getting the college on its feet. Little more attention was given to the qualifications of the laymen, who made up the majority of the board.[69] One of these laymen, Dr. Joshua W. Hering, commented many years later in *Recollections of My Life*, "There was not a real college man in the board . . . and

Joshua Webster Hering,
first college treasurer and charter trustee

we, therefore, had no conception of what was ahead of us in the way of work and difficulties. . . . If we had known in advance all the difficulties to be met and overcome, and all the dark places through which we were to pass, I doubt very much whether we would have had the courage and faith to undertake the work at all."[70] However, within the board of trustees were two who regularly assisted and advised Ward as the college slowly moved forward. These men were John Smith and Hering himself.

Joshua Webster Hering was born March 8, 1833, in Frederick County, Maryland. After receiving a limited educational foundation in the local schools, he served as an apprentice in a country store until age 18, when he came to Westminster to train in the mercantile establishment of Jacob Reese and Sons. In 1853 he studied for the medical profession under William A. Mathias, a Westminster physician, and in 1855 he was awarded the doctor of medicine degree from the University of Maryland. That year also saw his marriage to Margaret Henrietta Trumbo, a union that produced four children. (When his wife died in 1883, he remained a widower for five years, until his marriage to Catharine E. Armacost.) His medical practice grew rapidly and apparently made such demands on his strength and health that he retired in 1867 and moved to Virginia. His services were much in demand during the Civil War, especially following local engagements, including that of Gettysburg, when he assisted the army medics in aiding the wounded who were brought to the Old Union Church, which served as a hospital. (He was even temporarily under arrest during the Southern occupation of the town.) After a short stay in Virginia, he returned to Westminster, where he assumed the position of "cashier" (president) at the Union National Bank and where his services as a consulting physician were in constant demand, although he no longer practiced medicine on a regular basis. He gained such a reputation as a banker that in 1898 he was elected president of the Maryland Banker's Association. He also served four years as Carroll County senator in the Maryland Legislature, where he became the acknowledged leader of the Democratic Party, and, because of his financial acumen, for three terms (1899–1901, 1901–04, 1907–10) he served as comptroller of the treasury of Maryland. He was one of three gubernatorial appointees to the newly created Maryland Public Service Commission in 1910. It is reported that he declined nominations for both president of the Senate and governor. Active in the Methodist Protestant Church, he was superintendent of the local Sunday school for 25 years, president of the church's board of trustees, a member of the General Conference of the church for ten successive sessions, and president of the General Conference in 1892 and in 1896, the only layman to hold that office up to that time. He was also a charter member of the board of governors of the Westminster Theological Seminary when it was formed in 1882. Dr. Hering was a clear, forcible, and interesting speaker; few could equal his ability in gaining and holding the attention of an audience. From 1868 to 1913, he was an occasional lecturer in anatomy and physiology at the college. He served on the college board for 45 years, one of the longer terms for a trustee. He was treasurer of the board from 1868 to 1885, and in 1897 he succeeded Ward as president of the board, a post he held until his death on September 23, 1913. His devotion and service to the college were legendary.[71]

Two of the Fundamental Ordinances adopted by the trustees at their third meeting, on September 29, 1868, dealt with the great seal of the college and the privy seal. Ordinance IX stated, "The device of the Great Seal of this Institution shall be the college building, with the following verbal inscription: 'Western Maryland College. Incorporated March 1868. *Onare, et melior facere.*'" Ordinance X stated, "The device of the Privy Seal of this Institution shall be a Torch and Trumpet, with the following inscription: 'Western Maryland College. Incorporated March 1868.'" Joshua Hering, again in *Recollections of My Life*, paints an interesting picture of what transpired during the discussion of the seal that day:

> Some of the members of the Board thought as we were starting out to
> found a new college, we ought to make a departure from the old custom
> of Latin inscription in the Seal, and put it in plain English. And so

there was a warm discussion about it. Mr. Smith, the President, was in the chair. Those who knew John Smith knew him to be a man of strong intellectual force but limited education, a man of ponderous voice and positive convictions, and who could express himself with great force. He seemed intensely interested in their discussion about the Seal. Finally, he asked someone to take the chair and he came upon the floor and said, "I have listened with interest to this discussion and have my views about the subject. I don't know much about English and nothing at all about Latin," and then raising his ponderous fist, he brought it down on the table with a bang. "But I do think there ought to be a little Latin in the Seal." And that settled the matter. The Board voted to stick to the Latin.

What followed after that is rather curious. There is no trustee record of the seals actually being made, but the privy seal exists today and is still used. The great seal as described in Ordinance IX, on the other hand, must not have met with too much favor, for the faculty recommended that the motto be changed; the board instead directed them to correct and retain it. The next time it was discussed, according to the minutes, was on June 14, 1871, as a report of the Local Committee; this committee recommended that Ordinance IX be amended to read,

> *The device of the Great Seal of this Institution shall be an open volume in the centre, inscribed "Biblia Sacra (Holy Book)," a volume standing upright on each side, one inscribed "Platonis Opera (Works of Plato)," and the other "Novum Organum (philosophical treatise by Francis Bacon)." At the top a cloud with a hand projecting through it, surrounded by rays of light falling directly upon the centre volume, with the motto below "E Tenebris in Lucem Voco (I call you out of darkness into light)." Around the edge of the Seal "Sigillum Collegii Mariae-Terrae Occidentalis (Seal of Western Maryland College). Instit. A.D. 1868."*

The Local Committee, consisting of Smith, Ward, and Hering, apparently felt they were acting appropriately under Ordinance XIII to superintend "the business interests of the college" by effecting a new seal for those purposes. And they were able to convince the other trustees of their wisdom. There is nothing to suggest who actually designed the seal and came up with the motto, but one might suppose that the new professor of ancient languages, James W. Reese (1838–1917), had something to do with it, for he later described the seal very carefully and explained its subtle meanings.[72]

31

STUDENT LIFE

Although the amenities of life in the immediate post–Civil War era were nothing like those after the turn of the 20th century, by almost any standard, life at Western Maryland College was rather harsh for the students. Until 1871, the boarding students all lived in the four-story Main Building, separated by sex. They slept in large dormitories, sometimes 30 to a room, and ate somewhat meager meals served in one large room where they were again segregated by sex and chaperoned by faculty. Professors taught—or, more correctly, heard "recitations" of textbooks by the students—in cramped, often ill-equipped classrooms. Of course, there was no running water, no electricity, no central heating, and no indoor plumbing. Wills noted that these latter "inconveniences" were accepted as normal, since the students came from homes where these things did not exist. Water was provided by a well and a cistern and, when they went dry, carried from nearby springs. Heating was provided by stoves in each room, which posed a danger of fire, as did the kerosene lamps that provided meager lighting.[73] Ward commented in his diary (September 23, 1868) on the furnishings of the building, which were overseen by Professor Zimmerman and his wife: "Prof. Zimmerman and his excellent wife deserve great praise for the perfect and beautiful system they have established both in the collegiate and household affairs of the institution. Every visitor is charmed with the good and orderly manner in which things are now conducted." It should be noted, however, that student complaints led to some temporary changes in the stewardship of the dining room during 1869 and again in 1870. The Zimmermans left the college, perhaps partially because of this unpleasantness, in June 1871.[74]

Student life was also carefully governed; great effort was made to regulate students' lives at every turn. The faculty soon implemented a long list of Rules of Deportment and imposed a demerit system. Rules included the following:

4. *Do not attend any place of amusement, or public exhibition, without the advice or consent of the Principal.*
6. *In passing from one part of the building to another, do not rush, but proceed in a regular and orderly manner.*
13. *Make no improper use of the blackboards.*
15. *Never associate or converse with any student of the opposite sex, except in the presence and hearing of a teacher, without special, proper permission. [The rules were later amended and reordered, and this one, in a revised form prohibiting any conversation between the sexes, became known as the "infamous" Rule 11.]*
17. *Do not prompt, either by word or gesture, any student during recitation.*

21. *Do not attempt to pass any letter, book or other article, to any student of the opposite sex, except through the hands of the Principal or Vice Principal.*

25. *Let all time allotted to study be spent in study.*

Gaps in coverage of possible offenses were covered by such rules as these:

18. *If you should inadvertently or unintentionally have violated any rule, seek the earliest opportunity of candidly confessing and making suitable amends, that you may secure pardon.*

23. *Do not take advantage of any possible omissions in these rules to act in any respect contrary to your own sense of right.*[75]

To encourage obedience of the rules, an inspection system was in place for many years. Teachers took turns serving as inspectors, checking each room several times each evening to be sure that students were studying during the appropriate study hours, which ended at 10 P.M. with "lights out." One of the more difficult, indeed impossible, rules to enforce was that which forbade interaction between the sexes. The students always found ways to circumvent the rules, but these called for deception, alertness, and inventiveness. If the violators were caught, severe penalties were imposed, often suspension or even expulsion. By 21st-century standards, it is amazing, and rather amusing, to note the extent to which 19th-century adults would go to prohibit adolescents from "co-mingling." In February 1870, the board of trustees even passed a resolution: "Resolved, That it is the sense of this Board of Trustees that the Faculty of the Western Maryland College should use their utmost vigilance in preventing any improper commingling of the sexes of this institution, and that the Board will hold the Faculty responsible for the faithful performance of the spirit of this resolution." The faculty had gone on record the previous June in support of this concept, even extending it to themselves: "Resolved, that it shall be deemed improper for the teachers in the male or female department to manifest any greater interest toward each other than is permitted by the rules of the Institution between male and female students." This public statement was apparently deemed necessary after Daniel W. Hering, student and teacher of English and mathematics, and Susie H. Joyce, the vocal and instrumental music teacher, had demonstrated some "intimacy" in the book room (probably something as innocent as holding hands), and some of the female students had complained.[76] After much discussion and many apologies for their indiscretion, Hering and Joyce received certificates of good standing (or letters of recommendation) from Principal Ward, as they were leaving the faculty that June, he to study at Yale, and she because she was not rehired.[77] Wills commented, "This effort to regulate the conduct of the students . . . led to a watchfulness, that, on the part of tactless, suspicious, or domineering teachers, was little else than espionage, and caused frequent clashes between teachers and students, as many entries in Ward's diary testify."[78] Ward certainly approved of this restrictive *in loco parentis*, for he stated clearly in his diary (November 27, 1870): "Experience teaches us the importance of the strictest vigilance over the conduct of students at all times except when they are entirely removed from our jurisdiction by their parents taking them to their homes. We must not hereafter allow even their parents to give them permission to visit places, other than their homes, when they are taken from under the restraints of our discipline."

One outlet for youthful exuberance was the literary societies. When the college opened, the Irving Literary Society was given a room for its weekly meetings in the tower of the Main Building, which the students dubbed "Angel's Roost." This society was composed of men and women—under proper faculty supervision, of course. After a year, however, the women desired their own society, which would give them more opportunities to pursue their own interests, and so the Browning Society (named for Elizabeth Barrett Browning at the suggestion of Mary Ward '71) was formed during the school year 1868–69, and the Irving Society became strictly male.[79] The first literary publication of the college was the *Irving Literary Gazette*, which appeared in February 1868, with Maggie A. Fowler, principal of the Preparatory Department, as "editress." Three pages were filled with short essays and poems, some advertisements for local businesses, and a list of the Irving Society members and officers. The back page served as an advertisement for the college, including a list of expenses, a list of the faculty and board of directors, and a general description of the location and building. The *Gazette* continued for only three issues in 1868 and then suspended publication for 13 years.[80] Indeed, the Irving Society temporarily disbanded in December 1869, due to indifference of the members. (One wonders if the now all-male society needed the young women to keep them organized and on track.) Soon, as the college grew, it would reappear. The Browning Society, meanwhile, provided several interesting entertainments consisting of tableaux, music, and literary readings, some held in the college Chapel Room and others at the Odd Fellows Hall in town. (The Odd Fellows Hall was the largest venue in Westminster other than the court house; it opened in 1858 and provided rooms for plays, club meetings, concerts, lectures, and movies in the early 20th century. One of the most notable speakers was Frederick Douglass, who came to Westminster to speak in October 1870. Curiously, there is no record that any student or faculty member attended.)

Students also attended events in the town as they arose and, of course, if given permission. On November 5, 1870, Ward reported in his diary that "quite a number of the college students visited, with my permission and sanction, the Menagerie today, I having been previously assured by the Managers that no Circus Performances would be connected with it. The Exhibition was, I am told by those who attended, very interesting and instructive. Specimens of all the prominent species of the animal kingdom were exhibited, and explanations given of their localities, habits, etc."

James Reese noted that it might normally have been expected that some difficulties would arise between "town and gown" because such were common in the history of higher education and had been so for centuries, but this was not the case in Westminster.[81] No complaint was ever lodged against the college because of student disorderly conduct in the town during these early days. This may have been because of the disciplinary "tight hand" that had been imposed. Hazing of new students was also firmly discouraged from the beginning; it was traditional for new students to receive a courteous welcome by the "old" students. Reese noted in his 1893 article with pride: "In the twenty-six years during which young men and young women have been educated at Western Maryland College, with a town at hand not free from the usual propensity to gossip, no whisper of scandal has been heard. Silence, surely, was never more eloquent." As we shall see, however, this was not quite true.

FACULTY AND ADMINISTRATION

A perusal of the faculty minutes of 1868–70 (which are sometimes difficult to read, as they are handwritten in rather flowery script and have suffered some water damage) suggests that the lives of the faculty members of the fledgling institution were almost as regulated as those of the students. They met at least weekly, usually on Friday afternoons or evenings, and responded to a roll call (even though there were only ten of them). They spent several meetings in the fall of 1869 dealing with the deportment of their student charges and creating the Rules of Deportment, which seemed to increase and be modified steadily as new offenses occurred. These were published in subsequent catalogs and posted in the Main Building and eventually in each student's room. By September 1870, a detailed demerit system was also drawn up and approved and soon put into effect with almost Draconian efficiency. A list of some offenses and their demerits follows (and suggests the nature of what a 19th-century faculty considered important to the well-being of the students *and* the institution):

Absence from any stated exercise *3*
Absence from college premises *5*

Disorder *1–150*

Communication in any manner between the
*   male and female departments*.................................... *20*

Disrespect to college officers *1–150*

Failure to prepare recitation *5*

Use of profane or indecent language............................. *10*

Use of intoxicating liquor *1–150*

Playing games of chance... *25*

Smoking within the building... *5*

Carrying or using a firearm on the premises.................. *25*

Failure to extinguish lights at 10 o'clock P.M. *5*

Going into any part of the building or grounds appropriated to others..... *25*

Prompting during a recitation....................................... *5*

Leaving things out of order in the building *5*

Ballplaying or throwing stones on the premises.............. *5*

The maximum number of demerits that could be accrued in any one session was 150; after that, the student would be expelled. Most of the subsequent faculty meetings were taken up with dealing with infractions and imposing demerits. The demerit report for each week would be compiled at the regular faculty meeting and read to the students the following Friday afternoon at prayers, each student's name, offense, and penalty outlined for all to hear. Students given significant demerits were also called before the faculty, or the principal, to explain themselves and offer apologies. One particular incident in 1870 required two meetings, on December 1 and 3, before it was resolved. The previous Thanksgiving Day had seen some student disorder, and the entire faculty (including the part-time lecturers) had been called into special session at 7 P.M. to deal with it. The disorder was caused by certain male students taking advantage of the absence of the faculty to visit the female side of the house and to disarrange the study room and dormitory. The 15 young men were summoned. By lengthy interrogation it was determined who did what, and they received demerits ranging from 25 to 75. On December 5 the faculty was called back into session to deal with a matter brought by Professor Zimmerman, the college steward. Apparently, someone had broken into the food storeroom to steal some crackers, jelly, and preserves. Two male students were charged, and they appeared before the faculty the next day, confessing their fault, praying for forgiveness and leniency, and promising better conduct in the future. On December 8 this matter was resolved, one boy getting 25 demerits and the other 10.[82]

Occasionally, the faculty would deal with petitions from students, such as one requesting a school holiday the day after Thanksgiving (denied).

James W. Reese,
professor of classics for 42 years

Because of the obvious transportation difficulties of the time, Thanksgiving Day was a holiday from studies, but the students could not leave the campus to go anywhere unless given permission from their parents *and* the faculty. A petition from students to witness a local parade was also denied. A request to attend a concert in town was approved, but the request that the male students be allowed to circulate among the female students afterward was, of course, denied. Faculty also approved (or disapproved) all proposed changes in student academic schedules, dealt with the death from typhoid fever of a theological student by carefully planning the procession of students and faculty following the coffin to the depot, granted weekend and day leaves for individual students after permission had been granted by parents, and granted themselves leaves for weekend activities and trips to Baltimore (some were even denied). Other issues included whether Miss Hance, the Ladies Department preceptress, could have a key to the Chapel Room, and whether a teacher could have an extra half hour for an examination. More curiously, the faculty set the dates and times of the various holidays, classes, and examinations, often with only a week or so of notice. One can only wonder how the students arranged transportation home without knowing when the college would go into recess.

In February 1870, the faculty was called upon to interview a candidate for a teaching position in ancient languages and found him incompetent.

The position was ultimately filled by a local minister, James W. Reese. Born in Carroll County on October 3, 1838, James Reese was the youngest son of Jacob Reese and the grandson of David Fisher, one of the oldest citizens and largest landowners in the community. He prepared for college by attending St. Timothy's Hall in Catonsville, Maryland, where his classmates included Edward, Junius, and J. Wilkes Booth. At 17 he entered Princeton College, graduating in 1859. A serious and critical student, he won honors and the distinction of being elected class orator; he delivered the classical oration on Commencement Day. He was offered the post of tutor at Princeton but declined it to prepare for the Episcopal ministry. He entered the General Theological Seminary of the Episcopal Church in New York in 1860 and graduated in 1863. He was ordained in September of that year in Annapolis, and from January 1864 until 1870 he was rector of Ascension Church in Westminster. He married Mary Pauline Perry in 1868. It was this same James Reese who, as master of the Door to Virtue Masonic Lodge, laid the cornerstone of the first building of Western Maryland College. He was elected worshipful master of the lodge for 21 consecutive terms and also held various high offices in Maryland Masonry. On February 28, 1870, having been elected to the post by the trustees, he began his teaching career as professor of ancient languages and literature at the college, a position he would hold with great success for nearly 42 years.[83] His election to the faculty was not without incident, however. Several members of the board of trustees and the faculty opposed his appointment because he was not a Methodist Protestant. Apparently, the more liberal Ward was able to convince trustees Hering, Smith, and Yingling that such objection was "not worthy of notice," perhaps pointing out the special clause in the charter specifically forbidding such a religious requirement, and Reese was duly elected.[84] He was known for his bright mind, extensive store of information, and pleasant disposition, which made him a valued member of the faculty and the community.

FINANCES

When the board of trustees took over the newly chartered institution, it carried a debt of $17,361.58. As college agent, Ward was trying to raise funds from the churches and individuals in the conference (by December 15, 1868, he had received donations and pledges of $4,638.42), and the institution eked out an existence, almost totally depending on tuition and fees from students. Ward noted in his diary of August 12, 1869, that Methodist Protestants were increasingly referring to the college as "our college." This was probably due to his good work and fine reputation, but he happily turned over his duties as college agent to Rev. Peter Light Wilson (one of Buell's original board of directors) in the spring of 1869, preferring to resume a more pastoral and educational role in college affairs. Wilson held the position until 1876 and was rather successful at raising funds and obtaining students for the college. In 1872, however, Ward expressed some dissatisfaction with Wilson's efforts when Wilson claimed to have collected over $10,000 but nothing had yet reached the college. Apparently, the funds were pledged but not paid, and Ward was afraid that this "success" that Wilson touted would discourage others from giving.[85] (Wilson was succeeded by Rev. J. W. Charlton for one year, and then by Rev. J. B. Walker from 1877 to 1882.) Enrollments fluctuated during the academic year as students came and went (some of the men to go home to help with the farming), so guaranteed income was problematic. But in the first few years, the college seemed to catch on. After the first-year enrollment of 70, the following year (1868–69) showed only 63 students enrolled. But in 1869–70 there were 123 students listed, now by Male and Female departments; 50 were in the Collegiate program (33 men and 17 women), and the remainder were in the preparatory (19) and grammar schools (54). By 1870–71, enrollment had grown to 140, with 66 enrolled in the college (42 men and 24 women) and 74 in the preparatory (22) and grammar schools (52). The number of faculty remained relatively constant, but its makeup changed frequently. In the years 1868–71, 15 individuals filled the ten positions, and only three people (Ward, Zimmerman, and Hance) were there for all three years. Wills commented that it was impossible to establish a stable, competent faculty given the low salaries and restricted conditions under which they had to work and live.[86] The faculty salaries for each of the two sessions during 1868–69 were as follows:

J. T. Ward, principal and professor..$450
William Zimmerman, vice principal and professor $300
Daniel Hering, student/professor $100
William H. Ogg, student/preparatory principal............................$100
Anna S. Hance, preceptress of Ladies Department........................$150
Susie H. Joyce, teacher of music..$150

All except Ward lived in the college building and boarded there, as well.

Those who could be hired at such meager salaries were generally men and women of little formal scholarship or ability or, more likely, young people with ability and education who moved on to better-paying positions as soon as they obtained some teaching experience. Unfortunately, this situation would maintain for quite a few years.

To pay these salaries and meet other regular expenses, student fees were assessed:

Board, washing, fuel, and lights .... *$90.00 per session*

Tuition in the Preparatory Department.................... *$15.00 per session*
Tuition in the Scientific Department .... *$22.50 per session*
Tuition in the Scientific and Classical Department... *$30.00 per session*

Numerous extra charges were listed, for example, for instrumental music ($25), oil painting instruction ($20), ornamental wax flowers and fruit ($10), and ornamental needlework ($10). Having set the charges, the board anxiously awaited enrollments each session, hoping at least to break even, which did not always happen.

The minutes of the board for January 1870 reported that the college's gross indebtedness was now $26,009.65, reflecting additional borrowing to complete the Main Building and furnish it. Income for the year had been $4,420.12 from donations that were applied to the debt to reduce it to $21,589.53. The fall term's receipts from all fees for 123 students were $5,353.98, and all expenses were $5,204.33, leaving a profit for the term of $149.65. In the spring term the debt increased somewhat, because receipts did not quite cover expenditures. In June 1870 it was announced that the Maryland Legislature, which had been approached for a subsidy, had approved an initial grant of $3,000, with an additional $1,090 to be awarded annually thereafter. This helped to reduce the debt to $19,941.20. The real need was for an endowment, but that could not be established until the debt was paid off.

The town of Westminster was changing and growing, as well, affecting enrollments, especially in the preparatory school. Ward notes in his diary on September 27, 1869: "I could not avoid observing, as I walked the well-lighted street this evening, and witnessed the number of pedestrians on the pavements and vehicles in the street, the wonderful change since I came to reside here. I suppose the population of Westminster has increased three-fold within five years, and business of every kind appears to be prospering. Four new and commodious church edifices have been erected within that time, our college established, and other important public interests that were unknown before."

MAJOR EVENTS

Even though no students were eligible to receive degrees until 1871, a program of commencement activities was planned each year, and the events were well attended. The general program for the 1869 Commencement was well documented by Ward. A general announcement in the local paper outlined the "schedule of exercises":

1. *Public examination of the students by the faculty, June 7–15; visitors admitted 10–12 A.M. and 1–3 P.M.*

2. *Sabbath services on Sunday, June 13, at the Methodist Protestant Church; sermons delivered to the ladies of the Browning Society in the morning and to the men of the Irving Society in the evening*

3. *Anniversary exercises for the Literary Societies at the Lutheran Church on Monday and Tuesday evenings, June 14–15*

4. *Oration by Dr. Lawrence Bates before the Irving Society and a poem delivered by Dr. David Wilson before the Browning Society on Wednesday, June 16*

5. *Commencement exercises in the Lutheran Church, including awarding of prizes by the examining committee, 10:30 A.M., Thursday, June 17*

6. *Reception of the patrons and friends of the institution by the principal and faculty in the college building, 8–10 P.M., June 17*

The public was invited to attend all events. Ward noted that 250 people passed through the college building during the reception and were serenaded by the Westminster Brass Band to the great delight of all in attendance.[87]

In late June of 1869, the board was polled and agreed to award the first honorary degree, a doctor of divinity, to Daniel Evans Reese (1810–77), a charter member of the board and one of a family of gifted and devoted ministers in the Maryland Annual Conference. He had served as president of the Maryland Conference and attended three General Conferences of the church.

CONCLUSION

The decade from 1861 to 1870 was a momentous one for the United States; the country had experienced a divisive civil war, rapid technological change, and the beginning of significant social change. Western Maryland College during this time had been envisioned by Fayette Buell; brought to actuality by the realistic and almost superhuman efforts of J. T. Ward; rescued from insolvency by the Methodist Protestant Church through its patronage and the creation of a self-perpetuating, autonomous board of trustees; chartered by the State of Maryland; and kept alive in spite of great financial stress. In his diary of October 4, 1870, Ward commented: "We cannot reasonably complain of slowness of progress; I know not of any college that, within so short a time, made greater advancement upon so meager a beginning, and if we patiently persevere, looking to and trusting in God, we may hope that either we, or those who come after us, will yet see this college stand among the finest in the land." In spite of this optimism, as it entered the next decade, the college would encounter even more stress.

CHAPTER 1 ENDNOTES

1. Warner, *Carroll County*, 30–31.
2. Chandler, *Pilgrimage of Faith*, 4.
3. Drinkhouse, *History of Methodist Reform*, 252–67.
4. Chandler, *Pilgrimage of Faith*, 6–8.
5. Rowland Watts in 1900 *Aloha*, 22–23.
6. Chandler, *Pilgrimage of Faith*, 10.
7. Wills, *History of Western Maryland College*, vol. 1, 5–6.
8. Warner, *Carroll County*, 58.
9. Wills, *History of Western Maryland College*, vol. 1, 6–7.
10. James Reese in 1893 *Aloha*, 26.
11. *Western Maryland College Monthly*, July 1890, 430.
12. Wills, *History of Western Maryland College*, vol. 1, 160.
13. Sketch of Dr. Ward, Ward Papers, college archives.
14. Ward, *A Brief History*, 1.
15. Ibid., 4.
16. Ibid., 1.
17. Ibid., 4.1.
18. Ibid., 4.3.
19. Ibid., 6–7.
20. *Western Maryland College Monthly*, July 1890, 430; Schofield and Crain, *Formative Years*, 5.
21. Wills, *History of Western Maryland College*, vol. 1, 14.
22. Memorial, Ward Papers; Pollitt, *Biographies*; Schofield, Notes; "Western Maryland Railroad History," *Carroll County Times*, July 27, 2003, E1.
23. Pollitt, *Biographies*; WMC Catalogs.
24. Ward, Diaries, September 6, 1866.
25. Ward, *Brief History*, 5–6.
26. James Reese in 1893 *Aloha*, 25.
27. Ibid.
28. Wills, *History of Western Maryland College*, vol. 1, 12–13.
29. Tributes to Dr. Joshua Hering, *WMC Bulletin*, 1908, 26.
30. Ward, Diaries, September 8, 1866; Wills, *History of Western Maryland College*, vol. 1, 18–19.
31. Wills, *History of Western Maryland College*, vol. 1, 19.
32. Annual Conference minutes, March 1867, 14.
33. Ibid.
34. Ward, *Brief History*, 14.
35. WMC *First Annual Circular*.
36. Wills, *History of Western Maryland College*, vol. 2, 69–70.
37. Unidentified newspaper clipping, college archives.
38. Ward, Diaries, September 12, 1867.
39. Ibid., September 1, 1867.
40. Ibid., July 5, 1867.
41. Wills, *History of Western Maryland College*, vol. 1, 25.
42. Ward, *Brief History*, 23.
43. Wills, *History of Western Maryland College*, vol. 1, 26–27.
44. Alumni Record, 1905, Dickinson College, Carlisle, PA, 194–95.
45. Daniel W. Hering, Remarks at the 50th Anniversary of the College, commemorative booklet, June 13, 1917.
46. Ibid.
47. Wills, *History of Western Maryland College*, vol. 1, 28–29.
48. Schofield and Crain, *Formative Years*, 14.
49. Ward, *Brief History*, 20.
50. Wills, *History of Western Maryland College*, vol. 1, 30; Reese, 1893 *Aloha*, 26.
51. Ward, *Brief History*, 21.
52. Lewis, Papers, *The Methodist Protestant*, March 18, 1903, 2.
53. Schofield and Crain, *Formative Years*, 7.
54. WMC board of trustees minutes, 1968.
55. *First Annual Catalogue*, 1868.
56. WMC board of trustees minutes, June 25, 1868.
57. Ward, *Outline*, 10–12.
58. *First Annual Catalogue*, 1868, 4.
59. Ward, *Brief History*, 22–24.
60. Ward, Diaries, August 4, 1882.
61. Pollitt, *Biographies*, 27.
62. Wills, *History of Western Maryland College*, vol. 1, 36.
63. WMC board of trustees minutes, January 26, 1870.
64. Pollitt, *Biographies*; Wills, *History of Western Maryland College*, vol. 1, 36.
65. Ward, Diaries, August 4, 1882.
66. Buell letter, *American Sentinel*, June 17, 1911.
67. Wills, *History of Western Maryland College*, vol. 1, 37–38.
68. Ibid., 37.
69. Ibid., 31.
70. Hering, *Recollections*.
71. Schofield and Crain, *Formative Years*, 8; Pollitt, *Biographies*; dedication, 1900 *Aloha*, 9–11; Lewis Papers, "Recognition."
72. Wills, *History of Western Maryland College*, vol. 2, 10.
73. Article in Ward's unpublished scrapbooks, college archives.
74. Ward, Diaries; WMC faculty minutes.
75. *Third Annual Catalogue*, 1870–71, 15–17.

C H A P T E R 1 E N D N O T E S

76. WMC faculty minutes, June 4, 1869.
77. Ward, Diaries, June 10, 1869.
78. Wills, *History of Western Maryland College,* vol. 1, 40.
79. Schofield and Crain, *Formative Years,* 14.
80. Makosky, *Western Maryland College,* 10.
81. 1893 *Aloha,* 28.
82. WMC faculty minutes, December 1870.
83. Shadrack Simpson in 1896 *Aloha,* 10–11.
84. Schofield and Crain, *Formative Years,* 17.
85. Ward, Diaries, March 27, 1872.
86. Wills, *History of Western Maryland College,* vol. 1, 42.
87. Ward, Diaries, June 17, 1869.

MAJOR WORLD EVENTS

1861

Abraham Lincoln is inaugurated 16th U.S. president.
Kansas becomes a U.S. state.
U.S. Civil War breaks out with attack on Fort Sumter.
Albert, prince consort of Britain's Queen Victoria, dies.
Dickens publishes *Great Expectations.*
Alfred North Whitehead is born.
Wagner's opera *Tännhauser* is a scandal in Paris.

1862

Victor Hugo publishes *Les Miserables.*
Manet paints *La Musique aux Tuileries.*
Claude Debussy is born.
Battle of Antietam.

1863

Lincoln issues Emancipation Proclamation.
West Virginia becomes a U.S. state.
Battle of Gettysburg.
Lincoln delivers Gettysburg Address.
Longfellow publishes *Tales of a Wayside Inn.*
J. S. Mill publishes *Utilitarianism.*
U.S. National Academy of Sciences is founded.

1864

Gen. Sherman marches through Georgia.
Louis Pasteur invents pasteurization.
Lincoln is reelected president.
Nevada becomes a U.S. state.
Nathaniel Hawthorne is born.
Tolstoi publishes *War and Peace.*
Stephen Foster is born.

1865

U.S. Civil War ends with surrender at Appomattox.
Matthew Arnold publishes *Essays in Criticism.*
Schubert's *Unfinished Symphony* is performed in Vienna.
Yale University opens first Department of Fine Arts in U.S.
Wagner's opera *Tristan and Isolde* is performed in Munich.
Lewis Carroll publishes *Alice's Adventures in Wonderland.*
Abraham Lincoln is assassinated; is succeeded by Andrew Johnson.
Thirteenth Amendment to U.S. Constitution abolishes slavery.

1866
Dostoevsky publishes *Crime and Punishment.*
Alfred Nobel invents dynamite.
H. G. Wells is born.
Degas begins to paint his ballet scenes.

1867
Nebraska becomes a U.S. state.
Russia sells Alaska to U.S. for $7,200,000.
Ibsen publishes *Peer Gynt.*
Karl Marx publishes *Das Kapital.*
Marie Curie is born.
Livingston explores the Congo.
Pierre Michaux begins to manufacture bicycles.
Johann Strauss II composes *The Blue Danube Waltz.*
Queensbury Rules of boxing are published in London.
Mark Twain publishes *The Celebrated Jumping Frog.*

1868
President Johnson is impeached.
Louisa M. Alcott publishes *Little Women.*
Brahms composes *A German Requiem.*
First U.S. professional baseball club, Cincinnati Red Stockings, is founded.
Tchaikovsky composes Symphony no. 1.

1869
Ulysses S. Grant is inaugurated 18th U.S. president.
Mark Twain publishes *The Innocents Abroad.*
Bret Harte publishes *The Outcasts of Poker Flat.*
Francis Galton publishes *Hereditary Genius.*
Princeton and Rutgers originate intercollegiate football.
Frank Lloyd Wright is born.
Suez Canal is opened.
First transcontinental railroad is completed.

1870
Nikolai Lenin is born.
Jules Verne publishes *Twenty Thousand Leagues under the Sea.*
Tchaikovsky composes *Romeo and Juliet* overture.
John D. Rockefeller founds Standard Oil Company.
Telegraph is invented.

First known photograph of the Main Building; note Owings Hall addition (1872).

THE COLLEGE MOVES FORWARD

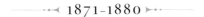

···◄ 1871–1880 ►···

The country was making strides toward recovery after the disastrous Civil War, although the process of reconstruction was slow. Some amazing and sometimes terrifying things were happening, which kept people talking and anxiously reading the newspapers of the era. Chicago suffered its devastating fire, the Brooklyn Bridge was opened, impressionist painting made its appearance in France, the telephone was invented, Edison invented the phonograph and electric lights, and Carnegie developed the first large steel furnace. It was a new age of discovery, and life was surely changing for Americans.

As the college entered a new decade and its fifth year of operation, it faced over $20,000 in debt, but its enrollments were holding steady. Indeed, the number of enrollees in the college program increased from 66 to 87 in one year and averaged about 74 for the decade, ranging from 56 to 87. There was a rather significant drop in enrollments for two years (1876–78) in the college and the preparatory school, but this was no doubt caused by a "marked depression and disturbance of industry"[1] from 1873 to 1879, the longest period of economic contraction in the country's history at that time. The preparatory school continued to be successful and to enlist 30%–45%

of total enrollees. This program, not at all unique to collegiate institutions of the time, enabled the college to survive financially while not requiring too much outlay of funds. It also provided a steady flow of students into the college program. During the four critical years of the depression, total enrollment dropped from 131 to 85, college enrollees slipping from 82 to 56 and preparatory enrollments from 49 to 29. By the end of the decade, enrollments had bounced back to fairly normal levels (82 in the college and 44 in the preparatory school). One other statistic appears at first to be alarming but was perhaps normal for colleges of the era: For the ten graduating classes from 1871 to 1880, only 30% of the entering women and 24% of the entering men graduated with their classmates. (Specific classes, of course, varied, the 1871 class holding the record; 50% of men and 50% of women received the AB degree with their class that year.) When the college opened, 80% of the students (in all divisions) were, not surprisingly, from Westminster or the immediate vicinity. Ten years later, local students were about 20%. The college was becoming more well known in the state.

BUILDINGS AND GROUNDS

To meet the needs of the growing enrollment, especially of students desiring to board in the college, the Local Committee (Ward, Smith, and Hering) recommended to the board of trustees on June 14, 1871, that an addition be appended to the Main Building. They felt that the additional students that could thus be accommodated would justify the increase in debt. This was quickly agreed to,[2] and between July and the following January a building four stories high, 37 feet wide, and 50 feet long was attached to the middle of the rear of the Main Building. This provided more student bedrooms, a chapel, recitation rooms, and a hall for the societies; and each teacher had his or her own apartment. There was a room to accommodate sick students, and separation of the sexes could be managed more easily than when everyone lived and recited in one building. It was reported to the trustees that the principal's room was so designed that students could gain access without ever crossing the path of a member of the opposite sex. Wills remarked, "The records of these early days could lead one to believe that the chief duty of the teachers was, not to teach, but to prevent any communication between the sexes except when a teacher was present."[3] The building cost about $6,000, which was borrowed; and the charge for board, lodging, washing, fuel and light, which had been reduced from $90 to $80 a few years earlier, was raised back to $90, the extra money allocated to pay off the cost of the building and the interest incurred by the new mortgage. The building was completed and occupied on January 24, 1872, and the college could now accommodate 50 more boarders, for a total of 100.

By the end of the decade as student enrollments began to grow again, additional space for boarders (especially theological students) was needed, and the trustees rented some housing near the campus. They were not yet in a financial position to build another building.

FINANCES

The net indebtedness during this decade oscillated between $20,000 and $30,000, the latter figure caused by erection of the new building and occasional deficits in operating budgets caused by low enrollments in the middle of the decade. In January 1872, Treasurer Hering reported that the net indebtedness was $26,900.55, of which $9,300 was owed to John Smith for his original and subsequent loans, plus interest of $1,265.56. Fortunately, Smith was a patient man who believed fervently in the college and would not see it fail. In June of that year the debt was reduced slightly to $26,409; the total operating revenue for the year (receipts minus expenses) was $968.52. There was still serious concern over how to eliminate the debt. However, the college agent had been successful in selling a number of scholarships providing three years' free tuition for a $100 donation. (Even though this appeared to be a loss—a year's tuition was $60—the plan meant the money, which could be invested and earn interest, was in hand; and it ensured that the student would be enrolled for three years, when enrollments were otherwise unpredictable.) The trustees also resolved to advertise the college more extensively in the local newspapers.

In 1873 Mrs. Tamsey A. Reese of Talbot County gave $500 to the college to start an endowment fund. And in 1875 the Maryland Annual Conference voted almost unanimously to rescue the college from its debt by assessing all the churches in the conference proportionately, the money to be payable over five years. Unfortunately, by July 1876, the conference agent reported that although 2 churches had paid their five-year assessment, 12 had paid only their annual amount, many had not paid all of their annual amount, and 19 had paid nothing at all.[4] The Methodist Protestant Church had again stepped back from the brink of commitment to the college.

On July 6, 1871, Ward had noted in his diary, "To me it seems perfectly amazing that the churches, particularly of the MD. Conference, do not rally to *this* enterprize and establish it beyond a doubt. But if they intend to do so, they move very slowly." He often wrote such comments when he was frustrated with the "embarrassing" financial condition of the college and the lack of support from the Methodist Protestant Church. On August 5 of the same year, he remarked,

Thus far the college has had paying students enough to meet current expenses, but the debt with which we started is nearly the same and we have increased the amount by the permanent improvements . . . and still more by borrowing the money for the additional building. . . . I cannot be sanguine of ultimate success until I see a spirit of co-operative liberality [by men and women of means within the church]. . . . I am led to believe that one reason for the apparent apathy on the part of the Methodist Protestants is their want of confidence in the permanent continuance of the denomination, many having an idea that it must ere long be merged into some other. . . . If the MP Church will not sustain [the college], I should rejoice to see it sustained by some other evangelical denomination, although my connection with it might cease.

The Maryland Legislature provided some much needed support in April 1878 through what came to be called a Senatorial Scholarship program. The bill provided $2,600 a year for two years as free tuition for 26 students (one from each senatorial district in the state) and $5,200 a year for the room, board, and books for those students. The scholarships were awarded after a competitive examination, and the student pledged to teach for two years following graduation. The state had previously, in 1870 and again in 1874, awarded ten scholarships to Western Maryland College, but this program was much better for all concerned, as it provided for all of a student's expenses, and the college benefited because actual costs were always somewhat less than the financial stipend, resulting in a positive balance for the college budget.[5] Wills noted that it is doubtful whether the college could have survived without some form of state aid. "Certainly, to do so," he wrote, "it would have had to find more money than it ever got from those to whom it had a right to look for support. . . . Except for occasional appropriations devoted to special purposes, the college has returned to the State, in board and tuition of students, value received for every cent it has got from the State. . . . The public receives incalculably more than the cost to the taxpayers. Generally, a high grade of student gets a college education which he could not get without the scholarship, and therefore makes a better citizen."[6]

The minutes of the meetings of the board of trustees throughout the decade are filled with comments about trying to pay off the debt and with schemes for doing so. In obvious frustration at not seeing the debt diminish appreciably, Ward in 1876 even offered to step aside if the board felt it would be in the best interests of the institution. At one point, nine board members pledged $2,100 toward the debt, and a year later, in 1879, a major debt reduction plan was put into effect (including the denial of a request for faculty raises); pledges and notes were obtained in the amount of $25,000. But at the end of the decade, the debt was still $22,300.

FACULTY AND ADMINISTRATION

While the number of faculty remained fairly constant during this decade (usually seven or eight full-time and three part-time lecturers), its makeup continued to change yearly. Natural science professor and vice principal William Zimmerman left in 1871—along with his wife, the stewardess—to become vice president of Washington College. He was succeeded as vice principal by James K. Nichols [1870–75] and as science teacher by Robert L. Brockett [1870–82], a Harvard graduate. Other names that appear in the faculty listing are Thomas Gatch [mathematics, 1870–76], H. C. Cushing [belles lettres, 1875–80], and George W. Devilbiss '75 [belles lettres and mathematics, 1875–83]. In his remarks at the college's 50th anniversary celebration, Daniel Hering remembered Prof. Gatch as a bit of a martinet, as he was trained in a military school and brought some rather severe methods of discipline to his teaching and his year as vice president [1875–76] (before becoming president of Frederick College); however, those methods gave a form and stability to the administration of the college that perhaps were needed. William Ogg '74 was appointed principal of the Preparatory Department upon his graduation, but he died August 6, 1875, at the age of 28 (his death shocking the campus and causing the faculty to place in the minutes a special memorial page),[7] and was replaced by Devilbiss. Lottie Owings (1839–94) was appointed preceptress in 1873, held the position for a year, then returned in 1878 and remained until 1894.

A singular honor was conferred upon James Reese when the trustees voted in June 1873 to confer upon him the honorary degree of doctor of philosophy (a second honorary PhD was awarded in 1878 to Rev. George B. McElroy, DD, president of Adrian College). Immediately after receiving notification of his new degree, the Rev. Dr. Reese departed for an extended tour of Europe, returning in late September, when the Webster Society, a new literary society named for Daniel Webster, welcomed him back with a reception, during which he gave a brief narrative of his tour. On October 30 of that year, he gave the first lecture of the season, entitled "Homer's *Iliad*: Why So Generally Regarded as the Masterpiece of Ancient Literature." Ward commented on the speech in his diary for October 31: "I doubt whether there are many men living who could have said so much so well, in thirty minutes, on such a subject."[8]

Ward brought honor to himself and to the fledgling college when Adrian College (the Methodist Protestant Church's "other" college, in Michigan) awarded him the honorary degree of doctor of divinity in June 1871. In his diary entry for the day he received notification of the honor (June 27), in typical self-deprecating fashion, he "prayed God may enable me to make myself more worthy of the title they have given me than I am now." Showing some humor at now being addressed as Dr. Ward, he noted on July 2, "If I could not take this lesson from the incident, I should consider myself entitled to the D.D. only as meaning *Decidedly Dull*." In 1873 his administrative title was changed from principal to president, and Nichols was named vice president.[9]

As the school year 1871–72 was beginning, the 51-year-old Ward was beginning to wear down a bit. In his diary he noted, "Were it not that the good Lord favors me with excellent health, I could not endure the amount of labor and care required now in my position. I have not time to attempt a description of the varied duties, responsibilities and perplexities of these days, but God knows all and 'tis He that sustains me amid all, or I should sink." He went on to note that he had had to deal with a report from John Smith regarding a rumor running through town that there was too much "intercourse" allowed between students in the Male and Female departments. In October he reported having to deal with a recalcitrant male student, trying in vain to "persuade him . . . to renounce his foolish course of resistance to wholesome restraint." The student had responded with insolence but the next day had come to his office to apologize and to beg forgiveness and pardon for his insolent manner. After some discussion and promises from the young man to behave himself, Ward allowed him to remain at the college (at least until his father ordered him home), even though the faculty had voted for his immediate expulsion. In December he had to deal with public drunkenness of the grammar school tutor and college German teacher, as well as the fact that several students had visited taverns in town and been intoxicated. The Local Committee met at Mr. Smith's house and took action to remove the teacher immediately because of his "disgraceful conduct."[10] The following Monday morning found Ward teaching German in place of the discharged teacher and anxiously wondering where he could find a replacement German teacher who would also teach preparatory English. And on Tuesday he was investigating the case of several students who had been discovered playing cards and being boisterous the previous Saturday evening. He commented, "At no time since my connection with the college have I felt more anxiety about its internal affairs than I do now."[11]

Two other names deserve mention here, not because they were faculty

Young students T. H. Lewis (on the left)
and W. R. McDaniel

members or administrators, but because they would soon play significant roles in the history of the college. In 1871, Thomas Hamilton Lewis (1852–1929), a native of Dover, Delaware, who was raised in Easton, Maryland, enrolled in the college's theological course. He graduated four years later as valedictorian of the class of 1875 and became a highly respected Methodist Protestant clergyman, the founding president of the Westminster Theological Seminary in 1882, and the president of Western Maryland College in 1886. William Roberts McDaniel (1861–1942), a native of McDaniel, a village near St. Michaels, Maryland, and a graduate of the high school there, enrolled in the college as a sophomore in 1877 and was one of the first to receive a Maryland Senatorial Scholarship when they were created a year later. He would graduate as salutatorian of the class of 1880, briefly become a high school teacher, pursue graduate work in mathematics at the newly formed Johns Hopkins University (joining fellow graduate students Woodrow Wilson and John Dewey), and return to the Western Maryland campus as professor of mathematics in 1885. We will hear much more about these two gentlemen as the college's history unfolds.

On May 29, 1874, Ward expressed his ongoing concern for the well-being of the college, noting that the faculty commanded the respect and confidence of the public and the students and expressing his fear that this might not continue to be the case if teachers left for better-paying positions. The effects of the depression were being felt, and enrollments and collection of fees were in danger. The principal of the preparatory school resigned in June, saying that his resignation would allow the trustees to fill his place with someone who would serve for less salary. The trustees even considered asking Vice President–Professor Nichols to resign, as well, so they could fill his positions with someone at a smaller salary; he continued in both positions for about a year longer but resigned in April 1875 to return to the itinerant ministry. Ward was forced to reduce faculty salaries for the year 1876–77, the year of the worst enrollments, to meet the lowered tuition income. At the June 1876 meeting, the board of trustees approved the following yearly salaries:

President...*$1,000*
Professor of mathematics... *$400 and board*
Preceptress.. *$300 and board*
Music teacher .... *$250 and board*
Professor of ancient languages...*$900*
Professor of natural sciences and French *$1,150*

Not surprisingly, Ward encountered difficulty in persuading some of the faculty to remain at these lowered salaries; however, only one person left. Even these lowered salaries were not always paid on time. Ward wrote in his diary,

This afternoon, Prof. Brockett made known to me the distressing fact that he is entirely destitute of money. . . . Some time ago I loaned him $25, and if I could do so consistent with other obligations, I would gladly loan or give him all he needs. As it is, I can only pray for him as I do for myself in such straits.[12]

Schofield commented on Ward's generosity: "Every year some of the parents neglected to send money for students to return home at holiday time, and he always loaned them the necessary amount—loans that were not always repaid. Perhaps he was not a shrewd businessman, but he was something more rare and greatly-to-be-desired, a good and unselfish person."[13]

As the day-to-day operation of the institution became more complex, the trustees decided in 1876 to expand the Local Committee (which assisted the president in making many decisions) from three to seven. The members appointed in addition to Ward, Smith, and Hering were Isaac Baile [1868–93], Joshua Yingling, J. K. Longwell [1868–96], and E. O. Grimes.[14]

As noted, the faculty was kept very busy, beyond hearing the recitations of their students in numerous classes, with meetings at least weekly, usually on Thursday or Friday. The minutes of those meetings reveal that an extraordinary amount of time seems to have been spent on approving requests from students to leave the campus for various and sundry reasons. Most of the remainder of the time was spent dealing with disciplinary problems as reported by the faculty. The reasons for discipline fell into two categories:

(1) collegiate students running afoul of the various rules regarding curfews and contact with members of the opposite sex, and (2) preparatory student boarders playing pranks and engaging in mischief not unexpected from adolescents, mostly male and living away from home. Most of the former were dealt with within the demerit system, with admonitions handed out freely to abstain from further such behavior. Schofield commented, "Without attempting to explain it . . . one must say that from the beginning young ladies and young gentlemen did form romantic attachments, some of which led to long and happy marriages. Perhaps risking twenty demerits to see your true love could be taken as an assurance of sincerity."[15]

Many of the latter problems were cause for suspensions or meetings with parents. The pranks and other "unseemly behavior" included nailing down the lid of a desk, throwing coal ashes down the stairs, ringing the college bell during the night, trying to remove the transom above the door of a bedroom, and removing the clapper from the bell. Such activities were bound to occur in a situation where young men of diverse ages (ranging from about 14 to perhaps 25) were living together under constant, rather repressive, supervision; but rules had to be obeyed, and the faculty had to enforce them, given their charge and the lack of any assistance from persons especially assigned or trained to do so (as in any modern college's student affairs office). Each case demanded considerable discussion, sometimes several special meetings, and appropriate demerits. In several instances in 1874, a preparatory student, one Dennis Smith, son of John Smith, the board chairman, appeared before the faculty to explain his defiant and unrepentant behavior. Eventually, the faculty voted unanimously to suspend him from the college. The next day they reconsidered and reinstated him, after he agreed to sign a long statement acknowledging his wrongdoing and promising to behave better. A year later, things had deteriorated again, and John Smith asked and was allowed to attend a faculty meeting to hear the report of young Dennis's deportment.[16] Although enrolled in various parts of the college from 1867 to 1878, Dennis Smith, considered a member of the class of 1880, unfortunately did not graduate.

Other items, such as the programs for the literary society, also came under faculty review, and in March 1875, a petition from the Browning Literary Society to have a drama at its anniversary meeting in June "was not granted on the ground that the exercises of that occasion are intended to be of a more dignified character."[17] In another example of faculty business, the petition from a number of students for a holiday on February 22, Washington's birthday, led the faculty to decide that the proper way to celebrate the occasion was by having Washington's Farewell Address read by Thomas Hamilton Lewis, a respected member of the senior class.

CURRICULUM

The curricula for the college and the preparatory department (the grammar school now subsumed into this department as a "third class") were beginning to be codified; in the catalog for 1871–72, the courses of study were carefully spelled out. The preparatory program included grammar, geography, reading, penmanship, composition, world and United States history, Latin, elementary Greek, rhetoric, arithmetic and algebra, declamation, and map drawing. It was noted that "every act of disobedience to every established rule of the Institution will be demerited, and every unexcused absence from recitation, or failure to recite a lesson assigned, will be demerited." Certificates of distinction were to be awarded at the end of the year to those with the required averages in deportment and studies.

Each year of the four-year collegiate undergraduate program continued to have emphasis on belles lettres, mathematics, ancient and modern languages, and the physical sciences. Everything except French and German was required for the AB degree. Of particular note was the program outlined for women students. Without any official, published explanation for the distinction, the AB degree program in the Ladies Department was only three years, the freshman, junior, and senior years carefully outlined. Wills commented that when women "studied the same subject [as the men] the content was often 'watered down' to suit the supposed mental inferiority of the women."[18] For instance, in mathematics, while men were required to complete algebra, geometry, trigonometry, analytical geometry, and both differential and integral calculus, women were required to study only arithmetic, algebra, geometry, and trigonometry. In the ancient languages, women did not go as far as men and were not permitted to study Greek, but they did have to complete studies in French not required of men. The three-year degree program for women continued in effect until 1886.

From about 1870 on, a theological course was offered as a supplement to the regular degree programs, especially for those preparing for the ministry. Students pursued the studies of the regular course, but a period in each day was assigned to recitation to the president on such theological textbooks as had been prescribed. The program was under the immediate direction of Rev. Augustus Webster, DD, Ward's old mentor, and the books the students read were all drawn from the course of study outlined in the Constitution and Discipline of the M.P. Church. The number of theological students varied from 6 to 13 over the decade, and the individuals committed to the program seemed to be respected on campus. By 1880 there was a movement afoot in the conference to create a true school of theology within Western Maryland

College, and with the growth of the college, it became obvious that a separate building would be necessary. During the next decade, further plans would evolve to meet the needs of the conference in a different way.

Requirements for admission to the college were formally established in 1872 and required each student applying for admission to present himself or herself to the president, who would introduce the prospective student to various members of the faculty, each of whom would conduct an examination in his field. The teacher would indicate whether the examination was satisfactory and into what class the student was to enter. Following this placement procedure, the student would return to the president, settle his or her account, and receive a certificate of admission to each class for which qualifications had been met.

The term *recitation* perhaps needs some explanation. In the catalogs beginning about 1870 there is a discussion of what it meant—for example: "The method of recitation from day to day is adopted from the best colleges. The old plan of asking questions is done away, so far as practicable, the student being allowed to choose his own language in giving his views of the subject of study, no interruption being made by the professor except where the author is abstruse or difficult to be understood. In this way the student is trained into the important habit of thinking for himself and relying on his own effort."[19] Apparently, students were assigned reading material, and then they recited each day on its meaning, giving as close to a direct regurgitation of the text as possible. They even found ways of reading the text back to the teacher without being detected.[20] It also seems apparent that the professor did not lecture on the material or give opinions, only correcting the student's "interpretation" and regurgitation of the material as necessary. Wills noted that even science laboratories followed this pattern. A sentence in the catalog of the period describing the course in chemistry stated, "The pupil is allowed to perform experiments under the direction of the teacher. . . . Each pupil tries for himself the experiments which have previously been performed by the instructor, then furnishes a written analysis of the experiment and the deduction from it."[21]

Accompanying the regular classes and recitations, a series of lectures was given during the school year by the faculty; for 1878–79, they included the following:

Mental and Moral Philosophy, President Ward
Rhetoric and English Literature, Vice President Cushing
Astronomy, Chemistry, and Natural Philosophy, Professor Brockett
Philology, Classical Literature, and Antiquities, Professor Reese
Mathematics, Professor Devilbiss
Elocution, Professor Wright

Anatomy, Physiology, and Hygiene, Doctor Hering
Civil Law and Political Economy, R. B. Norment, Esq.

Also included in these early catalogs was a clear delineation of grading, merits, and awards. A grade between 1 and 10 was awarded, both in deportment and in recitation, each day. As in the Preparatory Department, disobedience to rules and absences were demerited according to the faculty regulations; "minor marks for imperfect recitations in part [were] indicated by tenths or hundredths of a unit, according to the judgment of the teacher concerned." Medals were awarded at the end of the year to the students with the highest averages, gold medals going to the man and woman who showed the best record in deportment, and silver medals for excellence in belles lettres, natural sciences, mathematics, languages, and music.[22] Behavior (especially as it related to contact with the opposite sex) seemed to be the primary concern in these early years.

When the college first opened and for a number of years thereafter, the faculty and administration did not see the need for a library in the work of the student, since the student's job was to learn the contents of the textbooks. After doing that, the student might go to a library for cultural or recreational reading. From the earliest days of the college, the only library available to the students was Ward's personal library, which included works on a great variety of subjects, from moral tracts to first editions of major novels. Ward had from his youth been a book collector and avid reader, and he had now carefully cataloged the books for easy reference. He and the students could find periodical material and works within anthologies by using his index of the library, organized by author, title, and subject. However, he concluded early on that he would not allow his books to be taken from his home by students, since many had been damaged or not returned at all. He made them available only in the college book room, where students could use them for reference.[23] In 1873, he noted that there were about 3,500 books (mostly his, but also those purchased for the college by the literary societies and friends) to which students had access. In 1874, the faculty adopted a resolution: "Whereas a well-selected and arranged library is indispensable to a literary institution. Therefore resolved: that measures be at once taken to secure such a collection of books for West. Md. College."[24] In June of that year, it was reported by the librarian, Edwin M. Wilmer (also the preparatory school principal that year), that letters had been sent to all of the ministers in the Methodist Conference, as well as to other friends of the college, requesting donation of books for the library, but the appeal had brought only two donations. He wrote in his report, "It has been a matter of no little surprise and indeed regret . . . that the results of a direct, personal appeal . . . to said body should have been so meagre, especially when it is considered how very little has been done by them as a body for the college and that the institution is acknowledged to be vital to the interests of the denomination and is the only school of higher learning within [its] jurisdiction."[25] Beginning in 1876, Ward, using his own funds, began purchasing the volumes of the ninth edition of the *Encyclopedia Britannica* for the college library. By 1878 the library contained about 4,000 volumes.[26]

At the 1874 Commencement, the college conferred its first master of arts degrees, referred to as "in course," although the students had taken no courses. Rather, the degrees were conferred a minimum of three years after receipt of the bachelor's degree, on those alumni applicants who had entered one of the learned professions (ministry, law, or medicine); become teachers or writers ("literati"); or submitted a thesis on a literary, philosophical, or scientific subject. A diploma would be issued upon payment of a fee of $10.[27] The faculty chose the topic for the thesis each year. For example, in 1877 men wrote on the topic "The English Revolution of 1688, Its Causes and Results," while women wrote on "A Critique on the Poems of Mrs. Browning." Curiously, no mention of this degree option is made in the catalogs of the college until 1883, and no list of recipients is printed anywhere (except in the minutes of the board of trustees when the degrees were approved each year) until the late 1890s, although current recipients of the bachelor's degree were listed in the catalog each year after 1871 and in summary lists of all graduates.

STUDENT LIFE

Upon the occasion of his 30th anniversary as a faculty member, William Roberts McDaniel would be remembered fondly by numerous people, including his former roommate Lewis A. Jarman, who would describe his old friend "Mac" as one of only four boys in the class of 1880 who lived in the college:

I have known him upon the classroom bench, . . . at the frugal board of the college inn, as a room-mate up in old No. 6, where on wooden slats and "hard and more" we slept, and grew wise under the rays of a coal oil lamp mellowed by a paper shade, and together roasted . . . [by the] hard coal stove; and where through the upper sash of the only window we beheld the grand panorama of the Blue Ridge, a joy to us unto this day; I was glad with him in his first love and wept with him in his first disappointment; have heard him orate under the cooling shades of the . . . chestnut tree, and declare "There shall be no Alps."[28]

Even under these rather primitive conditions, certainly more severe than those experienced in their homes, students seemed to thrive. McDaniel wrote home his impressions of Westminster and College Hill in the most glowing of terms, anticipating Jarman's thoughts:

> *He who has never surveyed the spectacle from our college windows, has yet to behold one of the most gorgeous landscapes the eye ever fell upon. . . . Seated at my own lofty window, which looks toward the long dark ranges of the Blue Ridge and Catoctin mountains towering in imposing grandeur . . . until receding from view they are seen no more, how often have I watched the sunset's pencil trace a fairy picture, as the majestic orb of day neared the horizon and touched the peaks with myriads of shimmering sunbeams, producing a scene of enchanting magnificence.*[29]

Perhaps the words are too flowery for 21st-century tastes, but they indicate the depth of emotion he and other students felt for the hill and its surrounding countryside.

In this decade, the need for another literary society resulted in the Webster Society for men being formed in 1871, joining the Irving (which had been quickly resuscitated) and the Browning societies. It was expected that each student would be a member of one of the societies, which held weekly meetings, sponsored speakers, debated topics of interest, and generally provided for social interaction outside the classroom.

Of course, there was still a strict ban on interaction between the sexes. Even the rather reasonable request from the Irving and Browning societies to have joint public entertainments every six weeks was denied by the faculty.[30] The catalogs of the era refer to the college's "Peculiar Feature" of providing "co-education of the sexes *in distinct departments.*" Parents could send their sons and daughters to the same institution, and while they would have the same instructors, their departments were kept entirely separate. The parents were further encouraged by the statement that "the Vice Principal, Preceptress and other members of the Faculty reside in the building, eat at the same table with the Students, and have a constant oversight of them."[31] By 1874–75, this "feature" was being touted as the "Peculiar Advantage" to parents, a term used as late as 1887. Wills noted that those brothers and sisters who were sent together were so hemmed in by the rules that it was rarely possible for them even to chat with one another except in the presence of a teacher.[32]

Among the various artifacts in the college archives are a number of volumes containing class histories and prophecies that were read during Commencement Week during a tree planting ceremony. Laboriously handwritten in "copper plate" script are numerous references to "affairs of the heart," which prove that regardless of all the rules prohibiting commingling of the sexes, the young people of that era fell in and out of love (or at least infatuation) just like any normal adolescents. The references are sometimes obscure inside jokes, but many are somewhat clever puns. For instance, in the first Class History, written in 1872, the beaux of Miss Clara Smith (daughter of the board chairman) were reported to be "Clara-fied." Several gentlemen in the class of 1874 were "Mollie-fied," an obvious reference to Miss Mollie Jones. But the best (worst?) series of puns is related to a young lady who apparently was interested in a young man named Moore. The entry is this: "This young lady is very much like the little boy who ate his cake and hadn't enough, for she always wanted Moore. She wanted more (Moore) at the table; she wanted more (Moore) in the parlor; and indeed the historian thinks that she must get enough of Moore, or she will surely have Moore for life. . . . And now the historian had better say 'No Moore.'"[33] John D. Makosky, in *Western Maryland College in the Nineteenth Century*, pointed out that further proof of these "covert" activities of the heart is that in the first ten years of its existence as a college, 44 women were graduated, and 34 were married, many to former college classmates.[34]

In November of 1871, it was agreed by the faculty to allow "reunion of the departments" in the parlor on the last Saturday night of every month. This was the creation of an event that would be called Parlor Night and become a treasured tradition in student life. The faculty did not consider this a "stated exercise" of the college, so students were not compelled to attend, but of course, most did, this being the one opportunity to meet and talk "legally" with a member of the opposite sex, under careful faculty supervision, of course. Parlor Night was held in the principal's parlor, where the female students would sit quietly (expectantly?) in chairs arranged in a circle and the young men would rotate behind the chairs, pausing for conversation, which, at least at the beginning, was limited to two minutes before a teacher-chaperone intervened.[35] After two years it became necessary for the faculty to amend the rules to remind students that the parlor was open only for this specific conversational opportunity (since dancing and card playing were at all times forbidden), and that "linking of arms, shaking hands, and promenading are forbidden."[36] Eventually, the still well-supervised students were allowed to mingle freely, talking in pairs or groups; couples were allowed to sit together but only for short periods of time.[37] In 1876 a suggested change in the monthly reunions was considered, to transform the event into a "reading circle" that would be beneficial and enjoyable. The faculty considered that the change would not only add to the interest in the event but also meet with the approval of students of both sexes. It was soon ascertained, however, that the unanimous sentiment of the male boarding students regarding the change was negative and that they would not participate, so the faculty, surprisingly but wisely, rescinded it.

Some examples from the faculty minutes suggest the degree of control the faculty had over the students' daily lives. On October 26, 1871, a request from Miss Price and Miss Simmons to visit Miss Yingling and "remain until Sunday was, on motion of Prof. Brockett granted so far as to allow them to make the visit and return by 10 o'clock, provided a teacher accompanies them."[38] It was decided that no excuse from any student would be accepted in which the spelling was incorrect.[39] The faculty granted a request from Thomas Hamilton Lewis (a freshman at the time) and Joseph Weigand (also a freshman) for one of the rooms in the new building (the addition to the Main Building, which had just opened), since they promised to furnish it themselves.[40] The minutes of June 5, 1873, include a petition from two students asking permission to burn their lights until 11 P.M. (an hour later than usual) during examination week in order to prepare for the examinations. The faculty approved the request and directed that all students wishing to do so should give their names to the vice principal. Faculty even had to approve petitions from students to miss classes due to illness. (One wonders what would have happened had they done otherwise.) Later in 1872, the faculty decided in its wisdom that 150 demerits for expulsion should be reduced to 100 (perhaps for easier bookkeeping), and that the list of demerits for other offenses be proportionately reduced.

Further regulations continued to be passed to constrict student activity, however:[41]

- At least three minutes were required between the starting of the Male and Female departments going to and from church on Sunday.
- Students were prohibited from going to their dormitory during study hours except for extreme necessity.
- No young men were permitted to play croquet with the young ladies of the institution. (There was even a "no-man's-land" between the men's campus and the women's campus, over which neither sex was allowed to pass.)
- Students were to be seated in the dining room and in the chapel by classes and in alphabetical order.
- Students were forbidden from depositing ashes from coal fires in wooden boxes.
- Taking of rides on Sunday for "mere purposes of pleasure" was forbidden.

Students apparently found ways to get around the regulations, to get into trouble, and especially to obtain intoxicating spirits, despite the many rules against such activity. The faculty called two special meetings to deal with an incident that occurred in the gentlemen's sitting room on Saturday, February 10, 1872. It was reported that two young men (one a college freshman, the other a preparatory student) were "beastly intoxicated" and "used language obscene, vulgar and blasphemous; offensive and insulting to the ladies in the adjoining room." It was further reported that one of the young men had pawned his clothes to buy drink. The culprits were called in one by one and examined at length. They eventually admitted being intoxicated, and, ultimately, one had his demerits increased to 100, while the other (who happened to be President Ward's nephew) was suspended for a term. The faculty went further, sending a letter to the president of the board of trustees, notifying him of the fact that the barkeeper in the Montour House had sold liquor to the young men in question and requesting action to prevent any future transactions.[42]

The year 1872 saw the formation of an alumni association. At the time, there were 13 degree recipients from two classes, although many other former students (referred to as *quondam*) were also considered alumni. The first officers of the association were William P. Wright '71, president; Mary M. Ward '71, secretary; and Anna R. Yingling '71, treasurer. An annual membership fee of $2 was assessed, but by 1879 so few alumni had paid it, it was reduced to $1 and then eventually eliminated. The association held a reunion, which included a business meeting and a banquet, each year during Commencement Week. For the first few years, an orator was selected to speak at the dinner; after 1878, the college president made an address.

One distinguished alumna of this era deserves mention, simply because she defied the norm. Sarah L. Whiteside, class of 1874, from Cassville, Pennsylvania, went on to receive her MD degree and became a physician in Portland, Oregon. She was the first of the college's women graduates to become a medical doctor and among the first three doctors of medicine the college prepared, in the first five classes.

Major Events

As mentioned earlier, commencement exercises were held beginning in June 1868, with prizes and other awards handed out each year, but there was no graduating class until 1871, when a more elaborate ceremony was planned by the faculty. A week of activities included literary society meetings and reunions, formal distribution of certificates of distinction to students in all classes, and a board of trustees meeting. Principal Ward gave the baccalaureate sermon

First graduating class (1871);
Mary Ward (Lewis) is on the left.

and on June 15 conferred the degrees at the well-attended Commencement, addressing the class in Latin. Diplomas, hand calligraphed in Baltimore, written in Latin, embossed with the great seal of the college, and bearing the signatures of all the members of the faculty, were awarded to three women (Imogene L. Mitten, Anna R. Yingling, and Mary M. Ward) and four men (Charles H. Baughman, William S. Crouse, Thomas O. Crouse, and Henry E. Norris). An evening reception followed the ceremony. The next week Ward attended the graduation exercises of the Frederick Female College (renamed Hood College in 1913) and noted that they were "far less creditable than those at Western Maryland College." Then on June 29, he represented the college at the Commencement of Pennsylvania College (renamed Gettysburg College in 1921), where he stated that he "gained much knowledge of college affairs."[43]

Beginning with Commencement Week of 1872, the Irving and Webster societies began to hold oratorical contests. Four speakers represented each society, and the orations were judged. As the college grew and an additional society for women was established, heated contests were held between the men's and women's groups, vying for trophies.

An event of a different sort, but equally momentous for the time, was a visit to the Westminster Agricultural Fair on October 1, 1873, by President Ulysses S. Grant. Classes at the college were suspended at eleven o'clock so students and professors could visit the fair and shake hands with the president. Later in the afternoon, Grant toured the town and briefly visited the college, where he was given a tour (presumably by Ward) and praised the magnificent view from College Hill and the beauty of Carroll County.[44]

For the Commencement of 1875, in which Thomas Hamilton Lewis graduated as valedictorian for the class of one woman and two men, something special was added. A large pavilion, paid for by voluntary contributions, was erected for the exercises (in the flat area near Main Street, where the President's House and McDaniel House now stand). It was reported that over 600 people sat inside and at least 200 outside.[45] Ward reported in his diary (June 16, 1875) that on the evening prior to the Commencement, the members of the M.P. Church choir and other friends gathered to honor T. H. Lewis on his graduation and to present him with a $100 gold watch as an expression of thanks for being the choir leader during his college days. Various people gave tributes to the young man, including his future father-in-law.[46] (Lewis married Mary Ward '71, Dr. Ward's only daughter, on his 25th birthday, December 11, 1877.) In those early days, there were two valedictorians (male and female) and two salutatorians (male and female). All gave short orations, the men in Latin and the women in French. Wills noted that "though the occasion was serious and so regarded, it had its humorous side—an audience of a thousand or more listening with apparently close attention to a young man and young woman talk each for five or more minutes in a language that few in the audience could understand."[47]

Even though students were not in residence at the time, the college participated in the grand celebration of the United States Centennial in July 1876. The following diary entries by Ward suggest the extent of the activity:

> *June 30, 1876: Afternoon in town sympathizing with the spirit of patriotism as the glorious Hundredth Anniversary of American Liberty approaches; bought flags for the decoration of college building and my residence, and stands and candles for the illumination on the evening of July 4.*

> *July 3, 1876: At the college until near midnight assisting in the making of a flag to float from the cupola of the college. I had ordered one from Baltimore, but learned this afternoon that it was impossible to obtain a flag in that city, by purchase or even by loan.*

> *July 4, 1876: The 100th Anniversary of American Independence grandly celebrated in Westminster by the firing of cannons and ringing of bells*

at sunrise, noon, sunset and midnight. . . . In the evening, the principal buildings, public and private of the city were brilliantly illuminated, Western Maryland College making among the most beautiful shows of any. The people of Carroll County turned out in such numbers that Westminster is supposed to have contained more persons during the day than ever on any day before. The order was almost perfect.

July 6, 1876*: The brilliant illumination of the college was at my own private expense, as was also the purchase of the material for the national flag. . . . I cut the stars with my own hand. . . . The celebration at Philadelphia was, of course, the grand celebration of the day, but I doubt whether that of Westminster was surpassed by any other place for appropriateness, enthusiasm and good order.*

At the 1879 Commencement, Hugh L. Elderdice '82 (1860–1938), who would become president of the Westminster Theological Seminary in 1897, and William McDaniel '80 were two of the three orators for the Webster Society. In 1880, McDaniel graduated as salutatorian in a class of four women and six men, and the Class Prophecy suggested that he would later become the college's president. One of his classmates was Joseph W. Smith, son of board chair John Smith, who would host the wedding of his youngest sister, Ada, to McDaniel in 1895. Joseph Smith would also become a joint partner in Smith and Reifsnider, prominent Westminster lumber dealer, in 1897.

CONCLUSION

The decade from 1871 to 1880 saw the college struggle to maintain enrollments through an economic depression and continue to struggle with a debt that was whittled down slightly but still impeded the college's expansion and viability. The college also continued to struggle with its relationship with the Methodist Protestant Church, as well as with its identity as it tinkered with its curriculum while adapting to a constantly changing and poorly paid faculty held together by a few stalwarts under the steady leadership of J. T. Ward. In spite of many repressive rules of conduct enforced with almost Draconian efficiency, students continued to enroll, some to complete their studies and graduate with AB degrees (there were 81 graduates between 1871 and 1880), and all to go forth into the world to spread the glad tidings of the wonderful college on the hill.

CHAPTER 2 ENDNOTES

1. Wells, *Recent Economic Changes*, 6.
2. WMC board of trustees minutes, 1871.
3. Wills, *History of Western Maryland College*, vol. 1, 43.
4. Schofield and Crain, *Formative Years*, 18.
5. Ibid., 22; Wills, *History of Western Maryland College*, vol. 1, 45.
6. Wills, *History of Western Maryland College*, vol. 1, 45.
7. WMC faculty minutes, September 30, 1875.
8. Ward, Diaries, October 31, 1873.
9. WMC board of trustees minutes, June 18, 1873.
10. Ward, Diaries, September 6, 1871, October 16–17, 1871,
11. Ibid., December 5, 1871.
12. Ibid., October 31, 1876.
13. Schofield and Crain, *Formative Years*, 21–22.
14. WMC board of trustees minutes, June 14, 1876.
15. Schofield and Crain, *Formative Years*, 13.
16. WMC faculty minutes, December 9, 10, 1874, November 24, 1875.
17. Ibid., March 18, 1875.
18. Wills, *History of Western Maryland College*, vol. 2, 28.
19. *WMC Catalogue*, 1869–70, 13.
20. Wills, *History of Western Maryland College*, vol. 2, 31.
21. Ibid.
22. *WMC Catalogue*, 1870–71, 19.
23. Ward, Diaries, September 6, 1873.
24. WMC faculty minutes, March 26, 1874.
25. Ibid., June 11, 1874.
26. Wills, *History of Western Maryland College*, vol. 2, 40.
27. WMC faculty minutes, October 16, 1873.
28. Anniversary program, 1915, college archives.
29. W. R. McDaniel, essay in *St. Michaels Comet*, St. Michaels, Maryland, 1878. McDaniel Papers, college archives.
30. WMC faculty minutes, October 16, 1873.
31. *WMC Catalogue*, 1872–73, 18.
32. Wills, *History of Western Maryland College*, vol. 2, 8.
33. WMC Class Histories, 1872, 1874, college archives.
34. Makosky, *Western Maryland College*, 22.
35. Ibid., 20.
36. WMC faculty minutes, April 10, 1874.
37. Wills, *History of Western Maryland College*, vol. 2, 70.
38. WMC faculty minutes, October 26, 1871.
39. Ibid., November 16, 1871.
40. Ibid., January 18, 1872.
41. Ibid., February 11, 1870; October 27, 1870; May 2, 1872; September 12, 1872; January 9, 1873; February 26, 1874.
42. Ibid., February 17–19, 1872.
43. Ward, Diaries, June 21, 29, 30, 1871.
44. Ibid., October 1, 1873.
45. Schofield and Crain, *Formative Years*, 14.
46. Ward, Diaries, June 16, 1875.
47. Wills, *History of Western Maryland College*, vol. 2, 54.

MAJOR WORLD EVENTS

1871

British Act of Parliament legalizes labor unions.

George Eliot publishes *Middlemarch*.

Charles Darwin publishes *The Descent of Man*.

P. T. Barnum opens his circus, *The Greatest Show on Earth*.

Chicago is devastated by the Great Fire.

1872

Grant is reelected U.S. president.

Jules Verne publishes *Around the World in Eighty Days*.

Whistler paints *The Artist's Mother*.

Brooklyn Bridge is opened.

1873

A republic is proclaimed in Spain after civil war.

Tolstoi publishes *Anna Karenina*.

Herbert Spencer publishes *The Study of Sociology*.

Color photographs are first developed.

1874

Disraeli becomes Britain's prime minister.

Winston Churchill is born.

First impressionist exhibition is held in Paris.

Monet paints *Impression: Sunrise*.

Brahms composes *Hungarian Dances*.

First zoo in U.S. opens in Philadelphia.

1875

Mark Twain publishes *The Adventures of Tom Sawyer*.

Mary Baker Eddy publishes *Science and Health*.

Bizet's opera *Carmen* is performed in Paris.

Gilbert and Sullivan produce first operetta, *Trial by Jury*.

1876
Colorado becomes a U.S. state.
New Ottoman constitution is proclaimed.
Brahms composes Symphony no. 1.
Alexander Graham Bell invents the telephone.
Johns Hopkins University opens in Baltimore.
U.S. National Baseball League is founded.
United States celebrates its Centennial.
A World Exhibition is held in Philadelphia.

1877
Rutherford B. Hayes is inaugurated 19th U.S. president.
Queen Victoria is proclaimed empress of India.
Saint-Saens's opera *Samson and Delila* is performed in Weimar.
Henry James publishes *The American.*
First public telephones are available in the U.S.
Suffrage movement begins.
Edison invents the phonograph.

1878
Thomas Hardy publishes *The Return of the Native.*
Gilbert and Sullivan produce *H.M.S. Pinafore.*
Electric street lighting is introduced in London.
World Exhibition is held in Paris.

1879
French Panama Canal company is formed.
Joseph Stalin is born.
Henrik Ibsen publishes *A Doll's House.*
Henry James publishes *Daisy Miller.*
Herbert Spencer publishes *Principles of Ethics.*

1880
Cologne Cathedral (begun in 1248) is completed.
Dostoevsky publishes *The Brothers Karamazov.*
Lew Wallace publishes *Ben Hur.*
Gilbert and Sullivan produce *The Pirates of Penzance.*
Edison and Swan independently devise the first practical electric lights.
Andrew Carnegie develops the first large steel furnace.
Canned fruits and meats first appear in stores.
The game of Bingo is developed.
Rodin sculpts *The Thinker.*

Yingling Gymnasium I (1889), a gift of Anna Yingling '71

C H A P T E R

THE COLLEGE GROWS

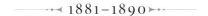

-‹ 1881–1890 ›-

Following the Civil War there developed in America a breed of businessmen who later became known as "robber barons" because of their financial double dealing and stock manipulation, which bilked naive investors and plundered companies. Other businessmen of the 1880s were not as greedy but still fiercely competitive. Individuals like James P. Morgan, Andrew Carnegie, John D. Rockefeller, and Henry Flagler managed the nation's resources; lowered the cost of oil, steel, and other goods, as well as transportation, for America's consumers; and created the modern corporation. While free enterprise had been an American gospel, an increasingly urbanized, industrialized economy began to encourage governmental attempts to regulate its unrestrained practices. Labor unions and federations were on the rise. The decade of the 1880s was also a time of some marvelous inventions, including hydroelectric power and electricity, as well as advances in medicine. In the arts, Gilbert and Sullivan were producing new operettas each year in London, to delighted audiences, and in 1882 Tchaikovsky composed his *1812 Overture*.

At the beginning of this decade, the college was 14 years old, had successfully graduated ten classes composed of 36 men (of 151 enrollees) and 45 women (of 152 enrollees), and was experiencing fairly stable enrollments again (after the precipitous drop in the mid-1870s). Because of the new mortgage to build the addition on the Main Building and several years of operating deficits caused by the enrollment declines, the outstanding debt, while it had fluctuated during the previous decade, was about the same as it had been ten years before. This continued to give President Ward and the trustees considerable cause for concern. But this decade saw some drastic changes in the institution and in the handling of the debt.

Enrollments ranged from a low of 110 (in 1883–84) to a high of 242 (in 1890–91), with consistent yearly increases from 1885 onward. The Preparatory Department still accounted for about 40% of the enrollment, but in both departments significant increases meant more income, which kept the operating budgets more stable. The college was becoming more well known and established as an institution, and its future seemed far less problematic.

FACULTY AND ADMINISTRATION

Several significant changes in the faculty, and especially the administration, during this decade contributed to the college's growth in enrollment, stature, and stability. The first of several important faculty additions occurred when Daniel Hering, the young student-teacher on the first faculty, returned to teach mathematics in January 1880. By this time he had graduated from the Sheffield Scientific School at Yale (where he went after two years at Western Maryland) and had spent two years at Johns Hopkins University in graduate study. The second important faculty hire was that of William McDaniel [1885–1942], class of 1880, who returned in 1881 as a tutor of Greek, Latin, and mathematics both in the preparatory school and in the college. He had spent the year 1880–81 as a teacher in Buckeystown, Maryland, fulfilling his Senatorial Scholarship obligation. He held the tutorial post for two years, after which he decided to enroll at Johns Hopkins University for graduate study in mathematics leading to a PhD. For almost two years he studied with one of the great mathematicians of the world, James Joseph Sylvester, and was well on his way to the doctorate.

Meanwhile, at Western Maryland, Prof. William J. Thomas had been hired in the fall of 1884 to teach mathematics when Daniel Hering resigned to become chair of the mathematics department at Western Union University of Pennsylvania (now the University of Pittsburgh) at more than double his $800 WMC salary. (Hering went from Pittsburgh to the chair of the Physics Department of the University of the City of New York [now New York University] in 1886.) But Thomas fell ill of typhoid in mid-February of

1885, and a week later Ward sent word to McDaniel, asking him to fill in for the ailing teacher until the end of the term. In his letter Ward noted, "[Prof. Thomas] could send no substitute who would be more acceptable to us than yourself, and I trust you will come just as soon as you can arrange to do so." McDaniel readily agreed, temporarily abandoning his studies, and arrived February 28 to take over Thomas's classes. On March 9, Thomas died, and McDaniel was formally named professor of mathematics, a post he would hold (both actively and titularly) until his death in 1942. Almost immediately, he began to make his mark on the campus; in September 1885, he was elected secretary of the faculty, a post he would hold until 1906, when he was named vice president of the college.

The year 1882 also saw the return to the campus of T. H. Lewis (1852–1929), class of 1875, who had been elected by the Maryland Annual Conference to be principal of the theological school being formed within the college. After completing his baccalaureate studies and formal ordination in the Methodist Protestant Church, Lewis had embarked upon his chosen ministerial career, taking a pastorate in Cumberland for two years. In 1877 he was called to a more conspicuous position as assistant to the venerable Dr. Augustus Webster at St. John's Independent Church in Baltimore. (Besides being J. T. Ward's early mentor, Webster had been professor of theology at the college, had laid out the course of study for the theologues, and was a driving force in the Maryland Annual Conference.) After Webster's retirement from his post, Lewis soon was in the leadership position. When he withdrew from St. John's in 1882, it was only because he saw a new and challenging outlet for his talents. He saw the need for special training for ministers, beyond the "theological course" he himself had pursued as a college student, and quickly set forth to create a true seminary. Along with his wife, Mary Ward, and their daughter, Miriam, he moved in with the Wards on Pennsylvania Avenue in August and began work on a larger scheme than originally envisioned by the conference.

Still another familiar face returned to the campus in 1882 when William Zimmerman [1867–71, 1882–83], the former vice principal and science professor, was successfully lured back by Ward to teach science when Prof. Robert Brockett resigned after 13 years on the faculty in a variety of roles. Zimmerman came from Chestertown, where he had been vice principal at Washington College for 12 years, and was hired at the unusually high salary of $1,100. He possessed some scientific equipment, which he brought with him to build a strong science program. He gave public lectures involving various scientific experiments and quickly enthralled the students with his enthusiasm. During the ensuing year, however, rumors began to circulate that he was expounding ideas at variance with the Bible (presumably concepts related to evolution, a relatively new theory propounded by Darwin not many years before). Summaries of the lectures were published in the *Irving Literary Gazette* for May 1883, including the comment, "Scientifical investigation can not but make a very forcible impression upon an attentively searching mind. . . . Every important movement of the day, practically scientifical principles in some way effect."[1] A three-member committee of the board of trustees was appointed to interview the professor, to "ascertain whether there is any foundation for reports that had reached the board as to his teachings tending toward skepticism."[2] As a result of their interview and Zimmerman's answers, especially to the question, "Do you believe in the divine inspiration and authority of the Sacred Scriptures?" they became convinced that the rumors were true and reported this to the board at a special meeting on July 13. Ward supported Zimmerman and felt that he should be retained but did not press the matter with the trustees.[3] Since there was no such thing as tenure at this time, the board simply chose not to reelect Zimmerman to his post and instead elected, from among 40 candidates, Rev. Shadrack Simpson as professor of natural sciences and French. Ward noted in his diary,

> *Meeting of the Board of Trustees in the M.P. Book Room. All applicants for Teacher positions were fairly presented, Professor Zimmerman among the rest. I bore my testimony emphatically to his Christian character and faithfulness. The Committee who had visited him in June could not agree with me that he was "sound in all essential points of Christian doctrine." I regret that he could not satisfy them as he did me, but I presume I differ with the Committee as to what points are essential. If Professor Zimmerman is not sound on the points upon which salvation depends, he has certainly deceived me. That he has peculiar views on other points and views that I could not endorse, is true; and some of these points are important, but not as I think essential.*[4]

As one might expect, some of the students were outraged that their favorite professor had not been rehired. Indeed, members of the freshman class gave Zimmerman two pieces of scientific equipment costing $30, instead of presenting them to the college as originally intended. By the end of the month, articles appeared in the local newspapers suggesting that the college was "pursuing a ruinous policy" in not reelecting Zimmerman. "It remains to be seen whether this policy will be for the good of the college," one said. Ward wondered the same thing.[5] Students writing in the *Irving Literary Gazette* upon their return to college noted, "We are glad that Prof. Zimmerman is still occupying his residence near the campus grounds. . . . Although he remained with us but one year, he made many lasting friends, who sincerely regret his absense [sic]."[6] The former professor, who lived just off the campus (about where the Fine Art Building now stands), quickly opened his own school in his home, presumably in retaliation for not being reelected, a move that Ward worried would draw local students away from the college. By October the situation had only grown worse. Ward described it in his diary:

Almost every day since Prof. Zimmerman opened his school near the College has developed some circumstance going to show antagonism on the part of the Prof. and his students toward the College. I have carefully avoided and advised all at the College to avoid everything that would tend to encourage resistance, hoping that Prof. Z. would himself take measures to keep his students in their proper place. Instead of this however, they are evidently not prevented by him from trespassing on the College premises and endeavoring to annoy and raise disturbance; and such of the College students as he knew last year and has influence over are encouraged and to all appearances invited and enticed by him to be at his house when they should be attending to their studies at the College. I did not think Prof. Z. could be guilty of such conduct, but so it is. He certainly ought to know that it is wrong, and must ultimately result in harm to himself. If I had even suspected that he was capable of such conduct, I should never have taken the part I did in inducing him to come to Westminster, nor have differed as I did from the Trustees of our College when they took the position that he was not such a man as we could rely upon. His course, since his non-election by the Trustees, is certainly calculated to prove that they knew him better than I did.[7]

Problems continued throughout the year, and Ward often noted the spiteful way Zimmerman was treating the college. However, Zimmerman apparently closed down his school at the end of the academic year and moved to Baltimore. In fact, Ward noted in his diary of October 18, 1884, that he had met with Zimmerman in Baltimore and had some friendly conversation with him, agreeing to forget the past unpleasant occurrences and to "let bygones be bygones." In 1888, the *WMC Monthly* reported that Prof. Zimmerman, "well known to many old students," had been elected to a professorship in physics and modern languages in the Maryland Agriculture College (later the undergraduate college of the University of Maryland),[8] a post he held until 1899. He died in Baltimore in 1921.

The turmoil and subsequent bad publicity brought on by the Zimmerman incident caused the trustees to reexamine their position, and they passed several clarifying resolutions, one of which was passed a month before Zimmerman's actual dismissal:

The Western Maryland College is distinctly a Christian College. By this declaration it is not affirmed or intended to be understood that the Western Maryland College is a sectarian institution. It aims to deal fairly with all, and respects the convictions of those who are not in doctrinal accord with its authorities. It receives students without imposing any religious test or qualification, and admits them without distinction of religious belief to all the privileges and honors of the school. Its professors and tutors have been chosen in the past, and will be chosen in the future, on account of their fitness for their respective departments, and not on account of their ecclesiastical preferences. No coercion or improper influences of any kind has ever been practiced or contemplated. They are to worship wherever their convenience or sense of duty may seem to require. . . . But while this liberty is freely accorded to teachers and students, it is required that nothing be taught in the college derogatory to the claims of the Christian religion, or that tends by declaration or innuendo to question the inspiration and authority of the Holy Scriptures. . . . The professors and tutors of this institution, therefore, are expected to teach what legitimately belongs to their respective departments, and not to go outside of their duties to distract the minds of their Pupils.[9]

Shadrack Simpson, AM (1849–1912) [1883–1900] was born in Rockingham, North Carolina, graduated from high school, and attended Trinity College (now Duke University).[10] He was one whose "claim to fame was his ability to get positions and qualify himself for them afterwards."[11] He was elected to the presidency of Yadkin College in North Carolina (another of the Methodist Protestant colleges, a coeducational junior college) before he had even graduated from Trinity, which he did in 1873. He served in that role for 11 years before taking the position at Western Maryland. Ward reported, "[He is] unpretentious as to his abilities to fill the position, but says, 'I will do the best I can to render faithful service.'"[12] Simpson's hesitancy to comment on his qualifications may have been due to the fact that he (apparently) had never taken a course in natural science. (The curious situation of Simpson and his lack of preparation for his various positions was noted many years later in "Ripley's Believe It or Not.")[13] But eager to prepare himself for the task, Simpson requested of Ward a letter of introduction to President Daniel Coit Gilman of Johns Hopkins University to "make arrangements for availing himself of the advantages which the University affords for higher instruction in the branches of Natural Science which he teaches."[14] For two years Simpson studied part-time with the celebrated chemist Dr. Ira Remson; he was an eager student and used to great advantage the university library and the scientific apparatus available to him. The training was apparently

Male faculty 1890–91: Simpson, Reese, and Lewis are seated
right to left; McDaniel is standing at far left.

sufficient to prepare him for his work, for he soon seems to have gained the respect of the faculty and students and especially Ward. In October 1883, Rev. Simpson preached at the local M.P. Church, and Ward was unimpressed with the sermon, noting, "I think it probable that Bro. Simpson is better qualified for efficiency in the Class Room than in the pulpit."[15] In 1885, Ward commented in his diary about Simpson, "If it please God so to ordain, I should like him to succeed me as President of the college."[16]

The year 1883 saw the departure of George Devilbiss '75 to become principal of the Anne Arundel Academy for young ladies and gentlemen. Devilbiss had served capably as a tutor, as principal of the preparatory school, and as vice president of the college for a year or so. The new vice president was Rev. B. F. Benson, whom Ward lured from a pastorate to be his assistant in charge of day-to-day operations for three years.

On January 27, 1886, after making a full presentation to the board of trustees of the present state of the college (which included enrollment and financial deficits and a continuing debt), President Ward asked to be released from the presidency (something he had done at least once before without success). His health had not been good (he had been seriously ill

Portrait of President James Thomas Ward

with pneumonia for two months during the spring of 1883), and he was getting tired. Just before his illness, he had made yet another appeal at the M.P. Annual Conference for financial support for the college, noting in his diary, "Good words for a cause are important, but they alone will not build or otherwise carry forward the cause, and I am heartily sick of men who are ever talking and never doing anything else. . . . It is simply because there are so many who do not co-operate that we lack means to push on the work."[17] He felt that his retirement was "for the good of the college," that the time had come to appoint a younger man to the position. This time, the board agreed, quickly nominating and unanimously electing T. H. Lewis to succeed Ward, who would continue as professor of mental and moral science and as secretary of the board of trustees.[18] The same day, the board of governors of the new Westminster Theological Seminary elected Ward as its second president, succeeding Lewis. The remainder of the academic year was spent in preparing for the transition, which formally occurred on July 1. After 19 years as the college's founding president, Ward must have had mixed feelings about what was taking place. But a sense of nostalgia creeps into his diary entries only occasionally; one noteworthy comment was made on February 2: "I signed about 100 reports to parents and guardians of the standing students. This I have done four times every year for twenty years. . . . I have signed my name over 8000 times in this way." Another was made on June 18, after his last commencement: "In thinking over all that has transpired, I feel deeply sensible of many errors and imperfections, but I magnify the grace of God that has enabled me to do whatever of good I may have done toward the founding of an institution which I trust will long continue to His glory and the benefit of mankind." He must have felt gratified at the response to his retirement. The attorney general of Maryland, Charles B. Roberts, wrote, "The knowledge of your contemplated change will cause profound regret to a large body of the best citizens of the State, and especially of this community."[19] And James A. Diffenbaugh '74 of the state board of education, wrote, "Among the most potent factors in producing the good results with which the college is to be credited, I reckon your personal character, example, and influence. Deeply indebted to you myself for many valuable lessons, I know that . . . I echo only the common sentiment of those who have had the advantage of your teachings."[20]

In June 1888, the board of trustees formally named Ward emeritus professor of mental and moral science. A month later, on July 28, he received notification that he had been named a fellow of the Society of Science, Letters and Art in London. The Latin diploma was dated May 8. Eligible fellows were university graduates, fellows of learned societies, and others eminent or engaged in science, literature, or art or interested in those pursuits. Thereafter, in the college catalog the letters FSSc appeared after his name.

Honor also came to the departing seminary founder and soon-to-be college president when he learned on June 25, 1885, that he had been awarded the doctor of divinity degree by Adrian College, perhaps one of the youngest men (at age 33) in the country to be so honored. Ward noted in his diary that Lewis was very deserving of the honor (which Ward had received 14 years earlier). In June 1886, as he was preparing to take office, President-elect Lewis [1886–1920] met with the board of trustees and presented his plan for the future of the college. (One wonders how much of this he discussed with his father-in-law, Ward, with whom he resided until August 30.) He recommended that the board dispense with the January meeting and convene only in June; that four committees be created to deal with specific matters: Executive (the former Local Committee), Finance, Auditing, and Degrees; and that phase two of the men's dormitory be completed and changes be made to the interior of the Main Building, along with the addition of a heating system throughout the structure. The trustees readily adopted these recommendations, amended the fundamental ordinances as necessary to reflect the changes, elected members to the new committees, elected Lewis as an honorary member of the board, and, in a final action, voted to "disapprove of students dancing in the college buildings and order the discontinuance of the practice."[21] Everything was duly recorded in the minutes by Ward, who was reelected secretary. On June 12, 1886, President-elect Lewis and his wife, Mary, held a reception for the students and faculty of the college, greeting everyone in the parlor of the Main Building, after which Prof. McDaniel conducted everyone to the dining hall, where welcoming toasts were given by President Ward ("The Past History of the College"), Vice President Benson ("The Good Order of the Students of 1885–86"), Lewis Jarman '80 ("The Old Students"), and Prof. James Reese ("The Outlook"); and Dr. Lewis responded.

Several other noteworthy events involving faculty and administration concluded the decade. In April 1888, Prof. McDaniel published a little book, *Club Swinging by Note*, in Baltimore after a year's work. It was described as follows: "[McDaniel] has given particular attention to gymnastics and has utilized his knowledge of mathematics and music by inventing this remarkably novel and ingenious method of teaching classes to swing a series of movements in unison and to a musical accompaniment. . . . It makes instruction in club swinging . . . a pleasure instead of a drudgery, and it is so clear and useful that the wonder is that it was not invented before."[22] It grew out of the athletic program he had introduced at the college in 1886, after studying anatomy, hygiene, and gymnastics for five weeks with Dr. D. A.

Thomas Hamilton Lewis,
second president

Sargent at the Summer School of Physical Culture at Harvard University;[23] in the book he carefully explained his system of exercises with Indian clubs, accompanied by music. He used his program and book when he was invited to teach the system at the Harvard Summer School in 1888. During the summer of 1890, he was invited to teach physical culture and club swinging in the Monteagle Summer School. The exercise involved in the many aspects of club swinging was popular with the students, and exhibitions of the activity by both men and women were an integral part of the public exercises of the college for many years. Ward even commented in his diary on October 25, 1886, "I fear the students are giving more attention to the Calisthenics and Gymnastic exercises—all well enough in their place—than to their intellectual advancement." McDaniel felt strongly that "physical culture" should be a part of everyone's life and gave a scholarly lecture on this to the student body on October 7, 1887, which was published in the *Monthly* in November. In it he concluded, "Physical culture, like all true culture means training, means discipline, means growth, development, improvement and refinement, excellence and worth."[24] He practiced what he preached, for in May 1886 he bought a bicycle (a "wheel," as it was then called, since it had one very large front wheel and a small rear wheel), not knowing how to ride it. Apparently with some difficulty and to the amusement of some of his colleagues, he eventually taught himself, and by September he had

McDaniel and club swinging class
in the basement of the Main Building

become an expert bicyclist; he formed a bicycle club on campus and began leading excursions into the countryside.[25] In 1888 he was also involved in the formation of the Tennis Club, which he served as president for some years. In 1889, H. G. Watson was hired to be director of the gymnasium and to take over the calisthenics program for McDaniel, who was moving on to other things. By 1890, physical exercise and activities in the gymnasium had become a part of the college's daily routine, as evidenced by the hiring of Katharine M. Smith to be director of the women's gymnasium. She would soon be principal of the primary school in Levine Hall and later preceptress in the college.

The decade saw another faculty death when Franklin H. Schaeffer '83, tutor in Latin and Greek and principal of the preparatory school from 1885, died of throat cancer January 7, 1889.

The activities of the faculty during the decade continued to be focused on student deportment, although as the college's enrollments grew, attempts were made to streamline the rather cumbersome disciplinary procedures. One incident will suffice to suggest how far-reaching the arm of the faculty could be when it came to the rules for deportment. In April 1882 during the Easter recess, a young female student attended a ball at the Odd Fellows Hall in Westminster and stayed out until 4 A.M. Even though she was at home with her parents and under their supervision during the holiday, the faculty awarded her 25 demerits for "abuse of visiting privileges and improper conduct." Curiously, the following fall, a hazing incident involving an upperclassman brandishing a pistol resulted in only 26 demerits.

In February 1890, a young woman (the daughter of a minister) was suspended for a month for walking into town with a young gentleman of Westminster instead of going to church. Four days later, after a session between President Lewis and her father, the faculty reversed the suspension but required her to sign a pledge promising no further violation of the rules (a favorite disciplinary tool). She was also given 40 demerits and forbidden to leave the campus for one month, and her misdeed and its consequences were announced to all the women students. It should be noted that, if a student appeared repentant and formally petitioned for leniency, the faculty usually backed down, reduced the demerits or the suspension, and gave the malefactor a second chance.

According to the faculty minutes, in December 1883 a committee consisting of Dr. Reese, Miss Lottie Owings (the preceptress), and Vice President Benson was formed to consider the "advisability of joint recitations or exercises by the Male and Female departments of the college." In October 1884, a group of students petitioned the faculty to form a joint male and female Shakespeare Society; the request was denied, the faculty declaring that it had no authority to establish any coeducational activity within the college. In April 1885 Vice President Benson requested comments from each professor on the "practicability of joint recitations of males and females in their departments." In January 1886 the board of trustees considered the issue and sent back some questions regarding coeducational recitations, but the faculty was not of one mind on the issue and could not provide answers. These were the first attempts to bring the two departments together into a single college, but that would not happen for decades.

Faculty salaries remained quite low, particularly in comparison with other colleges of the time. It was mentioned earlier that Daniel Hering left for a much larger salary ($1,800) in 1884. The great mathematician Sylvester, with whom McDaniel studied briefly at Johns Hopkins (before Sylvester returned to England to the Savilian Professorship at Oxford), earned at least $5,000. In 1889, WMC professors Reese and Simpson, both of whom lived off campus, each received $900; professors T. F. Rinehart [music, 1886–93] and McDaniel, who resided and boarded on campus, earned $450 and $550, respectively; the preceptress, Lottie Owings, received $450 plus room and board; and the five remaining staff members (assistants, preparatory school teachers, and the teachers of art and music) averaged $310 per year. President Lewis's salary for 1889–90 was $2,000 (plus his house). Because of the low salaries, younger faculty members continued to stay only a few years (McDaniel and Owings being the exceptions).

BUILDINGS AND GROUNDS

In March 1881, an M.P. Conference Committee reported, "There seems to be a growing need for an early provision to be made to teach systematic theology." As noted, the following March formation of a school of theology within the college was approved by the conference and the college board of trustees, and T. H. Lewis was elected to be its first principal. He was directed to begin at once the preparatory work necessary to begin instruction in September 1882. Lewis and Ward both saw an immediate need for a separate residence and classroom facility for the additional students, and in May the college's board of trustees approved the purchase of five acres of land contiguous to the college property on which to build a theological building. The board agreed to raise $2,000 for the enterprise and to deed the property back to the conference if and when the new seminary was established. It was also agreed that the theological students could attend classes and lectures in the college for free; that the college would provide free heat, light, and washing; and that the college would provide board for two students for two years. The building was completed during the summer and the school formally inaugurated in September. However, in March 1883 Lewis reported to the conference that it was totally impractical to carry out the school as a department of the college and recommended that the theological school become a separate entity known as the Westminster Theological Seminary of the Methodist Protestant Church and that a board of governors be appointed for the new institution. These recommendations were adopted by the conference, the Maryland General Assembly incorporated the seminary in April 1884, and from that time forward, the two institutions have been totally separate, although in the early days some college faculty also occasionally taught in the seminary. Three members of the initial board of governors, consisting of three ministers and two laymen, were also members of the college board, including Dr. Joshua W. Hering, who assumed the role of treasurer of the new institution (relinquishing his post as treasurer of the college's board of trustees in 1885).

At the May 1882 meeting of the board, Ward proposed building a new college dormitory for men, a free-standing building just west of the Main Building. This would eliminate the necessity of renting rooms in town for the young men, of using the attic of the Main Building (which was unsafe), and of assigning as many as six students to a room designed for two, as had been done for several years. The project was approved, and Ward set forth to raise funds from individual subscriptions. Funding for the building came in slowly, and so the board authorized Ward to erect "a building such as can be put under roof for the money already raised [about $1,000] and continue

Westminster Theological Seminary
(1882–83)

the effort to raise more money, finishing portion by portion according to the means received."[26] On August 21, 1882, the cornerstone for the new building was laid in a simple ceremony that was later reported in the local newspaper, the *Democratic Advocate*:

> *Dr. J. T. Murray . . . in the name of the Holy Trinity poured a bottle of water upon the foundation stone, giving the building a distinctive title. As agreed by the Trustees present [John Smith and Joshua Hering], in honor of the President of the College, it was given the name Ward Hall. As the intention of the well-deserved compliment was kept secret, its sudden revelation had a peculiar effect upon the President. It was an electric disturbance to his composure, and greatly enjoyed by those who had planned to fix an honor upon him, against which he would have protested if he had not been caught with guile.*[27]

This event happened to take place on Dr. Ward's 62nd birthday, and so, after the ceremony, everyone adjourned to his home for a party, where another surprise was planned for him. When refreshments were served, his plate contained a leather case containing an engraved gold watch shaped like a turnip. The present was a gift from his wife, daughter, son-in-law, and grandchildren, whose initials were engraved inside. The newspaper commented, "The Doctor, concluding that it would serve him better to mark the hours than as an esculent, did not eat it." Commenting on the events of the day, Ward noted in his diary, "Altogether this Birth Day Party and its incidents constitute one of the most pleasant episodes of my life."

Ward Hall (phase one) rose quickly, and 32 men moved in on February 20, 1883. Once the male resident students were installed in the new dormitory, the interior of the Main Building was again modified to provide more rooms for recitations and for the literary societies. A music room was also fitted out. The women students continued to occupy the Main Building and its annex. Two years later, after additional fund-raising, the second half of Ward Hall was begun; it was completed in 1886. It was the first building to have an internal furnace for heating. The rooms in the Main Building and its annex were heated by small (and dangerous) coal stoves in the rooms until a central heating system with radiators in each room was installed in 1887; three eight-horsepower boilers with draft regulations, safety valves, and water and steam gauges then maintained the indoor temperature at 70 degrees even in zero weather.[28]

In June 1883, Vice President Devilbiss sent a letter to the trustees recommending the building of an ice house to keep fresh meats, butter, and milk. This was approved, and the structure, which had a capacity of 34 tons of ice buried in the pit beneath the house, was erected in 1884. It served its function well until the advent of electricity.[29]

Soon after Lewis became president, as enrollments continued to rise, additional student housing, an expanded dining room and kitchen, and a larger auditorium were needed. Lewis recommended to the board the erection of a new building at a cost of about $6,000. Ultimately, $7,000 was borrowed, and an addition 104 feet by 39 feet was erected to the east of the Main Building during the summer of 1887 and occupied in September. A new dining room 75 feet by 36 feet occupied the lower level and seated 250 students at tables of six or eight (men on the north side, women on the south side, and professors in the middle). Adjoining it were a kitchen, dish room, and pantries. Above the dining room was an auditorium 98 feet by 37 feet with a stage 37 feet by 20 feet and with nine windows on each side. It was designed to seat 1,000 people and would house the commencement exercises, weekly orations and recitals, and society entertainments. The third floor provided space for 20 rooms for women students, as well as an infirmary. The building was formally opened on October 28 and was named for the venerable and longtime chairman of

Ward Hall I, a men's dormitory (1883)

the board of trustees and generous benefactor, John Smith of Wakefield. The old dining room in the Main Building became a classroom for McDaniel's classes in mathematics and calisthenics.

Once Smith Hall was completed, President Lewis launched a more extensive building program to accommodate the ever increasing student enrollments. When he took office in 1886, the total enrollment in all programs of the college was 135. In each of the four succeeding years enrollments rose dramatically: 1887–88, 165; 1888–89, 180; 1889–90, 218; and 1890–91, 242. In June 1888, he recommended building a new and separate facility to house the primary and preparatory school. He also noted the need for a president's house (he and his family, including three small children, lived in an apartment in the Main Building)[30] and additional classroom space. A year later, he was able to report that the Baker family of Buckeystown in Frederick County had pledged $4,000 to build the President's House. (The donors were W. G. Baker, Mrs. Charles F. Thomas, Joseph D. Baker, and Daniel Baker, who honored their parents Mr. and Mrs. C. A. Baker with the gift. Daniel and Joseph had been students at the college, and Mrs. Thomas's daughter was in the class of 1893.)[31] Anna Yingling '71 (1852–90), daughter of charter trustee Joshua Yingling [1868–82], had offered another $4,000 to build a gymnasium (for which she would receive a life annuity of $200 per year).

Yingling Gymnasium was completed and opened in October 1889, and the President's House was completed in December of the same year. Both were designed by Jackson Gott of Baltimore. As these were being completed, Lewis and McDaniel designed a new multifunction annex to the west of the

College dining room in Smith Hall (1887)

First college library, in Hering Hall (1890);
the first foreign student (from Japan) is standing between the bookcases.

Main Building, to match Smith Hall to the east. Lewis's recommended plan
was quickly approved by the trustees (as were most of his recommendations
and plans), and the building was erected and formally opened in the summer
of 1890. It was named Hering Hall in honor of the first treasurer of the board
of trustees and longtime member of the Local Committee, Joshua Hering
(who had been awarded an honorary AM degree in 1885). On the first floor
of Hering Hall were two large rooms for the Preparatory Department, a
chemistry laboratory, and a boiler room. The second floor comprised the
president's office and five recitation rooms, which opened onto porches
front and back. The third floor provided for a new and larger library, 80 feet
by 30 feet, which included an encyclopedia (a gift of Ward), mineral cases,
bookshelves, and reading tables; the room was also to be used for parlor
receptions. The remaining parts of the building provided dormitory rooms
for the senior men and an apartment for Prof. McDaniel. While this building
was being erected, a tower was added to the front of the Main Building to
house a central stairwell so the old one could be removed and the rooms
made larger. A covered porch 273 feet long, designed by Gott, was built
across the whole front of the building, giving it a very unified appearance.[32]

In 1888, the *Monthly* also noted that four acres of land had been
purchased from Daniel Geiman, whose farm adjoined the college property, so
that the college grounds were extended about 125 feet to the north,[33] where
Albert Norman Ward Hall and the Gill complex are now located. Part of the
new property was so level that with only minimal preparation it could be

turned into a ball field. One optimistic report noted,

> *The ground has been put in very good condition and will in the course
> of a few years be a first-class baseball field. A large fence and seating
> capacity for 300 will be erected in a few days. The management will
> sell season tickets to those desiring to witness the games; otherwise the
> admission will be 10 cents a game.*[34]

A few years later, an eighth-mile cinder running track would be added.[35]
Tennis courts were laid out east of Smith Hall in 1888. The students felt this
was one of the most important land acquisitions made by the college.

FINANCES

Debt was still a major issue for most of this decade. In 1881 the debt was
$30,489; this was successfully reduced to $7,563 through a subscription
program generated by the efforts of the agent, Rev. J. B. Walker. The Maryland
Annual Conference had assessed ten cents per member for the college, and it
was hoped this would raise an additional $1,200–$1,500. But the debt began
to grow again, until by 1886 it was $10,762. Although the Local Committee
had recommended to the board of trustees in 1880 that the college should
be self-sustaining without the necessity of asking for state aid and "should
demonstrate its ability to maintain a respectable life without it," funds from the
State of Maryland were nevertheless much appreciated and, in fact, necessary.
There was great relief within the board and administration when the state
scholarship appropriation to the college was renewed in 1880 (while the one
to St. John's College was not). It was reported that the "standing of Western
Maryland College in the Legislature was of a highly satisfactory character, it
being referred to by Senators and Delegates as an institution worthy of state
aid . . . in view of the educational work which it has and is accomplishing."[36]
When Governor Hamilton withheld his signature from the scholarship bill
in the spring of 1882, it had serious implications for the WMC budget. In
June of 1883 the board minutes stated, "Patronage [from the M.P. Church]
and Economy must continue to be the conspicuous objects in our business
management due to the loss of the state scholarship funds." Fortunately, by
1886, state funding was restored, and the college received $1,300 a year for two
years in addition to the scholarships.

When Lewis became president in 1886, his first priority was elimination
of the long-standing debt. Four thousand dollars was raised on a loan without
interest to fund the floating debt so that all current receipts might be used for
current expenditures. That loan was paid off a year later. Lewis mounted a

vigorous campaign among the M.P. churches and other friends and, because he was well known in the conference, was successful in raising money and attracting more students to the college, which brought in more income. The resources of the college were carefully managed and all surpluses applied to the debt. By 1890 the debt was paid off, and several new buildings had been erected, as well. Two notes for $1,000 each, held by John Smith and the Westminster Savings Institution (now BB&T), were the last to be paid, and Lewis proudly framed those as a symbol of his successful debt reduction campaign. (They are still in the college archives.) He noted in his annual report to the board and the M.P. Annual Conference for 1890 that the Local Committee had in 1878 made the following statement: "That the receipts from the school could ever pay the College debt or any part of it, is what neither the Board of Trustees nor the Church have ever expected."[37] He pointed out that 1886's debt of $10,762 *had* been reduced largely out of net operating budgets, and an additional $15,000 from receipts had been spent on improvements. He noted that this was possible because the enrollment was the largest it had ever been (218), in spite of a severe crop failure on the Eastern Shore, which had always provided many students, and the number of boarders had increased by 25% over the previous year, to 116. He went on to say, "The contradiction of this saying of the board has been paralleled in the whole history of the college which has persisted in living in spite of the fact that it has had no endowment, a fact unheard of before in the history of colleges." That being said, the trustees immediately authorized the mortgage of $15,000 to build Hering Hall and make other improvements. Such indebtedness was now considered sound business practice, as the college was growing rapidly, and the need for space to accommodate the students and the educational process was paramount. It was also now time to build an endowment for the future. Lewis contemplated asking the Methodist Protestant Church for direct financial assistance rather than just patronage and moral support.

CURRICULUM

For the first half of the decade, the classical curriculum was maintained with little change. However, with the new president, a number of curricular innovations were put into place. One of the most noticeable was the introduction in 1886 of a new academic calendar with three terms of study instead of two. The first term that year began September 7 and concluded December 3. The second began December 7, concluding on March 11, and the third began March 15 and ended June 6. Curiously, no mention is made of this change in either the trustee or the faculty minutes, so one is led to believe that President Lewis simply changed the calendar on his own. He may have discussed it with some faculty (including, no doubt, McDaniel, who had a mind for such details), but the change was never formally approved by either body.

In 1885, the faculty recommended to the board of trustees that a fourth year be added to the bachelor's degree requirement for women, so as to raise the standards in the Female Department. The trustees agreed, and the 1885–86 catalog, announcing the program for 1886–87, lists a four-year program for the AB degree without mentioning the gender of the student. Four distinct programs are outlined: a Preparatory Course (designed to prepare students for college or business), a Collegiate Course (a three-year course for female students leading to a Testimonial of Graduation but not to a degree), a Collegiate Course (leading to the AB degree), and a Normal Course (a one-year course to prepare students for teaching). It is also interesting to note that in that catalog the college faculty is listed only once, not separately for the Male and Female departments. The "peculiar advantage" of the separate departments is still described, but the departments are no longer delineated. In 1887, another "course of study" was listed: a primary course that would lead into the preparatory course. It has been suggested that Mary Ward Lewis, noting that the public schools were not particularly good, had encouraged her husband to install a primary department, so their children could be better educated. The course enrolled 14 students during 1886–87, including Miriam Lewis '96 and her sister Clara '98, in a class held in the Main Building.

Schofield pointed out that the faculty had for some time wanted to raise the requirements for graduation, and certainly the four-year degree program for women was a step in that direction. But entering students were sometimes not well prepared for collegiate work. When it was suggested that the Greek requirement for entrance and graduation be lowered, Dr. Reese remarked, "I am so thoroughly convinced that it would be unwise in itself and hurtful to the students, that I would not favor even agitating the question." Rather, he proposed that students take more Greek, as well as more English, mathematics, and Latin. While that suggestion was not adopted, neither was the Greek requirement diminished. In 1885, the faculty adopted a policy of requiring an average grade of 7 out of 10 in all subjects for graduation. The catalog stated that exceptions to this rule would no longer be made.[38]

Of course, classes were still segregated by gender, and the structure of the students' day was rather rigid, as the weekly schedule of recitations (printed in the catalog for 1883–84) attests. For each half-hour period, classes for men (M) and women (F) in each year were outlined:

| 24 | | *Western Maryland College* | | | | |

Weekly Schedule of Recitations in Collegiate Department.

TIME.	DEP'T OF STUDY.	MONDAY.	TUESDAY.	WEDNESDAY.	THURSDAY.	FRIDAY.
9 to 9½	Belles-Lettres. Anct. Lang. Nat. Sci. and French. Mathematics.	F. Fr. (Hist.) M.Sr.(Greek) M. Jr. (Nat. Sci.) M. Fresh.	M. Junior. F. Sr.(Myth.) M.Sr.(Greek) F. Fr. (Nat. Sci.) M. Fresh.	F. Fr. (Hist.) M.Sr.(Latin.) M. Jr. (Nat. Sci.) M. Fresh.	F. Fr. (Rhet.) M. Jr. M Sr.(Latin.) F. Jr. (Nat. Sci.) M. Fresh.	F. Fr. (Hist.) M. Jr. (Nat. Sci.) M. Fresh.
9½ to 10	Belles-Lettres. Anct. Langs. Nat. Sci. and French. Math.	M. Senior. F.Sr.(Latin.) M. Jr (Nat. Sci) M. Fresh.	F. Jr.(Latin.) F.Fr.(Fr'nch) M. Fresh.	Soph.(Latin.) F.Jr.(Bo 'ny) M. Junior. M. Fresh.	F. Jr.(Latin.) F. Sr. (Nat. Sci.) M. Fresh.	M. Jr. (Nat. Sci) M. Fresh.
10 to 10½	Anct. Lang. Nat. Sci. & Fren. Math.	M.Jr.(Greek) F.Jr (Fr'nch) Sophomore.	M.Sr.(Greek) F. Jr· (Nat. Sci,) Sophs.	F.Sr. (Latin.) F. Fr. (Nat. Sci·) Sophs.	Soph.(Greek) F.Jr.(Fr'nch)	F.Jr.French Sophs.
10½ to 11	Belles-Lettres. Anct. Lang, Nat. Sci, and French. Math.	M.Fr.(Latin.) F. Sr. (Nat. Sci.) Sophomores.	F. Fr. (Rhet.) M.Jr. (Greek) F.Sr (Fr'nch) Sophs.	M.Jr.(Latin.) F.Fr.(Fr'nch) Sophs.	M.Fr. (Latin) F.Sr.(Fr'nch)	F. Fr. (Rhet.) F. Sr. (Nat. Sci.) Sophs.
11 to 11½	Belles Lettres & M. & M. Sci. Anct. Lang. Nat. Sci and French. Math.	M. Sr. (Moral Phil.) Soph. (Latin) F. Fr. (Nat. Sci.) F. Junior.	M.Fr. (Latin) M. Sr. (Nat. Sci.) F. Junior.	F. Sr.(Myth.) M.Fr.(Latin) M. Sr. (Nat. Sci.) F. Junior.	F. Sr. (Myth.) M. Jun. (Lat) M. Sr. (Nat. Sci.) F. Junior.	F. Jr. (Nat. (Sci.)
11½ to 12	M. and M. Sci. Anct. Lang. Nat. Sci. & Fren. Math.	M.Jr.(Greek) F.Fr(Fr'nch) F. Seniors.	M. Junior. S ph.(Latin,) M. Sr. (Nat. Sci.) F. Senior.	Soph. (Latin) M. Sr. (Nat. Sci.) F. Senior.	M. Junior. Soph.(Gree) M. Sr. (Nat. Sci.) F. Senior.	F.Sr.(Fr'nch)
1 to 1½	Belles-Lettres. Anct Lang. Nat. Sci & Fren. Math.	F. Fresh.	F. Senior. F. Fresh.	F. Senior. F.Jr.(Fr'nch) F. Fresh.	F. Senior. M.Jr.(Latin.) F. Fresh.	F. Junior. F. Fresh.
1½ to 2	Belles-Lettres. Anct Lang. Nat. Sci. and French. Math.	Soph. (Nat. Sci.) F. Fresh.	Soph. (Nat. Sci.) F. Fresh.	M. Fr. (Nat. Sci.) F. Fresh.	M.Fr.(Greek) F.Jr.(Bot'ny) F. Fresh.	Soph. (Nat. Sci.) F. Fresh.
2 to 2½	M. and M. Sci. Belles-Lettres. Nat. Sci. & Fren. Math.	F. Junior. M. Senior.	F. Jr. (Nat. Sci.) M. Senior.	F. Junior. M. Fresh. Soph. (Nat. Sci.) M. Junior.	M.Sr.(Latin.) M. Junior.	Exercises in Elocution.
2½ to 3	M. and M. Sci Belles-Lettres. Nat. Sci. and French. Math.	F. Senior. Soph. M. Fr. (Nat. Sci.) M. Junior.	F. Senior. Soph. M. Fr. (Nat. Sci.)			Literary Societies.

Also stated for the first time in the 1883 catalog were the requirements for the master of arts degree. While the degree had been conferred since 1874, its availability had never been stated publicly. Each year the trustees approved, upon recommendation of the faculty, those students who met the stipulations of the degree. For example, William McDaniel, who graduated in 1880 and entered upon a teaching career, applied for and was awarded his AM degree in 1883 (along with four other members of his class), the year he concluded his two years as tutor at the college and set off to Johns Hopkins to pursue the PhD.

An interesting curriculum proposal came from the trustees to the faculty in 1888, when a culinary department was suggested. There apparently was concern in some circles that female graduates were unable to find husbands after graduation because they had no instruction in cooking. A column in the *WMC Monthly*, perhaps written by Ward, commented, "These dear girls have abundant opportunities for learning how to cook at their homes," and continued, "No class of young ladies are more desired as wives by intelligent men than those who are educated at our colleges."[39] The culinary arts were not added to the curriculum (at least not until home economics became a course offering in 1921).

As noted, by 1886 a "normal" course for the preparation of teachers had been established. The courses were taught first by James Diffenbaugh, who was joined by Edward Reisler '72 for a year or two. Diffenbaugh also gave a series of pedagogical lectures during May 1888, such as "The Art of Teaching—From the Ancients to Pestalozzi" and "The Mission of the Teacher." In 1890, a regular college lecture series was created, with lectures on Thursday evenings given alternately by members of the faculty and invited speakers from Baltimore, such as "Ethics of Expression" by Dr. Lewis, "The Koohinoor [sic] Diamond" by Dr. Reese, "Youth and Wealth" by President Newell (well-known educator and principal of the State Normal School at Towson), "Facts and Fancies of Evolution" by Prof. Simpson, "Piano Music and Its Development" by Prof. Rinehart, and "The Sun" by Prof. McDaniel. During May 1890, McDaniel also gave a series of lectures on the history of mathematics to the junior class (with seniors also invited).

Under President Lewis's leadership, the curriculum of the college was gradually moving away from the traditional, classical "lockstep" program for all students toward a program that would provide students with some choice at certain stages. Lewis commented to the board of trustees in 1889 that he felt such a modification would help retain students; the next decade would see this change.

STUDENT LIFE

While still tightly governed by numerous rules, regulations, and faculty oversight, the students of this decade seemed to find more ways to "expand their horizons" and enjoy their college experience. This was perhaps due to the gradually increasing enrollments, which brought more students with more diverse backgrounds into the college. Parlor Night was still a popular activity and was now held in the library each month. The *WMC Monthly* of October 1887 noted,

> *The first monthly social assembly, or "parlor night" as it is known in College parlance, took place on the evening of September 24th. . . . The sociable was really in the form of a reception by the resident members of the Faculty, who at the opening formed a group in the center of the room. The students, after paying their respects, with the usual handshaking and exchange of greetings, collected in parties about the room, which by this time presented a very animated scene. The old students were happy in recounting to each other the pleasures of the vacation just over, and at the same time endeavored to make new students have just the best time possible. It is needless to say the occasion was one of enjoyment to all, and gave a pleasant foretaste of what is to follow each succeeding month.*[40]

Reporting on the November 26, 1887, Parlor Night, the *Monthly* noted that it would be "especially remembered as the occasion upon which Dr. Lewis' baby [Marjorie] was baptized." The child's grandfather, Dr. Ward, performed the ceremony, and the happy family was presented with a silver cup and a silver spoon. After this special event, the evening "proceeded in the same old way, ever new and agreeable to the students as the 'red letter' evening of the month."[41]

The literary societies continued to flourish, with regular meetings and programs, and played an increasing role in the student social life. In January 1882, responding to the gradually increasing student population, the Philomathean Society for women was formed, bringing the number of societies to four. By now, the "Preparatorians" (the 43 students in the preparatory school) were included, but the "Primarians" (the students in the primary school formed in 1887) had their own society, the St. Nicholas Society. For the men's groups (Irving and Webster), oratory was a key activity, which culminated in a contest during Commencement Week, the prize being the Merrill Trophy, given in 1888 by A. H. Merrill of Vanderbilt University, who had been a Western Maryland faculty member in elocution [1883–86]. The ladies' groups (Browning and Philomathean) contested in the composition and reading of essays and vied for the Newell Trophy, given in 1889 by M. A. Newell, president of the State Normal

School at Towson. The societies' anniversary celebrations were significant occasions during the year, and all parts of the programs were subject to faculty approval. In February 1885, an edict was sent forth: "No dancing on the stage during the performance." An interesting situation resulted from repeated requests by the Webster Society for permission to perform *Ten Nights in a Bar Room* at its anniversary celebration in 1888. The classic play was written by T. S. Arthur, a popular writer during the Civil War era, and had been described as the *Uncle Tom's Cabin* of the antebellum temperance movement in the United States because of its look at the 19th-century tavern and its premise that "liquor selling is the way to ruin." Curiously, given the religious nature of the institution and its leaders (many of whom were Methodist Protestant clergy) and the regulations forbidding use of alcohol on campus, the WMC faculty were reluctant to allow the play to be presented, giving final approval only after it was agreed that "all objectionable parts be stricken."[42] One can only wonder what was objectionable and what was left to perform.

About the time Dr. Lewis took office, dissatisfaction with the *Irving Literary Gazette*, which had been resurrected in February 1881, arose among the other literary societies. This led to the suggestion that the publication be produced by all four societies, but when the Irving Society balked, the other three groups began to produce the *Portfolio*. From December 1886 until June 1887 there were two college periodicals serving a school of about 135 students, 77 of them in the college. As student editors and the faculty realized that this was not in anyone's best interest, the *WMC Monthly* was created in October 1887, and the rival society publications were discontinued. The students were unable to agree on who should be in charge of the *Monthly*, however, and appealed to the faculty, which appointed Prof. Reese editor-in-chief; in October 1888 the editorship was turned over to the students and alternated between the two male societies, Irving and Webster. To obtain a suggestion of the diverse contents of this publication, one needs only to look at any single issue, for instance vol. 2, no. 7 (April 1889). Included were an opening editorial that discussed the YMCA and the growing interest in baseball; essays entitled "The Literary Appetite," "The Carotid Artery of the Sea," "Sinbad Dreams Again," "Influence of America on Japan," and "Robert Burns"; articles dealing with the junior reception, scholarship grades, Friday afternoon exercises, and the Hopkins Hospital; and regular columns: "Alumni Notes," "Quondam Students," "Exchanges," "College World," "Seminary Items," "Locals," and one by Dr. Ward. "Locals" included all the campus news, good-natured teasing of individuals, and gossip. Anything of interest to the student body of the time was included. Many times these were puns on students' names involving declarations of interest in members of the opposite sex. The following occur within two pages of the November 1889 *Monthly* and involve a Mr. Jones and a Miss Hering: "What kind of fish is Jones' favorite? Why Hering, of course." "Nowadays, Jona(e)s is not swallowed by a Whale(y), but instead, is caught by a Hering." "We much regretted to hear this week that our brilliant Sophomore, Mr. Jones, had lost his he(a)ring." "Jones is willing to give away *his* ring. What he wants is *Hering*."[43] Apparently, these suggestions of affection were deemed harmless by the faculty, for they continued for years, even after the students could actually speak openly to one another on campus.

The *Monthly* is a wonderful source for descriptions of campus holiday observances in the late 19th century. For instance, while students did not return to their homes for Thanksgiving in those days, campus-wide activities helped celebrate the day. No classes were held, and some students slept in, while others went to church or into town. At about two o'clock the dinner bell rang, and the students flocked to the dining hall for a meal that is reported to have lasted until 4:30 P.M. The menu for 1887 (printed especially for the occasion and placed at each plate) was as follows:

Stewed Oysters

Crackers   Pickles

Boiled Haddock with Cream Sauce

Bread and Butter

Cold Slaw

Baked Wild Duck, stuffed with Onions

Celery   Cranberries

Roast Turkey

Parsnips   Mashed Potatoes

Saur Kraut

Mince Pie   Coffee

The rest of the day was spent in relaxation. At 7 P.M. the literary societies met, and everyone marched in to the Browning Society's anniversary performance in Smith Hall auditorium, forming a large and appreciative audience for the addresses, piano and vocal solos and duets, readings, and a farce in two acts entitled "Ladies at Home, or Gentlemen, We Can Do Without You" performed by 8 of the members. The program concluded with a pyramid of human sunflowers formed by 14 young ladies, each wearing a sunflower mask and a green gown, who sang a number of songs.[44]

In December of the same year, before the Christmas recess, on the night of the Webster Society anniversary, a Christmas tree (apparently the first for the campus) was erected in the calisthenics room in the basement of the Main Building. During the afternoon the students secretly took humorous little gifts for one another to the room, where they were labeled by a faculty member and tied onto the tree. After the anniversary program (similar in format to the Browning program at Thanksgiving) was performed by the 37 members, the whole college community hurried down to the room where the tree stood, and the presents were handed out to much merriment. Dr. Lewis received a small horse on wheels that nodded its head, and Preceptress Lottie Owings was given a tiny china tea service because she had been a "good girl." The highlight of the evening was when each male student was given a slip of paper containing a young lady's name, after which he marched to the dining room to pick up two dishes of ice cream, sought out the lady upon his return, and shared the rest of the evening with her in talk and refreshment.[45]

The long Easter weekend of 1890 was celebrated from Friday through Monday by about half of the students, those who had not returned to their homes for the holiday. The activities began on Thursday evening with the Webster Society anniversary celebration. (Each year the societies drew dates for their anniversary celebrations, so they were held at different times from year to year.) The highlight of the evening was a performance of "Damon and Pythias." Friday evening was devoted to a gymnastic demonstration of chest expanders, dumbbell exercises, club swinging, parallel bars, and fancy stepping. It was remarked that "the advancement that has been made in one year in physical training is simply wonderful, and reflects credit upon all of those that took part." Saturday a baseball game was played, and everyone in attendance enjoyed a reception for both teams afterward. Sunday the students attended the church of their choice, either in the morning or evening. Monday afternoon for about an hour the young ladies gave an impromptu musical entertainment before supper.[46]

In April 1888, a tradition was born when the junior class gave a supper for the senior class. A description of the event appeared in the *Monthly*:

It was a brilliant occasion, and will always be remembered by those present as an important epoch in their college career. . . . A few minutes after the [junior] class had assembled in the library, which had been prepared for the occasion, the Seniors made their appearance, a little after seven. After being introduced by Miss L. B. Taylor, the hostess of the Juniors, a few minutes glided by in pleasant conversation; and when all were invited by the hostess to supper, each gentleman, as previously arranged, escorted his lady to the designated seat in what is known as the ladies parlor. After wending its way along ground ordinarily sacred from the intrusion of male feet, the procession, led by the hostess and Miss Lottie [Owings], reached the desired room. Soon after grace was said by Dr. Lewis, merriment and laughter held the fort. . . . The menu was one of exceptional merit. Not only was that which was traced upon it pleasant to behold, but the menu itself was unique in its makeup. It was printed on fringed bolting cloth with satin back, and united at the top by artistic stitches. . . . The menu, to which ample justice was done by all:

Chicken Salad

Broiled Shad   Sirloin Steak

Cold Ham   Shad Roe

Saratoga Chips   Sliced Tomatoes

Chow-Chow

Muffins   Tea   Coffee

Maryland Biscuits

Cold Bread   Chocolate

Vanilla Ice Cream   Orange Ice

Chocolate Ice Cream   Jelly

Cake   Fruit

The supper lasted about two hours and a half, and, after preserving the menu as a memento of the occasion, each one discussed the merits of the Junior ladies as cooks. The Class of '89 should consider itself honored in possessing so many noble types of women. All the cakes, bread, and several other niceties were prepared by their own hands, and it was surmised that even the fish were caught by the boys. . . . Next came the toasts. . . . The Juniors not only had the pleasure and honor to give a reception to the graduating class, but they had the honor of establishing a custom which is to be known as the Junior Supper in future years. Just before ten o'clock all dispersed to their respective rooms to dream of Minnehaha and others.[47]

Another tradition was launched in the mid-1880s, the handing down of the Sophomore Cane. The *Monthly* of February 1889 reported the event for the first time, but it had been going on for a few years by then. Here is the account of the event as given by the president of the junior class:

The custom originated several years ago. It became necessary to have something to represent that great organization, the Sophomore Class. As the sovereigns of monarchies had a crown as a symbol of their authority and influence, as the president of every organization of prominence has a gavel, . . . a cane was procured and placed in the care of the President of the class. That cane was transferred from year to year and from class to class until the class of '90 became Sophomores. . . . If the President of the Sophomore Class will now come forward, I will present the cane to him. In the name of the class of '90 and by its authority, I now transfer the cane to your care. Always bear in mind what a great responsibility rests upon you in assuming possession of it.[48]

Schofield noted that the cane presented in 1889 was actually a replacement for the original cane. The first cane was made of ebony with a head of solid silver. The top was engraved with the words "Presented by the Class of '83" and on one of the plane surfaces was inscribed a quotation from Virgil's *Aeneid*: "Olim Meminisse habit" ("This, too, will be remembered with joy"). The replacement cane, which is in the college archives, is a gold-headed ebony cane engraved with "The gift of '93" together with a quotation in Greek. This cane is partially adorned with small gold and enameled pins representing the classes from 1894 to 1921, when apparently the tradition ceased.[49] The class of 1936, upon discovering the cane, affixed a small brass shield with its class numerals to it, but this revived tradition did not carry on. The formal ceremony of passing on the cane also seems to have ceased fairly quickly, even though the class pins continued to be affixed; perhaps the significance of the cane changed over the 30 or so years of its use.[50]

Regular Friday afternoon recitals and declamations in Smith Hall (presented one week by freshmen and sophomores, another week by juniors, with senior orations and other musical performances interspersed) provided more cultural entertainment for the students. On February 1, 1889, the program included the presentation of three student essays, three orations, a vocal solo, and a piano duet of waltzes played by professors Rinehart and McDaniel. (In addition to his many other talents, McDaniel was an accomplished pianist.) Music was beginning to play an important role on the campus. In April 1888 a chorus of 30 members was organized under the direction of Mrs. A. J. Carnes, and by November a college Glee Club was organized and directed by Prof. Rinehart.

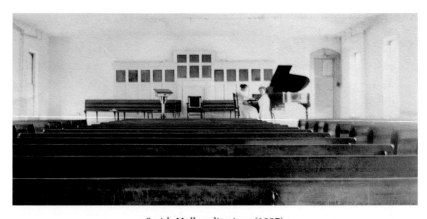

Smith Hall auditorium (1887)

In a more informal pastime, the boys of all ages enjoyed sledding down the back hill behind Ward Hall when the winter provided sufficient snow. Pranks of all kinds were also the norm; some boys enjoyed throwing water out of the windows and doing things that caused damage to the new dormitory.[51] A new form of "physical culture" had also evolved: climbing the fire escape of the dormitory by moonlight. The *Monthly* noted, "Music has not yet been introduced. Professors excluded."[52] Perhaps related to these nefarious activities is the fact that students were still obliged to extinguish their lamps at 10 P.M. A special privilege was granted the senior boarding students in November 1889, when the faculty allowed them to burn their lights until 11 P.M. Monday through Friday (but not on weekends). Alas, some of the senior men abused this privilege, and it was rescinded the following February. To enable the students to have more time for study, the faculty generously voted in September 1889 that men would have additional required study hours on Saturday morning from 7 to 8 A.M. Study hours for the young ladies were from 8 to 9 P.M. Saturday evening. Students were reminded that smoking in the college buildings during any study hours was prohibited.[53]

Perhaps the most important student activity of the decade took place in April 1888, when the Western Maryland College Base Ball Association was formally organized, uniforms were designed, and a playing schedule of three games with New Windsor College (renamed Blue Ridge College in 1912) was proposed. Intercollegiate athletics had formally come to the college. The men had played baseball informally during both fall and spring since the beginning of the decade,[54] but their activities were not truly sanctioned. In 1881, Dr. Ward had commented in his diary:

> A number of students went to New Windsor today to play a match game of baseball with the students of the college there. I regard it as a dangerous game. Only a few days ago one of the students . . . was injured by a ball striking him in the throat so that he is unable to speak above a whisper. Frequent accidents occur in playing this game and yet young men will play.[55]

The first game of the Association was played on April 14 in New Windsor. "Our boys were defeated [15–7], a result not at all unexpected, considering that they had had no practice whatever this season."[56] After the game, the teams shared dinner before the visiting WMC team boarded the train for Westminster. A week later, the Western Maryland Nine played the Westminster Stars on Reservoir Hill and won by a score of 23–21. By the next game, on May 5, a suitable home field had been temporarily secured on a two-acre piece of ground down the hill from the college (near what is now Green Street). Much work and effort were put into making the diamond and clearing the outfield of stones and rubbish. Again, the college Nine prevailed, 26–18, this time against another Westminster team. On May 12, the New Windsor team arrived in the morning, toured the campus, joined the college students for dinner at 1:30 P.M., and then everyone hurried over to the playing field for the game, which lasted only three innings before it was called because of rain, with New Windsor ahead 6–4. The visitors were invited back to the campus to the Smith Hall auditorium, where an impromptu musical entertainment was provided by several students and Prof. Rinehart, after which Prof. McDaniel had four of his classes demonstrate calisthenics movements, club swinging, and marching. Following some student recitations, the New Windsor captain gave a speech expressing thanks for the kindness shown them, and the students then accompanied the visitors to the train depot for their return trip. Five more games with other teams completed the season. The following year, the team showed marked improvement, playing games against St. John's College, Pennsylvania College, Union Mills, and Westminster and winning each.[57] In 1890, lacking a pitcher, the WMC team formed a combination team with New Windsor and scheduled games with Pennsylvania College, Mt. St. Mary's College, Union Mills, Johns Hopkins, and others, winning about half of the games that weather allowed.[58] The *Irving Literary Gazette* commented on the spirit of the contests (and perhaps of the era in which they were played) when it reported, "The game was notable for the gentlemanly behavior of those playing. Not an angry word was spoken during the entire game, and all left the grounds feeling glad they had attended."[59]

One final aspect of student life must be mentioned, for it was the beginning of a small but significant part of the student body. The first foreign-born student, Misao Tsune Hirata from Yokohama, Japan, arrived on campus in 1886 and provided a different perspective on the world for the college students of that era. Prior to his retirement, Dr. Ward had made arrangements for her enrollment, which was sponsored by Frederick C. Klein '80, a Methodist Protestant minister stationed in Japan. Perhaps Dr. Lewis had some concern about how well prepared she would be for college studies, but she was able to do very well both academically and socially during her four years on campus. At the 1890 Commencement, she wore her native costume and made a moving speech, "Farewell to America," in which she said that her Western Maryland days would be remembered fondly forever. It was reported in the *Democratic Advocate* that Miss Hirata had made many friends during her stay in America and that she was returning to her native land to engage in missionary work.[60] Since her enrollment, a steady stream of students from foreign countries worldwide have enrolled at the college and broadened the horizons of their fellow students.[61]

Major Events

The decade witnessed a number of major events on campus, many to break ground for or dedicate new buildings. On October 28, 1887, Smith Hall was formally opened with great fanfare. The *Monthly* reported that "in spite of the weather which was wet and disagreeable, a large and brilliant audience assembled in the Auditorium, then for the first time used," and enjoyed a program that included four musical presentations (piano and vocal) by faculty members T. F. Rinehart and Mrs. A. J. Carnes, several addresses and recitations by students, and three exhibitions of calisthenics led by W. R. McDaniel: club swinging by the young ladies, dumbbells by the young men, and marching by the young ladies.[62]

Commencement Week of 1888 featured many of the usual events and some new ones. A complete description of the week will provide a clear picture of this most important time in the college calendar of the period. A calisthenics exhibition was presented on Saturday evening under the direction of Prof. McDaniel and consisted of ten different activities, all performed to music provided by piano, organ, and drums. Figure marching by 32 young men "uniformed in neatly fitting shirts trimmed with blue and pants with blue belts" showed precision of step and a very soldierly appearance. Club swinging was a big feature of the program. The young women "executed some of the most intricate swings and twists such as would have done credit to professionals, and the skill with which the club continually passed from one hand to the other was marvelous." The Cane Drill and Broom Brigade provided an entertaining conclusion to the evening, since the ladies wore flannel dresses, with dusting caps to match, and carried dust pans.[63] The Baccalaureate Service, with President Lewis preaching the sermon, was held the next day, for the first time on campus in the new auditorium. That evening, the Christian associations of the college held a service in the M.P. Church.

On Monday an art exhibition was opened in the art studio on the third floor of the Main Building under the direction of the new art instructor, Miss Olivia Rinehart, niece of the celebrated sculptor William H. Rinehart and a fine artist in her own right. Over 165 pieces were on exhibition, including drawings, water colors, oils, decorative painting, and embroidery by students and local artists. They were judged by a teacher from the Maryland Institute of Art and Design.

Tuesday morning was devoted to the awarding of prizes and the reading of grades. When Prof. McDaniel, secretary of the faculty, read the grades for the year, the students sat in profound silence except when some brilliant record deserved a round of applause. Medals were awarded to the students in each class who had attained a grade of 9 or better in all their studies, and certificates of deportment were handed to those students who had managed to attain a behavior grade of 10 for the year. The literary societies held their reunions (of former members and alumni) on Tuesday afternoon, featuring lengthy programs of readings and music. On Tuesday evening another new feature was unveiled. The men of the Irving and Webster societies continued with the annual oratorical contest, but for the first time, the ladies of the Browning and Philomathean societies also competed in the composition and reading of essays. Each of the four societies was represented by two individuals. A large and appreciative audience enjoyed the contest, which was enlivened by music from the Westminster Cornet Band played at intervals throughout the evening.

Wednesday morning the class of '88 held its Class Day exercises. This event was always expected to be humorous, indeed sometimes ridiculous, and spoofed many of the college traditions. "Reading of the Grades" was a burlesque on the official announcement by the faculty of the students' scholastic standing and deportment. A Class History included all who had ever been a part of the class and was full of dry wit. The Class Prophecy described the future of those soon to be "torn from the tender embrace of their alma mater." And, finally, the *Class Annals* (forerunner of the yearbook) were presented to the faculty to be preserved in the archives, and a brass shield containing the class motto and the names of the graduates was presented to the college. (The brass shields hung first in Old Main, then in the lower level of Alumni Hall for many years but were moved to the narthex of Baker Memorial Chapel when Alumni Hall was renovated in 1979.) Wednesday evening a large audience gathered to hear the annual oration before the societies, given that year by the Hon. Milton G. Urner of Frederick, whose topic was "Individual Responsibility." The eloquent speech was well received and "tended to impress deeply the moral lessons of which it was so full." At last, the great Commencement Day arrived, on Thursday, and the ceremony was held in the new Smith Hall auditorium. It featured a number of musical performances, addresses by the valedictorians and salutatorians, and an address to the graduating class by President Lewis, who also conferred the degrees. The 21st year of Western Maryland College was officially concluded.[64]

In March of 1889, the teachers of Carroll County held an "institute" (an in-service?) in Smith Hall, with Western Maryland students presenting a program of music, recitations, and calisthenics. In attendance was the state superintendent of schools, M. Alexander Newell, who noted that the college might justly be called the leading college in the state because it gave equal attention to all sides of education: physical, mental, moral, and athletic. (Newell was simultaneously the founding principal of the State Normal School at Towson from 1866 to 1890.)

The new Yingling Gymnasium was formally opened on October 29, 1889.

Interior of Yingling Gymnasium I;
note indoor track and Indian clubs.

The main floor had horizontal and parallel bars, rings, ladders, ropes, and other equipment. The suspended indoor track (33 laps to a mile) could also be used for seating above the main floor. The basement contained bathrooms and would eventually be fitted out with showers for the male students. Two hundred and fifty people, including Anna Yingling, whose generous donation had made the building possible, walked from the Main Building to the entrance of the gymnasium, where the doors were thrown open to reveal the brightly gas-lit and spacious facility, touted as the largest of its kind in the state. During the dedication ceremonies, President Lewis noted that the "purpose . . . is not to make acrobats or even athletes of the students, but to develop them into strong and healthy men and women. Daily systematic exercise will be given to all, as the course is compulsory." The evening's program featured demonstrations of Baltimore's finest amateur gymnasts, as well as various calisthenics demonstrations by the college students.[65] A sad footnote to the event is that Anna Yingling died the following August 16 at the age of 38.

Once the President's House was completed, in December 1889, President Lewis and his family quickly moved in. Several days later, on the 18th (a very inclement night, it was reported), the Lewises held a reception and supper for the faculty and boarding students. "Our host laid aside his official garb and showed how genial the true man could be. He seemed a boy again, just for the night," reported the *Monthly*. Of special importance to the students that evening was the fact that the young gentlemen were allowed to select their partners for the evening and then escort the young ladies to the house. They were received in the parlor, then proceeded to the library, and from there to a general inspection of the house. Every spot in the house seemed to be full, and the students passed the time in each other's company until ten o'clock. "Truly, it was a grand and glorious occasion," according to the *Monthly*.[66] The *Monthly* also reported that several times during the college year the Lewises entertained groups of students at the house, for picnics, receptions, and ice cream socials. During the next 31 years, the Lewises would raise six children in the house, all of whom would attend the school and the college (Miriam '96, Clara Ward '98, Thomas Hubert '02, Marjorie '06, Hamilton Ward '08, and Elizabeth Ray '19).

President's House (1889)

CONCLUSION

The decade from 1881 to 1890 saw many remarkable and significant changes in the college, the most important being the retirement of the founding president, J. T. Ward, and the selection of Thomas H. Lewis as his successor. Ward at 66 was tired and ready for the less demanding role in the new seminary. He had given 20 years of his life, as well as a great deal of his personal wealth (inherited from his father), to the institution he helped to establish and nurtured through many trying times. He was not as strong a businessman as his successor, but he was truly a wonderful human being. Lewis's careful planning, debt reduction and elimination, and extraordinary skill at managing money led to a flurry of building projects to accommodate the ever growing institution. He obviously had the confidence and respect of the board of trustees, so that the college moved forward quickly to become recognized as a significant institution in the state. Lewis, a brilliant man with many capabilities, was ably assisted by a gradually improving faculty, but especially by the young William McDaniel, a Renaissance man with many abilities and interests and much enthusiasm. As the college entered the last decade of the 19th century, it could look forward to strengthening its curriculum, faculty, and endowment in preparation for the new century to come.

CHAPTER 3 ENDNOTES

1. *Irving Literary Gazette*, May 1883, 4.
2. WMC board of trustees minutes, June 20, 1883.
3. Ward, Diaries, July 7, 1883.
4. Ibid., July 13, 1883.
5. Ibid., July 30, 1883.
6. *Irving Literary Gazette*, September 1883, 4.
7. Ward, Diaries, October 3, 1883.
8. *WMC Monthly*, February 1888, 75.
9. WMC board of trustees minutes, June 20, 1883.
10. *Irving Literary Gazette*, September 1883, 2.
11. Schofield and Crain, *Formative Years*, 30.
12. Ward, Diaries, August 24, 1883.
13. "Ripley's Believe It or Not," August 10, 1969, King Features Syndicate.
14. Ward, Diaries, September 19, 1883.
15. Ibid., October 28, 1883.
16. Ibid., June 1885.
17. Ibid., March 16, 1883.
18. WMC board of trustees minutes, January 27, 1886.
19. Letter from Charles Roberts, Ward Papers.
20. Letter from James Diffenbaugh, Ward Papers.
21. WMC board of trustees minutes, June 1886.
22. *WMC Monthly*, November 1888, 172.
23. Ibid., October 1887, 4.
24. Ibid., November 1887, 20–23.
25. *Irving Literary Gazette*, May 1886, 5; September 1886, 5.
26. Ward, Diaries, August 15, 1882.
27. *Democratic Advocate*, Westminster, Maryland, August 25, 1882.
28. Schofield and Crain, *Formative Years*, 39.
29. WMC board of trustees minutes, June 17, 1883; Schofield and Crain, *Formative Years*, 25.
30. Schofield and Crain, *Formative Years*, 34.
31. Ibid., 40.
32. *WMC Monthly*; WMC board of trustees minutes.
33. *WMC Monthly*, December 1888, 194.
34. Ibid., May 1889, 276.
35. 1901 *Aloha*, 139.
36. WMC board of trustees minutes, June 16, 1880.
37. *WMC Monthly*, April 1890, 402.
38. Schofield and Crain, *Formative Years*, 32.
39. *WMC Monthly*, December 1888, 188.
40. Page 13.
41. November 1887, 43.
42. WMC faculty minutes, December 1888.
43. Pages 326–27.
44. *WMC Monthly*, December 1887, 45.
45. Ibid., January 1888, 60.
46. Ibid., May 1890, 420.
47. May 1888, 121–22.
48. Page 228.
49. Schofield and Crain, *Formative Years*, 51–52.
50. *WMC Magazine*, October 1965, 15.
51. *WMC Monthly*, November 1888, 171.
52. Ibid., October 1889, 310.
53. WMC faculty minutes, November 1889.
54. Makosky, *Western Maryland College*, 13.
55. May 21, 1881.
56. *WMC Monthly*, May 1888, 121.
57. Ibid., June/July, 1889, 295.
58. Ibid., June/July, 1890, 434–35.
59. Makosky, *Western Maryland College*, 13.
60. *Democratic Advocate*, Westminster, Maryland, June 20, 1890.
61. Schofield and Crain, *Formative Years*, 50–51.
62. November 1887, 25.
63. *WMC Monthly*, June/July 1888, 140–41.
64. Ibid., June/July 1888, 140–50.
65. Ibid., November 1889, 324.
66. Ibid., January 1890, 358.

MAJOR WORLD EVENTS

1881

London has a population of 3.3 million, Paris 2.2 million, New York 1.2 million.
James A. Garfield is inaugurated as 20th U.S. president.
Garfield is assassinated a few months later; succeeded by Chester A. Arthur.
Henry James publishes *Portrait of a Lady.*
Monet paints *Sunshine and Snow.*
Brahms composes *Academic Festival Overture.*

1882

Robert Louis Stevenson publishes *Treasure Island.*
Henrik Ibsen publishes *An Enemy of the People.*
Longfellow dies.
Tchaikovsky composes *1812 Overture.*
World Exhibition is held in Moscow.
American Baseball Association founded.

1883

Karl Marx dies.
John Maynard Keynes is born.
Renoir paints *Umbrellas.*
Metropolitan Opera House opens in New York.
First skyscraper (ten stories) is built in Chicago.
Frontiersman W. F. Cody organizes his "Wild West Show."

1884

Mark Twain publishes *Huckleberry Finn.*
Rodin sculpts *The Burghers of Calais.*
Charles Parsons invents first practical steam turbine engine.
Gold is discovered near Johannesburg, South Africa.
London opens the first underground railroad system.

1885

Grover Cleveland is inaugurated as 22nd U.S. president.
Francis Galton proves the individuality of fingerprints.
Gilbert and Sullivan produce *The Mikado.*

1886

First Indian National Congress meets.
Statue of Liberty is dedicated in New York.
R. L. Stevenson publishes *Dr. Jekyll and Mr. Hyde.*
American Federation of Labor is founded.
Canadian Pacific Railway is completed.

1887

Queen Victoria celebrates her Golden Jubilee.
Arthur Conan Doyle publishes *A Study in Scarlet*, the first of the Sherlock Holmes mysteries.
Strindberg publishes *The Father*.
Stainer composes the oratorio *The Crucifixion*.
Verdi's opera *Otello* opens in Milan.
Hannibal Goodwin invents celluloid film.

1888

Van Gogh paints *The Yellow Chair*.
Rimsky-Korsakov composes *Sheherazade*.
George Eastman perfects the Kodak box camera.
J. B. Dunlop invents the pneumatic tire.
"Jack the Ripper" murders six women in London.
Lawn Tennis Association founded.
Nikola Tesla constructs first electric motor.

1889

Benjamin Harrison is inaugurated as 23rd U.S. president.
Adolf Hitler is born.
T. H. Huxley publishes "Agnosticism," having coined the word 20 years earlier.
Eiffel designs the 1,056-foot-high tower for the Paris World Exhibition.
Catholic University opens in Washington.
A punch card system, the first automated data-processing system, is created by Herman Hollerith.

1890

Swiss government introduces social insurance.
Idaho and Wyoming become U.S. states.
Luxembourg is separated from the Netherlands.
Oscar Wilde publishes *The Picture of Dorian Gray*.
First motion picture films are shown in New York.
Rubber gloves are first used in surgery (at Johns Hopkins Hospital).
First entirely steel-framed building is erected in Chicago.

*Alumni Hall (1899) is seen through the Ward Memorial Arch (1898);
the Reifsnider mansion (1873) is in the background.*

C H A P T E R

A DECADE OF SIGNIFICANT CHANGES

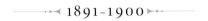

◁ 1 8 9 1 - 1 9 0 0 ▷

The last decade of the 19th century in America witnessed phenomenal technological innovations, a mid-decade economic recession, an explosion of literary and musical compositions from Europe, and a war with Spain. The papers were full of the exploits of Theodore Roosevelt; the inventiveness of Edison, Marconi, and Ford; and the creativity of Monet, George Bernard Shaw, Oscar Wilde, and Tchaikovsky. It was the so-called Gay Nineties. A relatively few large firms came to dominate the American business scene, and the Sherman Anti-Trust Act sought to control the activities of the large corporations, especially those of the robber barons. Spurred on by increasing affluence in the country, U.S. colleges and universities were growing, and some new ones were being created. The December 1891 "College World" column in the *WMC Monthly* reported that Princeton was approaching 1,000 students, the University of Michigan had 2,750, Harvard had 2,663, and Johns Hopkins had 138 graduate students enrolled.[1] The new University of Chicago (founded by John D. Rockefeller) opened in September 1892 with facilities to accommodate 600 students. Brown University went coeducational. By 1896, there were 27 universities and colleges in the United States that registered over a thousand students, and ground had just been broken for the new American

University in Washington, D.C.[2] College presidential salaries were averaging $10,000, with David Jordan at Stanford making $15,000 (the highest in the U.S.).[3] At Western Maryland College in 1894, President Lewis's salary was $2,000, even as major changes were taking place in the administration, curriculum, enrollment, and facilities. He was working very hard, and that was beginning to affect his health.

FACULTY AND ADMINISTRATION

As the college opened for its 25th year, in 1891, 16 of the original 34 trustees were still active; not surprisingly, by the end of the decade, only 10 would be. Most significantly, John Smith of Wakefield, the venerable and conscientious board president since the founding of the college, died on March 13, 1892, at the age of 85. He had been most generous to the college, often anonymously when funds were needed to keep the institution afloat. His wise counsel, dedication, and singular support would be greatly missed. He was lovingly eulogized by J. T. Ward as one who "took the deepest interest in the success of the college, which, through all the years he had done so much to promote," and Ward noted the impossibility of appreciating all that Smith had done for the college, especially in its earliest days, as a member of the Local Committee.[4] He was succeeded by his son Joseph W. Smith '80 [1892–1922]. Isaac C. Baile, another founding trustee, who had joined Smith in lending funds for the initial college building, and who had served as treasurer or assistant treasurer for 17 years, also died in 1892 and was succeeded on the board by his son Nathan H. Baile [1893–1926]. In June 1892, J. T. Ward (now the seminary president) was elected president of the board of trustees, and President Lewis was elected secretary (the traditional role of the WMC president).

Since he had become president, the years had taken their toll on Lewis. He had spent much time and energy reducing and then eliminating the debt, attracting more students, revamping the curriculum, handling the college finances, and planning and supervising the erection of four buildings. As he was the sole administrator of the college, he felt the "weight of responsibility so much."[5] The frenetic pace, coupled with some physical weakness, caused him to consider resigning the presidency in June 1891. When he apprised the board of his health concern, it voted to give him whatever time off he needed to rest and be free of responsibilities and agreed to give him whatever help he needed upon his return.[6] Some of the trustees even funded a trip around the world for the ailing president, a journey he commenced in September 1891. Dr. Reese was appointed acting president in his absence. Lewis crossed the United States,

*President Lewis seated in a rickshaw (at the right)
on a trip to Japan (1891)*

stopping in Denver, Salt Lake City, and San Francisco. Then he went by steamer, via Hawaii, to Japan (the chief object of his trip). He visited the leading cities of India, crossed Asia to the Suez Canal, and toured Egypt. Finally, he toured the principal cities of Europe, returning in mid-February after five months.[7]

In November 1891, Lewis responded to a letter from McDaniel that had reached him in Japan. It gives further insight into his physical and mental state:

The moment I recognized your writing, I thought, "It has come at last. Now I'll have to go back to the fires." But you so pleasantly relieved and entertained me that I was quite ashamed of myself for my fears. Really, I cannot help it. If I were compelled to go back to college work this moment, I think I might become desperate. Somehow I cannot bring myself to endure the thought. . . . I am somewhat ashamed of the fact that I am unable to look to my work as yet with pleasure. The experiences of last year gave me a terrible wrench and my gorge still rises when I think of some individuals. . . . I have just reveled in the rest and balm of the ocean; its great caps seemed so restful and its every motion hushed me to repose. And then I landed and day after day the pleasures and wonders of this land have unrolled themselves before me crowding out every care and filling my mind with the constant joy of change. . . . I am perfectly dazed with what I have seen. The month I spent here is certainly the most wonderful of my life.[8]

In January, big plans were made to welcome President Lewis back from his round-the-world trip. First there would be a general reception by the students and faculty, then a luncheon would be held for the students with

Lewis, and finally a supper would be given by the faculty for Lewis and invited guests. The college buildings were to be illuminated on the evening of his arrival, and a group of faculty would greet him at the railroad station. His return on February 9 must have been a very special event, indeed.[9] Soon thereafter, accompanied by Mrs. Lewis, he sailed for Bermuda to spend the winter. It was reported that his health continued to improve. The faculty did not ignore the acting president, Dr. Reese, however; it passed a resolution of appreciation and commendation for his efforts while Lewis was away.[10]

Keeping its promise to provide Lewis with some administrative help, in June 1894 the board elected, on Lewis's nomination, William McDaniel as treasurer of the board (i.e., the college) to take over some of the duties theretofore handled by the president. (This was the first time that a trustee had not served as treasurer, but the change was accepted, perhaps gratefully, by the trustees.) The college administration now consisted of two people.

Sadness fell upon the campus community on June 19, 1894, when word reached Westminster that Miss Lottie Owings had died after a dangerous operation at the age of 54. She had served for 20 years (actively for 15, while also tending to her invalid mother) as preceptress and later director of the primary school, and was much beloved, especially by the female students. The board noted that "her counsel, her patience, her tact, her wise discriminating judgment were invaluable."[11] Indeed, she had been awarded an honorary master of arts degree ten years earlier. She was eulogized in the *Monthly* with this statement: "Of the influence of her completely rounded character, and the example of her noble womanhood, death cannot deprive us."[12] Shortly thereafter, the trustees voted to name the Main Hall addition (built in 1871) Owings Hall in her memory. Four months later, on October 14, 1894, the campus learned of the death of John Byrd Whaley '89, who had completed studies at the Westminster Theological Seminary in 1891, gone on to the University of Chicago for two years of additional doctoral work, and just been elected professor of biblical literature at the college in June 1894. The locally well-known and respected 27-year-old theologian died after an illness of several weeks, never having taken up the post at his alma mater.[13]

In 1896, President Lewis reported that the college had eight faculty members and three additional teachers in art and music; the primary and preparatory schools had three teachers, as well. By the end of the decade, the faculty had grown by two, and of the ten faculty members, three held earned PhD degrees. (The first faculty member to hold an earned doctorate was George Washington Ward '90, professor of history and political science, who joined the faculty in 1891 and earned his PhD at Johns Hopkins in 1897.)

On March 4, 1897, Western Maryland College lost the most important figure in its founding when former president Dr. J. T. Ward died at his home at the age of 76. At the funeral service, Prof. McDaniel, secretary of the faculty, read a memorial statement that had been adopted by the faculty. It said, in part,

> We are saddened by the withdrawal of his familiar and inspiring presence. We miss his words of cheer, his hearty expression of interest and encouragement in our work. . . . The biography of Dr. Ward is a part, and a large part, of the history of the college, and the college is itself his monument. His name, his character, his influence, his abilities carried it safely through the early years of struggle and, at times almost of despair, and the reputation which it bears today among the schools of Maryland is built upon the deep and solid foundation laid during his presidency.[14]

On the evening of June 16, during Commencement Week, when a number of former students had returned to the campus, a Service of Commemoration of the life, character, and services of Dr. Ward was held, with Prof. Reese presiding. A year later, Ward's niece, Mrs. Ulie Norment Hurley, made a gift of $1,000 to erect a memorial gateway to the college grounds in his memory. It was built over the drive leading to the top of the hill, near the President's House, and stood there until the summer of 1936, when it was moved to its present location. Sometime after Ward's burial in the Westminster Cemetery, a large monument surmounted by a marble sphere was erected in the center of the family plot. Engraved on it are these words: "A Tribute from some of his college students who revered and loved him in life and will ever cherish his memory. 'For he was a good man and full of Holy Ghost and of Faith.'"

An interesting footnote is that Ward was never named president emeritus. When he retired in 1886, he had been named emeritus professor of mental and moral science, but, strangely, the emeritus administrative title was never forthcoming. He was always referred to as the ex-president. At the meeting of the board in June 1895, a trustee offered a belated resolution to remedy this, suggesting that Ward should be named president emeritus and that a small salary be paid him. The board minutes report only that the resolution was withdrawn without a vote, perhaps at Ward's request; he may have felt that he did not need the emeritus stipend because of his position as president of the seminary.

At its meeting in June 1897, the board of trustees elected Joshua Hering as its president. Hering had been a charter trustee, of course, and treasurer for 17 years (1868–85); he would serve as board president for 16 years, until his death in 1913.[15]

The position of dean (really dean of men) was created in 1896 and filled by George W. Ward '90 (also the history teacher), who lived on campus on the male side to match the preceptress on the female side (the title dean of women would

A gathering of faculty on the steps in front
of the Main Building, c. 1895

not come into use until 1918). The decade also saw a number of faculty changes and additions. Prof. Thomas Rinehart [music, 1886–93] left to go to Adrian College and was replaced by Miss Mary Eugenia Lewis, who remained until 1900. The following people also joined the faculty as the college grew: William Black [1891–1901] in classics; Rowland Watts [1894–1904] in mathematics and science (to teach those courses given up by McDaniel when he became treasurer); Ferdinand Bonnotte, PhD [1897–1932] in foreign languages; Leon Sampaix [1898–1905] in piano; and George Wills [1898–1904, 1922–44], the first full-time English teacher. In June 1900, Shadrack Simpson, who had received a PhD in chemistry from Johns Hopkins in 1898, resigned to become secretary (superintendent) of the Carroll County school board. His daughter, Iona Jewell Simpson (1881–1969), attended the primary and preparatory schools of the college and graduated as valedictorian of the class of 1899. She went on to be the first woman named assistant superintendent of schools of Maryland, a post she held from 1925 to 1942.

Shadrack Simpson in laboratory

As this decade closed, the ever present and always busy President Lewis was accorded another honor, when his bust was created in marble by Miss Grace Lee Rinehart '95, a student at the Maryland Institute of Art. While a student at the college, she had studied pencil drawing and oil painting with the art teacher, her sister, Miss Olivia Rinehart [1887–98], and then gone on to study sculpture, following in the footsteps of her distinguished uncle, Carroll County native William H. Rinehart (for whom the Rinehart School of Sculpture at the Maryland Institute College of Art is named). The bust was presented to the Alumni Association in June 1899 by the young accomplished sculptor, and a picture of it appeared in the 1900 *Aloha*.[16] (It was also pictured in an alumni publication at least 75 years later, but unfortunately, its present location is unknown.)

Buildings and Grounds

This decade saw nine buildings added to the small campus. The primary school, established in 1886, had no rooms for its exclusive use, so in 1891 the trustees decided to erect a building for the school on the Main Street Kreitzer property, which abutted the college property. Most of the money for this project was given by trustee Dr. Charles Billingslea [1872–1918], and the structure was named Levine Hall in memory of his young son, James Levine Billingslea, who had died suddenly on June 15, 1890, of complications from measles.[17] (The child was the grandson of John Smith, Dr. Billingslea having married Smith's daughter Clara.) Hubert Lewis, the president's son and a fellow student of the six-year-old Levine in the primary school, laid the cornerstone at a formal ceremony.[18] By 1898, President Lewis reported to the board that interest in the community for continuance of the primary school was waning (perhaps due to the development of and improvement in the local public elementary schools), and that the school was running at a loss of about $500 a year. Noting that the school was "undertaken in the first place only as a duty to the community," he recommended its closure. The board agreed, and the program was gradually phased out. Levine Hall was then enlarged (at a cost of $4,580) with another floor of classrooms and dormitory rooms to accommodate the preparatory school, which took occupancy in 1900.

The next new building was erected in 1892 behind the Main Building, to provide a facility for the YMCA and YWCA. The *Monthly* reported that there was a reading room on the first floor and a nicely furnished hall on the second floor for weekly devotional and prayer meetings. The furnishings, including a Brussels carpet, an organ, and cane-bottom chairs, were purchased by funds

Levine Hall (1891), the primary school;
enlarged in 1900 to house the preparatory school

raised mainly among the faculty and students.[19] Prior to this, a room in the Main Building had been set aside for the groups' use.

On February 19, 1893, a violent windstorm raced through Westminster, removing the roof of Smith Hall. The young women living there were unhurt and were promptly quartered for the night in the society rooms and the library.[20] The damages were soon repaired at a cost of about $700, but this led Lewis to recommend adding a story to Smith Hall (above the auditorium) to provide additional sleeping rooms, and also a tower at the corner to complete the front perspective of the complex to match the Hering Hall–Ward Hall arrangement at the other end. This was accomplished with dispatch using the surplus for the year of $7,113.[21]

In October 1894, it was announced that a gift of $5,000 for a campus chapel had been made by William G. Baker, a college trustee [1877–1922]. A senior member of the firm Daniel Baker and Sons of Buckeystown, Baker gave the chapel as a thank-you offering for the successful recovery of his son, William G. Baker Jr., who had suffered a critical illness and surgery in the summer following his graduation as valedictorian of the class of 1894. The building, designed by Jackson Gott, was completed in nine months and formally dedicated on May 12, 1895, a major event of the decade. (A detailed history of Baker Chapel, *A Grateful Memory*, was prepared and published for the 100th anniversary of the building,

*Western Maryland College c. 1900; note the towers and
porches across the front facade and Ward Hall II.*

in 1995, by Dr. Ira G. Zepp Jr., professor emeritus of religious studies.)

That same summer, Ward Hall (which had been remodeled several times during its 13-year existence) was razed and a new and larger Ward Hall built in its place, connected to Hering Hall, at a cost of $6,779 (using many of the materials from the old building). When the students returned to the campus in the fall, they were astonished to find the old building gone and the new building ready for occupancy. The construction could be done quickly because the old building had no plumbing and only very basic electricity. The *Monthly* described the new residence hall:

> *The building is divided into two sections, the main one containing twenty-six dormitories [rooms], and the lower or preparatory section, twelve. . . . The rooms are nice and neat, lighted with two large windows, and containing each a wardrobe, table, chairs, and a pretty iron bedstead [for two], as also a washstand of the same material. On the ground floor are the Preparatory and Freshman rooms, and five study rooms, which are rented to town students. . . . The main entrance is a wide flight of steps with a broad rail, and faces the gymnasium. Over the door is placed the name "Ward Hall" in carved letters, the idea being that this building, replacing as it does the structure erected through the efforts of our revered ex-President, could do no better than bear his name.*[22]

Several homes were built for professors during the latter years of the decade. Three were erected on lots purchased on College Avenue beyond Baker Chapel, and in 1896 one was built behind the President's House for the college treasurer, William McDaniel, for $2,500. It should be mentioned, however, that McDaniel paid $500 for the heating and plumbing in the house (and paid a yearly rent of $150). On November 21, 1895, he had married Ada Smith, youngest daughter of the stalwart first president of the board. The marriage occurred at noon at the Main Street home of her brother Joseph Smith, who presented her in marriage. The college faculty attended, and Prof. William Black was the best man. President Lewis performed the ceremony, after which a luncheon was served to all in attendance before they escorted the couple to the railway station (where 100 students also waited to see them off), from which they left for a honeymoon trip to Atlanta.[23] Soon after the couple moved into their new home, they held a reception for the faculty and students, and the home was pronounced "one of the most attractive buildings on the hill."[24]

Early in the decade (about 1891), there was a movement among the alumni to build a campus building envisioned as providing a large hall for Alumni Association meetings, smaller meeting rooms and libraries for the literary societies, and some dormitory space for students. The Alumni Association started a campaign to raise $5,000, but funds from the 363 living alumni were slow to materialize. It became obvious to President Lewis that it would be impossible for the alumni to carry out the project alone, and so to make the dream a reality, he reconfigured the plans to include an auditorium seating 1,000 people, as well as meeting rooms for the Alumni Association and the literary societies. At the June 1896 meeting of the board, he proposed that the foundations for this new building be immediately laid, using the money already collected, and a broad-based campaign be launched to collect the estimated $20,000 needed for completion, with work on the building to move along as money was collected.[25]

The *Monthly* reported on the November cornerstone laying ceremony: *A great throng of citizens of Westminster and the surrounding country, with many persons from a distance interested in Western Maryland College gathered around the foundation walls of the prospective alumni hall Tuesday afternoon to witness the laying of the corner-stone. . . . [The program consisted of] an opening prayer by Rev. Dr. J. T. Ward [his last official appearance], remarks by Mayor Joseph W. Smith '80 . . . [and] Senator J. W. Hering, of the board of trustees. . . . President D. C. Gilman of Johns Hopkins University was on the program for an address, but was unable to be present, and Dr. Griffin, Dean of the University, spoke in his stead. Rev. James W. Reese, Ph.D., Professor of Ancient Languages of Western Maryland College, acted as worshipful master of the [Door to Virtue Masonic] lodge, and conducted the laying of the stone, giving great impressiveness to the beautiful ceremony.*[26]

Among the numerous things deposited in the cornerstone were the charter and Fundamental Ordinances of the college, a historical sketch of the college, a list of all the students connected with the college during the first 25 years, a college catalog, copies of various local newspapers and college periodicals, and the Bible that President Lewis had carried with him on his tour around the world. The ceremony was concluded with a reception for Dean Griffin at the President's House. The *Monthly* went on to describe the prospective building in great detail, noting that it was to be 82 feet by 108 feet, the lower levels containing classrooms for the preparatory school and rooms for the societies, with rooms planned for alumni gatherings and committee meetings, as well as a banquet hall with an orchestra balcony. The main auditorium located on the floor above was to be 65 by 75 feet in the form of an amphitheater with a half-circle raked stage, the rear of which would be a raised corridor surrounded by Ionic columns. Theater seats were to be placed around the back of the stage, as well. It was to be in the Italian Renaissance style.[27]

By June 1897, Alumni Hall, as it was named, was up to the first floor at an expense of $5,000 (of which alumni had paid $4,500). In October 1897, the board authorized a mortgage of $25,000 to finish the building and pay off some earlier debts. It also authorized 20-year bonds and requested authorization from the legislature to issue them. By June 1898, President Lewis reported having sold $23,300 in bonds, and he was given the go-ahead to finish Alumni Hall at a total cost of $24,000. The building was finished in 1899 just in time for Commencement, and its dedication was a major event of the Commencement weekend and the decade. It immediately became a popular spot for large town and church gatherings. Indeed, as the century came to a close, the auditorium was being used by so many state and local groups that some trustees felt it should be kept strictly for college use. However, they did not prevail, and the building remained Westminster's "civic auditorium" for almost 75 years.

By June 1899, with a surplus of $13,175 in hand, President Lewis recommended, and the board approved, an addition to Smith Hall to provide even more sleeping rooms, as well as an expansion of the dining hall and kitchen. (This addition would be further expanded in the next decade and named McKinstry Hall.) It was completed at a cost of $4,942.

Finally, in June 1900, a small addition (about five feet) to Owings Hall, costing $1,388, was approved to provide apartments for the director of the gymnasium and the steward, as well as a women's bath and toilet room on the third floor.[28]

FINANCES

By June 1893, Lewis had turned his attention to the most pressing need of the college: the endowment fund. The board created a Finance Committee to manage such a fund, which had been created and now stood at $1,814 (including $500 seed money, the 1873 gift of Mrs. Tamsey Reese, and a $500 anonymous gift from John Smith in 1890).[29] By 1897 the fund had grown to $2,127, but Lewis knew that it would have to grow more quickly for the college to keep pace with its competitors. He noted quite forthrightly in his annual report to the board,

> We desire to have the reputation of being progressive, efficient, and at the same time preserve undisturbed our old time reputation for good moral and Christian influences. There can be no doubt that the condition of colleges is undergoing a change. What once answered will no longer meet the competition of rival schools springing up in every direction. It remains to be seen whether we can keep up our record in the van of progress while at the same time withdrawing so considerable a part of our revenue for material improvements. The history of the College is exceptional, not only paying its way, but paying for its plant out of current receipts. I think we shall not be able to keep this up. . . . The Trustees could properly it seems to me at this time make a formal appeal to be published in the church papers representing the absolute necessity for liberality on the part of the friends of the College to meet this new state of things. The College is too great to be allowed to wane, but its greatness already attained will be seriously endangered unless help comes from without.[30]

Enrollments continued to grow in almost every year of the decade, as they had since Lewis became president. In 1890–91, 242 students were enrolled (154 in the college, 75 in the precollege programs, and 13 special students); the following year the number increased by 1, the collegiate enrollment dropping to 148 but the precollegiate number rising to 87, and 8 special students. During 1892–93, the enrollments rose sharply, to 262, primarily because of the preparatory school. However, in his June 1894 report (the first to be typewritten), Lewis reported enrollments for the 1893–94 year down by 22, the first drop in eight years. He attributed this to the "stringency of the times," a mid-decade economic downturn, during which many colleges were having the same problem. The decrease was in special students and the collegiate enrollment, especially the senior class (36 in 1893, 20 in 1894). But he was pleased to report that the Department of Music was flourishing under Miss Lewis (who had taken over the program the previous September). He also presented faculty salaries for approval:

President Lewis *$2,000*
Prof. Reese *$900*
Prof. Simpson *$900*
Prof. McDaniel.. *$900 and board*
                    (because of his 12-month service as treasurer)
Prof. Black *$600*
Prof. Ward *$425*
Prof. Watson *$600*
Prof. Watts *$700*
Prof. Whaley *$600*

All other special subject instructors: $300–$500 and board

To meet this payroll and other college expenses, student fees (raised slightly when Lewis became president and not changed significantly since 1886) were increased to the following for 1896–97:

- *tuition, board, room, heat, light, and laundry—$200/year*
- *college tuition alone—$45/year*
- *preparatory school tuition alone—$30/year*
- *instrumental music, vocal music, and art—$45/year for special students*

At a special meeting of the board in April 1895, where the $30,000 budget for the coming year was discussed, Lewis noted, in conjunction with other financial matters, that more than one-fourth of all enrolled students (in the primary school, preparatory school, and college) were paying no tuition at all, because they were children of Methodist ministers, other local clergy, or faculty. This practice had been in effect since the beginning of the college, but he was questioning its continuance for obvious reasons. He recommended charging ministers half the regular tuition. The next year, in another move to save money, he recommended creating a creamery on campus (his recommendation was ultimately rejected as impractical). He also proposed to build the college's own electric system, and that was approved. The generator was added to the heating-boiler room. His report of this 1897 venture gives insight into his analytical mind:

We were compelled to put in our own Electric Light plant or abandon the use of electricity. The Westminster Company which began to furnish us light two years before at a rate suggested by them of $375 a year, informed us that they could not afford to continue the supply at the same rate, and we must pay in the future, $600 a year . . . to have 200 lights wired and burn 150 at any one time. The result was we contracted with the Maryland Manufacturing and Construction Company of Baltimore to put in a dynamo and engine capable of supplying us with 350 lights, for $1,325.00. Additional expense was incurred in wiring outdoor connections, making the total amount expended . . . $1,404.65. The *plant has never been out of order since the first night it began to run, and the quality of light has been all that we could desire. . . . More remarkable is the financial outcome. . . . Instead of paying $375 . . . or $600 . . . our whole expense of running the plant for this year, including coal, oil, and service of engineer over the previous cost of the watchman who was dispensed with because the engineer served in both capacities, was $230.00. We could add to this amount about ten percent on the cost of the plant for wear and tear, $132.50, and still be $12.30 a year better off than we were under the old rate, and $237.50 better off than we would have been under the new rate. But in fact if our plant only lasts us four years we can make money by buying a new plant every four years.*[31]

His careful calculations and shrewd suggestions indicate how, in the previous decade, he had been able to amass surpluses each year to liquidate the debt in four years. As Schofield pointed out, "Perhaps there could be no better illustration of the degree of difference that separates us from that period than the pride President Lewis obviously took in saving $12.30 a year."[32]

By the end of the decade, Prof. McDaniel's services were even more appreciated, and his salary had increased to $1,400 (he was no longer receiving board since he was married and living in his new home). President Lewis refused a $1,000 raise, but the board overruled him. It was now truly time to take a major step forward with the endowment, and Lewis had a plan for doing so in the new century.

CURRICULUM

In 1892, a revised entrance examination was put into place for all new students. It included short-answer questions in addition to longer, essay questions in English, grammar, arithmetic, algebra, and Latin. Blanche Murchison '95, who transferred to the college from North Carolina as a junior, wrote of her reactions to these exams in the *Monthly*: "The anxiety of the next day is never to be forgotten. How I went from one room to another where I was greeted by grave professors and a paper with the questions on it or pointed to the blackboard whereon was written the examinations which were to decide my fate. For two whole days was I in anxious suspense, being weighed in the balances. But luckily for me my weight was found sufficient to admit me to the desired class."[33]

At a special meeting in April 1894, the board of trustees approved the first major change in the college curriculum since its inception. Instead of the single basic course for the degree, all students would take the same course only for the first two years. At the beginning of the junior year, students would select from three degree routes: scientific, historical, or classical. In the scientific course, Greek and calculus would be omitted in favor of French or German and advanced physics in the junior year, and Greek and Latin would be dropped in favor of French or German and advanced chemistry in the senior year. The historical students would omit calculus in their junior year and Latin in their senior year to take economics, history, and government. The classical course would remain the same as in previous years (but with additional Greek and Latin). This more flexible program was met with enthusiasm by the students. In June 1896, 38 students graduated: 25 in the scientific course, and 13 in the classical. Four graduates (including President Lewis's daughter Miriam) had started in the primary department of the college when it began in 1886 and had spent ten years on the campus.

Curiously, the faculty continued its long-standing practice of allowing petitioning students to drop courses and substitute others for them, so that while the rigid degree requirements were specifically stated in the catalog, in practice, degrees were conferred on students with fairly diverse, somewhat individually tailored, programs. This was particularly true of the Latin and Greek requirements, as well as some of the mathematics. To a certain degree, the students enjoyed a bit of an elective system before it was actually introduced.

President Lewis proposed to the faculty in 1898 a new grading system, to replace the numerical one (based on 10) used since 1867. He suggested that letter grades be used, related to the old system as follows: A = 9 or greater; B = 8 to 9; C = 7 to 8; D = below 7. No F was proposed at that time, and the faculty agreed to the plan.[34] The faculty minutes are full of discussions of individual students' progress, including their diligence of study and attendance at classes. They suggest plenty of hands-on guidance, much testing during the term, and second chances (because of illness or poor performance) through reexamination to show mastery of material, so that theoretically no student should fail to graduate. (Therefore, perhaps no F grade was needed.) By 1895 the faculty considered having faculty advisers for each student, mentors who would keep the student's entire academic record and absences and counsel them on their deficiencies, striving for the best scholarship from each student. Unfortunately, a few more years would pass before they put the idea into practice.

Continuing and expanding on earlier programs, a regular lecture series was maintained each year, with faculty members and outside lecturers speaking in rotation. A noteworthy lecture given by Prof. McDaniel in February 1891 was "The Moon," which followed up on his earlier lecture "The Sun." He also gave one on Orion in 1894.[35] (The handwritten manuscripts of these lectures, and others given by him, reside in the college archives.)

In the winter series for 1897, Prof. Basil Gildersleeves of Johns Hopkins

University gave an illustrated lecture on Athens using a "magic lantern," and distinguished archaeologist Percy Meredith Reese lectured on ancient and modern Rome.[36] During the spring of 1898, Prof. Bonnotte gave a series of four lectures on French poetry, theater, and novels in March, and Prof. Reese gave four on Shakespeare in April.[37] A year later Dr. George Ward gave an illustrated lecture on campus and also in the community on "The Late War," speaking about Spain and commenting on the Spanish American War. This was one of the first times that a faculty member spoke in public about current and perhaps controversial events.[38]

Soon after Lewis returned from his 1891 trip around the world, he gave several talks about it, one in particular focusing on Hawaii. In 1899 he toured Maryland and several other southern states, speaking on "Our New Paradise" (Hawaii), the proceeds going to fund the seating in Alumni Hall.[39] Prof. Simpson gave a series of lectures on creation (including one rather strangely entitled "Creation and Numerology"), showing what science teaches about creation and noting that no conflict existed between true science and the account of creation given by Moses. "All truth must harmonize," he declared. Unlike the situation with his predecessor, William Zimmerman, in 1882, no public repercussions seem to have arisen.[40]

The facilities for teaching astronomy were enhanced with the gift of $1,000 from trustees W. H. Starr [1887–1901] and E. O. Grimes [1876–1922], both of Westminster, which was used to purchase a telescope. The instrument was ordered from Fauth and Company and was dedicated on November 20, 1891. A temporary home was built for it between Smith Hall and the seminary building, a spot that provided a clear view of the heavens. Schofield noted that the telescope presumably remained in that temporary housing until Yingling Gymnasium was converted into Yingling Science Hall (with an observatory) in 1904. It would be moved to the observatory at the top of Lewis Hall in 1914.[41]

Another major addition to the college was the valuable library of over 4,000 books that was willed to the college by J. T. Ward upon his death in 1897. Over the college's 30 years, the books had often been loaned to students, but now they reposed in the college library. (During the centennial celebration of the college in 1967, most of the Ward collection, which had been scattered throughout the library over the years, was reassembled, and today most of the books are shelved in special cases in the Hoover Library Board Room near the college archives.)

In a further attempt to push the college into the mainstream of American higher education at the turn of the century, Dean George Ward was sent by President Lewis to New York City to attend a meeting of the Association of Colleges and Preparatory Schools of the Middle States and Maryland in December 1898.

STUDENT LIFE

As the decade began, a new campus activity was created that was much appreciated by the students. The *Monthly* described it:

"Our Sunday School" . . . is one of the new things at Western Maryland. Owing to the large number of those wishing to attend Sunday School, it was necessary to withdraw from the church in town, and to begin the College Church. There are about one hundred and fifty members divided into twelve classes. A very impressive and interesting order of services has been prepared especially for this purpose, and all enjoy the Sabbath Morning hour spent in chapel. The Officers of the Sunday School are as follows: . . . Professor McDaniel, Superintendent; Miss Edna Tagg ['93], Secretary; Mr. W. H. Litsinger ['93], Treasurer; Mr. W. B. Judefind [director of the Men's Gymnasium], Chorister; and Miss C. C. Coghill ['92], Organist.[42]

The Sunday school would continue for many years, and Prof. McDaniel would serve as its superintendent for more than 25 years. Everyone always looked forward to the special and elaborate Christmas programs that were put on by the Sunday school and designed by McDaniel. They included special music, readings, and a Christmas message in a variety of worship forms. Originally held in the Smith Hall auditorium, the event was moved to Baker Chapel after it was built. The service for December 1900 was described in the *Monthly* and shows the nature of the special event:

Several weeks previous to the appointed time, the program had been arranged and completed by the untiring efforts of Prof. McDaniel . . . and those to whom special parts were assigned entered into the work with the determination to make the Christmas of 1900 a grand success. . . . The celebration took place in Baker Chapel, on December 16th, at 8 o'clock, and long before the hour of worship the house was well filled. Upon entering the chapel one beheld a large tree. . . . Laurel and ivy also were twined over the windows and around the choir loft. . . . The special feature of the evening was "The Lighting of the Advent Tree," after an old German custom. The tree was trimmed with unlighted candles, and as the scholars, representing the different classes repeated Bible verses suitable to the occasion, the candles were lighted, and by the time the last verse was recited, the tree was a blaze of fire. Then the carols pealed forth. . . . Dr. Lewis delivered a short address . . . and . . . the choir dismissed us with an anthem. Thus ended one of the most impressive services ever held.[43]

A number of other innovations in student life occurred during this decade, not the least of which was the first publication of a yearbook, in 1893.

A rare opportunity for male and female students to
"co-mingle" on the college lawn

Heretofore, each graduating class had produced a handwritten *Annal*, or class summary and prophecy, which was filed with the college (all are now in the archives). The editors of the new publication noted, "With the advent of this volume, Western Maryland ruthlessly brushes off the time-honored cobwebs of custom and assumes a place in the list of Educational Institutions publishing Annuals. The Class of '93, with its characteristic energy, has decided to relegate the reticence of past years to the realms of oblivion, and is thus responsible for this innovation."[44] The yearbook was called *The Aloha* as a result of a lecture on Honolulu by Dr. Lewis given after his trip: "*Aloha*. Could any syllable breathe more delicious music or suggest more tender significance? . . . It is a greeting and a farewell; it expresses the feeling of the heart whether that be the ordinary courtesy of hospitality or the tender sympathy of personal affection. . . . If you pay a visit, your first word is *aloha*, and with *aloha* you bow yourself out."[45] The book was dedicated "with loving esteem" to J. T. Ward. It included a historical sketch of the college written by Dr. Reese, a list of the board of trustees and faculty (without pictures), a class history, small pictures of each '93 class member (one page for men and another for women), class statistics, a class prophecy, the class ode and yells, descriptions of each literary society and other organizations, reports on the athletics of the year, and some original

A co-ed dormitory room c. 1900;
note the pennants and postcard collection.

poetry. Pictures of presidents Lewis and Ward and a sketch of the Old Main complex rounded out the book. When the idea of a published annual was first presented to the faculty for approval, the faculty (as might be expected) agreed but required that all material be censored by them. The seniors balked at such an oversight of their "memories," and after due consideration, and intercession by Dr. Reese, the faculty backed down and allowed the students to publish what they wanted.[46] They even allowed pictures to be taken of male and female students together,[47] although no such picture appeared in the annual. The book was a big success, but, apparently, even with 16 pages of advertisements, receipts did not match expenses, and so the next two classes did not attempt such a publication.

The class of 1896 took up the project again and published the second volume, which they called *Chick-a-Go-Runk*, taken from the class yell:

Chick-a-go-runk, go-runk, go-runk,
Rickety-rackety-rix;
Hi-yi-kickety-ki—
Ninety-six![48]

This yearbook was dedicated to Prof. Reese, Prof. McDaniel wrote the college sketch, and the book followed the same format as its predecessor but contained a few more pictures. Perhaps, even with 23 pages of advertisements, the book was again not a financial success, for no annual appeared again until 1899, when publication was resumed with the original name, *Aloha*. Similar publications continued through 1904.[49]

Student activity was still very much regulated by rules and careful faculty supervision. Several incidents suggest the depth of this intrusion. As late as the fall of 1899, the electric lights were still turned off at 10:30 P.M. Saturday breakfast was set for 8:00 A.M. with room inspections (a daily occurrence for years) at 7:45 "in order to secure attendance at this meal." Nightly room inspection was held at 9:45 P.M.

In February 1891 two young ladies were called before the faculty because they had had a photograph taken in which one of the women was wearing a boy's coat, vest, collar, necktie, and hat. After three long discussions of this behavior, the faculty restricted the girls from going to town except to church for a period of time. No reason was stated for this sanction, nor apparently were the questions ever raised of where the clothes had come from or why the picture had been taken in the first place. The so-called cross-dressing seemed to be the main issue.

In April 1891 the Glee Club appeared in a public ceremony in the town without first obtaining proper faculty permission. Since the faculty considered this behavior an egregious defiance of regulations, they proposed to expel all the participants from the college. After two weeks of discussion and the receipt of signed letters of apology, however, the matter was wisely dropped.

The students of the preparatory school continued to provide considerable fodder for faculty disciplinary action. Doors were being nailed shut, and windows were being broken. Indeed, two boys' behavior was so bad for so long that the faculty decided that they deserved a whipping and directed President Lewis to administer the punishment. The minutes later report that one boy received his whipping, but the other boy could not be found.[50] No further mention of his punishment was recorded.

In October 1892, eight senior men walked out of the dining room after breakfast without permission and went into town without permission, as well. The faculty spent two meetings developing a resolution that said in part, "Public demonstrations of dissatisfaction on the part of students cannot be tolerated, especially as they always have the right and opportunity to lay their complaint in a quiet and orderly way before the proper authority." (They may have had the right and opportunity to complain, but they probably felt that their complaints would be ignored by the faculty.) Beyond this, the faculty let the matter drop, except to send each of the young men a letter warning of serious consequences for further violations. Secretary McDaniel continued to be kept busy writing letters of reprimand to students and organizations, and President Lewis often followed these up with letters to the errant students' parents.

In March 1893 two men were reported for card playing. They were called before the faculty, told of the gravity of their offense, and given 25 demerits; their punishment was announced to the entire student body at the following chapel.[51]

In May 1893, President Lewis, probably acting on an anonymous tip, ordered a search of a woman's room and found a box of letters in a trunk. The letters showed that the young woman had been carrying on a clandestine correspondence with a young man. The plot began to thicken when another woman was also implicated. Apparently, the two women had even gone downtown between 9:15 and 10 P.M., to meet some young men of the town. They had also gone driving with them (in horse and buggy, of course). The faculty wasted no time in expelling both women, sending them home under the care of a teacher, and informing their parents that the college would no longer take care of them. So much for individual privacy. *In loco parentis* was taken very seriously.[52]

Somewhat curiously, the faculty denied a request to form a Prohibition Club in 1894 because it considered it "political" and the college didn't allow political groups to meet on campus. It was noted, however, that the faculty did agree with the cause of temperance.[53] Indeed, in December of that year a male student was found intoxicated on whiskey purchased in town, and he was suspended for a month. However, the suspension was lifted when he pledged to remain abstinent and his classmates pledged to keep him so.

The installation of electric lights in all the buildings in 1895 resulted in some students in Ward Hall tampering with them. President Lewis simply removed the lights from the building and required a signed pledge from the residents not to "interfere" with the lights and to report anyone who did.[54] An even more curious situation regarding the electrifying of the college arose in 1898. A parent wrote requesting that her son be excused from Sunday evening chapel services because the electric lights hurt his eyes. The faculty agreed, provided that the student secure a written statement from an "occulist" describing the injury to the boy in attending services where electric lights were used. Eventually, the young man presented a letter from an obliging occulist, and he was excused from chapel, but he and his parents were reminded that he would therefore not be allowed to attend evening activities in any public place that was electrified, and his movements would be carefully monitored.[55]

In 1897 a situation arose that suggests how parental reactions to collegiate discipline have changed in a hundred years. A young man was suspended for one week for going home in direct defiance of a faculty order. His parents disapproved of his action and in a letter expressed how "mortified" they were and begged the faculty for leniency. The faculty suspended the suspension "until similar action causes it to be put into effect." But the student was "campused" for the remainder of the term and could not leave Westminster for the remainder of the year except for specific college holidays. The parents wrote back expressing their thanks. (Twenty-first-century parents would no doubt defend their offspring to the hilt and probably sue the college!)

In reaction to student requests, the faculty revised the weekly Parlor Night slightly, to be held from 8:30 to 9:30 P.M. every Saturday evening, and said efforts would be made to prevent any prolonged interviews between special parties (a "problem" raised perhaps by jealous students?). The faculty noted that it saw no need to further change the rules and customs of Parlor Night that had worked so well for the past 30 years.

In 1895 the faculty received the first of a number of requests from students to form a Greek letter society on campus; it was denied. This was followed by one the following month to form a chapter of the Sigma Chi fraternity, which was also denied.[56]

In the fall of 1896, a rather difficult situation developed with a student. Caleb Wilson O'Connor, who had come to the preparatory school in 1890 at the age of ten, had been in lots of trouble during his earlier years, and he was again in difficulty as a college student. He had missed lots of classes, was apparently not studying, and was failing his courses. When in October he was called in to explain why he had determined not to study, he replied that "he had *not* determined *not* to study, but simply that he had just not studied!"[57] He was told that if he didn't improve, his guardian would be asked to withdraw him. (The previous year, he had been suspended and sent home, but his guardian had sent him right back, saying that he had no room for him at home.) Nothing changed. The boy was again reported for not studying, and the faculty voted to suspend him and to ask the guardian (in Ithaca, New York) to withdraw him by October 31. The guardian requested an extension until November 15, and Dr. Lewis agreed. By November 13, O'Connor had improved in conduct and class recitation slightly but not enough to encourage the faculty to lift the suspension, so they moved to send him home by November 28. However, the guardian again asked for an extension, until December 1, since he would not be at home until then. O'Connor left the campus as planned, and on December 11 he wrote a letter to the faculty, expressing his appreciation for the kindness they had shown to him. The story of Caleb O'Connor does not, however, end there. While he did not graduate with the class of 1899, as he should have, his love of the college was always there, perhaps since it had provided more of home and family to him than his guardian in New York. Some years later, after studying at the Yale Law School for three years (but without completing a degree), he composed and wrote the lyrics for the songs "Dear Western Maryland" and "Win, Western Maryland."

Win, Western Maryland

Win! Western Maryland, roll up the score;
We're here to win again, just as we have before;
And we will march on to victory—
Never give in;
We will fight for dear old Western Maryland,
To win! Win! Win!

In 1920, the college awarded the composer an honorary master of arts degree, which was presented by his old friend and mentor, William McDaniel. O'Connor made quite a name for himself as a composer or lyricist of over 200 songs, including a number of college fight songs such as Yale's "Down the Field,"[58] and was for many years a voice coach for announcers at NBC and in the Washington (D.C.) Academy of Speech.

The *WMC Monthly* had grown in stature and improved in content since its inception in 1886. Each issue contained many essays and poems, as well as news of the campus, the alumni, and the larger college world. J. T. Ward frequently published essays and poems under the byline "By an Old Contributor" until his death.[59] As the decade drew to a close, and the United States was embroiled in a war with Spain, which some saw as imperialistic, occasional editorials on the situation appeared. In the May 1898 issue, an editorial commented on the validity of Admiral Dewey's naval victory over the Spanish fleet in Manila. Generally, however, editorials and articles steered clear of anything controversial or related to the world at large. The faculty still demanded to see the contents of each issue before it was printed, but fairly regularly, the editor would "forget" to submit the copy to the censor, and the issue would go to press unedited. Each time, the editor would be called on the carpet for failing to follow the rules, and he would express abject apologies, promising "never again to violate the confidence reposed in him," until the next time.[60]

The literary societies continued their weekly meetings and annual anniversary celebrations, which gave great pleasure and entertainment to everyone on a campus that still did not permit dancing, dating, or even extended conversations between students of the opposite sex. A faculty Committee on the Society Anniversaries, however, felt it necessary to govern these events in 1892 by directing that at least half of the time should be devoted to literary works that were not dramatic. It went further to state, "Dramatic scenes that represent in the least degree gambling or drunkenness shall be forbidden."[61] The following year, the Webster Society asked permission for some women to take female parts in an upcoming drama, but the request was denied because of the college rules (and perhaps the faculty's bias against dramatic productions). One wonders if sometimes the faculty hid behind the rules rather than consider the requests in a rational manner. By the middle of the decade, however, joint anniversary celebrations of the male and female societies were allowed, to reduce the number and expense of similar events by rival groups, and some mix-gendered dramatic presentations were finally included, such as "The Rivals" and "She Stoops to Conquer." Three pages of the faculty minutes were devoted to the list of 17 regulations that governed those joint anniversary celebrations. Since men and women students were involved and it was essential to keep them from communicating except as vitally necessary, at least one faculty member was in attendance at each rehearsal, and the faculty said, "No talking will be allowed while rehearsing is going on."[62] While things had loosened up a bit by the end of the 19th century, many of the old conservative concerns were still very much present.

While no records have been kept of daily menus, one can occasionally glean from subtle comments and references made in the *Monthly* that the food served regularly to the students was less than gourmet and generally not plentiful. Apparently, a staple at meals was blackstrap molasses, which was often served over bread or potatoes for breakfast. A surprising note in the *Monthly* suggests that buckwheat cakes were served only on Thanksgiving morning.[63] When a special event was held, it almost always involved food, and one can surmise that those occasions and the accompanying refreshments were much appreciated by the students. Inclusion in the *Monthly* of the menus for special dinners probably suggests that these meals were very different from the ordinary fare. One example will suffice:

The Thanksgiving Dinner of 1890

Fried oysters, crackers, pickles
Stewed rabbit, roast pig,
sweet potatoes, sauerkraut
Cole slaw, parsnips and celery
Roast turkey, mashed potatoes, cranberries
Rolls and butter
Mince pie[64]

Another aspect of daily life and creature comfort was improved in 1897 when new iron single beds with wire mattresses were put in every dormitory room, replacing the iron double beds slept in by previous generations of students. It was reported that this move, at an expense of $1,143, was made in the interest of the health and comfort of the students. White enameled bedsteads were put in the men's rooms, and folding single beds (which made into a couch during the day) were placed in the Smith Hall women's dormitory.

An aspect of college life on the Hill that is rarely discussed or even documented is the weather and the winter temperatures the campus experienced. The *Monthly* of February 1899, however, reports on some horrendous weather the college community had to endure during the week of February 8–14. The snow accumulated to a depth of two feet; the maximum temperature reached in that interval was 24.5 degrees, and the lowest temperature recorded was minus 16. The coldest day was February 10, when the highest temperature for the day was minus 1 degree and the lowest was minus 13. Midway in the period a blinding snowstorm enveloped the whole eastern seaboard, and 17 inches of snow fell in two days, burying the college and all of Carroll County.[65]

A tradition of the era that marked the passage from freshman to sophomore year was held each year following the third-term final examinations, when everybody was ready for some fun. From accounts in the *Monthly*, apparently a straw man, symbolizing the first year just completed, was created and set on fire by the freshman men, and the sophomore men made every effort to stop this procedure. So various fake straw men were fired in other parts of

Senior Class trip to Pen Mar Park, properly chaperoned, of course

the campus to draw attention from the real straw man, which, in 1896, was hung near Hering Hall and set ablaze, after which the class orator announced the high status of the class of 1899 as it moved up the ranks of students. The "ceremony" concluded with the class yell:

Rah! Rah! Rah!
This we are,
Classis optima
Ac fortissima
'99, '99
Sis! Boom! Bah![66]

Over the years reference is often made to the annual senior class trip to Pen Mar Park, which in 1891 was held on the third Saturday in September. Apparently, this was very special, since few students had been there. After a hearty breakfast, the students (about half of the class of 1892) boarded the train (of the Western Maryland Railway, of course) and were conveyed up the mountain to High Rock observatory, enjoying the scenery along the way. The trip was enlivened by singing college songs and chanting class yells. The students enjoyed a lunch prepared by the college's culinary department at the park pavilion and spent the rest of the afternoon hiking around the area before departing for Westminster at 6 P.M. Chaperones for the day were Prof. William Black (Latin), Miss Kate Smith '81 (director of the women's gymnasium), and two students from the theological seminary.[67]

An outing to Fern Rock

Another destination for outings in this Victorian era was much closer to campus: Fern Rock, a shear cliff remnant of the quarry on the Diffenbaugh, later the Geiman, farm on the south side of Main Street (Taneytown Road). (The rock from the quarry would be used to form the foundation of the second Reifsnider house, which became the College Alumni House in 1969; and tradition says that the foundations of earlier buildings, including the Main Building, also were formed from stone quarried there.) Generations of students and some seminarians made trips down the road to Fern Rock, and botany classes studied the flora there. The quarry was relatively dry and a good place to take outings, explore, have picnics, and carve initials, some of which still exist. (The property was owned by James '31 and Margaret [Erb '33] Mann for many years and abuts Marbeth Hill, a residential area developed in the 1950s by Mrs. Mann's father.)[68]

In 1894 some of the women students founded a secret club known to everyone on the Hill as the JGC (which was only recently revealed to mean "Jeune Geist Club" not "Junior Girls Club," as was often suggested). Senior girls were favored for membership (indeed, apparently all senior girls were invited to join if they wished), but some juniors were also admitted to carry on the traditions. It has been described by former members as just a club to have fun, but the initiations were scary and "ghostlike." It was never considered a sorority, although it was apparently sanctioned by the college and given a space in Old Main to meet. The 1910 *Aloha* describes the rather macabre initiation of the new members:

Six of the juniors were given due notification that they had been chosen to share the awful secrets of J.G.C. . . . The victims try to study, to recite, to smile, to play tennis, but nothing is possible except thought of what is to come. It is ten-thirty P.M. The lights are out and the college is in darkness. At the foot of the steps leading up to the sky-parlor [the Main Tower room] wherein is the den of J.G.C. are those weeping ones kept company by their less fortunate class-mates. In deep sepulchral tones a name is called, and the owner bids farewell to those around her and tearfully makes her way through the Egyptian darkness up the winding stair to the door—that awful door! She knocks. The door opens. Only the shriek of agony is heard by those left below. The clank of chains, the shrieks of pain and cries for mercy, and then is heard the deep-toned voice reading the rules. Finally the last one is summoned from the arms of her loving friends to pass through the ordeals of J.G.C. Soon after this may be seen the transformed beings sitting round a table, enjoying life and thanking their stars that they have been through the mysteries of J.G.C.[69]

Music continued to be a major source of entertainment on the campus, in the society entertainments and anniversary celebrations and also on the Friday afternoon programs, interspersed among readings and orations. A men's Glee Club (11 members) had been formed (or re-formed) in 1891, and in 1892 a College Orchestra (11 members) had been created. The yearbook of 1896 reported that a Banjo and Guitar Club had also been formed (originally of both men and women but soon of only 8 men).[70] This group and the Glee Club even toured the Eastern Shore of Maryland together in December during the Christmas recess, staying in homes of alumni and performing in the local M.P. churches. They also performed at the YMCA Hall in Baltimore, at the Fireman's Hall in Westminster, and several times in concerts on campus.

From the beginnings of the college, oratorical contests had always been a big part of college activity, especially between the literary societies and at Commencement. In November 1898 a statewide intercollegiate Oratorical Association of Maryland Colleges was formed by St. John's College, Maryland Agricultural College, and Western Maryland College; and Prof. Reese (who had spearheaded the idea locally, along with Prof. George Ward) was elected president.[71] The first annual contest was held in Smith Hall on April 28, 1899, and Claude Cicero Douglas of Western Maryland was declared the winner. During the next eight contests, the Western Maryland orator (selected each year by the faculty) won six times.

By the beginning of the decade, a movement to establish a football team on campus was quite strong. An editorial in the December 1890 *Monthly* noted,

Among the many things which our college has long needed and which a number of the pupils have desired is a football team. It has been our privilege to enjoy, for some years, the sports of baseball and also, for quite some time, lawn tennis, but never have the students of W.M.C. had an opportunity to enjoy a game of football.[72]

The anonymous editor goes on, perhaps with a bit of sarcasm, to say,

But we may ask, whose fault is this? We cannot suppose the authorities of the college were for a moment opposed to such an amusement. For the authorities of the college so forcibly realized the importance of physical culture that they appropriated money to purchase a beautiful field, situated near the college, for the exclusive purpose of athletics. Thus it seems that it was negligence on the part of the students.

He concludes his comments with these words:

Football is fast becoming the popular game in college, and especially at this season, when it is too cold to play baseball. We have frequently been asked "Have you a football team at W.M.C.?" And it has always somewhat embarrassed us in being compelled to give a negative

answer. Not because it was in any degree dishonorable to be without a football team but because W.M.C. was so far behind the times in that respect.

Whether the editorial goaded the students into action or shamed the faculty and President Lewis out of their conservative lethargy is not known, but on October 31, 1891, the first WMC football game was played in Westminster, against Pennsylvania College. The results were less successful than one might have hoped. "Our boys, with little knowledge of the game and less hope of success, matched against a team superior to them in weight and general knowledge of the game, might well have given up in despair. But they were made of sterner stuff, and although they were defeated, the final score being 64–0, they fought nobly, and it was evident to the on-lookers that all they needed was practice," reported the *Monthly*. Presumably, they practiced for the next two weeks before playing Pennsylvania College again, in Gettysburg on November 14, but after a hearty lunch provided by the host team, the game ended in a 98–0 loss! The following week, however, New Windsor College came to Westminster for a game and went home the loser; WMC had its first football victory by a score of 66–0. Alas, the five-game season ended with more losses than wins for the fledgling team.[73] During the fall of 1892, apparently only one game was played, against Baltimore City College, and it resulted in a tie. The 1893 *Aloha* commented on the 1891–92 season: "Ignorance of the game excused no one, and enthusiasm fully atoned for inexperience. . . . True, indeed, many physiognomies suffered from violent collisions, and the grand march to chapel exercises revealed a variety of limps and hops. . . . Still our zeal did not lag, and we eagerly scanned the physique of every entering freshman, as he innocently knocked at our doors for admission. Material in abundance was found, but in a crude state. . . . We claim no superior excellence for our football team, but we are not ashamed of our beginning, and are confident that once firmly established, our college will win no meagre honors."[74] How prophetic!

In April 1892 an Athletic Association for the college was formed to organize more contests and intramural activities, even though Johns Hopkins University had just dropped football because they lost to everyone. In the fall of 1894, the association joined the Football Association of the Colleges of Maryland, and the college team began to play a few more games in the state. The team "played good ball under the efficient training and direction of [student-coach] Mr. Caleb H. Bowden, '92."[75]

In 1895, 13 of the college trustees signed an informal resolution opposing and discouraging intercollegiate athletic contests. This did not seem to dissuade the students (or the faculty who approved the games), however, and football matches, as well as baseball games, continued. Indeed, the faculty voted to continue football, by a vote of 8 to 4, over the trustee objection.[76] By 1897 the team was thought to be improving when it outscored Baltimore City College 26–6, but its other two games were losses. The baseball team fared even worse that year, winning only one game out of five, after being undefeated the previous year.[77] At the end of the 1897–98 school year, it was reported that the college was now part of the Inter-Collegiate Athletic Association of Maryland and the District of Columbia. Other colleges were expanding their athletic activities, as well. The year had not been a particularly good one for WMC athletics, however. Football had fielded its best team

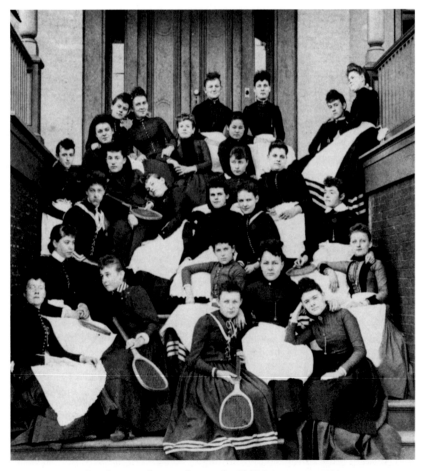

Co-ed tennis players relax on the Old Main steps c. 1900.

140

yet, but it had not been able to come up with many wins. The baseball team was described as not having done its best, and the track and field team (a newcomer to the ranks) had had "insuperable difficulties" due to lack of money and little support from the student body. An interesting and almost prescient comment concluded the year's review: "While we have not been winners, the year has not been unprofitable. The [Inter-Collegiate Athletic] Association has done much to eliminate the growing tendency with some of our colleges to practically employ a certain class of so called students whose only connection with the college is the semi-professional services they render to the athletic teams and have raised the whole plane of all college sports."[78]

While football and baseball were the predominant sports on campus, tennis, basketball, golf, and even croquet were played by interested students. A tennis club had been re-formed in the previous decade and continued to attract players from both the student body and the faculty. An intercollegiate tennis tournament was held on campus in May 1899, and the *Monthly* reported on the local tournament that led up to it: "We had quite a good deal of tennis on the hill and ought to make quite a good showing at the coming tournament."[79] (There was no report of the outcome.) In the fall of 1899, golf was introduced by Prof. William Black, who had become interested in it while on vacation. And so a golf club was formed of faculty and a few students with Black as president and William McDaniel on the executive committee. A golf course was laid out east of town, but because it was a distance from the campus, some of the men played in Geiman's pasture, which adjoined the campus to the west.[80] (This area would eventually become the college's nine-hole golf course.)

As competitive sports developed, the desire to have colors arose, and after much discussion, Schofield reported, black, red, and white were adopted in 1889. Apparently, these were soon discarded or forgotten, however, for an editorial in the *Monthly* of May 1892 asked, "Why is it that the students of Western Maryland College are satisfied to go on from year to year without colors? . . . I would rather have colors that I do not like, if a majority likes them, than to have none at all."[81] Perhaps spurred on by the editorial, the Athletic Association in January 1893 asked for faculty approval to adopt olive green and old gold as the official college colors. In true faculty form, a committee was appointed to look into the matter (again), and it reported back affirmatively. The faculty approved, and the college had its official colors. In January 1900, the colors again came under discussion when the problem arose of finding wool uniforms for the teams in the proper shades. Nevertheless, the faculty voted to keep the olive green and old gold and kept color standards and swatches in the Treasurer's Office for reference.[82]

Major Events

May 12, 1895, was the date set for special dedicatory ceremonies for the new Baker Chapel. Three services were held during the day, preceded by an organ recital given by Miss Mary Eugenia Lewis of the Department of Music. The organ (costing $1,000) had been the gift of an anonymous donor (possibly T. H. Lewis). At the morning service, President Lewis and professors Reese, Simpson, McDaniel, and G. Ward participated in the exercises. Dr. J. T. Ward preached the sermon. The consecration service was held at 3 P.M., with ministers of the local Methodist Protestant, Lutheran, and Methodist Episcopal churches participating. Daniel Baker of Baltimore presented the chapel to the college on behalf of his brother William G. Baker, and President Lewis conducted the ceremony of consecration. In the evening service, Dr. L. W. Bates of the theological seminary preached, student representatives of the YMCA and YWCA led opening exercises, and special music was provided by a choir of students and faculty. The white limestone building, with its 87-foot tower, seating capacity of 250, and antique oak furnishings, was described as the "crowning glory of Dr. Lewis's administration" and a gift much appreciated and needed by the college.[83]

While the first public conferring of degrees did not occur until June 15, 1871, President Ward had always noted each year's closing events as a "commencement," and thus the 1st Commencement was numbered as the 4th. This practice continued until Dr. Lewis took office and changed the numbering to more accurately reflect reality.[84] In 1895, then, the college celebrated its 28th year of existence and on June 9–13, its 25th Commencement. In honor of this milestone, many of the old traditions were continued, and some new ones were introduced, most notably the wearing of caps and gowns. The extravagance in dress for special occasions, especially by the young women, was causing concern among the faculty; another commencement meant another opportunity for a display of fancy silks, satins, and jewelry. After much discussion, Prof. Reese was directed by the faculty in January 1895 to survey other institutions regarding the use of academic costume. He reported that many of the leading colleges now required that academic regalia be worn by graduates, faculty, and administrative officers.[85] This national trend culminated in the creation of the Intercollegiate Commission in 1894 to prepare a code for American academic costume that was soon approved by almost all universities and colleges. It recommended and described gowns and hoods of differing style and decoration for the bachelor's, master's, and doctor's degrees. Reese's recommendation that the college follow these practices was soon adopted, and academic regalia were ordered for all participants in the 1895 ceremonies.

Commencement Week began with the Baccalaureate Service on June 9. The procession into Smith Hall auditorium to the strains of Martin Luther's stirring hymn "A Mighty Fortress Is Our God" must have been an impressive one, with everyone decked out in the new academic robes. This was the second time that Luther's stirring hymn had been used, and it would continue to be the processional hymn for all academic occasions at the college until 1973.[86] President Lewis preached the sermon to the graduates, and the music was furnished by the college's Choral Society.

Baker Chapel was dedicated in 1895; note faculty house just beyond.

Sunday afternoon and evening were set aside for two more religious services: an afternoon Praise Service conducted by Daniel Baker in the new Baker Chapel, and the Christian Associations Service in the Westminster Methodist Protestant Church that evening. On Monday afternoon the Elocution Contest took place in Smith Hall, with freshman and sophomore men and women vying for the Norment Medal (established in 1890 by Samuel Norment, a brother-in-law of J. T. Ward). That evening the Music Department faculty and students gave the Commencement concert. Featured soloist for the evening was Blanche Murchison '95, who sang and played the piano.[87] Tuesday was occupied by field sports and a tennis tournament in the morning, literary society reunions in the afternoon, with the oratorical contests between the societies in the evening. The Merrill and Newell trophies were awarded to the winning societies, represented by their best orators.[88]

Wednesday began with the humorous Class Day exercises at 9 A.M., after which class reunions were held, culminating in the annual alumni banquet in Yingling Gymnasium, attended by about 200 "old students" representing every graduating class since 1871. This was followed by a general class rally in Smith Hall, which featured two addresses, class yells, and the "college yell":

Rah—Rah—Rah!
Rah—Rah—Ree
Rah—Rah—Hullabaloo
W.M.C.—Rah![89]

The actual graduation exercises were held on Thursday morning in Smith Hall and began with the academic procession, during which the entire student body of 250 marched in singing the processional hymn. The seniors were last, with males marching on the right and females on the left. When they had filled the aisle, the lines stopped and turned to face each other, allowing the faculty to pass between them and onto the platform. The opening prayer was given by the Rev. Thomas O. Crouse, a member of the first graduating class. The salutation for the day was given by ex-President J. T. Ward, and the commemorative oration was delivered by Dr. Reese. Four members of the graduating class delivered addresses: The male valedictorian, William Roger Revelle, gave "The College, a Constructive Force," and the female salutatorian, Leila M. Reisler, gave "The Home and the State." Two other addresses were given by members chosen by the class: "The Religion of the Future" by Albert Norman Ward, the class president, and "The Expression of Thought" by Blanche Murchison. Music for the occasion was furnished by Itzel's Orchestra from Baltimore.[90] Schofield charmingly pointed out that on this particular day, taking part in the 25th Commencement were the first three presidents of the college *as unconscious symbols of the past, present, and future. . . . J. T. Ward must have felt gratitude that his "college enterprise" had become a strong and growing institution; T. H. Lewis must have felt gratitude that he had been able to carry through his ambitious program of building and debt retirement; and A. N. Ward, blissfully ignorant of future cares, was probably thinking of Miss Murchison.*[91]

On this occasion the college also conferred an honorary doctor of philosophy degree upon Daniel Hering. He was the student-teacher of mathematics and English on the first college faculty, in 1867, who had gone on to do graduate work at Johns Hopkins University and Yale University, returned to the college for a short time as professor of mathematics [1880–84], and later was professor of physics and applied mathematics in the Western Union University of Pennsylvania for a short time before becoming the chair of the Physics Department of the University of the City of New York (later renamed New York University) in 1886, eventually becoming dean of the graduate faculty there.[92]

This was the third and last time an honorary PhD degree would be conferred by the college. It had been agreed by the Intercollegiate Commission that the doctor of philosophy should be the paramount earned degree in the United States and should not in the future be conferred *honoris causa.* This rule maintains today.

In addition to Albert Norman Ward, who would become the third president of the college in 1920, and Blanche Murchison, who would become his wife in 1905 and the third first lady of the college, another member of the class of 1895, Nannie Camilla Lease, is worthy of mention because she would become a longtime member of the faculty in 1904.

From the 1895 Commencement onward, seniors were expected to wear the cap and gown during the third term (which began at the end of March) at all official functions, including the weekly Sunday evening chapel service. The ladies would enter the chapel two by two, followed by the men in pairs, who would be followed by President Lewis, the undergraduates having already assembled inside the chapel. This occurred in the third terms of 1896 and 1897. During the spring of 1897, it was decided to hold a more formal ceremony of investiture to mark the final term and the impending graduation. Dr. Reese, who had chaired the cap and gown committee in 1895, was appointed to draw up procedures for such a ceremony, and those he presented to the faculty in April 1897:

Your committee appointed to draw up and present a ceremonial for the Investiture of the Senior Class with Cap and Gown, respectfully suggests the following as a brief, simple and appropriate method of conducting said ceremony:

1. *The donning of Caps and Gowns shall take place on the first Monday morning of the third term and shall be connected with the Chapel exercises of that morning.*
2. *While the school is assembling for morning prayers, the Seniors remaining outside, shall don their vestments under the supervision of a member of the faculty designated for that purpose.*
3. *The class shall then march into the auditorium, men first, women next, investing officer last, all in the academic costume.*
4. *The Seniors shall proceed to seats reserved for them in the center of the room, and the investing officer to the stage where the rest of faculty are seated.*
5. *At the close of the hymn or anthem with which the devotional exercises open, the Senior Class will remain standing (the rest of the school being seated) and be addressed briefly, on the meaning and object of their investiture by the President or a member of the faculty previously selected for that purpose. The class will then be seated and the morning prayer proceed as usual. At the close the Class will march out in procession, the young women first.*
6. *The music to which the seniors march into the auditorium shall be the piece known as "Cap and Gown" [composed by Mrs. Fannie Pearson for the class], dedicated to the Class of '96.*

The report was approved and adopted.[93]

The first formal investiture was actually held on Monday, March 23, 1897,[94] a month before these guidelines were approved. No doubt the basic structure was followed, however, because the speaker for the occasion was Dr. Reese. The following year, Prof. McDaniel spoke at the investiture on March 21, and said to the seniors,

By this act of investiture you are here in the presence of these witnesses admitted to the noble company of scholars known as college-bred men and women. We who have entered these ranks before you and have been leading you on this journey extend to you the welcoming hand. . . . Like that other "evidence of things not seen" which you have in prospect your diploma—so too these vestments look back over the four years of your college course . . . and so too, they look forward through the coming years and are at once a promise and a pledge, that this same, earnest, faithful effort is still to be put forth in the pursuit of learning . . . and that your lives are consecrated to all that is noble, true, and good.[95]

In March 1899 the faculty also began appearing in regalia at the investiture ceremony.[96]

*Alumni Hall took about three years
to build and was dedicated in 1899.*

The last major event of the decade was one that had been eagerly anticipated for at least five years. Alumni Hall was finally completed and formally dedicated on the evening of June 13, 1899. The auditorium was filled for the event, which began with music by the College Orchestra, a welcome and short account of the building of the hall by President Lewis, and a brief speech by Maryland governor Lloyd Lowndes, who spoke of the contribution Western Maryland College had made to higher education in the state. Senator George L. Wellington spoke of the meaning of the opening of such a building to education, after which Dr. Joshua Hering, college board president, talked about the college's growth over its 30-year history. Prof. Reese spoke of the significance of the college and the power of enlightenment and referred to President Lewis's efficient administration. The ceremonies concluded with a piano solo by Prof. Sampaix. Thus ended one of the greatest days in the history of the college. The newspaper article describing the event noted, "We think it perfectly appropriate here to say that Westminster is proud of her college and appreciates the advantage of such an institution to the city. Let everybody speak the good word and do all they can to advance the college."[97]

One measure of a college's success is, of course, its graduates, and several distinguished graduates of this era have already been mentioned. However, it is appropriate to include a few others at this juncture, all of whom would go forth to be good ambassadors for the college in the years to come. In fairness, it should also be mentioned that some of their names crept into the faculty minutes because of occasional academic or social problems while they were students! Hugh L. Elderdice '82 became president of Westminster Theological Seminary in 1897; Sadie Kneller Miller '84 became a successful and published photojournalist in a time when women did not enter that field (she was named to the Maryland Women's Hall of Fame in 1988); John H. Cunningham '85 became a successful Westminster banker and later served as a college trustee [1914–65]; Amon Burgee '87 became a distinguished and much beloved Frederick educator; William G. Baker '94 became a successful stock broker in Baltimore and founded the Baker-Watts investment company; Charles Forlines '97 also became president of Westminster Theological Seminary, in 1935; and James Henry Straughn '99 became a Methodist Protestant minister, bishop of the Methodist Church, a WMC trustee for 59 years [1915–74], and board chairman for 20 years.

CONCLUSION

The last decade of the 19th century was a very significant one for the college. The institution grew in size of both student body (reaching a high of 278 in 1899) and faculty and staff (20 in 1900); it grew in campus acreage as new properties were purchased; and it certainly grew in physical presence as at least nine new buildings were erected, including Alumni Hall, Baker Chapel, and the second Ward Hall. The college was becoming well established and well respected in Maryland, and it was gradually changing its curriculum and customs to come in line with other respected institutions of higher learning. While it had debt, the debt was both reasonable and expected as the institution grew and invested in its future; the college was financially sound after struggling through its early years with weighty deficit and debt, but it truly needed an endowment. As the new century beckoned, the time was ripe for new goals and further expansion.

CHAPTER 4 ENDNOTES

1. Page 15.
2. *WMC Monthly*, May 1896, 14–15.
3. Ibid., May 1892, 14.
4. Ibid., May 1892, 4–6.
5. Ward, Diaries, December 6, 1986.
6. WMC board of trustees minutes, June 1891.
7. *WMC Monthly*, March 1892, 22.
8. Letter from Lewis to McDaniel, Lewis Papers, college archives.
9. *WMC Monthly*, March 1892, 15–16.
10. WMC faculty minutes, February 12, 1892.
11. WMC board of trustees minutes, June 20, 1894.
12. June 1895, 17.
13. *WMC Monthly*, November 1894, 10–12.
14. WMC faculty minutes, March 5, 1897.
15. WMC board of trustees minutes, June 1897.
16. Pages 14–15.
17. Wills, *History of Western Maryland College*, vol. 2, 8–9; obituary in Billingslea family book.
18. Schofield and Crain, *Formative Years*, 41.
19. April 1893, 12.
20. James Reese, 1893 *Aloha*, 31.
21. WMC board of trustees minutes, June 1893.
22. October 1895, 15.
23. *WMC Monthly*, December 1895, 22.
24. Ibid., March 1896, 21.
25. Schofield and Crain, *Formative Years*, 57.
26. November 1896, 21.
27. Pages 21–23.
28. Bruce Jones, *A History of Western Maryland College Buildings and Grounds*, unpublished manuscript, 1975, 23.
29. WMC board of trustees minutes, June 1893.
30. Ibid., June 16, 1897.
31. Ibid., 59.
32. Schofield and Crain, *Formative Years*, 60.
33. October 1893, 9.
34. WMC faculty minutes, November 18, 1898.
35. *WMC Monthly*, February 1894, 18.
36. Ibid., January 1897, 23.
37. Ibid., April 1898, 16, 24.
38. Ibid., March 1899, 20.
39. Ibid., January 1899, 23.
40. Ibid., May 1892, 2.
41. Schofield and Crain, *Formative Years*, 55.
42. October 1891, 13.
43. January 1901, 22–23.
44. Page 15.
45. 1893 *Aloha*, 10.
46. WMC faculty minutes, January 6, 1893.
47. Ibid., February 10, 1893.
48. 1896 *Aloha*, 15.
49. Wills, *History of Western Maryland College*, vol. 2, 56.
50. WMC faculty minutes, March 6, 1891.
51. Ibid., March 3, 1893.
52. Ibid., May 1, 1893.
53. Ibid., October 19, 1894.
54. Ibid., February 15, 1895.
55. Ibid., February 18; March 11, 1898.
56. Ibid., September 27; October 25, 1895.
57. Ibid., October 14, 1896.
58. Interview, Judith Schiff, Yale University archivist.
59. *WMC Monthly*, December 1890.
60. WMC faculty minutes, December 7, 1891.
61. Ibid., April 29, 1892.
62. Ibid., November 23, 1894.
63. December 1896, 22.
64. *WMC Monthly*, January 1891, 9–10.
65. Page 14.
66. *WMC Monthly*, June/July 1896, 30.
67. Ibid., 1892.
68. *The Hill*, March 1973, 12.
69. Page 154.
70. Pages 133–40.
71. WMC faculty minutes, November 25, 1898.
72. Pages 1–2.
73. *WMC Monthly*, December 1891, 17–18.
74. Page 159.
75. *WMC Monthly*, June/July 1895, 8.
76. WMC faculty minutes, September 15, 1895.
77. *WMC Monthly*, June/July 1897, 10–11.
78. Ibid., June/July 1898, 45–47.
79. April 1899, 19.
80. Wills, *History of Western Maryland College*, vol. 2, 64–65.
81. Page 2.
82. WMC faculty minutes, January 12, 1900.
83. *WMC Monthly*, June 1895, 52–53.
84. Schofield and Crain, *Formative Years*, 53–54.
85. WMC faculty minutes, January 11, 1895; March 8, 1895.
86. Schofield and Crain, *Formative Years*, 54.
87. Event program in McDaniel scrapbook for 1895, college archives.
88. *WMC Monthly*, June 1895, 59.
89. *WMC Monthly*, June 1895, 59; 1895 Commencement Summary publication in McDaniel scrapbook.
90. Ibid.
91. Schofield and Crain, *Formative Years*, 55.
92. Ibid., 54–55.
93. WMC faculty minutes, April 23, 1897.
94. Schofield and Crain, *Formative Years*, 67.
95. McDaniel Investiture Speech, 1898, college archives.
96. WMC faculty minutes, March 1899.
97. *WMC Monthly*, June/July 1899, 21–22.

MAJOR WORLD EVENTS

1891
Triple Alliance (Germany, Austria, Italy) is renewed for 12 years.
Thomas Hardy publishes *Tess of the d'Urbervilles*.
Rudyard Kipling publishes *The Light That Failed*.
Mahler composes Symphony no. 1.
Trans-Siberian railroad construction begins.
Widespread famine plagues Russia.
Earthquake in Japan kills 10,000 people.

1892
First automatic telephone switchboard is introduced.
Monet begins his series of pictures on the Rouen Cathedral.
Tchaikovsky composes *The Nutcracker*.
Gladstone becomes prime minister in Great Britain.
Ibsen publishes *The Master Builder*.
Rudolf Diesel patents his internal combustion engine.

1893
A World Exhibition is held in Chicago.
Hawaii is proclaimed a republic; annexed to the U.S.
Pinero publishes *The Second Mrs. Tanqueray*.
Grover Cleveland is inaugurated as 24th U.S. president.
Dvorak composes Symphony no. 5, *From the New World*.
Henry Ford builds his first car.

1894
Uganda becomes a British protectorate.
Czar Alexander III dies; Nicholas II succeeds him in Russia.
Rudyard Kipling publishes *The Jungle Book*.
Bernard Shaw publishes *Arms and the Man*.
Edison opens his Kinetoscope Parlor in New York.
Louis Lumière invents the cinematograph.
Death duties (inheritance taxes) are introduced in Britain.

1895
Chinese-Japanese War ends.
Cuba fights Spain for independence.
H. G. Wells publishes *The Time Machine*.
Roentgen discovers X-rays.
Marconi invents radio telegraphy.
Auguste and Louis Lumière invent the motion-picture camera.
First U.S. Open Golf Championship is held.

1896

Utah becomes a U.S. state.
Chekhov publishes *The Sea Gull*.
Five annual Nobel prizes are established.
Puccini's opera *La Boheme* is performed in Turin.
First modern Olympic Games are held in Athens.
Klondike gold rush begins in Canada.

1897

Kipling publishes *Captains Courageous*.
Edmund Rostand publishes *Cyrano de Bergerac*.
The first American comic strip, "Katzenjammer Kids," is begun by Rudolph Dirks.
Pissaro paints *Boulevard des Italiens*.
Brahms dies.
William McKinley is inaugurated as 25th U.S. president.
Gustav Mahler becomes conductor of the Vienna Opera.
J. J. Thomason discovers electrons.
Britain's Queen Victoria celebrates her Diamond Jubilee.
A World Exhibition is held in Brussels.

1898

U.S. declares war on Spain over Cuba.
Henry James publishes *The Turn of the Screw*.
H. G. Wells publishes *The War of the Worlds*.
Pierre and Marie Curie discover radium and plutonium.
Sir William Ramsay discovers the inert gases xenon, krypton, and neon.
Photographs are first taken using artificial light.

1899

Philippines demand independence from the U.S.
Oscar Wilde publishes *The Importance of Being Earnest*.
John Dewey publishes *School and Society*.
Sound is magnetically recorded for the first time.
Rutherford discovers alpha and beta rays in radioactive atoms.

1900

The first trial flight of the Zeppelin occurs.
The Commonwealth of Australia is created.
Sigmund Freud publishes *The Interpretation of Dreams*.
Wilhelm Wundt publishes *Comparative Psychology*.
McKinley is reelected U.S. president.
Puccini's opera *Tosca* is performed in Rome.
Max Planc formulates quantum theory.

Yingling Science Hall (the old gymnasium was remodeled,
adding an observatory dome) (1904)

C H A P T E R

YEARS OF RECOGNITION AND EXPANSION

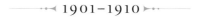

—◄ 1901–1910 ►—

The world and the college had entered the 20th century, although there was much debate about exactly when it began (1900 or 1901), as there would be a century later when the new millennium rolled around. England's Queen Victoria died in 1901, and with her death came the end of an era worldwide; she was succeeded by Edward VII, who would reign until 1910 (and give his name to the Edwardian era). The world was still in turmoil, with the Boer War and other skirmishes around the globe; tsarist Russia was trying to contain its serfs, not recognizing the coming revolution. And Albert Einstein formulated his special theory of relativity in 1905, in Germany.

In the United States, President William McKinley was assassinated in 1901 and was succeeded by Theodore Roosevelt. Also in 1901, Marconi sent telegraphed messages across the ocean. The first powered airplane flight by the Wright brothers took place in 1903. Work was begun on the Panama Canal in 1904. The U.S. Pure Food and Drug Act was passed in 1906. That same year, San Francisco suffered a massive earthquake in which 700 people died. Oklahoma entered the union as the 46th state in 1907. The Panic of 1907 caused a run on the banks (and a temporary economic downturn) until J. P. Morgan imported $100 million in gold from Europe. Admiral Peary reached

153

the North Pole in 1909, and Halley's comet was observed in 1910.

Soon after the turn of the century, in 1902, the following was true:[1]
- The average life expectancy in the U.S. was 47 years.
- Only 14% of U.S. homes had a bathtub.
- Only 8% of U.S. homes had a telephone.
- There were 8,000 cars in the U.S. but only 144 miles of paved road.
- The maximum speed limit in most cities was 10 mph.
- The average U.S. worker earned between $200 and $400 per year. A competent accountant could expect to earn $2,000, a dentist $2,500.
- Sugar cost 4¢ a pound, eggs 14¢ a dozen, coffee 15¢ a pound.
- The five leading causes of death in the U.S. were: (1) pneumonia and influenza, (2) tuberculosis, (3) diarrhea, (4) heart disease, (5) stroke.
- 10% of U.S. adults could not read or write.
- There were only 230 reported murders in the entire U.S.

In Westminster, at Western Maryland College, Dr. Joshua Hering was the only charter trustee still living by 1910. In recognition of his service to the state as a senator and comptroller, he received the honorary LLD degree in 1900 from St. Johns College. During this decade, he served three terms as comptroller of the State of Maryland, and in 1910 he was appointed to the Public Service Commission at the age of 77.

On the campus as in the town, electricity had become more common. Refrigeration was now in place, so the ice house was eliminated in 1907 (it had fallen in, anyway). The pit was filled in and the roof remounted, and it became a well-loved gazebo, or summer house, which later was given the name Carpe Diem (Seize the Day). During this decade the college did indeed "seize the moment" to move forward in several ways.

FACULTY AND ADMINISTRATION

While several people stand out as being important to the college during the decade, certainly Thomas Hamilton Lewis leads the list. In 1900, he had been president for 14 years and was suffering from ill health. However, during this decade he assumed several challenging roles that forever changed him and the college.

In 1901, in his report to the board of trustees, Lewis noted that he was completing 15 years as president and suggested that the board should think of replacing him, that the time had come for someone else to carry the work, perhaps with more success. "My time of usefulness here has about run its course," he said.[2] He had long seen the need for an endowment for the college. He proposed that he embark on a major endowment campaign during the 1901–2 academic year, canvassing the Sunday schools and churches of the M.P. district in a general appeal for funds. This, of course, met with the wholehearted approval of the board, which appointed Prof. McDaniel as acting president while Lewis was away from campus. Dr. H. L. Elderdice, the seminary president, agreed to fill the pulpit at Sunday evening chapel.

Lewis had barely returned from his endowment crusade when, in the summer of 1902, Adrian College (another M.P. college, a sister school, so to speak) wrote to Lewis requesting that he leave WMC and become Adrian's president. A letter dated July 26, from the Adrian Executive Committee, forcefully stated, "Unless Adrian College can secure the services of a man of known executive ability who will inspire confidence and secure the unanimous cooperation of the Methodist Protestant Church, the condition of Adrian College is indeed desperate." After visiting the college in Michigan and inspecting the situation, Lewis wrote to Dr. Hering, the WMC board president, reporting, "Adrian is in a somewhat disorganized condition . . . is without a president and in a very serious financial condition . . . [and on] very unstable footing." Instead of relocating, Lewis recommended to the WMC board that he work with both colleges, with a "corps of helpers" in each place (specifically, McDaniel at WMC). Adrian would pay his traveling expenses as he commuted back and forth to Michigan and would pay the expenses to fill his classroom place at WMC. The college board agreed to Lewis's plan, and he became president of Adrian College, as well as WMC, for two years (1902–4). The students were proud that this spoke well of the college and of Lewis, but many were afraid that he would stay at Adrian and leave WMC permanently.[3] Lewis was replaced in the philosophy classroom by Bartlett B. James '91, a Baltimore Congregational minister with a PhD from Johns Hopkins. During the first term, Lewis went back and forth every week, but after that he spent one week a month in Michigan. McDaniel, on whom fell the day-to-day operation when Lewis was away, told of being asked so often, "Is Dr. Lewis at home?" "When is Dr. Lewis coming home?" "When is Dr. Lewis going to Adrian?" "Will Dr. Lewis be here this week?" that he thought his only recourse was to wear a placard with the answers to those questions printed on it. Then he would only have to point to the proper answer. It seemed that as secretary of the faculty and acting president, he was expected to know everything.[4]

After the two-year stint in this unique dual presidency, Lewis reported, "I believe Adrian will now go on its course successfully." During his short presidency there, he had reduced the debt from $51,000 to about $40,000, reduced the yearly operating costs by half (by taking no salary himself and letting a number of faculty go, including former WMC music teacher T. F. Rinehart), seen the endowment fund grow, and increased the number of students from 77 to about 125. He had energized the student body and the faculty and had seen a 50% increase in the funds from the M.P. Church. A new president, Rev. Brayman W. Anthony, DD, had been elected to succeed him. Adrian was not totally out of the woods, and Lewis may have been a bit too sanguine about its future financial affairs, but he had rescued the college from closure, and his presidency at Adrian was always recognized as a significant one in that college's history.[5]

Lewis announced in January 1906 that he was worn down and needed a rest (perhaps he was on the verge of a nervous breakdown). He again suggested that he should resign, now after 20 years as president. He considered himself too old (at 53) for the most effective service. The trustees would not hear of it and instead gave him a year's leave of absence at full pay to travel and investigate new educational methods at home and abroad. Prof. McDaniel was formally elected vice president, so he could officially act (again) as president (at a salary of $1,800 and his house). Lewis did not prepare a president's report for the board for 1906 because he was too ill, nor did he preside at Commencement. Dr. Hering acted in his stead and at the ceremony announced the recent election of Prof. McDaniel as vice president and acting president. That announcement was met with great delight of the student body, faculty, and alumni. Samuel Schofield, who was a student (1914–19) during Lewis's last decade as president, commented after the 1906–7 year, "It is very likely that the students found the acting president more approachable than Dr. Lewis who, though brilliant and dedicated, never had his father-in-law's happy relationship with his student body."[6] The 1902 yearbook commented on Dr. Lewis's son, Thomas Hubert Lewis, by saying he "has inherited a little of the genius and all of the self-confidence and self-importance of his illustrious sire." Perhaps the most telling comment about Lewis's stern and autocratic manner was provided by his wife. Agnes Reese '11, once reminisced, "I recall hearing the mother of one of the town girls tell Mrs. Lewis she had heard that Dr. Lewis was known as 'the Sunshine of the South.' Mrs. Lewis's placid rejoinder was that she thought it was a pity he had not reserved a little more sunshine for home consumption."[7]

The year 1906–7 was quite a successful one for the college. Upon his return, Lewis noted in his annual report,

I have learned that the past year has been one of the most prosperous the college has ever enjoyed. . . . This is no surprise to me, because I have been long convinced that we have in Vice President McDaniel a man equal to any responsibility the board might put upon him.[8]

President
T. H. Lewis

Vice President and Treasurer
W. R. McDaniel

The trustees formally acknowledged McDaniel's efforts with a salary raise, a vacation stipend of $250, and a resolution:

Whereas, . . . Professor William R. McDaniel was called to the Office of the Vice President, to take charge of the administration of the college during the absence of President Lewis, and

Whereas, he readily responded to the call of duty, and entered immediately upon the arduous labors which he has continued during the entire year, therefore:

Resolved, That the board of trustees hereby express their gratitude to Professor McDaniel for his loyalty to this post of highest responsibility, for his diligence and diplomacy in meeting and mastering the puzzling problems of daily discipline, for his conscientious care in identifying himself with the minutest details of financial operations, and for his exalted character as a Christian gentleman whose precept and example have kept the moral tone of the student body up to the high standard which has long been the pride of our patrons and the glory of our college.[9]

Upon assuming the vice presidency, McDaniel finally gave up his post as faculty secretary, which he had held since 1885. He was succeeded until 1911 by Irving A. Fields, professor of chemistry and biology [1906–11], who was followed by Edwin A. Warfield, professor of English [1904–22], until his death in 1922.

President Lewis returned from his second sabbatical on April 23, 1907, apparently rested and healthier. All the male students marched to the train station after dinner to meet him after his long and eventful trip abroad and greet him with the college yell. Lewis shook the hands of the class presidents, stepped into a carriage, and drove to the college, where he was given an ovation by the student body. A recital in Alumni Hall was followed by a gala reception in the banquet room in his honor.[10]

In June 1907, the trustees again directed the president to devote his time to raising the endowment; McDaniel would continue as acting president for another year. That same year, Lewis was appointed to the Maryland State Board of Education by the governor, and Washington College conferred on him the honorary LLD degree. As the decade closed, plans were under way by the trustees to celebrate his 25th anniversary as president, in 1911.

Over the decade, the faculty continued to change frequently. Thirty-two people had filled an annual average of 11 faculty positions, with only about five individuals (including Reese, McDaniel, and Bonnotte) having any extended tenure. Leaving for other, perhaps better-paying, positions in this decade were William Black [1891–1901], Rowland Watts [1894–1904], and George Ward '90 [1891–1905]. As a student writer philosophically put it, "In a faculty of twenty-two persons, somebody is always getting married, or securing a better position, . . . or making a change for some other reason. We think the college has been fortunate in keeping teachers."[11] Dr. Ward was certainly leaving for a better position: the principalship of the State Normal School at Towson.[12]

During this decade there was an average of three PhDs on the faculty each year (although the people changed periodically). The Science Department was growing to include chemistry, biology, geology, and physics and was usually staffed by two people. Over the decade, ten science teachers were hired, but five (several of whom held PhDs) stayed only one year, probably because of the low salaries. German (now a distinct area of study) was taught by four different people in four years.

New faculty who came during the decade and stayed included Nannie C. Lease '95 [1904–37], who returned to the college to teach speech and direct women's physical education (replacing Mary Belle Cochran '95, who left after seven years). Lease had taught at Adrian during Lewis's two years there. Rev. Edwin Warfield '82 (PhD Yale) [1904–22] returned to the campus to teach English, replacing George Wills (who left after six years but would return in 1922 upon Warfield's death). James Widdowson [1908–18] was hired to teach pedagogy in 1908.

In September 1906, the faculty minutes noted the presence of a part-time registrar, Mrs. F. M. Handy [1901–10], who was also serving as librarian.

When she left, the president's daughter, Clara Ward Lewis '98 [1910–19], was hired as college librarian.

A new preceptress, Margaret Minerva Robinson (1857–1945) [1908–28] joined the college in 1908, after each of her three predecessors had left due to marriage after only a year or two of service. She was a graduate of the State Normal School in 1876 and is credited with establishing high schools in Berlin on the Eastern Shore and in both Baltimore and Harford counties. In 1889 she opened the Girls' High School in Frederick (the Boys' High School, for many years headed by Amon Burgee '87, was established in 1897). According to Carolyn Stegman in *Women of Achievement in Maryland History*, "She regarded this position [of preceptress] as a serious responsibility to the college women entrusted to her care and guidance. Since women were being given the opportunity to attend college, Robinson wanted them to excel in not only academics but also character."[13] The college conferred an honorary MA on her the following year. (This seemed to have been a fairly common practice. Apparently, the board of trustees felt that the preceptress and dean of men should hold master's degrees, and they were given one early in their tenure if they did not already hold an advanced degree; Owings, Black, and Robinson received one.)

Most weekly faculty meetings continued to deal with three subjects: (1) permission for students to go places (usually home or to visit a relative or friend, occasionally to attend some event or a meal); (2) class standing or academic problems and attendance problems (with exams scheduled as needed); and (3) "disorders"—misbehavior in class, dining room, chapel, etc., or violations of Rule 11. Passing notes between boys and girls was rather flagrant and was usually punished with ten demerits and no Parlor Night; many students played intermediary by passing a note (referred to as "kindness of bearer," or KOB) between parties.[14] A modification in the faculty's weekly agenda occurred in 1906. The faculty minutes noted that they would no longer reflect requests for leave of absence from the college because those would now be in the hands of the dean and the preceptress (a move away from total faculty control of the students and perhaps one the faculty was happy to make).[15]

BUILDINGS AND GROUNDS

The property between Levine Hall and Union Street was purchased for $1,500, and most of the lots along College Avenue were now owned by the college.[16] In 1903, Prof. Simpson's house on College Avenue was purchased for $3,000.[17] (Later in the decade that property became the site for the new Library and Administration Building.)

A view of the campus from Westminster c. 1910;
note the houses along College Avenue.

The first building project of the decade was a small extension of Owings Hall so that the whole first floor could be used as an infirmary, the second floor being living rooms for staff people, and the third floor adding a girl's bathroom. This was duly completed, with new plumbing, at a cost of $1,388.34.[18]

In 1902, William G. Baker and Daniel Baker gave $600 for four stained-glass windows for Baker Chapel. They were Romanesque in shape, 9 by 15 feet, and recreated four famous paintings: "The Annunciation by Gabriel to the Virgin" (Hoffman), "Madonna and Child" (Rafael), "The Light of the World" (Holman Hunt), and "Christ in the Temple" (Hoffman). There is no record of who actually decided on the subjects of the windows, but one can assume that Dr. Lewis's ideas played a large part in the decision. (Lewis was a good friend to the Baker family and probably solicited the gift.) The windows were created for the chapel by H.T. Gernhardt and Co. of Baltimore.[19] A year later, the picture "Christ and the Young Ruler" (after Hoffman) was put in place above the Baker Chapel altar, a gift of George W. Albaugh, a local businessman. The artist for the painting was Miss F. L. Thomson of Washington.[20]

As the college grew, it needed a larger gymnasium and a science building. A new gym was planned in 1904, to be erected behind Old Main near the YMCA building (it would later be named Yingling Gymnasium, after Lewis Hall was built). Construction was somewhat delayed, but the building was completed and finally put into use on October 10, 1904, at a contract price of $6,450. The two-story brick building was 43 feet wide and 75 feet long and almost touched the rear of Owings Hall. It was equipped with all the latest paraphernalia, including two bowling alleys. Suspended 12 feet above the playing floor was a wooden inclined track 5 feet wide, with a railing and banked turns. Thirty-three laps made a mile. The gym was reported to hold 500 spectators for events and games.[21] The ground floor had a bathroom, including six showers for the men, as well as a locker room and a boiler for hot water. The gym was connected to Owings Hall by a bridge for the young

Yingling Gymnasium II (1904)

Interior of Yingling Gymnasium II; note the suspended indoor track.

161

ladies' use; the men entered by a lower-level door. Of course, the gym was never used by men and women students at the same time.[22]

Soon after the new gymnasium was planned, Yingling Gymnasium was remodeled and fitted as Yingling Science Hall at a cost of $2,066. The first floor now held a recitation room and two laboratories for physics. The second floor provided similar facilities for chemistry and biology. In the front tower was a small classroom, over which was added the observatory dome,[23] and the telescope was moved there from its temporary site north of Smith Hall.

In 1905 the faculty approved a request from the senior class to spend as much as $125 on a stained-glass window for the alumni room in Alumni Hall, instead of a class plaque. It was approved if it would conform to a design adopted by the faculty with the names of the class members on a brass plate by the side of the window.[24] This plan would be continued by the next six classes (1906–11) until seven windows depicting the seven medieval liberal arts—the trivium (grammar, rhetoric, and logic) and the quadrivium (music, geometry, astronomy, and arithmetic)—were installed. (Although the windows are still in place, they are usually covered by scenery in the Dorothy Elderdice Understage; the brass plaques denoting the members of the class were removed during the renovation of Alumni Hall in 1978–79 and are now stored in the college archives.)

The athletic field, which had been expanded in 1902, was rebuilt and improved by 1904. The students pledged $300 to help pay for the grading. It was declared to be "second to none in the State," for it boasted a one-fifth-mile track.[25] Two years later the Athletic Association carried the improvement plans further by erecting an eight-foot-high board fence around the entire field and re-sodding the field, which apparently was necessary due to the rocky nature of the area.[26]

View of Yingling Gymnasium II, Ward Hall II,
and Lewis Hall from back campus c. 1915

Library and Administration Building (1909)

An extension to the Smith Hall addition was built in 1907 to provide eight additional rooms for women at a cost of $3,098.24. At Dr. Lewis's suggestion it was named for Miss Mamie McKinstry '79, who had written on the flyleaf of her Bible that she wished to leave a $5,000 legacy to Western Maryland College.[27] On her death in 1891, the will was contested by her brother and, because of a technicality, was declared invalid, although the court of appeals noted that this defeated "the plain and perfectly manifest intention of Miss McKinstry." The college board recognized her intention as if it had been carried out, although no money was forthcoming, and named the building in her memory.[28]

A growing student body and changing educational methods brought on the need for an expanded library to replace the space provided in Hering Hall, and so a combined Library and Administration Building was planned and ground broken next to Baker Chapel at the Commencement of 1908. It was completed in November 1909 at a cost of $50,984, of which $25,000 was contributed by the state legislature. Designed by Jackson Gott in the neoclassical and Beaux Arts styles popular at the time,[29] it was built of Indiana limestone and gray, hydraulic-pressed brick and faced with Roman Doric–style stone columns. It had a frontage of 65 feet, a depth of 50 feet, and

*Reading room on the second floor of the library;
administrative offices were on the main floor.*

was three stories high. It was considered the "most ornate of all the college group."[30] The main floor contained offices for the president and treasurer, a large meeting room for use by the faculty and the board, a bookstore, and a museum. On the floor below were rooms for the Browning and Philomathean societies and storage rooms. The second floor contained the library, with a large reading room, 30 by 60 feet; and stack area, 20 by 60 feet; a mezzanine floor; and a capacity for 25,000 volumes. The interior was paneled in weathered oak.[31] The trustees met in the board room of this building for the first time on June 14, 1910.

A note about Jackson Gott (1829–1909) is appropriate here, for the buildings he designed for Western Maryland College represent "the work of a master in his prime. They also represent the largest collection of Gott's work anywhere; all of the [existing] buildings . . . have been placed on the National Register of Historic Places. [Yingling Science Hall and the Old Main building were razed before the National Register designation.] . . . The endurance of five of seven works on a campus so pressed for space indicates that they were well-conceived and well built."[32]

A new heating plant was approved in June 1909, to be located down the hill below the new

Architect Jackson Gott

164

administration building, near Union Street, at a cost of $21,186.71. The building contained steam boilers and steam-powered generators for electricity for the campus. A new steam line was run to the old plant behind Old Main and out to the other buildings.[33]

At the end of the decade, Dr. Lewis suggested that, as the campus was changing and new buildings were springing up, perhaps a campus plan for the future was in order, and some attention should be given to landscaping. The Olmsted brothers from New York were hired to give some suggestions for campus landscape and beautification (the project apparently funded by Daniel Baker). Their report, which remains in the Olmsted archives in the Library of Congress, was submitted in 1911,[34] but it was not acted upon due to lack of funds.

Student Life

As the century opened, there was little change in the rather oppressive control by the faculty over the students' lives. The college rules and regulations announced in 1902 bear a striking similarity to those presented to the students 35 years earlier. A few examples will suffice:

- *Special permission is required for those who wish to be absent from the premises during any hours except from 3:00 to 6:00 P.M. Students receiving special permission of absence must report at the 9:45 inspection. Young ladies must be accompanied by a teacher. No student shall at any time visit any hotel, restaurant, or other place of entertainment, nor attend any exhibition or place of amusement without the permission of the faculty.*
- *During school hours students must remain in their rooms except when called to recitation.*
- *The portion of the campus east of the Ladies' Walk is appropriated to the use of the female students; that west of the Boys' Walk to the use of the male students. No student is allowed to use the Campus between the walks.*
- *Communication between the [male and female] departments, except in the presence of and with the consent of a teacher, is strictly forbidden.*
- *Young gentlemen are not to accompany young ladies either to or from town at any time.*
- *No young lady is to have the company of a young gentleman of the college while she is away from college on a visiting privilege.*

> • *All business letters, books, packages, and the like, which are to be transferred from one department to another, must pass through the hands of the Preceptress.*

The faculty was still approving student requests to attend all sorts of events and entertainments, often on the day of the event. One wonders how hostesses could ever prepare for such events as dinners and teas, not knowing whether the invited students would be given permission to attend. On Monday, November 23, 1903, the faculty decided that the young men would not be allowed to send flowers to the young ladies for Thanksgiving dinner later in the week because of the difficulties involved (whatever they were).

In November 1902, however, the faculty definitely was not consulted when Miss Lillian May Lindsay, a day student and member of the senior class, participated in a special evening elocution class, then dashed off to meet Mr. Dohnea C. Nygren x'95,[35] who was waiting in a carriage to drive her to the Centenary Methodist Episcopal parsonage, where they were married. They then drove to his parents' home and sent a note to her parents informing them of the marriage; the latter were deeply distressed that she would not complete her education (married women did not attend college).

During the decade numerous requests were made to the faculty by students to change the church they attended each Sunday. Even though the catalog clearly stated that the students were required to attend divine service on Sunday morning at some church in Westminster and that church affiliations would be scrupulously respected, requests to change churches (even with parents' consent) were often denied because no one else at the college attended that church or because there was no chaperone to accompany the student. In one instance, a request to attend the Lutheran Church was denied, but the young lady was informed that she could attend the Reformed Church because a teacher went there and could escort her. Although this was a clear violation of its rules, the college administration seems never to have been questioned on it by the parents.[36]

The campus Sunday school, which met each Sunday at 8:30 A.M. in Baker Chapel, continued to thrive under Prof. McDaniel's leadership, and most students participated.[37] Of special interest was the Christmas service, held the last Sunday evening before the Christmas recess in 1902. After the traditional music and readings, and an address given by seminary president H. L. Elderdice in Dr. Lewis's absence, Prof. McDaniel announced that the assembled crowd was going to hear a Christmas message from a "graphophone" (probably some form of radio or amplified telephone) provided by a Mr. Wentz from town. Soon everyone recognized that the voice was that of Dr. Lewis, who was a hundred miles away but had arranged to speak via the new technology.[38]

As expected, the rigid rules continued to be tested by preparatory and collegiate students. Two men were suspended for two weeks in April 1902 for being on the grounds of the women's section and conversing with two women who were in a window. The women were given 50 demerits each and deprived of all privileges for the remainder of the year; they also had to change rooms.[39] When the two men returned to campus, they were denied the privilege of being with the young ladies after dinner. Two weeks later, because of their good behavior, the women's privileges were restored, but a suggestion by Dean Ward on behalf of the men for similar treatment was denied. Two weeks after that, their privileges were finally restored.[40] Generally, male students were presumed to be more guilty than female students jointly involved in such nefarious activities.

The faculty minutes speak a number of times of students having problems getting back to the college, since almost everyone depended on public transportation at that time. Boats and trains sometimes ran late or not at all. The faculty was not very sympathetic to these problems, however, and still gave out demerits for lateness, missing chapel, and such. Traveling by train could also get you into trouble. Four young male students were each given 25 demerits for playing cards on the train from Westminster.[41] Ten demerits each were awarded to two women and two men for walking together to campus from the train; they were also deprived of Parlor Night for the month.[42]

The students' daily schedule was carefully laid out, as well:

6:40 A.M.	*Rising bell*
7:00 A.M.	*Breakfast*
7:45–8:45 A.M.	*Study*
8:45 A.M.	*Chapel*
9:00 A.M.–2:20 P.M.	*Study and recitation*
11:40 A.M.	*Luncheon*
6:00 P.M.	*Dinner*
7:00–9:45 P.M.	*Study*
9:45 P.M.	*Inspection*
10:00 P.M.	*Lights out and silence*

By 1905 the class schedule had been changed to provide for four 40-minute periods for recitation after lunch (instead of the three 45-minute periods of the earlier schedule), ending the day at 3:25 P.M.[43]

A student of the period, C. Milton Wright '06 (Harford County superintendent of schools 1915–45, succeeding his uncle Charles T. Wright '77, who was superintendent for 14 years), recorded his memories of college life of this decade:

I never studied so hard as I did that first year in college. We had

*dormitory inspection six nights a week and had to be in our rooms . . .
for study and another inspection to see if you were still there. . . . Classes
for me were always 5 hour periods a day and then opportunity for
participation in athletics from 3:30 until 6 P.M. when supper bell rang.
. . . On Sunday everyone was required to attend Chapel Sunday School
and then go down town to the church of his choice; also attendance
was expected at Chapel service on Sunday night. On Monday morning
each student answered at roll call "Church and Chapel" or else he had
some explaining to do to the Dean. . . . In those days the college had no
indoor toilet facilities but a large frame building over a deep pit which
was located just back of Ward Hall served its purpose well. For want of
a better name we called it No. 10. One day as I went to visit the place
with ice from a frozen rain storm covering the ground, I fell on the slope
and struck my head and the cut bothered me for several days.*[44]

Perhaps Wright went to the infirmary of the day. By 1900, it had been
expanded to provide three rooms for men and three for women in Old Main
and Owings Hall. A $1 charge was assessed of all boarding students for the
services of a physician and attention in the infirmary. A local physician visited
the college once each day to attend to the sick students.[45] They must have been
pleased that such a facility was available in 1904 when pinkeye, tonsillitis,
grippe, and mumps were "making ravages of the school," keeping the doctor
and nurses busy and the infirmary full.[46]

Certainly, food continued to be an issue with students. The 1903 *Aloha*
spoofed a faculty meeting in which Prof. Charles Holton (Men's Gymnasium
director, 1900–4) noted, "The students seem to be kicking about such light
meals. This morning I bought six pounds of sausage for two hundred students,
and some were still unsatisfied." Dr. Lewis responded, "How much a pound
did it cost you?" Holton replied, "It was a little bit strong when I got it, and I
only had to pay three cents." Miss Mary Belle Cochran (teacher of elocution,
1897–1904) observed, "That's right dear, I think, but if Prof. Holton can get
another half-pound at the rate of two cents a pound, I move you that he buy
an extra half-pound, making an abundance of six and a half pounds, and if
that isn't plenty for two hundred students, then I don't know." Later, Holton
noted, "I bought two gallons of strap [blackstrap molasses] last month and we
still have some left. I got that cheap strap and it 'works' a lot. The students can't
eat it very well." Dr. George B. Hussey (professor of Latin and Greek, 1901–3)
noted, "I wish the next that he would buy would be a little bit thicker, because
this thin molasses gets in my whiskers. . . . If Prof. Holton intends to have hash
for lunch tomorrow, I would like to say that I know where there's a dog."[47]

The students mentioned food again in the 1904 *Aloha*, when they defined

"Shadow Soup" as "the Menu for Luncheon, especially on Mondays and Saturdays. Consisting of water with two or three pieces of potato in it." Other definitions followed: "Shakin' Jimmie: One of W.M.C.'s famous desserts, too complex to be described." "Mixed Drink: Milk and Water, of which we are given one glass at breakfast and luncheon." "Strap: The outward form of that invisible force predominant in human nature."[48]

They seemed to make up for the meager daily diet at special feasts. Thanksgiving dinner for 1909 certainly did not lack for filling carbohydrates: oyster soup, baked ham, potatoes, roast young turkey, stuffing, giblet gravy, candied sweet potatoes, creamed peas, potato salad, crackers, mince pie, cheese, and coffee. A request to serve unfermented grape juice at the Junior Banquet of 1910 was not approved because of the additional cost.[49] The meal seemed not to suffer for lack of the grape juice, as the juniors and seniors dined on roast chicken, lamb croquettes, french fried potatoes, new beets, peas, Waldorf salad, ice cream, and cakes.

An interesting article in the *Monthly* included statistics that at least partially refuted the students' perception that they were undernourished. Entitled "What Have We Eaten?" it reported that, during the 1900–1 school year, 200 people had consumed 24,696 pounds of flour, 4,564 pounds of butter, 976 pounds of coffee and tea, 9,076 pounds of sugar, 19,307 pounds of beef, 5,908 pounds of veal, 2,085 pounds of lamb, 6,381 pounds of fresh pork and sausage, 4,815 pounds of ham and breakfast bacon, 3,047 pounds of fish, and 3,538 pounds of fowls. Soups, vegetables, and desserts were not tabulated. Eleven people prepared and served the food, which required 50 tons of coal to feed the stoves.[50]

Early in the decade, the faculty discussed how the students should be occupied on Friday and Saturday nights (certainly, they could not be left to their own devices). President Lewis suggested, and the faculty approved, a short Parlor Night each Saturday followed by a study hour![51] This replaced the longer parlor session held less frequently in earlier years. This quaint 19th-century tradition carried over into the 20th century for several decades. Wright remembered the weekly event:

> It may seem queer to those who read this but while WMC was coed, the boys and girls were kept entirely separate. They attended separate classes, ate at separate tables and were allowed no communication whatever except under the eyes of the Dean who had charge of the girls. The only exception to this was a parlor session on Saturday night at which time each girl arranged a chair beside her and one boy at a time was allowed to talk to her. The boy could be run off by another boy at any time and of course the most popular girls were constantly

*in demand and many talked to a dozen or more [boys] during the
evening. The more unattractive girls might get stuck with only one boy
who didn't have much to say and both were in great misery for a whole
evening. Girls were not allowed downtown even to church without a
chaperone who tagged along everywhere they went to prevent them
from talking with boys.*[52]

Parlor Night was also a regular topic of essays and humor in the *Monthly*,
usually in jest, but always descriptive of the weekly event. A short description
suggests the trauma the ritual could impose on young college women:

*The "Parlor" bell rings promptly at eight o'clock, and sad to say many a
corn is trodden upon, many a temper lost in the rush for the best places.
After this you are uncomfortably seated and trembling for fear you'll
be "left." You find that you didn't jam and push hard enough and you
are "left" all by yourself with a few members of a sympathetic faculty
looking on.*[53]

The 1904 *Aloha* also gives a definition from the student perspective:

*[Parlor Night] indirectly affects Monday's recitations as the whole of
Saturday is taken up in preparing for it. For the girls, it necessitates
many trips to the trunk hall, a search in magazines for witty sayings,
an hour spent on the path after each meal smiling at several boys to
ward against "getting stuck" in Parlor. For the boys it necessitates hours
pressing out trousers, and a great deal of practice on the latest fashion
of combing the hair.*[54]

A bit of a twist in the normal Parlor Night ritual occurred on January
16, 1904, when, in honor of Leap Year, the men were invited in first and were
seated, then the women were let in and sought men for conversations. It was
reported that the evening was "a great success, at least for the girls!" but some
of the male "wallflowers" were less happy.[55]

As the decade continued, things began to loosen up just a bit for the
students. In 1903 the faculty officially approved mothers as appropriate
chaperones for their daughters. Henceforth, young ladies were allowed to go
into town with their visiting mothers rather than strictly with teachers.[56]

The faculty also allowed four young women to see young gentlemen of
the visiting baseball team (after their parents made the request), although,
of course, the visits were under proper supervision.[57] In 1906 a Mr. Ford (a
nonstudent) was granted the privilege of calling on a Miss Tophan (a student
in the preparatory school), the length and time of the call to be determined
by the preceptress.[58]

By 1909–10, young women were regularly given permission to be "called
on" with proper chaperonage, via the preceptress's office. However, "dating"

The location of many "Parlor Nights"
in Hering Hall

was not allowed. A request from a young man to take a young lady to dinner at the Hotel Westminster and to accompany her to the Thanksgiving entertainment was not granted. He could call on her on campus, however, "under the usual regulations."[59]

In 1907 women were given permission to leave campus unchaperoned for short periods on Wednesday and Friday afternoons. This privilege was sometimes suspended for punishment.[60] In June 1908, senior boys and girls were allowed to walk together after supper until 8 o'clock, proper chaperones being provided.[61] On special occasions, such as a reception at the President's House or Thanksgiving dinner or the Junior Banquet, men and women could mingle freely, but always with teachers present.[62]

Curiously, the senior ladies were not given permission to attend the Stockton Literary Society's 26th anniversary celebration at the seminary (next door) because it was a purely social function.[63]

Students of the era found things off campus in which to be involved, and the faculty became more lenient in allowing participation. One young man was given a leave of absence in April 1904 to take a position at the St. Louis World's Fair. And in March 1905, some students were permitted to attend the inauguration of President Theodore Roosevelt in Washington. The faculty also approved the request of Charles W. Sanderson '08 to open a moving picture business in town on the condition that the establishment be open only on Saturday afternoons and evenings until 9:30 P.M.

One of the major events of the decade occurred in February 1904: the great Baltimore fire. Wright described the event (which began on Sunday, February 7, and went on for most of the following week) and how students became involved in it:

It was during my days at WMC in 1904 that the Baltimore fire occurred. We went to the tower [of Old Main] to watch the flames all night, 30 miles away. On Saturday about 20 boys boarded a train for Baltimore. I never have regretted that trip. Such a scene of desolation I have never seen; almost half a mile in every direction was fallen brick and ashes with a hundred smoldering fires still raging. Here and there was a pumper engine which had been caught in the flames. From what is now Howard Street to East Baltimore was all in ruins. We stayed all day walking around the perimeter of the fire and wondering whether Baltimore could ever rise again from the ashes. We returned to college late that evening, tired and hungry, but with a feeling that we had witnessed the results of one of man's greatest enemies—a tragedy of the century.[64]

Other students of later renown attended the college during this decade. Mabel Goshelle Garrison (Siemonn) (1886–1963) from Baltimore graduated in 1903. The 1903 *Aloha* described her singing: "To hear her sing, ah-h! one's soul, one's musical being, one's only being, is thrilled, touched to the quick by her bird-like notes."[65] While a student, however, Miss Garrison was often demerited for violations of Rule 11. She was also campused for a term for overstaying her time away from campus in Baltimore and reprimanded for rowdiness and talking in class.[66] After her vocal studies on campus with Miss Emma Schott, she went on to study at the Peabody Conservatory, made her debut in *Mignon* at the Boston Opera House in 1912, and became a star of the Metropolitan Opera and "one of the three most famous coloraturas." Concerts, record contracts, and a world tour rounded out her professional career, after which she taught voice at Smith College.[67] Her alma mater awarded her an honorary DFA degree in 1953.

Robert Joshua Gill (1889–1983) arrived on the campus in 1903, as a student first in the preparatory school (1903–6) and then in the college (1906–10). He was the grandson of charter trustee Joshua Yingling [1868–82], the nephew of the college's first benefactress, Anna Yingling, and the son of Rev. John M. Gill x'83. In February 1906, while still a preparatory student, Robert Gill was given 25 demerits for violation of Rule 11, and a letter was sent to his father. In the winter of 1907, as a college freshman, he was given an indefinite suspension from the college for disrespect and insubordination during an evening inspection.[68] He returned a few weeks later, however, to participate in spring sports. In his senior year, he was captain of the football team and manager of the baseball team. In the 1910 yearbook, he was described as "one of the most level-headed fellows in the college and . . . a natural leader among the fellows; . . . has excelled both in athletics and studies." He graduated as male valedictorian of the 1910 class and went on to the University of Virginia to receive his law degree and be tapped for Phi Beta Kappa. He became a successful corporate lawyer, as well as an army brigadier general. He later served the college as a trustee [1925–83; chairman 1963–68] and in 1947 received an honorary LLD degree. He is most remembered as one of the major sources of funds for the 1939 gymnasium that bore his name, as well as for his sizable estate, which partially funded the Robert Joshua Gill Physical Education Learning Center, which opened in 1984.

Mabel Garrison and Robert Gill were both very involved in activities outside the classroom, as were many other students of the era. Milton Wright was a member of the YMCA, which, in addition to holding Bible and mission studies each week, offered an hour-long service each Sunday at 4 P.M., usually addressed by a seminary student. A joint meeting with the YWCA was sometimes held before supper. Often the YMCA students would walk the two miles to the County Alms House (now the Carroll County Farm Museum) and hold services for the inmates.[69] They also assisted with funerals for the old people at the alms house. Wright recalled,

> *Well do I remember one of those funerals during a blizzard. We got the coffin on the big two-horse sled and like crows we sat on the wagon surrounding it, traveled to the Westminster Cemetery and proceeded with the burial. The minister was a most eccentric seminary student who wanted to take this opportunity to convince us of his great spiritual knowledge. At the grave the temperature was about zero and the snow was swirling all about us. The student prayed and prayed and prayed until someone told him to stop before we all froze. After the long grave service we all took turns shoveling the dirt to fill the grave and returned to college with ears and feet almost frozen.[70]*

Athletics were beginning to play a major role in students' lives, as sports programs slowly grew. The faculty continued to approve the playing of each game, as well as the players to be involved, since there was not yet a formal schedule of games for any sport. In the spring of 1901 an Athletic Carnival was held on campus for track and field events and a baseball game. A new eighth-mile track had been built and graded by the students under the direction of the athletic director, C. A. Holton. A baseball game with the University of Maryland ended in a 6–12 loss. Two weeks later the relay team went to Philadelphia for the Penn Relays, where over 600 runners participated in 30 events. The WMC team finished a strong third in a relay race with Johns Hopkins, St. John's, Gallaudet, and University of Maryland.[71]

Concerning the 1902 football season, the 1903 *Aloha* reported, "Never before has there been shown such interest, and never has there been achieved

College track team 1906; H. C. "Curly" Byrd x'09,
later University of Maryland president, is seated on far right.

Student gymnastics outside Ward Hall II; Yingling Gymnasium II is in background,
and at the left is the privy called No. 10.

such success."[72] Nine games were played, five were won, and the game with rival Johns Hopkins ended in a 6–6 tie.[73] Elias O. Grimes, a local businessman and WMC trustee [1876–1922], paid for new uniforms for the football team in recognition of their successful 1902 season.[74] By this time, the trustees had appropriated $100 for athletics.

In September 1903, the faculty approved a season of football games that was submitted by the manager.[75] The college team played Gallaudet (6–0 win), Columbian (6–0 win), Baltimore Medical (5–6 loss), Mt. St. Mary's (17–0 win), Maryland University (18–0 win), Delaware (16–6 win), Maryland Agriculture College (0–6 loss), and St. John's College (0–6 loss). They defeated some of their old rivals and gave their opponents a good game even when they lost.[76]

The first open track and field meet at the college was held on Saturday, May 23, 1903, when athletes from the United States Naval Academy, Johns Hopkins University, Gallaudet College, Maryland Agricultural College, Western High School, the Maryland Athletic Club, the Baltimore Athletic Club, the YMCAs of Baltimore and Washington, and a number of the Baltimore preparatory schools came to the campus for the day. The college was represented in each event and faced many of her old rivals.[77]

In April 1904 the lack of a proper playing field for baseball (the team had practiced on the tennis courts) and the loss of all games thus far that spring made the faculty reconsider whether to continue the team and games. By the end of the seven-game season, the team had won only two, both against teams from the Maryland National Guard.[78] The athletic fields were improved later that year by the student body, funded by a collection of $200 from the students themselves, as well as another $200 contributed by alumni and matching money ($400) from the college. The work did not progress rapidly due to bad weather, but it was finished in time for the alumni baseball game during Commencement Week. Although the relay team was unable to go to the Penn Relays in Philadelphia because of a lack of funds, great interest was taken in track and field activities. Plans continued for a fifth-mile track the circumference of the field, a fence around the field, and a line of bleachers (with dressing rooms underneath) the length of the north side, all of which was projected to cost an additional $800, for which another appeal was made.[79]

In December 1904, the Athletic Association requested permission to give a "pay entertainment" in Smith Hall to raise money to pay the football coach of the fall season, Dr. Milton Whitehurst. It was ultimately approved and slated for mid-February.[80] Apparently, the entertainment, a minstrel show, was so popular and professionally done that permission was given to repeat it the following night and again in March at the Odd Fellows Hall in town.[81]

A new Intercollegiate Athletic League was formed in October 1905; the college ultimately voted to ratify the constitution and to join it on October 30. The faculty had been reluctant to join any such league before, probably seeing it as a loss of power over the college program.[82] Perhaps the new athletic league helped in scheduling games, for in the spring of 1906 the baseball team attracted about 50 boys to practice, and the team played 12 games, including contests with the Maryland Athletic Club, George Washington University, Washington College, Gallaudet College, St. John's College, and Maryland Agricultural College. By the following spring, the team had new uniforms, was winning more games, and was hoping for the league pennant. Finances were still a problem, however, and the team manager, J. Hunt Hendrickson '07, noted that if substantial aid was not forthcoming from private donors, they would not be able to afford the services of the team coach, Dr. Whitehurst, during the latter part of the season.[83]

The football season of fall 1909 was the most successful so far. The team defeated Mercersburg and Mt. Washington for the first time in the college's history. The score of 47–0 against Mt. St. Mary's was the largest ever made by a WMC team. Led by Captain Robert Gill and coached by A. M. Cottrell, the team was defeated only twice and overall scored four times as many points as its opponents. Also on the team was Carl C. Twigg '11, who would be the captain for 1910. A highlight of the Mt. St. Mary's game was the "brilliant long forward pass from Twigg to Gill and Chandler Sprague '12. This was used many times and netted gains of from thirty to seventy yards."[84] The team statistics suggest that football a century ago had less brute force than modern football. The average height of the 17 players in 1909 was 5-11, the average weight was only 159 pounds, the average age was 20, and the average number of years playing football was two.[85]

The 1910 baseball team consisted of ten players and was managed by Gill. They played what was described as the "most pretentious schedule the college has ever had": 19 games with such schools as Villanova, Catholic, Eastern, Mt. St. Mary's, Washington, Dickinson, Lebanon Valley, Bloomsburg, Susquehanna, Delaware, Maryland Agricultural, and Gettysburg.[86]

Students followed these athletic contests with great interest. They also created class yells that were "presented" at these contests and other class functions, along with the college yell. One set, for the various curricula chosen by the class of 1904, will suggest their nature and sophistication.[87] Readers can supply their own translations:

Class Yell
Gee-roar, gee-rar, gee-rar-rar-roar!
Twentieth century year, No. 4!

Mille nongenti quattuor
Χιλιοι ευλκοσιοι τεττγρλ
Dix neuf cent quatre!
Neunzehn hundert und vier!
νυν πλελσκευζομεν
ινλ υπερισΧϖμεν
Videbimus et vincemus
Ac adire manebimus!
Gee-hee, gee-rar, gee-ha, gee-roar!
Rah for the Class of 1904!

Modern Language Yell

Zip pel let te! A lak ka rire!
Die grossen und die starken, wir,
Nous surpassons la scientifique
Et l'historique, et la classique.
Modern Language—evermore,
Western Maryland—1904.

Historical Yell

Quoniam jacta est alea
Fiat justitia
Ruat caelum
Fortitudine omnia et jure
Nobis commendant se.
Et his solum
Historialibus summus honor
Est habere palmam in 1904.

Classical Yell

Heus, heus, what's the row?
'Tis the climax coming now.
Known afar, of mighty fame,
Semper summum is our name.
Εσμεν εν α ριθμ ω των
Εκαστοτε επ ακρων.
Latin, German, French and Greek
Are the classics which we seek,
Edepol, ecce,—classis cor—
Classical, Classical, 1904.

177

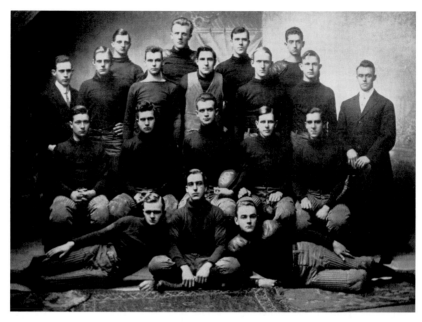

1909 football team captained by R. J. Gill,
in the center with the ball

Also following the traditions of the past, the class of 1904 had separate class colors (gold, green, and blue), a class motto (Non Omnis Moriar), and a class flower (Maréchal Niel rose). There was also a class song, a class poem, and a class ode. The students of this time did not have lots of other distractions and things to fill their time, so they wrote—essays, poems, songs, yells, and so forth.

The June 1901 *Monthly* included the words to a song written by trustee Laurence Webster Bates [1868–1901] a few years earlier that had been sent to the college (perhaps by his son after Bates's death) for consideration as a possible Alma Mater. The eight stanzas were to be sung to the tune of "Maryland, My Maryland" (or "O Tannenbaum"). The first verse and chorus were

Of Alma Mater we will sing,
Stately Western Maryland;
And make the blue arched welkin ring,
Stately Western Maryland.
With boys and girls her halls we'll crowd,
Of whom the State may well be proud,
And all shall sing her praises loud,
Stately Western Maryland.

Chorus:
Shout, Shout it out with loud acclaim
Good Old Western Maryland;
Long and glorious be her reign,
Grand Old Western Maryland.[88]

The other verses informally speak of baseball grounds, Parlor Night, Latin "ponies" (disallowed translations used to cheat in class translation), classroom cheating, and future vocational pursuits. It apparently was tentatively adopted as the college's alma mater, for it was sung as such at the Mid-Winter Alumni Banquet on February 3, 1905, where Governor Edwin Warfield was the featured speaker.

Oratorical contests, which began in 1899 when the college joined the Maryland Oratorical Society, brought a measure of success and pride to a number of WMC students. Each year the faculty selected the participants for the Intercollegiate Oratorical Contest. Many votes were taken until the final six speakers were selected. In the 30 contests held during the life of the association, the college won first place 17 times and second place 9 times. This is not surprising given the emphasis on oratory at the college since its beginnings. Students received instruction in oratory in their English and elocution classes, practiced it in their literary society debates, and demonstrated their developing skills in the Friday afternoon exercises (a regular part of the schedule until the college grew too large and the curriculum was expanded). The men's Irving and Webster societies continued to vie for the Merrill trophy in oratory at Commencement until 1931.[89]

The literary societies continued to be the mainstay of social activity on campus, with their joint anniversary celebrations on Thanksgiving and Washington's Birthday and other presentations during the year. In January 1901, the Browning and Philomathean societies presented Gilbert and Sullivan's *Mikado* in Alumni Hall, assisted by the faculty. The auditorium was full, in spite of a heavy snowstorm that day, and the show was considered a great success, culturally and financially. By request, it was repeated the following afternoon. The performance was a benefit to furnish the societies' new rooms.[90] In 1909, these women's societies were given still newer quarters in the new Library and Administration Building ("leased" in the same manner as the rooms in Alumni Hall had been in 1899 by the men's literary societies).

The *Monthly* still provided an outlet for literary expression; each issue had its campus news portion (local news, alumni news, exchanges, and athletics) and its longer literary section. The May 1901 issue included such articles as "The Self-Realization of the Race" by George H. Myers (the oration that had won him second place in the Maryland Oratorical Association contest);

a long poem entitled "The Loyalty of Mi" by Fergus '03 (a pen name); "An Afternoon Adventure" by Edward Barber '01; "The Nobility of Labor" by Van '03; a poem, "Twilight," and an essay, "A Plea for the Jew," by Levin Insley '04; a poem, "To Doris," by Mantis, '03; "A Consolation" by Marcella Grace Tracey '02; "Memory" by James Dawson Williams '02; "The Uplifting Force in Man" by Xela '01; and three short essays, "A Wasted Manhood," "Compensation," and "The Value of Appreciation," by H. (perhaps the editor-in-chief, Gideon I. Humphreys '02).

As the college grew, additional organizations were created to meet students' needs and interests. By the end of the decade, the 1910 *Aloha* listed the following with their members: YMCA, YWCA, Girls Athletic Association, the *Monthly*, Bachelor's Club, Law Club, Mandolin Club, Cliff Dwellers, Glee Club, Eastern Shore Club, Southern Club, Dramatics, JGC, and three others (perhaps local "fraternities" with very small memberships) designated cryptically AFA, FOB, and AGM. These were in addition to the various

Yingling Gymnasium I and Ward Hall II seen through the Ward Memorial Arch

intercollegiate athletic teams and the several intramural basketball teams. (The Bachelor's Club—not to be confused with the Bachelor Fraternity formed in the 1920s—was formed in 1903 with the caveat that "members must *pretend* not to be interested in girls.")[91]

Another student honor (the first of many now awarded at the Honors Convocation each year) was created in 1905 when the Bates Prize for best all-around college man was established by Edward Bayley Bates '98 in memory of his father, Rev. Laurence Webster Bates, DD. The award, originally a gold medal but in modern times a medallion and stipend, was based on four criteria: character, scholarship, standing and influence in the class, and athletic record. Roger Jay Whiteford '06 was its first recipient. Whiteford, the male valedictorian of his class, became a lawyer, served as a WMC trustee [1934–65], received an honorary LLD degree in 1943, and had a campus residence hall named for him and his wife in 1968. He and his son, Joseph S. Whiteford '43 (honorary DMus 1959), donated Baker Memorial Chapel's Whiteford Organ in 1958.

The classes of 1900–04 each published an annual, retaining the name *Aloha*. Each annual contained pictures and listings of all the classes, class histories, reports of organizations and athletic teams, and attempts at humor (lost on modern readers, who do not know the context). Of special interest is the inclusion of class member statistics in the 1902, 1903, and 1904 *Aloha*s, which give a profile of the students of a century ago. For instance, the 16 men in the class of 1902 reported the following:[92]

Average age: 21 (range from 18 to 27)
Average weight: 145 pounds (range from 120 to 175)
Average height: 5 ft. 9 in. (range from 5 ft. 6 in. to 6 ft.)
Average shoe size: 6.5 (range from 5 to 7.5)
Politics: 8 Republicans, 6 Democrats, 2 Progressives
Religion: 7 Methodist Episcopal, 5 Methodist Protestant, 1 Methodist Church South, 2 Episcopal, 1 German Reform
Future profession: 7 lawyers, 3 doctors, 1 preacher, 1 teacher, 1 engineer, 2 businessmen, 1 undecided

The 14 women reported these data:

Average age: 20 (range from 18 to 23)
Average weight: 129 pounds (range from 105 to 145)
Average height: 5 ft. 6 in. (range from 5 ft. 2 in. to 5 ft. 10 in.)
Average shoe size: 4.5 (range from 3 to 5.5)
Politics: 3 Republicans, 9 Democrats, 2 Progressives
Religion: 6 Methodist Episcopal, 2 Methodist Protestant, 1 Presbyterian, 2 Episcopal, 1 Catholic, 2 undeclared

*Future profession: 4 teachers, 1 physician, 1 secretary, 2 housekeepers, 1
missionary, 5 undeclared*

There was no yearbook from 1904 until 1910, except for a small, suede-backed *Class Book* in 1907 containing only write-ups and pictures of class members but nothing about college life. It sold for 75¢. In the years without an annual, the classes apparently determined that it was not financially feasible to publish one (there was no financial assistance from the college). Furthermore, a faculty committee recommended not publishing one on the grounds that recent *Aloha*s did not "render any service to the college" or to the class. Perhaps picking up the challenge to do something better, the class of 1910 requested permission to publish an annual and received it from the faculty, with the usual admonitions about taste and decorum.

The 1910 yearbook was dedicated to William G. Baker Jr. '94, of Baker, Watts and Company in Baltimore, in recognition of his efforts as chairman of the Western Maryland College Alumni Committee that had successfully completed a campaign to raise $10,000 for the college's endowment. The editors stated in the preface that they wanted to reestablish a worthy custom and to portray in lasting form the remembrances of their college course. What followed was the traditional layout of pictures (more of them, as photography had improved), individual class member write-ups, descriptions of all the campus organizations and their members, detailed reports of athletic endeavors, and many spoofs of college life and personnel.

The last page of the yearbook contained a seemingly innocuous poem entitled "Vale." The first letters of each line, however, formed an acrostic that spelled out, reading down: "DOC LEWIS IS A HORSE'S ASS." Soon after the yearbook was distributed, giggling erupted all over campus. The "offense" was discovered by the faculty, and the editors, Early H. Moser, Thomas S. Englar, and Robert J. Gill, were obliged to apologize, although they admitted no wrongdoing: "We, the undersigned, . . . do hereby repudiate the poem therein entitled 'Vale' and containing an acrostic shameful and indecent. The acrostic was not our work and we desire publicly to apologize for its appearance in the book." A bit later the five female members of the staff collectively submitted a long handwritten note disavowing any knowledge of the poem (and by implication, suggesting that the male editors were responsible). "We, the undersigned, absolutely disclaim all connection with or knowledge of the disgraceful and shameful matter in the Aloha. . . . We assure the faculty that we are entirely innocent of all questionable matter that went into the Aloha." Both letters were attached to the faculty minutes for posterity, along with the statement from the faculty read to the class on June 15, just prior to their Commencement, which recorded its "indignant condemnation of those responsible for the publication" because of the "outrageous violations of propriety, respect, and even decency."[93] No one was ever formally called to task and no official faculty action was taken, but Dr. Lewis suspended publication of the yearbook for six years (punishment applied not to the perpetrators but to their successors). College folklore has it that the author of the poem, who slipped it into the copy sent to the printer at the last possible moment, was the associate editor Robert Gill, who in later years grinned broadly but said nothing whenever he was asked about the incident. The next yearbook appeared in 1916 and included a veiled reference to the 1910 incident.

Other campus high jinks were reported in the yearbooks or faculty minutes. The Halloween celebration in 1901 saw some "disorder": Masked young ladies had paraded in the halls at 2 A.M. and tied the female teachers' doors shut. A faculty committee was appointed to investigate, of course, and a week later the faculty voted unanimously that the president reprimand the young ladies involved and express "the faculty's condemnation of the whole affair." No demerits were awarded, since it apparently was too hard to determine exactly who was responsible. The faculty also recommended abolishing the Halloween entertainment, which had been an annual presentation by the sophomore class, and putting something else on in its place.[94]

The 1902 *Aloha* reported on a student uprising on campus, likening it to a "true Revolutionary War." It seems that in December 1900, the college administration announced that the Christmas recess would end on Wednesday, January 2. After several secret meetings, the junior women decided to defy the rules and extend their vacation until the following Monday. When Dr. Lewis discovered the insurrection on January 4, he called the faculty together to discuss the situation, and the result was a stern letter sent to all absent parties by Secretary McDaniel:

> *In view of the fact that all the young ladies of the Junior Class have, as it appears, absented themselves by common consent from college exercises during this week, college having reopened on January 2nd, the faculty expresses its disapproval of this concerted action to interfere with the work of the class and order the following notice to be sent: These young ladies must make up by examinations the work they have missed before attending any recitations of the class. The first examination will be on Tuesday, January 8th at 9 o'clock in psychology, the first two chapters being the amount assigned. Those failing to appear at these examinations will be examined when they do return, and charged for their examination at catalogue rates.*[95]

Submission followed speedily as the students humbly returned.

Attendance at classes had become a problem during the decade, so a faculty committee was appointed (several times) to study it; the committee suggested abolishing demerits for unexcused absences and instituting 40-minute required study hours, one session for each missed class. For more than three unexcused absences, three study hours and appropriate confinement to campus would be required. Apparently, that didn't work well, however, because in 1907, the committee recommended lowering a course grade a fraction of a point for various absences (excused or not).[96] In January 1910, the absence officer reported that in the fall term, 64 students had made 435 absences from class, and of those, 16 students had been absent 10 or more times for a total of 281. The football players had on average 18.9 absences each.[97]

On a more positive note, a student-initiated optional Honor System Association was proposed by 35 male students of the YMCA in December 1903. It was soon approved by the faculty and was put into operation in 1904. The *Monthly* described it as an "entire success."[98] The members who signed on pledged to take their exams on their honor, and exams were given in an "honor room" without a proctor. In December 1904, the faculty voted to add a penalty for cheating (in addition to a zero for the exam): The names of the cheaters would be read out before the school. By 1905, perhaps inspired by this faculty edict, all but 15 male students had signed pledges, and the faculty voted to continue it. This was the first such honor system at the college, although it was apparently only for the men of the campus; no mention is made of women participating.

Milton Wright concluded his comments about student life with a remembrance of his Commencement:

I learned to love Western Maryland and spent three happy years there. It was sad to part with those I had learned to work with during those years and some of the friendships I made have continued to this day. . . . Graduation day came at last in June of 1906 and sorry to say I was one of the very few who had no one of my family to see me graduate. The President, Dr. Thomas H. Lewis, the stern old man, handed me my diploma and commented on my college career and the fact that I was the oldest member of my class.[99]

A college scrapbook was instituted in 1904, a simple thing, at first consisting of large pieces of paper folded to 18x12 size and tied with string. It was designed to be a depository for newspaper clippings about alumni, wedding invitations, greeting cards from alumni, business literature, and such—anything of a personal nature about the college's far-flung alumni. It became a historical record of former students, as well as a record of one's contemporaries to be perused by visiting alumni. (Today, it provides a wealth of information of the early students of the college; it is in the college archives.)

CURRICULUM

As the decade opened, the college courses became organized into departments for the first time: Philosophy, English, Latin, Greek, French, German, Mathematics and Astronomy, Chemistry and Geology, Physics and Biology, and History and Political Science. In addition were listed "Supplementary Courses" in piano, pipe organ, voice, art, and elocution.

The curriculum was becoming a bit less rigid. Greek was dropped as an entrance requirement for the preparatory school; and all students in the collegiate program could now substitute French or German for Greek, although Greek was still a viable offering. President Lewis had claimed in his 1898 presidential report that the course of study was so enriched by the three choices of areas of concentration that it was "all that a student should ask." In February 1901, he reported that there had been a meeting of college presidents with the state superintendent of education to design a course of study for the high schools that would mesh with the entrance requirements of the colleges.

Following its long-standing policy, the faculty continued to approve rather strange changes and substitutions in courses. For example, a sophomore woman was allowed to substitute an extra year of mathematics for Latin, because it was considered to be "equivalent," and besides, they reasoned—curiously—she was

Physics class in Yingling Science Hall lecture room;
its seating was moved to Lewis Recitation Hall.

prepared for mathematics and not for Latin. Another was allowed to substitute music for botany, and a third dropped Latin for drawing.[100] However, the faculty denied several student requests to change from one course program to another (e.g., from Modern Languages to Historical). It was noted that it would be too difficult to meet the different requirements, and, having selected a program, students were not allowed any further choice of subjects.

Physical education was made a graduation requirement, and a gymnasium fee for all students was imposed to support the athletic program. When one student asked to be excused from gym because of his health, the faculty suggested that he give up smoking instead and attend gym regularly to improve his health.[101]

The faculty met in June 1901 to discuss academic deficiencies and required reexamination in the fall or retaking a failed course the following year. No one appears to have been dismissed outright for academic reasons, but several were sent home permanently because of demerits for deportment.

New rules for graduation honors were established in March 1901. Students receiving honorable mention (a 9 or better grade in all courses) in a full curriculum, or an average of 9.4 in the senior and junior years, or the senior, sophomore, and freshman years, would graduate summa cum laude. Those who received honorable mention only in the senior year would graduate cum laude. In February 1905 the faculty approved a new grading plan: A = 9.5–10; B = 9–9.5; C = 8–9; D = 7–8; E = below 7.

The old master of arts degree (awarded after three years for professional standing but without any course work) was no longer listed in the catalog as an option after 1903 (and was totally discontinued after 1906). At President Lewis's urging, the board dropped that honorific because other colleges were doing the same thing; the master's degree was fast becoming an earned degree.

In 1908 Lewis recommended establishing a course in pedagogy for prospective teachers. This was not the first time such a course had been offered (in 1886–87 and 1887–88, the county school examiner, James Diffenbaugh, had lectured on the art of teaching). But this new formal program began a long association with teacher education in Maryland. By June Lewis reported that a course of study for teachers had been planned and that Professor James Widdowson had been hired and 52 students enrolled in the program for the fall term. This supplementary "normal course" was needed for students who wanted to teach or held a State Senatorial Scholarship.

The library was regularly adding books and other research tools. The 1907 "viewbook" reported that the library had about 6,000 volumes "carefully selected with regard to practical usefulness and useableness. The Library is kept open every day from 9 A.M. to 5 P.M. with a librarian always in attendance. . . . Research is the key-note of the education of the twentieth century." Completion of the new library was a major improvement to the changing and growing educational program; it was ready for occupation in 1909. In his report to the trustees in 1910, the president said,

> We have a collection of about eight thousand well selected books, besides two or three thousand government publications. Our books have been purchased new and with special reference to the needs of our students. I know that there is less dead material in our library than in most libraries. It is my purpose to keep our library up to the demand of our school, and I think we should spend about one thousand dollars this summer in purchasing books.[102]

By the end of the decade, Lewis reported to the board that the entrance requirements for the preparatory school had been raised to satisfy the New York Board of Regents; the same work in Latin and mathematics was now required of both boys and girls. A year of calculus was included in the collegiate scientific course, as well as a course in mechanical drawing to prepare students for engineering school. The rest of the scientific course had been adjusted to prepare students for entry into medical schools (especially Johns Hopkins) without any conditions.

In June 1910, Lewis commented on the status of coeducation in the country, noting that several colleges had abandoned the plan because the number of male students had dropped when females were enrolled. He noted, however, that WMC statistics were just the opposite, with slightly more men than women enrolled. (McDaniel had also commented on this in his 1903 speech to the NYC alumni.) In the 40 years since the first Commencement, in 1871, the college had graduated 781 students, 377 men and 404 women, only 18 classes having more women than men. Although more men enrolled in the college, more women graduated.

The issue of coeducation had been raised earlier when A. D. Melvin, the college representative and endowment secretary, wrote a letter to the trustees in 1902 noting that in his visits to churches and families, he had found that a number of people were afraid of coeducation, thinking of the college as a "mixed school" and obviously not understanding how WMC operated. There was also some concern that the standards were too high for admission and graduation for women. This did not seem to dissuade women from enrolling, however, as Lewis later pointed out. The issue also found its way into the *Monthly* occasionally, in articles and editorials such as "Why Educate Women?"[103] Strangely, the Commencement speaker for 1905, Governor Edwin Warfield, gave a rather mixed message regarding higher education. "His advice to the girls was to go home and help their mothers and not to marry until they are twenty-six; to the boys he said 'help your fathers do the harvesting.'" He did go on to say that he expected to hear great things of them at some future day and wished them success.[104] Perhaps he was simply expressing the prevailing mood about college education, particularly for women, a century ago, at least among the male population.

FINANCES

Enrollments for the decade fluctuated between 217 and 246, with an average of 234, boarders making up about 75%–80% of the student body. Males slightly outnumbered females each year, but the ratio of men to women was always fairly even, as noted. Since the college was almost totally tuition driven, any significant drop in student enrollments or boarders meant a corresponding drop in revenues. The financial panic of 1907 caused enrollments to drop to their lowest point in the decade, but they had rebounded to the average by the end of the decade. Tuition and room and board remained $225 per year (tuition was $15 per term for day students). In June 1903 Lewis reported to the board his thinking that student numbers were not growing because more students were choosing to take a "partial course" or a certificate program in art or music, and because the college was requiring more of students in the way of examinations and grades than some other schools (especially for women). Perhaps all of these reasons explain the graduation statistics for the class of 1904, as an example. Of the 74 students enrolled in the collegiate class in 1900, only 28 (38%) completed the AB degree four years later, while 46 are listed as *quondam* students. Similar statistics could be provided for every class in this decade. Lewis recommended that the board study the situation.

As the decade opened, Lewis reported a debt of $20,300 and embarked on his 1901–2 campaign to canvas the churches and Sunday schools of the district with a general appeal for the endowment. He noted that this campaign might not add a lot to the endowment, but it would educate people to the college's need and lay the groundwork for a larger fund-raising effort. In February 1902, he made some specific recommendations to the board on how to build the endowment:

> 1. *To ask the Maryland Conference (M.P. Church) to lay a permanent annual assessment on the district of $1,500 for the college endowment. [This request had been made earlier, but the conference wanted it to be a voluntary contribution from the churches—which in the past produced limited results.]*

2. *To have the conference select ten men and place an insurance policy of $5,000 on each of them for the benefit of the college endowment [the annual premium would amount to about $1,500].*

3. *To supplement the plan by soliciting friends of the college to take out insurance polices in favor of the college, paying their own premiums. [This was becoming a popular fund-raising technique of colleges.]*

4. *To ask those people who held bonds [for the debt] to give them up, with the understanding that $1,000 each year would go into the endowment fund until the bond was redeemed.*

5. *To employ someone to work full-time as a field representative of the college, visiting the churches to keep the assessment interest alive and to encourage people to put the college in their wills.*[105]

Upon his return from the endowment campaign, Lewis reported that he had visited 73 churches and addressed 20 Sunday schools and had received $745.13 from the Sunday schools and $518.50 from the churches and other sources for his efforts.[106] The conference had approved the district assessment (the first such direct action by the church), and Dr. Melvin had been appointed endowment secretary for a three-year period. The endowment fund now held $4,639.35 in a savings account, and he suggested that it be prudently invested. The board agreed. By 1903, $1,339 (the first significant money) had begun to arrive from the conference assessments, and the endowment had grown to $6,062.

In 1903, Lewis reviewed his 17-year presidency. He cited enrollments, which averaged 233 (with a high of 278), noting that 1,313 students had enrolled during the period, and 393 had graduated. He recalled that when he took office, the debt was $15,385 at 6% interest, and at that moment, it was $17,200 at 2%. He reported total receipts of $590,155.98 and total expenditures for land, buildings, and improvements of $197,713.83. An astonishing $203,775.89 had been saved from earnings over the period, but only $29,234 had been forthcoming in gifts, $19,500 of that from seven people. He especially noted that no one, including former trustees, had left the college anything in a will. "Our people feel no disposition to help the college because they think the college needs no help. . . . Our success is our sin," he said. He also noted again the church's reluctance to help: "Neither I nor any man can make a college for the Church without the Church to help. . . . I feel deeply and sincerely the risk the Church is assuming with regard to this institution, and I fear the result."[107] Clearly, he felt the strain of trying to keep the college on course and financially stable without much help from his church.

By June 1905, the endowment had grown to $13,332 and Lewis wryly noted that the college itself was contributing surplus funds in the same amount as the church. That same year, the Alumni Association proposed to raise $15,000 for the endowment, and the board voted to undertake raising a like amount during the year. It's not clear whether anything came of the board vote, but in appreciation of the Alumni Association's proposal, the trustees voted that the association should elect seven members to be known as the Board of Alumni Visitors, who would attend all regular and special trustee meetings. The board also elected Lewis treasurer of the endowment fund. By June 1908, the association reported pledges of $7,450 and collections of $2,520 in this campaign.

By June 1909 the endowment campaign had raised $50,095 (paid in and invested) with $2,000 more in pledges. It had been a success, especially with Alumni Association help and the money pledged from the churches. Not surprisingly, Lewis was proud, happy, and relieved. But certainly not complacent. He immediately recommended to the board that it set a new goal of $250,000, and it agreed.

The number of full-time faculty stayed fairly consistent at 9 during the decade, with 11 preparatory school teachers and assistants in art and music. Faculty salaries remained constant, except for a $100 reduction per person in early 1907 due to the national financial downturn, after which they were first returned to previous levels and then raised a bit, in June 1907, with Reese, McDaniel, Bonnotte, and Warfield each receiving $1,200; others averaged $500. The cost of faculty salaries varied from $15,000 to $20,000 per year during the decade.

In June 1909 Lewis suggested raising tuition and board rates and ceasing the free tuition for ministerial sons and daughters in favor of a one-third reduction in fees, noting that 45 students had paid no tuition the previous year, although they did pay room and board. This was one of the few Lewis recommendations the board did not approve; the increase did not happen until 1914, when those costs were raised $25, to an annual fee of $250.

While the State of Maryland did appropriate $25,000 for the new Library and Administration Building in 1908, annual state funding was still problematic. At the groundbreaking for the building after the 1908 Commencement, Governor Austin L. Crothers was present and responded to Lewis's remarks by saying that he was confident in the success of the president and the institution. However, his words did not match his actions, for he had cut in half the appropriation made to the college that year by the legislature, and during the following year, when the legislature appropriated $25,000 to cover the deficiency of the previous year, he not only did not allow that to stand but cut $9,000 from the compensatory grant for the scholarships for state students.[108]

Apparently, in 1910, the issue of state aid to private church-related colleges was raised by the state senator from Carroll County, Johnzie E. Beasman, leading Dr. Lewis to respond, referring in writing publicly to a private conversation they had had regarding the denominational status of the college. Lewis stated that the college was founded by the Methodist Protestant Church as its duty "to do something for the education of the young." He noted that all the college's property had been paid for by Methodist Protestants, except for a few contributions from outside friends, and one gift from the legislature. He felt that that was what was meant when it was said by the Methodists and others that a denomination "founded a college." (It is interesting to note that he glossed over J. T. Ward's failed initial efforts to get the church involved in the college's founding, as well as the fact that the annual conference of the church had contributed little to the college directly, for either buildings or upkeep. Indeed, only in this decade had the churches finally come forth with fairly significant contributions via the conference assessment. Perhaps he was hopeful, as his father-in-law had been, of "shaming" the church into a more active financial role.) He went on to liken the college to St. John's College and Washington College with regard to its charter and pointed out that there were no theological or "denominational" courses taught in the college. He strongly stated that the college was a liberal and public-spirited institution, contributing thousands of dollars to local businesses and workmen for supplies and building construction. He said that the students who had received State Senatorial Scholarships over 30-some years had gone forth to teach and served the state handsomely, noting that "the State is being amply repaid in the service they render for the cost of their education." He concluded that, while the college was a "denominational" school, the state was not helping that denomination at all. On the contrary, the "denomination is helping the State by establishing an institution of learning and by making the way to higher efficiency accessible to a larger number of young people."[109] This is an interesting foreshadowing of legal discussions to come 50 years later.

Major Events

The first wedding in the Baker Chapel was on January 5, 1904, when Miriam Lewis '96 married Herbert Veasey, in a ceremony performed by her father. It is interesting that it took ten years to hold a wedding in the "new" chapel.

In 1907 a testimonial dinner for Prof. James Reese served as the Mid-Winter Banquet of the Alumni Association. Unfortunately, Reese could not attend, but that did not stop the many tributes to the professor of 37 years, including one from his former student William McDaniel. It was proposed that evening, as an expression of the high esteem in which the professor was held by all his former students, that a portrait be commissioned by the association and painted by Oscar Hallwig, Baltimore portrait painter. Subscriptions were obtained from many alumni, and the portrait was unveiled at the 1907 Commencement as a surprise for Reese.

Former students, when sending in donations, commented about Reese:

- *I am sure every WMC student has the tenderest memories and deepest regard for Prof. Reese as a teacher and friend.*
- *Of the many men I have met and known . . . there is no one whom I remember with greater pleasure, or delight more to honor, than Dr. Reese.*
- *I love to think of that refined and gentle manner with which he always greeted us. The memory of it should give every Western Maryland graduate a sweeter and better life.*[110]

The *Monthly* went on to describe the unveiling:

One of the most interesting and pleasing incidents of the commencement was the unveiling and presentation of a beautiful life-size portrait of Prof. James W. Reese, Ph.D., who has been the professor of the Latin and Greek languages at the college for more than 37 years, having begun his connection with the institution before its first commencement. The presentation speech was made by William G. Baker, Jr., '94 of Baltimore, retiring president of the Alumni Association. In view of Professor Reese's long and valuable services to the college, he was presented a handsome sum of money voted by the trustees. Prof. Reese was greatly surprised and deeply moved by these evidences of appreciation and affection, and on rising to express his gratitude, he took refuge in the Latin tongue to conceal his emotion and spoke impromptu in this language.[111]

As Schofield pointed out, "Many faculty members have since been honored, but no others are known to have been startled into a Latin response."[112] The picture originally hung in the Alumni Association Room in Alumni Hall and now hangs in the Hoover Library Board Room.

Three years later, on February 16, 1910, a date chosen because it marked the close of his 40th year at the college, the Alumni Association again honored Prof. Reese at its Mid-Winter Banquet, and this time he was able to attend. The banquet was held at the Hotel Belvedere in Baltimore, and with Steinwald's orchestra playing "Dear Western Maryland" many times, Reese was joined by many old friends, including Daniel Hering. The toastmaster was Dr. Joshua

Portrait of James W. Reese,
first emeritus professor

Hering, boyhood friend of the honoree and WMC board president. Numerous toasts were given and responded to by various individuals. President Lewis (one of Reese's many former students) paid glowing tribute, declaring that the professor gave the college its first advance in the educational world. "When we think of that peculiar and powerful helpfulness we call scholarship," he said, "we bow the knee first of all to James W. Reese, and without a trace of envy or reservation give him our 'Ave Caesar!'" Reese's long affiliation with the Masons was recognized, and the town of Westminster presented him with a silver loving cup. After long and hearty applause, Reese finally responded in "that gentle, genial way which is so characteristic of him."[113]

The faculty also recognized Dr. Reese's completion of 40 years' service with a resolution: "Forty years of eminently faithful and successful teaching, of wholesome and lasting moral influence over the students, and of support and extension of the good name and fame of the college."[114]

The Commencement of June 17, 1908, was especially memorable because of a special honor accorded another of the college's stalwart leaders. First, Governor Crothers spoke, and those in attendance were gratified to hear him say in his remarks, "I have for years observed the work done by this great school. In scope it is second to none. Its reputation through Maryland is first class. Its graduates show in their lives of usefulness the advantages derived from their course in the college."[115] The governor later handed out diplomas.

Joshua W. Hering,
trustee chair and lecturer in anatomy and physiology

During the ceremony, the Bates Prize went to G. Frank Thomas of Adamstown, Maryland, who also received from Prof. Reese the gold medal from the State Intercollegiate Oratorical Contest, the eighth time in ten contests that the medal was won by a Western Marylander. President Lewis then unveiled a life-size portrait of Joshua Hering commissioned by the trustees in honor of the "last of the glorious company of 33 worthy men" who founded the college 42 years before. Dr. Hering responded by recalling the history of the college and its many difficult times. He saluted his friends and fellows on the board who had passed on, noting, "Only I have survived. Why I do not know, but I do know that soon . . . I will join them, and this portrait only will remain. If that portrait could speak, I would have it through all the years say to you that as God has been with us, may He ever abide, and may the watchword of the college continue to be 'Onward and upward.'"[116] The portrait now hangs in the Board Room in Hoover Library.

Following the Commencement, the audience left the auditorium and gathered at the site of the new Library and Administration Building. President Lewis used the same spade that was used to break ground for Smith Hall (his first building as president) and suggested that this might be the last building he would build on the campus. The governor also dug a spade of earth, and then Dr. Hering did the same. A testimonial banquet for Dr. Hering was held a week later, on June 24, 1908, and was attended by Governor Crothers, various state politicos, trustees, and friends. Dr. Reese was the toastmaster. His toast was followed by addresses from 11 other friends. In the concluding years of the decade, these two significant individuals in the history of the college were quite appropriately recognized for their long service.

Conclusion

The first decade of the 20th century was a significant one for the college. Its president was away for half of that time: several extended periods on endowment campaign solicitations, two years as the part-time president of Adrian College, and a year on a health leave, traveling abroad. Acting in his stead during all those absences was his loyal and able vice president, William McDaniel. During the decade, the faculty continued to change and improve, not only in new faces but also in academic training. Several new and needed buildings were erected, including a new gymnasium, a refitted science facility, and a Library and Administration Building. The student body continued to grow slowly and expand its interests into a number of new clubs, successful athletic teams, and oratorical contests. The restrictions on social intercourse among students were beginning to loosen a bit. The college's endowment grew almost exponentially, so that by the end of the decade it stood at $55,000 and was projected to double in the next decade, with a long-term goal of $250,000. It had been a busy and productive decade for many people at the college. The next decade would see some new faces and new buildings, as well as a winding down of an era marked by the extraordinary 34-year presidency of Thomas Hamilton Lewis.

CHAPTER 5 ENDNOTES

1. The Timeshare Beat, www.thetimeshare beat.com/yourworld/1902.htm.
2. WMC board of trustees minutes, June 11, 1901.
3. 1903 *Aloha*, 17.
4. McDaniel speech to NYC alumni, 1903, college archives.
5. A. Douglas MacNaughton, *A History of Adrian College*, 1994, 245–49.
6. Schofield and Crain, *Formative Years*, 74.
7. Lewis Papers, college archives.
8. WMC board of trustees minutes, June 11, 1907.
9. Ibid.
10. *WMC Monthly*, May 1907, 22–23.
11. Ibid., August 1901, 3.
12. Ibid., June 1905, 30.
13. Stegman, *Women of Achievement*, 81.
14. WMC faculty minutes, April 27, 1906.
15. October 12, 1906.
16. WMC board of trustees minutes, June 11, 1901.
17. Ibid., June 16, 1903.
18. Schofield and Crain, *Formative Years*, 60.
19. *WMC Monthly*, October 1902, 20–21.
20. *WMC Monthly*, May 1903, 20.
21. 1904 *Aloha*, 147.
22. *WMC Monthly*, April 1904, 22–23; November 1904, 21.
23. *WMC Catalogue* 1909–10, 24.
24. WMC faculty minutes, March 17, 1905.
25. 1904 *Aloha*, 148.
26. *WMC Monthly*, March 1906, 32.
27. WMC board of trustees minutes, June 1907.
28. Schofield and Crain, *Formative Years*, 74.
29. Pick, *A Brief History of Campus Planning*, 9.
30. *WMC Catalogue* 1910–11, 27.
31. *WMC Monthly*, November 1909, 12; Wills, *History of Western Maryland College*, 11.
32. Pick, *A Brief History of Campus Planning*, 9–10.
33. Schofield and Crain, *Formative Years*, 77.
34. Ibid., 78.
35. "x" preceding the class year indicates the expected year of graduation for a student who didn't graduate; e.g., "x'95" in this chapter indicates that the student was expected to graduate in 1895 but didn't.
36. WMC faculty minutes, April 18, 1902.
37. 1904 *Aloha*, 21.
38. *WMC Monthly*, January 1902, 20.
39. WMC faculty minutes, April 21, 1902.
40. Ibid., May 2, 16, 29, 1902.
41. Ibid., May 25, 1906.
42. Ibid., May 4, 1901.
43. Ibid., September 19, 1905.
44. Wright, *Memoir*.
45. WMC faculty minutes, September 21, 1900.
46. *WMC Monthly*, February/March 1904, 18.
47. Page 197.
48. Pages 197–98.
49. WMC faculty minutes, April 15, 1910.
50. August 1901, 7.
51. WMC faculty minutes, October 18, 1901.
52. Wright, *Memoir*.
53. *WMC Monthly*, February 1908, 26.
54. Page 198.
55. *WMC Monthly*, February/March 1904, 19.
56. WMC faculty minutes, June 5, 1903.
57. Ibid., May 8, 1903.
58. Ibid., October 5, 1906.
59. Ibid., November. 19, 1909.
60. Ibid., October 25, 1907.
61. Ibid., June 5, 1908.
62. Wills, *History of Western Maryland College*, vol. 2, 71.
63. WMC faculty minutes, April 23, 1909.
64. Wright, *Memoir*.
65. Page 42.
66. WMC faculty minutes, March 14, 1902.
67. Stegman, *Women of Achievement*, 268.
68. WMC faculty minutes, January 18, 1907.
69. 1904 *Aloha*, 23.
70. Wright, *Memoir*.
71. *WMC Monthly*, May 1901, 21–24.
72. 1903 *Aloha*, 142.
73. *WMC Monthly*, December 1902, 20–22.
74. Ibid., November 1902, 20–21.
75. WMC faculty minutes, September 18, 1903.
76. *WMC Monthly*, November 1903, 20–23; December 1903, 19–21.
77. Ibid., May 1903, 20.
78. *WMC Monthly*, May 1904, 31–32.
79. 1904 *Aloha*, 148.
80. WMC faculty minutes, December 13, 1904.
81. *WMC Monthly*, February 1905, 23.
82. WMC faculty minutes, October 19, 1905.
83. *WMC Monthly*, May 1907, 27–30.
84. Ibid., December 1909, 18.
85. 1910 *Aloha*, 124–27.
86. Ibid., 128–29.
87. 1904 *Aloha*, 54.
88. Pages 9–10.
89. Wills, *History of Western Maryland College*, vol. 2, 47.
90. *WMC Monthly*, February 1901, 20.
91. Ibid., November 1903, 25.
92. 1902 *Aloha*, 70–73.
93. WMC faculty minutes, May 6, 1910.
94. Ibid., November 1, 1901.

CHAPTER 5 ENDNOTES

95. Ibid., January 4, 1901.
96. Ibid., May 10, 1907.
97. Ibid., January 7, 1910.
98. January 1904, 19.
99. Wright, *Memoir*.
100. WMC faculty minutes, September 7, 1900.
101. Ibid., February 20, 1901.
102. WMC board of trustees minutes, June 14, 1910.
103. January 1905, 22.
104. *WMC Monthly*, June 1905, 29.
105. WMC board of trustees minutes, February 25, 1902.
106. Wills, *History of Western Maryland College*, vol. 2, 14.
107. WMC board of trustees minutes, June 16, 1903.
108. Schofield and Crain, *Formative Years*, 75.
109. Letter to the editor, March 1, 1910.
110. *WMC Monthly*, June 1907, 24–26.
111. June 1907, 18, 24.
112. Page 84.
113. *WMC Monthly*, March 1910, 1–2.
114. WMC faculty minutes, February 25, 1910.
115. *WMC Monthly*, June 1908, 17.
116. Ibid., June 1908, 20–21.

MAJOR WORLD EVENTS

1901

Queen Victoria dies; she is succeeded by son Edward VII.

Ragtime jazz develops in the United States.

Rachmaninoff composes Piano Concerto no. 2.

Max Planck announces laws of radiation.

J. P. Morgan organizes the U.S. Steel Corporation.

President William McKinley is assassinated; he is succeeded by Theodore Roosevelt.

1902

Coal strike hits the U.S., May–October.

Beatrix Potter publishes *Peter Rabbit.*

Triple Alliance between Germany, Austria, and Italy is renewed for six more years.

Arthur Conan Doyle publishes *The Hound of the Baskervilles.*

Enrico Caruso makes his first phonograph recording.

Monet paints *Waterloo Bridge.*

1903

G. B. Shaw publishes *Man and Superman.*

Jack London publishes *The Call of the Wild.*

The first Tour de France bicycle race is held.

The first post-season baseball series is held.

Orville and Wilbur Wright successfully fly a powered airplane.

The film *The Great Train Robbery* is made, the longest to date: 12 minutes.

Coronation durbar for Edward VII, king and emperor, is held in Delhi, India.

Henry Ford founds the Ford Motor Company with capital of $100,000.

1904

Russo-Japanese War breaks out.

J. M. Barrie publishes *Peter Pan.*

The Broadway subway opens in New York City.

The World Exposition and first American Olympics are held in St. Louis.

Work begins on the Panama Canal by the U.S.

Helen Keller graduates from Radcliffe College.

Sigmund Freud publishes *The Psychopathology of Everyday Life.*

1905

Theodore Roosevelt is inaugurated as president for second term.

Shaw publishes *Major Barbara.*

Debussy composes *La Mer.*

Franz Lehár composes *The Merry Widow.*

Albert Einstein formulates special theory of relativity.

Ty Cobb begins his major league baseball career.

1906

John Galsworthy publishes *A Man of Property*.
O Henry publishes *The Four Million*.
Upton Sinclair publishes *The Jungle*, revealing conditions in the Chicago stockyards.
U.S. Pure Food and Drug Act passed, a result of *The Jungle*.
San Francisco earthquake kills 700 and causes $400 million in property loss.

1907

Oklahoma becomes 46th state of the U.S.
William James publishes *Pragmatism*.
The first cubist exhibition is in Paris.
Ivan Pavlov studies conditioned reflexes.
Immigration to the U.S. is restricted by law.
The first Ziegfeld Follies is staged in New York.
Rasputin gains influence at the court of Czar Nicholas II.
Louis Lumière develops a process for color photography.
Mother's Day is officially established for the second Sunday in May.

1908

Union of South Africa is established.
The Ford Motor Company produces the first Model T; eventually, 15 million would be sold.
William Howard Taft is elected 27th U.S. president.
Isadora Duncan becomes popular interpreter of dance.
Fountain pens become popular.
Wilbur Wright flies 30 miles in 40 minutes.

1909

Ferenc Molnár publishes *Liliom*.
Picasso paints *Harlequin*.
Arnold Schönberg composes *Three Piano Pieces*.
U.S. explorer Robert E. Peary reaches North Pole.
Women are admitted to German universities.

1910

E. M. Forster publishes *Howard's End*.
Mark Twain (b. 1835) dies.
Puccini composes *The Girl of the Golden West*.
The weekend becomes popular in the U.S.
Marie Curie publishes *Treatise on Radiography*.
England's King Edward VII dies; is succeeded by son George V.
Frank Lloyd Wright becomes well known in Europe for his domestic architecture.
The South American tango gains immense popularity in Europe and the U.S.

Lewis Recitation Hall (1914)

C H A P T E R

THE END OF A MEMORABLE ERA

1911–1920

This decade was a difficult one for the world, for the nation, and for the college. The world was plunged into World War I, in which the country was engaged for several years. This affected the country's finances and lifestyle and changed the way people lived. The S.S. *Titanic* sank in 1912, on its maiden voyage, drowning 1,513 people. A federal income tax became law in 1913, via the 16th Amendment. Automobiles became more commonplace as a result of Henry Ford's assembly line techniques. The first transcontinental telephone call was placed in 1915. The United States tried unsuccessfully to legislate prohibition. Women's suffrage became a serious national issue, leading to the approval in 1920 of the 19th Amendment. The League of Nations, proposed by President Woodrow Wilson, was doomed to failure when the United States Senate voted against joining.

The college saw some of its male students and faculty go off to war, as either enlistees or draftees during 1917–18; some of these men sacrificed their lives. As a result of the war, male college students were trained for military service. Through it all the college continued to prosper, although the number of students sharply fluctuated from year to year and state appropriations, even for committed scholarships, could not be counted on. Remarkably, the endowment continued to grow (along with alumni giving and help from the church), and the campus continued to expand, both in acreage and with new buildings. The rules governing student life relaxed a bit as student governance developed. The curriculum also was loosened up to provide more course selection. During the decade, the college said good-bye to the last surviving charter trustee and the first professor emeritus, celebrated its 50th anniversary and its 50th commencement, celebrated William McDaniel's 30th year on the faculty and Thomas Hamilton Lewis's 25th year as president, and, in 1920, witnessed the completion of the Lewis presidency.

FACULTY AND ADMINISTRATION

As in the previous decade, T. H. Lewis dominated the scene as the autocratic president whose many suggestions for the good of the college were almost always ratified by the board of trustees. But during this ten-year span, the work and life of William Roberts McDaniel, his trusted and dependable vice president, were also recognized in several ways. About a third of the faculty continued to turn over fairly frequently, as young professors arrived for a year or two and then moved on to better-paying jobs. The problem was certainly recognized, but not until the end of the decade could the financial status of the college permit higher salaries that would lure and retain good, well-educated faculty.

There were exceptions, of course, in such educators as Nannie Lease '95 [elocution, 1904–37], Margaret Robinson [dean of women, 1908–28], Ferdinand Bonnotte [French and German, 1897–1932], Edwin A. Warfield '82 [English, 1904–22], James Widdowson [philosophy and pedagogy, 1908–18], and Harry Ryder [Latin and Greek, 1911–19], who continued their good work through most or all of the decade. They were joined during this period by such stalwarts as Fannie Stover '89 [dean of women, 1911–37], Walter B. Yount [Latin and Greek, 1912–31], Elise Dorst [music, 1914–28], Maude Gesner [music, 1917–55], Carl L. Schaeffer '14 [physics, 1919–59], Mabel Harris '01 [music, 1919–42], and Samuel B. Schofield '19 [chemistry and biology, 1919–66]. James Widdowson resigned his post in 1918 to become principal of the Normal School at Frostburg. Western Maryland faculty seemed to be good candidates for normal school leadership positions.

By mid-decade, the level of faculty training had increased. In 1916, there were four PhDs on the campus, from Johns Hopkins, Columbia, Yale, and Boston universities. All the other academic instructors held earned master's degrees from such institutions as Columbia, Chicago, and Virginia, and additional study had been undertaken at Columbia, Wisconsin, Cornell, Pittsburgh, George Washington, and the Peabody Conservatory. The total staff numbered 26, including 14 full-time academic faculty, 9 teachers of special subjects (art, music, elocution, physical training, etc.), and 3 preparatory school teachers.

In 1918, President Lewis recommended to the board that the title of preceptress be changed to dean of women, presumably to conform to general practice in other institutions. It was approved, and the incumbent became Dean Robinson.[1]

The first professor to remain long enough to retire was, of course, James William Reese (1838–1917), who joined the faculty in 1871 and retired from active service in 1912, when he was named the college's first professor emeritus. The *Monthly* noted, "To the college at large it is not extravagant to say that Professor Reese, more than any other one man, gave [the college] its first real advance into educational reputation. He shaped its ideals, gave direction and character to its curricula . . . so that the college quickly gained and has never lost a position of respectability in the educational world."[2] He was also remembered for having laid the cornerstones of most of the college buildings in Masonic ceremonies. In recognition of almost 42 years of continuous and distinguished service (during which he occasionally acted as president in the early years), he was retired at full salary ($1,200), which he received until his death five years later on March 30, 1917. His death was mourned by everyone associated with the college, because this gentle, scholarly man epitomized the educational program and life of the early college. The students reporting on his death in the *Monthly* said of him,

> *Unquestionably, one of the finest results of Prof. Reese's teaching was the regard he inspired for scholarship and the incentive he gave toward accuracy and thoroughness in study. His knowledge was not make-believe, or bluff. It was genuine learning, not pedantry, and every student who had the privilege of reciting to Dr. Reese or listening to his lectures never again had a sneer for scholarship, but only respect for it and a stimulus toward it.*[3]

In 1918, the board erected a tablet in his honor, which is now in Baker Chapel.

In the fall of 1915, all faculty members were required, for the first time, to sign a "loyalty oath" to the college, agreeing not to discuss items of faculty concern, to uphold the rules of the college, and to report all violations of the rules for appropriate disciplinary action. Everyone signed the sheet, which was included in the faculty minutes,[4] but one wonders what precipitated such an action. Perhaps there was some problem or internal discussion (insurrection?), and President Lewis was heading it off before it grew. But given that there was no such thing as tenure at this time, and faculty could be fired for any reason, one might assume the problem was not too serious.

The board of trustees continued to change occasionally, as the life trustees either died or resigned. During this decade the board had three presidents. The last living charter trustee and third chair, Dr. Joshua Hering, died on September 23, 1913, at the age of 80, having served 16 years as board president. President Lewis eulogized his life as "filled with unremitting and beneficent toil, one singularly free from storm and stress." At its next meeting, on June 9, 1914, the board elected Dr. Charles Billingslea (1840–1918) [1872–1918], a prominent Westminster dentist, as its president. Billingslea had long ties with the early history of the college, not only as the elected replacement for Fayette Buell on the board in 1872 but also because he had married Clara Smith, daughter of the venerable John Smith. The Billingsleas had also given the primary (later preparatory) school building in memory of their son James Levine in 1891. On July 6, 1918, four years after he was elected president, Dr. Billingslea died after an illness of one month and was succeeded as president by Elias Oliver Grimes (1838–1922) [1876–1922], a local wholesaler. Other prominent individuals named to the board in this era were T. W. Mather Sr. [1910–24], L. Irving Pollitt '89 [1913–53], John Cunningham '85 [1914–65], J. H. Straughn '99 [1915–74] (who would later become a bishop of the Methodist Church and serve as board chair for 20 years; he holds the record for trustee longevity, with 59 years), and William G. Baker Jr. '94 [1918–44].

Word reached Westminster in 1913 that Fayette Buell had died on January 1 at the age of 79 in Williamstown, New Jersey. He had previously resided in Philadelphia for about 30 years. He was survived by six children and his wife, Ellen (who continued to live in Philadelphia until her death on November 18, 1932, at the age of 95). Buell, his wife, and four of his children (Ellen, Ellis, Gertrude, and Hayward) were buried in the Westminster Cemetery.

In 1917, upon the death of another trustee from Carroll County, President Lewis suggested changing the charter (by request of the legislature) to remove the clause requiring that one-third of the trustees be county residents. According to the board minutes, he felt that it gave "too local a character to the college, besides preventing it from availing itself of the service of men from all parts of the State."

In a highly unusual move, but one of which everyone heartily approved, the board elected William McDaniel to board membership in 1911. It is rare for a faculty member to be a trustee of the same institution, but the election spoke volumes about the esteem in which McDaniel was held by the trustees. At that same meeting the board voted to confer upon him the honorary degree of doctor of science. It was conferred the next day at the

Commencement exercises, which also celebrated the 25th anniversary of the Lewis presidency. Trustee and seminary president Hugh Latimer Elderdice '82 [1898–1938] presented McDaniel to Lewis for the degree by saying, in part, "Every alumnus, every student and every friend of Western Maryland College will rejoice in the decree of the board of trustees which calls you to bestow upon him the high dignity and the well earned honor of Doctor of Science." The president commented, "I do it with greatest pleasure, because you have been efficient in so many things, you have been faithful in all things, scholar, teacher, administrator, counselor, Christian gentleman."[5] Prolonged applause followed the conferring of the degree, which was long overdue (given the conferring of the PhD on Reese two years after he joined the faculty) and made up, at least in part, for the Johns Hopkins PhD degree McDaniel was never able to finish because he heeded the call to serve his alma mater and never returned to graduate school. It was a singular honor, and certainly a surprise, for a unique and highly respected pillar of the college.

On the occasion of Dr. McDaniel's 25th anniversary as superintendent of the Sunday school (which he founded), the students presented him with a special resolution of appreciation as a Christmas gift in December 1916, following yet another inspiring Christmas service in Baker Chapel. The resolution noted his wise and inspired leadership and the hundreds of young people he had touched.[6]

In recognition of his 25 years as president, T. H. Lewis was honored at the February 25, 1911, Alumni Banquet, held at a Baltimore hotel, where he and Mrs. Lewis were presented with a beautiful silver fruit bowl and tray, designed by Jenkins & Jenkins of Baltimore in repoussé style. (They are now in the college archives.) There were many short and witty speeches, and "Dear Western Maryland," composed by Caleb O'Connor x'98, was sung enthusiastically by the banqueters:

Dear Western Maryland

Dear Western Maryland
Fearless and Bold
We're here to cheer to victory
The Green and the Gold
And we will always
Be Loyal to Thee
We'll love thee ever
Dear Old WMC.

The event broke up just in time for the Westminster contingent to catch the midnight train.[7] The *Monthly* of June 1911 included a reprint of an article that had appeared in the *Baltimore Sun* on June 4, in which the college and

Portrait of President Thomas Hamilton Lewis

Lewis were profiled. He was further honored at the 1911 Commencement, when his portrait, commissioned by the trustees, was unveiled. It was presented by McDaniel, who said of the honoree, "Ripe scholar, gifted preacher, skilled educator, wise counselor—persistent in purpose, energetic in action, fertile in resources."[8] The painting had been executed by Marie DeFord Keller and was unveiled by the president's little granddaughter, Mary Hamilton Veasey. (The portrait now hangs in the Board Room in the Hoover Library.) Lewis was honored a second time in 1911 when he was awarded the honorary doctor of divinity degree from Victoria University in Canada on the occasion of its 75th Charter Day Anniversary on October 9.

During the decade, it was apparent that Lewis was wearing down, although he kept up his full calendar of activities. Early on, in 1912, he discussed with the board a possible restructuring of the college administration, involving the appointment of two vice presidents to help with the day-to-day operation. The board agreed to the proposal, and Lewis appointed Rev. Albert Norman Ward '95, who had been elected to the board the previous year, to be the new vice president. Ward was able to leave his pastoral duties in Denton, Maryland, and assume the office in the spring of 1913; he then began to take a general survey of local conditions, as well as visit other institutions and seek out prospective students.[9] He quickly won the respect, love, and loyalty of the student body because of his character and cheerful disposition. However, he resigned April 1, 1917, to return to the pastorate. No reason was recorded, and Lewis reported it with disappointment, noting that he would miss the help but did not want to make another "administrative experiment." He was feeling the burdens of the office, and again he offered his resignation:

> It may be that the only way out of the difficulty would be to elect another president. Perhaps if one were given full power and complete control it might work better results. Accordingly, I wish to make it possible and easy for the board to exercise its best judgment without embarrassment, and I place my resignation at your service.[10]

In December 1914, a potentially significant event occurred that could have changed the college forever. The board of trustees met in special session to consider a possible relationship with Maryland State University (which was being formed from the loosely connected professional schools in Baltimore and an undergraduate liberal arts college). Such a movement to create a more centralized and administered state university had been in the works since 1907, when St. John's College had been approached to be the undergraduate school; negotiations regarding that affiliation had broken down, perhaps because of the university's debts. Callcott, in his *History of the University of Maryland*, commented on the situation:

The Johns Hopkins served the scholars, proprietary schools served the professions, the Maryland Agricultural College served the farmers, state normal schools provided teachers, and such private institutions as Washington, St. John's, Loyola, Western Maryland, St. Mary's, Morgan, and Goucher served for regular collegiate training. The general assembly had fallen into the peculiar custom of providing regular appropriations to almost all of these institutions. . . . Generally the established colleges considered the idea of a state university unnecessary and socialistic.[11]

Wills described the state's new concept of a university, citing the laws of Maryland:

In 1914, the Maryland Legislature passed an Act "to create and incorporate the Maryland State University, to provide for the affiliating therewith of other universities, colleges, academies, schools, hospitals, laboratories, or similar bodies corporate, institutions and associations in this state. . . ." The proposed university would be so constituted "that as many of the educational and kindred institutions of this state as shall desire so to do may become affiliated with the said . . . University."[12]

Now Western Maryland College was approached to become the liberal arts base for the university. After much discussion the board passed the following resolution:

Resolved, that this college enter into affiliation with the proposed Maryland State University according to the terms of the Charter of said university and that the President of the College is hereby authorized to sign the contract effecting this affiliation, provided such contract shall contain a provision for withdrawal of the college from the arrangement upon giving proper notice.[13]

Lewis was offered the provostship of the new university in early 1915 and concluded that "the call is one from which I could not turn away without the most serious reason."[14] He asked the board to accept his (qualified) resignation so that, if he decided to accept the offer, he would be free to do so. The board agreed. In a letter to the new board of regents of the university, Lewis noted that he was highly honored by being offered the position, but he had heard that "some apprehension has been expressed that it is unwise to place a minister of the Gospel in this position, as being likely to interfere with the broadest development of the university." He went on to say that he had been a preacher all his life and that he would not conceal or lay aside his clergy position. Interestingly, he also noted that the proposed salary for the new position was "considerably less than I now receive [$3,000]." In June 1916, Lewis reported to the board that "finding the conditions of the new position offered me not such as I believed promised success, I declined it."[15] With his withdrawal, the

college's potential affiliation seems also to have
been withdrawn, for nothing more is said about
it in the board minutes. (The university regents
then turned their sights to the small land-grant
institution in College Park, Maryland Agricultural
College—chartered in 1856, expanded under the
Morrill Land Grant Act of 1862, and perhaps the
only school willing to make the transition, because
it would be in its best interests to do so. It was
absorbed into the new university in 1920 as the
undergraduate campus and college.)

In March 1918, Lewis volunteered his services
to the War Work Council of the YMCA and became
director of religious work at Camp Wadsworth
in Spartansburg, South Carolina. He spent three
months doing that and in June was given an open-
ended leave of absence by the board to continue the
work. In his absence, McDaniel acted as president (at
the president's salary for April and May, while Lewis

*T. H. Lewis in uniform
(1918)*

drew no salary). Lewis's daughter, Clara Lewis Richmond (the college librarian,
who had recently married Capt. Leon Richmond) took over the management of
the dining hall for the period. Lewis apparently continued this work on a part-
time basis after June and through the summer. The *Monthly* carried a picture of
him in a military uniform, as well as an article by him describing the work and
his satisfaction in it. "No pastor or religious worker ever had a better chance to
do the biggest thing on earth. The men are right there . . . and they are facing
the most serious experience of their lives; and they have no other place to find
what they need. . . . Never have I seen a job as big as this, and everything in me
rises up to meet it."[16] For the 1918 Commencement, he returned to the campus
on a leave of absence from Camp Wadsworth and appeared at several of the
events, including the Commencement exercises themselves, in his regulation
olive green military uniform instead of his cap and gown.

While Lewis had offered his resignation to the board several times over
his long presidency, as he approached his 67th birthday in 1919, he formally
recommended that a committee be appointed to select his successor, to take
office not later than July 1, 1920. The board members politely ignored him, as
they had each time before. Finally, in February 1920, he thanked them for their
confidence and the compliment of continuing to do nothing, but he insisted
that they now must do something, and so a six-member committee was
appointed. At the June meeting of the board, the committee reported that they

had approached Dr. McDaniel, "whose splendid services to the college through a series of years marked him as the one outstanding man to succeed Dr. Lewis." When approached, McDaniel, who was 57 at the time, "after graciously and heartily expressing his appreciation of the offer, felt forced, by reason of the condition of his health, to decline the position." (He had been ill all through the spring of 1920 and had received treatment at Johns Hopkins Hospital, probably for the onset of Parkinson's disease, which would plague him for the next 20 years.) The committee then nominated A. N. Ward as Lewis's successor. The report and nomination were adopted unanimously (after one more attempt to encourage McDaniel to take the office, which he declined). After resigning WMC's vice presidency in 1917, Ward had become chancellor of Kansas City University in 1918. He had just succeeded in raising the entire amount necessary to clear that institution of a $100,000 debt. It is not clear whether he had actually been asked if he wanted the WMC president's job (although one can assume that some communication must have taken place), but it is interesting that the board notified him of his election one day and invited him to be present at the Commencement exercises the next day. The salary of the incoming president was $4,000 (the same amount Lewis had been receiving since 1918); Vice President McDaniel's salary was $3,000.[17]

Lewis officially retired June 30, 1920, but not before numerous statements of appreciation and recognition had been expressed. The selection committee noted a "deep sense of regret at the severing of the official relations which through all the long years have been so uniformly harmonious and happy and which have resulted in such marked progress to the institution we all love. May heaven's richest blessings go with him to the new field to which he has been called by the denomination of which he is an honored and commanding minister of the Gospel."[18] The board elected him president emeritus and approved a resolution "that the proceeds or income of the $25,000 surplus [reported earlier in the meeting] . . . be affixed to the position as a salary during the incumbent's lifetime." The faculty resolution adopted on June 11 expressed its

> *appreciation of, and admiration for the long and successful period of President Lewis' administration of the college, how that from a small plant of inadequate buildings, and a few acres he has developed comfortable and commodious living apartments, and professors homes; lecture halls and laboratories hard to duplicate among the small colleges; and a great public hall that a university might well envy; and broad acres for future developments; how under his wise and just administration, the student body has grown to its present gratifying number, and a splendid amount of endowment has been amassed.[19]*

Upon the completion of his 34-year presidency, Lewis was elected president of the General Conference of the Methodist Protestant Church, a post he had previously held from 1908 to 1912, and in which he remained until 1927, when he succeeded Dr. Frank T. Benson '84 [trustee 1906–29] as editor of the *Methodist Protestant*.

BUILDINGS AND GROUNDS

The preliminary campus plan prepared by the Olmsted Brothers (and apparently funded by Daniel Baker) was presented in June 1911 and included a number of suggestions: some new buildings, removal of the wings to the Main Building, and a new and grander entrance to the college to make a noticeable separation between the college and the town. Peter Gallagher, an Olmsted associate, even suggested razing the President's House and moving Baker Chapel to that site. He also suggested covering some of the buildings in ivy and planting dogwoods and magnolias to add color to the campus. The project would cost $1,000; but only $300 of the Baker money remained. The board voted to have the Executive Committee proceed with Olmsted's plan as they deemed wise,[20] but nothing seems to have been done with it. In part, this was because of the need for a more definitive master plan that included a much-needed laboratory and recitation building, and because of Lewis's perception that the Olmsted firm was uninterested in

moving forward. Indeed, Lewis abruptly broke ties between the college and the Olmsteds in October 1912, although he returned to them in 1913 for some further advice, some of which was eventually followed in the placement of Lewis Hall. While that was the last paid contribution of the Olmsteds to the campus plan, their many suggestions would be discussed and debated in future decades. At this juncture, however, there were more urgent uses for the money.[21]

Continuing the tradition begun in 1905, of each graduating class contributing a stained-glass window for Alumni Hall, the class of 1912 began a new series of windows by purchasing a stained-glass window for the rear of the stage. Again, the gift of a window would be made by each class, until 1920, and these windows would depict the nine Greek muses—Calliope, Clio, Erato, Euterpe,

Greek muse Clio

*Daisy chain formed for Class Day
during Commencement Week*

Melpomene, Polyhymnia, Terpsichore, Thalea, and Uranea—when all were in place. The dedication of the class of 1917 window during Class Day exercises was described in the *Monthly*:

> We all then adjourned to Alumni Hall and had not long to wait before the Class came in walking between two long chains of daisies carried by girls and boys of the lower classes. Murray Benson, president of the Class of 1917, presented a window dedicated to History [Clio], in behalf of the class, to the college. Dr. Lewis accepted the window. Yells and songs were given and the program ended.[22]

President Lewis suggested a new classroom (recitation) building in June 1912, to combine all rooms and laboratories in one place. In 1913, the board voted to go ahead with the project as soon as possible, and Lewis was named chair of the Building Committee. Since no funds for such a project were readily available, fund-raising was begun, including organizing a Ladies Auxiliary to make appeals to the townspeople. The M.P. Conference opened its church pulpits for a $10,000 campaign, with Vice President Ward doing the promotion. Lewis noted, "It will be a good way to get close to the friends of the college and also to try out [Ward's] own inventions [ideas]."[23] The design of the new building was by Montgomery Anderson of Baltimore, as Jackson Gott was terminally ill. (Gott and Anderson presumably had some professional connections, because they certainly had similar ideas about design.) The contract for the building was finally let in the spring of 1914. The original idea of moving Yingling Science Hall back behind the new building was discarded when it was determined that it would cost too much, so it was torn down and the new building built in its place.[24]

A member of the class of 1917, F. Murray Benson, remembered the razing of Yingling Science Hall:

After the roof of the building had been removed and the interior pretty well gutted, a great number of the male students went into the building at night and proceeded to batter down the walls. I'm afraid that it was hoped that this prank might embarrass the college but it had the opposite result—the wreckers were paid on a per diem basis and the college actually saved money.[25]

As construction of the new classroom building was under way, the matter of its name became a bit of an issue within the board. Apparently, as early as June 1914 Daniel Baker had made a motion to name the building after Lewis, but Lewis, who was also secretary of the board, had omitted the motion from the minutes. At a special meeting the following December, Baker reiterated his motion, and, of course, it carried. This time, it appeared in the minutes of the meeting. The Thomas Hamilton Lewis Recitation Hall, erected on the

Lewis Recitation Hall (1914) was named for the incumbent president.

213

site of the older Yingling Science Hall, was the largest single building to be constructed on the campus. Built of red brick faced in Indiana limestone, it was surmounted by an observatory dome. It was 123 feet long, 63 feet wide, and three stories high. Each floor had a wide center hallway, off of which were 17 recitation rooms, 23 by 25 feet, and 3 large laboratories. The first floor contained the physics laboratory, while the third floor housed the biology and chemistry laboratories. It was fitted out "in the most modern way with tablet arm chairs, composition black boards, and usual appliances."[26] The building was connected to Hering Hall by a covered brick walkway entering the second floor, to make for easy and dry access by the young ladies into the women's part of the building. The men would enter the building by the south-porticoed first-floor entrance and attend segregated classes in that end of the building. In the center of each hallway were double oak doors, separating the halves of the building. Until coeducational classes became more commonplace a decade later, the doors would be opened only to admit a student of the opposite sex to attend a class too small to be offered twice. A student commented on the new facility, "It stands in bright relief against the days when we gathered wisdom sitting in shadowy cellars, or in some unused cranny of the dormitory, which needed no other qualification than having two doors in opposite walls, that

Home of the first ROTC commandant (1919); later the Dean's Cottage

The new building of the Westminster Theological Seminary (1920),
later acquired by the college

the traffic regulations might be enforced. Perhaps some of us feel a sentimental regret to know that the old haunts [in the Main Building] have been abandoned, and the memories that lurked about them dispossessed of their habitat."[27] Lewis Hall was formally dedicated at the 45th Commencement, in June 1915, and the naming tablet was unveiled by Miss Mary Veasey, granddaughter of Dr. Lewis, who had unveiled his portrait at the 1911 Commencement.

Once Yingling Science Hall was demolished, Lewis recommended that the name be transferred to the new gymnasium to carry on the benefactor's name and to recognize the original gift of Anna Yingling, which was for the first gymnasium.[28]

In 1915, as enrollments began to fall off, Lewis was frustrated that there were no extra funds in the treasury for repairs and remodeling of facilities. Ward Hall needed considerable work, and the Main Building needed painting. He also felt that the entrance to the college needed to be upgraded, and he recommended that a low wall be built leading up to the Ward Arch. (This was prophetic in light of the low wall announcing the college name that would be built near the relocated arch in 2004, a gift of trustee Catherine Schumann Kiddoo '46.)

The only other building built during the decade was a small faculty cottage built in 1919 at a cost of about $4,000, for the use of the commandant of the new Reserve Officers Training Corps (ROTC) program. It was located south of Lewis Hall and somewhat behind the President's House. It would house the ROTC head until the 1930s.

The trustees were always alert to possible campus expansion. In 1911, a property adjacent to the college campus and facing Union Street was purchased for $2,000. In 1920, upon the death of W. H. Geiman, the 65-acre farm to the west of the college suddenly came on the market, and the board authorized Lewis to purchase it for $26,201. This expanded the campus to about 90 acres. It was formally deeded on March 31, 1920, using endowment funds. The purchase agreement allowed Charles Geiman to lease back part of the farm, while a portion would be used for new athletic fields. At the June meeting, the alumni visitors to the board stressed the urgent need for improving the fields, and the Buildings and Grounds Committee was empowered to act.[29]

While not, of course, part of the college, the seminary next door was also growing, and a new and larger facility was needed, so a $50,000 campaign was launched by President Elderdice immediately following the college's Jubilee campaign. Sufficient funds were collected or pledged that the old building (built in 1882 and added to several times over the succeeding years) was razed in the summer of 1919, using WMC student help, and the new building, in a rather ornate Tudor Gothic style (designed by Paul Reese of Westminster), was begun on the same spot in late September. Seminary classes were crowded into every available space in the college for that

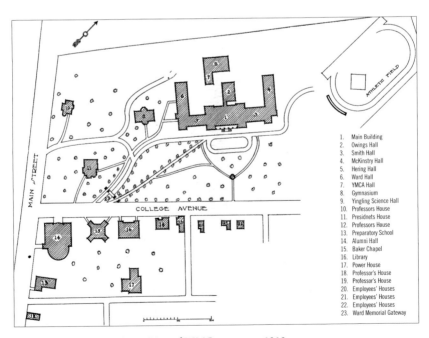

1. Main Building
2. Owings Hall
3. Smith Hall
4. McKinstry Hall
5. Hering Hall
6. Ward Hall
7. YMCA Hall
8. Gymnasium
9. Yingling Science Hall
10. Professors House
11. Presidnets House
12. Professors House
13. Preparatory School
14. Alumni Hall
15. Baker Chapel
16. Library
17. Power House
18. Professor's House
19. Professor's House
20. Employees' Houses
21. Employees' Houses
22. Employees' Houses
23. Ward Memorial Gateway

Map of WMC campus c. 1910

academic year with the hope that the new building would be ready by the following September. It was actually opened in October 1920 and formally dedicated December 17, 1920. Over the doorway was inscribed in gothic letters, "Blessed be thy coming in and blessed be thy going out." The tower room above the fourth floor was used for prayer and meditation. Daniel Baker soon thereafter gave $500 toward a new home for the seminary president, which was built in the same dark red brick (and landscaped) in 1923–24 at a cost of $25,000, and occupied by the Elderdice family in April 1924. A source of considerable controversy at the time was the stone cross on the tower of the seminary building, which seemed to some Methodist Protestants to be a Roman Catholic symbol and not appropriate for an M.P. seminary. President Elderdice defended its placement and allayed prejudices by pointing out that it was a Celtic cross—not a Latin or Roman cross—and eventually the issue died down. In *Pilgrimage of Faith*, Chandler wrote, "Elderdice could never have dreamed that a similar controversy would develop in protests against the college's removal of that same cross in the 1960s [actually 1974]."[30]

STUDENT LIFE

Things were slowly changing in the life of the students. During this decade an opportunity for self-governance arose, restrictions on student comings and goings were loosened, and, of course, World War I changed many lives forever. Students were also plagued with epidemics. The college closed three weeks early in December 1910 because of a scarlet fever epidemic; another outbreak in January produced no serious cases. In 1916–17, an epidemic of measles arose and threatened to close the college.

The faculty still held control of the discipline, although this would gradually begin to change. A Mr. Jones was given three demerits for whistling in the dining hall in 1911. Female day students were regularly given demerits for visiting boarding students in their rooms. Occasional hazing antics, which apparently were rather frequent as sophomores initiated freshmen into the college, were dealt with by two- to four-week suspensions. The advent of the automobile was creating a whole new set of problems: Two women each received 25 demerits for communicating from their windows with some young people who had come onto the campus in an automobile between 9 and 10 P.M. one evening (those wicked townies!). And two men were reported for driving around the circle in front of the Main Building and near the women's end of the complex. They claimed they were just out for a ride and were eventually excused. Two students of the opposite sex met in a residence downtown and were reported. Neither denied the offense, and the man was suspended for two weeks and denied parlor privileges for the rest of the term. The woman was given 50 demerits and deprived of permission for any absence from the college in the future. In June 1915 a male student was suspended indefinitely for "immorality"; the specific details, which were never stated in writing, were presented to the faculty with the comment that it "seemed to be so well founded as to leave little, if any, ground for doubt." There was no hearing, and the student was given no opportunity to defend himself.[31]

In 1917 two senior men were reported for going to town every free period during the day and later boasting that they had been playing pool. Their attendance at meals had also been irregular (absence from meals was considered a serious violation of college rules). Vice President Ward, then in charge of male students' discipline (the students thought of him as the dean of men), was directed to warn them about their conduct and threaten them with being confined to campus if it did not cease. One of the young men was the son of a prominent M.P. minister (and trustee of the college) and president of his class who would later become a distinguished Baltimore lawyer, a trustee of the college himself, and chair of the board for 14 years, Murray Benson.[32] In May 1917 the faculty dealt with two junior men who left the dining room one morning disapproving of the breakfast they had been served. They had

Annual Halloween party in Yingling Gymnasium II, c. 1914

been refused permission to leave by a faculty person on duty but angrily left anyway. The faculty directed them to apologize to the faculty member, but one man refused. At the faculty's next meeting, the incident was again reported, and the recalcitrant young man was ordered to see the president to explain his actions. Apparently, President Lewis helped him to see the light, and he duly apologized. The young man was Fred Garrigus Holloway '18, who would become the fourth president of the college.

One final incident suggests the conservative mindset of the faculty of the era. In December 1917, five senior women were each given 50 demerits for attending a murder trial at the Carroll County courthouse without permission. It was considered a very serious offense, and they were required to acknowledge publicly the "wrongness of their act." Apparently, the issue was not that they had failed to obtain permission (by this time women could at times leave the campus in groups without a chaperone) but rather that they were women attending a murder trial.

There were lots of infractions of the rules, especially Rule 11 and others governing men and women being together. The faculty and administration must have been "eagle eyed" and omnipresent to observe the many "misbehaviors." One can only wonder how many students they did not catch, given the average eight to ten infractions they dealt with each week.

One amusing, perhaps apocryphal, story of life of this era tells of a somewhat desperate senior man who informed President Lewis that the Lord had revealed to him in a dream that he would marry a classmate. Therefore, would the president please permit him to meet and talk with this young lady immediately? The matter was urgent. "Very well," Dr. Lewis replied, "you will have my permission, just as soon as the Lord sends me the same dream."

Parlor Night continued unabated, but as we shall see, some major improvements were in the offing. In the early years of the decade, the traditional procedures continued to be followed. Philip Myers '16 described the weekly event during his first year on campus in 1912:

> Promptly at seven we presented ourselves with dignity and decorum at our entrance to Parlor. . . . This room was furnished [with] two chairs here, two chairs there, . . . not quite touching but all within easy hearing distance of each other. . . . We new stags advanced, under the prompting of the old-timers, toward the middle of the room where the professor who "had to take parlor [an assigned faculty duty]" was standing. . . . Gravely we shook hands with him . . . and the ladies of the resident faculty, and were turned over to one of the girls who served on the reception committee. These girls, I found, were ones who could boast of no "strike" of their own, had no false pride, and were therefore

219

free to foment such affairs for others. If you had ambition to speak to a certain girl whom you saw in the hopeful and waiting crowd at the foot of the stairs at the girls' entrance, you breathed her name to your guide. Then she led you forward and passed the word to the one so signally honored. Thus joined, you led her toward a pair of chairs. . . . Just as you were getting slightly more at ease with the girl whose acquaintance you were trying to cultivate, one of the reception committee, dragging a gawking boy, would step up to your pair of chairs. As you found your feet, she would murmur, "Miss Jones, Mr. Smith," and fade with you in tow. There was nothing you could do about it. When she asked for your next choice you did have the privilege of walking with her once around the entire room and then returning to the original Miss Jones to finish the predicate of your interrupted sentence, but this would definitely be taken as having a strike on her. . . . A sure way to receive a box of fudge was to ask for the same girl three weeks in succession. . . . However, you could not work it too often in the same year. It branded you as fickle and commercial. . . . After 8 o'clock the girls' social life went into seclusion for a seven day period, but the boys were free to go to town until 9:45 and sin as thoroughly as the limited time would permit. If they accepted the inevitable three demerits for missing last inspection a more thorough job could be done.[33]

Inspections of each student's room were made Monday through Friday evenings between 7:00 and 9:45. Traditionally, the professor "on call" would make the first inspection soon after the 7 P.M. bell, the last at the 9:45 bell, and another somewhere in between, remaining in the building on the top floor to be available to students who needed academic help. The students soon became accustomed to the habits of the various faculty inspectors. At one point, Prof. Leon Richmond was calling on Miss Clara Lewis and so was known for making his first and second inspections one immediately after the other, then rushing off to see Clara, returning precisely at 9:45 to finish his inspecting before returning to her again. The boys, noting this pattern, were able to rush downtown to see a movie after the first two inspections and still return before the final bell.[34]

Murray Benson '17, recalled campus life this way:

During our stay at the college the old practice of separation of the sexes was rigidly enforced. . . . After meals the boys would gather on their side of the campus and smile across the dividing roadway at the ladies of their choice, known then as "strikes." This practice was not without its elements of danger as some less romantic souls were apt to go to the windows of Hering Hall and toss paper bags filled with water on the lovelorn suitors. Love, however, found a way and many notes, then known as "K.O.B.'s" found their way to the ladies' dormitories, sometimes by way of the waiters in the dining room. . . . Sometimes baskets of food, candy or ice cream were pulled up to the dormitory windows by means of ropes dropped for the purpose. I have never ceased to be amazed at the number of marriages that resulted from these difficult courtships.[35]

The honor system was now a permanent institution at the college, although only for men until 1913, when the women requested a similar system, which was approved. Schofield reported that the Honor League was administered by a committee of three seniors, two juniors, and one sophomore, all elected by their peers; and that it seemed to work well,[36] at least until an instance of flagrant cheating in 1916. The students required that the guilty senior retake his examinations, be deprived of wearing the cap and gown until Commencement, and be graduated without class standing; and that the decision be publicly announced. The faculty felt that the penalty was not severe enough and suggested that in the future such offenses should merit expulsion.[37]

The students felt they were ready for additional self-governance. Upperclassmen had been preserving order in the halls on Friday and Saturday evenings, and they had been permitted to go into town those same evenings without permission, so long as they were back by the 9:45 P.M. inspection. These relaxed rules had worked well, and more self-discipline opportunities were now sought by the students:

When the Honor System was first suggested it was a step in the dark but, now that we have made that step and find ourselves in a higher and better position than before, it is becoming time for us to make another step. That step is Student Government. Student Government does not mean student license. It means that the students have a chance to develop their sense of honor and to govern themselves in a democratic manner . . . which would raise the standard of the college, and be beneficial to both students and faculty.[38]

Apparently with the encouragement of Vice President Ward, a Student Government Association was proposed by the men early in 1917; in May of that year, after Ward had resigned, Prof. Richmond called together the male student body to discuss a plan:

Before the meeting closed, a committee consisting of representatives from each class had been elected by the respective classes, with Professor Richmond from the faculty, to form a constitution to be submitted to the faculty. . . . After burning much mid-night oil, the committee finally submitted their plan to the faculty on May 18, for approval. After passing this body without a single change, it was presented to the male college students on May 23, when it was voted upon and accepted. The same evening the election for President and representatives to the Board of Governors was held, and the following morning . . . at eight o'clock, the new system went into effect.[39]

While the students were jubilant at the prospect of self-governance, President Lewis was not enthusiastic:

There are grave dangers in the execution of such a scheme. Gettysburg College tried it I have been informed and abandoned it. Other schools have tried it and found it successful. There are undoubtedly some matters of discipline such as inspection and disorder in the halls which could be much better managed by the students themselves. The difficulty is that they do not desire this particularly, nor will they be content with this. And when students undertake to govern an institution it is difficult to restrain their administration within proper bounds.[40]

He nevertheless recommended its acceptance by the board, and a trial run was approved. At the end of four weeks it was reported to be a great success. The first president of the Boys' Student League was Joshua W. Miles '18 (later a trustee and board chair). The students felt that such a program created a greater sense of responsibility in the student body and more enjoyable social hours between the sexes. Because the upperclass students were necessarily in charge of the behavior of the younger students, the program also inaugurated the "wonderfully becoming freshman cap of a prescribed color and style."[41] The caps seem to have been created as a symbol of class spirit; the sophomores also began to wear a "strikingly individual hat."[42] Thus was born on the campus self-governance *and* the freshman beanie.

By the fall of 1917, a Student Government League for women had also been established, using the same general constitution as the men's league. The result was that the students, through their leagues' board of governors, policed themselves and awarded demerits for misbehavior, subject to faculty approval of their report each week. The faculty approved some minor alterations to the Parlor Night procedures but specified that a plan needed to be devised so couples would be prevented from sitting together for the entire hour. Soon such details were turned over to the students. By the spring of 1918, the two leagues had been given general oversight of all the "meetings of the two sexes, and to see that the spirit and meaning of the regulations are observed. They shall also have authority to make suggestions from time to time as to special features for making these meetings more interesting for all."[43] Student reaction to the changes was swift and positive:

Since that day many interesting things have happened and to notice the affairs that now take place on College Hill reminds one of living in a new world—or at least a different college. The girls' path is no longer forbidden ground; the time honored "K.O.B." has lost its charm and even its use, for now with parlor every day in the week the "strikes" find ample time for private business interviews; the faculty inspector is no longer seen on the boys halls making his three rounds each night, for now the student reports his own absences.[44]

Perhaps due to the burgeoning spirit of self-governance, student attention turned to national politics, and Republican and Democratic Clubs were formed in October 1916, reacting to the coming national election. Rousing meetings were held to discuss the qualifications of the candidates, Woodrow Wilson and Charles Evans Hughes, and a debate between the two clubs was held on November 7. This was followed by a campus vote, in which Wilson received 93 "electoral" votes and Hughes 53.[45]

The arts were certainly not ignored on the campus. A College Orchestra was formed in fall 1913 and consisted of 8 members, including students, faculty (Dr. Bonnotte on flute), and 2 seminary students. It was directed by Lester Langdon '16. They practiced twice a week in Smith Hall and made their debut at the Philomathean/Webster Anniversary performance on February 19, 1914. The catalog for 1910–11 proudly states that "the Department of Music is provided with fourteen pianos for practice, all recently purchased new, a Chickering Concert Grand used in recitals, a Chickering Parlor Grand, and a

College Choir in Baker Chapel

two-manual pipe organ made by Brown." The 1916 *Aloha* pictures and names the members of the 26-voice College Choir, the 28-voice male Glee Club, and the orchestra, which by this time had 11 members. Names of musical participants familiar to alumni of a later era include Philip Myers, Sara Smith '18, Henry L. Darner '16 [trustee 1957–73], and Murray Benson. Myers noted that singing in the choir provided a wonderful opportunity for passing KOBs, hidden in sheet music, without Miss Mathilde Rimbach [1908–12], the director, catching on. He referred to this as "enlisting in the college postal service." Still another musical opportunity was begun by Dr. McDaniel in this decade; he entertained students on occasional Sunday evenings with Victrola concerts. Some focused on sacred music, while others were more general: male voices, female voices (including an aria by Mabel Garrison), orchestra, opera, violin. There was even a small printed program for each event.[46]

Following the "unfortunate incident" with the 1910 yearbook, the next class permitted to publish an *Aloha* was that of 1916—"after a sleep of six years," it was noted in the foreword. The faculty response to the class's request to publish was that the cost could not exceed $600 and the book would sell for $2.25, with the college contributing $25 if necessary. This appears to be the first college subsidy for an annual, however small. The class did quite well, and the book took on a format (with improved photographs taken by the art editor, Philip Myers) that later yearbooks would follow. It was dedicated to Vice President Ward. Because of the 1910 acrostic incident, the faculty, which had to pass on each bit of written copy, was wary of any poetry. Myers had written what he termed a "tender offering of appreciation of Mother Royer" (proprietor of a popular eating establishment just off campus) entitled "How We Beat Yale and Harvard":

> We don't compete with Harvard,
> We number not with Yale;
> When we glance at their equipment
> Our own seems like a jail. . . .
>
> This "Alma Mater" seems to be
> Their main-spring of religion.
> Because they've ONE, they swell themselves
> Just like a pouter pigeon!
>
> I wish to state a simple fact,
> (I'm talking like a lawyer)
> We've beat them here, for we have TWO–
> W. M. and MOTHER ROYER![47]

Participants in the first intersociety debate (L to R): C. E. Moylan '17, S. A. Owen '19, F. G. Holloway '18, E. M. Pusey '19, J. W. Miles Jr. '18, T. L. Hooper '17

The faculty analyzed it carefully and could find no hidden meanings in it. After all the male faculty members had again scrutinized it for objectionable material, Dr. McDaniel called in Myers and told him, "We can't find anything wrong, or hidden in your verses. Will you give us your word of honor that you have not concealed something that we have not been able to discover?" Myers noted, "It was a moment of real triumph [over the faculty] as with light heart I granted them this boon."[48]

The 1916 *Aloha* was the only annual to be published in this decade, however; another would not appear until 1922. To provide a less formal way of recognizing and recording those classes that did not publish yearbooks, the *Monthly* usually devoted its June issue to class member biographies, prophecies, poems, and informal memories, with a few pictures of the class and the college buildings.

The literary societies continued their normal activities, providing a reasonably high level of entertainment and academic discourse for the campus under the watchful eye of the faculty. They also published the *Western Maryland College Monthly*. In December 1915 the men's societies asked permission to organize a debating league. They submitted a constitution to the faculty, which approved it, and were soon sponsoring debates on campus. The first public intersociety debate was held in March 1916, and the topic was "Resolved: That the President of the United States should be elected for a term of six years and should not be eligible for reelection." Prof. Widdowson and Dr. Warfield acted as coaches for the Irving and Webster debaters. On

March 16, 1917, the topic was "Resolved: That the United States should adopt a system of compulsory military training." Fred Holloway, Charles "Chris" Moylan '17, and Joshua Miles were debaters in these events. A note about the Intercollegiate Oratorical Contests is in order here because Lester Alvin Twigg '16 won the competition in 1915 and was selected to represent the college again in 1916. However, at the request of two of the contesting colleges, he was not permitted to compete because of his remarkable oratorical skills, and he was replaced by J. Leas Green '16, who nevertheless won first place. Western Maryland orators captured 13 first places and 7 second places in 22 competitions (through 1920).[49] Twigg went on to be appointed professor of oratory at the University of Mississippi.

Sports continued to occupy male students, football in the fall and baseball in the spring. Basketball was played between classes during the winter, but there were movements afoot to make it intercollegiate, and by the end of the decade, there was renewed interest in making it a major sport on campus. Tennis and track and field drew small numbers, although their players participated in some intercollegiate contests. (The captain of the tennis team in 1916–17 was Hugh Elderdice Jr. '17, who would later be a WMC chemistry professor [1929–61].) Women were able to participate in intramural basketball, as is evidenced by the sophomore, freshman, and prep teams in 1916, all coached by Marjorie Lewis '06 [1911–24], director of the women's gymnasium (and daughter of President Lewis). The faculty continued to approve all scheduled games and each game's roster, as well as giving permission for the team to leave the campus (with explicit hours for return). The football teams played about ten games each fall and completed most seasons with an even record of wins and losses. During the war years, the teams were limited a bit in numbers but still performed.

The *Monthly* of the era, written as it was by students, always tried to put on a brave face and provide some inspiration even in the face of defeat. In the fall of 1910, the team traveled 300 miles to play Virginia Polytechnic Institute and lost the game 0–13. The *Monthly* reported, "It was a game of which we may well be proud, and to be defeated by this team, truly was no disgrace."[50] In other issues, losses are explained away because of injuries, lack of practice, too little time for practice, or no place to practice. The forward pass was becoming a staple of the game, for it is mentioned as being used to advantage in several games. Carl C. "Molly" Twigg '11 was famous for his ability to throw the forward pass; indeed, some say he "invented" it. Myers wrote, "His enthusiasm for football was sincere and his ability in playing was far above average. . . . With his huge hand wrapped around the ball he could hurl it with remarkable accuracy toward the speeding end who hopefully raced down the field. His explanation . . . was that in his lazy youth on the mountain farm where he was raised [in Twiggtown, Allegany County, Maryland], it was easier to throw a stone at a wandering cow than it was to climb up and down grades in pursuit of her."[51] Twigg stayed on at the college after graduation to coach the football team and direct the men's gymnasium for two years. The 1911 football season was marred by the untimely death of a visiting football player from Davis and Elkins College, William L. Merryman, who received a fatal injury to his head during a game on October 17. The young man was transported to Baltimore immediately but died that night. There was some question of whether the remainder of the season should be cancelled, but only one game, the next week, with Baltimore Polytechnic Institute, was omitted. The 1916 season saw seven wins and three losses, the team playing a difficult schedule and scoring only five points less than the leading team in the state. Some scores were very lopsided: WMC 61, Eastern 0; WMC 40, Mt. St. Mary's 3. Unfortunately, the team lost to Fordham 20–0, as well as to Hopkins, 21–0. During the 1917 season, the team played six games and won five, with such scores as 50–0 and 40–0. The game against St. John's, played at home on October 27, was graphically described in the *Monthly*:

> *Band was playing, colors flying, voices raising, St. John's goose frying, as we eagerly cheered the boys on. What a battle that was! Who could forget it? It was hard fought, but the bleeding faces and bruised limbs of the wearers of the gold and green, the cracked voices and parched lips of the supporters of the gold and green, all linked by the common chain of determination brought a victory not soon forgotten. The snake dance which ensued lasted fully an hour, and our hearts were overflowing. The conquereds' tears were suppressed more easily than the tears of joy of the victors. We were happy.*[52]

Baseball of the decade had about the same level of success, if not slightly worse. Of special interest are the several games played against the Baltimore Orioles of the Eastern League. The 1911 game was lost to this professional team by a score of 1–3, and it was claimed that "the game was practically a victory for the school." The game featured superb pitching by the versatile athlete Captain Molly Twigg, who held the Orioles to six hits. The 1916 baseball schedule included ten intercollegiate games with such schools as Lebanon Valley, Maryland Agricultural College, Washington, Mt. St. Mary's, St. John's, and Delaware. The team was scheduled (and approved) to travel on a five-day tour into Virginia in April to play Virginia Military Institute, Hampden-Sidney College, Washington and Lee, and Virginia Polytechnic Institute, but the trip did not materialize, probably because it would have been too expensive. The *Monthly* reported that the team won three games and lost seven. But, optimistic to the end, it claimed, "Our team showed a wonderful

Grandstand of the fenced athletic field, north of Old Main

improvement over the last few years. So marked has been the improvement that the teams can hardly be compared."[53]

For years the football field was "affectionately" known as the "stone pile," and for years, freshman male students (non-football players) were commandeered by the sophomores to pick up stones on the field (which was laid out approximately where Albert Norman Ward Hall stands today, on the crest of the Hill). Picking gangs were formed into lines stretching across the field, and they would walk it, stooping to pick up the thousands of loose stones that covered it. Myers remembered this back-breaking activity:

This rare treat was repeated day after day without noticeably smoothing the texture of the field. It was really most discouraging, especially the afternoon after a rain, when, it seemed, boulders that had been covered with the thin topsoil, leered at us and defied us to dislodge them. If we puffed and strained and were successful, then we had to bring dirt from some remote spot and fill in the hole. It was all "for the team" and our loyalty was at least as strong as our backs. . . . During my college life, the top of that hill must have been lowered some twelve to eighteen inches, well into bedrock.[54]

At the students' request, the athletic fee was raised in 1914 from $5 to $10 since more money was needed to run the various growing athletic programs.

In recognition of the 50th anniversary of the college, a student's Volunteer Publicity Association was formed to contact possible future students for the college. By May 1916 this had become part of a Student Enrollment Campaign, to enroll the largest number of students in the history of the college as part of the celebration (and to attack the trend of dwindling enrollments during the years 1915–18). A committee of faculty was appointed, and the students were organized by counties, with faculty supervision; they were charged to go home on holidays and seek out potential students, boasting about the college and its special advantages. A copy of the *Monthly*, the *Aloha*, and a brochure listing the faculty and their training and expertise would be sent to each high school in the state; high school seniors would be invited to the campus for a special day; the faculty would canvass the counties as well, after commencement. Most of the "special day," May 13, was abandoned because a proposed baseball game did not materialize, but several events did go off, and some visitors did attend. Dr. Ward canvassed the state instead of the faculty (because Dr. McDaniel and Dr. Warfield were both ill for extended periods), and the students did come back with hundreds of names of prospective students. Prof. Richmond summarized the various activities of the spring for the *Monthly*, ending with, "Let the fiftieth anniversary of the college mark the beginning of a period of new growth for the college. Everyone, trustees, faculty, Alumni, and Student Body get together and Boost."[55] The work apparently paid off, because enrollment grew from 214 in 1917–18 to 274 in 1918–19.

In 1914, with the onset of the war in Europe, new concerns affected life in the "outside world." However, as Myers remembered,

It took quite some time for the disturbance . . . to cause more than a ripple of interest in life on The Hill. We were too self-centered, and of course, far too remote to have more than superficial knowledge of what was going on. What caused that going on we thought was none of our business, if we thought of it at all. Gradually our thoughts became colored, or lightly tinged, by the world-shaking events, and in the end we became violently partisan.[56]

During the two years that the United States was directly involved in the world war in Europe, the normal functioning of the college was disrupted in several ways. Enrollments dropped, in part from lack of new students and in part from students leaving to enter the armed forces as draftees or enlistees. Some faculty members were affected in the same way, and presenting courses was at times problematic. Murray Benson recalled this unsettling time:

The dreams, plans and ambitions of the Class of 1917 were brought to a complete halt. The only certainty was the war. What was to be its outcome and who would survive were open questions only to be answered by future events. Such was the atmosphere at Commencement in 1917. Practically every man was in the service within a matter of weeks. . . . One week after delivering what was then called an "oration" on Alumni Hall stage . . . [I was] peeling potatoes and onions in the mess shack of Company H of the First Maryland Infantry.[57]

Organizations on campus, as well as individuals, became involved in various aspects of the war effort (rolling surgical dressings for the Red Cross, conserving food and fuel, working with the YMCA fund-raising effort to help refugees and orphans in Europe, etc.), and, of course, a number of alumni were also involved in one way or another. In June 1919, a complete list of alumni involved in the war was published; it included 169 names (6 were ministers like T. H. Lewis and H. L. Elderdice, who assisted with the YMCA work). Four men made the supreme sacrifice: John A. Alexander '17, C. C. Billingslea '96, Alwin Roberts x'10, and J. W. Welch '12. The veterans were honored at the "Victory Commencement" of 1919. Lewis also suggested to the board that a suitable memorial to the students and alumni of the college be created on campus,[58] although none now exists.

At the annual meeting of the board on June 15, 1920, Murray Benson appeared before the body to offer $250 from his class to establish a medal in memory of classmate John A. Alexander, who had died in 1918 in the service of his country. Alexander, from Taneytown, had stayed on at the college to fill in for the enlisted professor of physics, Richmond, and then entered the aeronautical school at Cornell in April preparatory to entering the U.S. Aviation Corps. He was killed six months later. The class wished it to be a medal for excellence in athletics, in memory of this fine athlete. At the same meeting three representatives of the Browning Literary Society, Mrs. Frank Mitten, Carrie Rinehart Wantz '96, and Mollie Shriver '96, presented $250 to found a medal to be known as the Mary Ward Lewis Prize, to be given to the best all-around senior college girl (a parallel to the Bates Prize for the boys). Mrs. Lewis was being honored as she had suggested the name "Browning" for the society when it was founded in 1871. Both prizes were accepted and approved with thanks.[59]

In his report to the board in June 1919, Lewis commented on the food being served the students. He stated that no complaints had been forthcoming, but rumors persisted that the students didn't think they were getting their money's worth. He noted that, instead of a dining hall superintendent and steward, he and his daughter Clara (also the librarian) had been doing those jobs, giving constant attention to the dining room at no additional cost to the college. The costs for cooking and baking by three people amounted to $66 a month, and other "purchases are made with the most careful attention to details, and we never waste anything." At least by this time the college was not losing money on its boarders anymore (as it had in 1917), even if the students still didn't feel they were being adequately fed. A reference is made in the *Monthly* to Mother Royer's, a store and restaurant just off campus on the corner of Main and Union streets that had been established during the previous decade. Apparently, male students had begun to find their way there with some frequency for additional sources of nourishment such as caramel sandwiches (six-by-two-inch slices of raisin-studded coffee cake enclosing chocolate fudge), grilled cheese sandwiches, chocolate and banana pies, cereal, and milk.[60] Myers noted of Mrs. Royer, "Four years of scolding by Mother Royer had hardened us to her words, for by that time we knew the soft maternal heart she was covering up. If she did not scold you, she did not like you enough to let you put it on the cuff, and if you could not get credit between allowances, how could you live?" He went on to tell a story of his frequent visits downtown to see an alumna, Miss Azalea Shipley '14, and his later night raids on Mother Royer's pantry. She would ask him when he was going to get married, noting, "I've been feeding you to keep you alive for her. She's a nice girl." Mr. Myers and Miss Shipley were married by Dr. Lewis in Baker Chapel on September 29, 1917, and Mother Royer was one of the guests.[61]

Myers also commented on the meals served on campus:

The meals themselves sustained life, but they were uninspired. . . . Luby [gravy] had the remarkable characteristic of always having the same taste [and color] no matter what meat—or even fish—was being served. Its saving grace was its availability. It was always there. It was always hot, and once you learned to douse the really excellent freshly baked bread with it, you could be assured of a pleasant pressure against your belt, regardless of the other components of the meal. Coffee and tea were served three times a day. A pint of milk for a table of ten was all that could be expected. . . . Sunday evening supper almost invariably consisted of cold biscuits and twenty sardines served on a platter that would readily have held a twenty pound turkey. The theory was two per person, but it never worked out that way. Two boys usually got ten each. . . .[62]

The winter weather plagued students, particularly in 1918, when a "good old fashioned winter with all the snow and ice of a genuine winter" arrived. But they also seemed to enjoy it sometimes, for "coasting parties" are described in the *Monthly*. Of course, accidents could happen. A sled ran into a telephone pole and almost everyone on the sled was hurt, but not seriously. The cold weather also played havoc with the college heating bills. To conserve coal for the war effort, the heating of all unnecessary rooms was discontinued. Sunday chapel was held in Smith Hall rather than Baker Chapel, and the heating elsewhere was used "very judicially." Lights were turned off at ten P.M.[63]

Life on campus, especially in Ward Hall for the men, was still not the most pleasant experience. Myers described room 107 of Ward Hall upon his arrival as a freshman in September 1912:

> The room was about fourteen feet in all directions, including up, was illuminated by a single bulb hanging unshaded from a cord in the exact middle of the ceiling, and was furnished with two folding beds, a double built-in wardrobe, a table, two kitchen chairs, two chiffoners [sic] and a small bookcase hanging from the wall between the windows. The trim was painted a pallid gray. The white plastered walls were unadorned. [It] was a place unspoiled by beauty in any form.[64]

Another student commented in the *Monthly*: "Why live at home when you can be just as uncomfortable in Ward Hall? We have two wash rooms with occasional hot water, fuses are frequently blown out, and it has been actually known to happen that the rooms were swept."[65] The *Monthly* also reported on the great excitement when fire broke out in a Ward Hall room about 11 one night. The fire was soon extinguished, but everything in the room was destroyed. A strong wind was blowing that evening, so the fire could have easily spread to the rest of the dormitory, as well as to the other connecting buildings.[66]

Lindsay Sapp '24 wrote a short essay in which he describes the dormitory life and the hazing of a freshman male:

> Life in a dormitory is, as a rule, a very pleasant life, though it is full of surprises, some of them not so pleasant. . . . The hours actually spent in his room are small, mostly while sleeping. Here is where the freshman receives one of the unpleasant surprises. About twelve P.M., some considerate sophomores kindly throw a bucket or two of water over him and his bed. They do this in order to prevent the new student from becoming sleepy-headed and also to save him the long walk over to take a shower-bath. Any person who makes the mistake of thinking that the study-hour from 7:15 to 9:15 is the time to study, is somewhat rudely taught otherwise. This is the time for fun, for those who do not have to study. The whole gang files in the room of the one who thinks he has to study, and the fun commences. One of the most important phases of this is the sweat-bath. In the bath, the patient or victim is gently placed in bed and there is placed over him and tucked around him, every sheet, blanket and quilt in the hall. All the boys who can, then climb on top, where they find a wonderfully soft seat. After an hour or so, what is left of the victim is pulled out and deposited on the fire-escape in order to cool off. He is usually rather hot-headed, after being pulled out.[67]

A final note on life on campus during this decade relates to the plumbing facilities for men. In it Myers replicates and expands upon Milton Wright's memories of "No. 10" a decade earlier:

> The transition from the original fresh air to indoor plumbing facilities which had taken place many years before my arrival on the Hill had not been too successful. Showers and toilets for boys were all in the basement of the gymnasium. To enjoy the use of either it was necessary to leave the dormitory and cross an open quadrangle swept by winds that had nothing to break their keenness for the twenty-five miles that lay between us and the Blue Ridge Mountains. [It was] a bitter experience in winter time; it was never to be undertaken alone if possible. As a desire for cleanliness or a cosmic urge came upon a boy, he would roam up and down the halls calling, "Who wants to go to number ten?" Usually in a matter of only a few minutes he had sufficient company for the perilous journey. If it was a bathing party, all took with them their socks which were thrown on the floor of the shower and trod upon in wine-making fashion while soaping of bodies was in progress. Toilet stalls and showers faced each other in a chummy manner, so that the steam-filled room was often the scene of some of the very best bull sessions. The arrangement, while not the most convenient, worked reasonably well when good health was ours, although I have often wondered how we escaped pneumonia coming from the hot shower through the zero weather back to our rooms.[68]

In June 1912, Rev. Harry D. Mitchell, perhaps uniquely, was awarded both the AB degree (which he had been unable to finish with his 1898 class) and the honorary doctor of divinity. An honorary master of arts degree had been conferred on Fannie Grove Stover '89, preceptress at Kee Mar College in Hagerstown, in 1910 and another was conferred on Caleb O'Connor, composer of many of the college songs, in 1920.

The *Alumni Bulletin*, created by the Alumni Association, was approved in 1914. Its first edition was published in March 1914 and was designed to provide more information about alumni for alumni than the short and often incomplete column in the *Monthly*. One alumna of note, Sadie Kneller Miller '85, was reported in 1914 as sailing for England to cover the coronation of George V, after which she was headed for Russia to study the prison system. The *Monthly* noted, "Mrs. Miller holds a unique place in journalistic circles. She was the first woman base-ball reporter, the only photographer who has been admitted into Indian Head and to the torpedo station at Newport, the only woman to photograph a National Convention, to receive permission to make photographs in the Dead letter office, the Philadelphia Mint and the routine life of the cadets both at Annapolis and West Point."[69] She died November 21, 1920, of a thrombosis at the age of 53.

CURRICULUM

During this decade some gradual changes took place in the curriculum of the college. A two-tiered preparatory school program (lower sub-freshman and upper sub-freshman) had, by 1920, expanded to three levels, including a middle sub-freshman class, all designed to prepare students to enter the freshman class of the college. The boy boarders roomed in Levine Hall, while the girls roomed in the Main Building. All boarders took their meals in the college dining room. The 1920 class roster for the preparatory school lists students from Puerto Rico, Singapore, Pennsylvania, Delaware, Mississippi, New York, Virginia, New Jersey, South Carolina, Alabama, and, of course, towns all over Maryland.

The supplementary programs in piano, harmony, musical history, voice, expression, and education enrolled about 150 students yearly, although many were enrolled in the regular college program, as well. Some of these programs had been around for a while and, as they expanded, formed the basis for developing departments with excellent reputations, especially after 1920.[70]

It has been noted that elocution and oratory played a big part of the curricular and extracurricular life of the campus. After 1904, much of this activity was directed by Nannie Lease, who had studied at the Emerson College of Oratory in Boston after her Western Maryland education. For the next 33 years she would guide students through the trials and tribulations of Friday afternoon Smith Hall "appearances," in which each student performed a "piece" each term. She also prepared special students for the more daunting Friday evening recitals of "readings." Myers remembered Miss Lease and her methods: She would work with students individually, line by line, encouraging them to get the right inflection in each word or phrase, admonishing them to "warm it up" or "make it human." "As she mouthed 'warm it up,' she stood with her left foot advanced, toe held high above the floor, her weight supported entirely by her right leg. That was her stance while anyone recited. When she wanted to emphasize a word her long foot would come down flat on the floor with a SMACK that at first scared me into paying attention, and later offered much opportunity for mimicry in extra-curricular activities." One of his "pieces" was an excerpt from O Henry that he memorized and recited in less than half the time allotted, one breath per paragraph. "She could not make me repeat for I had spoken every word of the text, and she knew it. She had held the book while I raced and had become almost cross-eyed trying to keep up with me."[71]

By 1913 the faculty had approved the requirement of a graduation thesis for all seniors. Subjects would be chosen by the students with faculty approval. Theses would be 2,500–4,000 words with full bibliographical references.

A six-member faculty committee would judge them, and a copy of each would be filed in the college library. The best theses would be chosen for public delivery at Commencement. (The theses are still lodged in the college archives.) Some titles from Commencement programs suggest the nature of these writings: "The Economic Importance of the Earthworm"; "Qualitative Analysis in the Dye Industry"; "The Modern Short Story, a Distinct Form of Literary Art"; "The Policy of the United States in regard to Freedom of the Seas"; "The Seventeen Year Locust"; "The Oyster Industry of the Chesapeake Bay"; and "Substitutes for Leather."

The *Monthly* included a description of the college science program in 1914, suggesting that a more modern approach was being taken. The Chemistry Department was teaching independence, whereby each student had to work out his own experiment without help from professors or other students. He was given an unknown solution and salts and had to find out all that was therein contained and report it in tabulated form. There was always something new to be discovered in each day's work; it was not "all cut and dried beforehand." In biology, zoology was holding students' interest, and various phyla were studied; botany provided study of bacteria and yeasts, as well as the lives of Pasteur and Lister.[72]

Related to this was the description of the science laboratories in the catalog of 1914–15:

Physics laboratory, first floor of Lewis Recitation Hall (1914)

The Chemical Laboratory [in the new Lewis Hall] is fitted up with the usual modern arrangements for individual work—separate tables and drawers supplied with gas and water, and a good collection of working apparatus. Similar provision is made for the Department of Physics.... The biological laboratory is equipped with all the regular apparatus necessary for doing thorough work in morphology, embryology and histology. It includes compound and simple microscopes, a microtome, paraffin bath and the usual accessories of glassware, reagents, etc. There is a working collection of several hundred zoological specimens, representing the important classes of vertebrates and invertebrates.[73]

A later *Monthly* featured the historical course in several essays by professors and students. One gave insight into the curriculum of this program, which usually attracted about two-thirds of the students in each class:

The great advantage of this course is that we learn to think of each event, not as a mere fact as we did before, but that everything in History has a cause and result and plays its part in a continuous story which is truly as interesting as any dime novel. The men who before seemed to us as merely great and rather uninteresting, now take on new light. . . . Only members of the Historical course have experienced the thrill of delving into the secrets of the Congressional Globe and American Historical Reports, thus getting knowledge first hand instead of taking some one else's word for it. Economics and Politics must not be slighted. From the first we learn the Value of Money, which all people should know at this time and from the latter, how Congressmen are elected and their work after they are elected and find, they are not, as we thought sublime figureheads but mere men. Perhaps the greatest advantage of this course is to show us how much we don't know.[74]

It is clear that the rote recitation form of teaching of an earlier generation was gradually being supplanted by individual study and library research.

In 1917, after the entry of the United States into World War I, the college was selected by the government as a site for a unit of the Student Army Training Corps, established on campus during the fall of 1918. Schofield, who was a student at the time, remembered that an "aura of military discipline prevailed on campus. Students returning to college that fall found that they would be 'in the army now.' . . . Even the boys who could not be in the SATC because they were under age or 4-F had to buy uniforms and drill with the rest."[75] After the armistice in November, the program was quickly phased out by the end of the fall term. While it was functioning, the physical training and discipline of the men was put under the direction of the military staff. Lewis reported to the board that he had mixed feelings about the SATC because it "divided control and made study almost impossible," but there were also aspects of the military discipline of which he approved.

In the November 1919 issue of the *Monthly*, the editor, William J. Kindley, explained part of why there had been no editions of the publication between May 18, 1918 (when the editor was Samuel Schofield) and that issue:

> *The whole situation among colleges changed at once with the advent of the Students Army Training Corps. . . . Outside duties had small chance of being attended to while the whole student body was organized on the basis of an army camp. The college exercises even had to take second place, and it is believed that the December examinations showed a larger percentage of failures than has ever been known at the college. . . .*
>
> *It will perhaps seem a small matter to get out a publication like this, but in fact it involves a great deal of labor. . . . Advertisements do not come voluntarily. . . . This involved not only time, but absence from the campus which was subject to the military pass.*[76]

After the SATC was disbanded, in December 1918, the *Monthly* found itself in debt, and the price of paper, ink, and labor had drastically increased. These financial problems, coupled with the inexperience of the staff, led the editorial leadership to discontinue publication for the school year 1918–19.

At the 1918 board meeting, Lewis's recommendation that military training become part of the curriculum and compulsory for men was adopted. When the war was over, the government formed the ROTC, and the college was again selected for a unit, one of the first in the nation. In the application, Lewis noted that there was still equipment on campus from the earlier program. In 1919, Capt. Leon H. Richmond, former professor of physics [1913–17] and Lewis's son-in-law, returned to the campus as the commanding officer of the new ROTC detachment. By the fall of 1919, the unit had been formed; it consisted of two cadet companies of six squads each, commanded by cadet second lieutenants. A battalion commander with the rank of first lieutenant was put in command of the whole corps. Students with some experience studied the parts and function of the rifle, as well as infantry combat principles. Less experienced recruits learned army organization, close-order drill, and the manual of arms. Of the ROTC program Lewis commented, "The military training does not occupy the time of the students to an extent that interferes with their studies. The physical benefits are pronounced and the discipline has never been so good. We earnestly hope we may be able to continue this corps."[77] The program required 100 males to be enrolled, and the college had to post a $11,500 bond for the government property on campus.

Apparently, Capt. Richmond was popular with the male students, perhaps because he already knew the campus and the type of school it was. Schofield reported that he worked hard and made a favorable impression on the War Department, so that from 1920 to 1924 Western Maryland College was designated a "Military College" in the *Army List and Directory*. A later researcher, John D. Kraus, noted this anomaly while studying the development of military colleges and commented that he felt Western Maryland was essentially a civilian institution that got drawn into the "war environment" for a brief period. After Lewis's retirement, the military aura on campus subsided, although the ROTC program would continue to the present day, with occasional modifications.[78]

In the fall of 1918, a Department of Home Economics was approved by the board, but no mention of it appears in the catalog until 1921, when Corinne Troy was hired as an instructor.

In 1919 the faculty and board approved some minor curricular changes. The first two years' work remained much the same, except German and French now became options like Greek, which seemed to be catching on again. In the last two years, the number of required subjects in each program was reduced. The next decade would see major revisions of the curricula, which had remained relatively unchanged for 25 years.

FINANCES

For a college as tuition driven as Western Maryland, this decade proved to be a worrisome one for the administration and trustees. Enrollments were rather stable during the first half of the decade, maintaining an average of 234 and reaching a maximum of 256 by 1914. Then they plummeted, first to 239, then to 219, then to 214, hitting a low in 1917 of 213. Equally distressing, the number of boarders decreased proportionately. The four years from 1915 to 1919 were difficult ones, made more so by the war effort, which affected everyone.

To compensate for the loss in tuition and board, the trustees, at Lewis's urging, did the only thing they could do. They raised fees. After many years of maintaining a total fee structure of $225, in 1914 the board increased it to $250. In 1917, because of rising food costs during the war years and because the college was losing money on its boarders, Lewis suggested raising the fees again, to $300; he reluctantly agreed to a $25 increase and to shortening the school year by two weeks, instead. (He wanted to open two weeks late and close two weeks early but settled for a two-week-late start.) It is difficult to tell whether this was carried out, for the catalogs do not reflect adjustments in the calendar, and schedules could have been further adjusted due to the war and the SATC. In June 1919, the board reluctantly approved an increase to $300 for the 1919–20 school year ($75 for tuition and $225 for room, board, and laundry). Lewis noted, as he had on numerous occasions, that the college was giving 14 scholarships worth a total of $1,173 to children of ministers and suggested that these be officially listed as scholarships to head off criticism of the rising rates. The rising fees may have had something to do with the enrollment drops, but by the end of the decade, as mentioned, enrollment rebounded to 274, the second-highest enrollment in the college's history (278 enrolled in 1898–99), with 233 boarders (the largest number ever). This rise may have been due in part to the SATC program during the fall of 1918, but it maintained after that program disappeared four months later.

Graduation rates were improving, as well. The class of 1916, for example, produced 37 graduates and 20 quondam. Over the decade, graduating classes ranged from 26 to 42, with the average being 35. (Three of the ten classes had more men than women, reflecting the slight imbalance in enrollments; the 1919–20 college census showed 122 male and 150 female students.)

Not unexpectedly, the annual college budget, which averaged about $50,000 each year over the decade, grew slightly in most years, faculty salaries being about half of total expenses. In 1910, full professors earned $1,200, while assistants averaged about $700. (In 1912, the board voted to give faculty members their college housing rent free to offset rising costs of living.) By 1919, full professors were receiving $1,300, and the others averaged $800. The last two years of the decade were exceptionally prosperous, given rising enrollment and the increase in fees, so that there was a $25,000 surplus in 1920. Consequently, Lewis paid 5% bonuses to the faculty twice during the year, in December and June—something almost unheard of in higher education and probably never done again.

Probably just as vexing as the fluctuating enrollments, the state appropriations did not always come through. In 1913, Lewis reported that the state appropriation for scholarships was $4,500, but the legislation to provide $3,100 for maintenance was cut. In 1914, he reported that the appropriation should have been $15,000 but was cut to $10,000 ($3,100 for scholarships and $6,900 for general use). He noted that the state funding had again diminished in 1914–15, with $3,700 received for scholarships instead of the required $12,100. (The state also owed the college $10,850 for the building appropriation for Lewis Hall and would owe another $5,425 after July 1.) In June 1916, the president reported that no money from the state had been forthcoming except $1,000 for the county scholarships. It was known that the state had a deficiency of revenues and would have to float some bonds to get money. (The same problem would occur in later decades.) All of these defaults caused the college to borrow funds several times for short periods to meet operating expenses. It was expected, however, that WMC would receive $22,700 in 1917. The bill was approved, and the governor had signed it.

More encouraging to the administration and trustees was the ever increasing endowment. In 1910, it stood at $55,200, and by mid-decade it had grown to $92,000. With the Jubilee Campaign aiming to raise $50,000 by 1917 on the one hand, but a world war on the other, the endowment grew more slowly than had been hoped. By 1919, however, it had reached $162,000, and at the time of Lewis's retirement in 1920, it had grown to $257,521 (including the newly purchased Geiman property).

In anticipation of the 50th anniversary, a special committee of the Alumni Association was given permission to approach the Rockefeller Foundation for a $50,000 grant, with the understanding that if it was forthcoming, the college would raise a like amount. The application was made and a visit to the foundation followed, but the committee was turned down. The Jubilee Campaign was begun in 1916 and completed in 1918 (with a total of $50,657 in pledges over three years, of which $29,513 had been paid). By 1919, the fund had grown to $50,944. During the campaign, the M.P. Church Conference promised $5,000, but by 1917 it had raised only $3,535, with pledges of more to come.

At one point during the fund-raising, Lewis bemoaned the fact that of 1,002 graduates up to 1917, only 140 had contributed to the Jubilee Campaign, which at that point stood at $26,233.[79] The board acknowledged that Dr. McDaniel's illness and Vice President Ward's abrupt resignation had kept the campaign from being carried out in a proper and modern fashion, but they pressed on until the goal was reached in 1919.

MAJOR EVENTS

The June 1911 Commencement also was the occasion for honoring Lewis's 25th anniversary as president. Board President Hering presided at the anniversary celebration, which formed the latter portion of the Commencement proceedings. It featured an address by Dr. Ira Remsen, president of Johns Hopkins University, and congratulatory addresses by Prof. James Reese for the faculty, William Clark Coulbourn '11 for the students, Lynn R. Meekins '82 for the alumni, and Daniel Baker for the trustees. The state board of education, of which Lewis was chairman, was represented by Col. William S. Powell, who spoke of his board colleague as "a man among men, an educator among educators, but such a delightful, loving companion that we want to testify before you, our good feelings to him on this . . . most momentous occasion in his life, and present a slight token of our regard in the shape of a loving cup." After all the congratulatory remarks, Lewis responded, "When one is obliged to be perfectly frank with himself and sits listening to such remarks as have been made, he is obliged to say, not half is true, but I like to hear it. . . . We appreciate the spirit in which they are spoken." He spoke of the special help given by the trustees and quipped, "I cannot but remind them and remind you, who are so kind in your feeling and expression today, that it has been necessary in these years twice for the board to relieve me of my duty, and on one occasion, at least, it was reported that I had lost my mind. I hope I have not gone that far in decay; but certainly there is intensity of effort and of responsibility in such a position that wears one down." Of the faculty, he noted, "We are very democratic, and I don't get half the things done in the faculty that the students have an idea I do . . . I think our faculty has always been independent in its judgment. . . . I would not have it otherwise, and I don't think we could have a strong school if it were otherwise." Of his health and longevity in office, he commented, "It is a wonder to me that I am here, not only because it is a long stretch of time but because it is a marvel to me that my slight physical strength has lasted so long. . . . I cannot imagine that any business in this world would have attracted me so that I could have stayed in it twenty-five years." He concluded with an interesting introspective statement: "The work of a college president was never my choice, never has been, never has appealed to me as an ideal vocation. I came to it under the stress that seemed to be a crisis. I have remained in it because I could not get out of it; but if I had been allowed to choose my own way, I know I should not have become a college president. But I am thankful to feel today that my work has been appreciated at such a value. . . . To have been of any use in any capacity is a cause for profound gratitude. . . . It is a joyful occasion for me and will be appreciated by me as long as I live."[80]

A Commencement dinner continued the festivities, for which L. Irving Pollitt, the president of the Alumni Association, was the toastmaster. Governor Crothers was present and brought greetings; a special song, "Fair Western Maryland," composed especially for the occasion by Dr. Warfield, was sung; and several more speeches followed by various trustees and alumni. Lewis responded by climbing onto a chair to be heard and saying, "This is an occasion which has grown to such a great proportion that no individual can appropriate it to himself. It belongs to the future of our dear college. . . . While I am glad to be made the occasion of such an inspiring outbreak . . . of interest and enthusiasm, I have too much sense to think that I am the center and the circumference of it. I am only too glad to think that you mean by this demonstration a new fidelity, a new enthusiasm, a new interest in every way and a new pride in your institution . . . and I am glad to hail the dawn of what I believe and what I think we all believe to be a new day for our dear college."[81]

It should be noted that the Commencement Week festivities included the President's Reception the evening before the Commencement exercises, to which were invited all who had ever been students at the college. It took place on the lawn of the President's House at 7:30 P.M. and fully 500 people expressed their congratulations to Dr. and Mrs. Lewis while an orchestra played throughout the evening and refreshments were served.

Dr. McDaniel was honored for 30 years of service on the faculty [1885–1915] by being feted at the 12th Annual Mid-Winter Banquet of the Alumni Association held in the Palm Room of the Emerson Hotel in Baltimore on February 19, 1915. After a sumptuous dinner featuring broiled bluefish, lobster patties, and roast turkey, association president Lynn Meekins presided over the program, and Irving Pollitt was toastmaster. Letters were read from a number of alumni and friends who could not be present, including Governor P. L. Goldsborough, Daniel Hering, Charles Billingslea, Caleb O'Connor, and President Lewis. The president, who was in Greensboro, North Carolina, at the time, concluded his long congratulatory letter with these words: "Doctor McDaniel is one of those rare men who can do many things better than other people, and I do not know any gift he possesses that he has not given to the progress of Western Maryland College. . . . 'Well done, good and faithful servant.'"[82]

A number of short speeches of congratulation and fond memory were given, including one by J. Bibb Mills '95, who recalled the following:

I think one reason why Prof. McDaniel was so good to me in putting me through in mathematics was because I used to come up from downtown in seeing young ladies home about fifteen steps behind Dr. McDaniel [who was downtown visiting his future wife, Ada Smith], and he could not be too hard on Bibb because Bibb knew too much.[83]

The banquet was also reported by K. Roberts Greenfield '11: "What we should like to tell no one who was not there as a member of the family, could feel, or appreciate. The banquet was a love feast. . . . We took the occasion to demonstrate to him how he is beloved among us. Representatives were there of nearly all of the thirty classes whom he has put through the mathematical hopper, and converted into friends, if not into Newtons. . . . It was the glow of this unanimous feeling among us that made the evening heartwarming and delightful." Caleb O'Connor composed a five-stanza poem for the occasion, including the following (the second stanza is prophetic):

Up in old Westminster, there's a college on the Hill,
 And the strongest rooter for the dear old place is BILL;
Everybody knows who Bill is, by the thorny path,
 He has made us struggle through, with that infernal Math.

The time is coming when old Western Maryland, on the hill,
 Will cover all the top of it, and keep on growing still;
And the biggest building up there, and better than them all,
 Will be the one from Billy's boys, and called McDaniel Hall.
"God Bless Billy Mac!"[84]

A song was written (attributed to Dr. Thomas O. Crouse '71) especially for the occasion, as well, and was sung to the tune of "Tipperary":

'Twas a long way through Western Maryland,
 'Twas a long way, you know;
Seemed a hard way through college,
 In the days of long ago;
But tonight we greet McDaniel,
 "Billy Mac." Factotum there,
With joy we hail our Alma Mater,
 For our hearts are still there.

Dr. McDaniel responded with some charming reminiscences and this statement about his life: "Surely the lines have fallen to me in pleasant places and if I had it all to do over again, I would want to be Professor of Mathematics and I would want to be on the faculty of Western Maryland College."

Besides the many verbal tokens of affection, the McDaniels were presented with a silver tea service of colonial design, inscribed,

1885–1915
Presented to
Dr. William R. McDaniel
By the Alumni of Western Maryland College
In Recognition of Fidelity to Duty
And as a Token of Affection.

(The service remained in McDaniel's family until 2003, when it was graciously given to the college by his grandson, Dr. William McDaniel Herr, on the celebration of renaming the college in Dr. McDaniel's honor.)

The year 1917 marked the 50th anniversary of the founding of the college, but plans for marking the event were almost abandoned due to the state of war between Germany and the United States and the feeling of some that college commencements should be simple if held at all. Some colleges closed early, and some handed out diplomas without a ceremony.

*Metropolitan Opera star Mabel Garrison '03 performed
during the college's 50th anniversary (1917).*

The trustees debated the propriety of holding a Jubilee celebration under the circumstances; they decided to go ahead with the event but perhaps scale it down a bit. The annual debates and elocution contests for the Merrill and Newell trophies were held, as well as Class Day. The baccalaureate sermon was preached by President Lewis, as usual, and a larger gathering heard Bishop J. W. Hamilton of the Methodist Episcopal Church in the evening. On Monday, the literary society reunions were held, and on Tuesday the board of trustees met. A highlight of the celebration was a musical recital in Alumni Hall by Mabel Garrison, who offered the recital as her contribution to the endowment fund of the college. The Metropolitan Opera star, accompanied on the piano by her husband, George Siemonn, performed 20 art songs and arias. Each group of songs received great applause, which she acknowledged, and several times she was showered with roses. She added several encores to the program, which finally ended with her rendition of "Dixie." At the conclusion of the concert, her classmates from 1903 rushed to the stage and mobbed her, giving the college yell and a special one improvised for the occasion that ended with "Mabel, Mabel, Mabel!"[85]

The Commencement of the semi-centennial was held on June 13, with an academic procession consisting of alumni and old students, present students, trustees, the graduating class, presidents of other Maryland colleges, other guests, and the faculty. They entered Alumni Hall to the strains of "A Mighty Fortress," the traditional processional hymn, played by the orchestra and sung by the students. Commencement orations were given by six seniors, including Murray Benson (later a distinguished Baltimore lawyer and college trustee [1936–63], board chair [1949–63], and honorary LLD [1955]) and Charles E. G. Moylan (later a distinguished lawyer and judge, college trustee [1948–69], honorary LLD [1952], and recipient of the first Alumnus of the Year Award in 1968). The degrees were conferred by Governor Emerson C. Harrington, and after two selections by the orchestra, the anniversary celebration began. Congratulatory addresses were given by Johns Hopkins University president Frank J. Goodnow; Daniel Hering, now graduate dean emeritus of New York University; Mary Belle Cochran '95, professor of expression at Vassar College and former WMC faculty member [1897–1904], representing the alumnae; James D. Williams '02, Washington, D.C., attorney, representing the alumni; and Murray Benson representing the student body. The event concluded with the reading by Rev. Thomas Crouse of a Jubilee Poem composed by David Roger Englar '03. Daniel Hering's comments were particularly interesting, as he reflected on the early history of the college, of which he was a part as a member of the first faculty. He marveled that the college had survived so long without an endowment and encouraged all present to support the institution and invest in it. "The day of miracles is past and we are confident that a new day is at hand, when the efforts of this loyal body supported by the administration will procure an endowment which will so far relieve the college of anxiety and the stress of mere living, that it can live always to better purpose."[86]

The Jubilee Poem included the following stanzas (among 15):

War's dreadful echoes scarce were still,
  His countless graves were newly made,
When, on this consecrated hill,
  An humble cornerstone was laid.
But Peace, and Freedom, hand in hand,
  Who blessed our Alma Mater's birth
Have bred in Western Maryland
  Unselfish aims and honest worth.

For, after fifty peaceful years,
The age-long struggle flames again;
Once more the earth is drenched with tears
Of women, and the blood of men
O Alma Mater, wise and just
Be steadfast in the future years!
You shall go on when we are dust,
And other laughter, other tears

Shall be, where we have laughed and wept.
Still may your children carry on
The simple faith that you have kept,
In ages after we are gone.

Three years later, in 1920, the 50th Commencement of the college was held, and President Lewis's official retirement was recognized. The annual investiture ceremony, which always preceded the graduation by about ten weeks, was held on April 6, and in a departure from tradition, the speaker was not a faculty member but the president's wife, Mary Ward Lewis, a member of the first graduating class, in 1871. Mrs. Lewis opened her remarks to the 26 seniors with a rather curious statement that perhaps reflects the status of women of the time (or perhaps her 42-year relationship with her husband):

I am here today to represent the first President of the College, Rev. James Thomas Ward, D.D. of precious memory, and to do the bidding of our president of today, also beloved, whose pleasure has been the law of my life for many years; and also the representative of the First Graduating Class, to speak to you as the First to the Fiftieth.

She continued, "Great changes have taken place. The women are about to be enfranchised and the men must help them bear the new burdens which they have so long sought." She also noted, "My world has not been as large as yours, nor my opportunity so great; for College Hill has been the world for me. I have always been here. . . ." (She had never accompanied her husband on his trips abroad.) She concluded, "Receive now from the First Class the benediction of good wishes and firm hopes that you may prove worthy to have received your great blessings, and when one of you shall stand here to give God-speed to the members of the One Hundredth class may you have the joy that I have."[87]

During Commencement Week, the usual activities prevailed, including the Class Day exercises (during which the last of the Alumni Hall "muse" windows was unveiled and presented), the freshman class cremation of classical texts, President Lewis's baccalaureate sermon, the literary societies'

*Women students gather for the annual Rose Cup ceremony
in front of Old Main c. 1920.*

reunions and contests, and the annual business meeting of the Alumni Association. As had been the custom for many years, the congregations of the local Methodist Episcopal, Methodist Protestant, Reformed, and Lutheran churches were invited to attend the Baccalaureate Service in Alumni Hall, instead of holding their own services that morning, as a union of faith. Given that the entire college student body, the faculty, many alumni, and relatives of the graduates were also in attendance, it must have been a rather full auditorium. During the Commencement exercises on Wednesday, June 16, the four surviving members of the class of 1871 were honored with remarks, and each received a commemorative diploma marking the 50th graduation. (This was done at the 100th Commencement, in 1970, for the class of 1920.) The address to the graduates was given by Rev. Crouse, DD; the diplomas were presented to the graduates by Mary Ward Lewis; and a commemorative address was given by Dr. James W. Chapman, chairman of the Baltimore City Board of School Commissioners. The alumni dinner following the Commencement was held in the college dining room, where 400 alumni were served. It was billed as the "greatest dinner event the college has ever known. No selected speakers and no speech more than five minutes. No collection and no begging. No sermonizing and no instruction. Just joyful reunion and good food." The dinner cost $1.50 per person.[88] It must have been a high point of the year and the decade, and certainly for Thomas Hamilton Lewis as he concluded his 34-year presidency.

CONCLUSION

It had been a turbulent decade for everyone, and the college had come through some very difficult times. Enrollments and finances had fluctuated, so that stability was problematic. Lives had been disturbed or ended by World War I, and a new era of military preparedness arose. Student life had begun to change as self-governance took root and the faculty gradually gave up some of its control. The curriculum and teaching had been enhanced by the erection of a new and modern classroom and laboratory building. The endowment had grown significantly, and the college, by the end of the decade, was in a better position financially than it had ever been. Significant milestones had been celebrated, and difficult times and losses had been endured. The torch was about to be passed from an older, conservative, Victorian-style administration to a younger, more liberal, and forward-thinking leadership. The college was about to enter a new era.

Chapter 6 Endnotes

1. WMC board of trustees minutes, June 1918.
2. October 1912, 1–3.
3. June 1917, 33.
4. September 18, 1915.
5. Transcript of the 1911 Commencement proceedings, commemorative booklet celebrating Lewis's 25th anniversary as president, college archives.
6. *WMC Monthly*, January 1917, 10–11.
7. Ibid., March 1911, 13–14.
8. Transcript of the 1911 Commencement proceedings, commemorative booklet celebrating Lewis's 25th anniversary as president, college archives.
9. WMC board of trustees minutes, June 13, 1913.
10. Ibid., June 12, 1917.
11. Page 276.
12. Wills, *History of Western Maryland College*, vol. 2, 16.
13. WMC board of trustees minutes, December 1914; Schofield and Crain, *Formative Years*, 80.
14. WMC board of trustees minutes, January 19, 1915.
15. Ibid., June 1916.
16. May 1918, 2–5.
17. WMC board of trustees minutes, June 1920.
18. Ibid.
19. WMC faculty minutes, June 11, 1920.
20. WMC board of trustees minutes, June 1911.
21. Pick, *A Brief History of Campus Planning*, 12–15.
22. June 1917, 38.
23. WMC board of trustees minutes, June 9, 1914.
24. Ibid., June 1914.
25. *WMC Magazine*, June 1962, 8.
26. *WMC Catalogue*, 1914–15, 27–28.
27. *WMC Monthly*, January 1915, 15.
28. WMC board of trustees minutes, June 9, 1914.
29. Ibid., February 11, 1920, June 1920.
30. Chandler, *Pilgrimage of Faith*, 66–70.
31. WMC faculty minutes, October 13, 1911; October 11, 1912; November 1, 1913; May 20, 1914; November 13, 20, 1914; June 10, 1915.
32. Ibid., January 19, 1917.
33. Myers, *Fearless and Bold*, 6–7.
34. Ibid., 19.
35. *WMC Magazine*, June 1962, 8.
36. Pages 82–83.
37. WMC faculty minutes, March 28, 1916.
38. *WMC Monthly*, March 1915, 10.
39. Ibid., June 1917, 34.
40. WMC board of trustees minutes, June 1917.
41. Schofield and Crain, *Formative Years*, 93.
42. *WMC Monthly*, December 1917, 19.
43. WMC faculty minutes, February 15, 1918.
44. *WMC Monthly*, June 1918, 35.
45. Ibid., November 1916, 31.
46. Ibid., March 1918, 19; event program in McDaniel scrapbook for 1895, college archives.
47. 1916 *Aloha*, 149.
48. Myers, *Fearless and Bold*, 28–29.
49. 1916 *Aloha*, 134.
50. *WMC Monthly*, January 11, 1911, 23.
51. Myers, *Fearless and Bold*, 9–10.
52. December 1917, 14.
53. *WMC Monthly*, April 1911, 18; June 1916, 29.
54. Myers, *Fearless and Bold*, 8.
55. *WMC Monthly*, May 1916, 9.
56. Page 24.
57. *WMC Magazine*, June 1962, 8.
58. WMC board of trustees minutes, June 10, 1919.
59. Ibid., June 15, 1920.
60. *WMC Monthly*, February 1918, 17; April 1920, 11; *The Hill*, April 1973, 5–6.
61. Myers, *Fearless and Bold*, 23.
62. Page 3.
63. *WMC Monthly*, February 1918, 17–18.
64. Page 2.
65. January 1917, 6.
66. February 1917.
67. *WMC Monthly*, November 15, 1920, 9.
68. Pages 17–18.
69. March 1914, 15.
70. Wills, *History of Western Maryland College*, vol. 2, 32.
71. Myers, *Fearless and Bold*, 11–12.
72. March 1914, 14–15.
73. Pages 28–29.
74. March 1918, 7.
75. Schofield and Crain, *Formative Years*, 91.
76. Page 13.
77. WMC board of trustees minutes, June 10, 1919.
78. Schofield and Crain, *Formative Years*, 91–92.
79. WMC board of trustees minutes, June 1917.
80. Transcript of the 1911 Commencement proceedings, commemorative booklet celebrating Lewis's 25th anniversary as president, college archives.
81. Ibid., 34–37.
82. Commemorative booklet of the McDaniel celebration, 1915, 16, college archives.
83. Ibid.
84. Ibid.
85. Commemorative booklet, 50th anniversary celebration, June 13, 1917, college archives.
86. Ibid.
87. 50th Commencement Program and Report, college archives.
88. Golden Commencement Announcement to Alumni, 3, college archives.

MAJOR WORLD EVENTS

1911

Turkish-Italian War begins.
Revolution takes place in central China.
Edith Wharton publishes *Ethan Frome.*
Ernest Rutherford formulates his theory of atomic structure.
Irving Berlin composes *Alexander's Ragtime Band.*
Richard Strauss composes the opera *Der Rosenkavalier.*
Roald Admundsen reaches the South Pole.

1912

Arizona and New Mexico become U.S. states.
S.S. *Titanic* sinks on her maiden voyage after colliding with an iceberg.
Carl Jung publishes *The Theory of Psychoanalysis.*
Ravel composes his ballet *Daphnis et Chloé.*
R. F. Scott reaches the South Pole.
F. W. Woolworth Company is founded.

1913

U.S. Federal Reserve System is established.
Willa Cather publishes *O Pioneers!*
G. B. Shaw publishes play *Pygmalion.*
Zippers become popular.
Federal income tax is introduced in the U.S. through the 16th Amendment.
Woodrow Wilson is inaugurated as 28th president of the U.S.

1914

World War I breaks out when Archduke Ferdinand of Austria is assassinated.
Almost 10.5 million immigrants enter U.S. from southern and eastern Europe (1905–14).
John B. Watson publishes *Behavior: An Introduction to Comparative Psychology.*
Joyce Kilmer publishes the poem "Trees."
E. R. Burroughs publishes *Tarzan of the Apes.*
Booth Tarkington publishes *Penrod.*
Panama Canal opens.
U.S. Federal Trade Commission is established.

1915

Somerset Maugham publishes *Of Human Bondage.*
Motorized taxis appear.
Classic New Orleans jazz is popular.
Albert Einstein postulates his general theory of relativity.
First transcontinental telephone call is made, between Alexander Graham Bell and Thomas A. Watson.
Margaret Sanger is jailed for writing her first book on birth control, *Family Limitation.*

1916

James Joyce publishes *Portrait of the Artist as a Young Man*.
Martin Buber publishes *The Spirit of Judaism*.
Jazz sweeps the U.S.
Woodrow Wilson is reelected president over Charles Evans Hughes.
Pancho Villa crosses border with guerillas and raids Columbus, New Mexico.
Carl Sandburg publishes *Chicago Poems*.
First Rose Bowl Game is played, between Washington State University and Brown University.

1917

Charlie Chaplin, American film star, receives yearly salary of $1 million.
Four women are arrested for picketing at the White House in support of women's suffrage.
Allies execute Mata Hari as a spy.
T. S. Eliot publishes *Prufrock and Other Observations*.
Jung publishes *Psychology of the Unconscious*.
Sigmund Freud publishes *Introduction to Psychoanalysis*.
Bobbed hair for women sweeps Britain and United States.

1918

World War I ends with Armistice, November 11.
Ex-Czar Nicholas II and his family are executed in Russia.
Bertrand Russell publishes *Mysticism and Logic*.
Leonard Bernstein is born; Claude Debussy dies.
Daylight Saving Time is introduced in the United States.

1919

Radio Corporation of America (RCA) is founded.
Pablo Picasso paints *Pierrot et Harlequin*.
Rutherford demonstrates that the atom is not the final building block of the universe.
Peace Conference is held at Versailles; President Wilson presides over first League of Nations.
Bauhaus, in Weimar, Germany, revolutionizes teaching of painting, sculpture, architecture.

1920

The 19th Amendment gives women the right to vote.
U.S. Senate votes against joining the League of Nations.
The Hague is selected as the seat of the International Court of Justice.
Earthquake in Kansu province, China, claims 200,000 victims.
World population numbers 1,811,000,000.
Hermann Rorschach devises the "inkblot" psychological test.
In the United States almost 9 million motor vehicles are licensed.
Adolph Hitler announces his 25-point program in Munich.
Gandhi emerges as India's leader in its struggle for independence.
The 1920 census reports the U.S. population to be 117,823,165.

McDaniel Hall, a women's dormitory, was opened in 1924.

C H A P T E R

SWEEPING CHANGES

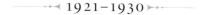

1921–1930

It was the Roaring Twenties. The United States, in particular, was experiencing an era of almost unprecedented development in relative isolation from the rest of the world. Scientific discoveries, assembly-line production, silent (and then "talking") motion pictures, and advances in aviation were the talk of the era. Entertainment abounded, with some of the most famous plays and musicals of the 20th century, not to mention novels, classical music, poetry, and art, being produced in this decade. Flappers were dancing the Charleston, playing mah-jongg, doing crossword puzzles, enjoying comic strips, and singing popular songs.

In 1923, the following occurred:
- Time *magazine was founded.*
- *The DuPont Company began production of cellophane.*
- *Jacob Schick patented his first electric razor.*
- *Yankee Stadium opened in New York.*
- *The price of a Ford automobile dropped to $290, down from $950 in 1909.*
- *Ethel, John, and Lionel Barrymore all starred in separate plays on Broadway.*

- *A round-trip ticket on the Western Maryland Railroad from Westminster to Pen-Mar on July 4 cost $1.10.*

It was an era of hedonism, high spirits, and optimism until October 28, 1929, when the New York stock market crashed, bringing on a gradual worldwide economic crisis.

At Western Maryland College, the faculty and students experienced an almost immediate whirlwind of activity and change when Albert Norman Ward assumed the presidency in July 1920. A product of the late 19th century, he was, nevertheless, a 20th-century thinker and visionary who saw the need for major improvements in curriculum, student life and discipline, and college facilities. This decade would witness the most sweeping changes in the history of the college to that time.

FACULTY AND ADMINISTRATION

Albert Norman Ward '95 (1871–1935) [1920–35] was born near Jarrettsville, Harford County, Maryland, November 27, 1871, one of a number of children of John T. and Elizabeth Mellor Ward. (He was not related to J. T. Ward.) His father was a farmer and merchant who gave young Norman his first training in business. His mother taught him to appreciate the beauty in nature and literature. After studying in the county public schools, he headed for Towson State Normal School, where he spent a year preparing to become a teacher before enrolling at Western Maryland to prepare for the Methodist Protestant ministry. During his college years, he evidenced a love for literature and was a member of the Irving Society, editor-in-chief of the *Monthly*, active in the YMCA, and president of his class. At his graduation in 1895, he was one of the four student orators (giving "The Religion of the Future"), along with the young lady who would become his wife in 1905, Blanche Murchison, from North Carolina. Ward was received into the Maryland Annual Conference of the Methodist Protestant Church in 1895 and ordained in 1897. During an eight-year pastorate in Washington, D.C., he also attended George Washington University, where he received a master of arts degree in English literature in 1901 and continued his studies in English and history until 1904. He held several other successful pastorates in Maryland (Baltimore, Denton, Salisbury), as well as one in Seattle, Washington (1906–9), where he planned and oversaw the building of a church considered to be one of the finest on the Pacific Coast. He served his alma mater as vice president from 1913 to 1916, and from 1918 to 1920 was chancellor of Kansas City University (which later failed; some felt that had he

Albert Norman Ward,
third president

remained there, the school could have been saved).[1] In 1920 he received the honorary doctor of divinity degree from both Adrian College and Otterbein College in Ohio. A year later, Kansas City University conferred upon him the doctor of laws degree. He assumed the college presidency in late July 1920, coming east from Kansas with his wife and five-year-old son, Albert Norman Jr. Dr. McDaniel ably filled in until he arrived.

Ward's formal presidential inauguration (the first to be held at the college) was planned for February 18, 1921, with McDaniel in charge. However, McDaniel's health forced him and his wife to sail for Bermuda in January for a month's recuperation, so the inaugural ceremony was postponed until the 1921 Commencement. (A year later, McDaniel was again too ill to attend meetings, but he gained strength by the fall. By the end of that year, he gave up his classroom duties altogether.)

The new president had been a trustee of the college from 1905 to 1911, and he was reelected to the board at the June 14, 1921, meeting. At that same meeting President Emeritus Lewis tried to resign from the board, but the trustees would not accept his resignation, and he remained on the board until his death in 1929.

The decade saw the deaths of several prominent board members, including Daniel Baker [1901–21], F. K. Herr [1901–21], Joseph W. Smith '80 [1892–1922] (the last direct link with John Smith of Wakefield), T. W. Mather

Sr. [1910–24], Nathan Baile [1893–1926], F. T. Little [1896–1928], Frank T. Benson '84 [1906–29], Joshua W. Miles Sr. '78 [1886–1929], and Thomas Crouse [1903–29] (of the first graduating class).

New trustees elected to replace them included J. Pearre Wantz [1922–51], Daniel MacLea [1924–52], Robert Gill '10 [1924–83], William J. Thompson [1926–44], T. W. Mather Jr. [1927–64], R. L. Shipley [1927–47] (father of future art professor M. Louise Shipley '30), J. N. Link '25 [1929–71], and E. C. Makosky [1929–55] (father of future dean and English professor John D. Makosky '25 and grandfather of future physics instructor Edmund E. Makosky '62).

As in the previous decade, the board leadership changed fairly regularly. At the June 13, 1922, meeting, Rev. Frank Little [1896–1928] was elected board president, replacing E. O. Grimes [1876–1922], who wished to step down after three years as president and who died a month later. Upon Little's death, the board in 1929 elected James H. Straughn '99 [1915–74] as president, a post he would hold for 20 years (even after he was elected bishop of the Methodist Church in 1939). He would ultimately hold the record for board membership longevity, actively serving for 59 years.

The board of trustees dealt with many things during this decade, but one issue was particularly reminiscent of a situation from the previous decade. The leaders of American University approached President Ward about moving WMC to Washington, D.C., where it would become the undergraduate college of the university. Founded by Methodists in the late 1890s, American University was originally established as a graduate university (like Johns Hopkins), but by 1923, creation of an undergraduate college of liberal arts was seen as crucial if it were to survive. The Western Maryland trustees carefully considered this move in January and February of 1924 and appointed a committee to give further consideration to the many details.[2] On June 9, 1924, they decided not to make the move. The move would require selling the Westminster property, and they questioned whether a buyer would be forthcoming. Perhaps even more important, WMC would lose its identity within the university. Western Maryland College would continue to go it alone.

In 1922 the board approved a $1,500 lifetime annual salary for President Emeritus Lewis. This replaced the earlier pension allowance approved in 1920. Lewis continued to draw this stipend until his death, on June 29, 1929, at his home in Washington, D.C. He was survived by his widow, Mary Ward Lewis, their six children (Miriam Lewis Veasey '96, Clara Ward Lewis Richmond '98, Thomas Hamilton Lewis Jr. '02, Marjorie Lewis '06, Hamilton Ward Lewis '08, and Elizabeth Ray Lewis '19) and seven grandchildren. His funeral was held in Baker Chapel, with burial in the Westminster Cemetery.

Not unexpectedly, he was eulogized by the board, the faculty, the students via the *Gold Bug* (the student newspaper), and the alumni via the new *Alumni Quarterly*.[3] Perhaps the most insightful description of his life was written for the Maryland Annual Conference minutes by his successor in 1930. Ward described Lewis as "the most remarkable man that the Methodist Protestant Church has produced. He now takes his place with the immortal great men of a great church. . . . He was the greatest preacher that the Methodist Protestant Church has produced." In Ward's view, "This prince among preachers has not been excelled in all Methodism during the past one hundred years. His was an eloquence that stood out in a grandeur and nobility all its own. . . . In his great moments, he reached the sublimest heights in pulpit oratory." Thinking to the future, perhaps, Ward noted, "He was a conspicuous leader in the movement towards the union of Methodism. He made the greatest contribution to Methodist union that has been made by any man in the three Methodisms. . . . He blazed the path—the only path—by which the union of Methodism will come." Speaking of him as an educator and college president, Ward remembered, "In his earlier years he had a will of iron, that when aroused could brook no opposition, and often he was misunderstood. He was so sure he was right that he often impatiently brushed aside his opponents [perhaps Ward was giving voice to his own frustration during his vice-presidential years, which may have led to his resignation?]; but back of that stern demeanor and the fury of the crusader battling for a cause there was a heart of a child and the gentleness of a woman. . . . He despised all sham and all duplicity and could take blows as well as give them, but had ever the forgiving spirit. His students feared him, but respected him, and in after years loved him. . . . To many of us he will always be Master and Teacher." However, John Makosky, who knew Lewis through his trustee father, Eugene Makosky, remembered that the former president (sometimes called "Stone Face" by the students because of his granite-hewn features) was a fire-and-brimstone preacher and administrator who instilled fear (as well as respect) in the college community: "He had no rapport with the students at all. The institution in 1920 when he left was as near like what it had been in the latter 19th century as he could make it."[4] Makosky observed, however, that it was a different era. "President Lewis was doing a job at which he was enormously competent, and he knew it. His concept of the job did not include being pals with *any*body—students or faculty—and his natural disposition accentuated this remoteness."[5]

The progressive (and approachable) new president began spearheading major changes in curriculum, student life, and financial and campus planning. During the decade, enrollment steadily increased from a low of 214

(1920–21) to a high of 422 (1927–28). This doubling of the student body in ten years required a major increase in faculty and staff to provide the courses in a broadened curriculum. Sadly, several stalwarts were taken from the faculty by death. Dr. Edwin Warfield, professor of English since 1904, died suddenly in 1922. In September 1929, Dr. Herbert Taylor Stephens, professor of philosophy and Bible and Sunday school superintendent, died suddenly after nine years at the college. New faces began appearing on the faculty each year. In 1920–21, the faculty numbered 11, with 9 teachers of special areas (art, music, speech, military science, etc.). In 1922–23, the total teaching staff numbered 29 (of which only 2 held a PhD and 3 had no graduate training), and by 1929–30, there were 37 faculty (4 PhDs and 21 with earned master's), including the instructors for the special areas, which were now integrated into the curriculum for credit (and sometimes as a major). The faculty had almost doubled to match the student body's growth.

During this decade, history was taught by Bartlett B. James '91 [1920–24], who was succeeded by James B. Ranck [1924–29]. When Ranck transferred to Hood College upon completion of his PhD at Hopkins, he was succeeded by the legendary and memorable Theodore Marshall Whitfield [1929–72], also a fresh PhD from Hopkins. Years later, in 1985, John D. Makosky '25 wrote some reflections on his college education (1922–25), which gave some perspective on the teaching of history in this decade:

> I came to WMC as a sophomore transfer student in 1922 [from Webb Institute in New Jersey]. For anyone lucky enough to have had excellent previous schooling, the college was a soft touch. . . . The professor of history, for instance (Doctorate from Hopkins), used the recitation system. He selected a text with short sections, each headed by a large black title. He glanced at the title, then at his roll-book, and commanded, "Miss Allnutt, tell us about the Missouri Compromise." As he looked out at the mountains during the recitation and called on the students in strict alphabetical order, girls first, it was easy to predict one's section a few minutes in advance and prepare. Even that much scholarship wasn't necessary; I once read him a section (I think it was The Wilmot Proviso) verbatim, simplifying a couple of sentence structures and throwing in a few "ers." Dr. James said, "Excellent recitation, Mr. Makosky." . . . In October of my senior year . . . the above mentioned history professor, learned but pedagogically impotent, was called to a chair in the newly-formed [undergraduate college of] American University. President Ward found a young man fresh from the M.A. to take his place. James B. Ranck was a born teacher. His classes were discussions and arguments, lively from bell to bell. One looked forward to each meeting as an

exciting happening. He was a bright, well-schooled teacher, lively and enthusiastic. He drew us out, listened to us, never talked down to us.[6]

Upon Dr. McDaniel's retirement from the classroom (he would carry the title of professor of mathematics until his death), Bertha I. Hart '21 [1921–29] took over the math classes. When she left in 1929, she was succeeded by the legendary Clyde A. Spicer [1929–69]. Both Whitfield and Spicer were young Virginians, graduates of the University of Richmond, and roommates at Johns Hopkins, where they both received their PhD in 1929 before coming to the college to remain for 40 or more years.

George S. Wills [1922–44] returned to the Hill to teach English, replacing Dr. Warfield. Ironically, Warfield had replaced Wills when he left in 1904 to teach at Baltimore Polytechnic Institute. Wills chaired the English Department for many years. Joining him in English was Dean W. Hendrickson [1926–58]. Makosky later reflected fondly on Wills's effect on him:

Professor Wills [was] the only person in the [English] department in my sophomore year, and the only English teacher I had at WMC. Tall, slender, with a magnificent bearded head, he had great dignity and "presence," but was capable of warmth, kindness and humor. In literature courses his method was textual clarification, occasionally illumined by digressions of insight and wisdom. If these classes were rather dull, two others were quite the reverse. In "Old English" we learned to read Anglo-Saxon, grasped the significance of enriching ingredients, comprehended the full history of our language, saw it as a vital growing organism; it was an experience no future English teacher should miss. In "Argumentation" we were challenged by Wills' knowledge of world problems, his definition of issues, his insistence on logic, his revelations of tactics in debate. In summation, one of the crucial experiences of my life was the contact with the wisdom, the character, and the personal impressiveness of George S. Wills. . . . I thought, if I can join the qualities of these two men [Wills and Ranck], I have found what I should like to do with my life.[7]

In an effort to build the education program to meet the needs of the schools in the state, President Ward hired Alvey Michael Isanogle [1920–46] to revamp and expand that department. His salary was $1,500, of which $500 was paid by the Carroll County Board of Education to provide a "teachers' class" for the county. His name would be remembered by legions of students. His sister Mamie was hired to run the dining hall and the infirmary on the fourth floor of McDaniel Hall, and in 1924 his wife, Anna Houck Isanogle, was named the first full-time college registrar, grade reporting having been carried out in Vice President McDaniel's office up to that time. Mary Olive

Ebaugh joined the education faculty in 1926 and served until 1941. She was joined in the latter part of the decade by Sara E. Smith '18 [1926–67], who had returned to the campus to teach chemistry and science education but eventually concentrated her efforts in education.

Samuel Schofield had been hired to teach chemistry immediately following his graduation, but in 1924 he returned to graduate school to work on a doctorate. He was temporarily replaced by Frederick Warren and his sister Ruth Warren '24. Biology was taught by Arthur E. Woodhead [1918–24], who was succeeded by Lloyd M. Bertholf [1924–48]. At first part-time, Bertholf soon became full-time, completed his Hopkins PhD, and eventually served as dean of the faculty. In 1927 the need for additional instruction in biology was met with the appointment of Cloyd Bennighof [1927–52]. Additional teaching in chemistry was provided by Hugh Elderdice Jr. [1929–61].

Physics was taught exclusively by Carl Schaeffer '14 [1919–59] until Frederick M. Miller [1927–37] joined him. Miller also served as dean of men [1928–37] and taught some mathematics. Schaeffer had gone on to earn a bachelor of science in engineering from Johns Hopkins and, upon his return to the college in 1919, soon employed his talents not only in the physics and geology classroom but also as surveyor of the Geiman property. Schaeffer also assumed the role of faculty secretary in 1922, upon Dr. Warfield's death, and would remain in that position until 1947. Later, he oversaw installation of the college's sewer system and establishment of the veterans housing ("Vetville") after World War II.[8] When Dr. McDaniel became too infirm to continue the treasurer's duties, Schaeffer was named assistant treasurer; he assumed the treasurer's position in 1942, upon McDaniel's death.

In physical education Faith Millard [1920–29] became the first full-time director of physical culture for women, and Hugh Barnett Speir '22 [1922–44] came on board to direct the men's activities and coach. During her tenure, Millard developed a well-rounded program of women's physical education and organized the first women's intercollegiate teams.[9] In 1926 Richard C. Harlow was hired from Colgate University to take over as director of athletics and coach several sports, especially football. By the end of the decade, Marie Parker [1929–63] had replaced Millard, who left to get married, and Roselda Todd '28 [1930–65] returned to the Hill in women's athletics.

The arts began to establish a true foothold on the campus as music, art, and dramatic art became full-fledged areas of study for credit in the collegiate program. Dorothy Elderdice '11 was hired in dramatic arts and speech but stayed only one year [1922–23] before leaving for New York to pursue further studies. She returned to the Hill in 1927 to teach speech and religious drama for almost 30 years in the Westminster Theological Seminary. Soon another

The college faculty, 1923

well-remembered face made its appearance when Esther Smith came to teach speech and dramatic art in 1926. She left two years later for further study in New York but returned in 1930 to remain for the next 40 years as a beloved Western Maryland teacher. In music Maude Gesner continued keyboard instruction in her studio in McDaniel Hall (at the end of what came to be known as "Onion Hall" because of her penchant for baking onions at night), assisted by Mabel Harris '01 [1919–42]. Ruth Sherman Jones [1928–35], a former supervisor of music in Montgomery County schools, joined the faculty in voice and as director of the College Choir and Glee Club, replacing Elise Dorst [1914–28], who was forced to resign because of illness.

Two other new faces in 1921 were Corinne Troy in the newly established Home Economics Department and Minnie M. Ward '12 in the library [1921–61]. Miss Troy left in 1925 for another position in Albany, New York, but returned in 1929 to marry Samuel Schofield and would fill in from time to time in home economics for the next 30 years. Miss Ward (A. N. Ward's niece) would spend the next 40 years presiding over an ever-growing library.

Margaret Julia "Moxie" Snader '25 returned to the campus as a part-time instructor in French [1925–27] but joined the faculty full-time in 1930 and remained until her retirement in 1963.

Margaret Robinson, who had been preceptress and then dean of women since 1908, resigned in 1928 and was replaced by Fannie Grove Stover. Mrs. Stover had been preceptress at Kee Mar College in Hagerstown, returned to Western Maryland to teach in the preparatory school, taught home economics, and most recently had been assistant dean to Miss Robinson. She would hold the post of dean until 1937. A student of the early 1920s, Sarah E. Corkran Smith '23 (1903–2006), recalled that Miss Robinson looked rather "forbidding" but was really very nice, although she was a bit "nosy" and wanted to know all about you. The women students could fool Miss Robinson, but they were much more afraid of Mrs. Stover, whom they couldn't dupe as easily.[10] Virginia Holland Nicoll '29 remembered that while Miss Robinson could be very strict, the students preferred her methods to those of Mrs. Stover, who didn't get along as well with the students.[11]

Theophilus Kenoley "T. K." Harrison '01 was hired to be the college's business manager (as well as the Alumni Association executive secretary) in 1930. This was the first time the alumni office was located on the campus and maintained by a college employee.[12] Harrison would hold the post until he retired in 1949. In 1925, Helen Ohler was hired to assist President Ward during the financial campaign. She would remain on campus as secretary to the president until August 1972.

Honors were awarded to some of the faculty, bringing prestige to the college. In 1921, Prof. Ferdinand Bonnotte received a special honor, Palms of the French Academy with the title "Officer of the Academy," as a "reward for his long and good service as a French Teacher in a foreign country."[13] At the 1923 Alumni Banquet, he was the honored guest in recognition of his 25 years at WMC. Nearly 300 attended, representing almost all classes since 1871.

As the faculty grew and began to have more permanency (although tenure was not yet awarded), issues of faculty morale began to arise. The Faculty Club was formed in 1924 with George Wills as its first president. Meeting monthly for socializing and educational discourse, the members heard such lectures as "Some Literary Studies of Southern Writers" (by Wills), "Presidents I Have Known" (by Bartlett James), and "German Rationalism" (by Herbert Stephens). By the end of the decade, a faculty committee consisting of professors Isanogle, Schofield, and Schaeffer was appointed to study the feasibility of a teacher pension fund. The trustees also discussed creating a retirement fund for faculty at its June 1929 meeting and approved an internal program funded by $200,000 accumulated from several sources and invested to provide retirement income for those faculty teaching at least 30 years. Under the new president, an expansion of faculty governance ensued via a number of appointed committees: Admissions, Athletics, Catalog, Extension Work, Schedule, Library, Student Activities, and so forth. The administrative work was thus spread among these standing committees, some of which still functioned many years later.

During the fall term of 1922, President Ward fell ill (probably with a chronic heart condition) and was out of service for some of the term. His illness recurred during spring term of 1927, requiring a stay in the University of Maryland Hospital; Vice President McDaniel filled in for several months and presided at the 1927 Commencement. When the trustees were apprised of the situation at the June meeting, they insisted that McDaniel be given assistance by an Executive Council (Isanogle and Schaeffer), which functioned until Ward's return in the fall.[14]

Prior to 1922 the academic program of the college (indeed, all aspects of college life) was overseen by the president and the faculty, but Ward felt that more direction could be given via a College Studies Committee, to which he appointed Alvey Isanogle, George Wills, Arthur Woodhead, and Samuel Schofield in 1922. The committee dealt with such things as grading systems, course loads, student requests to drop and add courses, academic standards, and eligibility standards for athletes. It met frequently and reported its actions to the faculty at their now-monthly meeting.

More administrative changes occurred in 1928, when, for the first time, an academic dean (in contrast to the student deans) was appointed. Prof. Schofield was named dean of the college (at a salary of $2,600), and at the same time Prof. Isanogle was named dean of the School of Education (at a salary of $3,200). The College Studies Committee then ceased to exist. Ward also expressed his desire to expand the college program to include a School of Religious Education in the near future. Two years later this had not yet occurred, and he expressed to the board (in his President's Report for 1930) his regret that limited finances had stalled the project. Soon after Schofield's appointment, the professorial academic ranks were more carefully established and adjusted to fall in line with those of other institutions. Until this time, the primary instructor in a given academic area or department carried the title of professor, with an occasional assistant being named. Ranks did not correlate to either academic preparation or previous classroom experience. After 1928, the traditional ranks of professor, associate professor, assistant professor, and instructor were established, and appointments began to be made according to degrees and experience. Faculty salaries gradually increased, but President Ward knew that they would have to improve much more if the college were to keep its accreditation. At the June 1929 board meeting, he presented "The Financial Needs of a College of Liberal Arts of 500 Students." This was obviously an outgrowth of his intense studies of liberal arts institutions, which would evolve into a monograph and in 1930 a nationwide conference on funding for small liberal arts colleges. In his projections, he gave what he proposed to be appropriate salary ranges for the various WMC faculty ranks: full professor, $3,500–$5,000; associate professor, $2,500–$3,200; assistant professor, $2,000–$2,500; and instructor, $1,400–$1,800. He also proposed reducing the faculty teaching load to an average of 12 semester hours per week, 9 hours for department heads. He noted that this would require an additional $3 million of endowment and would cost the 1929–30 students $520 tuition per year. Of course, his proposals could not be implemented at that time; these goals were not met for another 25 years.

Samuel Biggs Schofield (1898–1984) played a significant role in the college's development in this decade and the future. He came from Cecil County, on Maryland's Eastern Shore, in 1914 on a state scholarship, which allowed him to complete his high school work in the prep school and then graduate from the college in 1919 with specializations in chemistry and biology. During his college years he was editor of the *Monthly*, member of the Irving Society, class president, and even played a bit of football as a freshman until he broke his collar bone. Upon graduation, he left to take a teaching position in Grasonville, Queen Anne's County, a post he held for only three weeks before accepting a position tendered by President Lewis to return to the college as an instructor in biology. The following year Dr. Ward asked him to become dean of men. Schofield wrote of himself in his new appointment, "For a young man who had just graduated from the college in 1919 to act in such a capacity, dealing with other young men, some of whom had known him as a student, was not an easy task, but somewhat reluctantly he undertook it for a few years."[15] By 1921, he was titled professor of chemistry. In 1924 he took a leave of absence for almost four years to attend Princeton University for graduate studies leading to a PhD in chemistry, specializing in gases. He had virtually completed all the course work, as well as the research for the dissertation, by 1928, when he discovered that someone else had just published the same results, which in that era (unlike the present day) made Schofield's research redundant, and completion of the degree would now require a new research project. He felt that he did not have the time or inclination to start over and returned to the campus with a master of arts degree. Even without his completed doctorate, he was well qualified to present and expand the chemistry curriculum and to lead others in the curriculum revision that was ongoing throughout the decade. He would continue to be dean of the college until 1938, when he was appointed dean of administration, a post he held until 1963. In 1929 he married Corinne Troy, a former home economics instructor, and they had one daughter, Corinne Schofield (Lescallette) '52.

Samuel Biggs Schofield, dean

Curriculum

In February 1921, President Ward reported to a special meeting of the board of trustees (his first official meeting with them as president) that a revision in the course of study was necessary immediately. He noted that Dr. Lewis had also seen the need but had not been able to (or perhaps couldn't bring himself to) effect the needed changes. The other colleges in Maryland had been surveyed as to their requirements, and it was found that WMC was requiring more of its faculty and students than the accrediting agencies recommended.[16] A faculty committee was already studying college curricula in other institutions, as well as what the state high schools were doing.

To accomplish the revision, he submitted a proposal for new entrance requirements: 2 units in mathematics, 3 units in English, 2 in foreign language, and 1 in history, in addition to electives chosen from mathematics, foreign languages, history, geography, sciences, and business, to total 15 units. In order to bring the college more in line with the majority of colleges in the United States (and following the elective system instituted by President Charles W. Eliot at Harvard), Latin and Greek would no longer be required. While there would not yet be much election of courses in the freshman or sophomore years, the third and fourth years were to be much more elective. Eight group majors were offered: biology or chemistry; education (listed as a major for only one year); English; history or political science; home economics; Latin or Greek; mathematics or physics; and French, German, or Spanish. The four-year major course in home economics was added to meet a growing demand. The revision of the curriculum and system of instruction as outlined was approved by the trustees on the spot. By the regular June meeting of the board, Ward reported that the students were in favor of the new curriculum, including the new home economics program, which still needed to be equipped. Approval was also given to awarding college credit for work in music, art, and expression (speech) for the first time.[17]

The education program was growing to meet public school staffing needs under the direction of Alvey Isanogle. Isanogle was a graduate of St. John's College in Annapolis and received his master's degree from Johns Hopkins in 1924. Ward envisioned building the Education Department into a full-fledged School of Education. By 1924 graduates were "sought eagerly by the county superintendents." Out of a class of 65 in 1924, 50 were prepared to teach in the Maryland public high schools. Ward recommended offering the bachelor of science degree in education to attract students preparing to teach who had finished the two-year training at Towson State Normal School or the newly opened Salisbury State Normal School. Students would enter for two years of additional work leading to the BS.[18] Action on this was not taken, however, and Isanogle fashioned a program within the bachelor of arts structure that met the certification needs of students. For one year early in the decade, a major in education was listed in the catalog, and for a very short

Home economics laboratory, c. 1925

time in mid-decade there were even offerings in elementary education. Soon after his arrival on campus, Isanogle saw the need for an extension program for public school teachers and established a program in Westminster and Cumberland to provide course work beyond the "normal" training. Generally, the courses were academic rather than professional work, to strengthen teachers' background in content. By 1929, the education programs had grown so much that the School of Education was approved and established with Isanogle as dean.

Isanogle developed a system for obtaining feedback on how newly trained teachers from the college were doing in their classrooms. He would call on the various county superintendents to ask about these first-year teachers and make suggestions that would help them if needed. Similar information was sought from school principals, and he followed up with a conference with each teacher. Apparently, the program worked well in most instances and was appreciated by the school systems. Of course, by being out in the field, Isanogle was also able to assess the needs of various school systems and recommend his graduates for positions as they became available. This soon led to recruitment activity on campus by representatives from the counties. Prof. Isanogle was well known and respected across the state, and his recommended graduates were always sought.[19] By 1926 it was reported that Western Maryland was preparing more high school teachers than any other college in the state (the state normal schools prepared only elementary teachers). Student teaching was being done in the Carroll County schools.[20]

At the board meeting in 1922, it was reported that the General Education Board of the State of Maryland had visited the college to examine it and its programs. The state board reported favorably on the college but noted the need for a larger endowment and increased faculty salaries (which it noted were less than the salaries of pastors of average churches).

Schofield and Crain reported an interesting story of how the college came to be formally accredited for the first time. Apparently, Prof. Isanogle, while studying part-time at Johns Hopkins in the fall of 1921, noticed a meeting being held in Gilman Hall. His curiosity led him to sit in on the session and to find out that it was the annual meeting of a section of the Association of Colleges and Preparatory Schools of the Middle States and Maryland, the accrediting body for the area institutions. With Ward's blessing and encouragement, Isanogle and his wife, Anna, prepared a detailed application for an examination by the association. A year later, in November 1922, Dr. Adam LeRoy Jones of Columbia University conducted the accreditation visit.[21]

By this time, accreditation agencies were coming into their own in acceptance and prestige, and the Middle States Association had adopted higher standards for accreditation than it had used previously. Its governing body reported that those higher standards had revealed some "startling deficiencies" in many colleges of the region. As a result of Jones's examination, however, the Middle States Association gave WMC the best rating it could and placed the school on a list of approved colleges, which recommended that graduates be accepted by university graduate schools. The association informed President Ward, however, that in its next survey it would be looking for a $500,000 endowment, higher faculty salaries, and more equipment. Ward promised the association to make every effort to correct the deficiencies as soon as possible with board support.[22]

By 1924, with the initial accreditation process behind him, Ward reported to the board, "The Standardizing Agencies look with disfavor upon preparatory schools directly connected with colleges. Colleges having preparatory schools lend themselves easily to the temptation of permitting a short cut into the college." He went on to propose scaling down the college's preparatory school toward its final elimination (which occurred in June 1926).[23]

During the academic year 1922–23 a new freshman advisory system was put into place, and for the following year a new organization of freshman courses was established. Because the first year is the most critical one in the life of a college student, the plan gave attention to all the activities, academic and social, of the freshman year. Faculty advisors were carefully chosen and taught special courses for their advisees that dealt with methods of study, time management, and sources of academic help, for example. From this experience it was hoped that the new students would see more clearly the academic path before them and how to trod it successfully.[24] In the fall of 1925 a Freshmen Orientation Week was established for the first time, with Prof. Isanogle as chairman. It included lots of speeches, testing, receptions, orientation to college practices and traditions, medical examinations, and course selection. The schedule was modified from year to year, but the general format remained essentially the same for years.

The curriculum continued to be rethought and revised throughout the decade; in 1926, a rather detailed description of the total college program was stated in the catalog. The program's basic principles were (1) freer election of courses, (2) all college work offered on a semester basis, (3) a closer coordination of the first two years of college work with that done in high schools, and (4) ongoing revision to meet the changing needs of modern life. The revision also sought a more unified curriculum and a more careful differentiation between the work of the first two years and the work of the last two years. Special freshman courses had been developed, careful advising had been established, and a broad program of work requiring 17 semester hours

ROTC battalion on Hoffa Field, 1923;
note seminary and gym in background.

each semester was laid out for the first two years. At the end of the sophomore year, a general examination of the work over the first two years would be given. The last two years would build on the foundation of the first two, allowing for more advanced work in the student's elected major and including preparation for professional work or graduate school.[25] The sophomore comprehensive examinations, given in late April each year by the Education Department, consisted of two parts: a general examination covering the work that a student should have completed in high school, the work usually required of students during the first two years of college, and general current and cultural knowledge; and two special examinations over subjects in which the student had some depth of knowledge. The names of the students with the ten highest scores each year were published in the college newspaper, the *Gold Bug*. The results of these examinations, along with the high school record, were used to determine the direction of the student's future college work, as well as vocation and employment. Also introduced gradually (with final implementation for the class of 1930) was a grade point system (A = 3 points, B = 2, etc.) and a minimum requirement of 136 semester hours and 136 points to graduate. A grade point average of 2.2 was required for summa cum laude, 2.0 for cum laude, and 1.8 for honorable mention,[26] suggesting that relatively few high grades were given in this era. Indeed, there are references in the faculty minutes to discussions about grading and the paucity of A grades given.

The home economics program was growing and expanding and was, by 1926, using two rooms in the McDaniel Hall basement for a "practice house." For two weeks at a time, three students ran the house on a budget of $15 for eating and entertaining (including an informal and a formal dinner).[27]

In 1930 the War Department designated the college a "Distinguished

College in Military Science" in the region. Dean Schofield was also pleased to note in his report to the board that the standards of the college were gradually rising due to the higher quality of both the faculty and the students. He went on to say,

> Western Maryland has been unusually successful in the field of competitive athletics for men during the present year. . . . Our standards for admission for all students are higher than ever before, and while reaching high places in athletic competition the same boys stood above average for athletes at Western Maryland and their grades for the most part have been creditable. . . . It may be added that the captain of the 1929 football squad will graduate creditably this year and that the captain-elect of the 1930 squad may receive some academic honors at his graduation in 1931.[28]

STUDENT LIFE

In his reflections, John Makosky remembered the nonacademic part of his college life:

> The kind of academic program [I found upon enrolling in 1922] gave me a great deal of leisure. What to do with it? Athletics were out—four years of high school track, a year of college basketball and tennis had left me a back that precluded organized sport. The WMC social ideal was the separation of the sexes—not 100% effective, but "contact time" held to a minimum. Result—my sophomore leisure was dedicated largely to mischief. I must have matured over the year, because my junior leisure was somewhat more creditable. I joined with two or three kindred spirits in founding intercollegiate debating; an excellent college activity that prospered for 20 years but perished in the World War II gas shortage. Secret societies were forbidden by college law, so I became a charter member of two such fraternities. The first [Gamma Beta Chi], founded as a "share-the-food boxes from home" group, was created in my sophomore spring, forgotten over the summer, later revived after the second organization broke the college rules to smithereens. This group was founded by a chap [G. Hall Duncan x'26] who knew what a fraternity could be. We immediately realized that we must impress the college with our value to the institution. Our first big project was the college newspaper [The Black and White], which three of us produced weekly throughout my junior year. At the end of the year we turned it over to the college as an established publication. [It was renamed The Gold Bug.] Among

smaller projects of my last two years were a deputation team [called the Black and White Flying Squadron] that represented the college in a dozen or so high schools (I was the speaker on Social Life—I now wonder what I could have found to say), a medal to be awarded annually in honor of Lynn Gruber, a fraternity brother killed in a sledding accident, and The Bicker Session. This last was a group of serious upperclassmen who spent late night hours discussing—some evenings with professors as guests—the problems of improving the college. I wrote a summary of our "findings," not very complimentary; these were mimeographed and mailed to all faculty and board members on our commencement day. I still wonder how I ever ended up teaching at WMC.

Makosky concluded his reflections about the college of the early 1920s with these words:

Looking back, I can see that the WMC of the early '20's was far from the academic institution it now is. But the relaxed life on the campus allowed one to make friends, to talk out the great problems, to find oneself. I studied under, and made friends of, two great teachers. I found a vocation that was perfect for me—I could not have been so happy in any other. And I found a classmate [M. Gertrude Jones '25] I wanted to marry! What's a college for, anyway? Perhaps a very good college after all.[29]

The statement about the "peculiar advantage" of the college (that men and women could both attend and never see each other) appeared in the catalog until the 1923–24 edition. (It was also made clear that students did not recite together except where the classes were small.) Thereafter, the statement was eliminated (although there is no record of trustee approval), and one

A bird's-eye view of the campus, looking north from Main Street, c. 1917

can assume that a gradual, though unheralded, move toward coeducational classes was under way by mid-decade, as Makosky's comments about his history class, above, attest.

President Ward noted in his President's Report of 1924, "We are living in a different age from any that has proceeded it, and the colleges . . . have felt the changed viewpoint." Noting that other colleges had seen the need to modify the rules and methods of discipline that prevailed before World War I, WMC had moved cautiously and slowly, but the results were good. More freedom on campus, which involved more and freer intermingling of the sexes in social activities, was proving beneficial. Girls were still carefully supervised, "much more so than they want, to be sure," and there was still "no safer place for a girl than the campus of Western Maryland College."[30]

Ward realized early on that student restraints needed to be lifted, and he gradually set out to make the lives of students more pleasant, even a few months after taking office. In January 1921, boys were allowed to take girls to an oyster supper at the Methodist Episcopal Church. The *Monthly* reported a female student's reaction: "A shock when we heard we could go? Words will never express it. Most of the girls were paralyzed at the news and with such suddenness too. . . . The men called for the young ladies in mission parlor promptly at two [and] escorted them to the supper. . . . It was dark . . . when everyone left for college, getting up here about seven o'clock in time for a Smith Hall recital. . . . I can still see couples coming up past Alumni Hall and on up the path, dark and not a chaperone for every two. We really thought we were terribly wicked."[31] On April 24, Dr. Ward announced more privileges. Boys and girls could now mingle (without loitering) on campus, exclusive of class hours, until 7 P.M. each evening. The "campus" was defined as from the front of the Main Building to Alumni Hall. It was reported that at first the boys were somewhat hesitant to cross the former "no-man's-land." A young man could now call upon a young lady in various parlors once or twice a week, as well as at the general parlor on Saturday night.

Blanche Ford Bowlsbey '27 (1906–2006) remembered the Sunday evening services in Baker Chapel, where the women entered by the main door and sat on the left near the organ, while the men entered by the side door near Alumni Hall and sat on the right. For a half hour after chapel, students could mingle freely, and the young women could hardly get out the door for all the boys gathered around it. Bowlsbey also described the rules under which women could go downtown unchaperoned. As freshmen, six girls had to go together after signing out. By sophomore year, a group of four was required, and by junior year, two girls could go by themselves. Only when one was a senior could she go downtown alone, now that she was an "adult."[32] Ward promised that if the students successfully accepted the responsibilities of the new privileges, he would be willing to grant further ones. It would not be too long before the formal "parlor" was disbanded as an unnecessary anachronism. Indeed, the 1922 *Aloha* pictured the "social parlor" and commented, "The onward march of progress has taken from us the hallowed spot where our social affairs waxed and waned; where we sometimes knew joy and sometimes sorrow, but where we always knew when the hour of seven had arrived. Scene of the balmy days of 'strikes,' we bid thee a fond farewell. Though thou art gone, thy spirit lingers on."[33] In the fall of 1925, the president announced the end of Wednesday and Saturday morning chapels. Instead, a general assembly would be held each Wednesday at 11:20 A.M. to hear speakers and highlight student activities. A *Gold Bug* editorial of the same year proudly announced, "The old days of autocracy have past [sic]. Democracy in all its pomp and glory, has been enthroned on College Hill; and it is here to stay. No more will force and 'Don't' rule WMC."[34] It might also be noted that, for the first time in a WMC yearbook, the 1925 *Aloha* pictured couples together, unchaperoned. Included among them is a picture of John Makosky and Gertrude Jones.

Curiously, while many restraints on student activity were being lifted, others were being put into place. In October 1922 the faculty voted not to allow boarding students to keep automobiles in Westminster after January 1. No specific reason was recorded, but one can infer that parking on campus was becoming a problem. In the fall of 1923, the faculty again banned automobiles for boarding students (perhaps the previous year's prohibition had not gone over well). By 1926, finding parking for day students' cars had also become a problem. At its meeting of September 29, 1923, the faculty approved the requirement that all students would report for 15 minutes of sitting-up exercises each morning. These would begin October 2. When a number of young men refused to participate for the first three days, they were demerited, and after a meeting with the dean of men, they agreed to go along. Since nothing more is said about this enforced exercise regimen, one can assume that it eventually died out for lack of interest.

The students' negative reaction to the food continued, as might be expected. Several students of the decade remembered being served chicken, mutton, and liver (but not much beef), vegetables (grown on the college farm), and sweet and sticky blackstrap molasses poured over bread. In the Smith Hall dining room, the students changed tables every week, a senior sitting at one end and a faculty member at the other. The food, served family style, was brought in on platters and in bowls and was usually not enough to serve the table without refills (if available). One dinner was, apparently, especially memorable. The local *Democratic Advocate* reported on January 26, 1924, that the students had staged a total boycott of the dining room on January 15 as a result of being served pickled souse the previous Saturday evening. Dr. Ward was not at all pleased by the hunger strike, noting, "I feel like spanking them! When students pay $400 a year for everything, including room, board and tuition, they can't expect fancy meals." However, he discussed the problem with student leaders and with the dietician, Mrs. Lilly, who presented a sample mid-week menu of fried scrapple for breakfast, fried bologna for lunch, and fried fresh sausage for dinner. The students' response to this was that "the breakfast bacon was burned, the bologna was thin and tough, the cereal a mysterious mush, and the sausage an unfamiliar-looking mixture." A rare treat at breakfast was hotcakes and syrup. One rather strange breakfast, however, was served on January 23, 1925, when the dietician overslept, so hot dogs were cooked for the meal.[35] Thanksgiving, Christmas, and Easter meals were more expansive and festive, with more "trimmings." Former students remembered that they were not "overly fed" and depended upon "care packages" from home. One commented, "The food wasn't great!"[36] The 1922 *Aloha* noted, however, that, unlike an earlier time, students no longer had to bring their own utensils and napkin rings to college to use in the dining hall. With the completion of the new dining hall in 1929, food service at the college changed radically. Breakfast and lunch were served cafeteria style, while the evening meal was served by waiters as before.

Students of the 21st century are often amazed at hearing of the student life of 75 or more years ago. Earle T. Hawkins '23 described in the *Monthly* what boys did in their idle time. He reported that they listened to the Victrola, played games of rook or checkers, went to Parlor Night, enjoyed outdoor sports in good weather, went to the movies downtown, and headed for Ford's Inn (out New Windsor Road) and Mother Royer's for food. (In 1926, it was reported that Mother Royer was ill with heart problems, and the students were concerned that her famous hamburg and egg sandwiches would not be available. Her daughters, "Little Margaret" and Nellie '17, filled in for her, continuing to feed 50–60 hungry students on occasion.) Saturday morning was devoted to room cleaning in preparation for the weekly inspection.[37] Doing one's laundry also filled some time. An unnamed student described the college laundry as the "button-extractor" (among other, less complimentary names). "If you have a blue shirt, and you would prefer a green one, allow the college laundry to work its will. . . . It is well to procure those garments of nocturnal retirement complete in one segment, as after several launderings, those made up of two component parts have difficulty at arranging a meeting—the various members having been minimized by the refining influence of the laundry."[38] Girls held parties for friends and classmates, and

Sarah Corkran Smith admitted that she and her friends even played cards (still very much forbidden on campus) in their room late at night, but only after locking the door and covering the transom to hide the after-hours light from the proctors. (Electric lighting was provided only from 6 A.M. to 10:30 P.M., after which students were forced to switch to coal oil lamps, with which they were not totally happy.) After a branch post office was established on campus in the fall of 1922 in the Library and Administration Building, one can assume that students enjoyed picking up their mail and having the opportunity to meet others and talk (like a "little parlor").

Ginna Wilson Shockley '27 remembered dorm life on the third floor of Smith Hall:

> As a freshman in the fall of 1923, I had a room in Smith Hall with a window over the porch roof. Since we were confined to our rooms for study hours 7 to 9 P.M. with Mrs. Stover checking, we dared not be seen in the hall. Blanche Ford Bowlsbey '27 was two doors down, so I would go out the window and walk down the roof to her window for a visit. It was a quick exit when the knock came for room check, and I was forced to scamper back to my room before Mrs. Stover reached number 56.

Of these antics, Bowlsbey commented that the roof had a dangerous pitch, and in later years they "shuddered to think that with one false step we could have ended as a pile of mush on the road."[39]

As the decade progressed, concern increased about the viability and relevance of the literary societies. While the YMCA and YWCA continued to flourish, the four old societies, which had been the source of most of the social and cultural activities for 50 years, were no longer meeting the needs of the students. A *Gold Bug* editorial asked, "Do we want the literary societies to continue? . . . A feeling of electiveness seems to have permeated the minds of all. . . . To contend that just one type of society can be made tasteful to the entire student body is foolish and illogical."[40] Soon, small groups of students banded together to provide a different type of social activity and comradeship, and the administration and faculty were powerless to stop them. While the request from male students to form chapters of national fraternities had been refused several times in the past, local groups for both men and women began to spring up, joining the purely social, women's JGC, which had been around for 25 years and was accepted, perhaps grudgingly, by the powers that be. Editorials in the *Gold Bug* appeared with some regularity in support of fraternities and sororities, but still they were officially banned. Makosky wryly noted the founding in 1922 of Gamma Beta Chi as a social group for men, in his reminiscences quoted earlier. The group formally announced itself in April 1924 by stating that its purpose was "to cooperate with the rest of the student body for the furtherance of all forms of college life."[41] The young men soon found it useful to rent a room off campus, in the Davis Building on Main Street, above the Star movie theater, where they could hold parties and dances; they invited everyone to a masquerade ball to celebrate Halloween in October 1924.

In November 1923, Makosky helped found the Black and White Club, with the avowed purpose of forming a fraternity that would be officially recognized on campus for its service, as well as its social aspects: "to foster a more perfect fellowship among the student body of this college; to strive for a bigger and better school thru bigger and better men." As he noted later, "The purpose was to be so valuable to the college that the club would be recognized as no liability, but an asset—even a necessity. A newspaper was planned as . . . one step in making the college change its mind about secret societies."[42] By 1924 the club had taken the Greek name Pi Alpha Alpha. In February 1924, the Bachelors, or Alpha Gamma Tau, was formed; and in 1925, a group of preministerial students formed a "preachers club" to help the college "be more intensely Christian," which took the name Delta Pi Alpha. The women also formed groups, the first, in 1922, being the WW Club (for "Why Worry?" although some apparently thought it meant "Wild Women"), which would become Sigma Sigma Tau in 1936. The JUG ("Justice, Unity, Good Fellowship") Club, formed secretly in the fall of 1923 and made public on campus in February 1924, took the name Delta Sigma Kappa a year later. Phi Alpha Mu was formed in 1926.

While the college officially stated as late as 1931 that no sororities or fraternities were allowed on campus, eight thriving social and service groups with lofty ideals met weekly, pledged new members, held social events, announced and reported their activities in the *Gold Bug*, entertained faculty and administrators, and proudly listed their members and their respective crests and symbols in the annual yearbook of 1924 and thereafter. By mid-decade the groups were pressuring the faculty and trustees for formal recognition, and various organizations sent signed petitions to this effect. The Bachelor's Club noted in its June 1925 petition, reported in the board of trustees minutes, "If we are to fully compete with other schools in our progress towards that higher goal of success, the need of such organizations is very obvious. . . . We lack the social spirit among the students which is the outstanding factor among student life in other institutions. . . . While we are progressing in other ways should we not take our opportunity in progressing along this line?" The WW Club went further and petitioned for a chapter of a national sorority, Pi Beta Phi. The trustees appointed a committee to study the matter at their June 1925 meeting, and *three years later* concluded that introducing national fraternities and sororities on the campus would not be wise because it would lead to the establishment of private fraternity houses and additional expenses for students. The local organizations that already existed on campus were apparently tacitly accepted, although no formal approval seems to have been given. An interesting sidelight to the discussion about these new groups is that in February 1926, the WW Club asked permission to award a cup to the organization with the best scholarship. The faculty thanked the group for the thought but turned it down, citing too many existing awards. Perhaps this was a gentle rebuke of the social groups that existed without faculty approval.

Apparently, in the early years, new members were added to the fraternities by a fairly simple process. Harry O. Smith '30, who joined the Black and White Club as a freshman in 1926, described the process he remembered. Members would suggest to a committee the names of college men they knew and deemed of high quality. The membership committee in turn would present a slate of nominees to the chapter for a vote, and those elected would be verbally invited to join. There was no formal rushing, bidding, pledging, or hazing.[43] This was probably not the case with all groups, for a 1926 WW Club newsletter to its alumnae refers to "pledge stunts" and "ordeals to be passed through" by the pledges. And what amounted to an inter-sorority council had been formed to firm up rules for rushing and bidding and establish dates for rush and initiation activities.

An article in the October 20, 1926, *Gold Bug* commented on the various social groups on campus: The Bachelors were considered the varsity training club and met in Alumni Hall. The members of Gamma Beta Chi were hard-working and studious men but also "social butterflies" who met downtown. The Black and White Club had persuaded the student body that they were the "intelligentsia" of the campus. Delta Pi Alpha was the group of prospective clergymen who met "when the spirit called them." The women of Delta Sigma Kappa met in McDaniel Hall and considered themselves to be the best on campus. The WW Club also met in McDaniel Hall and were a hearty group with prestige. The JGC was conspicuously absent and apparently was not considered in the same category as the other groups.

Several groups associated with students' home areas were formed, as well. There was a North Carolina Club, a Harford County (MD) Club, a Frederick County (MD) Club, a Dorchester County (MD) Club, and the WAGs (drawing students from Washington, Allegany, and Garrett counties; sometimes called the Mountaineers).

Other ongoing extracurricular activities included the College Players (first formed under the direction of Dorothy Elderdice and continued under

The College Orchestra, including French professor Bonnotte,
seated second from left, c. 1925

Esther Smith), the men's and women's student government organizations, the orchestra, the choir, the debating society, and the Jesters. This last male group presented musical and comedy programs on and off campus and in 1923–24 was under the general direction of Samuel Schofield while John Makosky figured prominently as both a comedian and a mandolin player. In early May the Jesters were joined by the Powder Puffs, a recently formed campus female singing group, to present a concert over station WGBA in Baltimore. Dr. Ward delivered an address appealing for contributions from alumni and friends, and 12 songs were performed by the groups and individuals. During the event, many people telephoned and telegraphed their good wishes and encouragement.

As Makosky noted, the need for a weekly school newspaper as a vehicle for student expression was keenly felt, and the Black and White Club had been formed partly for that purpose. On January 22, 1924, the *Black and White*, vol. 1, no. 1, appeared. Sterling Edwards was editor, John Makosky news editor, G. Hall Duncan sports editor, and Charles Bish business manager. An editorial explained the reason for the club's formation and its proposed activities in addition to the newspaper. Included in subsequent issues were weekly schedules of campus activities (including the meeting of the Black and White Club in room 140, Ward Hall), sports scores, an occasional article on the history of the college, and many advertisements to fund the newspaper (a financial success), including announcements by the Opera House of "High

Class Vaudeville," a showing of *Birth of a Nation*, and a production of the play *Way Down East*. In March the newspaper created a furor on campus by denouncing the "degrading and childish" initiation rites of the JGC. The editor claimed that the group served no purpose, had no value to the college, and should turn itself into a purposeful organization. Not surprisingly, many letters to the editor and rebuttals from JGC members followed. The issue was revived in the fall when the new editor commented, "The initiates of JGC, supposedly clever, intelligent, promising, and upstanding young [senior] women, have disgraced themselves, their classmates, and the college in the eyes of every beholder of their shameful conduct. . . . The initiation should not be flaunted in the eyes of the college again."[44] With this first fall issue of 1925 the newspaper was turned over to the college, a new staff was created, and the name was changed from the *Black and White* (from the riddle "What's black and white and read all over?") to the *Gold Bug*, after a naming contest among the students. Makosky commented on this transition:

> *In May 1924, Bish, Edwards, and I went to Dr. Ward with a plan to turn the newspaper over to the college with its financial problems solved for the future. . . . Dr. Ward accepted gracefully for the college—We have always thought that he took into account that we were all juniors and wanted to make sure that we wouldn't next year be printing a self-supported and thus completely independent series of comments on the college and the administration; the probability, however, is that he, too, saw that the college needed a newspaper.*[45]

With the success of the *Gold Bug* now assured and the realization that funding for two college publications was problematic, the student body met in Smith Hall in October 1926 and unanimously voted to discontinue the *Western Maryland College Monthly* and to merge its staff with that of the *Gold Bug*. This was brought on in part by lack of student interest in writing for the literary side of the *Monthly*. The merger was quickly brought about, and the weekly *Gold Bug* continued to provide a place for written expression by students, although not in the same form. The monthly publication, after 39 years, had lost its relevance to a changing college. The weekly publication usually contained campus news; at least one page of "humor" ("This piano reminds me of Asia Minor. It is quite ancient, for a fact, and it's got a dead C in it");[46] and a column devoted to "College Chatter," which included announcements of parties and small events on campus and noted who had visited whom off campus. Much space was also given over to various sports events, as well as musical and dramatic productions. There were many advertisements, including large ones for Chesterfield cigarettes.

Throughout the decade hazing of freshmen continued to "evolve" and

⤙ CHAPTER 7 ⤚

be tacitly sanctioned by the college. Whereas earlier decades had seen efforts to stamp out hazing, a well-organized program of rules and regulations now held sway. During the decade the term "Rat" came to be applied to freshman men, and even the new women students underwent some weeks of "indoctrination." Rules for new women students in 1926 required that their hair must not be curled, they must go to breakfast, they must wear black stockings and green bows in the left shoulder, they must carry dictionaries, and they must not have any pictures of men in their room. The men were required to wear red ties, part their hair on the right, and carry matches; they were not allowed to converse with or date women students or wear knickers.[47] The *Gold Bug* of October 3, 1929, presented 19 rules for freshman men and reported on the bonfire and "entertainment" (songs and skits) that had been coerced out of the young students, goaded on by the sophomores. While each year, the sophomore class tried to be more "clever" in their requirements, the general tone of the rules was to harass the "frosh" without much real introduction to the college. For example, the men of the class of '33 "must not wear knickers except with green socks," "must not smoke on campus, except in rooms," "must not pass under the 'sacred arch,'" "must learn all the inscriptions on Lewis Hall," "must learn the names of all Varsity football men and their positions," and "must wear 'Rat Caps and Ties' at all times except on Sunday." The only positive requirement was that the students were expected to "acquaint themselves with the principles of the Honor System and the student government." Freshman members of the football team were exempt from the rat rules.

The editors of the 1926 *Aloha* reflected on the hazing of the entering class during the fall of 1922, remembering that the "boys were manhandled, boards were freely used." There had been freshman punishment nights and "paddling parties." But they also noted that "the hazing was always given and received in good spirit and 'Freshie' soon found himself acclimated to his new environment." That may not have been entirely true, for in March 1926, an incident occurred that could have escalated into tragedy. A freshman, Charles Foutz x'29, son of a well-known Westminster doctor, apparently took two pistols to a hazing event because he did not approve of the methods of the sophomores and wished to frighten them out of their plan. Foutz was promptly suspended by the student council for bringing the firearms to campus. A local paper reported the incident and quoted Dr. Foutz: "It was merely a joke. Charles does not approve of the hazing methods employed at the school. He did object to being struck by boards. He took to the school a pistol which lacked its magazine and another containing several blank cartridges."[48] The young Foutz was reinstated when the facts of the case were presented to Dr. Ward (who noted that the council had exceeded its authority since hazing was prohibited at the college) and continued his studies, later managing the college bookstore for many years. By February 1927, hazing had apparently gotten more out of hand, and President Ward announced in chapel that it would no longer be tolerated. The sophomores promptly responded by paddling and clipping the hair of eight freshman day students. Freshman hazing, often physical and especially of men, would continue in various forms and for extended periods of time (often well into the second semester) until World War II, and "rat rules" would remain in effect for freshmen until the 1960s, when enough entering students refused to cooperate, and the practice finally died out.

The absence of dancing on the WMC campus had become a sore point with students. A *Gold Bug* editorial of February 1924 noted that all the other state colleges allowed it. Dancing, the paper noted, was a "prominent form of recreation" and would be "beneficial to the mental, moral, and physical life of the college."[49] President Ward several times discussed the issue with the trustees. He even went so far as to survey students and parents (including many Methodist ministers), finding that 95% wanted it. Armed with these data, he again broached the subject in 1929, but the board still would not permit dancing on campus. After 1925, the *Gold Bug* regularly contained reports of fraternity dances and parties held away from the campus. The first Military Ball was held at the downtown Gamma Beta Chi Club in 1927.

In a similar vein, women students began to demand the right to smoke, part of larger freedoms being demanded at the time. President Ward stated to the board that "many young women seem to think that they have just as much right to smoke as men, and so they have."[50] The trustees turned down the request.

When the weather turned snowy, students enjoyed sledding or "coasting" on boards and mattresses down the back hill of the campus to the athletic field. One student described the experience: "Swish! Walk a mile." They also occasionally sledded down Main Street hill, striving to get the longest run all the way to the railroad tracks in the center of town. On Saturday, January 10, 1925, tragedy struck when a double-decker bobsled carrying seven students and faculty collided with an automobile at Union Street at about 10:15 P.M. Deep ruts in the snow prevented both sled and automobile from turning to avoid the crash. Lynn F. Gruber '26 (1902–25) was in front steering the sled and received such severe head and neck injuries that he died without regaining consciousness soon after reaching the University of Maryland Hospital in Baltimore. Mathematics teacher Bertha Hart '21 was seriously injured, as was Merillat C. Wills, daughter of Prof. Wills; both women were transported to

Maryland General Hospital in Baltimore early Sunday morning. (Hart, whose jaw was crushed and leg fractured, did not return to her classroom until November.) Chemistry instructor Ruth Warren '24 and Adelaide Shriver of Taneytown (a nonstudent) received cuts and bruises, while history professor James Ranck's nose was badly broken. Only Frederick Warren, dean of men, escaped without injury, although he was rendered temporarily unconscious.[51] A local newspaper reported Dean Warren's account of the accident: "There was no chance to escape when the automobile came in sight. . . . We hardly had time to realize what was happening before the crash came. I lay no blame on the driver of the car. He was keeping to the right, and our swerve to the left made the accident unavoidable."[52] Scores of students and instructors were sledding that evening, and many came to the assistance of the injured, including football coach Kenneth Shroyer, who pulled Gruber from under the automobile. Gruber's death cast a pall over the campus, for he was a popular student and center on the football team; he was preparing to enter the Methodist Protestant ministry upon graduation. In May 1925, the Black and White Club, of which he was a member, established the Lynn F. Gruber Medal for proficiency in extracurricular activities. It has been awarded each year since then to a graduating senior. A month after the accident, a toboggan slide and ski track were constructed down the back hill of the campus, and students sped down them without incident or injury.

That tragic student death was not the only one the campus faced in this decade. In April 1923, just a few weeks prior to his graduation, Randall Otho Stone committed suicide by hanging himself from the balcony of the gymnasium.[53] He had been editor-in-chief of the *Monthly*, president of the class of 1923, and captain of the ROTC company, and his sudden death was a severe shock to his classmates. In December 1926, J. Edward McKinstry '27, an active and popular member of the senior class, was killed when struck by an automobile while he was walking near a friend's home in Baltimore County. In November 1927, during his freshman year, Joseph Stevens Mills '31 fell out of a third-story window in Owings Hall, suffering a broken back and subsequent paralysis. He was removed to Maryland General Hospital and then to his parents' home in Alabama, where his condition gradually worsened; he died October 26, 1928. He was the son of J. Bibb Mills '95. Two members of the class of 1930 also died before their graduation: Elizabeth Ohler Gillelan (of double pneumonia) and Edgar Howarth Covington. The decade also witnessed several bouts of serious illness on the campus. In the spring of 1921, a case of diphtheria closed the campus for a few days, and all men were vaccinated. Pneumonia also plagued students from time to time, particularly in 1923. In January 1929, influenza struck the campus, and the infirmaries were full. And in 1930, epidemics of scarlet fever and mumps plagued the residence halls. In a time before antibiotics and penicillin, such illnesses were more readily accepted as facts of life.

On March 20, 1925, history was made when a U.S. presidential inaugural address was broadcast live by radio. The *Aloha* staff arranged for speakers to be installed in Alumni Hall so that the college community could gather and hear the address by President Coolidge.

In any society, customs and traditions often evolve gradually without formal or official action to create them. Such was apparently the case with the college's Alma Mater. The song that had been in use for some years (since about 1901), sung to the tune of "Maryland, My Maryland," seems to have been gradually supplanted during this decade by a new song entitled "Western Maryland! Hail, All Hail!" (adaptation attributed to Dr. Herbert L. Rich, professor of chemistry [1902–4] in the *Gold Bug*):

College Ties can ne'er be broken
Formed at W.M.C.
Far surpassing wealth unspoken
Ever may they be.

Chorus:
Western Maryland! Hail, all Hail!
Echo softly from each heart.
We'll be ever loyal to thee
'Til we from life shall part.

When our college days are over
Round our hearts shall cling
Memories of our Alma Mater,
Every day shall bring.

But our life is swiftly passing,
Soon its course is run.
What e'er our lot we'll ever cherish,
Friendships here begun.[54]

In student handbooks (first published in 1913), the old Alma Mater is included along with the new song until 1924, when the new song is called the Alma Mater (it is also so listed in the 1925 *Aloha*) and the old one is not included. One can surmise that the former song had been difficult to sing (some of the lines were quite "tongue twisting": "And make the blue arched welkin ring" and "Shall haunt us whate'er else beguiles"), and many of the

Homecoming c. 1925; note the Geiman farm buildings in the background.

verses describing student life and memories may have been deemed no longer applicable or relevant to the 20th-century college. Whatever the reasons, the new Alma Mater, sung to the tune (slightly modified) of "Far Above Cayuga's Waters" (the Cornell University Alma Mater), was adopted by mutual consent and remains the college's song to this day (with a few modifications in 2003 to reflect the new college name).

The origin of the long-standing name for the athletic teams, Green Terrors, has been debated for decades, but the most definitive centers on a football game in 1923. For the first three decades of the sport, a local athletic hero could have been called "a worthy wearer of the green and gold" and the team was referred to as "the Methodists," "the Marylanders," or "our boys."[55] In October 1923, at a game with Washington and Lee University in Lexington, Virginia, the WMC team, under Coach Ken Shroyer, was called by their opponents the "Green Terrors" because they were a "rugged, battling crew with indomitable fighting spirit."[56] The name apparently was considered appropriate, as recorded in a story by Preston Grace '26:

After one of the games two players of the opposing team were heard discussing the merits of the Terror squad. One said he could not see the reason for the name, "Green Terrors." The other one, nursing a black eye, said that they sure were "Terrors," but for the life of him he could not see the connection of the "Green" because they were anything but green. This is a fair example of how they strike "Terror" in the hearts of the foe.[57]

Although not officially recorded as a tradition, the "kicking post" on the corner of College Avenue and Main Street by Alumni Hall seems to have played a part in many students' lives, especially the women, for it marked the boundary of the campus beyond which they could not legally walk. A student of 1924 wrote, "We draw nigh the time-honored telegraph pole at the corner, where there is a sacred rite to be performed. As we land some resounding kicks on its well worn base, our minds are filled with visions of the future . . . as we see mentally the crowd of souvenir hunters feverishly tearing splinters from it because we were known to have kicked it in the past."[58]

A May Day celebration had been held on campus for some years, usually in mid-May rather than on or near May 1. *The Black and White* of May 15, 1924, noted that all classes and the preparatory school participated in various dances. The 1927 May Day event featured a king and queen as well as the traditional May Pole Dance.[59] By 1928 the ceremony settled into the format that was maintained for the next 40 years: a queen, duchesses, heralds, a May Pole dance, and a program or pageant.

Class songs continued to be popular and are recorded in the yearbooks of the decade, although the traditional yells seem to have begun to die out during this time, the last recorded yell appearing in the 1923 *Aloha*:

Ray! Ree! Row! Rah!
Ray! Sis! Boom! Bah!
Ou polla, alla pollou,
We're the class that's tried and true.
Est altissimum, ac nobilissimum,
Always true to W.M.C.
Semper memor, nihil compar,
Nineteen hundred and twenty three.

The 1925 *Aloha* contains only the class song, but Katherine Richards Tillman '25 shared the class yell with her son, H. Richards Tillman, who wrote it down:

Boom Chic a lac
Boom Chic a lac
Rickity Ax
Rickity Ax
Co Ax
Co Ax
Wha Who Wha
Wha Who Wha
We are the Class that is alive:
19 Hundred and 25

On the other hand, certain activities were created during this decade that would become traditions for 50 years. Since about 1920, the spring farewell events for senior women included the Rose Cup ceremony, held in the summer house (Carpe Diem), where each senior received a rose from an underclass student. At times this was accompanied by a pageant and music, but the ceremony would be modified as the years passed. On the evening of May 27, 1926, the freshman women created a new activity honoring the seniors, which they called Lantern Chain. Carrying green and gold lanterns, the freshman women formed lines and escorted the senior girls to Hoffa Field. Then they marched around in the darkness forming the class numerals visible by their lanterns. Several songs were sung, and then the freshmen formed a *W* and an *M* and sang, "Adieu to seniors," after which they escorted the seniors back to the dormitories. Each lantern was autographed by a senior, and the lanterns were then packed away to be used the following year.[60] This soon became a much-loved spring tradition for the college women. The 1926 *Aloha* reported the establishment of a college ring that year, as well as the start (or continuation) of the tradition of caroling prior to the Christmas holiday break. Alas, one long-standing tradition was discontinued in 1928 when the Oratorical Association disbanded. No longer would there be an oratorical contest among the colleges of Maryland. Another 19th-century college activity had outlived its usefulness.

The decade saw many changes in the athletic program of the college. The *Monthly* duly reported the various sports and early on declared that too much attention was being paid to football and baseball and that basketball deserved more attention. For the first half of the decade, the various teams produced mediocre records, with a few unexpected successes from time to time. The 1921 football team played eight games but won only one, against Drexel 14–0. The basketball team was forced to play its local games in the armory downtown, since Yingling Gymnasium was much too small for intercollegiate competition. The 1921 baseball team played eight games and won two. A rifle team was formed in 1922 and competed rather successfully with 11 other colleges, each firing on its own range and exchanging its scores by telegraph. A few actual matches were held at the University of Maryland. In the winter of 1924, the college became the first in Maryland to field a wrestling team, under Coach Harvey Hall. Apparently, the team made a fine showing at West Virginia University, although they lost 25–0. Soccer also made its appearance on the Hill, when a freshman club team with no coach played the midshipmen of Navy (1–1), Franklin and Marshall (2–3), and Franklin High School (2–0). The following year, 1925, with a player-coach, the team played four games, winning all four. The subsequent season showed a 3–5–1 record.[61]

All of this began to change by mid-decade. The football team, under Coach Shroyer, had its best season in some years, winning seven of nine games, and seven players were named to the All-Maryland Team. Baseball had a better season than before, and soccer, track, and tennis were drawing increased interest from the student body. As the athletic program grew, the Alumni Advisory Committee on Athletics, headed by Robert Gill, determined that a player eligibility code was needed to stave off problems that were beginning to crop up in larger institutions. The code was published in the *Alumni Bulletin*[62] within a larger article about Western Maryland athletics, one of several written by guest columnist W. Wilson Wingate '18, sportswriter for the *Baltimore Sun*. In December 1925 the popular Shroyer refused to sign a new contract as head coach and director of athletics, a post he had held since 1922. He was offered a salary raise but declined to continue (it was thought that he was moving to a larger school, in Pennsylvania). Ward and Gill (who had just been elected a trustee) set out to find a new football coach and athletic director, and they found him in the person of Richard Cresson Harlow (BS '11; MS Pennsylvania State College, where he had been an All-American tackle). The new coach and athletic director, hired at a salary of $3,000

Coach Richard Harlow

(only slightly less than President Ward's), was also an ornithologist and had previously been at Colgate and earlier at Hamilton. He was formally introduced to the student body at a special morning assembly on April 13, 1926, and spoke on what was needed for good athletics: sportsmanship, cooperation, study, determination, and courage on the field.[63]

By the fall, Harlow had raised soccer to varsity status, and the football team was rated one of the strongest in the state. It beat Loyola of Baltimore in Baltimore Stadium 33–0, and the students had to be discouraged from tearing down the goalposts. The following week, it beat Bucknell 40–0. At the end of the season, the Terrors had racked up 206 points to their opponents' 30, beating Gettysburg, Dickinson, Swarthmore, Washington, Loyola, and Bucknell. Their only loss was to Holy Cross, 14–20, which was considered a moral victory because the Terrors had more first downs and completed passes and gained more yards. Unfortunately, all the games had been played at sites off campus, and the students complained about having to travel to the games in Baltimore and elsewhere. It was evident that Harlow had made the Western Maryland football team into one of the best in college history—indeed, probably the best team in the East. Robert Gill continued his support for the football program by hosting a dinner for all the members of the team in Baltimore. The team was ranked by the *New York Times* along with the University of Chicago, Drake, Fordham, University of Georgia, Georgia Tech, and Tulane. One of the stalwarts of the team, Orville E. "Greasy" Neal '29, was tapped to play in the Shrine East-West game in California. In January 1927 the college joined the Eastern Colleges Athletic Conference, which included Gettysburg, Dickinson, Franklin and Marshall, Muhlenberg, and Ursinus. During this era four football players qualified for All-America honors: Paul L. Bates '31 in 1929 and 1930, Charles Havens '30 in 1929, Orville Neal in 1926, and Nathan Weinstock x'29 in 1927.

Under the coaching of Faith Millard, the girls' varsity basketball team began to make strides, as well. Playing Gettysburg, Towson Normal School, Bryn Mawr, Frostburg Normal, and several club teams, the 1926 team won ten games and lost three, amassing 392 points to their opponents' 253. One of the stalwart members of the team was Roselda Todd '28. They continued their winning streak during the remainder of the decade.

In the spring of 1927, Harlow introduced boxing to the campus, and the first intercollegiate match was held March 12 with the University of Pennsylvania in Philadelphia. Harlow took over the baseball team, as well as the boxing team. His assistant with the football team was H. Barnett Spear '22, who was also the basketball coach. A newly formed club team in lacrosse won its first game 3–2. In March 1930, Gill announced that Harlow had signed a five-year contract, much to everyone's relief and joy. While the Trustee records listed Harlow's salary as $3,000, his contract (found in the college archives) actually guaranteed $6,000, the additional compensation being paid by the Athletic Association, which included Gill, C. Twigg '11, J. F. Reese '13, and W. F. Thomas '98.

On November 11, 1927, the Terror football team played an All-Army team (composed of players from a number of regional army bases) in a game in Baltimore Stadium before 23,000 screaming spectators. Army had been favored to win because three of the Terror players were injured, but all three ultimately played, and Army lost the game 48–0. Maj. Gen. Douglas MacArthur, a friend of Gill from the Rainbow Division in World War I, presented the engraved sterling silver trophy to Capt. "Greasy" Neal at the end of the game, the first of its kind ever won by a WMC team.[64] (The MacArthur Cup is safely preserved in the college archives. It may not have been totally coincidental that the college awarded an honorary LLD degree to Gen. MacArthur in 1929.) The 1927 season concluded with the Terrors winning all but the first game (Washington and Jefferson 15–6), scoring 213 points to their opponents' 21. Nathan Weinstock would go on to be line coach at George Washington University and head coach at the University of Baltimore in 1929. He was also selected to play on the All-East Team in the 1928 Shrine East-West game and was considered one of the best football players and best tackles in the history of WMC football. Charles Havens was called "one of the greatest fighting centers in the country." Orville Neal was described as one who "has spread fear to the hearts of all WMC's opponents" and a great All-American captain.[65]

The 1927 soccer team ended the season with 4 wins, 4 losses, and 2 ties. In the winter of the 1927–28 year, wrestling opened its first intercollegiate season. The basketball team ended its season with 12 wins, 9 losses and was ranked the second-best team in the state.

The 1928 football season, Harlow's third, was not quite as successful, the team losing to both Temple and University of Maryland. But the soccer team made great strides, also losing only two games, to Army (the best team in the East) in a game under lights at West Point and to Baltimore Polytechnic, and winning six matches with such schools as Towson, Franklin and Marshall, Lafayette, and Haverford. The 1929 season ended 5–4–1, one of the losses to Penn State. One of the players of this era was Harry O. Smith '30, about whom a story is told that he kicked a ball into the opponent's goal from his own goal box almost 100 yards away. Smith, a large man with a very strong foot, verified this feat but noted modestly that he had the wind with him.[66]

The fall of 1929 saw the football team, captained by Charles Havens, go undefeated in all 11 games, scoring 184 points against opponents' 19. The team allowed only three touchdowns. On the schedule that year were University of Baltimore (34–0), Georgetown (7–0), Temple (23–0), Albright (21–6), St. John's (20–0), Loyola (35–7), Mt. St. Mary's (6–0), St. Francis (PA) (7–0), Muhlenberg (7–0), and University of Maryland (12–0). Four of the games were played in Baltimore Stadium. Havens was named to several All-American teams, Paul Bates was named to several All-East teams, many players were named to the All-Maryland team, and Charles "Rip" Engle also played. Engle was also captain of the small 1930 basketball team, which won one game.

1929 undefeated football team;
Capt. Charlie Havens is in the middle of the front row.

An article entitled "Harlow—A Hum-Dinger Coach," written by Will Wedge for the *New York Sun* in October 1929 (and reprinted in the *WMC Bulletin*) said of the coach and the team,

> *Harlow is football coach at Western Maryland. He has never been blessed with extraordinary material. His team is a light squad this season, average weight 168-pounds. He has developed two splendid players: Capt. Charlie Havens, 185-pound center, from Rome, N.Y., and Paul Bates, 178-pound end from Los Angeles. How does this tiny academic school off in the woods come to have players from such distant spots as the Empire State and the Pacific Coast? Friendship is the answer—the friendship Harlow has built up during the last eighteen years. Men who have played with or under Harlow delight in recommending boys to his tutelage. . . . Havens, the captain, is high in all his classwork. He was advised to go to Western Maryland by an old Colgate friend of Harlow. High school boys from other states who know a little football are thankfully received at W.M.C., for football is not played in the high schools of the State of Maryland, soccer being the only game allowed. Paul Bates picked Western Maryland because he attended Franklin High School, Los Angeles, coached by Frank Hess, a fullback at Colgate under Harlow's reign there. Charles Engle, another W.M. end, came to Harlow for football guidance and counsel because his uncle played the other tackle on the team at Penn State when Harlow won All-American recognition there. . . . Harlow takes his W.M. footballers a-hunting bird eggs as part of the early field routine. A lot of the boys have become enthusiastic amateur naturalists. . . . Harlow teaches his boys something besides football. Among other things, he teaches them never to swear. Swearing frightens birds. No naturalists are cussers and Harlow can't see that cussing helps on the football field. . . . Harlow's teams are well conditioned above all else. They have to be with a limited number of subs.*[67]

The 1929 boxing season ended with wins in six of eight meets, and the team placed third in the intercollegiate matches held at Pennsylvania State College in March. At that meet Harlow was elected president of the Eastern Intercollegiate Boxing Association, and during that same winter Western Maryland was admitted to the prestigious Intercollegiate Boxing League, joining the Naval Academy, Penn State, Syracuse, Pennsylvania, Virginia, and Boston.

In four years Richard Harlow had put Western Maryland College on the athletic map in both football and boxing and had elevated the role of athletics on campus higher than anyone dreamed possible.

Buildings and Grounds

At that special meeting of the board on February 18, 1921, President Ward recommended beginning a special campaign to raise $35,000 to create a new athletic field on the recently purchased Geiman farm. Not surprisingly, given the alumni pressure, the project was approved, and the campaign was soon under way. Perhaps equally unsurprising, by June $24,000 had been collected from many alumni long frustrated by the limited athletic facilities of the college, and so the contract was let, with the new complex to be finished by the end of the summer. Delays slowed its completion, so that it was not formally dedicated until the 1922 Commencement. The catalog for 1921–22 declared the field "one of the most complete and up-to-date athletic fields in the eastern part of the United States. The field contains over five acres; . . . a quarter-mile running track, fourteen feet wide, with a hundred yard straightaway; proper watering facilities, and ample space is provided for tennis courts. The field will be fully equipped for all branches of sport . . . for both men and women."[68] Soon after it was dedicated in special ceremonies featuring a spectacular pageant, it was announced that, because of a $6,000 contribution from Arthur P. Hoffa toward the erection of the grandstand, the new athletic field would be named Hoffa Field. By the time everything was completed, the whole project cost $50,000.

At the same meeting, Ward proposed a regrouping of buildings as part of a plan for a "Greater Western Maryland." Seven new buildings were in the plan, as well as an enlargement of Lewis Hall. The grouping (two new dormitories for men and two for women, a gymnasium, a science hall, and a religious education building) would front on to Main Street, with Lewis Hall the main focus. The other buildings would be built around the old Main Building, and when the whole grouping was complete, the Main Building would come down, leaving a quadrangle inside the grouping. The board approved this ambitious plan and decided that the first of the new buildings to be constructed would be a dormitory to accommodate 125 women, because the space was urgently needed. Ward envisioned the new building as also providing an infirmary for women, rooms for the Home Economics Department, a social parlor, and a few rooms for teachers. He went further to explain how the building could be paid for. Scholarships would be sold at the rate of $75 per year, and if 1,200 were sold, the building could go forward. This plan was approved, and by September 600 scholarships had been sold. The board authorized moving ahead with the building and further authorized the borrowing of $85,000. Six months later, the architect Montgomery Anderson had designed a building, and the Southern Steel Construction Company had been awarded the contract, for

*Artist's rendering of President A. N. Ward's campus plan
for a "Greater Western Maryland"*

$110,622. When heating, wiring, plumbing, and furnishings were factored in, the cost would ultimately be about $140,000. Early on, it was decided to name the building for Dr. McDaniel, perhaps at the urging of the alumni who had prophesied such a building name a decade earlier. As Ward said in the campaign prospectus for the building, "He gave his life to this school, and in honoring him in the way we propose, we do honor to ourselves." In October 1922, at the opening of McDaniel Hall, McDaniel was again lauded in the *Monthly* as one who "plays an important part in the forward trend of affairs of the college." He "has been, and is, one of the foremost men in directing the advance towards the Greater Western Maryland." He has "a personality which prompts the admiration of learned men, the respect of students, and the love of all."[69]

In 1921, the board decided that after Mr. Geiman's lease ran out in April, the Geiman property should be stocked and run as a farm to supply the college. The initial cost of $1,500 provided 2 horses, 5–6 cows, 40–50 pigs, chickens, and such.[70] At the board meeting the following year, it was reported that the farm had shown a profit of $123, or a 4.73% gain on the investment of the $26,000 purchase price. In 1930 the board considered the purchase of another farm, as the Geiman farm (a good portion of which had been made into the athletic field) was inadequate for the college's growing needs.

In March 1922 Miss Troy and Mrs. Stover opened a tearoom on the ground floor of Hering Hall to the delight of students and faculty. The profits were to go to the Student Loan Fund.[71] Later, the tearoom location would be occupied by a grill.

During the summer of 1922, Terrace Hill, the grand mansion of Westminster built in 1873, owned by the John L. Reifsnider Sr. family and situated across Main Street from Alumni Hall, came on the market, with an asking price of $19,000. After several months of offers and counteroffers, the college was able to purchase the property for $15,000. It was noted prophetically at the June 1923 board meeting that this property "likely will prove a valuable asset in the future." At the same time, two lots on Union Street were purchased from the Rinehart estate for $1,500 each. During the academic year 1922–23, the mansion was rented out for $900. In the June 1923 issue of the *Monthly*, an advertisement appeared for the Gray Gables Inn (the remodeled mansion), serving à la carte breakfast from 8 to 9 o'clock, and special dinner and à la carte service from noon to 8 P.M. The inn was run by Mrs. George Wills, and the Wills family moved into the house and lived there for several years. Later, Mrs. Louise Hamrick, the college dietician, and then Mrs. Edwin Miller were the managers. The inn was the scene of many student group activities, which were reported in the *Gold Bug* during the latter part of the decade.[72] An editorial in the *Gold Bug* of November 1929 commented that the College Inn (as it was called after further refurbishment) was quite suitable for all social functions, including club teas and banquets. It was also a place to entertain overnight guests, since it was equipped in such a modern and luxurious fashion. The students were enjoying it because it was a place to supplement the usual lunch or dinner fare or get a complete breakfast after arising late. The *WMC Bulletin* commented, "Alumni and

Reifsnider mansion, "Terrace Hill,"
purchased by the college in 1922

friends will find here exceptional accommodations, for short or long periods in all the seasons. Open fireplaces and comfy chairs when the air is chilly, . . . benches, trees and breezes when it is warm; and good food at the right prices always."[73] The inn would continue until the mid-1930s. Since that time the house has been used for a variety of purposes and has had several names.

In May 1924, the trustees' Buildings and Grounds Committee surveyed the campus and reported the following items:

- *Old Main was in good shape, but no money should be spent to paint it, since it would "soon" be razed in the new college building plan.*
- *There was a need for a new gymnasium and dining room to accommodate the growing student body.*
- *The reception hall in McDaniel Hall needed furnishing.*
- *The seminary building and property might be obtained if the seminary moved closer to Pennsylvania Avenue—this would allow the college campus to be united more harmoniously.*[74]

The State of Maryland appropriated $125,000 for a science building in 1924, provided the college raise $250,000 for its endowment. Following a successful endowment campaign, this funding was released, and plans for a new science building and dining hall were under way. The board authorized an additional borrowing of $85,000 in May 1928 so construction could begin. Science Hall was completed by June 1929 at a total cost of $177,506.88. The building contained a kitchen and offices in the basement, a dining room to hold all the boarding students on the first floor, classrooms and a small assembly room on the second floor, classrooms and a biology laboratory on the third floor, and several departmental offices distributed on the second and third floors. Schofield pointed out that in order to receive the state appropriation, Maryland law required that the college give a mortgage to the state for the land on which the building stood. This mortgage contained a clause requiring the college to return the money to the state if the building were used for any purpose other than a science building.[75]

Science Hall was completed in 1929.

With a remaining debt on the building of $79,865.57, President Ward asked the state for help, arguing that WMC prepared the most high school teachers in the state (equal in number to those prepared by all the other Maryland colleges and universities combined), but Governor Ritchie, a good friend of the college, wrote back that it would not be possible for the state to issue bonds for a private institution (the others being Washington College and St. Johns College).[76]

In 1926, when the preparatory school closed, Levine Hall became a dormitory for senior men and was used as such for 13 years.

The first of several exchanges of property between the college and the City of Westminster took place in 1929, when College Avenue, a city-owned street that connected Main Street and Pennsylvania Avenue and ran in front of Alumni Hall, Baker Chapel, and the Library and Administration Building, was turned over to the college in exchange for a triangular piece of property in front of the Reifsnider mansion, so that New Windsor Road could be extended to Main Street (Taneytown Road).[77] The irony in this transfer is that most of the triangular property would be traded back to the college in 2002 for another piece of college property along Uniontown Road when that road was widened and became the main exiting road from the city.

FINANCES

From September 1920 to June 1930, enrollment had steadily grown, from a low of 214 to a high of 422, with an average of 356. Male enrollment had grown from a low of 87 to a high of 190, with an average of 161, and female enrollment from a low of 127 to a high of 240, with an average of 195. These figures did not include enrollments of the preparatory school (which closed in 1926), in the education extension program (which grew from 57 in 1921 to a high of 110 in 1930), or in supplementary and special courses (about 30 at mid-decade).

President Ward reported in February 1921 that the enrollment (in both the college and the preparatory school) for the past year was the largest in college history: 297, with 237 boarders. Students were clamoring for enrollment, and some had to be turned away. Indeed, 12 students had already applied for the 1921–22 session (students didn't apply a year in advance in those days). By the June meeting, he felt that the college could easily grow by 200 students, because the demand was so great. A year later, boarding students had to be limited to 335 (175 girls and 160 boys) due to space, the first time that had happened. The old parlor, or social room, was fitted out to house 20 girls during the school year. Clearly, the college was on the rise.

Also on the rise were costs, and so increases were approved in tuition, room, and board in 1921, from $300 to $350, and again in 1922, to $400. These were the first increases in a number of years and were overdue. Two years later, in 1924, fees were again raised, to $500, since the previous tuition covered only 39% of costs of education; fees remained stable for the remainder of the decade.

At a special board meeting called for December 16, 1921, a financial campaign for $400,000 was approved: a $250,000 general appeal, $150,000 from foundations and the M.P. Church. It was allocated as $85,000 to pay off the debt on McDaniel Hall, $100,000 for a new boys' dormitory, $50,000 for a gymnasium or science hall, and $165,000 to the general endowment.[78]

At the June 1922 board meeting, Ward, perhaps emboldened by the success of the fund-raising for McDaniel Hall, recommended that the campaign goal be raised to $600,000, with $200,000 hoped for from the Methodist Protestant Church and $400,000 from a general campaign. The board approved the recommendation. A new dining hall was now in the long-range scheme. Ward also reported that he had appealed to the Maryland Annual Conference, which approved a campaign to raise an annual amount of $1 per member in each church or charge. In addition, the General Conference of the church (of which, not coincidentally, T. H. Lewis was president) had, for the first time, placed the college in the denominational budget for the coming quadrennium. Finally, some significant support might be forthcoming from the church that claimed the college as "its own."

A year later, as the campaign was getting into full swing, the president recommended that the goal of the campaign be raised to $1,100,000, to build two new boys' dormitories, another girls' dormitory, a dining hall, a gymnasium, a science hall, and additions to Lewis Hall, the Library and Administration Building, and Alumni Hall; provide more houses for professors; liquidate the McDaniel Hall debt; and put $350,000 in the endowment. In his presidential report to the board in 1924, Ward proposed enlarging the college to 500 boarding students. A special event was held on November 20, 1925, when Mabel Garrison returned once again to present a gala concert as her contribution to the campaign fund.[79]

Throughout the decade, the emphasis was on building the endowment while also building new buildings. When Ward assumed the presidency, the endowment was about $275,000; throughout the next several years, campaigns would bring in funds, and it continued to grow on its own, so that by 1924 it stood at $330,672. But Ward had a goal of raising it to $500,000, the minimum to keep the college's accreditation. He knew that this would also bolster a request for a grant from the Rockefeller Foundation's General

Education Board. At a special meeting of the college board in December 1924, it was reported that the General Education Board would give $125,000 to the college for the endowment if the college raised an additional $375,000 for the endowment by December 31, 1928. The board approved moving forward. Ultimately, the college was able do this, with a slight time extension, so that the endowment rose by almost $500,000 by 1929, to a total of $826,937. By the end of the decade, it stood at $861,823, a remarkable growth given the building projects undertaken at the same time.

President Ward reported to the board in 1929:

The campaign to raise $500,000 for endowment has been successfully concluded. The appropriation of the General Education Board has been paid over in full to us. [But] in bringing the campaign to a successful conclusion, in order to secure the appropriation of the General Education Board, I had to assume personally [by borrowing] $7,340. Of this amount $5,196 have been paid, leaving an unpaid balance of $2,144. I propose to put on a vigorous campaign for the collection of these outstanding subscriptions, but I am not hopeful of the outcome. It looks as if I shall have to add that much to my own personal subscription.[80]

In talks with the Rockefeller Foundation, it had been suggested to Ward that if the income from the endowment were used to raise faculty salaries immediately, the foundation would consider a $10,000 grant in future years to assist in that need. Ward told the board, "I strongly urge that in every way possible we shall do our best toward placing this college in the very front rank of the colleges in this section."[81] This was approved, and faculty salaries began to rise, although not as fast as Ward wished. At the beginning of the decade, the average faculty salary was $1,485, and by 1930 the average was $2,500, reflecting about a $100 raise each year. About three-fourths of the faculty lived in rooms (or houses) on campus and received their meals, as well. Perhaps not surprising for the times, female faculty were paid about two-thirds of the salaries of the male faculty. In 1921 the total of all faculty salaries was $31,200, but by 1930 the budget amount was over $100,000, reflecting both the doubling of the teaching staff and the rising salaries.

Another measure of institutional growth was the rising yearly budget, which reflected anticipated expenses (based on projected income). At the beginning of the decade, the budget was about $85,000; by mid-decade, it had grown to about $138,000, and by 1930, it was over $150,000.

State support for the college was always somewhat unreliable, and in June 1921 Ward expressed concern to the board about possible cuts in state aid. He was concerned that the college remain full (indeed, it was almost overflowing and needed more space) to offset any decrease in state aid. Ten years later, he reported that the state appropriation was $50,000, whereas in 1925 it had been $22,700. The state actually increased its aid over the decade, to keep pace with the rising costs of state scholarships for tuition, room, and board.

The college was the beneficiary of two bequests during the latter years of the decade. Mrs. Harriet Brooks Jones left the college $10,000 to endow a scholarship in memory of her husband, Harry Clary Jones, who had been a student at the college in the 1880s. (He had later graduated from Johns Hopkins, in 1889, received his PhD in chemistry there in 1892, and was professor of physical chemistry there until his death in 1916.) A scholarship in chemistry and another in physics were created for rising senior students in those fields. The second scholarship gift, of $15,000, came from Miss Grace Lee (the Lee Scholarship), along with a valuable mineral collection to be known as the John W. Lee Collection. The class of 1929, at the suggestion of its Commencement speaker, Roger Whiteford '06, erected the flag pole on the campus in front of Old Main at a cost of $116.27. Whiteford donated the first flag, and the 1929 class paid for replacements, at least for a while.[82]

By the end of the decade, Albert Norman Ward, the visionary, looked ahead to an extended "Greater Western Maryland, 1929–1939" with a goal of 500 students. In his report to the trustees in 1929, he commented on the financial needs to implement this ten-year program and proposed raising admissions standards, lowering faculty loads, establishing four grades of faculty rank, establishing sabbatical leaves for faculty, providing money for attendance at professional meetings, and establishing a pension system. A year earlier, he had proposed and received approval for still another increase in the large campaign goal, to make it $4 million, $2 million for the many buildings in the plan and $2 million for the endowment.

Interestingly, the first comprehensive audit of the college's books was done in fall 1928, by Wooden & Benson. A new set of books and bookkeeping processes were set up to go into effect in September 1929.[83]

Major Events

The first major event of the new administration was the 51st Commencement in 1921, which included the inauguration of Albert Norman Ward as the college's third president. It took place on Wednesday, June 15, 1921, in Alumni Hall and began with the usual orations. The women's valedictory was given by Bertha I. Hart, who would take over the mathematics classes from Dr. McDaniel the following September. An address by Johns Hopkins University president Frank J. Goodnow followed.

Then the presidential inauguration began, with greetings by Rev. Frank T. Little representing the trustees, Hon. Robert R. Carman '03 representing the alumni, Otwald Bryan Langrall '21 representing the students, Samuel M. North representing the Maryland State Department of Education, and James M. Cain of Yale University representing the score of visiting delegates from other colleges and universities. President Emeritus Lewis presented Dr. Ward as the new president, and Ward responded by noting his indebtedness to his predecessor, his love for the college, and his plan to carry on the good work through clear vision and devotion to service. The ceremony then went on with the awarding of undergraduate honors and degrees, Governor Albert C. Ritchie handing out the diplomas. Surrounding this main event during the week were the usual oratorical contests, music recitals, Class Day exercises, president's reception, freshman class classics "cremation," Baccalaureate Service, Christian Associations Service, and society reunions. Also packed into Tuesday were the annual meeting of the board of trustees, an outdoor production of Shakespeare's *Much Ado about Nothing* attended by over 500 people, and a performance of Handel's *Messiah* by the college Choral Club and local church choirs (a combined chorus of over 200 voices), accompanied by an orchestra, all under the direction of Miss Elise Dorst. An admission of $1 was charged to begin an organ fund for Alumni Hall. Following the Commencement exercises, an alumni dinner and association business meeting concluded the day.[84]

The following year, on Saturday, June 10, a warm and sunny day, the formal dedication of Hoffa Field was held before an audience of 5,000. In keeping with the great optimism that abounded in the country at the time, that World War I was to be the "war to end all wars," Dorothy Elderdice had written

Hoffa Field dedicatory pageant, 1922;
Martha Manahan '23 is third from left.

The Sheathing of the Sword: A Pageant of Peace, a community drama featuring 1,000 participants, to follow the formal dedication. Governor Ritchie made a short congratulatory address, expressing the hope that future generations of students at the college would win many victories on the new field. Charles R. Miller '81, an old baseball player, presented a baseball and bat to Paul H. Frantz, captain of the 1923 baseball team. W. P. Roberts '03, a former football player, presented a football to John A. Hafer, captain of the 1922 football team. J. Samuel Turner '09, former track and field athlete, presented a track symbol to Frederick S. Waesche, captain of the 1923 track team. Then a fanfare of trumpets heralded the arrival of "Peace" attended by representatives of the four ages, Ancient, Medieval, Modern, and Future. "Prosperity" and "Progress" entered to music provided by the Westminster Band, seated on a dais in the center of the field. Events of world peace were then presented, including the restoration of the Olympic Games; the Roman Pax Augusta; and the birth of Jesus, the Prince of Peace. Other victories for peace featured 250 young girls singing an international hymn, a ceremonial Indian dance by 100 girls, and a Pan American number. The finale, proclaiming "Peace Universal," featured schoolchildren dancing and singing and the freeing of white doves.[85]

On February 7, 1930, hundreds of alumni gathered at the Lord Baltimore Hotel in Baltimore for the 25th Annual Mid-Winter Banquet and to celebrate the 50th anniversary of the graduation of William McDaniel: "Fifty years, fifty glorious years filled to the limit with service and sacrifice, fifty years crowned with noteworthy achievement, fifty years blessed with the interest and affection of his associates, fifty years as an Alumnus of Western Maryland College."[86] The toastmaster for the evening was Charles E. Moylan '17, music was provided by the Bob Iula Orchestra, and special guests for the evening included the 1929 championship football team, including Charlie Havens, Paul Bates, and Charles Engle. A number of alumni, including Charles Miller, fondly remembered McDaniel with kind words and reminiscences of days gone by. Dr. McDaniel was presented with a large volume of testimonial letters from alumni, and his formal portrait, painted by William Wirtz, was unveiled by his three-year-old grandson, Ober S. Herr Jr. It was to hang in the lobby of McDaniel Hall. After all the words had been spoken about him, McDaniel took the podium and remarked, "It is good to be living!" He thanked the Alumni Association for again honoring him as it had 15 years before, "when I felt you had paid me all the honor you could, and more than was my due." He then told a little story on himself:

> *[All of this] quite overwhelms me and my first impulse would be to tell you how unworthy I feel myself of it all, and I would, but for a bit of experience that comes back to me from my very early school days; I*

Portrait of Vice President
William Roberts McDaniel

recall the incident quite vividly. I was once reciting in High School and by some chance gave an answer that exceeded the teacher's expectation, whereupon he proceeded to compliment the diligent study which that answer seemed to indicate. Conscious it was due more to good fortune than to diligent study, I was about to disabuse his mind of the impression he had, when the shrewd boy who sat next to me brought me up with a sharp nudge, and whispered, "Don't spoil it." And so I presume it would be equally rash on this occasion for me to insist that this all is a piece of good fortune rather than a reward for real merit. It is your verdict, and I must not spoil it.

He concluded his remarks by paying tribute to each of the three college presidents he had served and saluted President Ward for "great deeds already accomplished and those yet to be. . . . Great things for a Greater Western Maryland."[87]

An event occurred in March 1930 that, while not directly related to the campus or the college, certainly gave the college stature and publicity and placed it at the forefront of liberal arts colleges in the United States because of the prominent efforts of President Ward. Ward had been active for several years in rejuvenating interest in and funding for the liberal arts in America, and he had been the driving force behind the planning for a conference held in Chicago at which representatives of all liberal arts colleges across the country were present. The conference featured addresses by the presidents of Carleton College, Duke University, and Franklin College; the U.S. secretary of the interior; and the executive secretary of the Association of American Colleges. It was called to consider the relation of the college of liberal arts to higher education in the United States in 1930, and to set forth collectively the needs of colleges of liberal arts in order that they could function better. Also discussed were plans by which an appeal might be made to the American people for the financial resources necessary for the liberal arts colleges to serve the million students then in college, as well as those expected in future years. Ward had written a pamphlet (in 1929) entitled *Making Provision for the College of Liberal Arts—The Small College*, which had been published and distributed to the delegates nationwide. The document approached the subject from the small college viewpoint, showing the status of such institutions in the field of higher education. It did not attack the larger institutions of learning but outlined how the smaller colleges were providing a significant service in educating those students being turned away from the larger schools and explained why they should be funded more generously. Following the conference, which was reported to President Herbert Hoover, Hoover wrote to Dr. Ward, heartily endorsing the liberal arts college movement:

I am glad to learn that a movement is being organized to preserve the more vital of the smaller colleges, which have been suffering from the competition of the great universities. The small college is irreplaceable in many of the services it renders and the inspiration it gives. There is a great need for such institutions, for in them is preserved to a high degree that personal relationship of teacher and student so difficult to maintain in the universities. They develop character and provide a rounded cultural equipment to students who do not wish professional specialization. I warmly commend the effort to maintain these institutions, which have played and should still play so large a part in the development of leaders of American Life.[88]

A final major event of the decade occurred following the 1930 Commencement. The Alumni Association met in Alumni Hall to conduct its annual meeting and to induct the newest alumni into its fold. On this occasion Dr. and Mrs. Ward were celebrating the 35th anniversary of their graduation from the college and their 25th wedding anniversary, and Ward was celebrating his 10th year as president. Mrs. Ward was presented with a basket of flowers by her classmate Nannie Lease, and Murray Benson, now the editor of the *Alumni Quarterly*, presented Dr. Ward with an engraved gold seal of the college. In his remarks Benson noted, "Few men can boast of so consistent a record of unselfish public as has been yours." He highlighted Ward's many accomplishments over the past ten years and then stated, "You have been variously hailed as a visionary, a dreamer, a builder of castles in the air, a promoter, an enthusiast, a genius. Upon the authority of the record of your great accomplishments during this busy decade, we hail you as an intensely practical man. . . . You have refused to let us look behind as you have led us forward. You have refused to rest upon the laurels already won. You have taught us to think upon a higher level and in larger terms. You have captured our imagination with a plan for a yet greater Western Maryland College that completely eclipses all that we have now. We've been growing steadily and surely but we have only grown that we might grow more."[89]

Conclusion

The decade had been one of great activity and forward movement for the college. The curriculum had been modernized and standardized; the college had received regional accreditation; extracurricular activities had been extended to include fraternities and sororities, while older, 19th-century-style societies were gradually fading away; student government and student life

Aerial view of the campus c. 1923

had been enhanced with the liberalization of student rules; a new athletic field, new women's dormitory, and new science building and dining hall had been erected; a successful campaign for $625,000 had raised the endowment from $250,000 to nearly $900,000; the college's enrollment had doubled; the faculty had doubled and was better paid and better prepared academically to handle the curriculum than ever before; and the college's athletic teams were becoming known as significant adversaries on the East Coast. Albert Norman Ward had returned to his alma mater to find an established institution with an honorable history, one that had maintained the standards of education of an earlier time and was highly regarded within the State of Maryland. He had arrived when a revolution in higher education was taking place in America and new standards were replacing old ones. He had, as Benson noted in his 1930 laudatory address, "set to work to transform 'ancient good' into 'modern good.'" The history of this decade is one of transformation or metamorphosis for the college, as it reinvented itself for the 20th century. It was now poised to move forward to achieve Ward's goal of a "Greater Western Maryland."

C H A P T E R *7* E N D N O T E S

1. Minutes, Maryland Annual Conference, 1935, 130.
2. WMC President's Report, 1924, 24–26.
3. WMC board of trustees minutes, May 31, 1930; WMC faculty minutes, October 7, 1929; *Gold Bug*, October 3, 1929, 1; *Alumni Quarterly*, September 1929, 3.
4. *The Hill,* February 1973, 9.
5. Ibid., June 1973, 31.
6. John Makosky, *English Department Newsletter*, May 1985, 1, college archives.
7. Ibid.
8. Schofield and Crain, *Formative Years*, 100.
9. Wills, *History of Western Maryland College*, vol. 2, 59.
10. Interview, Sarah Corkran Smith, July 16, 2003.
11. Interview, Virginia Holland Nicoll, July 16, 2003.
12. Schofield and Crain, *Formative Years*, 120.
13. *WMC Monthly*, April 15, 1921, 5.
14. WMC board of trustees minutes, June 1927.
15. Schofield and Crain, *Formative Years*, 96–97.
16. WMC board of trustees minutes, February 18, 1921.
17. Ibid., June 14, 1921.
18. WMC President's Report, 1924, 2, 5.
19. Schofield and Crain, *Formative Years*, 97, 99.
20. *Gold Bug*, November 2, 1926, 2.
21. Schofield and Crain, *Formative Years*, 99–100.
22. WMC board of trustees minutes, June 13, 1922.
23. WMC President's Report, 1924, 5–6.
24. *WMC Bulletin*, July 1923, 2.
25. *WMC Catalogue* 1925–26, 29–33.
26. *WMC Bulletin*, June 1927, 2.
27. *Gold Bug*, November 2, 1926, 1.
28. Schofield, Report to Board, 1930.
29. Makosky, *English Department Newsletter*, May 1985, 1, college archives.
30. Page 7.
31. January 15, 1921, 19.
32. Interview, Blanche Ford Bowlsbey, June 2002.
33. Page 26.
34. *Gold Bug*, February 17, 1925, 2.
35. 1925 *Aloha*, 253.
36. Interviews, Bowlsbey, Nicoll, and S. C. Smith.
37. April 15, 1920, 11.
38. *WMC Monthly*, October 28, 1924, 11.
39. *The Hill*, Spring 1999, 33.
40. February 26, 1924, 2.
41. *Gold Bug*, April 22, 1924, 3.
42. Ibid., November 14, 1947, 3.
43. Interview, Harry O. Smith, September 1998.
44. *Gold Bug*, October 7, 1924, 2.

45. Ibid., November 14, 1947, 5.
46. Ibid., March 10, 1925, 3.
47. *Gold Bug*, September 28, October 15, 1926.
48. *American Sentinel*, March 12, 1926.
49. February 12, 1924, 5.
50. WMC President's Report, 1929, 6.
51. *Gold Bug*, January 13, 1925, 1.
52. *Democratic Advocate*, January 16, 1925.
53. *Carroll County Times*, April 27, 1923.
54. May 2, 1935, 2.
55. *WMC Monthly*, December 1908, 17; 1916 *Aloha*, 100.
56. 1924 *Aloha*, 165; 1925 *Aloha*, 157.
57. *WMC Monthly*, December 1925, 29.
58. Ibid., March 1924, 8.
59. *Gold Bug*, May 4, 1927, 1.
60. Ibid., June 1, 1926, 2, 4.
61. Soccer records, 2005, Homer Earll.
62. May 7, 1925, 2.
63. *Gold Bug*, April 13, 1926, 1; *WMC Bulletin*, November 7, 1929.
64. *Gold Bug*, November 17, 1927, 1.
65. 1928 *Aloha*, 142.
66. Interview, H. O. Smith, September 1998.
67. *WMC Bulletin*, November 7, 1929, 3.
68. Page 32.
69. October 1922, 5.
70. WMC board of trustees minutes, February 18, 1921.
71. Schofield and Crain, *Formative Years*, 100; WMC board of trustees minutes, June 1922.
72. *The Hill*, April 1973, 6.
73. November 7, 1929, 7.
74. WMC board of trustees minutes, June 1924.
75. Page 110.
76. WMC President's Report, 1929, 2–5.
77. Ibid., 10–11.
78. WMC board of trustees minutes, December 16, 1921.
79. Schofield and Crain, *Formative Years*, 103.
80. WMC board of trustees minutes, June 1, 1929.
81. Ibid., June 1922.
82. Schofield and Crain, *Formative Years*, 114.
83. WMC President's Report, 1929, 2.
84. *Democratic Advocate*, June 1921; Commencement program 1921, college archives.
85. *American Sentinel*, June 16, 1922.
86. *Alumni Quarterly*, vol. 1, no. 2, Banquet Issue, 1930, 1.
87. *Alumni Quarterly*, May 1930, 4.
88. Hoover letter, 1930, Ward Papers, college archives.
89. *Alumni Quarterly*, Summer Issue 1930, 5.

MAJOR WORLD EVENTS

1921

Warren G. Harding is inaugurated as 29th U.S. president.
Hitler's storm troopers begin to terrorize political opponents.
Somerset Maugham publishes his play *The Circle*.
Lytton Strachey publishes *Queen Victoria*.
Enrico Caruso, famous operatic tenor, dies.
Chromosome theory of heredity is postulated by Thomas Hunt Morgan.
Albert Einstein wins Nobel Prize for his discovery of the photoelectric effect.
Sacco and Vanzetti are found guilty of murder.

1922

Mussolini forms fascist government in Italy.
Soviet states form the USSR.
T. S. Eliot publishes "The Wasteland."
James Joyce publishes *Ulysses*.
Irving Berlin composes "April Showers."

1923

Teapot Dome oil scandal occurs.
Centers of Tokyo and Yokohama are destroyed by earthquake; 120,000 dead.
George Gershwin composes "Rhapsody in Blue."
John Maynard Keynes publishes *A Tract on Monetary Reform*.
President Harding dies and is succeeded by Vice President Calvin Coolidge.

1924

J. Edgar Hoover is appointed director of the Federal Bureau of Investigation.
Leopold and Loeb are sentenced to life imprisonment for kidnap-slaying.
Lenin, founder of the USSR, dies.
Sean O'Casey publishes his play *Juno and the Paycock*.
Pablo Picasso enters his abstract period.
George Gershwin composes the show *Lady Be Good*.
Mah-jongg becomes a worldwide craze.

1925

The Charleston becomes the fashionable dance.
Hitler reorganizes the Nazi Party and publishes *Mein Kampf*.
Noel Coward publishes his play *Hay Fever*.
John T. Scopes is tried for teaching evolution in Tennessee, defended by Clarence Darrow.
Theodore Dreiser publishes *An American Tragedy*.
Edna Ferber publishes *So Big*, which wins the Pulitzer Prize.
F. Scott Fitzgerald publishes *The Great Gatsby*.
Crossword puzzles become popular.

1926

Gene Tunney wins heavyweight boxing championship from Jack Dempsey.
"Jelly Roll" Morton's first recordings of jazz appear.
The Book-of-the-Month Club is founded.
Sarah Lawrence College is founded in Bronxville, New York.
Ernest Hemingway publishes *The Sun Also Rises*.
Kodak produces the first 16mm movie film.
A. A. Milne publishes *Winnie-the-Pooh*.

1927

Sinclair Lewis publishes *Elmer Gantry*.
I. P. Pavlov publishes *Conditioned Reflexes*.
Jerome Kern and Oscar Hammerstein II produce *Show Boat*.
Willa Cather publishes *Death Comes for the Archbishop*.
The Holland Tunnel connecting New York and New Jersey opens.
The first talking motion picture is released: *The Jazz Singer* starring Al Jolson.
Charles Lindberg flies a monoplane, *Spirit of St. Louis*, from New York to Paris in 33.5 hours.
Thornton Wilder publishes *The Bridge of San Luis Rey*, which wins the Pulitzer Prize.

1928

The New English Dictionary (begun in 1888) is completed in ten volumes.
Amelia Earhart is first woman to fly across the Atlantic.
The first Mickey Mouse films are produced by Walt Disney.
George Gershwin composes "An American in Paris."
Alexander Fleming discovers penicillin.

1929

Herbert Hoover is inaugurated as 31st U.S. president.
Ernest Hemingway publishes *A Farewell to Arms*.
Georgia O'Keeffe paints *Black Flower and Blue Larkspur*.
Einstein postulates his unified field theory.
Chicago endures the St. Valentine's Day Massacre.
The U.S. Stock Exchange collapses on October 28, "Black Friday"; world economic crisis begins.
Bell Laboratories experiments with color television.

1930

Marc Connelly publishes the play *Green Pastures*.
Noel Coward publishes the play *Private Lives*.
Robert Frost publishes *Collected Poems*.
Maxwell Anderson publishes the play *Elizabeth the Queen*.
Grant Wood paints *American Gothic*.
Pluto is discovered by C. W. Tombaugh of Lowell Laboratory and made the ninth planet.
Comic strips grow in popularity in the U.S.; "Blondie" is a particular favorite.

The Ward Memorial Arch was razed and rebuilt
on the corner of Main and Union streets in 1936–37.

C H A P T E R

THE DEPRESSION YEARS

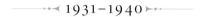

1931–1940

The world was enduring an economic depression. In the United States, drastic measures were eventually taken by newly elected president Franklin Roosevelt, which gradually put people back to work and the economy on the upswing. The repeal of prohibition, the Social Security Act of 1935, and the rise of organized labor made people feel a bit more optimistic about their lives and their futures. Europe was more in turmoil, as Hitler rose to power and by 1939 led Germany into World War II; refugees from Europe began to flow into the United States to escape the carnage. By the end of the decade, the economy had rebounded, Roosevelt had been reelected to an unprecedented third term, and concerns were rising about possible involvement in the European conflict.

At the college in Westminster, a number of cost-cutting measures were put in place early in the decade to balance the budget. Enrollments grew steadily, so that by the end of the decade, the college was 30% larger than in 1930. The faculty expanded slightly, and teaching qualifications improved. To house the larger student body, new dormitories were needed, as well as other facilities, and President Ward's plan for a Greater Western Maryland slowly continued to be implemented. Even though the college underwent a significant change in leadership due to President Ward's sudden death in mid-decade, it continued to march forward, raise its standards, and strengthen its already fine reputation.

FACULTY AND ADMINISTRATION

The faculty saw a number of changes brought on by resignations, retirements, and death. Walter B. Yount, professor of classics since 1912, died in 1932 after a year's illness. He had been president of Bridgewater College and a professor at Blue Ridge College in New Windsor before coming to Western Maryland. Ferdinand Bonnotte, known affectionately as "Jobby," longtime and admired professor of foreign languages [1897–1932], retired but, curiously, was not named professor emeritus, although he was awarded a retirement stipend of $600 per year, subject to yearly renewal by the board. He died in February 1935. In 1940 the venerable Nannie Lease, who had first come to the campus in 1904 to teach elocution and direct the women's gymnasium and who completed her tenure as professor of speech, retired at a monthly stipend of $60, again subject to yearly renewal. She, however, was named professor emerita and would remain so until her death, in 1958.[1] Retirement, at least for faculty members, was an economically tenuous and uncertain time until a fully funded pension program was implemented (along with Social Security) in the next decade.

New faculty who came to the campus during the decade and remained for an extended period included Frank B. Hurt [social sciences, 1930–65], Addie Belle Robb [history, 1930–48], Philip S. Royer [music, 1930–67], Roselda F. Todd [physical education, 1930–65], Evelyn L. Mudge [education, 1931–49], Evelyn Wingate (Wenner) [English, 1931–69], Milson C. Raver [physics, public relations, 1932–44], Joseph C. Willen [languages, 1933–66], Charles W. Havens [physical education, coach, 1934–57], John D. Makosky [English, 1934–73], Bruce E. Ferguson '35 [physical education, coach, 1935–56], Alfred deLong [music, 1936–69], James P. Earp [sociology, 1938–73], Helen Gray [home economics, 1938–64], William R. Ridington [classics, 1938–73], M. Louise Shipley '30 [art, 1938–72], Daisy W. Smith [home economics, 1938–63], and Oliver K. Spangler [music, 1938–73]. Over the decade the faculty grew from 50 to 56, and the number holding doctoral degrees increased from 4 to 16.

Several administrative changes also occurred. Fannie Stover, a longtime fixture on the campus, first as preparatory school teacher and principal in 1911, then campus social director, then assistant dean of women under Margaret Robinson in 1918, and finally dean of women in 1929, retired in 1937 and was awarded a $50 monthly stipend, which she received until her death only a year later. She was replaced by her assistant, Bertha S. Adkins [1934–42]. Frederick M. Miller, who had been dean of men from 1928 to 1937, was replaced by L. Forrest Free [1937–52], who would serve for the next 15 years. In 1939, Samuel Schofield, the dean of the college, changed roles and titles and assumed the newly created post of dean of administration. Taking on the new title of dean of faculty was Lloyd Bertholf, who had been dean of freshmen for 6 years.

Three stalwart staff members also died during this decade. Harvey A. Stone, superintendent of buildings and grounds for 48 years, died on November 18, 1934, after a short illness. His will bequeathed much of his property to the college. The newly created park and pavilion on the western edge of the campus were named for him as a memorial to his humble and loving service to the college.[2] The following year, the new power plant built on Union Street and put into use on February 27, 1935, was also named for him. Louise Bates Fisher '22 (1902–38), an honor graduate of the college, later a Latin teacher in Salisbury, Maryland, had returned to her alma mater in 1932 to be assistant registrar and editor of the *WMC Bulletin*. She died on January 11, 1938, after an appendectomy. Anna Isanogle, the college registrar (for 15 years) and wife of Dean Alvey Isanogle, died on October 14, 1938, after a short illness. In her memory, her husband made a gift of $5,000 toward the renovation of Levine Hall for music, and the recital hall was named the Isanogle Room.[3] Mrs. Isanogle was succeeded as registrar by Martha Manahan '23 [1938–66], the first woman to receive a WMC degree in home economics[4] and a home demonstration agent in Howard County. She had returned to the campus the preceding April as Mrs. Isanogle's assistant, following Miss Fisher's death. Cora Virginia Perry '36 [1938–77] was then named assistant registrar.

The most significant administrative change was brought about by the sudden death of President Ward on September 22, 1935, while preaching in the Bethel Presbyterian Church in Harford County, Maryland. While his death was unexpected, his health had not been good, and he had been seriously ill during the spring of 1932. The Sunday evening service at Bethel was a sort of homecoming for him; his immediate family were all present and witnessed his collapse in the pulpit due to a massive heart attack. The funeral service was conducted in Alumni Hall on September 25, and the large auditorium was crowded with representatives of the civic, religious, and educational life of the state, including Maryland governor Harry W. Nice. Pallbearers were professors Bertholf, Elderdice, Havens, Little, Makosky, Schaeffer, Schofield, and Speir. Members of the board of trustees were honorary pallbearers. Burial was in the Westminster Cemetery.[5] Eulogies were written by many groups and individuals. One said of him,

He believed and frequently expressed his faith that education is the

greatest asset of democracy and ignorance is its greatest foe. The faculty was inspired in finding in him a friend and a leader. A true estimate of his character by one who knew best designates him as a man of vision, of pre-vision, re-vision, and pro-vision. The problems of the depression were met with courage by increasing employment through building construction, meeting reduced income with changing contracts and aiding students whose families had met with reverses. Without his large-heartedness, many who would have been compelled to leave college were enabled to graduate. His building of the college as an institution was balanced by his personal consideration of the individuals within the faculty and the student body.[6]

The editor of the *Gold Bug*, Rosalie Silberstein '36, called him a "builder": of buildings, landscapes, educational opportunities, and character.[7] The faculty's memorial resolution noted his prominence in educational circles and the honorary doctor of laws that George Washington University had conferred on him in 1932. It also said of him, "None knew him but to love him; none named him but to praise him."[8]

Because of Ward's untimely death, the start of college classes was delayed until September 26, and, because Dr. McDaniel was not physically able to act as president as he had done so many times before, an Administrative Committee consisting of Dean Schofield, Dean Isanogle, and Assistant Treasurer Carl Schaeffer was appointed by the board of trustees to deal with the daily operation of the college until a new president could be chosen. By this time Dr. McDaniel was also too ill to continue his daily work in the treasurer's office, and Schaeffer was authorized to sign all checks, with countersignatures by the board president or vice president.[9] In October, McDaniel formally submitted his resignation, but the board would not accept it, noting that there was "no immediate urgency" to do so and that the "fine relationship now existing shall continue."[10] McDaniel's health continued to deteriorate for the next six years, and he spent much time in bed. But he did not lose his interest in happenings on the campus. On game days he sometimes sat at an upstairs bedroom window looking down at Hoffa Field while his old friend and former student Caleb O'Connor described the plays to him.[11] In November 1940 illness forced him and his wife, Ada, to move to their daughter Dorothy's home on Ridge Road, leaving the cottage that had been built for him on campus 45 years before. In a letter to the trustees, he again submitted his resignation as treasurer, thanking Prof. Schaeffer for carrying on so ably in his stead. The board refused to accept the resignation and reelected him but reduced his salary to $2,400 at his request.

At a special meeting on November 8, 1935, the board of trustees elected

Portrait of President Albert Norman Ward

Fred Garrigus Holloway,
fourth president

Fred Garrigus Holloway '18 (1898–1988) [1935–47] the college's fourth president, at a salary of $4,000. The trustees' presidential selection committee had received 15 (nonclergy) nominations for the office from various sources, including several college presidents and deans holding the PhD degree, but they chose someone they knew, who was also a Methodist minister. (Ordination was never a requirement for the presidency, only a tradition.) Holloway assumed the office on December 1 and was presented to the students and faculty the following day.

President Holloway was born March 28, 1898, in Newark, New Jersey, the son of Alice Garrigus and Frank D. Holloway. He entered Western Maryland College in 1914, receiving his AB in classics in 1918. He then attended Westminster Theological Seminary for one year before transferring to Drew Theological Seminary, where he received the bachelor of divinity degree in 1921. He also received a master of divinity degree on a special fellowship there. He married Winifred Jackson (1902–88) in 1923, and they had two sons, William J. '46 and Fred G. Jr. '47. Holloway served Methodist Protestant churches in Wilmington, Delaware; Baltimore; and Arlington, Virginia, before returning to the seminary in Westminster in 1927 to become professor of biblical languages, a post he held until he was elected president of the seminary in 1932. In that same year, the college conferred upon him the doctor of divinity degree. Three years later he returned to his undergraduate alma mater as president, following in the footsteps of the seminary's founding president, Thomas Hamilton Lewis. Holloway brought to the seminary and to the college a "unique combination of scholarly and literary gifts united with exceptional administrative skills."[12] Dickinson College honored him in 1936 by conferring on him an honorary doctor of laws degree.

The campus was saddened to learn of the death of Mary Ward Lewis on July 24, 1935, at the home of her daughter, Miriam Lewis Veasey '96, in Orlando, Florida. Daughter of the first president and widow of the second, as well as a member of the first graduating class, in 1871, Mrs. Lewis was eulogized by President Ward during funeral services on July 26 in Baker Chapel. Her close friend Miss Carrie Mourer '88 noted, "She sacrificed greatly to bring Western Maryland College through a critical time. . . . Mrs. Lewis taught some of the primary grades, advised in the culinary department and led the social life on the hill, besides attending to her duties of wife and mother. She was a rare entertainer and like her father . . . had an appropriate story or poem or quotation for any occasion. . . . There are . . . not many left of her generation and of her old-fashioned hospitality and geniality." She was buried beside her husband in the Westminster Cemetery and was survived by her four daughters and two sons.[13]

The board of trustees was very concerned for the welfare of Blanche Ward, widow of President Ward, following his sudden death, and appointed a committee to make recommendations. She continued to live in the President's House until spring vacation (the Holloways graciously remained in the seminary president's home not far away), and then she moved to the West Virginia Cottage on the edge of the campus for a few months before occupying the small cottage behind the President's House originally built for the ROTC commandant (after her death it housed the dean of men). President Ward's salary was continued through December, and then Mrs. Ward was paid a salary of $100 a month, with duties to be arranged by President Holloway, including planning campus gardens and redecorating buildings. At the annual board meeting on June 5, 1937, she was elected the first woman member of the board, a post she held for only a year before her death on July 13, 1938. It should be noted that President Ward had been encouraging the board to elect a woman and as early as 1934 had made such a nomination, which was not accepted.

The board of trustees welcomed some new faces during this decade, as well. Roger J. Whiteford '06 [1934–65], F. Murray Benson '17 [1936–63], William W. Chase '23 [1937–57], and Miriam Baynes Matthews '98 [1939–73] were among the group replacing such stalwarts as Lynn R. Meekins '82 [1922–33]; 50-year trustee Clarence F. Norment Sr. [1886–1937]; and Hugh Elderdice Sr. [1898–1938], who had died. Special honor came to board president James Straughn when he was selected as one of two bishops of the newly formed Methodist Church by the Methodist Protestant Church representatives at the Uniting Conference of Methodism in Kansas City, Missouri, in May 1938. Under discussion for years, and strongly encouraged by both President Lewis and President Ward, the unification was the merger of three Methodist denominations: the Methodist Protestant Church (1830); the Methodist Episcopal Church, South (1845); and the original Methodist Episcopal Church, founded by John Wesley. The new "Methodist Church" consisted of more than seven million members and had ten seminaries (of which the Westminster Theological Seminary was but one, instead of being the only seminary of the small Methodist Protestant Church).[14] Similarly, Western Maryland College, one of two schools related in some way to the Methodist Protestant Church, now joined a host of other Methodist-related institutions, including Goucher College, Duke University, Syracuse University, Northwestern University, Dickinson College, Emory University, Southern Methodist University, American University, and the University of Southern California, all seeking funding and support from the new larger church, which could provide more "patronage" for the many colleges related to it.[15]

CURRICULUM

With continued emphasis from President Ward and regular prodding from such faculty leaders as Dean Schofield and Dr. Bertholf, the college's curriculum saw ongoing revision during this decade. The faculty minutes record discussion of different curricular systems (including a four-course plan and the "Harvard system"), new methods of teaching, and common problems in the classroom. An innovative Curriculum Revision Committee, which included six seniors, six juniors, and four sophomores was appointed by Dean Schofield to get ideas for consideration by the faculty. The faculty for freshman courses met regularly with Dr. Bertholf, the dean of freshmen, and out of their discussions evolved a How to Study course given to all freshmen through the English Department.

By 1939, the requirements for a new bachelor of science degree were included. The degree was offered in biology, chemistry, and physics. The only significant difference between the BA and the BS was that for the BS ten more semester hours of work in the major were required and the basic requirements in social science were reduced somewhat. By this time the basic liberal arts requirements had been formalized; rather than being specified for each of the four years, they consisted of 60 semester hours of study distributed as follows: English composition and literature, 12 hours; science, 9 hours; foreign language, 12 hours; social studies, 15 hours; religious education, 3 hours; psychology, 3 hours; fine arts, 2 hours; and physical education, 4 hours. Military science was also required of all freshman and sophomore men.

Additions to the college curriculum also appeared during the decade. "Speech" was renamed and expanded to become "dramatic art," and business administration courses were added to economics. Physical education, in conjunction with biology, was now a possible major field, and coaching classes were open to both men and women. By the end of the decade, sociology would be separated from social sciences and become its own department, just as economics was in 1931.

Esther Smith [1926–70], who had helped transform the area of elocution and speech into dramatic art, fondly recalled Nannie Lease in an (undated) article in the *Carroll County Evening Sun*: "She was a lovely lady with a keen mind and a warm sense of values. I owe her much, because she instantly believed in me, trusted my ideas and gave me freedom to take her dream and turn it into mine. . . . I loved her for that." As dramatic art gradually grew under her direction, Miss Smith was keenly aware of the need for better stage facilities. Miss Lease had for some time directed one Shakespearean play each year, but out of doors and during the day. Miss Smith wanted to use the Alumni Hall stage for productions. She approached President Ward about putting curtains on the stage, and he agreed. Once the beautiful olive green proscenium curtains and cyclorama were in place by January 1933, she approached Ward about stage lighting. Years later, she told the amusing story of what happened next:

"Oh, Miss Smith," he said, "we can't afford any more expense." I knew it would be better not to argue, so I thanked him again for what he had done and quietly left his office. The next weekend, I packed my bag and headed for New York City. I knew plays closed practically every week and there must be some secondhand place where you could buy old stage lights cheap. So after several inquiries, I was directed to some God-forsaken place where I found a theater warehouse and bought, second or third hand, two floods, two spots, a balcony spot, two sets of footlights, and overhead strips. I paid for them myself, and got the entire set-up for an unbelievably low price. I was pleased as punch! Early the next week, I had another conference with Dr. Ward and told him what I had done and asked him if, by any chance, he would like to buy them from me. (The curtain man had estimated a lighting plan for Dr. Ward at a price of several thousand dollars.) When I told him I could let him have them for $200, his eyes gave a little twinkle and then a big smile, and he began to break. "Miss Smith," he said. "You win! Promise to let

me have a private preview when you get them set up." So much for those
years of trials and tribulations, when we had very little equipment. . . .
I remember our first stage dimmer—it was a crock of salt water and
open-ended electrical wires. We were brash enough to try anything. But
we actually achieved some remarkable effects in our production of "Alice
in Wonderland" with this primitive use of courage and imagination.[16]

President Ward's dream of establishing a School of Religious Education
was realized in 1931 when continuing-education programs were created
primarily for ministers and for those preparing to be directors of religious
education in the churches. Dr. Lawrence C. Little [1931–45] was hired as the
dean of the school. Little was a graduate of Davidson College, with a master's
degree from Duke University. He would go on to receive his PhD from Yale in
the philosophy of education in 1942. He came to the college from the post of
executive secretary of the Department of Religious Education of the Methodist
Protestant Church, was very active in religious education societies, and would
remain at the college as a professor of philosophy and religion until 1945, even
after the School of Religious Education was phased out in 1937 (perhaps a
casualty of the Depression) and courses in religious education were dropped
(by 1940). While he was on the campus, he also served as the coordinator of
the various religious activities and organizations.

As part of the home economics program, a nursery school was established
in March 1934, with Helen Gray as director, and operated during the second
semester in the Management House, which was now located in the West
Virginia Cottage, a brick house down the slope from the seminary. The
senior home economics majors, after completing their home management
practice sessions, staffed the school in the remodeled and refitted house for
the remainder of the term. Sixteen youngsters, children of faculty and staff
members, as well as of local residents, were enrolled in the morning program
and ranged in age from one and a half to four and a half years.[17]

In 1932 a summer session was established. Two five-week terms were held,
offering courses in biology, chemistry, education, English, French, history,
mathematics, physical and health education, physics, and social sciences. For
two years, during the second summer term, courses in religious education were
also offered for pastors, directors of religious education, seminary students,
church school teachers, and laymen.[18] This additional term proved effective
and produced more student enrollments; during the first summer 126 students
enrolled, and by 1938 the number had grown to 247. The summer session has
continued to the present day as a useful and financially successful adjunct to
the regular two-semester schedule. During the Depression, it provided a source
of additional income for a number of faculty members.

*Top of the Hill with Old Main and Smith Hall at right,
McDaniel Hall at left*

In a further effort to raise standards and improve student learning, the faculty instituted mid-term grades in 1930. The perennial problem of student absences from class continued to be discussed throughout the decade, and by 1936, a Committee on Absences was appointed, with Clyde Spicer appointed the absence officer to administer a number of rules. An interesting discussion took place in April 1936 when the faculty considered the possibility of eliminating classes on Saturday morning (when many of the absences occurred). Saturday classes, however, continued for another 30 years. In 1933 comprehensive examinations were instituted for those seniors desiring to graduate with honors, beginning with the class of 1935. These examinations would be in two parts: a three-hour examination in one's major and a two-and-one-half-hour examination in two student-selected subjects. The dreaded sophomore comprehensives were eliminated in 1938 because the results were not being used effectively, and the standardized test was no longer widely used. The students had generally done well on that test, however, in 1932 standing in the upper fifth of the 138 colleges giving the test and scoring highest in the areas of fine arts, history, and literature.[19] In 1937 a Committee on Admissions and Standards was created to consider student work and standards for academic success and failure. President Holloway reported to the trustees that the college had denied admission to 73 students from an applicant pool of 288 for the entering class of 1937, which was also the largest entering class in the college's history: 172. (The admission process had rarely turned anyone away until the dormitories became too crowded to admit more students.) Apparently, the process of raising standards worked fairly well, for in February 1939, the faculty discussed the reasons fewer A grades had been given the previous semester and what an A grade should mean. (This grade "deflation" contrasts with the grade "inflation" colleges faced in the latter 20th and early 21st centuries.) By 1940, the students were noting and reacting to the rising standards and commenting in the *Gold Bug* on the superiority of women students over the men, at least as reflected by the names on the Dean's List. They even took to task those 20 or so men they considered "nothing but a detriment to the college" because of their behavior and lack of academic ambition.[20]

Richard W. Kiefer, of the class of 1934 (a later graduate of Duke University Law School, prominent Baltimore lawyer, and college trustee [1967–2002]), who *earned* his A grades and graduated summa cum laude, remembered a class in modern European history with Dr. Whitfield in his senior year:

People took his courses with some trepidation because he liked to pick out a student in a classroom period and question him or her about a particular matter. It resembled an attorney's cross-examination of a witness. . . . During this particular period, the college (as had other colleges) adopted a policy of no formal final examinations at the end of the semester or year. A professor gave quizzes at any time and determined a person's grades from classroom performance, quizzes, and term papers. As we drew near the end of the semester, I had a strong hunch I should memorize all of the kings and queens of England from the time of William the Conqueror in the 11th century to the present. I did exactly that, and the next morning, when the Modern European History class convened, Dr. Whitfield announced that he knew what mark he was going to give every student except Mr. Kiefer. Then he said he would take the time right then and there to give me an oral quiz. The 20 or so other students settled back to enjoy the fun since they were not involved. Dr. Whitfield asked me to name ten European countries and their capitals. This was easy. . . . Then he said, "Mr. Kiefer, name all of the kings and queens who reigned in England from William the Conqueror to the present." You could hear my classmates gasp. Who in the world could do that? Well, I made it seem hard and took time to think a bit before naming each one. When I had finished, Dr. Whitfield said, "That will be all." The best part for me, however, was the reaction of the students. As soon as the class ended, they surrounded me to congratulate me and ask how in hell I could have known that kind of information. I think Dr. Whitfield wondered the same thing. I just smiled, made no explanation, and went on to my next class. Incidentally, I got an A.[21]

Cora Virginia Perry remembered those days, as well, especially the testing: "We didn't have final exams. We had 'unannounced cumulative quizzes.' Mr. Elderdice, my chemistry professor, would say, 'We've reached the end of our unit, so we'll have our first unannounced quiz tomorrow.'"[22]

David C. Osborn '42 remembered his professors and classes, especially during his freshman year. He was impressed that Dr. Bertholf came to the dormitory, sat on the floor with the freshman boys, and answered questions about life. He recalled Miss Robb lecturing at high speed, while Dr. Whitfield asked questions about the text and interspersed the discussion with personal thoughts and stories. He also remembered Dr. Wills, who taught him freshman English: "He liked to say that he never knew that damyankee was two words until he was 21. For a final exam he stood up and wrote, 'Outline the text' on the chalkboard." And Osborn fondly remembered Miss Snader: "[She] enjoyed preparing drama productions that she presented in competition with three other colleges and to which she invited the French ambassador as judge. WMC won the competition each year. I was allowed to kiss the heroine in the senior year while saying in French 'All the stars are falling.'"[23]

In 1935 the college began to award a master of arts degree (an earned degree in contrast to the honorific AM offered from 1874 to 1906). The 1935–36 catalog listed the requirements: a year of residency or equivalent; completion of 34 semester hours of course work; a problems or reading course in the field of the candidate's bachelor's degree major or minor that would lead to an essay or thesis (worth 6–10 hours); the remainder of the 34 hours taken in advanced (300 level or above) courses with a grade of B or better; and a general examination over two fields including the area of the essay or thesis. In each succeeding year until 1942, at least two and as many as five MA degrees were conferred. This program was short-lived, however; only 24 degrees were conferred before it was phased out in favor of a master of education degree program in 1940;[24] the first MEd was conferred in 1943.

At the annual meeting of the board of trustees in 1937, discussion focused on the three resolutions for raising the academic standards of the college, presented in Dr. Holloway's annual report:

- *To build as strong a faculty as possible, continuing efforts already being made in this regard.*
- *To develop a stronger student body, admitting "only such students as give promise of a successful career." [He noted that the college was now turning some applicants away and said that standards for remaining in school were also needed. He felt the college should strive to be better, not necessarily bigger.]*
- *To provide or improve the college facilities. [Specifically, he noted the*

need for a new gymnasium, more library space, and more comfortable
dorms, especially for men.]

The result of this discussion was approval to begin a campaign to raise
$250,000 for a new men's dormitory, a new field house, and an addition to
the library.[25]

Three efforts to improve the academic standing of the student body,
award student achievement, and stress higher standards occurred in this
decade when the Alpha Mu chapter of Beta Beta Beta, a national biological
honor society founded in 1922, was chartered and installed on campus in
February 1932, under the advisorship of Prof. Bertholf. This group met
regularly to hear scientific speakers and encourage scientific pursuits. In May
1935, a chapter of Tau Kappa Alpha, a national debating and public speaking
society, was established on campus, electing junior and senior members
who had participated in intercollegiate or intramural debates. Professors
Wills and Makosky advised the chapter. That same month, the Argonaut
Society was formed as a local academic honor society under the direction
of Dr. Bertholf. The name and Greek symbolism of Jason sailing the *Argo*
in search of the Golden Fleece were suggested by classics professor Edgar
Jenkins. The constitution for the society was formally ratified by the faculty
in January 1936. "Fellows" in the organization were those who graduated
cum laude or summa cum laude, but the activities of the group were carried
out by members known as "associates," who were candidates for graduation
honors or who had a B average in all their work at the college. The charter
group consisted of nine members who achieved graduation honors in
1935, but the first associate members, who were elected and initiated at the
first Argonaut banquet, held May 18, 1936, at the Carroll Inn, were Louise
Byerly, Marguerite Carrara, Cynthia Hales Gladden, Zaida McKenzie, Cora
Virginia Perry, Idamae Riley, Rosalie Silberstein, and Sterling Zimmerman.
Meetings were held monthly to hear reports of scholarly research, and the
year culminated in the induction banquet.[26]

STUDENT LIFE

Life at the college continued to improve from the students' point of view, as
societal rules were loosened and the young people were gradually treated
more as adults. Early in the decade President Ward apparently got tired of
waiting for the trustees to allow dancing on campus and quietly permitted
it himself. There is no record in any trustee minutes of it being officially
approved, but dances started to occur on campus, the first as the traditional

Halloween Party in 1930, given by the sophomore class. This was followed by the Junior Prom in February, an Inter-Fraternity Ball in March, the Military Ball in April, and the May Day Dance.[27] Dances were held in the Science Hall dining room and, after 1935, in the Girl's Gymnasium in Blanche Ward Hall, and have continued unabated (in some form) to the present day. Indeed, by 1934 the four fraternities and their Inter-Fraternity Council had set up a rotation for four campus-wide dances throughout the year: Fall, Christmas, Valentine's Day, and May Day. Smaller affairs like tea dances and fraternity hops were held in other venues, including McDaniel Lounge.[28]

Similarly, the question of whether fraternities and sororities were to be allowed on campus seems to have been answered by the students themselves. The clubs of the mid-1920s had evolved into local fraternities and sororities by the end of that decade, officially sanctioned or not. Although the catalog for 1930–31 specifically stated, "No fraternities are permitted in the college," there were four fully functioning local groups with Greek letters on the campus (and three sororities as well, two with Greek letters, in addition to the JGC). The catalog for the following year omits this statement, so one can conclude that the groups were in some way sanctioned, at least by the faculty and administration if not by the board of trustees. In the catalog of 1938–39 the

May Day festivities in the amphitheater in Harvey Stone Park,
back campus, c. 1936

323

six Greek-letter groups were finally mentioned and formally acknowledged as "social fraternities and sororities."

Life in the dormitories was still fairly spartan, as described by Richard Kiefer:

My father drove me to the Western Maryland Railroad station in Baltimore. I boarded the train and rode to Westminster with my trunk packed with clothes, sheets, blankets and other odds and ends. . . . My trunk and I got to the college some how [sic] and I found the room in the freshman dormitory, Owings Hall, to which I had been assigned. My roommate was Paul H. (Buddy) Myers ['34]. Our room was on the third floor, had two beds, two flat top desks, and a bureau. Each floor had a house proctor. Our house proctor was a football player named Harry (Hog) Benson, a hard, tough character who was guard on the football team. His major activity as proctor was to eat the goodies parents sent to the homesick children.

College life was a strange life at first, but we soon got accustomed to it. There were no showers in old Owings Hall, and we had to walk outside to Yingling Gym a couple a hundred feet away to take showers in the shower room in the basement. We walked down in bathrobes and slippers or only a towel around our waist. We went whether it was clear, raining, snowing, or freezing. We all ate in the dining room on the first floor of the new science classroom building. Meals were served by student waiters and waitresses who earned their board this way. At breakfast we sat at tables of our own choice, eating and leaving at will. Because of classroom schedules, lunch was cafeteria style. However, dinner was a different matter. Everybody gathered for 6 P.M. dinner and sat at an assigned table. Furthermore, girls wore dresses or blouses and skirts and men wore suits or jackets, ties, and shirts. All men students had to take R.O.T.C. for the first two years, and everyone had a uniform issued to him. It was permissible to wear the military uniform to dinner. This was important since there were some students who just did not own a suit. The dinner meal started with grace by Dean [Frederick] Miller, Dean of Men. Each student was assigned to a table for a period of six weeks, and the table seated ten people including at least one person from each class year. Also, each table had a faculty member or a senior student as head of the table. We could not leave the dining room until Dean Miller rang his bell, made whatever announcements he might have, and dismissed us.[29]

Apparently not everyone was as diligent about his dress as Kiefer, or maybe expectations deteriorated during his time on campus, for a *Gold*

Bug editorial of 1934 decried the slovenly dress of the male students and encouraged men to wear coats and ties to class and in the dining hall. The writer considered the habit of wearing athletic clothes, ragged apparel, linen trousers, and bedroom slippers unacceptable for college dress.[30]

Bedroom slippers and pajamas (and, of course, beanies) were required dress for freshman men for the annual pajama parade early in the fall, as part of their ongoing hazing, which was still in vogue. While freshman women seem to have been indoctrinated fairly quickly, men apparently needed more hazing, and regularly scheduled events such as the "color rush," the tug of war, the mud fight, the freshman-sophomore football game, and the traditional punishment paddling for breaking the rat rules continued during the decade. Some of the silly hazing traditions from earlier decades had been dropped by this time, although one *Gold Bug* editor bemoaned their passing.[31]

David Osborn recorded memories of his days at the college, especially during his freshman year:

Moving into McKinstry dorm [in 1938] gave no hint of the life that freshmen would lead in the months ahead. Little did I know that my colleagues on the second floor would regard those of us on the first as enemies, but wild nocturnal water battles ensured weekly, resulting in so much water flowing into the first floor corridor that it ran down on the bed of the college carpenter. A random bucket of water also came through our transom to soak carpets in our living quarters. Insulation was unheard of when McKinstry was built, with the result that bottles of ink from which I filled my Parker fountain pen froze solid on the coldest winter nights. On one such frigid night my roommate . . . came running in from a hazing initiation by his fraternity. Trotting several miles while clad only in King syrup and feathers, he had lost all of his body feathers, but sported a few on the top of his head. Whether bragging or not, I do not know, but he claimed to make excellent speed past the President's residence.[32]

Susannah Cockey Kiefer '33 and Kathleen Moore Raver '33 recalled some of the menus for the meals, which were under the direction of Mrs. Louise Hamrick, head dietician, who also ran the inn in Carroll Hall. Breakfast included scrapple with "strap" (that thick syrup to which generations of students had been subjected) poured over it. Creamed chipped beef on toast was another offering. While dinner menus varied (although served on a regular cycle) and featured meat such as pork chops, chicken, roast beef, and pork stew, the alumnae fondly remembered the baked goods, including pies and cakes, created by the resident baker. Later in the decade, in 1937, when Kathleen Moore returned to the campus as head dietician after training at

Johns Hopkins, she hired better cooks with restaurant experience, bought new kitchen equipment, added more vegetables to the daily fare, and created more diversity in the menus.[33] Also changed were the seating arrangements in the dining room. Students were no longer assigned to tables but could choose where they wished to sit and with whom. (Men and women were allowed to share the same table!) A *Gold Bug* editorial of February 19, 1938, took issue with this, noting that there was now a rush to gather at tables, and one did not get the opportunity to meet new friends across the classes. The *Gold Bug* later reported statistics on how much food was eaten by the boarding students in a month: 1,800 pounds of butter (for both eating and cooking), 100 large (two-and-one-half-pound) loaves of bread, and 6 tons of potatoes (425 pounds per day). It noted that for just a single meal, students consumed 1,500 hamburgers, 2,300 oysters, or 250 pounds of roast beef.[34] However, if the students were not sufficiently fed in the dining hall, they could stop in at the College Grille on the lower level of Old Main for sticky buns, cup cakes, cherry tarts, soups, sandwiches, and colas. Or they could wend their way downtown to Griffin's restaurant opposite the State Theatre, where light sandwiches, sodas, and sundaes cost 10¢–15¢, pies and soups went for 10¢, and a hot plate lunch cost 25¢.

Cora Virginia Perry remembered the women's curfew of the era:

When I was a student, after four years of 10 P.M. curfews, finally, on the last weekend of the college year, we seniors could stay out until midnight. It was then we discovered that everything in Westminster closed at 10 P.M., so there was nothing to do. We still wouldn't go in until the last minute, even if it meant sitting on the curb across the street, talking.[35]

Susannah Kiefer and Kathleen Raver also remembered some of the rules by which they were governed. As freshmen, they needed a junior or senior woman to accompany them as chaperone off campus. Freshman women could date, but a junior or senior couple had to go along with them. Students violating the "Victorian" rules were "campused" and their normal privileges temporarily removed. Kiefer and Raver remembered the dean of women, Fannie Stover, as someone who was difficult to deal with, had little understanding of young people, and would brook no protest or backtalk. They recalled the daily chapel between first and second periods in Smith Hall auditorium during their freshman year, for which students lined up alphabetically, men and women separate, and then filed in to be checked off by the professor in charge of attendance. A brief religious service was followed by announcements. Sunday service in Baker Chapel also required checking in, women at the door facing McDaniel Hall and men at the door facing Alumni Hall. Sunday services were moved to Alumni Hall in October 1932 to accommodate the growing student body, and a new attendance system with assigned seats was devised.[36] At about this same time, the 65-year-old requirement (established with the opening of the college) that all students attend a church in town on Sunday morning was abolished, as was the requirement to attend all concerts and lectures and daily chapels. President Ward encouraged students to attend, but they were now free to do so or not. The weekly chapels, now only on Sunday night and Monday morning, were still deemed necessary for the "successful integration" of the students.[37]

By 1930, the 60-year-old literary societies had combined into two, the Irving-Webster and the Browning-Philomathean. The groups continued to meet weekly for literary purposes and some oratory, but they were gradually holding less interest with the students; they quietly disappeared from the campus about 1935, no mention of them appearing in the catalogs or yearbooks after that date. The more social groups were popular, the fraternities averaging about 27 members and the sororities about 22 members per group. The women's groups met in McDaniel Hall, Delta Sigma Kappa and the WW Club in basement rooms and Phi Alpha Mu in a room on the third floor. The sororities and fraternities met on Tuesday evenings after dinner, a tradition that maintained until about 1970. Kiefer recalled his days as a fraternity member:

> When I was at [the college] from 1930 to 1934, there were no national men's fraternities, but there were four local fraternities, one of which was Gamma Beta Chi (GBX). Each fraternity was assigned a room in Alumni Hall, and the members could furnish it any way they planned, including a radio that could tune in the big bands playing at big hotels. At 10:30 every night all of the lights in all of the college buildings automatically went off to save expenses (times were tough for colleges like WMC). But, the lights in Alumni Hall were not part of the "lights out at 10:30," so fraternity members could go to the fraternity room after "lights out" to study, read, or whatever. In my sophomore year I was invited to join Gamma Beta Chi fraternity and did so.[38]

Two changes in the social organizations occurred in 1937 when the WW Club formally changed its named to Sigma Sigma Tau on November 2, and a second chapter of Gamma Beta Chi was formed on November 18 at the University of Baltimore.[39] This latter chapter seems to have been short-lived; nothing more appears about it. However, a second chapter would have made the fraternity a "national" organization, something the trustees very much wanted to avoid having at WMC. One wonders if they knew about it.

The students found new ways to amuse themselves as their lives became less structured. While May Day had always been the province of the women's

College Orchestra, 1939, conducted by Philip S. Royer '34

student government, in 1933 the male students put on a burlesque of May Day, set in ancient Rome, that spoofed all aspects of college life and personnel. Intramural Ping-Pong tournaments, staged by the fraternities, became the rage, and jigsaw puzzles kept people busy for hours in the lounges during the winter. For several years in the spring, the *Gold Bug* published its own spoof of college life with "The Old Mug."[40] In February 1936, the students were invited to the seminary next door to attend a production of *Ten Nights in a Bar Room* directed by Dorothy Elderdice. One can only wonder what the early college faculty would have thought of this production by *seminary* students, when they had denied permission for the Webster Society to perform it on the college campus in 1888. In November 1939 the students celebrated the official anniversary of Sadie Hawkins Day by holding a dance, the women inviting the men.

New clubs came into being during the decade, including the Chemists' Club (which evolved into Alpha Delta Lambda in 1939), the Art Club, the Camera Club, and the Men's Glee Club (45 voices) and Women's Glee Club (30 voices). This last group had existed for a while but was taken over by Alfred deLong when he arrived in 1936; he was accompanied on the piano by a colleague, Ethel Owen, whom he married in July 1937. Music had always held a large place on the campus, but its popularity grew in the latter part of this decade. The College Choir was expanded by deLong to about 50 voices and began to make radio broadcasts at Thanksgiving and Christmas, as well as performing regular concerts on campus, including a special production on Baccalaureate Sunday afternoon. The choir went on tour to New Jersey in

1939, ending with a concert at the World's Fair in New York. In 1940 they sang at a session of the General Conference of the Methodist Church in Atlantic City. Each Christmas, the choir joined the College Players in presenting a special program in Alumni Hall: a choral concert followed by a short play or nativity tableau. The College Orchestra, under the direction of Philip Royer, presented an annual spring concert and served as a training ground for student conductors in the music education program. The orchestra also regularly accompanied the All-County Chorus at the annual Carroll County Eisteddfod Music Festival held in Alumni Hall. The 1939 production was a concert version of *Martha* by Friedrich von Flotow. A ten-piece swing band known as Cap' Kidd and his Buccaneers, formed by Wilbur Kidd in the fall of 1939, was composed of students and regularly played for organizational dances, class hops, the Sadie Hawkins Dance, and home basketball games.

The YMCA and YWCA continued to provide a venue for religious and social activities, though the numbers of participants began to dwindle during the decade; by April of 1939 they were combined into a coeducational group named the Student Christian Association, advised by Dr. Little.

Cultural activities increased during the latter part of the decade, perhaps because arts groups sought work even with small remuneration, and probably because President Holloway saw them as an important adjunct to the college program. The Don Cossack Russian Male Chorus appeared in November 1935; an annual recital by music students from the Curtis Institute in Philadelphia was presented each spring after 1930; a joint recital by Westminster residents Caroline Wantz Taylor '26 and Virgil Fox, already an acclaimed organist, was scheduled for April 1936; and Walter Hampden, noted Shakespearean actor, appeared in November 1936. The five-year-old National Symphony from Washington, D.C., under the direction of Hans Kindler, made the first of many annual appearances on campus in Alumni Hall on November 17, 1936, with student tickets costing 25¢, while general admission was $1. The Stradivarius String Quartet performed the following spring, and the Trapp Family Singers were scheduled to appear in 1939–40.

In addition to these events, the College Players performed a series of plays throughout the year, including a Thanksgiving play, one-act plays by the junior class in the spring, and a Commencement play. Presented on the Alumni Hall stage were such favorites as *Noah* and *Pride and Prejudice*. Violin sonata recitals were given by Maude Gesner and Philip Royer almost every year, as were vocal recitals by Alfred deLong after 1936 and piano recitals by Oliver Spangler after 1938. The College Choir, under the direction of Ruth Sherman Jones [1928–36] continued to present classic oratorios each spring, including Mendelssohn's *St. Paul*, Handel's *Messiah*, and Haydn's *Creation*.

Scene from a production of Noah
in Alumni Hall in 1936

Intramural athletics grew in interest and participation during this decade, as the physical education faculty grew and was better trained and more attention was paid, especially by the athletic director, Richard Harlow. Professors H. Barnette Speir and Marie Parker organized the well-rounded program, which was designed to include everyone on campus if possible. In addition to the usual sports, volleyball, horseshoes, field hockey, and women's soccer were added in 1932. By 1934, 80% of the males on campus participated in one or more sports, and by the end of the decade the women's intramural program included field hockey, golf, archery, and tennis in the fall; badminton, basketball, and volleyball in the winter; and softball, tennis, archery, golf, and horseback riding in the spring.

Intercollegiate athletics were also pursued by many students. The soccer team, now firmly established, involved about 25 men each year and played between 8 and 13 games each season. They chalked up six winning records, three losing seasons, and one .500 season (4 wins and 4 losses). Their best record was achieved in 1935, when they showed 8 wins, 1 loss, and 2 ties. Opponents included Navy, University of Pennsylvania, Penn State, West Point, University of Maryland, Westchester Teachers College (PA), and Towson Normal School. Basketball did not fare as well, posting almost all losing seasons under three different coaches: Neil Stahley, Charles Havens, and Bruce Ferguson. The 1935 team listed ten players, which was about the average turnout for the sport. Tennis continued to have winning seasons, going undefeated in 15 matches in 1932. Frank Hurt became the coach in 1935, and he led the team to successes over such schools as St. Johns, Johns Hopkins, University of Maryland, Catawba, Catholic, Delaware, and Gettysburg. Baseball had a much more difficult time drawing student interest. Although it was in danger of dying out, the *Gold Bug* reported that the sport would not be dropped as an intercollegiate sport because there seemed to be enough interest in it.[41] However, it was not until 1933 that a team actually developed under a new coach, Carl "Molly" Twigg. The 1934 team recorded 4 wins and 3 losses. In 1936 Joseph Lipsky '35 took over as coach, and the team of 15 men played 12 games with 6 wins and 6 losses. The 1937 team was more successful, posting 11 wins and 6 losses. By the end of the decade, under coach Charlie Havens, who was followed by Bruce Ferguson, the team was usually .500 for the season. Lacrosse occasionally fielded a team of interested students for a few intercollegiate games, but usually it remained on intramural or club status.

Boxing, under Coach Harlow's tutelage, continued to draw interest from a small group of men who acquitted themselves well in intercollegiate matches with such teams as Bucknell, Navy, Army, Catholic, West Virginia, Penn State, and Villanova. The team was ranked nationally in 1931, had winning seasons in 1933 and 1934, and then began to drop off in the latter part of the decade, perhaps because Harlow was no longer the driving force. Outstanding boxers during the era, who often received national recognition for individual bouts at the Eastern Intercollegiate Boxing Tournament in March each year, included George Ekaitis '31, Ludwig "Tiny" Pincura '32, Bernard Kaplan '35, Andrew Gorski '35, Thomas Pontecorvo '36, and Anthony Ortenzi '38 (who became coach in 1940). The college was proud that Coach Havens (who succeeded Harlow) was elected vice president of the Intercollegiate Boxing Association in March 1939.

Kiefer remembered his boxing experience:

When I attended Western Maryland, I weighed approximately 145 pounds. I decided to go out for a place on the boxing squad. In those days boxing was a major sport at many colleges. Western Maryland had one of the leading teams in the Eastern Intercollegiate Association and had several Eastern Intercollegiate champions. We worked out regularly, beginning after the Christmas holidays until the end of the season, about three months later, when the intercollegiate championship bouts were held to pick a champion in each weight class. Dick Harlow, the well-known football coach, was also the boxing coach. In addition to the daily workout in the afternoon, most of us ran five miles or so early in the morning to help get into proper physical condition. The afternoon sessions consisted of rope skipping, shadow boxing, and three-minute sessions of punching a heavy bag suspended from the ceiling on a rope. Harlow also set up informal bouts. Harlow considered me a 135-pound boxer. Before each match there was a formal weighing process with a four-pound leeway. I had great trouble "making weight" as did some others. We practically fasted to get down to the acceptable weight. I fought in only three or four official bouts, two against the University of Maryland whose 135 pound boxer was an ex-Marine who had been the Marine Corps champion for seven years. I didn't stand a chance![42]

A new varsity sport, golf, was introduced in 1937 after the college built a nine-hole golf course. The first golf tournament was held on the Hill April 29, 1937, and involved teams from Catholic University, George Washington University, University of Maryland, St. John's College, and Western Maryland. The college team generally held its own, usually racking up a .500 season against its opponents. After a hiatus of 26 years, track reappeared in the 1930s. From 1902 to 1910 the college track team had been excellent. During the 1920s no full team was produced. Renewed interest in 1936 led to organization of a small team, and in 1937 marked improvement in interest and ability was shown. The 1937 *Aloha* reported the hope that by the end of the decade the college could look forward to regaining its prominence on the track.

The Terror football team continued to dominate athletic news for most of the decade, posting seven winning seasons, two losing seasons (1937 and 1939), and one .500 season (1931). Coming off the undefeated 1929 season, the Harlow team surpassed that effort in 1930 with a 9–0–1 record, amassing 246 points while giving up only 14 to their opponents. The 59–0 defeat of the University of Baltimore under the lights of Baltimore Stadium and the 7–0 defeat of the archrival University of Maryland ensured the state championship (and the Mayor Jackson Cup); Captain Paul Bates was named to the All-Maryland and All-Eastern teams. Following a 27-game undefeated streak (and the loss of some key players to graduation), the Terrors suffered their first loss, in 1931 to Georgetown. Other losses that year were to Washington and Jefferson, Boston College, and the University of Maryland. But the wins were decisive, with scores of 59–0 (St. John's), 40–0 (Johns Hopkins), 34–0 (Muhlenburg), and 20–0 (Mt. St. Mary's). The 1932 team gave up only 1 game, to Bucknell by a score of 13–14, winning 5 others and tying 1. Included on that team were Bill Shepherd x'35, Harold Kopp '33, Bruce Ferguson '35, John Olsh '35, Eugene Willis '34, Andrew G. Gorski '35, and Bernard Kaplan '35. Kaplan went on to play for the New York Giants

*1934 undefeated football team; Coach Harlow is at the right,
Bill Shepherd seated in the second row, center.*

in 1935, when the team was NFL Eastern Division champion, and retired
after the 1936 season. He returned to the NFL during World War II to play 3
games for the Philadelphia Eagles before retiring for good, having played 22
professional games.

The 1934 Terrors were again undefeated, finishing the year with a 8–0–1
record and scoring 209 points to the opponents' 12 (all in one game by
Westchester State Teachers). The only tie (0–0) was with Villanova. Significant
wins over Boston College (40–0)—a two-touchdown favorite—and Albright
(49–0) made the season especially memorable. Bill Shepherd led the nation
in scoring that year, with 133 points, and enabled the Terrors to rack up
significant wins against some of the best teams in the nation. Shepherd,
Andrew Gorski, Louis N. Kaplan '35, Joseph Lipsky, and Webster Lucas '35
were given All-America honors by the Associated Press. The final game of
the season, against Georgetown on December 1, was played in a blinding
rainstorm in Baltimore Stadium, and the win ensured that a number of
Terrors would be named to All-Maryland and All-East teams.

Following that eventful game, the front page of the *Baltimore Sun* the
next morning carried a banner front-page headline in two-inch-high letters
declaring, "Western Maryland Triumphs 13–0"[43] (possibly the last time a
WMC team's win would make the front page of the *Baltimore Sun*). The
article mentioned that between halves of the game, Coach Harlow received a
telegram from the president of the University of Miami inviting the Terrors
to play a New Year's Day game in Florida. Other eastern teams were possible

candidates for this special "Orange Blossom" game, including University of Maryland, Penn State, and Bucknell, but Western Maryland was the first choice. (Curiously, the *Gold Bug* published two weeks later never mentioned this offer, nor is there any comment about it in presidential reports or minutes of the trustees or faculty.) Although it might have been pleasant to play football in Florida in the winter, and it would most assuredly have added another win to the powerful team's record, Harlow declined the offer; this may have been for financial reasons (although one could imagine that Robert Gill would have found a way to get the team to Florida had it been necessary). However, it has also been conjectured by several people who remember the season and the people involved that Harlow probably did not see the Miami game as anything special and thought that sending his star player, Bill Shepherd, to play in the Shrine East-West game (then football's most prestigious college all-star game, played since 1926) on January 1 would be the best thing for the college's (and Shepherd's) athletic reputation.[44] As it transpired, Shepherd was the outstanding player of that game (where his teammate was Gerald R. Ford, University of Michigan all-star and later 38th U.S. president), playing 59 of the 60 minutes. When Shepherd left the game, he received a thunderous standing ovation from the sellout crowd of 55,000, even though his East team lost to the West 19–13. In a post-game column, Grantland Rice, the syndicated sports columnist for *Collier's* who selected the All-America teams, apologized for not including Shepherd, a triple-threat back who had been the country's leading scorer, on the 1934 team, acknowledging that Shepherd (who stood only 5-6 and weighed 142 pounds) was a better player than Navy's Fred Borries. The following summer, Shepherd went on to justify Rice's belated evaluation when he played on the College All-Star Team against the NFL Champion Chicago Bears and was the leading ground gainer, with 44 yards on 11 carries. He once told a sports reporter that his biggest thrills playing college football occurred in 1934 with the 40–0 win over Boston College and the 6–0 win over Bucknell (the team that ultimately went to Miami in January 1935 to beat Miami 26–0 in what would later be renamed the Orange Bowl). Shepherd went on to play in the NFL, spending six months with the Boston Redskins before joining the Detroit Lions, who won the NFL championship in 1935 with his help. He retired in 1940 after tearing his Achilles tendon.[45] He later worked for the Ford Motor Company. He was twice nominated for the National Football Hall of Fame. He died in 1967.

In January 1935, it was announced that Richard Harlow had been named head coach at Harvard University (the first nonalumnus to hold the job) and would be leaving Western Maryland. Twenty-two of his former players were now football coaches in high schools or colleges. His assistant, "Skip" Stahley, had left the year before to become head coach at the University of Delaware but after only one year moved on to Harvard as Harlow's assistant there. Charlie Havens replaced Stahley as assistant coach and in March 1935 was named head coach, replacing Harlow. A month later he named Bruce Ferguson his assistant.

When Dick Harlow left, he was much missed. It was noted in the 1932 *Aloha*, which was dedicated to him, that he was a man "whose efforts have raised Western Maryland from a position of comparative obscurity in athletics to a position of prominence and esteem." He was considered "an inspiring leader of men." The *Alumni Bulletin* noted, "Not only have the words 'Dick Harlow' indicated winning teams, but they have also symbolized a spirit of good, clean sportsmanship."[46] In 1936 he was named Football Coach of the Year by the American Football Coaches Association, the second awardee of that prestigious honor.

During the latter part of the decade two other football players qualified for the All-America honor: Bernard Kaplan in 1935 and Anthony Ortenzi in 1937.

An interesting footnote to and highlight of the otherwise lackluster 1937 football season was an innovation for the October 15 home game with Upsala College. A temporary lighting system was installed around Hoffa Field, and the game was played at night. Preceding the game, a parade of students and the band marched to the football field, and the game was played in the presence of Maryland governor Harry Nice. The Terrors wore specially made night uniforms of brilliant gold and light green. After the 28–0 drubbing they had received in 1936, the Upsala Vikings sought revenge. But the Terrors clicked for the first time that season and rolled over the visitors 19–0.[47]

In May 1938 the *Gold Bug* reported that the board of trustees had adopted a new policy for intercollegiate sports, especially football. Henceforth, eight games would be scheduled with the college's "natural rivals," colleges comparable in size to WMC in southern Pennsylvania and Maryland.[48] In May 1940 the college joined the newly formed Mason-Dixon Collegiate Conference, which included American University, Catholic University, University of Delaware, Johns Hopkins University, Loyola College, Mt. St. Mary's College, Towson State Teachers College, and Washington College. St. John's College had withdrawn from all intercollegiate athletics. This action continued the effort to bring WMC's athletic program more in line with those of other colleges of about the same size and locale. It also had the effect of downplaying football and putting a different, perhaps more balanced, perspective on athletics and athletes at the college.

Periodically, football rivalries get a bit out of hand, and such was the case with the long-standing relationship of WMC with the University of Maryland (until 1940, and then with Johns Hopkins to the present day). During the fall of 1939, presumably prior to the annual game with Maryland, a male WMC student was allegedly kidnapped by some of the university students. David Osborn recalled the incident and the retaliation:

> *Not wishing to involve the academic bureaucracy in such trivia, a select group of our men kidnapped one of their students and kept him for a week or so in an undesignated closet where he was fed regular meals sneaked out of the dining hall by the charitable minded. Not wishing to let this matter rest, our dorm was alerted about 1 A.M. one night by news that the University of Maryland had come back to retaliate. As inarticulate freshmen, we frankly did not know how to proceed with such an undeclared war, but the football stars upstairs came roaring to the rescue, each one ripping one of the vertical wooden supports from the banister as they rushed down the stairs. They said that they chased the intruders before they achieved their objective.*[49]

The campus continued to be saddened periodically by student deaths, especially those caused by uncontrollable diseases. William Hubbard '36 died of typhoid fever at his home in Easton in the summer of 1934. William Washington Rhodes III of Queenstown, Maryland, who had completed his freshman year at the college, died August 18, 1935, also of typhoid. M. Katherine Cissel '39 died during her senior year and was memorialized in February 1940 with a plaque in the Phi Alpha Mu clubroom. The community was also shocked to learn in May 1936 of the death in a shooting accident of Wilson Wingate, longtime and highly respected sports editor for the *Baltimore Sun* and later the *Baltimore News Post.* Wingate had always given full and fair treatment of his alma mater's athletics; he was the brother of English professor Evelyn Wingate (Wenner). The college witnessed the end of an era when Imogene Mitten Ensor '71, the last surviving member of the first graduating class, died on February 19, 1937, in New York City at the age of 86. She had furnished a room in Blanche Ward Hall, and her picture had been placed there. There were now few people who remembered the early days of the college or President J. T. Ward.

Early in this decade, an editorial in the *Gold Bug* remarked, "It is wonderful to think of the enormous changes that have come about during the lifetime of even an average student. What a lot he will have to tell his grandchildren!"[50] By the end of the decade, the list of changes included a world war, the Great Depression, the overthrow of Spanish royalty, the beginning of air travel, streamlined cars, unprecedented powers granted to a U.S. president, the collapse of the stock market, the adoption and rejection of prohibition, the organization of labor, and the development of the radio.

Buildings and Grounds

The decade saw a number of changes to the face of the campus, as several new buildings were erected, a number of small and older structures razed, several more renovated or refitted for new purposes, and the grounds improved. The campus was even expanded by 258 acres with the gift of a farm near Uniontown, Maryland, from Mr. and Mrs. Burrier L. Cookson, in return for an annuity of $75 per month for life. It was formally deeded on April 1, 1932, and noted that it had formerly been owned by a charter trustee of the college, Alfred Zollickoffer [1868–91]. This new addition proved very beneficial, as the farm supplied milk and other produce to the college for many years.[51] By 1934, the Geiman farm was taken out of service as a working farm because it was not producing revenue, the farm buildings were razed (with the exception of the springhouse, which remained until 2006) and the land incorporated into the campus for more athletic fields. Part of the farm on the western edge of the expanded campus was then designed as a park, with a large octagonal pavilion (containing huge stone fireplaces, a large stone table, and rustic benches) and an outdoor amphitheater. During the winter of 1935, a group of 25 men worked on the natural amphitheater under the auspices of the Civilian Work Administration. These men were paid 45¢ per hour for a 30-hour week for three months by the federal government. (They also worked on the foundation of the new Westminster High School on Longwell Avenue.)[52] The campus park was named for the longtime superintendent of buildings and grounds, Harvey A. Stone, as mentioned. Another important

Picnic pavilion in Harvey Stone Park, 1935

project was carried out under this federal program. A modern sewage and disposal system was designed for the campus and connected to the new city system. Carl Schaeffer was the engineer who oversaw the installation of this improved system, which has stood the test of time.[53] The men living in Ward Hall were delighted when showers were installed in the basement of that old dormitory during the summer of 1935, eliminating the necessity of traipsing over to Yingling Gymnasium in all kinds of weather.

During the summer of 1933, extensive improvements were made to the campus grounds. The houses located on College Avenue beyond the Library and Administration Building were razed, and the old city street extending to Pennsylvania Avenue was removed. Stone walls behind McDaniel Hall were built, a terraced garden was created in the protected angle of the dormitory's wings (named for and dedicated in 1934 to Minerva Robinson, longtime dean of women), the athletic fields improved, the tennis courts behind the seminary rebuilt and expanded, the outbuildings behind Carroll Hall (part of the former Reifsnider property) removed, and new shrubbery planted. This was all accomplished by a group of 27 male students recruited by President Ward and known as the WMC Conservation Corps. The group included Fred Malkus '34, Brady Bryson '35, and John Olsh '35. They were paid 25¢ an hour in addition to room and board for the summer, funded by the federal Civilian Conservation Corps program. They were under the general direction of T. K. Harrison, the business manager.[54] The summer of 1934 provided additional work for the students when the golf course was constructed on the Geiman farm. Workers on that detail included Olsh, Norman Ward Jr. '35, and Dennis Yingling '35. The course was completed and ready for play by June 1935.

Dormitories for both women and men were needed as the student body grew, and so in February 1934 the board approved the plans, drawn up by Charles M. Anderson and Eugene Adams, for a new women's dormitory, which ultimately cost $161,042. By June bids for the construction were opened and accepted, building began soon thereafter, and the following June at Commencement, the building was dedicated (although not occupied until the following fall), the trustees having named it Blanche Ward Hall in honor of President A. N. Ward's wife. The building was designed to house 160 women, besides including rooms for some faculty and a women's gymnasium fully equipped with lockers and showers. It also contained the first elevator in Carroll County, installed by the General Elevator Company for $5,000.[55]

In an effort to insulate the campus and obtain contiguous property, the board of trustees continued to purchase nearby properties and obtained five lots on Union Street in July 1934. At its annual meeting two years later, it formally adopted a policy of buying up all properties on the west side of

Blanche Ward Hall, a women's dormitory,
was opened in 1935.

Union Street as they became available. A portion of that land was used to build a new power plant, which was constructed simultaneously with Blanche Ward Dormitory at a cost of $48,289. The rest of the land was to be used for women's athletic activities, and some tennis courts were built in the area.

The Reifsnider property (aka Gray Gables Inn, College Inn) continued to be used for various purposes. By 1931, the Home Economics Department had taken over the second floor as its practice house (the first floor remained a tearoom). The upstairs apartment consisted of a living room, dining room, kitchen, two bathrooms, and five bedrooms. After several six-week practice periods, the bedrooms were made available to guests at the inn. The following year, the management of the inn was turned over to the home economics students, and the first floor was remodeled and refurnished. In 1934 the home economics practice was moved to the two-story West Virginia Cottage, rented from the seminary. Groups of five senior women lived in and ran the house for a six-week period. The inn continued its operations until 1937, when it was closed to the public because it was losing money for the college. Following its closure, the building was used for a year as a dormitory for women faculty members. It then became the administration building in the fall of 1938, housing the offices of the president, deans, treasurer, and registrar. The bookstore and post office, which had been located in the front part of the first floor of the Library and Administration Building, were moved in 1938 to the lower level of Old Main, where an expanded post office provided individual boxes for each student for the first time. All these moves provided much needed space for the library, which was growing to meet

*Levine Hall was remodeled to house
the Music Department in 1939–40.*

the academic demands of the larger student body. After Dr. Lewis's death in 1929 (and Mrs. Lewis's death in 1935), his entire library was eventually given to the college by his family and placed in this newly expanded space.

In April 1936, the board approved moving the Ward Arch from its location over the main college drive to the recently purchased property on the corner of Union and Main streets. Built in the days of horse and buggy travel, the arch was too narrow for modern automobile traffic. A local stone mason, Harry Ditman, and his crew carefully tore the arch down and devised a numbering system for the stones so that it could be reconstructed on the new site exactly as it had stood in its original place since 1898. After the numbered stones were laid out on the ground near the new site, an early snow covered them, and since the weather turned bitterly cold, reconstruction was postponed until spring. When the workmen returned to reerect the arch, they discovered that the weather had caused the markings on many of the stones to disappear. But a lunch bag saved the day! As it was being dismantled, Ditman had carefully sketched the arch and each stone, with its number, on his lunch bag, and his wife still had the bag. So the project was saved; each stone could be matched to the diagram and put in its proper place. The arch, with some iron grillwork additions to form gateways to the upper campus, was completed during the summer of 1937.[56]

Another fixture of the campus scene was removed in 1936. The bridge that had connected Hering Hall to Lewis Hall was removed because of concern about fire and rising insurance rates. This freed up some room in Hering Hall, and the home economics classrooms expanded into that space.[57] Owings Hall, the first addition to the Main Building (now traditionally called Old Main), had been considered less than desirable, indeed unsafe, dormitory space for some time, and so in 1939 it was razed, and with it the women's entry bridge connecting it to Yingling Gymnasium. With the new women's gymnasium in Blanche Ward Hall, the women no longer needed to share the old facility.

Levine Hall, which had served as a senior men's dormitory for some years, was remodeled and refitted to house the Music Department during 1939–40. The front door was moved to the town side of the building and the first floor redesigned to provide a recital hall and a studio for Maude Gesner (all funded by the $5,000 annuity from Alvey Isanogle). As new dormitories were being built, older student housing could be recycled for growing departments.

With a campaign to raise funds for a new men's dormitory (slated to cost about $150,000) and a field house ($75,000) well under way, the trustees moved forward with plans for both in April 1938. Ground was broken in special ceremonies in December 1938, and construction continued throughout the winter and spring. Cornerstones were laid at Commencement

Albert Norman Ward Hall,
a men's dormitory, was opened in 1939.

in June 1939, and the formal dedications were a highlight of Homecoming on November 18. The men students moved into the new dormitory on October 28, and the gymnasium was the site of a grand Homecoming Ball.

The men's dormitory was named in memory of Albert Norman Ward and designed with four sections, each containing four double bedrooms and a bath on each floor. The fourth floor of each section contained two larger rooms and a bath. Also included were an office for the dean of men, a student lounge, and a game room. The building was situated so that another building of similar design could be placed opposite it at some later date. The field house was named for Robert Gill, an outstanding athlete during his undergraduate days, a trustee since 1925, and a significant leader in the fund-raising efforts for the facility. The gymnasium had an 80-by-115-foot playing floor, which was called one of the finest gymnasium floors in the East. The folding bleachers that lined the walls provided seating for 1,000 spectators. The building also contained showers, locker rooms, a supply room, and offices for the athletic staff. By February 1940, the trustees had been alerted to parking problems around Gill Gymnasium and directed the administrators to work on a solution.

FINANCES

Enrollments grew from 462 to 598 over the decade, with graduating classes increasing from 64 (1931) to a high of 143 (1940), the average class 106. This 30% growth in the student body even during difficult economic times meant that the annual budget ($234,000 in 1931 and $297,000 in 1933) could continue to expand each year, even as the endowment, based primarily in the stock market, remained relatively stable. By 1934, the endowment had grown to $1,300,000. Included in that sum was a scholarship fund amounting to about $50,000 that could be used to help needy students. As enrollments increased, the number of females was gradually overtaking the number of males. President Holloway was concerned about this as early as 1936, because of the long-standing tradition of keeping the student body evenly divided, and recommended building better dormitory facilities for men. Once Albert Norman Ward Hall was built, male enrollments rose dramatically (at least until the United States entered World War II).

While things seemed to be going along fairly well with the college after the stock market crash, it was nevertheless necessary to reduce all faculty and staff salaries by 7.5% in the year 1932–33. (Only Richard Harlow's salary remained the same, at $3,000, because he was on a long-term contract.)[58] While some small changes occurred mid-decade, salaries then generally remained the same throughout the Depression. For example, a professor with a PhD was hired in 1929 at a salary of $2,300 (plus room and board). In 1931 he married and moved off campus, and his salary was adjusted to $2,650 (which, since he was now paying his own room and board, was not really an increase). The following year, his salary was reduced to $2,451 and remained there for the rest of the decade until it was finally increased to $2,500 in 1940. (After 11 years, taking inflation into account, he was probably worse off than when he was hired.) President Ward's salary was reduced by the same percentage; he received $4,162 for most of the decade. The highest-paid WMC faculty and administrators of the era received $3,145. The creation of the summer school in 1932, as mentioned earlier, provided extra income for the faculty involved, and also kept the buildings in use year-round. It should be noted that, during this time, faculty salaries were never firmly established until after fall enrollments were stabilized and the board's Executive Committee could study the financial situation and approve any increments. In earlier decades, the faculty salary list had been presented and approved at the June meeting of the full board, but now the list was deferred to fall. Faculty members of the era later remembered waiting for the first paycheck of the fall to see what they would be receiving each month and whether it was more or less than the previous year. During this decade, after the first reduction, the salaries were never less but rarely more.

An interesting discussion occurred within the board of trustees regarding presidential perquisites following Dr. Holloway's hiring as president in 1935. In addition to his $4,000 base salary, he was allotted $500 for entertainment; $750 for utilities; $550 for maid service; and additional funds to cover laundry, food, and automobile travel. At the same time, Vice President McDaniel was to receive funds for utilities (water, fuel, telephone, gas, and electricity), as well as milk and eggs. Apparently, before this time, all the president's and vice president's expenses had been paid out of their salaries (or perhaps some of them were taken care of within the college budget without formal allocation).[59]

By 1937, the faculty was pushing the administration and trustees to adopt a group insurance plan for sickness and accident insurance, as well as a pension program. President Holloway was given permission to study the issue of pensions, and the trustees discussed it but took no action, waiting to see what the federal government would do. After Social Security was established, some trustees, including President Holloway, felt that that would take care of pension needs. However, discussion of a pension plan for all college employees would continue.

When the decade began, the fees for students were held at $500 for the year ($150 for tuition and $350 for room, board, and laundry), as established in 1924. Early in 1938 President Holloway recommended raising the tuition by $50. He noted in his annual report that St. John's College's tuition was $250, Hood College's $250, Gettysburg's $325, Dickinson's $300, and American University's $250. The board did not enact the increase for 1938–39, however, probably fearing the loss of students, although the dormitories were full, almost to overflowing. In October of the same year, Holloway again recommended the tuition hike, noting that the University of Maryland (a state-funded school) was charging $125–$175, and both Johns Hopkins and Goucher were charging $450. Even more important was that the college was spending more for instruction (faculty salaries) than it was receiving in tuition. Finally, the trustees agreed and raised the tuition fee to $200 for the academic year 1939–40. The room and board fees were also adjusted to reflect the newer dormitories now favored by the students. Those living in Ward, McKinstry, and McDaniel halls continued to pay $350, while those living in Blanche Ward and Albert Norman Ward halls paid $415.

To meet the rising costs of sending their children to college, occasionally (perhaps more often than reported) parents would "barter" with the college (especially with A. N. Ward) for tuition. While cash would have met the regular bills, in some instances what was received in trade greatly enhanced the campus property. One example of this was the trade of trees and shrubbery for the campus in return for tuition, a bargain made by Chester Grier of Grier Brothers Nurseries of Bel Air, Harford County, Maryland, on behalf of his two daughters. Each spring more trees were planted. Once this project was completed and the two young women, Ruth (Klair) '35 and Elinore '36, had graduated, Elwood Grier, the other brother in the business, bartered more trees for tuition for his son, George x'39, and the planting continued through the spring of 1938, adding considerably to the appearance of the back campus and golf course. During the Depression, such bartering was not uncommon.[60]

The lack of assistance from the Methodist Protestant Church continued to be a sore issue (at least until Methodist unification at the end of the decade). Church contributions were minimal, and by the latter days of the decade, when the Depression worsened, they ceased altogether. In his report to the trustees for 1932, President Ward noted, "For several years we have received practically nothing from the Board of Education of the Methodist Protestant Church. This has been due to the financial depression in part, but more largely because of an unequal and unfair distribution of the Church Budget between missions and education." He went on to note that during his 12 years as president, the college had provided $100,000 worth of scholarships for prospective ministers and ministers' children. During the period 1928–32, the church had contributed a total of $750 to the college, while the college had contributed $40,000 in scholarships. He opined that the general feeling within the church was that, because of its careful management, the college could take care of itself. "The time has come when Western Maryland College should receive its proper recognition at the hands of the denomination which is sponsoring it." His final comment was somewhat surprising: "I sometimes think that I made a mistake in taking up the ministry as a life-work. If I had gone into business instead, I might have been able to build and endow this college myself."[61] A year later, he appealed to the church for a contribution of $3,000 to cover the interest on the bonds, but there is no record of it being paid. His comments and concerns sound very much like those of J. T. Ward and T. H. Lewis, both of whom had questioned the church's commitment to the college. (After unification, the college continued to host a number of church conferences during the summer, as it had for about 20 years, including the annual meeting of the newly formed Baltimore Conference.)

Even without help from the church, and even during the Depression, the college had been able to mount and successfully run a capital campaign to build the new men's dormitory and the new field house. Half of the goal of $250,000 was raised through individual pledges, amazingly, and the remaining funds were obtained over a period of years to replace funds borrowed from the endowment and local banks. A number of events were held specifically to obtain funds for the $75,000 field house. One of special interest was a football game on December 7, 1935, with the University of Maryland in Baltimore Stadium (a game not part of the regular schedule that year). University acting president Harry C. "Curly" Byrd x'09 graciously agreed to let all the proceeds of the game (normally split between the institutions) go to the field house fund. Another event designed to raise funds for the campaign was a faculty-administration performance of *Snow White* in May 1938.[62] Dr. Holloway was well known for his sense of humor, and no doubt he masterminded the production, being sure to cast all the parts with "appropriate" faculty members. A second performance was given the following January, again organized by the president.

Major Events

The entire college community gathered in McDaniel Lounge on Saturday evening, November 14, 1931, to hear a special radio program broadcast by NBC from 9 to 9:30 P.M. on the Liberal Arts College Movement. Giving the principal address was President Herbert Hoover. Dr. Ward was chairman of the Liberal Arts College Movement (he would resign that post in 1932)

Robinson Garden was created outside McDaniel Hall
in 1933–34 to honor the former dean of women.

and also spoke, as part of the concerted effort to interpret the needs, aims, and achievements of American liberal arts colleges. Other speakers included Dr. John H. Finley, associate editor of the *New York Times*; Dr. Robert L. Kelly, executive secretary of the Association of American Colleges; and Mrs. Thomas J. Preston (formerly Mrs. Grover Cleveland). The cheerleaders led the listeners in cheers and college songs before the broadcast, and a feeling of pride in the college and its president was evident.[63]

When Margaret Robinson was dean of women, she conceived the idea of planting a garden in the sheltered angle formed by the wings of McDaniel Hall. As long as she remained at the college (until 1928), she oversaw the planting and care of the flowers in that space, which came to be called Miss Robinson's Garden. After her retirement, others cared for it, but in the summer of 1933, during extensive improvements to the campus by the WMC Conservation Corps, it was decided to improve the garden and dedicate it to the woman who first laid it out. Three terraces formed the improved garden, with evergreens

Dean Margaret Robinson

and flowers bordering the building. Stone walks and steps formed the paths. Cut into the steep bank leading to the lowest level was a seat built of stones and overlooking the town. On June 2, 1934, Miss Robinson returned to the campus as guest of honor at the dedication of the garden named for her. President Ward made an address, and a Spanish well was positioned in the garden as a gift of the WW Club in memory of Louise Walters Werntz, who had been killed in an automobile accident in December 1930. The well was octagonal in shape, of white granite with wrought-iron trim. Although primarily ornamental, it concealed a drinking fountain. A second gift to the garden was a sundial presented by the members of Delta Sigma Kappa in honor of Miss Robinson. They hoped she would remember the many sunny hours spent with "her girls."[64]

The 1935 Commencement, on June 3, was a very special one for Albert Norman Ward. He and his wife were celebrating the 40th anniversary of their graduation from the college, their 35th wedding anniversary, his 15th anniversary as president of the college, and their only son's graduation from the college that day. The *Western Maryland College Bulletin* of May 1935 contained a number of congratulatory statements from friends, educators, churchmen, alumni, trustees, faculty, and students. The cornerstone of the new dormitory was laid on Saturday, prior to the annual dinner of the Alumni Association, which honored the Wards and celebrated the anniversaries. President Ward preached the baccalaureate sermon on Sunday morning, and on Monday, he conferred degrees on graduating seniors at the Commencement exercises, which featured an address by the eminent theologian Dr. Ralph W. Sockman of New York City. A portrait of Ward, painted by distinguished Washington artist Hans Schlereth as a gift of the board of trustees and the alumni, was unveiled by Albert Norman Ward Jr.[65] It was also announced by the trustees that the new women's dormitory would be named for Blanche Murchison Ward. Of special interest and delight to the alumni, among the seven honorary degrees awarded that day were a doctor of education bestowed upon Alvey Michael Isanogle and a doctor of literature given to George Stockton Wills. Isanogle was cited as a "successful teacher, writer, administrator; master in the field of secondary education" and lauded for making the college's education program one of the most outstanding in the nation, its graduates recognized throughout the region. Wills, longtime revered professor of English, was recognized for his devotion to literature and to his students and was called a "successful teacher of English, a master in that field."[66]

For many years the need for a pipe organ in Alumni Hall had been recognized, particularly after Sunday evening chapel services were moved there from Baker Chapel in 1932. A fund had been established to purchase

Alvey Michael Isanogle   *George Stockton Wills*

an instrument and had grown through the receipts of the various oratorio presentations by the College Choir. Finally, in 1935 the organ became a reality when J. E. Myers, a used organ dealer in Woodlawn, Baltimore, exchanged an instrument for scholarships for his two sons, Joseph C. Myers '34 and Raymond C. Myers '42. A special dedication service was held on November 10, 1935, presided over by Dean Schofield acting as president. Following the formal presentation, J. Norris Hering of Baltimore presented a recital that included selections from Bach, Byrd, Schumann, and Franck. The console of the organ was located on the north side of the balcony facing the stage, the pipes in chambers at the back of the balcony near the stairways.[67] The organ was a three-manual instrument with a 32-pedal keyboard; 869 pipes capable of producing 1,296 different tones; a set of chimes; and swell, great, and choir chambers.

April 25, 1936, was the date selected for the formal inauguration of President Holloway and was a significant day in the college's history, for it was the first presidential inauguration held strictly for that purpose at Western Maryland College. A committee composed of George Wills, James Straughn, Pearre Wantz, Samuel Schofield, and Lloyd Bertholf had carefully laid plans for the important occasion. One hundred twenty-two colleges, universities, and learned societies sent delegates to the ceremony, and, under the direction of Chief Marshal Theodore Whitfield, they formed an impressive and colorful academic procession as they marched from Science Hall toward Alumni Hall in the order of the founding of their institutions. They were followed by the faculty and trustees of the college, entering the hall to the strains of "A Mighty Fortress Is Our God," the college's traditional processional hymn. The address was given by Dr. Arlo Ayres Brown, president of Drew University; and board president Straughn delivered the charge of office to Dr. Holloway. As Holloway rose to deliver his inaugural address, he was given a standing ovation. He began his remarks by recounting the progress made by the institution under his three predecessors and pledged himself to a program of "extensive expansion and intensive expansion." He closed his address with the following words: "In receiving my charge as President of Western Maryland College, I pledge my utmost in the conscientious execution of my duties. I look upon my task as one which necessitates the utmost cooperation of the trustees, the alumni, the faculty, and the students. I want your friendship. I pledge you mine." The organist for the occasion was a young musical prodigy who was head of the Organ Department of the Peabody Conservatory in Baltimore and had already developed an international reputation: Virgil Fox. He played several classical numbers during the ceremonies, including the "Allegro from the Sixth Symphony" by Widor for the recessional. Immediately following the ceremony, the delegates, alumni, faculty, and friends gathered in McDaniel Lounge for a reception. At 1:30 P.M. a luncheon was held in the dining hall for the official representatives, the trustees, the faculty, and prominent alumni and friends of the college. Dr. Hugh Elderdice '82 served as toastmaster, and seven tributes to the new president were given by representatives of the trustees, faculty, student governments, alumni, and visiting delegates.[68]

Homecoming 1936 was scheduled (as it had been for several years) for Thanksgiving Day, November 26, and featured many activities for visiting alumni. The sororities and fraternities held open houses, and McDaniel Lounge served as alumni headquarters during the day. Prior to the 2 P.M. football game, the homecoming parade, led by the College Band, wended its way through Westminster to Hoffa Field. The Terrors faced Mt. St. Mary's and beat the Mountaineers 35–0. The big feature of the game was a touchdown run by Leroy "Monk" Campbell '38, All-Maryland back (later Carroll County sheriff, 1962–82). A new feature of homecoming was the selection of a queen by the student body; senior Mary Alice Wrigley was crowned during the half-time ceremonies. The Carroll Inn served a tray dinner from noon until the evening at a cost of $1, while the tearoom in Old Main served sandwiches throughout the day. Undergraduate boarders were served the traditional Thanksgiving turkey dinner with all the trimmings at 5 P.M., and the day ended

*Gill Gymnasium, the largest and best-equipped gym
in Maryland, was opened in 1939.*

with the performance by the College Players of Édouard Pailleron's *The Art of
Being Bored*, under the direction of Esther Smith, in Alumni Hall at 8 P.M. The
price of admission was 50¢.[69]

In early June 1937, the college played a large part in the Carroll County
Centennial Pageant, directed by Dorothy Elderdice. Several parades, a
horse show, games, a band contest, and a street carnival filled the five days
of special observance of the county's founding. During the pageant on
Hoffa Field on Wednesday at 2 P.M., the ROTC unit provided a color guard;
H. Barnette Speir '22 portrayed Francis Scott Key; the college choir, band,
and orchestra performed; members of the faculty portrayed the faculty
of the college of 1867; and a number of alumni represented aspects of a
symbolic Court of Yesterday, presided over by the Queen of Memory, Mrs.
Fred Holloway.[70]

Groundbreaking ceremonies for the new men's dormitory and the new
field house, located on the north end of the campus near each other, were
held on December 9, 1938, in conjunction with the annual banquet of the
Carroll County Western Maryland Club. In attendance was Governor-elect
Herbert R. O'Conor, who made a brief address paying tribute to the college's
contribution to the State of Maryland and pledging to do everything in his
power to assist the college in its future development. The major speaker of
the event was Harry C. Byrd, president of the University of Maryland. Byrd

noted the contributions that colleges like Western Maryland were making to modern civilization. He referred to his own brief student days at the college and acknowledged the significance that that year had for him. Perhaps he was also grateful that the college had conferred the honorary doctor of science in business administration on him the previous June. The College Orchestra under the direction of Prof. Philip Royer furnished music throughout the dinner. The groundbreaking ceremony was described in these words:

> The inclement weather made it impossible for the banqueters to go to the exact building sites. The reflection of the huge bonfires at the locations was clearly visible from the dining hall. As planned, the ground was broken for each building by a blast of dynamite. An electric wire had been connected with the dining hall, and with the pressing of the plunger by Governor-elect O'Conor, the intonation signaled the breaking of ground. The display of fireworks was given at a point visible from the dining room and was easily witnessed by the guests who were assembled. It was a beautiful and glorious and climactic finish to a great evening.[71]

The following June, at the 1939 Commencement, the cornerstones for both buildings were laid. Trustee Irving Pollitt presented the box that contained the materials to be deposited and read a list of the contents: a list of the contributors to the building fund; names of the board of trustees; names of members of the class of 1889, who were celebrating their 50th reunion; a copy of the WMC Bulletin for May 1939; and the pen used to sign the diplomas for the class of 1939.[72]

A major event for the campus community each December during this decade was the outdoor Nativity Play staged on the portico and terrace of the seminary building. This annual event, begun in 1930, was arranged and directed by Dorothy Elderdice, teacher of speech and religious drama at the seminary, with cooperation from the college. The college Sunday School Choir often provided the musical background of carols and selections from Christmas cantatas. The program each year provided live interpretations of well-known paintings such as Rossetti's Annunciation and Feuerstein's Nativity. The Madonna was often portrayed by a college student, with the parts of shepherds, magi, and angels taken by students from the seminary, the college, and local public schools. The pageant spread across the whole facade of the building; angels would appear in the windows and on the roof and parapets of the building, while "Gloria in Excelsis" rang out over the town from the tower. The effective staging, lighting, music, and costuming blended to produce an annual pageant for the community revealing the true meaning of Christmas. The programs continued until 1951.[73]

CONCLUSION

E ven in the midst of a severe economic depression, especially during the latter years of this decade, and having undergone a sudden change in leadership due to the unexpected death of its president, the college endured, prospered, and grew. Students continued to enroll in ever greater numbers, the faculty grew to meet the needs of the changing curriculum and the burgeoning academic community, and the standards of the college continued to rise, especially in the second half of the decade. Albert Norman Ward's vision of a "Greater Western Maryland College" was shared by Fred Garrigus Holloway, although neither would see the plan fully implemented. The college that had become well known beyond the state of Maryland for its football team's prowess was becoming equally well known for its strong academic programs as it entered the decade of the 1940s, over which hung a dark cloud of concern for world affairs.

CHAPTER 8 ENDNOTES

1. WMC board of trustees minutes, April 29, 1932; August 27, 1940.
2. *WMC Bulletin*, May 1935, 9.
3. WMC board of trustees minutes, October 14, 1938; September 2, 1939.
4. Schofield, Corinne Troy, *Newsletter*, Maryland Home Economics Association, vol. 10, no. 2, April 1939.
5. Minutes, Maryland Annual Conference, 1936, 131; Schofield and Crain, *Formative Years*, 122; Lewis Obituary, college archives.
6. Minutes, Maryland Annual Conference, 1936, 130–31.
7. *Gold Bug*, October 10, 1935, 2.
8. WMC faculty minutes, November 8, 1935.
9. WMC trustee Executive Committee minutes, September 23, 1935.
10. Minutes of a special meeting of the WMC board of trustees, October 3, 1935.
11. *WMC Bulletin*, December 1936, 12.
12. Chandler, *Pilgrimage of Faith*, 96–97.
13. *WMC Bulletin*, December 1935, 12.
14. Chandler, *Pilgrimage of Faith*, 113–14.
15. *Gold Bug*, May 12, 1938, 1.
16. *Carroll County Evening Sun*, undated, Historical Society of Carroll County archives.
17. *WMC Bulletin*, May 1937, 6; *Gold Bug*, March 3, 1938, 1; History of the Home Economics Department, college archives.
18. WMC summer school catalogs, 1932, 1933.
19. *Gold Bug*, October 20, 1932, 1.
20. Ibid., February 8, 1940, 1.
21. Kiefer, *Life and Times*, 71–72.
22. Carolyn Seaman Ingalls '67, *News From the Hill*, alumni magazine, May 1977, 6.
23. Osborn, letter to Coley, August 29, 2001, 2–4.
24. *WMC Catalogue* 1940–41, 28.
25. WMC board of trustees minutes, April 30, 1937.
26. Schofield and Crain, *Formative Years*, 117–18; *WMC Catalogue*, 1935–36, 36; *WMC Bulletin*, November 1936, 8.
27. 1931 *Aloha*, 218–19.
28. Interview, Brady Bryson, October 26, 2004.
29. Kiefer, *Life and Times*, 65–67.
30. May 3, 1934, 2.
31. *Gold Bug*, October 15, 1931, 2; October 6, 1932, 4.
32. Osborn, letter to Coley, August 29, 2001, 1.
33. Interview, Susannah Cockey Kiefer '33 and Kathleen Moore Raver '33, June 5, 2003.
34. *Gold Bug*, November 30, 1939, 1.
35. Carolyn Seaman Ingalls '67, *News From the Hill*, alumni magazine, May 1977, 6.
36. Interview, Kiefer and Raver, June 5, 2003.
37. *Gold Bug*, October 20, 1932, 2.
38. Kiefer, *Life and Times*, 70.
39. *Gold Bug*, November 11, 1937, 1; November 24, 1937, 4.
40. February 13, 1936.
41. March 24, 1932, 3.
42. Kiefer, *Life and Times*, 68.
43. *Baltimore Sun*, December 2, 1934, 1.
44. Interview, Bryson, October 26, 2004, for example.
45. *Cumberland Times*, November 18, 1992.
46. May 1935, 22.
47. 1938 *Aloha*, 116; *WMC Monthly*, October 1937, 7.
48. *Gold Bug*, May 12, 1938, 1.
49. Osborn, letter to Coley, August 29, 2001, 2.
50. January 11, 1934, 2.
51. Schofield and Crain, *Formative Years*, 113.
52. *Gold Bug*, January 11, 1935, 1.
53. *WMC Bulletin*, May 1934, 11; Schofield and Crain, *Formative Years*, 114.
54. *Gold Bug*, September 21, 1933; interview, Bryson, October 2004; Schofield and Crain, *Formative Years*, 114; *WMC Bulletin*, January 1934, 4.
55. WMC board of trustees minutes, February 8, 1934; September 12, 1934; *WMC Bulletin*, May 1935, 6.
56. Philip E. Uhrig remembrance; press release on McDaniel college logo; *WMC Bulletin*, May 1937, 6, college archives.
57. *Gold Bug*, September 21, 1936, 1.
58. WMC board of trustees minutes, September 23, 1932.
59. WMC trustee Executive Committee minutes, January 20, 1936; WMC board of trustees minutes, April 24, 1936.
60. Schofield and Crain, *Formative Years*, 113; interview, George Grier, 2002.
61. WMC President's Report, 1932, 8–10.
62. *Gold Bug*, May 12, 1938, 2.
63. *WMC Bulletin*, October 1931, 1; *Gold Bug*, November 12, 1931, 1.
64. *WMC Bulletin*, January 1934, 5; Schofield and Crain, *Formative Years*, 115.
65. Schofield and Crain, *Formative Years*, 119.
66. *WMC Bulletin*, December 1935, 15; degree citations, college archives.
67. Schofield and Crain, *Formative Years*, 119; *WMC Bulletin*, December 1935, 14.
68. *WMC Bulletin*, May 1936, 2.
69. *Gold Bug*, November 19, 1936; *WMC Bulletin*, November 1936, 12; 1937 *Aloha*, 112, 153.
70. *WMC Bulletin*, May 1937, 8.
71. Ibid., December 1938, 2–3.
72. Schofield and Crain, *Formative Years*, 129.
73. Chandler, *Pilgrimage of Faith*, 56–57; *WMC Bulletin*, December 1938, 4.

MAJOR WORLD EVENTS

1931

Pearl Buck publishes *The Good Earth*.
Robert Frost wins Pulitzer Prize for his *Collected Poems*.
Francis Scott Key's "Star Spangled Banner" becomes the national anthem.
Empire State Building is completed in New York City.

1932

Erskine Caldwell publishes *Tobacco Road*.
Ernest Hemingway publishes *Death in the Afternoon*.
Ferde Grofé composes *Grand Canyon Suite*.
Amelia Earhart becomes first woman to fly solo across Atlantic Ocean.
The Lindberg baby is kidnapped.
Franklin D. Roosevelt is elected 32nd president of the U.S. by a landslide.
Roosevelt introduces slogan "New Deal."

1933

U.S. Congress votes independence for Philippines.
Adolph Hitler is appointed German chancellor.
Jerome Kern's *Roberta* opens on Broadway.
Tennessee Valley Authority is created.
21st Amendment to U.S. Constitution repeals prohibition.
Eugene O'Neill's comedy *Ah, Wilderness* stars George M. Cohan.
Dinner at Eight and *Dr. Jekyll and Mr. Hyde* are popular films.
First concentration camps are erected by Nazis in Germany.

1934

German plebiscite votes Hitler as führer.
James Hilton's *Goodbye, Mr. Chips* is a best seller.
F. Scott Fitzgerald publishes *Tender Is the Night*.
Cole Porter's *Anything Goes* is a hit on Broadway.
FBI shoots John Dillinger, Public Enemy #1.

1935

T. S. Eliot publishes *Murder in the Cathedral*.
Clifford Odets publishes *Waiting for Lefty*.
Robert Sherwood publishes *The Petrified Forest*.
Sinclair Lewis publishes *It Can't Happen Here*.
The rumba becomes a popular dance.
American jurist Oliver Wendell Holmes dies.
President Roosevelt signs the U.S. Social Security Act.
Mutiny on the Bounty, *The 39 Steps*, and *Anna Karenina* are popular films.
George Gershwin's opera *Porgy and Bess* opens in New York.

1936
King George V of England dies; he is succeeded by his son Edward VIII, who later abdicates.
Roosevelt is reelected for a second presidential term.
Spanish Civil War begins.
Margaret Mitchell publishes *Gone with the Wind*.
Boulder Dam (later renamed Hoover Dam) is completed on Colorado River.
Henry Luce begins publishing *Life* magazine.
Floods sweep Johnstown, Pennsylvania.

1937
George VI's coronation is first radio broadcast heard worldwide.
Wallace Carothers patents nylon for the DuPont Company.
Wall Street stock market dip signals serious economic recession.
President Roosevelt signs U.S. Neutrality Act.
Insulin is used to control diabetes.
Amelia Earhart is lost on a Pacific flight.

1938
Marjorie Kinnan Rawlings publishes *The Yearling*.
Thornton Wilder publishes *Our Town*.
Benny Goodman's band brings a new style to jazz.
A 40-hour work week is established in the U.S.
U.S. Supreme Court rules that the University of Missouri must admit Negroes.
Howard Hughes flies around the world in 3 days, 19 hours, 17 minutes.

1939
World War II begins when Germany invades Poland.
George S. Kaufman and Moss Hart produce *The Man Who Came to Dinner*.
The Methodist Church unites into one church.
Artist Grandma Moses becomes famous in the U.S.
Aaron Copeland composes ballet *Billy the Kid*.
A baseball game is first televised in the U.S.
U.S. economy begins to recover.

1940
U.S. population is 132 million (including .5 million European refugees).
Duke Ellington becomes known as a composer and jazz pianist.
Carl Sandburg wins Pulitzer Prize for *Abraham Lincoln: The War Years*.
World War II continues in Europe; London Blitz begins.
Roosevelt is reelected for a third presidential term.
Ernest Hemingway publishes *For Whom the Bell Tolls*.
Penicillin is developed as a practical antibiotic.
First electron microscope is invented by RCA.

*McDaniel House (1896), residence of the McDaniel family,
became the home economics management house in 1940.*

C H A P T E R

9

THE WAR YEARS: MORE SIGNIFICANT CHANGES

The darkening clouds of potential world turmoil were increasing as the decade opened. In America, young citizens were being caught up in the world events and would continue to be for at least the next four years. It was a decade of a devastating world war and its aftermath, including rationing and wage freezes for Americans. But it was also a decade of profound discoveries: Enrico Fermi split the atom, which led to intensive atomic research and the Manhattan Project, and pencillin was shown to be successful in treating chronic diseases. In world politics, the United Nations was formed in 1946, replacing the League of Nations, and the North Atlantic Treaty Organization was formed in 1949. In Carroll County, Maryland, in a pumpkin patch owned by Whittaker Chambers, incriminating tapes were found, which led to the conviction of Alger Hiss for spying. It was also the era when the work of Noel Coward, T. S. Eliot, Thornton Wilder, John Steinbeck, James Michener, Ernest Hemingway, Arthur Miller, and Kurt Weill came to prominence. And people found memorable and welcome entertainment from Broadway productions such as Rodgers and Hammerstein's *Oklahoma* and *Carousel*, Irving Berlin's *Annie Get Your Gun*, Leonard Bernstein's *On the Town*, and Lerner and Loewe's *Brigadoon*. It was a decade of major contrasts socially, politically, culturally, and educationally.

At Western Maryland College, the decade saw a drastic decrease in male enrollments in 1943 and 1944, and with it a change in the campus life, which had been dominated by male athletic events and fraternity-sponsored dances and activities. The absence of male faces (and the corresponding drop in college revenues) was temporarily remedied when 300 men from all over the country arrived in the summer of 1943 to enroll in the Army Specialized Training Program, one of many accelerated educational programs for armed service personnel conducted on college and university campuses across the nation. But nine months later, those men were shipped off to the war, and the campus anxiously awaited peacetime, which came a year later. Following the war, many men, newly released from military service, headed back to college on the GI Bill, and Western Maryland accepted its share of those students, with enrollment growing to a maximum of 871 (double the lowest enrollment in 1943) before the decade was over. The college successfully handled the fluctuations, while enduring a number of significant internal changes.

FACULTY AND ADMINISTRATION

During the decade, the board of trustees experienced an unusually large turnover in membership; a third of the group changed. After Methodist unification, the board was also enlarged by two to include the bishops of the newly formed Baltimore and Peninsula Conferences. Sadly, the Baltimore Conference bishop, Adna Wright Leonard [1941–43], was killed in the summer of 1943 in a plane crash in Iceland while on a mission for President Roosevelt to the armed forces.[1] His successor was Charles Wesley Flint [1944–52]. Among the long-tenured trustees who died in office were S. R. Harris '74 [1897–1942], J. W. Kirk '83 [1900–43], Milton Zollickoffer [1901–44], William J. Thompson [1926–44], and Richard L. Shipley [1927–47]. Among those resigning from the board for health reasons were Fred P. Adkins [1919–42] and William G. Baker Jr. '94 [1918–44]. New members elected to the board as replacements were D. Roger Englar '03 [1942–48], Harry C. Adkins [1943–51], Lowell S. Ensor [1944–75], W. Lloyd Fisher [1946–94], J. Earl Cummings [1947–71], E. Cranston Riggin [1948–84], Charles E. Moylan '17 [1948–69], and D. Carlysle MacLea '22 [1949–75]. The board also welcomed another woman member (its third) when it elected Dorothy McDaniel Herr '18 [1945–74]. The election of women trustees had been an issue for several years before 1945, especially as vacancies occurred. It appears from the board minutes that the "old guard" of conservative male trustees were not going to be pressured into electing a woman, even when the nominating committee put forth women's names in response to the desire for accreditation by the American Association of University Women.[2] Bishop James Straughn continued to chair the board and assumed the title of "chairman" rather than "president" upon board action taken in 1943.[3] Over his yearly objections, based on his physical distance from campus (he was bishop of the Pittsburgh area), he was regularly nominated and unanimously reelected until April 1949, when his emphatic resignation was reluctantly accepted, after 20 years in the post; he had retired as bishop in 1948. He continued on the board until his death in 1974 at the age of 97. In recognition of his service as board trustee and chair and as bishop, he was awarded an honorary doctor of laws degree at the Commencement in 1949. (He had received an honorary doctor of divinity from the college in 1921.) The trustees also commissioned his portrait, which was painted by Hilda G. Taylor and now hangs in the Baker Chapel foyer.

Straughn was succeeded as chair by F. Murray Benson '17 (1895–1963) [1936–63], who was not the first in his family to serve as a trustee. His two grandfathers, Benjamin Franklin Benson [1883–1902] and Joshua T. Murray [1876–99]; his father, Frank Thomas Benson '84 [1906–29]; and his uncle, Thomas A. Murray [1905–35], preceded him. A Murray or a Benson had been a trustee for almost all the college's history; and B. F. Benson had also been vice president and professor of belles lettres in 1883–86. At the time of his election, Murray Benson was a member of the law firm of Tydings, Sauerwein, Benson, and Boyd in Baltimore; he was also on the board of trustees of the Westminster Theological Seminary.[4]

In this decade the college's charter was amended on several occasions: to change the title of the leader of the board; the name of the church after unification; and the wording describing the makeup of the board, from "twelve members of the clergy" to "one more than one-third . . . shall always be chosen from among the ministerial members of the Baltimore Conference or the Peninsula Conference of the Methodist Church." This allowed the board to expand its numbers as necessary while maintaining the ratio of laymen to clergy that had existed since1868.[5]

During this decade, some aspects of the college's past were brought to mind when the diaries of J. T. Ward (from 1866 to 1886) were presented to the college in 1947 by his granddaughter Miriam Lewis Veasey '96. (Copies were made for the family, and the originals were bound and placed in the college archives.) The diaries have proved invaluable to historians researching the early history of the college, as well as the post–Civil War era. They are all handwritten, of course, most in beautiful "copper plate" script in ink, which is still as fresh and clear as the day they were composed. In 2006, Ward's diaries covering 1889–95 were made available by his great grandson

Dr. Edwin Lewis and were placed in the archives. In May 1946, a portrait of Mary Ward Lewis was presented to the Alumni Association by the class of 1896 for inclusion in a proposed "historical museum" along with some other memorabilia from the Lewis presidency. The class, which included Mary Ward Lewis's daughter Miriam Lewis Veasey, requested that the college find a permanent site for such a museum.[6] Unfortunately, the museum was never created (the college archives not being created until the college centennial, in 1967), and the portrait and the ephemera (including souvenirs of Lewis's several trips abroad) have disappeared. There is a portrait of Mrs. Lewis in the archive collection, but it seems doubtful that it is the one presented in 1946.

The campus was deeply saddened to learn on April 19, 1942, that William Roberts McDaniel had died at the home of his daughter Dorothy (Herr) at the age of 80 years, 8 months. Students, faculty, trustees, alumni, and townspeople mourned the loss of this Renaissance man who had devoted his life to the service of his alma mater. Born just four months after the beginning of the American Civil War, he died four months after the beginning of World War II. Between these two world-shattering events, he lived a scholarly academic life in a world full of change and wonder. He saw the college grow from 59 students in 1877 (when he enrolled as sophomore) to 600; he saw the physical

Fall convocation 1941; seated behind President Holloway
(L to R): T. Whitfield, C. Spicer, C. Schaeffer, A. Isanogle, L. Bertholf, S. Schofield,
C. Little, G. Wills, P. Sadler, M. Ward, E. Schempp, W. Ridington

campus change from a single building (with the Owings Hall addition) to one with 17 buildings. In one capacity or another, he assisted the first four presidents of the college, and he was a propelling force for the growth and development of the institution for almost 65 years. Funeral services were held in Baker Chapel on April 22, conducted by President Holloway, assisted by seminary president Charles E. Forlines and McDaniel's pastor, Lowell Ensor. Members of the board of trustees served as honorary pall bearers, while his oldest faculty associates carried him to his grave in Westminster Cemetery, where he was buried in the John Smith family plot. In their memorial resolution, the trustees eulogized him in these most loving words:

> Were this minute for the eyes only of the personnel of the board of trustees as it is today, then it were better that it might never be inscribed. For there remains for those who knew and who loved him—and the two are, in his case, synonymous—a memory that neither written phrase nor spoken word may adequately express. But there will be others, of another day, who will ask: "Who was this Dr. McDaniel? Whence was he? What was he?" "We know he was a teacher, a Trustee, Faculty Secretary and College Treasurer. Others, conceivably, might have been some, even all, of these. Who was he?"[7]

A detailed biography follows, which describes him as an able policy maker, a great teacher, and the originator of the many progressive movements in the social life of the students and the curriculum of the college. It also mentions his active civic and community life (including twice being asked to become superintendent of the Carroll County schools) and his activity in Masonry and his church.

The resolution concludes with these poignant and prophetic words:

> Somehow or other, one feels that the life of William R. McDaniel will be interwoven into the destiny of Western Maryland College, as his life has been into every decade of its history. For while William R. McDaniel, the mortal, is gone, William R. McDaniel, the spirit, lives—and motivates the lives of others. It will continue to do so 'til time and eternity meet.

With McDaniel's death, the office of vice president was eliminated, and his role as treasurer was officially filled by Carl Schaeffer, who had been assistant treasurer for several years.[8] Upon taking on the full-time role as treasurer, Schaeffer gave up his teaching duties, and in 1947 he also gave up his post as secretary of the faculty, a position he had held for 25 years. He was succeeded by William Robbins Ridington [1938–73]. Other, more far-reaching administrative changes occurred later in the decade, the most important one being in the presidency.

In early spring 1947, President Holloway informed the board that he had been approached by Drew University to become the dean of its theological school (from which he had received his BD in 1921). At the April 1 board meeting, he formally tendered his resignation, effective June 30; he expressed regret that he had not accomplished everything he thought needed to be done, but he stated that he had given all his energies to the work and saw great things for the college's future. The trustees passed a resolution of appreciation for his service, saying, in part,

> President Holloway has maintained without reservation the great traditions of his predecessors. He has had an excellent, indeed a superior administration. He leaves the college of his own volition, possessing at the time not only the confidence and affection of his associates—the trustees, the faculty, the student body, the constituency—but their abiding gratitude and pursuing goodwill. It is a position of high estate and one could envy so fine a record.[9]

Four years before, the trustees had passed another resolution of commendation:

> We commend President Holloway for the very careful and thoughtful study he has made of the problems of the school for the [past] eight years... and upon the splendid record of achievement which he has established. We especially commend [him] for his very thoughtful and intelligent approach to the particular problems which have been presented by the war . . . [and] for his far-sighted view of the future of Western Maryland College.[10]

Fred Holloway had led the college through a very difficult time. In his annual report to the trustees in 1947, he noted,

> I doubt that any period in American higher education has presented so many different and unusual circumstances as the past twelve years. Between 1935 and 1939, we were coping with the problems of the depression, between '39 and '41 we were in the pre-war era, from '41 to '45 we were facing the varied and constantly changing problems of the war era. Since then we have met the floodtide of high education. . . . However, when everything is considered, I believe that we can proudly say that we are doing an honest educational job.

The formal portrait of President Holloway was immediately commissioned; it was unveiled by Dorothy McDaniel Herr at the fall meeting of the board in November 1947 and presented to the college at the 1948 Commencement. Holloway remained a member of the board for two more years, resigning a year after becoming president of Drew. (It has been speculated that he knew he would become president in 1948 upon the retirement of the incumbent, but that that could not be announced at the time of his departure.)

Portrait of President
Fred Garrigus Holloway

He was later remembered as one who devoted his life to education and the life of the mind, and as one who got the college "back on the academic track" when he became president. Perhaps he knew that in a year he would be named president of Drew. Perhaps he was also exhausted with trying to keep the finances of the small college in balance while confronting wildly fluctuating enrollments. Perhaps he was still smarting from the alumni backlash from his efforts to raise the college's academic standards by downsizing the football program after Coach Harlow left and his resistance to rebuilding the program after the war (although nothing of this is reported officially in minutes of either the board or the faculty). An article in the Drew *Alumni Magazine*, by John T. Cunningham, described a conversation he had with Holloway in 1950 regarding sports at Drew. When the possibility of football was raised, Holloway rather coldly announced that he was not about to take alumni pressure about university athletics, and there would be no football at Drew. A bit later he noted to the article's author, more calmly, "You could not have known that alumni fanatics drove me out of Western Maryland College after I proposed downsizing football. My wife and I suffered around-the-clock phone messages demanding that I leave. I did."[11]

What is curious about the statement is that the first downsizing of the football program had occurred in the years soon after Harlow left for Harvard. During the war, there was no football at all for three seasons, because there were not enough men available to play in any of the colleges. But apparently there was considerable alumni pressure *after* the war to reinstitute a football program similar to that of the Harlow era; furthermore, Harlow was planning on returning to Westminster in early 1948 (following his retirement from Harvard after 11 seasons (1934–43, 1945–47) for health reasons and possibly was "talking football" to his former players and some trustees (including, perhaps, Robert Gill). Holloway strongly resisted any move to rebuild the football program to the level of the Harlow era, preferring the college to focus its funds and energies toward improving its academic reputation.[12] Bishop Flint, commenting on the Holloway departure, said, "As an alumnus of Drew, I am very happy; as a trustee of Western Maryland, I am perplexed."[13] (This may suggest that some of the trustees, at least, were unaware of the pressures Holloway had been under.) Holloway and his family were feted at a farewell dinner on June 27. He would remain as president of Drew for 12 years before being elected bishop of the Methodist Church in 1960, serving the West Virginia area for 8 years, before retiring in 1968. For 4 years after that, as emeritus professor of modern English at Morris Harvey College in Charleston, West Virginia, he taught poetry, which was his love. He retired to Wilmington, Delaware, in 1972.

The eight-member trustee committee appointed in April to seek a new

Lowell Skinner Ensor,
fifth president

president, chaired by Murray Benson, presented its report two months later, at the June 25 meeting. Benson reported that the "committee had the pleasure and privilege of seriously considering a number of men of unquestioned character, intellect and ability. . . . The task was one of selection—not of elimination. We are pledged to silence as to our deliberations." However, rumors at the time, as well as some letters in the archives, suggest that serious consideration was given to several popular ministers in the Baltimore Conference, along with at least two nonclergy, one an alumnus who was already a college president. This was an interesting beginning of a move away from the tradition (never a requirement) that WMC presidents be Methodist clergy.[14] The committee's nominee was the Rev. Dr. Lowell Skinner Ensor (1907–75) [1947–72], who was 40 years old, a native of Baltimore, the son of the Rev. John T. and Birdie Skinner Ensor. He had attended Towson High School, graduated from Baltimore City College in 1923, received his BA from Johns Hopkins University in 1928, and gone on to Drew University, where he received his bachelor of divinity in 1931. He married Eloise Bittner that year, and they had one daughter, Caryl Jeanne '58. He served pastorates in Prince Frederick (1931–33) and Pikesville (1934–39) before coming to Westminster to the Methodist Episcopal Church in 1940. As pastor there he accomplished the unification of the two local Methodist churches (Centenary M.E. and Immanuel M.P.) after the Methodist unification in 1939. Western Maryland

College had conferred the honorary doctor of divinity on him in 1944, and he was elected a trustee the same year.[15] He assumed the office of president on July 1, 1947 (six days after he was formally elected), the first president who was not an alumnus and the first to come from the Methodist Episcopal rather than the Methodist Protestant tradition. It has been suggested that this appointment was significant, for it gave true substance to the Methodist unification and strengthened the college's position within its church affiliation.[16] In June 1950, Ensor received the honorary degree of doctor of humane letters from the University of Maryland, conferred by President Byrd.

Soon after President Ensor took office (at a salary of $6,500 and the usual benefits), Dr. Lloyd Bertholf, dean of the faculty for nine years and longtime professor of biology [1924–48], announced that he would be leaving the college on February 1, 1948, to become dean of the College of the Pacific in Stockton, California. Bertholf, who received his PhD in physiology from Johns Hopkins, had also been dean of freshmen [1933–39]. He had twice been president of the Maryland Association of Biology Teachers and in April 1946 had been elected national president of Beta Beta Beta, the college biology honor society. He was also an active churchman, having been lay delegate to the Methodist General Conference, president of the board of education for the Baltimore Conference, and an active member of the Westminster Methodist Church. He left with good feelings about the college he had seen evolve over his 23-year tenure, noting in his "Goodbye to the Hill," "She stands today, I firmly believe, on the threshold of a new advance. . . . Western Maryland is in a strategic position to advance in most any direction she chooses."[17] He would be going to a senior college with a graduate program, the oldest college in California, one also affiliated with the Methodist Church.[18] After ten years there, he was elected president of Illinois Wesleyan University in Bloomington, a post he held for ten years before retiring in 1968. He died in January 2003 at the age of 103.[19]

After requesting nominations from the faculty, Ensor appointed Dr. G. Franklin Stover [1946–49] to be the dean of faculty. (He candidly reported to the faculty that John Makosky had received many nominations but had not yet completed his doctorate.) Stover had been dean of education, which position was now abolished, for two years. He would continue to be professor and chair of the Education Department. He had come to the college from the Pennsylvania State Department of Education in Harrisburg, where he was a curriculum consultant. He was a graduate of Susquehanna University and received his master's degree from Pennsylvania State College and his EdD from Columbia University.[20]

Sixteen months later, in May 1949, Stover resigned as dean of the faculty. He noted that "the press of responsibility connected with both positions was too much for him to put the time on the education department which he feels it deserves."[21] President Ensor did not immediately name another dean, preferring to complete the year with the able assistance of faculty committee chairs. Soon after the conclusion of the academic year, John Makosky completed the doctor of education degree at Columbia and was immediately named dean of the faculty, a position he would hold for the next 20 years while simultaneously chairing the English Department. (It was said of Makosky many years later that he always considered administration a "step down" from the classroom but far too important to leave to professional administrators; since someone had to do it, it might as well be a "liberal artisan," which he certainly was.)[22] At the same time, Dr. Stover resigned his positions in the Education Department and accepted an appointment as dean of instruction at the Maryland State Teachers College at Towson.

During this decade, the post of dean of women was held by four different people: Bertha Adkins [1938–42], Katherine K. Carmichael [1942–44], Kathryn Huganir [1945–47], and Helen G. Howery [1946–65]. The latter three women also were members of the English Department. The college nurse, Mamie Isanogle, in charge of the infirmary in McDaniel Hall since 1922, retired in 1941. The sister of Alvey Isanogle, "Miss I.," as she was affectionately known, was described as gracious, sympathetic, versatile, competent, and cheerful.[23] She was replaced by Belle Eason Griffin, RN, for 6 years. When "Mom" Griffin retired in 1949, the post was turned over to Isabel Glenn for a year before M. Virginia Stoner arrived on the scene in 1950 to manage the new infirmary and care for the students' health for the next 23 years.

Milson C. Raver [1932–45], who had been hired to teach physics, was named director of public relations in 1942; he would also seek out prospective students. He held the post until February 1945, when he resigned to become executive secretary of the Maryland State Teachers Association. (His wife, Kathleen Moore Raver '33, the former dietician, returned to the Hill in 1941 as instructor in home economics for several years.) He was replaced by John Bayley Jones '41, a Methodist minister, who would continue in the public relations role, as well as teaching sociology and coaching the soccer team, until he returned to the pastorate in 1949. He was replaced by Philip E. Uhrig '52M [1949–81],[24] who took on the additional duties of director of alumni affairs after T. K. Harrison [1930–49] retired as college purchasing agent; manager of the bookstore, grille, and post office; and secretary of the Alumni Association. Harrison's duties as purchasing agent and bookstore manager were assumed by Charles R. Foutz Jr. [1949–61].

A word about T. K. Harrison is needed because so many early alumni were kept in contact with the institution through his efforts as alumni secretary for

26 years. He had a varied career, as an army officer, teacher, and businessman, working in the oil fields of Texas and with United Railways. He spent a year in Rio de Janeiro before returning to the campus as business manager for 19 years. Upon Harrison's retirement, President Ensor commented, "If no one could be found for a particular job it was usually turned over to T. K., and he has accepted his responsibilities with the same loyalty and gracious spirit for which he is known by so many alumni."[25] In 1969, the newly established Alumni House on the campus (the former Reifsnider home at 239 Main Street) was named Harrison House in his honor.

T. K. Harrison '01, business manager

Two significant retirements from the faculty occurred during the decade. Dr. George Stockton Wills, professor of English [1898–1900, 1901–4, 1922–44], retired in June 1944 at the age of 78, completing a 50-year teaching career, including service at Greensboro Women's College and the Baltimore Polytechnic Institute, in addition to his 27 years at Western Maryland. Born in 1866 in North Carolina, he received the bachelor and master of philosophy degrees at the University of North Carolina at Chapel Hill and the master of arts from Harvard. He was a member of Phi Beta Kappa, the first graduate student to write a master's thesis on an American author (Sidney Lanier), and the first English professor in the country to offer a college-level American literature course. In recognition of his inspired teaching, his many students surprised him by arranging to have his portrait painted (by Lloyd Embry of Washington) and presenting it to the college at the Alumni Banquet of 1941. Almost 500 people attended the banquet in his honor, to watch his grandson unveil the portrait that now hangs in the Wills English Seminar Room in Hill Hall.[26] Many former students and colleagues sent messages for the occasion, which were bound into a book. One from W. R. McDaniel thanked Wills for his visits during his prolonged illness and ended by saying, "While others are singing your praises, let me sum it all up by saying in a familiar phrase—you are a gentleman and a scholar." His most loyal student and colleague, John Makosky, noted, "I am a teacher because Professor Wills is a *great* teacher. . . . I still hold Professor Wills before me as the ideal—both professional and personal—which I seek to approach. I can conceive of no higher standard." The trustees named him professor emeritus and awarded him a pension of $100 per month (increased to $125 in 1949), approximately 40% of his annual salary. In the years following his retirement, Wills published, in two issues of the *Bulletin of the Historical Society of Carroll County, Maryland*, "History of Western Maryland College 1866–1951," the first definitive history of the institution.[27] The first volume focuses in some detail on the first 20 years of the college, while the second summarizes more quickly the next 65 years. Wills continued to teach an occasional course or seminar for the English Department for a number of years (his final class was in spring 1954), and the formally dressed gentleman with the white beard was often seen walking the campus until his death at the age of 89 in February 1956.[28]

The second retirement of note was that of Alvey Isanogle on August 31, 1946, at the age of 73. Isanogle had come to the college in 1920 to resurrect the Education Department and transform it into one that would put the college in the forefront of teacher education in Maryland. He was very successful in this, as the legions of teachers prepared under his guidance over 26 years could attest. After his first wife, Anna Houck Isanogle, died, he married Isabel Thompson in June 1944; Thompson had come to the college to teach biology in 1942. After retiring from the college as professor emeritus on a $125 monthly pension, Isanogle moved on to head the public junior college that was being formed in Hagerstown to provide another collegiate program for returning veterans on the GI Bill. He held that post until February 1949, by which time Hagerstown Junior College, the first of its kind in Maryland, was well established. Even though he no longer taught courses, Isanogle kept his ties with WMC. When Joseph Bailer arrived in 1949 to head the Education Department, Isanogle took him around the state and introduced him to the superintendents and principals who had aided the department in the past.[29] Affectionately known as "Piney," Isanogle died in January 1953. At the Alumni Banquet on May 30, 1953, his portrait was presented to the college, and it now hangs in the Education Department conference room. Speaking at the event was Earle T. Hawkins '23, LLD 1948, the president of Maryland State Teachers College at Towson, who reviewed Isanogle's many accomplishments and contributions to education in Maryland. He concluded by saying that Isanogle had been "most of all a friend and inspiration to many hundreds of Western Maryland graduates."[30] Wills commented that "no one was more influential than [Isanogle] in bringing the academic life out of the lingering pattern of the nineteenth century into touch with modern education."[31]

The Education Department also lost the services of Mary O. Ebaugh [1926–41] when she retired in 1941. Mabel B. Harris '19, longtime organ instructor [1919–41] in the Music Department, also retired in 1941. Both were awarded pensions ($25 per month) by the board, but only Ebaugh was named professor emerita. Ebaugh died eight months later. Edwin Schempp [1932–43] in economics resigned after 11 years on the faculty. Lawrence C. Little, who had directed the religious education program, left his position in philosophy and religion in 1945 to take a position in philosophy at the University of Pittsburgh. Addie Belle Robb [1930–48] resigned her position in history after 18 years to take care of her mother. Evelyn Mudge [1931–49] became chair of the Education Department at Hood College in Frederick in 1949.

Replacing these faculty stalwarts during the decade were a number of individuals who would become, through their long years of service, part of the fabric of the growing institution: Grace Murray [1942–51] in music, J. Lloyd Straughn [1942–53, 1959–73] in chemistry, R. Dewees Summers [1942–64] in physics, Isabel Thompson (Isanogle Royer) [1942–79] in biology, Thomas F. Marshall [1943–55] in English, W. Allan MacDonald [1945–57] in art history, Reuben S. Holthaus [1946–76] in philosophy and religion, Helen Howery in English, Elizabeth Simkins [1946–70] in library science and the library, Joseph W. Hendren [1947–66] in English, Mahlon F. Peck [1947–59] in physics, Harwell P. Sturdivant [1948–73] in biology, Joseph R. Bailer [1949–71] in education, Charles E. Crain [1949–78] in religion, and Olive R. Russell [1949–62] in psychology. One other professor, Dika Newlin, who stayed only four years [1945–49] lives on in stories (legends?) because she was quite a character. A child prodigy, pianist, and composer, she became the protégée of Arnold Schönberg, received a PhD from Columbia University, and premiered several of her compositions in piano recitals at WMC. She completed her teaching career of over 60 years at Virginia Commonwealth University.

Over the decade the faculty grew from 56 to 60, plus 8 special instructors. As many as 23 held an earned doctorate (PhD or EdD), another 35 held a master's degree, and 5 had a professional diploma or certificate. Various members of the faculty were becoming more active in statewide and regional professional associations and holding offices in them, bringing recognition to the college. Samuel Schofield received an honorary doctor of science degree from Dickinson College on May 5, 1949, at its Founder's Day exercises. He was recognized for his many years of outstanding service to science and higher education.[32]

President Holloway in Victory Garden

In the years leading up to the war, there was within the faculty and administration a diversity of opinion on whether the United States should join it, and during the war, on how we should conduct it once we were in it. A continuum of feelings existed, from strong pacifism on the part of Lawrence Little, Lloyd Bertholf, and Montgomery Schroyer, to strong nationalism from others. This divergence of views rarely seems to have erupted into any overt activity on the campus or in the community. German professor Joseph Willen, a native German who had become a U.S. citizen in the 1920s, was sometimes subjected to harassment in the community and in his neighborhood and suffered isolation and shunning from some of his colleagues. Other college friends were supportive of him and his family during this time, however, and he did not feel the need to leave the college or community.[33] Tolerance of differing philosophies appears to have been fostered fairly successfully by President Holloway at Western Maryland.

During the decade, the trustees finally addressed the issue of a faculty retirement pension plan, as well as sabbatical leaves, promotions in rank, and tenure. All would have a significant effect on the college's finances.

CURRICULUM

The war obviously had an effect on student enrollment, faculty, and thus the curriculum. In February 1943, the *WMC Bulletin* was produced as a small pamphlet that asked the question "Will Western Maryland continue its regular college curriculum during the war period?" The answer was an emphatic "Certainly!" The pamphlet went on to assure the reader that the college would still be preparing premedical, predental, and preministerial students, as well as teachers, and offering all the traditional liberal arts majors. It acknowledged that there would be some "special war-time courses" offered, as well, reflecting the world emergency and meeting an immediate need. These included Aeronautics (including flight simulation as part of a Civilian Pilot Training program) and Modern Japanese. Furthermore, special one- and two-year curricula were designed to provide students destined for the armed services with a foundation that would

17

Flight simulator, civilian pilot training

371

fit them for specialized service (and on which later studies could be built). Students could now enter medical school following a two-year intensive premed program approved by the American Medical Association.

As early as January 1942, the faculty had designed and were beginning to implement a three-year accelerated program to serve young men and women who wished to complete their college education prior to entering military service, were going into the scientific professions, or were preparing to fill teaching shortages in the public schools. To accomplish this acceleration, the college year was divided into four terms, two short (six and a half weeks) and two long. The long terms were essentially the regular semesters, while the short terms replaced the traditional summer sessions. Fourteen hours of credit could be earned in two short terms, and 36 hours in two long terms. The graduation requirement of 136 hours was maintained; a student could complete the bachelor's degree in three years (four short terms and six long terms). While this program per se was discontinued after the bulk of returning veterans had completed their work, it was still possible to accelerate using the summer sessions (which included a number of regular undergraduate courses) until the rise of the community colleges made such offerings less attractive to students and they were reduced or discontinued.

The 1944 *Aloha* described another temporary change in the normal college program:

> *In the annals of the history of Western Maryland College, July 12, 1943, will stand out as the beginning of an unprecedented phase of her growth and activities, because it was on that day that 300 young soldiers became her adopted students and alumni-to-be. What took place was happening on more than 225 campuses throughout the nation, for the largest educational project in the world was taking shape in America to meet the challenge of total war. It went by the name of the Army Specialized Training Program [ASTP], and its purpose was to provide the vitally needed specialists and technicians for the Army. Under this program thousands of Uncle Sam's brainiest soldiers, many of whom would never have been able to go to college in civilian life, were sent to the best universities in the land, with the Army paying for their tuition, food, clothes, books, and rooms, in addition to continuing their regular pay. Most of them were high school graduates under 22 years of age, embarking on a course that was to last almost two years, and from which they would emerge as specialists in civil, mechanical, electrical, chemical, sanitary, and marine engineering.*[34]

The cadets who came to Westminster to be part of AST Unit no. 3308 hailed from 39 states and the District of Columbia. All had had 13 weeks of basic army training in Washington, D.C., or Texas. Their preengineering studies included 24 hours of classroom work each week in mathematics, physics, chemistry, English, and American history. In addition, they had five hours of military courses and six hours of physical training. Laboratory work and the required 24 study hours brought the work week to over 50 hours. Platoons of 30 men marched to classes under the command of their leader, who turned the students over to the teacher for instruction; when the class was over, the platoon leader again took command, and the group marched off to the next class.[35] The regular college faculty taught the bulk of the courses (with a salary adjustment of $100 for the overload), and 15 additional instructors were hired to teach specialized areas outside the normal program. For example, Elizabeth Johnson Marshall, wife of newly hired English professor Thomas Marshall, was hired to teach mechanical drawing because of her architectural studies. Even regular faculty took on some new duties: English professor John Makosky was tapped to teach mathematics in the program because of his early training in engineering.[36]

The military staff had its offices in Yingling Gymnasium, while the cadets were housed in Albert Norman Ward Hall (in wooden double-decker beds made in the college shop, four cadets to a room) and Gill Gymnasium (in metal cots) and took their classes primarily in Lewis Hall. They ate in the

Cadets in Army Specialized Training Program march to classes in 1943.

college dining hall (where they found the food better than army food). At no time were they allowed to forget that they were soldiers. Reveille was at 6:15 A.M. and taps were blown at 10:15 P.M. These bugle calls soon became as familiar to the civilian students as the chimes of the town clock.[37] Attempts were made to provide some breaks in the normal routine, including some parties and dances on campus. The 19th Annual Military Ball was moved forward to December 11, so that the cadets could attend. In Westminster, local churches and civic groups also put on occasional dances and parties. Robert Peterson was a cadet from South Dakota who arrived in July and soon went to a Soroptimist-sponsored dance at the armory, where he met a local young lady named Pauline Dunn. They dated whenever possible for the next month or so, until he was about to be transferred to a medical corps program in Illinois. Before he left, they became engaged, and on April 1, 1944, they were married. After the war, Robert returned to his bride in Westminster, where he remained for the rest of his life. He was one of at least five ASTP students who returned to local brides in Westminster after the war.[38]

By the end of the second ASTP term, the group had diminished to 250 men. By the end of the third term, March 30, the war had escalated to the extent that ASTP cadets in engineering units (like the one at WMC) were called into active duty, their studies cut short as they marched off to war. The local unit had performed very well in its nine months on campus; on army achievement examinations the WMC cadets ranked seventh out of 47 units at colleges and universities. Beyond its significant service to the war effort, in Westminster the ASTP served as a buffer for the drop in enrollment and revenue in 1943–44. The government paid for renovations to accommodate the cadets, rent for use of the facilities, instruction by the faculty, medical services, and food, as well as a portion of the cost of heat, light, power, and administrative overhead. President Holloway described the venture this way: "While the contract is in no sense profit-making to the college, it does give us an opportunity to operate in this emergency period without any financial headaches. It does make it possible for us to hold our faculty and staff together."[39] The loss of the program earlier than planned posed a financial crisis, but after making adjustments, the college closed the year without a deficit.

In January 1944, there appeared in the *Gold Bug* an article by John Makosky that was designed to create some debate and discussion among the students and faculty. Entitled "Western Maryland—College or Country Club," the article began with a description of the college as a wonderful place for culture, athletics, courting, and parties. But as an educational institution, Makosky found it lacking, because the ideal of scholarship was not held very high. He claimed that students were distracted by a glut of activities that kept them from real scholarly work. Administrative softness, he said, had encouraged intellectual irresponsibility, allowing students to opt out of difficult courses and shy away from demanding professors. "Our students collectively have an aversion for study; as a result they go where they need do as little of it as possible." After giving lots of examples of poor student attitudes toward intellectual pursuits, he noted that students "take the college as they find it, and if an atmosphere of intellectual curiosity, of absorption in what is significant in the fields of study, if care and thoroughness and honesty in matters of the mind were what they encountered as they passed under the arch, there would be few dissenters from this way of life."[40] Makosky may have overstated the case a bit, but those who knew him can appreciate his wisdom and his analysis of the college of the 1940s; they will remember that, a few years later, when he was appointed dean, he tried to remedy some of the ills he described. For all his concerns, Makosky loved the college deeply and delighted in its early history, as evidenced by his little treatise, "Western Maryland College in the Nineteenth Century," first given as a lecture at the Faculty Club and then published as the *WMC Bulletin* for July 1940.

Perhaps stimulated by Makosky's article, the faculty made several attempts at raising standards and devising means of measuring and honoring academic achievement. Twice in the decade the specific requirements for degree honors (summa cum laude and cum laude) were changed. These had been rather regularly overhauled as grading patterns changed; the 1942 standards required computing the percentage of A and B grades obtained, and, for the highest honor, a departmental recommendation. By 1950, this rather cumbersome plan had been revised so that honors were based strictly on GPA: cum laude, 2.2 through 2.49; summa cum laude, 2.5 or better. (When the college adopted a 4.0 scale, the minimums became 3.2 and 3.5.)[41] In 1947, three-hour final examinations were again instituted in all courses over a four- or five-day period, and requiring comprehensive examinations in all departments was considered. Students were also being encouraged to take the Graduate Record Examination in preparation for graduate school admissions. A group of four faculty members (George Wills, Theodore Whitfield, Kathryn B. Hildebran, and Ann E. O'Rourk [1947–51]), all Phi Beta Kappans, submitted a request to the national organization of Phi Beta Kappa in 1949 for an investigatory visit to determine the viability of the college sheltering a chapter of the prestigious liberal arts honor society. Unfortunately, a month later they learned that Phi Beta Kappa would not make a visit during the next triennial cycle.[42] The letter from the Phi Beta Kappa secretary cited low faculty salaries, endowment, and library holdings as some of the reasons for the denial.

While the trustees were planning for the postwar years primarily from a bricks-and-mortar point of view, the faculty was charged with planning for the curricular and pedagogical needs of an influx of students, especially veterans, following the war. To that end they organized a variety of committees that eventually recommended needed changes or additions to current practice. The committees were Public Relations, Admissions, Physical Education, Library, Sciences, Humanities, Religion, Teaching Tools, and Guidance and Placement. The first two suggest areas of expansion to ensure a stable student body for the long-term future of the college, while the last suggests a need beginning to be felt by students across the country as employment opportunities were changing and expanding for both sexes. Recommendations included a traveling admissions officer, an office of guidance and placement (which was established within the dean of men's office), a printed guidance bulletin for advising students, an expanded library collection and a facility to house it, a foreign scholarships committee, and some new curricular organizations for study.

A survey of the catalogs of the decade reveals a few interesting curricular changes but about the same number of courses. In 1940–41, both French and German were offered as majors, but by 1943 and continuing into the 1950s, German was no longer a major. Greek and Latin had always been offered, but by 1950, they were listed under classics, which included some cultural history. Psychology was subsumed under sociology in 1940, but by 1943 it had evolved into its own department and major. Economics expanded during the decade to include business administration as a major, and by 1950 physical education could be a major when combined with another major field. Political science had always been considered part of history and offered only as a minor, but by 1951, it would become an area for majoring.

The bachelor of science was awarded for study in the sciences until 1950, when it was redesigned to be a more "professional" degree for those majoring in applied art, home economics, physical and health education, and public school music. The bachelor of arts degree was then awarded to all other majors in the college, including the various sciences. The master of education, which had replaced the master of arts in the previous decade, received another overhaul at the end of this decade and featured more "action research" for teachers, under the direction of Dr. Bailer, the new head of the Education Department.

In 1947, the Music Department became an associate member of the National Association of Schools of Music, ranking it among the best in the country. Eight staff members gave instruction in piano, voice, organ, and violin; organizations for students included a choir, glee club, orchestra, and band; and both faculty and students gave numerous recitals during the academic year in the newly renovated Levine Hall, which now boasted attractive practice rooms and a recital hall.

STUDENT LIFE

The bombing of Pearl Harbor on Sunday, December 7, 1941, brought the war directly to the United States. That "Day of Infamy" was remembered by Anna Rose Beasman (Anderson) '45, who described the chapel service that evening in Alumni Hall, and the days following:

> I so vividly remember the tone of that service—so different from the previous Sunday evenings when some student-assigned seats were empty. The five hundred and some faces expressing feelings of the unknown, fear, anxiety, and emptiness are still with me. . . . Our dear President Dr. Fred Holloway stood on that stage in Alumni Hall surrounded by his staff, humbly yet courageously calming our fears, knowing our campus lives had been changed that day. Our Monday morning classes with our beloved professors were of a somber aura, but we knew we must continue being the students aiming for a good education. Dr. John Makosky, English "prof," lacked his stern, serious demeanor and revealed to his young Freshmen that his heart was heavy, too. The usual babble in the dining hall was silenced with only the sounds of clinking knives and forks. Prayer service in Little Baker Chapel found the pews filled. . . .

> And then there were the football teams who would not see another fall season for "Heaven knows when"! My Li'l Abner (escort to the Sadie Hawkins dance in November) was Roland Blanchette, center on the Freshman team; he never returned to campus after the Christmas holiday. His name was one of the first to be announced "killed in action" in the European theater of war.[43]

Edward P. Furlow x'46, who entered college in 1942 but left for the army after only one year, provided some reminiscences of his freshman year during wartime:

> The fall of 1942 started off with the usual complement of freshmen, a bit more than two hundred. We had an approximate 40 to 60 ratio of boys to girls. It wasn't long after the start of the fall semester that a few of the male students began to disappear: volunteers to the military. Along toward the middle of the fall semester the male students were invited to a convocation at the Alumni Hall. We were to find out what Uncle Sam had in store for us. Four short talks were given by uniformed representatives of the army, army air corps, navy and the marines. They all said the same thing, "We Gotcha!" We were told that we could enlist in the reserves of one of the services and be allowed to complete our

freshman year. Or we could wait to be drafted which could happen at any time. . . . I chose the army and within a day or two had enlisted in the reserves. Those of us who signed up were able to finish the freshman year. I was even lucky enough to get in several weeks of summer school before the army remembered where I was. . . . Shortly after our arrival all of us freshmen, both male and female, were lectured by the Dean of Men [Forrest Free] on what behavior would be acceptable, and what would not be, at the college. . . . We would be considered to be adults. We would be expected, therefore, to behave as such. Thinking over his remarks from the vantage point of some fifty years later, this really did give us a lot of latitude, though the Dean certainly meant the opposite! . . . The girls, but not the boys, had to be in their dorms on weekday nights by ten, eleven on Saturdays. He suggested that it would be best if the campus authorities did not catch students smooching away after hours in any of the many dark nooks and corners that were abundant on the campus. . . .

One of my professors [Joseph Willen] taught both Spanish and German. He was of German or Austrian birth and, as you might expect, had a strong accent. He was unable to pronounce the English "th" which causes no problem in German but it was another story in teaching Castilian Spanish. . . . He also introduced me to German which later became useful when I found myself in Germany in WWII. I learned to conjugate a few verbs, acquire a modest vocabulary . . . and to learn to count in German. I was very fortunate to have him as a teacher. . . . [Another] of our professors [Cloyd L. Bennighof, assistant professor of biology] was a jolly, rotund sort, a bit on the short side. He carefully read each lecture to his class, word for word (including jokes that he had penned in the margin of his notes), all prepared years before and had been given many, many times. His true love, however, was the theater and occasionally we would be able to pry him off his written material and with obvious joy he would launch into an off-the-cuff lecture on a play that he had recently read or seen. He was one of the leading lights of the amateur theatrical group in Westminster. Probably he should have taught drama rather than biology. . . .

As the fall turned into winter, the disappearance of male students increased from a trickle to a steady stream. Fellows would lose their roommates and the remaining ones would room up with others who hadn't been drafted. During this period I believe I had three roommates.

After awhile, as more and more rooms became empty, we turned them into miniature gymnasiums using the extra mattresses as floor pads. We had a big time wrestling, boxing, fencing, etc. . . . One of the boys on my floor kept a large jug of cider in his wardrobe closet. He kept it stored there just a bit too long; it blew up one day all over his clothes and his room. What a stink! . . .

Dating facilities were practically non-existent. Sunday afternoon after the day's main meal was the usual get-together time. And for what? A walk in the countryside. We took walks. Did we ever! We must have covered Carroll County in every direction from the campus, in pairs, and foursomes, and maybe even threesomes. . . . I was in high clover on Sadie Hawkins Day, with two dates. One of the girls presented me with a lovely corsage for our afternoon date: one of carrots and celery. I was delighted. My other young lady escorted me to the movies that evening. Hot dog! We probably saw an Errol Flynn movie.[44]

After the war, the Alumni Association took careful note of those alumni who had served in some branch of the armed services and published all their names in a special edition of the *WMC Bulletin* in July–August 1945. A total of 884 alumni had served, including 17 men who also served in World War I. The number included 45 women, who served in the WAVES, WACS, and WAAC.

Of special note are those who gave their lives for their country: George Elmer Babylon '35, Claude Elmer Belt x'43, Harry Hartley Benson '34, Roland

Coeds line up during the Sadie Hawkins Dance in 1947.

Raymond Blanchette x'45, Donald Chant Bohn x'46, Robert Milton Brooks '39, Benjamin Ellsworth Cantwell '42, William James Connellee Jr. x'45, Thomas Joseph Coonan '21, Franklin Warfield Crowe '37, Nathan Gustavus Dorsey Jr. '40, James Frederick Draper Jr. '36, John Gilbert Eichler x'45, John Charles Fitzgerald '40, Royce Donald Gibson '42, Marion Eugene Gore x'44, Milton Humphreys Hendrickson '38 (son of Prof. Dean W. Hendrickson), Julian Dennard Hill x'43, Walter Lee Hoke '38, Leonard Calvin Humbert '38, William Shepherd Humphries '36, Fred Adam Kullmar Jr. x'44, Thomas Joseph Lavin Jr. x'43, John Francis Leatherwood '41, Carroll Rice Maddox '39, Robert Gordon McKnight '38, Peter Mergo '35, Levin James Newcomb Jr. '39, Joseph Oleair '39, Richard Gladstone Patten x'44, Edward Alfred Peters '39, William Fleming Potts x'44, David Long Quinn '19, Hugh Barnett Speir Jr. x'45 (son of Prof. Speir '22), William D. Tipton '10, William Edwin Warfield '29, and George Frederick Wathen '30.[45]

One of the many veterans who returned to college after the war wrote "My Room at College" for the *Gold Bug*, describing the conditions the first influx of students under the GI Bill had to endure. This was reminiscent of the way some of the ASTP students had been billeted in 1943:

> *It was the latest thing in the way of dormitory accommodations on the Hill: the main floor of Gill Gymnasium. . . . Five rows of surplus army cots, nine to a row, were lined up like soldiers on dress parade. The cots were paired off and between each pair, at the head was a dresser. Two desks, butted back to back, were at the foot of each pair of cots. A desk chair at each desk completed the accommodations. . . . Particularly noticeable were the acoustics. They were wonderful, magnifying each sound many times. This, as I soon learned, was not conducive to efficient study. Then those little demons of the insect world, the flies, made themselves known. They descended in swarms . . . and made life most uncomfortable. . . . Another feature which detracted from the livability of my room was the scarcity of toilet facilities. Only two wash bowls [in the locker rooms] served forty men. The rush and confusion as those forty men tried to shave and clean their teeth before breakfast can only be imagined by one who has ridden the rush-hour subways of New York. Even though my room had many disadvantages, it was comparative luxury to its forty occupants, men who spent the last several years of their lives in the mud of Europe, the steaming jungles of Pacific Islands, or in the cramped confines of a naval vessel. Plain and simple though the room was, it made possible for forty men the securing of the education for which they had fought so hard, and so, it has gained forever a place in Western Maryland history.[46]*

These men were able to move into the dormitories in early November as others dropped out of school; the gymnasium floor was then cleared and made available to the basketball team for the winter season.

Another veteran, who came back to the Hill after leaving it in 1943 during his freshman year, reported on campus life upon his return in 1946:

A 1940s room in Albert Norman Ward Hall

What surprised everybody, the student body, the administration, and even the citizens of Westminster, was the splendid attitude of the recently discharged military students. They adapted quite easily; they had seen worse housing, far worse, worse crowding, far worse, and a general attitude of "Let's get on with it" prevailed. There was concern on campus that the returnees would not be willing, nor would they abide by the code of conduct and rules and regulations that existed at the time of their departure some three years previously. . . . [But] discipline learned earlier, and in the military service, was the glue that held it all together on campus. . . .

One of the places down town that did draw the attention of all the students on campus was the movie house on Main Street (now the Carroll Arts Center). . . . Another off-campus location of quite some notoriety was the establishment of Margaret's and Earl's, most commonly referred as "Earl's." This establishment [formerly known as "Mother Royer's"] was located on the ground floor of the corner house at a bisection of Main Street and Union Street. It consisted of a front door on Main Street that led to a front room hardly larger than a billiard table. Crammed into this miniscule space was a pin ball machine, a soda fountain, and ice cream freezer. Stacked all over the walls, on shelves, and any other available space, were piles of edible sundries: cookie and cake packages, potato chips, chewing gum, dried fruit, cigarettes, and various sorts of other items that attracted a hungry group of college students. . . . [A] back room was lined on two sides with tables and booth-like seating, and at the far end against the wall was . . .

a juke box. . . . Students would crowd in, wall to wall, literally on top of one another, pushing and shoving, trying to play the pin ball machine, . . . shouting orders to Margaret and Earl who both stood behind the soda fountain, trying frantically to hear orders and fill them by passing milk shakes and toasted cheese sandwiches over the heads of those closest to the limited space at the serving counter. Everyone wanted something else, and everyone wanted it as quickly as possible. . . .

There was a strict no-alcohol rule in effect on the campus. No such beverages were permitted anyplace on campus. To be caught meant expulsion. This provided those returning veterans who desired to imbibe, with an excuse to go down town . . . [to] a spot on the extreme other end of town . . . called the "Pit." . . . The Pit became known as "Macho Haven" since only the men students went there. . . . The men were perfectly content to have a relatively secret place to which to retreat from the feminine world and concentrate on their own thoughts and engage in strictly manly conversations. . . . Those who went there knew the perils of returning to campus with the tell-tale smell of beer on their breaths, so every effort was made to conceal [it] . . . when they returned to campus.[47]

A letter to the editor of the *Gold Bug* in 1947 expressed the omnipresent complaint about the dining hall food and compared it to other nearby sources of food:

Students frequented the popular off-campus hangout Margaret and Earl's and danced in the back room, the Rainbow Inn.

I hate to bring up an old and very unpleasant topic. . . . My question is, "Does the fact that several hundred people must be fed three meals a day every day in the week for a major part of each year, and further, that these meals must conform to certain caloric and vitamin requirements, make it necessary that the food be inferior as to palatability?" . . . We have had a remarkable parade of dieticians, always a new one in the last few years. The food has its good spells, but on the whole it isn't very much like that made by mother or Nick the Greek or anybody else we know. . . . Yes, we all know about the increased costs and the scarcities and all that. But we're willing to pay enough (we just have to spend it in the nearest eaterie if we don't get full in the dining hall, anyway), and we do *pay enough. And more than enough, it seems to me. . . . Dinners at the three places closest to the Hill cost from $.65 to $.85; lunches (that is, at least as much or more than we get in the dining hall) cost about $.40; and breakfast in the Grille, with enough coffee, fruit juice, and doughnuts to satisfy most of us, we'll put at $.15 . . . [These prices, combined with room rents off campus, were about the same as room and board fees at the college: about $12.50–$13.00 per week.] Which would you rather have, Margaret and Earl's Friday night "steak, French fries, peas, salad, hot rolls, and coffee" or liver?* [48]

The problem of the constantly changing dietician and dining hall steward seems to have been solved with the appointment of Byron Rice in 1949. But students continued to haunt the off-campus eateries for additional nourishment, just as generations of students before them had done. A new spot opened near the campus in 1948: Baugher's Family Restaurant, on Main Street west of the campus. But a brisk business also went on in the dormitories, conducted by male and female student entrepreneurs (and groups) who went from floor to floor selling homemade sandwiches, pastries, fruit, and more. Laundry service and newspaper deliveries were also provided for a fee. [49]

Most campus activities continued in full force during this decade, even though the student body fluctuated in size from year to year. With the diminishing numbers of males on campus, however, the four fraternities closed their doors from 1943 until the spring of 1946. To provide a fraternal opportunity for the relatively few civilian men on campus, a group called the Hospians (Kappa Pi Alpha), a service-oriented male brotherhood, was created by Dean Free and three young men in December 1943. The group was not secret and was open to all. The 1944 *Aloha* noted of the group, "It is unique in that no other organization of its kind has existed at WMC." Included with the write-up were the pictures and names of the 22 men who joined that year. Once the four fraternities reorganized after the war, their yearly membership averaged about 45 men per group, with Gamma Beta Chi being the smallest (34) and Delta Pi Alpha the largest (55). In the fall of 1946, Pi Alpha Alpha and Alpha Gamma Tau moved into new clubrooms in the basement of Albert Norman Ward Hall, freeing up space in Alumni Hall for classrooms. All the fraternities purchased television sets and rented Coke machines for their clubrooms, which made them comfortable hangouts for the men and attractive places for women to visit when curfew allowed. The sororities continued in their traditional way throughout the decade, averaging about 35 members per year; the smallest group was Delta Sigma Kappa (30), and the largest was Phi Alpha Mu (40). During the decade, the members of the JGC decided to join the normal sorority structure. (This followed some drastic revisions in 1938, when the group reorganized, selected a sponsor, drafted a constitution, and began functioning like the other women's groups.) During 1942–43, the name was formally changed to Iota Gamma Chi (the Greek equivalent of JGC).[50]

At its 50th reunion, the class of 1950 produced doggerel that remembered their college days. Some of the verses suggest the life and times very well:

In September '46, we arrived on the Hill,
With varied ambitions we hoped to fulfill.
As eclectic a group as any group gets
With kids right out of high school and a whole lot of vets.

Some wore freshman beanies like good little sheep.
Most of the veterans just said, "Go take a leap!"
Most everyone was friendly and helpful too,
And you soon knew the Hill was the right place for you.

There were Saturday classes, although not for all,
And required Sunday chapel in Alumni Hall,
Which meant that most weekends were not very long.
We abided by rules and we followed the throng.

As freshmen, all girls were in their dorms by eight.
After freshman year they could stay out real late,
But "late" by the standards established back then
Meant girls "staying-out-late" could stay out 'til ten.

During sophomore year we pledged the Greeks.
Initiation week we all acted like freaks.
Gamma Betes, Bachelors, and Black and White
And Preachers all conjured weird fraternity rites.

Skulls, skunks, and even purple cows
Made it easy to spot pledged sorority gals.
Mismatched plaids, hair in curlers, odd socks and such
Made sorority pledges seem just a little bit nuts . . .

A great winter pastime on snowy days
Was sliding down the hill on dining hall trays.
A large piece of cardboard would serve just as well.
Coming back up the hill is what proved to be (difficult)! [51]

Several opportunities for honoring academic and leadership achievement were added during this decade. A new honor society for women, the Trumpeters, was formed on May 19, 1944, by Dean of Women Katherine Carmichael, aided by Addie Belle Robb, Evelyn Mudge, Evelyn Wenner, and Esther Smith. The goal was to recognize women campus leaders, who would be elected to membership at the end of their junior year based on their records of scholarship and service. The self-perpetuating group (which it was hoped would evolve into a chapter of Mortar Board) soon took on the project of assisting with freshman orientation and planning monthly birthday dinners, as well as the annual campus Christmas Dinner. The name recalled the verse in I Corinthians 14:8: "For if the trumpet give an uncertain sound, who shall prepare himself for battle?" The charter members of the group, all seniors in the class of 1944, were Cordelia Price (Turk), Dorothy Rovecamp (Edwards), Beverly Slacum (Agnoli), Margaret Ann Smith (Cassell), and Mary Turnley (Gipe).[52] They inducted the first juniors, from the class of 1945, on May 25: Catherine Ann Waring (Barnes), Helen Stoner (Dettbarn), Ruth Miles (Huber), Ruth Hausmann (Thomas), and Lillian Jackson (Martin).[53] The group has continued to elect an average of five students each year since then. The adviser to the group from 1944 to 1949 was Evelyn Mudge; Isabel Thompson Isanogle (Royer) succeeded her in 1949 and continued in the role for 23 years. In 1945, nine seniors (two men and seven women) were named to *Who's Who in American Colleges and Universities*, the first time Western Maryland was included in this nationally recognized listing. A chapter of the philosophy honor society, Alpha Kappa Alpha, was established in April 1950, with Dr. Reuben Holthaus as the advisor.

Related to the goal of honor societies was the ongoing attempt to establish (or reestablish after many years) an honor system on the campus. The Men's Student Government president in February 1941, Robert Faw, called a special assembly to discuss the possibility, and discussions and editorials in the *Gold Bug* followed; but no affirmative action was taken. An honor system was again a topic of debate in 1945. And three years after that, the faculty again raised the issue of student cheating, and a joint student-faculty group was appointed to consider

*Trumpeter Honor Society, 1945; (L to R) H. Stoner, C. Waring, E. Mudge (advisor),
R. Hausmann (standing), L. Jackson, R. Miles*

the possibility of establishing an honor system to control it. Two years later the discussions were still going on, with no conclusions being reached. A survey of the students, in which over half of the student body participated, resulted in favorable responses to such questions as "Do you disapprove of cheating?" "Are you willing to take some action against the situation?" "Would you say in which department and which courses cheating most frequently occurs?"; but to the question "Would you be willing to turn in the names of persons you have seen cheating?" the majority response was negative.[54] Cheating was a problem on campus, but an honor system to correct it was still a dream.

Perhaps related to the cheating problem was the perennial problem of student absence from class. Again in this decade the faculty spent inordinate amounts of time discussing absences and what to do about them, creating new and more stringent rules every year. They seemed surprised that most absences occurred in Saturday morning classes. A fine system was established in 1946, with a maximum number of "cuts" carefully spelled out; excesses had to be explained to the absence officer, who reported in 1946 that 348 unexcused absences during the year resulted in $642 being collected in fines of $2 and $5. The discussions continued during the following years.

The number of clubs and organizations continued to grow during the decade, especially after the return of the veterans. The various musical organizations, the Debating Society, Camera Club, Chess Club, International Relations Club, College Players, and College Radio Players provided opportunities for activity and enjoyment. There was also a group of professionally oriented clubs such as the Home Economics Club, the Economics Club, and the Art Symposium, which attracted majors in those fields. In February 1949 a chapter of Future Teachers of America, named for Alvey Isanogle, was established on campus under the direction of Dr. Stover. To round out the extracurricular options, there were church-related organizations, including the William G. Baker Sunday School, the Lutheran Student Association, the Canterbury Club, the Wesleyans, and the Wesleyanettes, as well as the Student Christian Association, which annually sponsored Religious Emphasis Week, featuring outside speakers.

While the war, travel restrictions, and limited budgets curtailed the number of cultural events presented on campus by outside groups (with a few exceptions, such as the Don Cossack Chorus and Dancers in 1947 and dancer Ted Shawn in 1949), the campus was, nevertheless, well entertained by individuals and groups within the college. The College Players regularly performed well-known plays, including *The Night of January 16*, *The Male Animal*, *Stage Door*, *Junior Miss*, *The Taming of the Shrew*, *The Skin of Our Teeth*, *Blithe Spirit*, *I Remember Mama*, *The Corn Is Green*, and *The Late George Apley*. The senior class of 1943, as a gift to their fellow students, produced a variety show, "Senior Follies," which was a huge success. This was followed in March 1946 by a Sophomore Follies entitled "Thanks for the Memories." These apparently continued intermittently until 1950, when they evolved into

College Radio Players present a program in 1947.

the Junior Follies. In addition to these dramatic events, the Music Department presented a regular schedule of recitals by students and faculty. Faculty regularly performing were Alfred deLong (voice); Philip Royer (violin); Oliver Spangler (piano); Helen Brainard (piano); and Dika Newlin (piano), who performed several original compositions. Of special note was the production of two operas. Haydn's *The Songstress* was given its second American performance in Alumni Hall as part of the college's 75th anniversary celebration on March 27, 1942. Philip Royer directed the production, assisted by other colleagues in the Music, Art, and Dramatic Art departments. The cast included Mary Frances Hawkins (Galbreath) '43, James Snodgrass '43, and Joseph Whiteford '43. In April 1949, the Kurt Weill opera *Down in the Valley* was produced by the College Players, the College Orchestra, and a chorus from the College Choir. It was the joint effort of Royer, deLong, Esther Smith, and Donald Bailey and starred William H. Simpson '51 and Kitty L. Olewiler (Kirsch) '51.

Esther Smith took a two-year leave of absence in 1944–46 to assist with the production of the play *Strange Fruit*, written by her sister, Lillian Smith (LitD, 1964), based on her novel of the same name. The play, which was produced and staged by José Ferrer, opened in November 1945 in Philadelphia and

Scene from the 1947 faculty production of Arsenic and Old Lace

received critical acclaim: "Finely produced, excellently acted, and possessed of some extremely forceful and interesting writing." Professor Smith had a small part in the play and assisted with the production details during the New York run.[55] During her absence, her work in dramatic art was carried on by Ruth Beth Watts, from the Theater Recreation Project in Dover, New Jersey. In December 1944 the students asked the faculty to put on a show, and Miss Watts suggested a production of the dark comedy *Arsenic and Old Lace*. The faculty quickly became absorbed in the project, and the play was performed March 17, 1947, to the great delight of all. Maude Gesner played one of the Brewster sisters, Lloyd Straughn played the nephew, Forrest Free played Teddy Brewster, and Alfred deLong played the insane and dangerous brother, Jonathan. Others taking roles were Carl Schaeffer, John Jones, Lloyd Bertholf, Alvey Isanogle, Thomas Marshall, Philip Royer, Clyde Spicer, and Cloyd Bennighof. Assisting with the production were the rest of the faculty and their spouses. It apparently was a huge success and a memorable evening, for alumni who saw the production as students still talk about it and remember it as one of the more hilarious moments in the college's history.

College life is always full of pranks, but in January 1949 one went a bit too far. Cecil Eby, a senior student slated to graduate in the spring, decided to perform a chemistry experiment and threw sodium into a toilet on the fourth floor of Albert Norman Ward Hall. The porcelain "crumpled like a sick elephant," he later recalled. According to eyewitnesses, Dean Schofield raced across the campus to view the waterfall cascading down the dormitory stairwell. Dean Free appeared and uttered one word to Eby: "Pack!" (No Honor and Conduct boards in those days!) Eby did, heading to Shepherd College to complete his bachelor's degree. But that is not the end of the story. He went on to Northwestern for a master's degree and then to the University of Pennsylvania for a PhD, which led him to a professorship in English at the University of Michigan, as well as Fulbright lectureships in Spain and Hungary. But he apparently still craved the Western Maryland degree, and he eventually petitioned the college to award it, based on his later accomplishments if not his prowess in chemistry. On May 21, 1988, in his doctoral gown and to great applause from the amused audience, Cecil DeGrotte Eby strode across the platform to receive the bachelor's diploma that had eluded him for almost 40 years.[56]

Not everything that went on was humorous. In March 1946, the student governments confronted the issue of race relations and surveyed the student body on its opinions. In a letter to the president that was forwarded to the trustees, the student government presidents, Henrietta T. Jones (Moore) '46 and John L. Dorsey '46, commented,

We of the Student Governments realize that the racial issue is one that affects not only the students of our college but other parties as well. We are well aware of the conditions that exist in the City of Westminster; we are aware of the probable criticism that will arise from certain members of the Alumni; we realize that the college has certain vested interests that must be protected; we realize that certain members of the board of trustees are not in sympathy with a liberal approach to the racial problem; and finally we are aware of the fact that we are but a passing generation of students and that the present administration is responsible not only to us, but to the many who we sincerely hope will follow in our footsteps. . . .

We who represent the students of Western Maryland College make the following recommendations in the interest of creating a well rounded education that has as its basis the Christian ideals of Protestantism as expressed by the Methodist Church to whom we are related, and finds its basis also in the ideals of democracy as expressed by our state and national governments from whom we receive a great deal of financial support.

- *We recommend that Western Maryland College be in the future a host of conferences of an inter-racial nature.*
- *We recommend that the facilities of Alumni Hall, McDaniel Lounge, and the dining hall be made available to these conferees.*
- *We further recommend in behalf of the veterans, that these conferees be permitted to use that portion of the dormitory facilities which are in the use of these men.*

The Executive Committee of the board of trustees considered these recommendations (based on positive responses from the students to the survey) and the possibility of hosting interracial conferences, but "because of the sharpness of opposition to the proposals" it did not approve the option.[57] The college would have to wait a few years to implement this first step toward integration.

A similar situation had occurred in 1942 when the trustees voted not to accept any American-born Japanese students, "although they were sympathetic to their needs." Two years later they reversed themselves and voted to accept Japanese-American students, particularly if they were women and Methodists.[58]

For a number of years there had coexisted on the campus a Men's Student Government and a Women's Student Government dating back to the first attempts to give the students more responsibility for their own campus life and discipline. Each elected its own officers, and each was in charge of some specific activities—for example, May Day was the province of the Women's Student Government. In 1948–49 the student governments merged into one all-campus governing body, the Student Government Association, with separate men's and women's councils. The SGA sponsored homecoming activities, a sports banquet, an athletic award assembly, and May Day. At least into the 1960s it was traditional for a male to be president and a female to be vice president. Interestingly, the editorship of the *Gold Bug* was held by a woman fairly regularly during this decade, even after the war. Almost all vestiges of a college divided along gender lines were gone, save only the assigned seating in chapel and assembly (eliminated when Baker Memorial Chapel was opened in 1958) and the student rosters issued by the registrar, which still separated men and women in all official documents.

Not unexpectedly, as almost all intercollegiate athletics were for men, athletics on the campus suffered during the four- to five-year hiatus caused by the war. The football team played three seasons (1940–42), the last one under a fill-in coach, Leroy Byham '26, while Coach Charlie Havens was in the army, before canceling the next three seasons. (In 1941 Robert E. Bricker '42 received All-America honors.) Following the war, and back under Coach Havens's direction, the reconstituted football team completed four winning seasons, becoming Maryland State Champion in 1946 (a 5–2 season) and Mason-Dixon Conference Champion in 1949 (a 7–1 season, the best since 1935, which ended with a spectacular win over Johns Hopkins, 35–7). The 1947 season was particularly interesting because it included one special game against Harvard, which was coached by Richard Harlow in his last

Students enjoy playing Ping-Pong and billiards in the recreation hall in 1946.

season. The game was played on September 27, 1947, in Harvard Bowl, and unfortunately was a rout, the Terrors losing 0–52 to a strong Crimson team (which included Robert F. Kennedy). Probably what is most remembered about the game is the famous Peter Arno cartoon in *The New Yorker*, which showed a distinguished Harvard alumnus encountering a hawker outside the bowl selling both Harvard and WMC memorabilia. The man in the bowler says, "Which *one*? Great heavens, are you *mad*?"[59] So much for the college's foray into the Ivy League!

The 1947 season is also remembered for its final game, played with longtime rival Johns Hopkins. On the night before the game, several WMC army veterans dreamed up a scheme to abduct two Johns Hopkins freshmen, bring them to campus, and hold them captive until the game. Mary Todd Griffiths '48 and Patricia Outerbridge Corrado '49 were the decoys who lured

"Which one? Great heavens, are you mad?"

the unsuspecting 18-year-old boys into their convertible, claiming they were going to a party at Goucher "with beer and women." A few miles away, the girls met their cohorts and turned over the captives. When everyone arrived back on campus, the hostages were led into a pep rally with ropes around their necks. Apparently, after the boys were properly humiliated and had their hair cut, they spent the night tied to beds in the men's dormitory, feasting on hamburgers and drinking beer (obviously illegal on all counts) before being transported back to Baltimore on the College Band bus and wheeled onto the field at halftime. "Hopkins came and took them to the other side of the field," said Griffiths in her 1997 remembrances of the event. "Today we'd probably end up in court with all kinds of law suits, but it was fun at the time and they were good sports."[60] The game ended in a 14–14 tie.

Soccer was able to continue for most of the decade, because it could muster enough men to play, but the team didn't do very well except in 1946, when it ended with a 4–4–1 record. In the absence of football, however, a soccer game between the Terrors and the ASTP was the featured event for the 1943 Homecoming. Coaching the team through much of the decade was John Bayley Jones '41, the director of public relations. He was succeeded by Philip Uhrig in 1949. Homer C. Earll '50 was named All-America (Honorable Mention) by the National Soccer Coaches Association in 1947; he was also named to the southern collegiate tryout team for the 1948 Olympics. The basketball team was able to keep functioning for all the years except 1943–45 and racked up four winning seasons and four losing ones. The coach, Bruce Ferguson, went off to the army and was replaced for one year by Charles "Rip" Engle '30, who also assisted Coach Havens with football for the 1941 season. (He apparently got his nickname as a child because his pants were often ripped.)[61] Engle's basketball squad had a 14–11 record. The following year Engle went off to Brown University and later to Pennsylvania State University, where he became a legendary football coach, amassing a record of 104 wins, 48 losses, and 4 ties. (His assistant at both Brown and Penn State was the equally legendary Joe Paterno.) In 1950 the *Gold Bug* noted, "Coach Ferguson needs more, and better, material to work with in order to produce a winner. . . . The athletic department is constantly on the lookout for athletes who excel in a sport other than football, but this isn't always possible. Consequently, these teams must take what they can get without any additional help."[62] The 1950 basketball season, while following the normal losing pattern (5–15) did showcase a spectacular player, Art Press '52, who in that season averaged 21.4 points per game and racked up 451 points for the season. More would be heard from him.

Spring sports fared little better than fall and winter sports, with the exception of tennis. Records report all winning seasons for the team whenever they played matches. Coach Frank Hurt was working his magic as usual. The golf team, often under the tutelage of John Makosky, did reasonably well in the few years it competed. The baseball team suffered many losses both before and after the war. Lacrosse made a comeback on an experimental basis in 1948 and scheduled a full slate of games in 1949 under student-coach Alvin Paul '50. The team played such worthy opponents as Penn State, Franklin and Marshall, Loyola, Hofstra, and VMI and completed the season with five wins and four losses. The 1950 season, under new coach Edward Sparrow, was not so successful, the season ending 1–10. The sport was rapidly growing in interest on the campus again, however.

Just prior to the war, fencing made itself known on campus for organized competition, and showed two wins, one loss, and one tie in its single season, but it was never picked up afterward. Boxing continued except for the 1943–44 year, when no men's varsity sports were fielded and only physical training was emphasized. Following the war, the team acquitted itself well against some tough opponents, often showing winning seasons. Upon Richard Harlow's return as a consultant to the sports program, the boxing team came under his tutelage again, in 1950, and showed signs of steady gain. Wrestling was also introduced but without much success.

While the war certainly had its impact on student life, things moved along fairly smoothly, even in the difficult years, and returned to relative normalcy following the war. Those who were students during this decade have many memories of special events and challenges but not of unusual deficiencies or deprivation. A *Gold Bug* editorial in 1950, by Lou Pietroforte, summarized the latter part of the decade:

Since the Spring of 1946, the writer has noticed several very prominent changes. First and foremost is the more liberal attitude taken by the administration toward student freedom. Believe it or not, the student body has gained more "social privileges" since then than it had during at least the previous ten years. . . . Among the students themselves . . . there has been a tremendous increase of the intangible thing called college spirit. Enthusiasm for student-sponsored activities has increased quite noticeably, and the various groups and organizations seem to have been outdoing themselves in presenting events which would be of general interest. A new type of person is behind these activities, one who goes all out for publicity, imagination, and originality. In short, one who has become conscious of the student body as a social unit. Even the old separate men's and women's student governments have been merged as a solid, unified organization. . . . Western Maryland is undergoing a change, an evolutionary kind, to be sure, but nevertheless, she is changing.[63]

Buildings and Grounds

The world war, fluctuating enrollments, limited finances, and governmental regulations made any major changes in the physical plant impossible for much of this decade. But significant planning went on in anticipation of the years after the war. Whenever possible, new parcels of adjacent property on Pennsylvania Avenue, Main Street, and Union Street were purchased to provide "insulation" and possible expansion of the campus, and renovations to several existing buildings were accomplished without too much cost.

The first of these renovations occurred in 1940, after the McDaniels vacated their campus home to move to Ridge Road. The house was soon transformed into the Home Economics management house, returning the West Virginia Cottage to the seminary, from which it had been rented for some years. McDaniel House (as it came to be called) served as the model home management laboratory and base for the child development nursery school until the programs were phased out in the early 1960s. The second renovation had to wait until after the war, but it was fairly quickly accomplished; the old stables and garages of the Reifsnider property were converted in 1947 to provide space for the Maintenance and Service Department. This enabled the maintenance area and shops to be removed from the basement of Old Main, a situation that had been a fire hazard for some time. The space opened up in Old Main was temporarily turned into a dormitory, where some of the men initially housed in Gill Gymnasium were moved in November 1947.[64] Edward M. Black [1934–64] was now the superintendent of buildings and grounds, replacing a man who, unfortunately, had been arrested for stealing funds. (The college requested restitution but did not prosecute the man.)[65]

The college suffered two fires during the decade, one in Yingling Gymnasium in 1946, and another in Lewis Hall on June 9, 1950. While the first apparently caused little damage and is only casually mentioned in reports, the latter, a late-night fire that was contained in the third-floor chemical storage room and the classroom below, caused damage estimated at $10,000. The potential for campus fires triggered considerable discussion among the trustees before they agreed, in 1941, to add a fire escape to Alumni Hall, something that had been requested for some time by students, especially the choir members, who sat in the balcony. Less of a hazard, but nevertheless an inconvenience, was the unexpected collapse of the dining hall ceiling in the spring of 1949. It was quickly replaced with Celotex (at a cost of $3,500, an unbudgeted item in a tight budget, Dr. Ensor noted in his annual report), which greatly reduced the noise in that busy room, to everyone's satisfaction.

In 1945 the trustees allocated $10,000 to renovate the President's House, which had not had much attention since it was built in 1889. Nothing was done, however, until a new president was about to come on the scene in 1947, and that triggered immediate action. By February 1948 the house had been rewired, a new radiator heating system installed, new hardwood floors laid on the first and second floors, an additional bathroom installed on the second floor, a breakfast room and lavatory created on the first floor, and the interior painted and papered. The house was finished for occupancy by the end of November. (Curiously, no record exists of where the Ensors lived from July until that time, nor does anyone seem to remember.) It was during this time of postwar renovations on campus that the Victorian "gingerbread" on Carroll Hall was removed.

The postwar years were very busy ones, as the college got back to normal and picked up plans for the future. It also reacted to the influx of students attending college on the GI Bill. In June 1946 the college received from trustee Walter H. Davis in the form of an annuity four acres (valued at $5,000) about three blocks from campus, between Schaeffer and Wimert avenues and Sullivan Road, as a site for a veterans' housing project, under the Mead-Lanham Act.[66] The site was surveyed and the buildings prepared under the direction of Carl Schaeffer. By February 1, the project had been sufficiently completed so that some married students could move in, and eventually 40 families of veterans (70 adults and 16 children) lived in eight one-story barracks, each of which had been turned into three apartments, and four barracks with four apartments each, just off campus. The area was soon dubbed "Vetville." Each apartment consisted of two bedrooms, a kitchen, a bathroom, a combined living and dining room, and large storage areas. Utilities included a kerosene space heater, a gas stove, a refrigerator, and a hot water heater. The buildings were faced

WWII veterans returning to college with their families lived off campus in Vetville.

with red brick composition shingles, and the trim was painted white.[67] For two years, 1946–48, temporary housing for 26 freshman women was provided in Cassell Hall, a rented facility at the fork of Main Street and Pennsylvania Avenue. Originally a private home of the Cassell family, it had been expanded into an "old ladies' home" run by the Methodist Episcopal Church and was now available as dormitory space. The girls had breakfast and dinner at the hall but ate lunch on campus. Helen Howery and her mother lived there and supervised the young women for two years.[68] (Soon thereafter, Cassell Hall was rented by the seminary for additional housing; it was finally razed and replaced by a gas station.)

Long-range plans for the postwar era had been developing since 1943, when a trustee committee, along with one from the faculty, began to consider the nature of the college at mid-century and what it would need after the war. Not surprisingly, this primarily took the form of a wish list of desired facilities; the college needed more space and more up-to-date buildings to house its students and program. The committee listed, in order, the following needs: a new chapel, an infirmary, a men's dormitory, housing for unmarried faculty, and a new library.[69] A year later it made more suggestions and attached some potential costs. One recommendation was that Old Main be moved to a more desirable location and renovated to be a student center. Another was to make the old library into an administration building once a new library was built. These renovations, as well as the proposed new buildings, were estimated to cost about $500,000. A short-term goal of $300,000 would provide for the chapel, infirmary, and men's dormitory. In 1945, the board approved some preliminary drawings for the infirmary and the dormitory. More discussion, planning, and redefining of priorities and campus plans continued for the rest of the decade and became formulated into the Mid-Century Campaign, which began in the fall of 1950.

A new infirmary became the first priority, and specific planning finally took shape during the Ensor administration when Mrs. W. J. Thompson made a gift in 1948 for such a building in memory of her husband, William J. Thompson, PhD, DD, a former trustee [1926–44], who died in 1944. In October 1948 the trustees were delighted to receive a $100,000 gift for a new chapel from the Baker family of Buckeystown (a new generation of the family that provided the funds for the original Baker Chapel in 1894). So another piece of the plan was falling into place, although it would take ten years to bring it to fruition. More funds still had to be gathered for the infirmary, but it was soon sited on the rear of the Reifsnider property across Main Street from the President's House. By the fall of 1949 enough money had been accumulated so that the contract was let to build the new building, which

The Thompson Infirmary was opened in 1950.

was slated to cost $70,000, exclusive of furnishings ($3,500–$4,000). The infirmary was completed in May 1950 and dedicated on May Day, when it was formally named for Dr. Thompson.

The college had owned the Cookson farm near Uniontown since 1932 and used it as a source of milk and food for the dining hall, as well as for general income, but in 1944 the board decided to sell the property, with the proceeds going toward the outstanding debt on Blanche Ward Hall. In 1950, the board approved purchase of the property at 203 Pennsylvania Avenue. The house was old and needed work, but it housed two apartments and could be used for faculty or student housing. It was contiguous to the college property, and its purchase was a logical one. A bit later, President Ensor learned that this was the house in which Fayette R. Buell held the classes of his 1860s school, which evolved into the college.[70]

As early as September 1945, overtures were made to the seminary about buying a small piece of land beyond the seminary president's home on which to build a men's dormitory facing Albert Norman Ward Hall. Seminary president Lester A. Welliver, however, had other plans; indeed, he had hopes of procuring some land from the college to pursue a much-needed expansion of the seminary. This tension continued in the early years of the Ensor presidency and was described by Chandler in his history of the seminary:

> Welliver's zeal to protect every inch of the seminary's seven acres made negotiations fruitless. Committees appointed to adjudicate the competing claims extended their debate over several years. Complicating the question was the hope some had of exchanging the seminary's acreage for a comparable tract of college land, perhaps at the back of the golf course, so that neither institution would be in the way of the other's expansion. Some suggested that since the college had given the seminary its land in the first place (in 1882), some flexibility on the seminary's part would be an appropriate sign of gratitude, but just what this might be no one could say. There was no real desire on either campus to make any concessions.[71]

The WMC trustee committee suggested several alternative solutions to the need for expansion of both institutions: (1) A joint library could be built. (2) The seminary could buy from the college the small triangle of land just past the seminary president's house and erect a building "in conformity with the architecture of Albert Norman Ward Hall and located as a part of the proposed quadrangle." (3) The seminary could build a new building across the road from the present building (where Rouzer Hall now stands) and continue to develop its property down to Pennsylvania Avenue. (4) The seminary could relocate at the extreme northern side of the campus along Pennsylvania Avenue or along the Taneytown Road (Main Street). The board considered these alternatives and unanimously disapproved any sale of land for alternative 2. While they had no say in the matter, they expressed the hope that the seminary would not pursue alternative 3 because they felt that there was not enough room there, and that the property would more logically fit into future college development since college property surrounded it. Alternative 4 was considered the most viable, with some exchange of land and money being possible.[72] By October 1949, Ensor reported that negotiations with the seminary had not led to any solutions or agreements, and so it was agreed to discontinue them. Meanwhile, the seminary was experiencing unprecedented prosperity (after some rather dismal years during the war), with enrollment in the school growing to 150. Support from the church was also growing. But enrollment growth demanded more space, even though the college was still providing classroom space, plus the chapel (for small rent), and the seminarians were still eating in the college dining room. The seminary was also now renting Cassell Hall for additional dormitory space. Seminary hopes were rising for a groundbreaking for new facilities in the near future.[73]

FINANCES

The wildly fluctuating enrollments during the decade made it difficult to keep the college budget balanced or even to foresee what was going to happen next. For the first two years, enrollment remained relatively stable, holding at about 600 each year, while the ratio of men to women slowly changed, from 47%–53% to 43%–57%, as more women were enrolled to compensate for the slightly decreasing number of men. The impact of the war was truly felt during 1942–43, when male enrollment dropped to 108 from the prior year's 262, and total number of students dropped to 435, women outnumbering men three to one. The following year, male numbers diminished even further, to 88, while female enrollments rose to 388, for a total of 476, a four-to-one ratio. That was the year, however, when the 300 ASTP students were enrolled, so the college was temporarily bursting at the seams. Numbers began to improve slightly the following year, and with the close of the war, they skyrocketed to a maximum of 871 students in 1946–47. Thus, the college saw a 100% increase, from 435 to 871, over five years. The highest men's enrollment, in 1947–48, was 482, of which half were veterans, while women's enrollment was reduced to fit the dormitory accommodations. By 1950, things were beginning to return to normal, with 703 enrollees, only 25% of the men veterans. The number in the graduating classes also varied dramatically, beginning the decade at 135, dropping to a low of 78, and rising to 217 by 1950. The average enrollment was 674, higher than in any previous decade, but the fluctuations made budgeting a nightmare. By the end of the decade, applications for admission were as numerous as ever. For the entering class in 1949, 822 applications were received, 245 were rejected, 577 were accepted, and 290 enrolled.[74] The entering class of 1950 would present much different statistics.

In order to keep pace with rising costs and rationing, the trustees, at the president's suggestion, increased the tuition every two years during the decade, from $200 to $280, to $300, to $350, to $400. Thus, in ten years tuition doubled. Simultaneously, room and board fees rose slightly, although not as regularly, from $400 to $500 on average over the decade, a 25% increase. Factoring in activities fees that were sometimes added on, the average cost of a boarder attending the college rose from about $650 in 1941 to approximately $950 by 1950, a 50% increase.

The tuition increases generated much-needed increases in faculty salaries over the decade. In 1940, the highest annual salary of $3,300 was paid to the various deans; the average faculty salary was about $2,500–$2,700; assistant professors received about $1,500. The president's salary was $5,000. By 1942, salaries had moved up a few hundred dollars overall, and in 1943, a new scale was proposed, which raised maximum salaries as follows: administrators, $4,000; professors, $3,500; associate professors, $3,000; assistant professors, $2,500; and instructors, $2,000. The president's salary was fixed at $6,000. More minor adjustments were made in 1945. President Ensor soon saw the need for additional increases, and in 1947 the scale was pushed up to maximums of $4,500, $3,500, $3,000, and $2,500. He pointed out in his report to the board that the faculty were teaching course overloads and were not being compensated as well as public school teachers. In April 1948, cost-of-living grants of $100 for nonresident faculty and $50 for resident faculty were approved. And in 1949, still another scale put maximum faculty salaries at $4,800, $3,900, $3,300, and $2,800. Thus, over the decade, most faculty salaries had doubled, as well. An examination of individual salaries shows, again, that women were paid less than men, because, it was reasoned, almost all of the women were single (and lived and boarded on campus) and did not have families to support.

A significant addition to the compensation package for faculty and staff was the adoption by the trustees in 1946 of a long-needed retirement program, one managed by the Teachers Insurance and Annuity Association in New York and partially funded by the Carnegie Corporation. Other colleges and universities had already become part of this growing pension program. The program required everyone to participate upon completion of two years' service at the college. The retirement age was set at 65, but it could be extended year by year to 70, by mutual agreement. Participants agreed to contribute 5% of their salary to the program, and that amount was matched by the college. Because some faculty and staff members had been at the college for years before this program took effect, the trustees also awarded a small monthly pension (1% of the monthly salary in 1946 for each year of service prior to inauguration of the TIAA plan) to make up for the years not vested in the pension plan.[75]

Another benefit for the faculty was formally approved in 1945, when a sabbatical leave program was formally established. Applicants could apply to the president and the trustee Executive Committee for a half-year sabbatical at full salary or a full-year sabbatical at half salary. The previous year, when M. J. Snader and Frank Hurt were both given half-year sabbaticals to pursue graduate work, they received only a quarter of their salaries. These appear to be the first paid leaves awarded by the college. Providing for such leaves became one more factor in the ever increasing college budget.

The concept of tenure for faculty did not arise until this decade (at least there is no record in the faculty or trustee minutes), but now two significant board actions led to its establishment. In 1944, at its spring meeting, the board amended its charter to eliminate annual election of faculty. Previously, as noted, faculty appointments were made yearly, subject to board approval, and anyone could be released from service without notice, reason, or due process. The 1944 action suggests that the board was moving toward tenure (although the word is not mentioned). Three years later, at its fall meeting, the statement on academic freedom and tenure of the American Association of University Professors was read and presumably accepted. Since then, tenure and the principle of academic freedom have been in force at the college. Granting tenure to a faculty member is a significant action that poses long-term financial considerations.

While not all details of the college budget are included in the trustee minutes, it is interesting to note the growth in income and expenses that took place in the 1940s compared to prior decades. For the 1940–41 year, Assistant Treasurer Schaeffer reported estimated income of $474,500 and estimated expenses of $473,300; the following year, he estimated the income at $481,783 and expenses at $479,543; for 1942–43, his estimates were $503,450 and $498,060.[76] The small difference between each year's income and expenses provided little cushion for unexpected expenses. Compounding the difficulties of the budget process later in the decade was the slowness of the U.S. government in paying the fees for the veterans enrolled under the GI Bill. The treasurer noted to the board in January 1947 that he had borrowed funds to cover expenses until the government payments were forthcoming. Funding from the State of Maryland seems to have been more timely; the college was receiving a $63,200 appropriation (up from $55,000 in 1943) to cover the scholarships annually awarded by the legislators.[77]

Support from the Methodist Church was still minuscule. President Holloway noted in his report to the board in October 1941 that the colleges in the area conferences all felt the need for more support from the church, but that more Methodists were attending Western Maryland than any of the other Methodist-related colleges (which included American University and Dickinson). He felt that the college needed to start a campaign in the churches (as had been done many times before) to gain more financial support. By 1943, he reported that the church had taken a "renewed interest in the college" and had appropriated $1,000, with the hope for more in future years. In 1947, a small amount of money was made available from the church, to be matched by the college, to provide assistance for faculty to attend scholarly and professional meetings. The fund would pay 50% of expenses up to $25.

As previously noted, early in the decade discussions were held on mounting a financial campaign to build a new infirmary, another men's dormitory, and some other structures.[78] In 1944 the committee set a goal of $500,000 to accomplish the building program (which was part of the Greater Western Maryland program originated by A. N. Ward two decades before). This was predicated on the successful and timely completion of the war. Limited fund-raising began in 1945 and resulted in the gifts for the Thompson Infirmary and the new chapel. President Ensor in November 1949 recommended a more ambitious effort, to be called the Mid-Century Campaign, to raise at least a million dollars,[79] and by March of the following year, half of that amount had been raised in two major gifts. Walter H. and Elizabeth Davis, a local businessman and trustee [1944–51] and his wife, gave $256,000, and another $250,000 came from Robert Gill, who at the time wished to remain anonymous. By April, the consultants Marts & Lundy had been engaged, and they recommended the formation of a board Development Committee to plan, supervise, and conduct the fund-raising effort. Working with architects Eugene Adams and Edward Rigg of Baltimore, the Building and Grounds Committee recommended a revision in the campus plan: to renovate Old Main, raze Smith and Hering halls, renovate Ward and McKinstry dormitories, build a new men's dormitory in line with Albert Norman Ward Hall (where Academic Hall now stands), and build the new Baker Chapel backing onto Main Street and facing Gill Gymnasium across the campus (behind McDaniel House, near the stone gates). Appropriate materials describing these plans were prepared, and the Mid-Century Campaign was launched.

A final event with financial implications occurred in the fall of 1948 when the Baltimore Colts professional football team approached the college about using the facilities (football field, gymnasium, dining room, and dormitories) for a six-week practice session beginning in summer 1949.[80] President Ensor was authorized by the trustees to proceed with the arrangements, which resulted in the first Colt camp. Ensor reported to the board at the fall meeting that the camp went well and he looked forward to a continued relationship with the team. The Colts continued to hold their practice camp on the campus for the next 18 years.

Major Events

The 75th anniversary of the college's founding was approaching in 1942, and it was agreed that the Diamond Jubilee was worthy of a gala celebration. There was some hesitation about holding such an event while the war was on, but plans went ahead to hold it in conjunction with the 1942 Commencement, just as the 50th anniversary celebration had been joined with the 1917 Commencement, also during wartime (and the Centennial would be celebrated during the Vietnam War). A committee of five trustees, two faculty, two alumni, and two students, headed by Irving Pollitt, was appointed to plan the weekend's activities. The celebration began on Friday evening, May 15, with a presentation by the College Players of *The Yellow Jacket*, directed by Esther Smith. The following morning, the Anniversary Convocation was held at 10:30 A.M. in Alumni Hall. In spite of rain, which canceled the colorful procession of faculty and 75 delegates from Old Main to Alumni Hall, spirits were undampened; attendees were welcomed by President Holloway and heard addresses by Dickinson president Fred P. Corson and the president of the American Council on Education, George F. Zook. During the ceremony, six honorary degrees were conferred; recipients included Charles R. Miller '81, D. Roger Englar '03, and Albert Buckner Coe '09. The printed program for the convocation included an "Anniversary Chronicle" by Nannie Lease, which highlighted the major events and personages in the college's history. A buffet luncheon in Blanche Ward Gymnasium was followed by conferences of various professional groups. Addressing and leading the groups were Charles Miller, business; Earle T. Hawkins '23, education; Miriam Lewis Veasey '96, homemaking; Roger Englar, law; C. Gardner Warner '24, medicine; and Albert Coe, ministry. Later in the afternoon the rained-out garden party was turned into a reception in McDaniel Lounge, which was followed by the Anniversary Dinner in the dining hall, attended by 450 people, including nine members of the Golden Jubilee Class of 1892, who graduated on the 25th anniversary of the college. The *Bulletin* (July/August 1942, p. 8) reported, "From the Pacific Coast, Florida, and the Canadian Border, loyal Alumni came to help make this occasion linger long in our memories." The evening concluded with the Diamond Jubilee Ball in Gill Gymnasium. The following morning, President Holloway preached the baccalaureate sermon in Alumni Hall; seniors, parents, and alumni enjoyed tea at 4:00 P.M. in McDaniel Lounge, and a vesper service was held at 8:00 P.M. On Monday, May 18, at 10 A.M. the 72nd Commencement was held in Alumni Hall with U.S. Senator Millard E. Tidings as the speaker.[81]

The anniversary celebration had actually begun three months earlier with the resumption of the Mid-Winter Alumni Banquet in Baltimore on February 6, with corresponding dinners in New York; Philadelphia; Indiana, Pennsylvania; Washington, D.C.; and Cumberland, Maryland. The Haydn opera later in the spring added to the celebration, and the traditional May Day, Lantern Chain, class teas, and club reunions all built enthusiasm for the 75th birthday party.[82] During the anniversary, alumni were reminded of the tremendous changes in the

Lantern Chain was a traditional spring ceremony.

college during seven and a half decades. Enrollment had increased from 70 in 1867 to 587 in 1942, faculty had grown from 7 to 56, campus acreage had expanded from 8 to 100, and buildings had increased from 1 to 14. Seven students were in the first graduating class (1871), and 140 graduated in 1942. The total number of graduates had increased from 258 in the 25th year to 1,034 in the 50th year and 3,011 in the 75th year. The college had come a very long way from the Ward-Buell dream in 1867.[83]

Because of World War II and the desire to move students through their degree programs as quickly as possible, it was decided to hold mid-year and summer graduation ceremonies, so the early graduates would not have to return to receive their degrees (many would not have been able to do so because of their military status). The first of five mid-winter convocations was held on Friday, February 11, 1944, in Alumni Hall. Attending were the faculty, the students of the college, the cadets in the ASTP unit, and relatives and friends of the graduates. The program followed the traditional format, the address being given by President Holloway. Three men and three women received bachelor of arts degrees, and a master of education and an honorary degree were conferred. During his remarks to the graduates, Holloway noted,

> You are unique. Yours is the first mid-year graduating class; the first class to hold a commencement with a temperature under 120 degrees F. Only twice before have fewer appeared in a graduating class . . . 1875 and 1884. It seems that relatively little attention is apparently being given you at this time. Apparently, I say, because there is no Senior Play, no Garden Party, no Baccalaureate Sermon, no Choir Concert, no orchestra, no lengthy address, no outside speaker, no lengthy ceremony. Actually you are being given a lot of attention. You are getting more attention per capita than any graduating class I have known!

He went on to comment on academic acceleration:

> Acceleration does not affect time; it affects only your use of it. I am not in favor of the acceleration of the college curriculum in normal times,

Deans Forrest Free and Helen Howery lead
the class of 1950 to their investiture.

but I am in favor of the acceleration of our use of time always. If it has taught you how valuable time is, and how to use it more frugally, your acceleration, in addition to equipping you sooner for useful work, has served an excellent educational objective.[84]

In 1945 a second mid-winter convocation was held, on January 31, and a summer convocation was held (in Baker Chapel) on August 31. At each, six graduates received bachelor of arts degrees. The practice continued until 1948, when it no longer seemed necessary. However, in addition to the annual spring commencement, degrees are still awarded in December and at the end of each summer, although not in a formal ceremony.

In May 1945, the 75th Commencement was held, although the country was still at war with Japan and the U.S. Office of Defense Transportation was restricting travel. President Holloway wrote this for the *WMC Bulletin*:

All of us rejoice in the good news of V-E Day. It makes us all the more anxious for the victorious end of the hostilities in the Far East. Hundreds of Western Marylanders are scattered throughout the earth. A steady flow

of letters tells of their anxiety to be back on College Hill. Regulations of the
O.D.T. compel us to conduct our Commencement activities on a purely
local basis. We regret that this is the case and will miss the many alumni
who normally come at this time of year. We hope that another twelve-
month period will ease the travel situation, so that we can once more
follow our normal commencement program with a great celebration.[85]

The 75th Commencement was a special one, nevertheless, since it
included some activities not normally a part of the weekend. It began on
Friday evening with the play *Papa Is All* given by the College Players in
Alumni Hall. Saturday focused on the seniors and their parents and featured
a reception in the Robinson Garden, a special dinner in the dining hall, and
a songfest in McDaniel Lounge to round out the evening. While there was no
Alumni Banquet, the Alumni Association was able to hold its annual business
meeting on Saturday afternoon. Sunday was a busy day, for, as in the two
preceding years, Baccalaureate and Commencement were held on the same
day, to minimize traveling.[86] President Holloway preached the baccalaureate
sermon at 10 A.M. The ceremony followed the traditional format, which
included the Commandments and Responses from the graduates, psalms
and scriptures, an anthem by the choir, and the processional and recessional
hymns: "A Mighty Fortress" and "O God, Our Help in Ages Past."[87] At 2 P.M.
the Commencement ceremony got under way, the speaker being Madame
Chu Shih-ming of the Chinese Embassy in Washington. Fifty-one women
and 14 men received diplomas, and three honorary degrees were conferred,
including one in absentia to the Rev. E. Pearce Hayes, a missionary in the
Far East.[88] Two members of the 1945 class would go on to serve the Alumni
Association in significant ways: Donna DuVall (Sellman) as director of
alumni affairs from 1970 to 1999 and Katherine Kaiser (Frantum) as president
of the association from 1986 to 1988.

A significant event occurred on Thursday, December 5, 1946, when a
special convocation was held in Alumni Hall to confer an honorary doctor
of laws degree on Supreme Court Justice Robert Houghwout Jackson. Justice
Jackson had served as chief of counsel for the United States in the prosecution
of the international war crimes trials in Nuremberg following World War II.
President Holloway cited Jackson in these words:

As the representative of the United States, you negotiated with the
representatives of the other great powers an unprecedented agreement
under which the first international military tribunal in history
was created and its procedure, a compromise among the widely
different procedures of the nations concerned, was determined. Your
understanding and patience in the problems involved contributed

greatly to the reaching of the agreement. Your ability in leading the prosecution of the greatest trial in history is everywhere accepted. Your profound and eloquent arguments were largely accepted by the tribunal and by the thinking people of the world as a basis for the future course of international law.[89]

In his address, Justice Jackson made some profound and prophetic comments about the world of that time and what the future might hold:

In the uncertainties of these days it is well to look ahead and see if any comfort can be had from the work that has been done at Nürnberg. After all, it is for you to take a long view of it because it will be twenty years from now, perhaps in 1965 or 1970, when you young people will be at the height of your powers, when you will be running the United States of America. This is significant because the danger of war is not tomorrow nor the next day. All of the people of the world want peace at this moment. No matter what country you visit you find the common people weary of flesh, their resources exhausted, and they

Justice Robert Jackson hears testimony during the Nuremburg trials in 1946; seen over his right shoulder is R. J. Gill '10.

are tired of war. They are disillusioned, too, and they know that war solves no problems. They know it brings disaster to the just and the unjust alike. So there is no imminent danger of war. The danger will be 25 or 30 years from now when the lessons of our experience will have been forgotten, when the people again will become restored and rested, and ambition may then seek ends that can be accomplished only by wars. . . . The one thing mankind needs to fear is man. And it is no longer primitive or illiterate man who represents a menace; it is the technically educated people, the competent people, who hold the secrets of destruction and can loose these forces upon the world. . . . Education, of course, brings knowledge, and knowledge is power, and power unrestrained by moral principle leads to catastrophe. . . . I would like you to think of the Nürnberg trial as an effort to teach some moral responsibility and to enforce some legal responsibility in international affairs. Moral responsibility seems more effective if there is some legal responsibility to strengthen it. We have tried to set up standards of conduct for nations and for men who control the destiny of peoples. . . . To have condemned these men without giving them a chance to be heard would always leave the impression that we were afraid of what they might say. By hearing them it became apparent from the very arguments made in their defenses how complete and inexcusable was their guilt and how ruthless men become when they have absolute power. It has been said that power always corrupts, and absolute power corrupts absolutely. These men had absolute power and destroyed the people's right to control their officials, and revelling in such power these men had come to the point where they had no sense of moral responsibility and no sense of legal responsibility. . . . Much more will have to be done to give peace a firm footing in the world. People will have to be alert to see that statesmen do not take advantage of trivial incidents to precipitate large crises and risk wars.[90]

On the platform that morning, the trustee presenting Jackson for the degree was Robert Gill, now a brigadier general. It was because of Gill that Justice Jackson came to the campus. Following his graduation from the college in 1910, Gill had enrolled in the University of Virginia Law School, where he received the bachelor of laws degree in 1913 and was elected to Phi Beta Kappa. He entered the practice of corporate law in Baltimore and became a member of the Maryland National Guard. He saw significant army service during World War I, commanding a mortar battery attached to the famous 42nd Rainbow Division, commanded by General Douglas MacArthur. He attracted the general's attention and eventually was attached to MacArthur's

Robert J. Gill

staff, leaving the service as a lieutenant colonel. He returned to private law practice for 24 years, until returning to active duty in 1942, directing the Army Specialized Training Programs for the Third Service Command in Baltimore before being assigned to Europe in 1944. Upon the German surrender, he was named chief of the Prisoner-of-War Division, in charge of the 23 prisoner-of-war camps in France and the 15 in Germany and supervising 2,852,000 prisoners. Just before he was to be mustered out following the war, he was tapped to become executive officer to Justice Jackson, the chief prosecutor. He supervised and organized the Nuremberg trials, arranged for the innovative simultaneous translations needed to make the trials run smoothly and efficiently, and dealt with the imprisonment of the Nazi war criminals. For his service at Nuremberg, he received the Legion of Merit and the Distinguished Service Medal from the United States and the Third Order of the White Lion from Czechoslovakia. He was also promoted to the rank of brigadier general on the recommendation of Justice Jackson. Jackson noted Gill's outstanding performance in the position of executive officer, which contributed "in vital measure to the success of the trials at Nürnberg."[91] It was because of this close personal relationship that Gill was able to persuade Jackson to come to the college to speak and receive the honorary degree. It was also because of all he had done that Gill himself was awarded an honorary doctor of laws degree at the 1947 Commencement the following May.

Once Lowell Ensor took office in July 1947, planning began immediately for his formal inauguration, scheduled for November 8. Dean Schofield chaired the small planning committee, which included trustees J. P. Wantz and Dorothy Herr, and faculty members R. Dewees Summers and Thomas F. Marshall. The 130 visiting delegates representing colleges, universities, and learned societies (including 18 presidents) registered in Science Hall and joined the faculty in the academic procession to Alumni Hall, where the formal ceremonies began at 10:30 A.M. A chill rain poured down all day, but the spirit of the occasion was not diminished. With the delegates, faculty, and trustees sitting on the stage in colorful academic regalia and the white-robed choir joining other students in the balcony, the remaining seats in the auditorium were filled to overflowing with alumni and friends of the college, making the total attendance over 1,000. Bishop Straughn presided, Oliver Spangler was at the organ, and Alfred deLong directed the choir, which sang three anthems interspersed throughout the ceremony. Delivering the invocation was Charles Wesley Flint, bishop of the Washington Area of the Methodist Church and a college trustee. The main address was given by Bishop Edwin Holt Hughes, a retired church leader and old friend of the new president. The white-haired and witty orator began by saying, "Lowell Ensor, I was 40 years old when you were born—not that anyone would know that unless it were advertised—so I give you counsel today because you have a great and challenging job ahead. What you do here may last thousands of years, but do not be of fearful heart for we develop as work develops."[92]

Holt went on to charge the new president with four more points: "Pay heed to the balance of the ledger," "Provide also for a balanced institution," "Continue here the primacy of the student," and "Go, and God be your comrade." Bishop Straughn then formally gave the charge to the new president, noting that it is the business of the president to "run" the institution, but in all probability it would "run" him. Then he commented on the various constituencies of the college, all of which would probably expect more of the president than any one man could do: the students, the faculty, the trustees, and the alumni. Calling attention to this last group, the bishop wryly stated, "Some of them will be your advocates. . . . But for many of the old grads there is one credential of love, you must every year produce a winning football team. They will not be greatly concerned where the material for this team comes from, or how they rate in the class room. 'We want a touchdown' is the battle cry. And so long as you can win—how sweet and lovely the world!" (One may wonder if the board chairman was really being facetious in this comment, given what may have transpired only a few months earlier with Ensor's predecessor.) He concluded his remarks by noting the long association of the college with the Methodist church and the college's founding on religious principles. He concluded his charge to Ensor by saying, "You, Sir, are the college and we feel we have a right to say that in you is Western Maryland. . . . God bless you in your new task."[93]

Ensor, in his response, paid homage to his four distinguished predecessors and what they had accomplished over the previous 80 years. He commented, "Only a fool would be willing to prophesy today with any degree of certainty what does lie before us . . . but whatever our modern world holds for us in the immediate or more distant future, I am convinced it has a place, a unique place, for Western Maryland College to run the race alongside its sister institutions in the arena of higher education." But he noted that, to run that race, attention must be given to the college facilities, to the curriculum as it related to the changing world, to the training of teachers, and to the college's relation to the church. He concluded by saying that the primary purpose of the college, in response to the demands of a world of moral law (perhaps reacting to Jackson's speech a year earlier?), is "to emphasize those high principles of

Lowell Ensor is inaugurated in 1947 as fifth president by
Bishop James Straughn, board chairman.

character and virtue without which the educated man becomes a distinct liability. . . . Our opportunities are superb, whether in the immediate present or in the more distant future; to their seizure will I direct my every energy."[94] A reception for all in attendance was held in McDaniel Lounge following the ceremony, and the visiting delegates were treated to a luncheon in the dining hall at 1 P.M. W. Edward Cushen '48 and Sarah Smith '48, presidents of the Men's and Women's Student Government, respectively, greeted the 450 guests at the luncheon. Other speakers included Hubert Burdette, the president of the Alumni Association; Dr. Thomas S. Pullen, state superintendent of schools; Murray Benson representing the trustees; and Dr. Henry W. Hanson, president of Gettysburg College.[95]

CONCLUSION

The decade was one of many uncertainties—about the war and about the viability of the college as its enrollments and finances were on a roller coaster of highs and lows. It saw many changes among the trustees, administration, and faculty, and the college mourned the loss of a number of its sons on battlefields across the world. But it was also a time when the faculty and staff found for the first time an element of stability in their lives, as tenure, pensions, sabbaticals, and gradually rising salaries encouraged many to remain at the college for their entire careers. The legacy of the decade would be that, with all the fluctuations and changes the college endured, it maintained and gradually improved its educational program for all who would attend, and realized what it needed to do for the future. The college, having successfully existed for 83 years, was now poised to celebrate the mid-20th century by embarking upon the largest financial campaign in its history, which would expand and improve its facilities and its programs to meet the many demands of the postwar era.

CHAPTER 9 ENDNOTES

1. Chandler, *Pilgrimage of Faith*, 123.
2. WMC board of trustees minutes, November 6, 1942; September 29, 1944.
3. Ibid., November 28, 1943.
4. Ibid., October 28, 1949.
5. WMC trustee Executive Committee minutes, May 31, 1941; *Fundamental Ordinances*, 1941.
6. *WMC Bulletin*, November 1946, 8.
7. WMC board of trustees minutes, November 6, 1942; *WMC Bulletin*, July/August 1942, 6–7.
8. WMC board of trustees minutes, April 24, 1942.
9. Ibid., April 1, 1947.
10. Ibid., April 16, 1943.
11. Summer 2004.
12. Interview, William Holloway, February 4, 2005.
13. WMC board of trustees minutes, April 1, 1947.
14. Interview, John D. Makosky, April 1985.
15. *WMC Bulletin*, July/August 1947, 2.
16. Interview, Makosky, 1985.
17. *Gold Bug*, January 16, 1948, 2.
18. Interview, Mabelyn Bertholf Westcot, 2002.
19. *Illinois Wesleyan University Bulletin*, undated.
20. *WMC Bulletin*, May 1948, 3.
21. *Gold Bug*, May 13, 1949, 4.
22. Richwine, memorial remarks, October 26, 1986, college archives.
23. *WMC Bulletin,* May 1934, 12.
24. "'52M" refers to the year in which he received a master's degree.
25. *WMC Bulletin*, July/August 1949, 3.
26. *Gold Bug*, December 6, 1940.
27. Vol. 2, no. 1, May 1949; vol. 2, no. 2, May 1952.
28. 1956 *Aloha*, 14; *WMC Bulletin*, November 1944, 3, 8; WMC trustee Executive Committee minutes, March 1944, March 1949.
29. Philip K. Blatz, "The WMC Education Department 1886–1986," 13, unpublished paper, 1986.
30. Schofield and Crain, *Formative Years*, 136.
31. Wills, *History of Western Maryland College*, vol. 2, 36.
32. *Gold Bug*, May 13, 1949, 1.
33. Interview, Erich Willen, February 26, 2005.
34. Page 96.
35. *Democratic Advocate*, July 16, 1943.
36. *Gold Bug*, October 1943, 2.
37. 1944 *Aloha*, 96; Holloway Report, October 1943.
38. Interview, Robert V. Peterson, 2004.
39. Holloway Report, October 1943; April 1944.
40. January 13, 1944, 2, 4.
41. WMC faculty minutes, February 2, 1942; February 6, 1950.
42. Ibid., December 5, 1949; January 9, 1950.
43. Letter from Anna Rose Beasman to President Joan Coley, October 3, 2001, college archives.
44. Edward P. Furlow, *Life on the Hill*, 1942–43, unpublished memoir, May 14, 2001, college archives.
45. *WMC Bulletin*, July/August 1946, 4.
46. October 30, 1946, 2.
47. K. Douglas Beakes, *The Legacies of Western Maryland College*, 24–26, 32–35, 41–43. Baltimore: Gateway Press, 2003. College archives.
48. March 6, 1947, 2–3.
49. *Gold Bug*, December 13, 1940, 2.
50. 1942, 1943 *Alohas*.
51. 1950 reunion poem, May 2000, college archives.
52. Schofield and Crain, *Formative Years*, 134.
53. Trumpeter reunion booklet, 1997, 1, college archives.
54. *Gold Bug*, May 16, 1950, 2.
55. Ibid., November 15, 1945, 1.
56. *The Hill*, August 1988, 46.
57. WMC trustee Executive Committee minutes, April 26, 1946.
58. Ibid., August 1, 1942; August 15, 1944.
59. September 27, 1947.
60. *The Hill*, Fall/Winter 1997–98, 21.
61. *WMC Bulletin*, July 1963, 16.
62. *Gold Bug*, February 28, 1950, 3.
63. Ibid., May 16, 1950, 2.
64. Interview, M. Lee Rice, February 25, 2005.
65. WMC trustee Executive Committee minutes, February 6, 1942.
66. WMC board of trustees minutes, July 2, 1946.
67. *WMC Bulletin*, October 1946; May 1947, 1, 5.
68. *Gold Bug*, September 26, 1946.
69. WMC board of trustees minutes, October 28, 1943.
70. Ensor Report, April 1950.
71. Chandler, *Pilgrimage of Faith*, 155.
72. WMC board of trustees minutes, October 22, 1948.
73. Chandler, *Pilgrimage of Faith*, 158–59.
74. WMC faculty minutes, October 28, 1949.
75. WMC board of trustees minutes, November 1, 1946.
76. Ibid., November 4, 1940; October 24, 1941; November 6, 1942.
77. WMC trustee Executive Committee minutes, March 18, 1949.

CHAPTER 9 ENDNOTES

78. WMC board of trustees minutes, October 28, 1943.
79. WMC trustee Executive Committee minutes, October 20, 1949.
80. WMC trustee Executive Committee minutes, October 22, 1948.
81. Commencement Program, 1942; Convocation Program, 1942.
82. *WMC Bulletin*, July/August 1942, 8.
83. Ibid., November 1941, 7.
84. *Gold Bug*, February 17, 1944, 1.
85. May 1945, 2.
86. Schofield and Crain, *Formative Years*, 132; WMC faculty minutes, April 5, 1943.
87. Program, Baccalaureate, May 27, 1945.
88. Program, Commencement, May 27, 1945; Schofield and Crain, *Formative Years*, 132.
89. Degree citation, college archives.
90. Robert H. Jackson, Convocation Address, *WMC Bulletin*, January 1947.
91. *War Department Bulletin*, January 23, 1946.
92. Margaret Dempsey, *Baltimore Evening Sun*, November 8, 1947.
93. *WMC Bulletin*, Inaugural Addresses, January 1948, 4–15.
94. Ibid., 17–23.
95. *Baltimore News Post*, November 8, 1947.

MAJOR WORLD EVENTS

1941
Germany invades Russia.

Shostakovich composes Symphony no. 7 during the siege of Leningrad.

Japanese bomb Pearl Harbor.

U.S. and Britain declare war on Japan December 8; later declare war on Germany and Italy.

Noel Coward publishes *Blithe Spirit.*

Winston Churchill gives his "blood, sweat and tears" speech.

Manhattan Project of intensive atomic research begins.

1942
Albert Camus publishes *The Stranger.*

C. S. Lewis publishes *The Screwtape Letters.*

Thornton Wilder publishes *The Skin of Our Teeth* and wins Pulitzer Prize.

Douglas MacArthur is appointed commander-in-chief of the Far East.

Enrico Fermi splits the atom.

The first automatic computer is developed in the U.S.

1943
President Roosevelt freezes wages, salaries, and prices to forestall inflation.

Jackson Pollock holds his first one-man show.

Penicillin is successfully used in treatment of chronic diseases.

Popular films included *Casablanca* and *Jane Eyre.*

U.S. War Labor Board orders coal mines nationalized when half million miners strike.

Shoe rationing, followed by rationing of meat, cheese, fats, and canned foods begins in U.S.

1944
Over 700 ships and 4,000 landing craft land in Normandy on D-Day.

Battle of the Bulge (Ardennes) begins.

Cost of living in U.S. rises almost 30%.

Franklin Roosevelt is elected to an unprecedented fourth presidential term.

Lillian Smith produces *Strange Fruit.*

Tennessee Williams produces *The Glass Menagerie.*

Leonard Bernstein composes musical comedy *On the Town.*

1945
President Franklin Roosevelt dies and is succeeded by Harry S. Truman.

Germany surrenders on May 8, V-E Day and is divided into four zones.

U.S. drops atomic bombs on Hiroshima and Nagasaki; Japan surrenders.

Nuremberg trials of Nazi war criminals begin.

United Nations is formed in October; League of Nations folds.

George Orwell publishes *Animal Farm.*

"Bebop" comes into fashion.

1946

UN General Assembly holds first session, in London.
Juan Perón is elected president of Argentina.
Churchill gives his "Iron Curtain" speech at Westminster College in Fulton, Missouri.
President Truman creates the Atomic Energy Commission.
Richard Byrd leads an expedition to the South Pole.
Lerner and Loewe produce *Brigadoon*.

1947

"Almost Like Being in Love" and "I'll Dance at Your Wedding" are popular songs.
Jackie Robinson becomes first Negro to sign a major league baseball contract.
More than one million war veterans enroll in colleges under the U.S. "GI Bill of Rights."
India is proclaimed independent and partitioned into India and Pakistan.
Tennessee Williams wins Pulitzer Prize for *A Streetcar Named Desire*.
European Recovery Program (Marshall Plan) is proposed.
The Diary of Anne Frank is published.
Dead Sea Scrolls are discovered in Wadi Qumran.
Bell Laboratories scientists invent the transistor.
Henry Ford dies, leaving a fortune of $625 million.

1948

Gandhi is assassinated.
Jewish state of Israel comes into existence.
Harry S. Truman is elected president, defeating Thomas Dewey.
Marshall Plan is approved by Congress: $17 billion in aid for European recovery.
U.S. Selective Service Act provides for a continued military draft.
Alfred Kinsey publishes *Sexual Behavior in the Human Male*.
The long-playing record is invented by Peter Goldmark.
Babe Ruth dies; Joe Louis retires from the boxing ring.

1949

China falls to communism.
Apartheid is established in South Africa.
George Orwell publishes *1984*.
Arthur Miller produces *Death of a Salesman*.
Rodgers and Hammerstein produce *South Pacific*.
Israel is admitted to the UN; its capital is moved from Tel Aviv to Jerusalem.

1950

Douglas MacArthur is appointed commander of UN forces in Korea.
Margaret Mead publishes *Social Anthropology*.
Truman instructs the Atomic Energy Commission to develop a hydrogen bomb.
North Korea invades South Korea; UN forces are ordered in to be peacekeepers.

Baker Memorial Chapel was dedicated in 1958.

CHAPTER 10

IMPORTANT PHYSICAL CHANGES ON THE HILL

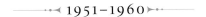

1951–1960

The world and society in general were in a state of flux. The Korean conflict occupied many minds early in the decade. King George VI in England died and was replaced by his daughter, Elizabeth II, while Josef Stalin in the USSR also succumbed and was replaced by Malenkov and then Khrushchev. In 1956 the Soviets occupied Hungary. Fidel Castro assumed control in Cuba. Hydrogen bomb testing threatened peace and survival. On the home front, McCarthyism reared its ugly head as communists were sought in every walk of life. Segregation was outlawed in the public schools, and the civil rights movement got under way. With the Soviet launching of *Sputnik*, America belatedly began a scientific revolution that included the establishment of NASA and a new approach nationwide to science and mathematics education. The explosive growth of television was providing Americans with new entertainment and more access to world news; Alaska and Hawaii joined the union; and Dwight Eisenhower was a two-term president, from 1953 to 1961. The world was changing faster than many people could accept.

On the local front, the college's enrollments were growing faster than could comfortably be accommodated. New facilities were needed, were being

419

built, or were on the drawing boards all during the decade. The top of the Hill changed radically as 19th-century buildings made way for 20th-century edifices and the seminary moved to Washington. Tuition and fees escalated just to keep pace with an inflationary spiral that affected everything. It was the era of the so-called silent generation, when students accepted rules and regulations and traditions without much question. It was also the time of white bucks, saddle shoes, bobby socks, and the bunny hop. By the end of the decade, rock and roll had supplanted Rodgers and Hammerstein, and Elvis was king!

FACULTY AND ADMINISTRATION

The board of trustees saw almost two-thirds of its number change in this period due to deaths and resignations. Familiar and active individuals such as Henry Gilligan '01 [1922–50], Harry C. Adkins '08 [1943–51], J. Pearre Wantz [1922–51], Walter H. Davis [1944–51], Irving Pollitt '89 [1913–53], John H. Baker [1923–54] (the last of the Baker family's collective 128 years of representation), Eugene C. Makosky [1929–55], William W. Chase '23 [1937–57], and Edgar A. Sexsmith [1938–59] were replaced by a new group that included William R. Winslow [1950–62], G. Russell Benson [1951–71], G. Frank Thomas [1951–65], Bishop G. Bromley Oxnam [1952–60], E. McClure Rouzer '07 [1952–72], O. B. Langrall '21 [1953–73], Alonzo G. Decker Sr. [1953–56], John M. Clayton Jr. '21 [1953–73], John A. Trader '20 [1955–72], T. Newell Cox [1956–65], Eugene C. Woodward [1956–80], Lewis F. Ransom '35 [1957–81], Daniel W. Justice [1957–62], John Bayley Jones '41 [1958–80], F. Kale Mathias '35 [1958–84], George A. Meyls '22 [1958–80], E. Dale Adkins Jr. [1959–71], Joshua W. Miles Jr. '18 [1959–76], and Allan W. Mund [1960–80]. In 1953, the board considered the issue of trustee life membership and approved creation of the designation "trustee emeritus" for those who had served at least ten years and could no longer attend meetings. In 1958, it was agreed that alumni visitors to the board should have more involvement and would be appointed to board committees.[1]

A third of the faculty also changed because of retirements, resignations, and deaths, although the number of full-time teachers remained fairly constant at about 55. Cloyd L. Bennighof [1927–52] in biology, Maude Gesner [1917–55] in music, and Dean W. Hendrickson [1925–58] in English all retired to emeritus status. Resignations were received from chemistry professor J. Lloyd Straughn [1942–74], who left in 1953 to work at Aeroprojects in West Chester, Pennsylvania, before returning to the

The college faculty 1950–51

faculty in 1959; Thomas F. Marshall [1943–55], who resigned to become chairman of the English Department at Kent State University in Ohio; and W. Allan MacDonald [1945–57], who left to become assistant director of the Baltimore Museum of Art (and soon after, chairman of the Art Department of George Washington University). New faces on the Hill were those of Arleen Heggemeier [1950–89] in music, Evelyn Smith (Hering Winfrey) [1951–55, 1966–94] in music, Jean Kerschner [1952–80] in biology, Joy Sleeper (Winfrey) [1952–59] in art and dramatic art, William M. David [1952–84] in sociology and political science, E. Robert Adkins [1953–57] in psychology, Ralph B. Price [1954–77] in economics, Gerald E. Cole [1955–84] in music, Richard B. Hovey [1955–61] in English, Karl L. Lockwood [1955–59] in chemistry, Eugene M. Nuss [1955–63] in education, Richard A. Clower '50 [1956–98] in physical education, L. Earl Griswold [1956–73] in sociology, Robert J. Waldorf [1957–65] in physical education, Richard A. Pugh Jr. [1957–62] in physical education, Ervin L. Szilagyi [1957–70] in art, William L. Tribby '56 [1958–61, 1963–79] in English and dramatic art, and Henry Natunewicz [1959–62] in psychology. Upon his arrival, the last-named individual was reported by the *Gold Bug* as having a varied record of study and degrees; he soon became well known on the campus for boasting in class about his adventures "hobnobbing" with celebrities. Eventually, his academic record became suspect, his eccentric classroom behavior was noted, and he was encouraged to leave the faculty.

On a more positive note, faculty members continued to be active in professional associations, bringing honor to the college. In 1953, Reuben Holthaus was elected president of Alpha Kappa Alpha, the national philosophy honor society. And Harwell Sturdivant was elected national president of Beta Beta Beta in 1960 (following in the footsteps of Lloyd Bertholf). Thomas Marshall was named a Fulbright lecturer in 1953 and spent the year teaching in Greece. In the fall of 1957, professors Jean Kerschner and John Makosky were selected to appear on WBAL-TV in Baltimore as part of a series focusing on colleges and teachers; on two successive Sundays in November, Kerschner talked about bees and their language, and Makosky spoke on George Bernard Shaw. In an effort to provide for more faculty governance and input into administrative decisions, in 1955 President Ensor created an Administrative Advisory Council, on which were three elected members of the faculty in addition to several administrators.[2]

Death claimed two faculty members during the decade. Fernanda Doria, a part-time teacher of music since 1946, after a distinguished career on the operatic stage in Europe and America, died in 1953 and left her entire music library to the college. This outstanding and unusual collection, including first editions and signed copies of musical works, was installed in a special room in Levine Hall, where it remained for many years until it was moved to the college archives. Margaret Wappler [1958–60] was completing her PhD in music at the University of Michigan when she was killed in an automobile accident in March 1960. Critically injured in the accident was Nancy L. Winkelman '51, who had returned to the Hill as assistant director of public relations [1958–73].

The campus was also saddened to learn of the deaths of three revered emeriti faculty. Dr. Alvey Michael Isanogle died on January 27, 1953, at the age of 80. (Two weeks later, his sister Mamie Isanogle, former college nurse, also died.) Dr. George Stockton Wills passed away February 27, 1956, at the age of 89, and Miss Nannie C. Lease died November 30, 1958, aged 84. A Wills Memorial Room was established in Science Hall to contain much of Prof. Wills's library, which was given to the college by his family. The Wills Room has moved within the building several times over the intervening years but is still used for seminars in the English Department. A fund for the purchase of books for the Dramatic Art Department was established in Miss Lease's memory.

Administrative changes during the decade included the resignation of L. Forrest Free [1937–52] as dean of men and mathematics professor to become dean of instruction at West Chester State College in Pennsylvania. His role as dean of men was assumed by William David, who held it for 11 years before taking on a full-time professorship in political science. Lucille Gishel Norman '44 [1953–57] joined the staff of the public relations office and assumed some duties as an admissions recruiter. When she left to lead the admissions program at Hood College, she was soon replaced by H. Kenneth Shook '52 [1959–75], who created the first separate office to deal with admissions (and later financial aid). He named Gloria E. Jones '58 as his assistant in 1960. Preston Yingling was named assistant superintendent of buildings and grounds in 1955. The housemother in Blanche Ward dormitory also changed. Nina Venables Veale '09 retired in 1954 after 13 years in the role [1941–54]. She was replaced by Mary L. Ewell [1954–57]. Veale was prevailed upon to return in 1957 and stayed through June 1958 before returning to her home in Salisbury. She was then succeeded by Henrietta P. Scott [1958–67].

There had been growing pressure from alumni and some trustees for a change in the athletic focus and staff; this was brought about by the resignations of Bruce Ferguson '35 and Charles Havens. Ferguson's role as basketball coach was filled by Richard Clower '50 [1956–98], and Havens's position as athletic director and football coach was filled by Robert J. Waldorf [1957–65]. Havens was much revered for his long service to the college and went on to teach in the Carroll County school system for 12 years, was active with the local fire company ambulance service, and assisted the city with its recreation program for many years. Prior to his death in 1996 at age 92, he was recognized a number of times for his service to the community. He was named to four sports halls of fame; joined a reunion of the 1951 undefeated football team at Homecoming 1981; was the college's Alumnus of the Year for 1982; and was honored in 1986 with a special testimonial dinner by his college classmates and former students, who established an award and a scholarship in his name.

After 40 years of association with the college as a physics professor and treasurer, Carl Schaeffer retired. He was replaced by his son, Philip B. Schaeffer '50 [1959–82]. The senior Schaeffer had assumed many roles at his alma mater, surveying the campus for electrical and sewer lines, assisting in the planning of new buildings, serving for seven years as assistant treasurer when William McDaniel was ill, teaching physics for 23 years, and keeping the books of the college in order for 17 years. He was given a testimonial dinner by the trustees upon his retirement as treasurer emeritus.

*Carl L. Schaeffer '14 (left) and son Philip B. Schaeffer '48
were consecutive college treasurers.*

CURRICULUM

The basic curriculum remained much the same as in previous years, except that political science was now an area in which students could major, and Russian was offered for the first time in 1959. By 1954, two "3-2" programs had been put in place with major universities: one in engineering in association with Johns Hopkins, and another in forestry with Duke. Students would spend three years on the Western Maryland campus completing their liberal arts requirements (for which they received the AB degree) and then two years at the university completing professional work (for which they received the BS degree). Relatively few students availed themselves of this arrangement, however; though they may have been drawn initially to the option, most found undergraduate life on the Hill so pleasant and valuable, they stayed for the regular four-year AB degree.

The college underwent its regular external evaluation by the Middle States Association of Colleges in March 1952; in preparation, the faculty adopted a new five-part statement of college purposes and objectives as the basis for its self-evaluation.[3] The evaluation report following the team visitation noted some weaknesses (not unexpected) in the program. It called on the board to give priority to increasing faculty and administrative salaries, to increasing fees for tuition and room and board, and to planning for an enlarged or new library to accommodate a larger collection. It also strongly suggested that all students be required to include a science (biology, chemistry, or physics) in their program, but not just biology as in the past. The music program was commended, as was the athletic program (considered excellent for the size of the college).[4] Also, after considerable discussion over several years and ultimately a campus visit by the association representative, the college received accreditation from the American Association of University Women in November 1953.

In another move to raise academic standards, the faculty voted in 1952 to require the Graduate Record Examination to be taken by all graduating seniors and a 50th percentile ranking to be achieved for graduation honors. The 167 seniors of 1953 were the first to take the tests, which were also used, of course, to assess the effectiveness of the various departments in the academic program. Collectively, students in 10 of the 14 departments for which there was an area test exceeded the 50th percentile, the highest area being the fine arts, which ranked in the 73rd percentile. Literature was close behind, in the 70th percentile. By 1956, students in economics and philosophy scored in the 80th percentile on average. Departments that did not generally score as high were encouraged to revise courses and prepare their students for the tests, and many successfully rose to the challenge. On the National Teachers Examination, given to all seniors entering the teaching profession, the 1953 group scored a collective average of 64th percentile on the general academic areas test and 65th percentile on the professional education component. These scores were replicated three years later.[5] Obviously, Western Maryland students were learning what they should and performing better than the national averages.

For the first time in decades, the faculty was involved in a major curriculum review during the years 1959–60. They proposed a new three-term calendar (reminiscent of the three-term calendar instituted by President Lewis in 1886 and maintained until 1926). Students would take three courses in each of three ten-week terms. Incorporated into the new plan was a required year-long course in western civilization. Courses in the humanities and social sciences would also be required, and all seniors would take a Great Issues course as a capstone to their degree. Finally, it was recommended that the home economics major be phased out in three years because the area was least related to the liberal arts (the two faculty staffing that department would soon be retiring). At the faculty meeting of May 9, 1960, the proposal was put to a vote and rejected. However, the decision to phase out the home ec major was approved, a required course in western civilization was added to the curriculum, and a faculty member was hired specifically to handle the latter.

A footnote to the home economics issue is that in January 1956, John D. Roop offered a piece of property to the college if it would institute a course in food engineering leading to a BS. The trustees declined the offer.

The master of education program had existed for about 15 years and had been redesigned by Dr. Joseph Bailer and Dean John Makosky in 1949. It had been refined into a successful program with some (perhaps) unique features. Instead of the traditional thesis as a culminating experience, a project of "action research" was instituted; action research came into being after World War II and focused on ways to improve teaching practices and classroom methodologies to ultimately improve student learning. In the Western Maryland program, action research was carried out in a school system, by an employee in that system, and approved by administrators in that system. Teachers analyzed a problem in theory and then tested the theory in practice in their own schools. As Makosky described it, "The second stage is this practical examination of the idea under the microscope of everyday teaching conditions. . . . The effort is not primarily to produce something new in the field of education research, but rather to face directly a challenging classroom situation in the life of the teacher-student himself and apply the best that is known to the problem—both in theory and practice." The study was scientific in its methods (including statistical analyses) but connected to reality. The third stage was the reporting, revising, concluding, and recording of observations.[6] The program required everyone to take two basic courses (Trends in American Thought, Introduction to Educational Research), courses in a content area, and courses in specialized education appropriate to the candidate's interests and needs. It would continue to attract educators (especially from the Baltimore area and southern Pennsylvania) wishing to do advanced work in education for the next 30 years. On average, 30 master's degrees were conferred each year during 1951–60. As few as 19 were awarded in 1953 and 1957, but 50 were granted in 1959.

STUDENT LIFE

With the uncertainty of the Korean conflict looming over their heads, the male students of the early part of this decade could not foresee what their futures held. However, a new policy for college students allowed some 200 WMC males to be deferred at least until they had completed their degrees. This, coupled with the fact that the GI Bill would cease on July 1, 1951, and fewer World War II veterans would be enrolled under that plan, meant that the college student body was somewhat back to normal in numbers and gender ratio. By the fall of 1951, Vetville housed only ten veteran families, the rest of the apartments being rented to seminarians and regular college students. However, in October 1952, President Ensor reported that a new GI Bill for Korean veterans was now in effect, and ten students enrolled under that plan.

In an effort to make the college experience more valuable for freshmen, 30 sophomores and juniors were recruited in 1954 to be student advisers (on a Freshman Advisory Council), each to work with 6 or 7 freshmen. As the student body continued gradually to expand, more rooms in McDaniel Hall were needed for women students, and the basement rooms facing onto Robinson Garden were renovated to become sorority rooms; these were larger and more conveniently located than those upstairs in the dormitory. When Daniel MacLea Hall was completed in 1956, Gamma Beta Chi and Delta Pi Alpha quickly moved into new clubrooms in its basement, releasing the old rooms in Alumni Hall for other use.

Fraternities and sororities continued to attract the majority of eligible students. Fraternities averaged 37 members (from 41 to 29) over the decade, the largest being Alpha Gamma Tau and Gamma Beta Chi and the smallest, Pi Alpha Alpha. Sororities averaged 40 members (from 57 to 20), the largest being Sigma Sigma Tau and the smallest, Iota Gamma Chi. The numbers in Greek organizations grew to a high of 369 in 1958–59. (Earlier in the decade, numbers had been as low as 247.) Generally, the percentage of Greek participation among eligible students averaged 65% (with a range of 58% to 75% over the ten-year period).

Other activities and organizations kept students busy, as well. Women could be majorettes or serve on the pompon squad (formed in 1955). They could perform in a variety of plays directed by Esther Smith, including the annual Christmas program, which alternately featured one-act plays and tableaux such as stained-glass windows and living sculptures. They could see one-act plays written by their classmates: *The Granny Knot* by George Gipe '56 (who went on to be a screenwriter in Hollywood) and *White Screens* by William Tribby '56 (who returned to the campus as an instructor in dramatic art two years later). They could attend presentations by such well-known celebrities as actress Cornelia Otis Skinner, actor Arnold Moss, organist Catherine Crozier, actress Ruth Draper, environmentalist Rachel Carson, and actor Charles Laughton. They could be entertained at several Alumni Hall assemblies by local resident Florence Keppel, former Metropolitan Opera soprano, accompanied by Oliver Spangler. They could watch their fellow students perform in such plays as *The Barretts of Wimpole Street; Our Town; Goodbye, My Fancy; Twelfth Night; Harvey; The Crucible; Separate Tables; The Diary of Anne Frank;* and *A Winter's Tale.*

*Esther Smith coaches a cast for a play
in the late 1950s.*

They could attend some of the many concerts and recitals presented by students and faculty in the Music Department, including the production in 1954 of *The Lowland Sea*, an opera jointly performed by the Dramatic Art and Music departments. They could sing in the men's and women's glee clubs, the College Octette (formed in 1950 with a student director), and the College Choir, which was now regularly joining the Baltimore and National Symphony orchestras for concerts featuring music from operas and operettas (*Cavalleria Rusticana* and *The Merry Widow*) or by Jerome Kern, Rodgers and Hammerstein, or Lerner and Loewe. In the spring of 1957, senior music major Betty Ely May '57 performed Brahms's Alto Rhapsody with the National Symphony in Constitution Hall (also in Alumni Hall), with a male chorus from the choir. Students could go to gallery art shows to see, for example, the work of James Snodgrass x'43 or the death masks of famous personages, a valuable set of which had been given to the college by Dr. Harry C. McComas in 1956. They could write for the new literary magazine, *Contrast*, founded in 1957, or for the *Gold Bug* or *Aloha*. And they could dance to the music of the Campus Capers, led by Richard Titlow '54, which provided music for parties and dances. Others in the Capers were Charles Bruno '56, Kirk Griffith x'57, Arnold Hayward '54, and William Ashburn '55.

In 1957, the Student Government decided that it would be appropriate to have a campus Christmas tree; a pine tree on the main road in front of the President's House and across from McDaniel Hall was selected and decorated. On a crisp December Sunday evening, after the choir and dramatic program

*The final scene from the Christmas pageant "Stained Glass Windows,"
created by Esther Smith*

in Alumni Hall, students gathered around the tree to hear Dr. Ensor make
some brief remarks about the symbolism of the tree before he turned the
switch that illuminated its many colored lights. Afterward everyone moved
to McDaniel Lounge for hot chocolate and cookies. A few years later, after
the plaza in front of Baker Memorial Chapel was landscaped, the two trees in
front were decorated as part of the campus Christmas observance, often with
a formal tree-lighting ceremony, a practice that continues today.

Students could attend the annual student-faculty basketball game,
sponsored by the Student Christian Association for the benefit of the World
Student Service Fund, and watch Lowell Ensor, Reuben Holthaus, Frank Hurt,
and Clyde Spicer, among others, demonstrate their athletic prowess. They
could attend Sunday Fellowship (the new name for the old Sunday school) or
the events of other religious groups, which now included the Jewish Student
Association and the Westminster Fellowship (Presbyterian). They could even
enroll in flying lessons at the local airport under the auspices of the new Flying
Club, sponsored by sociology professor and former pilot L. Earl Griswold.
Of course, they would be riotously entertained each spring by the Junior
Follies, a staple of campus activity from the early fifties on, which always
good-naturedly spoofed college traditions and personalities while bringing
the class together to work on a major project and raise some money to pay
for the Junior-Senior Prom. Some of these gems were cleverly entitled "Spree
of '53," "The Bore of '54," "Scalping the T.P.," "Willy Mack's Co-op," and "The
Making of Prudence Grunion."

In 1951 the board approved a request from students and alumni that the golf course and tennis courts be open for play on Sunday. During the fall of 1956, the golf course was improved and revamped, and six all-weather tennis courts were built. A year later a concrete floor was poured in the low-ceilinged basement of Gill Gymnasium to provide for a better rifle range, room for the wrestling team, and storage of equipment.[7]

Students gather for the tree lighting ceremony and caroling c. 1958.

In the fall of 1951, the dining hall steward, Byron "Barney" Rice, decided to rearrange the dining room, creating several long tables running the length of the room. This was supposed to make the waiters' job easier. The students reacted negatively, and the *Gold Bug* editor, L. Stanley Bowlsbey '52 (later dean of the graduate program) likened the arrangement to that of a prison.[8] Rice soon changed the arrangement back to tables for ten. Generally, while there was regular, and not unexpected, complaint about the dining hall food, one editorial in 1956 took a different tack. It opined, "Much of the food is very good, but there is not much of it. It is . . . foolish to suppose that one

Science Hall dining room, c. 1958

serving bowl of anything could ever serve as many as ten people. . . . There is a great deal prepared which simply is not appetizing enough to eat, and . . . there is seldom enough of what *is* appetizing enough to eat." It went on to list the variety of unappetizing foods, served especially at lunch, and concluded, "They simply are of a composition which does not inspire enthusiastic consumption. . . . Let us hope that the situation may improve."[9]

A parking problem still existed on campus, with 172 cars registered and 148 parking places to accommodate them in 1953; in 1954 the SGA created a traffic court to deal with parking fines. In March 1955, President Ensor announced that fraternity-sponsored off-campus parties could no longer serve beer, which quickly provoked angry reactions. The following year, the students again reacted when a sandwich salesman's car got stuck in the mud in the middle of the men's quadrangle between Albert Norman Ward and Daniel MacLea halls. Catcalls across the quad soon erupted, and the noise escalated. Firecrackers were set off, and one student was later disciplined for throwing a flaming roll of toilet paper from an upstairs window.[10] The police were called, as they would be on various occasions now that the men lived in close proximity to one another across the open quad.

The weather also posed problems from time to time. In October 1954, Hurricane Hazel tore up the eastern seaboard, uprooting trees and knocking out power on campus for a time. And in February 1958, an 18-inch snowfall (the heaviest since 1942) paralyzed the campus. The Sunday chapel service was cancelled, but classes went on as usual, with faculty getting there as best they could. (The story that sociology professor Earl Griswold rode his horse to campus from his farm west of town was debunked by Griswold himself. He did, however, ride his tractor.) Phone lines were dead, the grille was closed, and

Sledding down the hill, back campus, 1958

icicles hanging off the roof of McDaniel Hall were a hazard to walkers through Robinson Garden. The dean of women even permitted the coeds to wear slacks (a rare privilege) because of the cold. A snowplow got stuck in front of Science Hall and sat there for a week. Students who had gone home for the weekend straggled in as late as Thursday. Perhaps the worst part of the whole event for the boarding students was that there was no whipped cream for the Jello.[11]

Many alumni of the era have fond memories of life on campus during this era, and George Fringer '60 wrote about them for a Carroll County weekly newspaper:

> In the fall of 1956 I officially became a student at Western Maryland College. Freshman week was full of testing and orientation. . . . Evelyn Wenner was my advisor, and in later years she would become my favorite professor, teaching me English literature and novels. . . . Whenever I decided to socialize, it would be at "Old Main." You could eat your lunch here [Fringer was a "day hop"] and play the juke-box. At the time "Singin' the Blues" with Guy Mitchell and Pat Boone's vocal rendition of "April Love" were the top tunes. Besides food and drink, you could go to the bookstore and post office to conduct your necessary business. Among my early courses were French and Spanish. Biology was always informative with a detailed lecture by Harwell Sturdivant. . . . Theodore

Whitfield, history professor, was very dramatic in his presentation. He would pound his lectern whenever he wanted to make a point. One day he brought an umbrella to class, opened it up, and imitated Neville Chamberlain. . . . No one was ever bored. . . .

All freshmen wore "rat caps." These green and gold beanies were displayed at all times. Sophomores gloried in the power they wielded over these unfortunate first-year students. Until the annual tug-of-war took place at the homecoming football game, this headgear was part of your attire. If the freshman class won the battle, however, they were no longer beholden to anybody. . . .

My last two years were spent taking required education courses. Under the direction of Joseph Bailer, my teaching ambitions reached fruition. . . . Content courses, AV instruction, and practice teaching were compulsory. . . .

On a Monday morning, the last day of May in 1960, I received my diploma at graduation ceremonies in Alumni Hall. My diploma, signed by President Lowell S. Ensor and Secretary of the Faculty William Ridington, confirmed that I had graduated with a Bachelor's degree. A new chapter in life awaited me. . . . A 30-year [teaching] career began.[12]

Freshmen and sophomores participate in the Homecoming tug-of-war.

Toward the end of the decade, a number of innovations were put into place to give the student body more control over their lives. During 1958 a Judicial Board was created to handle serious discipline problems referred by the Men's and Women's Councils and academic dishonesty issues referred by faculty. This complemented the Student Life Council, also created in 1958, to consider all phases of student life and effect solutions to perceived problems. It was to help coordinate activities and the use of college facilities, especially the new student union building, which would be in use by 1959. Student leaders, faculty members, and key administrators served on the board and the council. The student government continued to function well through its several committees, including a Food Committee, which met frequently with Helen Harbaugh, the dietician [1944–66], and Byron Rice, the steward, to discuss menus and food service (the small quantities of food served, as well as such things as liver and "mounds of joy"). In the fall of 1958, the first of several leadership conferences was held with the theme "Helping the Hill"; it drew student leaders from across the campus for three days of discussions, panels, and development of resolutions for campus change.

Students of the era still sought sources of food off campus, and while Margaret and Earl's closed in the early 1950s, Baugher's Family Restaurant and Sharkey's Cove provided hearty and inexpensive fare to assuage night-time cravings. For more formal occasions, Thelma Hoffman's boarding house (later renamed Cockey's Tavern) on East Main Street served great quantities of food family style for banquets and special events.

Members of the freshman class looked forward to being entertained in groups of 25 by President and Mrs. Ensor in the special dining room on the lower level of Science Hall. Mrs. Harbaugh always supervised the almost weekly events, which featured a menu of steak, vegetables, and fancy ice creams. The first course was a surprise to most students: broiled grapefruit. Mrs. Harbaugh recalled many years later how it was made: "You cut the fruit in half, sprinkle brown sugar and butter over the top and a little bit of rum— we had to use artificial at the college, but it's even better with the real stuff! Put those under the broiler and they are delicious." She also remembered preparing meals for the Baltimore Colts: "They were birds. Artie Donovan always came to the dining room in his pajamas. The football players would get steaks and we'd ask each one how he wanted it cooked. Every one of them wanted them different. We had one man who wanted his steak taken right out of the refrigerator!"[13]

Perhaps the most far-reaching innovation of the decade was the proposed honor system, which had widespread support within the student body. Obviously, this was not the first honor code for the college, but for this generation of students it was unique; it was overwhelmingly accepted by them on April 27, 1960, and by the faculty on May 2.

As academic standards rose, so did concern for student behavior, and in 1954 a system of administrative warnings was created in lieu of fines for absences from classes, assemblies, and chapel. The system attempted to put more responsibility on the shoulders of the students while eliminating some of the more onerous rules of earlier generations. It attempted to emphasize cumulative good conduct rather than isolated infractions. The following year, a Dean's List of Campus Citizens was created, to which students were named based on their good scholarship, good attendance, good conduct in the dormitories, and good attitude toward the college. Those on the Dean's List were exempt from penalties for absence.[14]

In 1959 the faculty approved stricter rules for probation. They wanted to guard against admission of weak students and make it more difficult for students habitually in academic arrears to remain in the college. These moves gradually led to an academically stronger student body, from which exceptional students would emerge to garner special awards and scholarships. William H. Simpson '51 received a Rotary fellowship for a year's study at the University of Edinburgh. He was one of 111 students worldwide to receive the fellowship for advanced study that year. Some of those receiving Fulbright scholarships (eight in 1951–57) were Charles Immler '52 for graduate study in economics at the University of Sydney, Australia; Eugene Mechtly '52 for graduate work in physics in Innsbruck; Henry Ernst '53 for study in theology and philosophy at the University of Edinburgh; Richard F. Brenneman '55 for study of theology at Westphalian State University in Munster, Germany; and George Gipe '56 for study in English at the University of Glasgow. Another aspect of the changing and improving student body was the increasing number of foreign students on campus. In 1958, nine students from eight foreign countries (Arabia, Philippines, Japan, Syria, Guatemala, Korea, Indonesia, and Hungary) were integrated into the campus population and life, providing a diverse point of view about the world and its issues.

The ROTC program continued to grow during this decade. In 1951, it reached its all-time high of 210 cadets enrolled in the four-year program (the first two years were required of all freshman and sophomore men). Fifteen officers were commissioned that year. By the end of the decade, the number of commissions had more than doubled, and the program had grown commensurate with the growth in the college.

In 1952 a new college award was endowed by Dr. and Mrs. Felix Morley in memory of their son Felix Woodbridge "Woody" Morley, who had drowned at Gibson Island during the summer following his freshman year. The award has been given each year since "to that member of the Freshman Class who by his or her development on The Hill has most happily justified admission to the college community."[15] The third national honor society on the campus, Delta Omicron, was chartered in November 1957, to recognize superior work by women in music. It was the first chapter in Maryland. In the spring of 1960, a men's leadership society was formed, to complement the Trumpeters for women. It would evolve into a chapter of the national men's leadership society, Omicron Delta Kappa, during the next decade.

After the excellent showing of the football team following its rebuilding after World War II, the next decade witnessed far less success. Only three winning seasons in ten were recorded. The decade opened with 13 consecutive wins over two seasons including a rather spectacular undefeated (8–0) season in the fall of 1951, when the team gave up only 66 points while amassing 184 points against their opponents. That season the Terrors were the undisputed Mason-Dixon Champions; Victor Makovitch '52 and Martin "Mitch" Tullai '52 were named to 1951 All-America teams, and Tullai was also named to the Grey team for the Blue-Grey game, for which his coach was Rip Engle. However, the seasons to follow were disappointing.

President Ensor reported to the trustees at its meeting in April 1957 that some alumni, trustees, and administrators had "not been too happy about our athletic program during the past several years. The program . . . was in fact doing more to hurt our educational program and student morale than to strengthen it. Men were being invited to enroll and participate in athletics who were not qualified—so they were either dropped or became ineligible to play." The board considered whether to continue football at all but decided to

1951 undefeated football team coached by Charlie Havens

*Students celebrate Homecoming with a pep rally
and bonfire in the late 1950s.*

keep it if it were properly conducted. Limited aid would continue to be given to some athletes, but they would have to qualify on their academic ability and financial need, as well as their athletic ability.[16] A new football coaching staff took over in the fall of 1957, consisting of Robert Waldorf, athletic director and head coach (at a salary of $7,000, the same as senior administrators), and Richard A. Pugh and Robert Myers Jr., assistant coaches. Waldorf came to the college from Washington and Lee High School in Arlington, Virginia, where he had a record of 29 wins and 11 losses. He had also held coaching positions at Simpson College and Marquette University. Pugh joined the staff from a high school position in Lothian, Maryland. By the fall of 1959, the team had recorded a winning season (5–2–2). Receiving All-America honors for their individual records in football were Fred P. Burgee '61 (1958, 1959), Robert W. Butler '57 (1956), Fred A. Dilkes '61 (1959), and Gerard S. Miller '58 (1957).

Another well-known campus athletic personality in this era was James Boyer, who was assistant basketball coach and varsity baseball coach [1950–56], as well as athletic trainer. In mid-April 1951, Boyer turned the baseball team over to Julian Dyke '50 temporarily and went off to umpire major league baseball, which he had done for nine seasons (including the 1947 All-Star Game and the 1948 World Series). He retired from the American

League in 1951 and served the college ably until a heart attack took him out of service for some months in 1957. He returned to part-time work but died of a heart attack in 1959 at the age of 51. The Jim Boyer Memorial Award was established by his former players in 1962 and is presented annually to the most outstanding student baseball player. Charlie Havens coached baseball for the 1957 season, and Dick Pugh finished out the decade.

Soccer began the decade with four losing seasons; however, two players were named All-America: Albert T. Grimes Jr. '51 in 1950 and H. Richard Linton '54 in 1953. By 1954, the team had reversed its fortunes, showed a 7–2–1 record, and was tied for the Southern Division Middle Atlantic Conference title. Dennis Harmon '57 had sparked the team's effort and was named to the All-America team. The following year, he led the team (6–3–1) to the first Maryland championship in at least 20 years and received more All-America honors. Phil Uhrig's soccer team amassed a record of 8–2 in 1956, and both Harmon and Sam Reed '57 received All-America honors that year. Uhrig lost both of those stars to graduation but gained a Hungarian refugee powerhouse in George Varga '61. The remaining two seasons under Uhrig did not produce championships. He retired after nine seasons of coaching and turned the team over to Harmon for the 1959 season; the team went 9–1–1, one of the best records in college history. The October 30 game against Lycoming produced a 13–0 score, the highest for any WMC team. Varga was a standout player, making 34 goals in 11 games that year (a school and national record), with 9 in a single game, earning him All-America honors. The team received recognition and honors from the NCAA and the Middle Atlantic Conference; it was ranked among the top 25 teams in the United States and the top 5 teams in the South.[17]

The basketball team continued its streak of losing seasons under Coach Ferguson, with its best season in 1952, when it was 8–6 in the Mason-Dixon Conference and 9–10 overall. Leading scorer was Art Press '52, who scored over 1,500 points in his college career. In 1960, the team recorded its first winning season (11–9) since 1943 under new coach Dick Clower, posting significant wins over Mt. St. Mary's and Washington College. The team also played in its first Maryland tournament in a decade, having recorded an 8–6 record among Maryland schools. Things were definitely improving.

Lacrosse had not fared particularly well, either, showing such season records as 1–10 and 0–7. With waning student interest, the sport was discontinued in 1955. Jim Boyer's baseball team posted one winning season (9–6) during the decade, finishing second in the Mason-Dixon Conference in 1954, while the tennis team posted nearly all winning seasons, with such records as 12–4, 12–2, and 15–2. Frank Hurt's men seemed always to be able to do the job and do it well. The golf and rifle teams competed with average records.

*Terror mascot joins Dr. and Mrs. Ensor, daughter Caryl '58,
and Professor L. Straughn at a football game.*

Women's sports were still generally intramural, except that a basketball team played four intercollegiate games in 1953 and won all four. By 1959 the team was playing St. Joseph (Emmitsburg), College of Notre Dame (Baltimore), Goucher, Mt. St. Agnes (Baltimore), Villa Julie, and Towson. Slowly, women's intercollegiate athletics were beginning to develop. Physical education professor Roselda Todd '28 must have been pleased to see the women again playing other college teams, as she had had the opportunity to do as a student 30 years before, under Faith Millard.

A student of special historical interest enrolled in the college in September 1959. Whittaker Chambers (1901–61), a noted journalist, editor, and essayist, owned a farm north of Westminster for some years. It was there that the sensational "Pumpkin Papers" escapade took place (stolen microfilm was hidden in a hollowed-out pumpkin in a patch on Chambers's Carroll County farm), leading to the famous and controversial Alger Hiss trial, which also involved Senator Richard Nixon. Chambers's involvement in the Communist Party and his knowledge of Hiss's communist ties and activities ultimately led to Hiss being tried, convicted, and imprisoned for espionage. In 1959, after the publicity of the trial died down, Chambers enrolled at the college, hoping to complete his AB degree and begin working on a master's. In a conversation with Dean Makosky, Chambers was asked what he planned to do with his

MA. He replied that he had no idea but said, "I shall be different from what I am at this moment."[18] Chambers was quite serious in his studies. "It isn't only the question of an earned degree and the completion of something left unfinished [he had left Columbia University in 1924 to take his first journalism job]. I feel the crying need of formal, intensive training in history, philosophy, and economics."[19] He would not complete his degree, however, for he died unexpectedly on July 8, 1961, at the age of 60. During his two years of academic work at the college, he studied French, Greek, Latin, Spanish, and Russian at various levels and took courses in psychology, economics, biology, and European art, as well. Had he finished the AB, President Ensor intended to ask him to be the commencement speaker on the occasion of his graduation.

The campus was saddened to learn in 1954 of the death of Carlo J. Ortenzi '48, who had been killed in Korea in December 1950. He had been listed as "missing in action." Also killed in Korea was Robert D. Ebert '51. In January 1956, the community was shocked to learn of the tragic murder of Gaither Lee Fischbach, a freshman in the class of 1959, in front of his home in Baltimore. His class established a fund to endow a scholarship in his memory. In October 1958, word reached the college that Mrs. Nina Veale, longtime and beloved housemother in Blanche Ward Hall [1941–55, 1957–58], had died at her home in Salisbury.

The Washington Alumni Club gathered for lunch;
Caleb O'Connor is pictured second from left.

Word also reached the campus that Caleb Wilson Spofford O'Connor (1880–1956) x'98, '20M(hon), had died in Washington on April 3, 1956. He was described as being "heavy set and stocky and very bright and alive. He was quite a character. He had a lot of charisma, and he was a very loyal alum of the college." So dear was the college to O'Connor that, per his request, he was cremated and had his ashes sent to the college. President and Mrs. Ensor sprinkled them over the hill overlooking Hoffa Field.[20]

Nancy Winkelman '51, '69M, in an essay written 40 years after her college experience, recalled life in the 1950s:

> Those of us who came to college right after World War II graduated into the beginning of the Korean War. A good while later, I realized that we weren't the . . ."silent generation." Ours were The Interim Years. . . . One afternoon, as I went from Science Hall to Lewis Hall, no one was sitting on the bench or on the steps, and there was the kind of quiet that one remembers 40 years later. Outside McDaniel I heard radios. It was March, 1948, and President Harry S. Truman was making a speech. We didn't have televisions in every room then, in fact, in none of them, so everyone sat around a radio waiting to hear if Truman would reinstitute the draft. He did. . . . I've had the feeling that [members of that generation] weren't silent for lack of something to say; perhaps subconsciously they were just holding their collective breath waiting for the other shoe to drop. And, with Vietnam, it did.[21]

BUILDINGS AND GROUNDS

During the summer of 1952, the interior of Baker Chapel was completely renovated, the first major change in the building since its dedication in 1895. The pews were rebuilt and refinished, the old wainscoting was covered with paneling, the antiquated lighting was replaced by recessed floodlights and Early American fixtures, and the carpet was replaced for the first time. The chancel area was redesigned so that there was now an altar, a pulpit, and a lectern enclosed by an altar railing with kneelers. Some of the wide pine boards from the attic of the old Geiman farmhouse were used for the flooring of the two entryways, which were furnished with reproductions of an original communion table. The simplicity of the old Methodist Protestant tradition, with its central pulpit and no altar, had been replaced by the newer Methodist style, reflecting more of the Methodist Episcopal traditions. A secondhand, two-manual Moller organ, originally in the Towson Methodist Church, was installed in 1959 and used as a practice organ by music students for years.

Another major renovation was undertaken during the 1953 Christmas recess when the Alumni Hall interior was replastered and repainted. A radical departure from previous color schemes was used on the proscenium arch, which was painted in combinations of green, brown, and goldleaf, providing a striking focal point for the auditorium.

Bishop Oxnam wanted to move the seminary to Washington to a spot near the American University. By 1953, he had "persuaded" the seminary board (of which he had been immediately elected president upon his appointment to the Washington Area) to abandon the nine years of planning and discussion with the college about mutual expansion and property and focus on moving to Washington. As Chandler described the situation in *Pilgrimage of Faith*, "The Oxnam bulldozer was without subtleties." Seminary president Welliver was forced to accept the new plan and soon relinquished his office. The transfer of the seminary property to the college "after a satisfactory settlement" was made quickly. Chandler quoted Oxnam's diary concerning the bargaining:

> *I finally said, "What is the point of a long discussion? Ordinarily, a man never reveals the line to which he will retreat in negotiation but it seems to me since we are all Methodists and we all desire the same thing it would be better for me to state what I believe to be the value of the Seminary property." I then stated the value of the land, the buildings and faculty residences. They reached a total of slightly in excess of $200,000. General Gill, a former military leader and a real estate man of great wealth, said to the chairman [Murray Benson], "Would you mind if I whispered something to Bishop Oxnam?" He came to me and said, "Bishop, what do you say we settle this at $175,000?" I said, "I think that is excellent." It was done as quickly as that.*[22]

Even though it would not take title or possession of the buildings until the seminary moved to Washington in October 1958, the college now had property onto which it could expand. When the old seminary building became part of the college, it was named Elderdice Hall (in recognition of former seminary president and college trustee Hugh Elderdice Sr., who had overseen the building of the facility in 1920). It was soon remodeled and became the college's administration building in 1958–59. The board of trustees held its first meeting in the assembly room (formerly the seminary chapel) of the new facility on April 24, 1959.

Once it was clear that the property just north of the seminary and opposite Albert Norman Ward Hall was to become part of the college, a new and much needed men's dormitory was planned by architects O. Eugene Adams and Edward G. Rigg, and construction began. The men who lived in McKinstry and Ward halls had long been complaining about cracking

*Daniel MacLea Hall, a men's dormitory,
was opened in 1956.*

plaster, loose window frames, inadequate electrical service, and insufficient shower and lavatory facilities; they would have no regrets at leaving the old dormitories for a new one.[23] The new hall was named in memory of Daniel MacLea, longtime chairman of the trustees' Buildings and Grounds Committee [1924–52] and prominent Baltimore wholesale lumber merchant. The building was to be completed by the fall of 1955, but construction delays postponed its occupancy until January 3, 1956. It was funded in large measure by a state grant of $250,000, which had been approved by the legislature in an override of Governor Theodore McKeldin's veto.[24] The new dormitory, built to house 140 men and costing approximately $400,000, was formally dedicated on June 6, 1956.

A new and much larger chapel had been in the plans for three decades, and partial funding in the amount of $200,000 had been promised by the Baker family. After a major adjustment to the 1950 campus plan was presented and approved in 1955, the new chapel was sited on top of the hill, replacing Yingling Gymnasium, and detailed plans to raze the Old Main complex (and build a new student center and library) were made, at a proposed cost of $600,000.[25] In order to provide for the chapel's construction, McKinstry dormitory and Yingling Gym would have to be removed, and that was accomplished as soon as the new MacLea dormitory was opened. The Military Science Department, which had inhabited the old gymnasium since

443

Gill Gymnasium had been built, was now moved to renovated quarters in the basement of Albert Norman Ward Hall, with staff offices in the basement of Daniel MacLea Hall. The top of the Hill was beginning to change for the first time in 60 years.

All through the academic years 1956–58 the students watched the new Baker Memorial Chapel, built by Consolidated Engineering, slowly rise behind Old Main. A major event one day during the summer of 1957 was watching the largest crane ever put together in Carroll County raising the steeple to its place 113 feet above the porch. (The metal cross on the top of the steeple was 6 feet high and 3.5 feet wide.) The building was 149 feet long and 60 feet wide and seated 715 in the nave, 145 in the balcony, and 60 in the choir. It was completed at a cost of about $588,000 and formally dedicated in special ceremonies in April 1958. The three-manual organ, valued at the time at about $45,000, was designed by Joseph S. Whiteford '43 and constructed by the Aeolian-Skinner Organ Company of Boston, of which he was president. The organ consisted of four divisions: great, choir, swell, and pedal, with 38 ranks consisting of 2,310 pipes. The exterior case of the console came from the historic Bruton Parish Church in Williamsburg, Virginia. When the company installed a larger organ there, it was saved and refitted to house the new college chapel console. The white wood paneling in the chancel was designed to blend with that on the organ console. The carillonic bells were a product of Schulmerich Carillons and were designed to play the Westminster chimes on the quarter hour, strike the hour, and play the alma mater three times daily. The chimes can also be played from the organ console.[26]

Immediately after the chapel was dedicated, the seniors were slated to take the Graduate Record Examination in the large room in the basement, but some complained that it was a "sacred space" and should not be "secularized." President Ensor responded in the next *Gold Bug* (published after the examination) that education is "sacred" and educational activities, including examinations, were quite appropriate to take place in the chapel. The large space was soon subdivided to provide offices and classrooms for the Philosophy and Religion Department, as well as a large room seating 300–400. The appropriate name for the new chapel was discussed, and apparently Ensor announced that the new chapel would be known as Memorial Chapel to distinguish it from the older Baker Chapel. Time has shown that this designation didn't stick, and for decades the chapels have been called "Big Baker" and "Little Baker" because of their size. There are people who think the official name of the older, smaller chapel is Little Baker Chapel, perhaps named for the Little and Baker families.

The remaining buildings of the old central complex were slated for

Winslow Student Center was opened in 1959.

demolition, but before that could occur, homes had to be found for everything housed therein. The Art Department was moved to the old home of the seminary president, renamed Forlines House (after former seminary professor and president Charles E. Forlines '97). The Dean of Women's Office was removed to Elderdice Hall, to join administrative offices moved there from Carroll Hall in 1958. The Home Economics Department then moved to Carroll Hall (keeping McDaniel House as the home management laboratory). But a place to house the college post office, student grille, recreation hall, and student organization offices was still needed. This need was met by the design and construction of a student center (the first on the campus). It was first planned for a spot opposite the old seminary building (site of the present Decker College Center), but the steep hillside posed problems for the architects of the time, so it was redesigned as a split-level building on a flat piece of property below Lewis Hall, near the entrance to Hoffa Field off Main Street. Construction, at a cost of $255,000, went on throughout 1958–59, and the building was formally opened on Alumni Day in May 1959. It was named for trustee William R. Winslow. To provide easier access to this new building, the lower road behind the chapel was surfaced and extended all the way to Gill Gymnasium. With spaces now created for everything formerly housed in Old Main, Smith Hall, and Hering Hall, those final three 19th-century buildings were razed in the summer of 1959 (Ward Hall had been torn down the previous year). Amazingly, their cornerstones were salvaged by students, who returned them to the college for later incorporation into a monument, topped

The Old Main complex in front of Baker Memorial Chapel
was razed 1957–59.

by the Old Main bell, that was first built south of Baker Memorial Chapel and reconstructed in Memorial Plaza in 1991. The walnut newel posts from the Old Main stairwell were also salvaged, and in 1968 they were fashioned into maces that have since been carried by the marshals at the head of academic processions. The alumni plaques of the earliest classes, which hung in Smith Hall for years, were moved to the lower level of Alumni Hall to join the later class plaques in the Alumni Room. (When Alumni Hall was renovated and that room turned into the Elderdice Theatre, some of the plaques were moved to the narthex of Baker Memorial Chapel and the remaining ones stored safely in the archives.)

In the summer of 1958, more changes were made in the housing of the academic departments. Because the remainder of the mortgage ($58,524) on the Science Hall property had been forgiven by the state (at the urging of Senator Frederick Malkus '34),[27] the regulations governing its use as a science building were nullified. The Biology Department was moved to the second floor of Lewis Hall (where it had resided between 1914 and 1928), and the Mathematics Department was moved to the first floor of Lewis Hall, joining physics, making the entire building a science-oriented facility. The departments of Economics, Sociology, Foreign Languages, Classics, History, and Political Science were then moved to Science Hall, and the building was renamed Memorial Hall in memory of all the buildings in the Old Main complex. Those buildings were later described and pictured on a bronze bas relief mounted on top of the Old Main cornerstone, which was placed on the

446

site of the old complex, in front of Baker Memorial Chapel, in 1992.

By 1959, the need for an expanded or new library was becoming acute, particularly with the growing enrollment. Indeed, in April 1960, President Ensor proposed expanding the college by 300 students to accommodate the growing number of people seeking a college education, especially in Maryland.[28] The board moved forward with plans for a new building to be placed north of Baker Memorial Chapel, and a committee was appointed to plan the necessary fund-raising. Perhaps more important was the creation of a Development Committee of the board to study future financial needs and develop long-range plans for fund-raising. This coincided with appointment of the college's first development officer the following year. One of several fund-raising efforts toward the goal eventually set at $500,000 for the library was the several tours by the College Choir, which sang in Methodist churches around the state, from Cumberland to Salisbury, Washington to Hagerstown.

Following its long-standing policy, the college continued to purchase properties on its perimeter and now owned 15 properties on the west side of Union Street. Another off-campus property came into the college portfolio when the J.C. Penney building in downtown Westminster was bequeathed to the college by Mrs. Walter Davis (widow of the former trustee). Soon thereafter, a major fire destroyed the interior, but after $55,000 was spent to rebuild and renovate the building, it was rented and brought in about $15,000 yearly.[29]

In an attempt to be patriotic and also raise some funds, the trustees agreed to lease the basement of the Thompson Infirmary for at least three years to the U.S. Office of Defense Mobilization (Civil Defense) as a potential shelter from nuclear attack. The rent covered the utilities and the expenses of renovation. Ensor was assured by ODM director Dr. Arthur S. Flemming that the space would be used only for relocation of governmental agencies in emergency situations (when enemy planes were known to be approaching the U.S.).[30] Practice civil defense alerts were held periodically on campus, although the *Gold Bug* questioned whether they were needed.

Finances

During this ten-year span, enrollments grew by about 140, from a low in 1952–53 of 631 to a high of 774 in 1958–59. Annual totals averaged 685, with the balance between the sexes fairly well maintained. The entering class of 1950 (203) was a bit smaller than usual because the counties in Maryland not already requiring 12 years of education instituted the 12th grade that year, so there were fewer graduates to send off to college. During the next two years, enrollments dropped nationwide as much as 15%. At WMC the drop was only about 4%, and then enrollments rebounded and kept rising. Curiously, in 1955, the board decided to cap enrollment at 700, but in two years it had already exceeded that figure; it was ultimately capped by housing capacity. The entering class of 1958 numbered 246 (out of 955 applications) and the campus housing filled long before September. Female enrollments were 19 greater than residence spaces, so that many women had to be placed in rented rooms in houses adjacent to the campus. For the freshman class in 1955, 457 applications were received, 267 were accepted, and 122 enrolled. In 1957, 804 applications were received, 549 were accepted, and 252 were enrolled. By 1959, 1,170 applications were received, and 299 students, many more than expected, enrolled, pushing total enrollment to 764 (73 boarders more than available residence spaces) and requiring tripling in rooms.[31] (Some women students were again housed off campus, and every available spot on campus was utilized.) It was noted that the quality of male applicants was not as good as that of females.

The country was in an inflationary spiral, and college costs rose accordingly. Tuition rose 75% over the decade; room and board costs increased only 33%, but the total cost increase was 52%, from $950 in 1950–51 to $1,440 in 1959–60. After years of little or no increase prior to 1940, there were only 2 years over the next 20 when total costs did not rise by some amount (as little as $10 and as much as $130). Total costs were still considerably less than those for any of the other local and competing colleges, however. For instance, in 1954, when WMC costs were about $1,000, Goucher's were $1,725, Hood's were $1,435, St. John's were $1,500, and Gettysburg's totaled $1,125. Despite the increases, inflation was taking its toll on the budget, always stretched thin. Throughout the decade Carl Schaeffer, the treasurer and a conservative fiscal manager, regretfully reported to the board at its April meeting that there might be a small deficit in the year's final accounting, but he was always able to report at the fall meeting that the previous year had ended with a surplus (however small). It is interesting to note that by mid-decade, the college's annual budget exceeded $1 million.[32]

As should be expected, faculty salaries rose as tuition increased. In 1950 the average salary was about $3,500 in a range from $2,700 to $4,800. The following year saw $100 to $400 increases, but the inflationary spiral gripping the country eroded those increases. In 1952 a salary scale was proposed that paid professors $4,000–$5,500, associate professors $3,500–$4,500, assistant professors $3,000–$4,000, and instructors $2,100–$3,000. The president's salary was $7,500. By 1956 salaries ranged from $3,500 to $6,000 and averaged $4,900. By 1959–60 they had almost doubled, rising to a high of $8,400 and a low of $4,500. The 12-month deans earned $9,500, the athletic director received $7,500, and the president's salary was $12,000.[33] President Ensor noted that the National Education Association had reported in 1958 that the median salary for nonpublic college professors was $5,100, and the WMC average was $5,700. There was some satisfaction expressed that, for the first time, the college was slightly above the national average. The growth in salaries, much appreciated by the faculty, as expressed by letters to the trustees and president, can be attributed in part to a grant of $181,900 from the Ford Foundation for the endowment, the interest from which (about $7,200 yearly) was designated for improving faculty salaries over a ten-year period. The college also received a grant of $2,000 from the Esso Educational Fund.[34] A note to the president from Dean Makosky in 1959 suggests the financial status and attitude of the era: "[My wife] tells me that our salary has been materially increased. Thank you very much. Financially, my objective is to be able to live, in a quiet and unostentatious way, yet able to afford books and music and an occasionally luxury, without thought or worry about money. I feel that you are making this possible for us, and should like to express very real gratitude."[35]

In another effort to improve the financial status of the faculty and staff, the board in 1950 voted to include all college employees in the federal Social Security program.[36] In 1953, it voted to allow employees to participate in a new supplementary program of TIAA, called CREF, which allowed for more growth in the pension program. And in 1957, it instituted a major-medical expense program through TIAA, with 100% of premiums paid by the college when employees paid for a Blue Cross/Blue Shield base plan. (The total cost to the college that year for this significant benefit was $3,600.)

The endowment grew steadily throughout this period. From a total of $1,029,273 in 1951, it increased about $100,000 each year until it was slightly over $1,500,000 in 1956 and $1,822,762 by 1960. It grew through good management, compound interest, and some funds received during the Mid-Century Campaign (the bulk of the money was spent on buildings, debt management, and campus improvements) in the early years of the decade. Drawing off as little as 4% of the interest provided the college with $40,000–$70,000 for ongoing expenses. Another source of funding was the Living Endowment, really an annual fund by another name. Under the direction of Philip Uhrig, this fund steadily grew each year, as more alumni made contributions. From very small beginnings, and with the help of newly appointed class agents, it reported contributions of $10,722 in 1955 and $13,559 in 1956. In 1958 the name of the fund was changed to the Annual Alumni Fund, and it continued to bring in increasing funds to help meet the annual budgets. By 1959–60, alumni were contributing almost $25,000 annually.

At mid-decade a quiet but intensive solicitation was launched to raise $275,000 to pay for the seminary property and some of the debt on the chapel.

Throughout the decade a number of summer conferences (not to mention a well-attended summer school for undergraduate and graduate studies) drew thousands of campers and conferees to the campus and provided a steady income stream to offset expenses and inflation. The Baltimore Colts continued to hold their summer training camp on campus, drawing hundreds of fans to Westminster. Indeed, in later years a significant number of applicants would note that their first visit to the campus had been to see the Colts practice.

In 1953, the Maryland Association of Independent Colleges was formed by Hood, St. Johns, Washington, and Western Maryland to seek funds for higher education from Maryland businesses and industries. Ensor was elected its first president. Two years later he reported that the college's share of this effort for the year was $6,436. (This group would grow and be reconstituted as the Maryland Independent Colleges and Universities Association, MICUA.)

State support for the college continued unabated, rising from about $72,000 in 1951–52 to $95,000 in 1953–54, in payment for various scholarships. However, it remained at $95,000, which unfortunately was slightly less than the cost to educate the students holding the scholarships, for the rest of the decade. In 1957–58, a teacher education grant of $500 per student per year was established by the Maryland legislature; the program made 152 awards that year statewide, 71 to Western Maryland students.[37]

By far the most interesting and long-awaited funding came from the Methodist Church. In his report to the board in April 1953, President Ensor noted that the Baltimore Conference had contributed $4,000 annually for the previous five years, and that he was hoping for as much as $6,000 in the current year. Expressing the same sentiment voiced by each of his predecessors over the 85 years of the college's existence, he noted, "The time has come when more adequate support from the church is so absolutely essential. . . . It is my sincere hope that in the next few years the Church will take its share of the relationship more seriously in a material way."[38] The church appropriated $6,000 the next year and $7,000 the following year. By October 1956 Ensor could report that the church had contributed $9,125 with the hope of collecting $36,000 more for the college. Not quite reaching that goal, the next year's contributions totaled $24,242. This was followed by a grant of $26,328 in 1957–58, about $32,000 in 1958–59, and $35,966 in 1959–60.[39] Furthermore, the conference pledged to raise $350,000 for a new library. For the first time in the college's history, the Methodist Church was making a significant contribution to the college's well-being and ongoing existence.[40]

Major Events

The Mid-Century Convocation, the formal inauguration of the Mid-Century Advance Campaign, was held on Homecoming Day, November 18, 1950, in Alumni Hall. The program opened with an invocation by Dr. Fred Holloway and included a welcome by board chairman Murray Benson, greetings by Governor-elect McKeldin, and a discussion of the Western Maryland Fund goal ($1.5 million) by President Ensor, who said, "May she move upward and onward in the achievement of her goal in the months ahead." Roger J. Whiteford, chairman of the Mid-Century Advance Program, introduced the speaker for the occasion, J. Howard McGrath, attorney general of the United States. McGrath was actually pinch-hitting for the scheduled speaker, Vice President Alben W. Barkley, who had to back out because of illness. McGrath said, in part,

The importance of the small, private, independent college in our educational process cannot be overemphasized. It is surprising, but nevertheless true, that the larger percentage of the men and women listed in Who's Who *attended small, independent colleges, rather than large universities. . . . From all I have heard, read, and know about your institution, it has since its founding . . . in 1867 fulfilled the expectation of its founders and has served to provide the elements of a sound college education. . . . I salute you and wish you every success in your campaign.*[41]

Two weeks later McGrath's words were read into the *Congressional Record* by Senator Herbert R. O'Conor. During the convocation 28 leather-bound citations were awarded to distinguished alumni, including Brady O. Bryson '35 (Law), William Wiley Chase '23 (Medicine), R. Floyd Cromwell '22 (Education), Henry L. Darner '16 (Medicine), Charles A. Engle '30 (Athletic Coaching), Kent Roberts Greenfield '11 (History), T. K. Harrison '01 (College Service), Dorothy Herr '18 (Service to Community and Church), Lida Orem Meredith '19 (Medicine), Charles E. Moylan '17 (Law), William Byers Unger '20 (Teaching/Science), and John Thomas Ward '19 (Journalism). These awards appear to have been the forerunners of the Trustee Alumni Awards, given since 1975.

Rounding out the weekend of events were a Methodist Dinner in McDaniel Lounge attended by 100 Methodist leaders from Maryland; the homecoming game with Johns Hopkins (which the Terrors won 14–6), attended by some 4,000 alumni and friends in 650 cars jammed into the Hoffa Field bowl; the President's Luncheon for the distinguished guests including Senator and Mrs. Millard Tydings, Governor and Mrs. W. Preston Lane, and Senator O'Conor; the fall play, Oscar Wilde's *The Importance of Being Earnest*; the homecoming dance in Gill Gymnasium; and the Consecration Service on Sunday at 4:30

Dorothy McDaniel Herr '18 receives award at Mid-Century Convocation from Dean Makosky and President Ensor.

P.M., with Dr. Daniel Poling, a dynamic figure in American and international religious life, as the speaker.[42] Five lion cubs borrowed from the Baltimore Zoo joined the life-size Green Terror on a float in the homecoming parade. They were the hit of the parade, and even President Ensor had his picture taken with them before the Convocation.[43]

By the following May, the campaign was well enough along to hold a gala evening in Baltimore's Lyric Theatre on May 7 to highlight the needs and the success thus far. And on May 29 a dinner was held in Baltimore to celebrate reaching the $500,000 mark. By July 20, pledges and contributions totaled $1,028,026.05. The goal was in sight, and work continued through the following year.

Atty. Gen. McGrath and Dr. Ensor hold lion cubs.

The Commencement of 1953 brought back to the campus two distinguished women to receive honorary degrees (among six recipients). Mabel Garrison Siemonn, who was cited for reaching the top rung of the Metropolitan Opera with her "golden voice" and generously sharing her vocal talents with the college over the 50 years since her graduation, was honored with a doctor of fine arts. She was joined by former dean of women Bertha Adkins, who had gone on to be assistant chair of the national Republican Party. Adkins gave the Commencement address and received an honorary doctor of laws degree. Her qualities of leadership, integrity, and dependability were cited as having propelled her to national prominence. She would be named undersecretary for health, education, and welfare in the Eisenhower administration in 1958.

On October 23, 1954, during the halftime ceremonies of the football game between the Green Terrors and Hampton-Sydney, Richard Harlow was formally inducted into the National Football Hall of Fame, the premier society of collegiate players and coaches in the United States. He was one of 12 coaches and 40 players selected for the honor that year from across 25 campuses nationwide. He was escorted down the 50-yard line by an honor guard of his former players from both Western Maryland and Harvard. The former Terrors included Henry A. MacHamer '29, Richard Norris '29, Floyd "Goose" Doughty '33, J. Randolph Shilling '34, Eugene "Stoney" Willis '34, Donald Keyser x'35, and Louis Kaplan '35. Admiral John Brown, U.S. Navy retired, president of the National Foundation and Hall of Fame, who had been Harlow's commanding officer in the navy during World War II, made the presentation. The citation read, "Coach Richard C. Harlow has been granted highest honors of the National Football Hall of Fame, in recognition of his outstanding coaching ability as demonstrated in inter-collegiate competition, his sportsmanship, integrity,

Harlow is inducted into Hall of Fame.

character, and contribution to the sport of football."[44] Harlow was at the time the only living coach to have received the Alonzo Stagg Award (1949) and be named the U.S. football coaches and writers' Coach of the Year (1936).

Following the game (6–38), Harlow was honored at a testimonial dinner cosponsored by the college and Westminster service clubs, including the Rotary Club, of which he was a member. Testimonials were given by General Gill, who had been instrumental in bringing Harlow to the WMC campus in 1926; Charles Havens, an all-star former player and the present WMC coach; Nathan Weinstock, a standout player in Harlow's early days at WMC; T. William Mather Jr., a trustee and local businessman; Tim Russell, a former Harvard player; and President Ensor. Toastmaster for the evening was Judge Charles Moylan.

The formal dedication of Baker Memorial Chapel was held on Sunday, April 20, 1958, at 3:00 P.M. and was attended by a capacity crowd that included at least two alumnae who had attended the dedication of the first Baker Chapel in May 1895, 63 years earlier: Corinne Ford '95 and Emeritus Professor Nannie Lease. The ceremony began with an academic procession led by the College Choir and including the faculty, the trustees, the district superintendents of the Baltimore Conference, Westminster clergymen, delegates from neighboring collegiate institutions, and the senior class (which broke with tradition and wore their caps and gowns a day before they were formally invested). President Ensor presided, and Bishop Oxnam gave the dedicatory sermon. The invocation and benediction were given by former president Fred Holloway; David J. Harper '58, president of the Student Christian Association, read the scripture lesson. Board chair Murray Benson presented the building for dedication in memory of William G. Baker, Joseph D. Baker, Daniel Baker, and Sarah Baker Thomas. This was followed by the litany of dedication, led by retired bishop James Straughn. The choir, directed by Alfred deLong and accompanied by Oliver Spangler, sang several anthems, including Brahms's "How Lovely Is Thy Dwelling Place."[45] While the interior of the building was finished, the landscaping was incomplete, so wooden walkways had been constructed so that people (and the long procession) could get into the building.

Two weeks later, on May 4, in place of the regular chapel service, the Whiteford organ and carillon were dedicated in a ceremony that featured a silent procession of the seniors and choir, appropriate liturgy, and the first official sounds of the organ ("A Mighty Fortress"), played by Joseph

Homecoming Game on Hoffa Field in the 1950s

Whiteford, the designer and builder of the organ. The ceremonial part of the program included a presentation of the organ by its donor, trustee Roger J. Whiteford '06, "not only that it may become a part of the services in this chapel, but also that it may contribute to the musical education of our students." Following the litany and prayer of dedication, led by President Ensor, a recital was presented by Virgil Fox, organist at the Riverside Church in New York City since

Virgil Fox plays dedicatory recital.

1946. Fox had been to the campus many times, for he grew up in the Carroll County area and played briefly at a local church before moving to Baltimore. He had been the organist for the inauguration of President Holloway in 1936. Fox, who annually presented over 80 concerts, appeared in his customary red-lined cape and could be observed by the audience via a mirror above the console. Included on the program were Bach's "Sinfonia: Now Thank We All Our God" and "Toccata in F Major" and Reger's "Fantasy and Fugue on the Chorale: 'How Brightly Shines the Morning Star.'"[46] The recital attracted a huge crowd of alumni, friends, and townspeople, so that even with hundreds of additional seats placed in the undercroft, many, including some students, were unable to get into the building, a situation for which President Ensor apologized in the next issue of the *Gold Bug*.

On Alumni Day May 30, 1959, the much-needed Winslow Student Center was officially dedicated. Board chair Murray Benson presided, and President Ensor outlined the uses of the new building and spoke about William Winslow, the trustee for whom the building was named. Winslow was a successful businessman and farmer in Montgomery County, Maryland, and had been a generous benefactor to the college's scholarship fund, as well as providing much of the funding for the student center. Keys to the building were presented by Buildings and Grounds chairman Carlysle MacLea to Donna King '60, vice president of the Student Government Association, which had offices in the building; and to Charles Foutz, manager of the grille and bookstore on the lower floor of the building. The president of the Faculty Club, Dean of Women Helen Howery, also received a key to the faculty lounge on the upper floor of the split-level facility. After Chairman Benson formally dedicated the building—"to serve [the students'] social, recreational, and extra-curricular needs in an environment conducive to good fellowship, wholesome recreation, and constructive student activities"—everyone was invited inside for tours and refreshments.

The annual Alumni Banquet the next evening drew over 400 returning alumni, no doubt because a special award was to be presented to Professor Frank B. Hurt, longtime tennis coach and political science teacher. He was cited for his 24 years of service to the college as tennis coach and winning the respect and esteem of his many players, who had compiled an enviable record of 229 wins, 121 losses, and 2 ties. "The various ideas which you imparted have been just as valuable in our daily lives as they were on the

Frank Hurt is honored at Alumni Banquet.

tennis court. . . . We desire that our appreciation and veneration be known to all . . . who have the honor and privilege of knowing Frank B. Hurt," Alumni president Kale Mathias '35 noted.[47]

CONCLUSION

In an era that saw the end of the Korean War, the rise of McCarthyism, the civil rights movement, *Sputnik*, and expanded television coverage, the college also saw significant changes in its board of trustees, normal changes in the faculty, and some administrative changes. A 25% growth in the student body required more and expanded facilities to be built, including a men's dormitory, a new chapel, and a student center, as well as renovations of the seminary buildings, which were acquired when the seminary moved to Washington. Student life continued to evolve as more self-governance was established, including an Honor Code and a Student Life Council. The curriculum and academic calendar were given a careful and lengthy examination, out of which came some important changes. Perhaps the most significant change occurred in the college finances, brought on by an inflationary spiral that forced faculty salaries and food and heating costs to rise, and tuition and fees to rise dramatically to meet them. Fortunately, the endowment also saw an 80% increase, and the college embarked on its first comprehensive fund-raising campaign at mid-century. While maintaining the status quo in some ways, the college was becoming poised for major growth and many changes in the decade to come.

CHAPTER 10 ENDNOTES

1. WMC board of trustees minutes, October 30, 1953; WMC trustee Executive Committee minutes, October 24, 1958.
2. Ensor, Report, April 29, 1955.
3. WMC faculty minutes, December 3, 1951.
4. Ensor, Report, October 17, 1952.
5. Ibid., April 24, 1953; October 26, 1956.
6. *WMC Bulletin*, December 1958, 3, 10.
7. Ensor, Report, October 26, 1956; October 25, 1957.
8. *Gold Bug*, October 16, 1951, 2.
9. Ibid., February 28, 1956, 2.
10. Ibid., January 17, 1956, 2.
11. Ibid., February 28, 1958, 1–2.
12. *The Advocate of Westminster and Finksburg*, October 27, 2004, 8.
13. *The Hill*, Summer 2001, 27.
14. WMC faculty minutes, October 14, 1954; March 7, 1955.
15. *WMC Catalogue* description, 1957–58.
16. WMC board of trustees minutes, April 26, 1957.
17. *Gold Bug*, November 6, 1959, 3.
18. Sam Tanenhaus, *Whittaker Chambers: A Biography* (Random House, 1998), 511.
19. Whittaker Chambers, *Cold Friday* (Random House, 1964), xiii.
20. *The Hill*, August 1991, 7.
21. Ibid., August 1992, 20.
22. Chandler, *Pilgrimage of Faith*, 167–68.
23. *Gold Bug*, November 23, 1954, 1.
24. WMC board of trustees minutes, April 29, 1955.
25. Ibid., October 28, 1955.
26. Dedicatory Program; *WMC Bulletin*, April 1958, 5, 9.
27. Ensor, Report, April 25, 1958.
28. WMC board of trustees minutes, April 22, 1960.
29. Ensor, Report, April 30, 1954; April 29, 1955.
30. Ensor, letter to trustees, November 22, 1954; WMC trustee Executive Committee minutes, April 13, 1956.
31. Ensor, Report, April 29, 1955; October 27, 1957; April 24, 1959; October 30, 1959.
32. WMC board of trustees minutes, October 26, 1956.
33. WMC trustee Executive Committee minutes, September 18, 1959.
34. Ensor, Report, April 13, 1956.
35. Note to President Ensor, Ensor Papers.
36. WMC trustee Executive Committee minutes, December 11, 1950.
37. Ensor, Report, April 24, 1953; April 29, 1955; October 25, 1957.
38. Ibid., April 24, 1953.
39. Ibid., October 25, 1957; October 24, 1958; October 30, 1959; October 28, 1960.
40. Ibid., October 30, 1959.
41. *WMC Bulletin*, December 1950, 3.
42. Ibid., October 1950, 3; December 1950, 2.
43. *Gold Bug*, November 18, 1950, 7.
44. *WMC Bulletin*, November 1954, 9.
45. Chapel Dedication Program.
46. Organ Dedication Program.
47. *WMC Bulletin*, June 1959, 2.

MAJOR WORLD EVENTS

1951

22nd Amendment to U.S. Constitution limits presidents to two terms.
J. D. Salinger publishes *Catcher in the Rye.*
James Jones publishes *From Here to Eternity.*
Color television is first introduced in the U.S.
Rachel Carson publishes *The Sea around Us.*
Rodgers and Hammerstein produce *The King and I.*

1952

Dwight D. Eisenhower is elected U.S. president.
Agatha Christie publishes *The Mousetrap.*
First hydrogen bomb is exploded in the Pacific.
King George VI of England dies and is succeeded by his daughter, Elizabeth II.
Ernest Hemingway wins Pulitzer Prize for *The Old Man and the Sea.*
Norman Vincent Peale publishes *The Power of Positive Thinking.*
S.S. *United States* crosses the Atlantic in 3 days, 10 hours, and 40 minutes.

1953

Popular films are *Roman Holiday, From Here to Eternity,* and *The Robe.*
Stalin dies; is succeeded by Malenkov.
Arthur Miller publishes *The Crucible.*
Winston Churchill wins Nobel Prize for Literature.
Tennessee Williams publishes *Camino Real.*
B. F. Skinner publishes *Science and Human Behavior.*
Julius and Ethel Rosenberg are executed for espionage.
Korean armistice is signed.

1954

Tennessee Williams publishes *Cat on a Hot Tin Roof.*
Roger Bannister runs the mile in 3 minutes, 59.4 seconds.
J. R. R. Tolkien publishes *The Lord of the Rings.*
Popular films are *On the Waterfront* and *Rear Window.*
Dr. Jonas Salk, developer of anti-polio serum, begins inoculating schoolchildren.
U.S. Supreme Court rules that segregation by color in public schools is unconstitutional.
Senator Joseph McCarthy continues searching for communists, is soon formally censured.

1955

Negroes in Montgomery, Alabama, boycott the segregated city bus lines.
Popular films are *The Rose Tattoo, The Seven Year Itch,* and *Richard III.*
The musical comedy *Damn Yankees* opens on Broadway.
The Universal Copyright Convention takes effect.
Ultra-high-frequency waves are produced at MIT.

1956

Martin Luther King emerges as a leader of the campaign for desegregation.
Pakistan becomes an Islamic republic.
Dwight D. Eisenhower is reelected U.S. president.
Lerner and Loewe's *My Fair Lady* opens in New York.
Soviet troops march into Hungary.
Monaco's Prince Ranier marries American actress Grace Kelly.
Rock and roll music is in vogue.

1957

Dr. Seuss publishes *The Cat in the Hat.*
Jack Kerouac publishes *On the Road.*
Ayn Rand publishes *Atlas Shrugged.*
USSR launches *Sputnik I* and *II*, first earth satellites.
Eugene O'Neill's *Long Day's Journey into Night* wins Pulitzer Prize.

1958

European Common Market is established.
Popular songs include "Volare," "Catch a Falling Star," and "Chanson d'Amour."
Alaska becomes the 49th U.S. state.
Pope Pius XII dies, is succeeded by Pope John XXIII.
Popular films are *Cat on a Hot Tin Roof* and *Gigi.*
NASA is established to administer scientific exploration of space.
Rodgers and Hammerstein produce *Flower Drum Song.*

1959

DeGaulle is proclaimed president of the Fifth Republic in France.
Hawaii becomes 50th U.S. state.
First Ecumenical Council since 1870 is called by Pope John XXIII.
Popular films are *Anatomy of a Murder*, *La Dolce Vita*, and *Ben Hur.*
Bill Mauldin wins Pulitzer Prize (his second) for his cartoons.
Books and plays include *The Status Seekers*, *Advise and Consent*, and *The Miracle Worker.*

1960

U.S. population is at 179,323,000; the gross national product is $502.6 billion.
Breshnev becomes president of USSR.
Robert Bolt publishes *A Man for All Seasons.*
Harper Lee publishes *To Kill a Mockingbird.*
John F. Kennedy is elected U.S. president.
Lionel Bart produces musical play *Oliver!*
Popular songs include "Let's Do the Twist" and "Never on Sunday."
U.S. nuclear submarine *Triton* circumnavigates the world under water.
Popular films include *Exodus*, *Psycho*, *The Entertainer*, and *The Apartment.*

Entryway to the Lewis Hall of Science (1966)

CHAPTER 11

A CENTENNIAL CELEBRATION
IN TURBULENT TIMES

◦◄ 1961–1970 ►◦

The world and society in general were now in an even greater state of flux. The Vietnam War occupied many minds during the decade. The civil rights movement continued, and Martin Luther King Jr. received the Nobel Peace Prize. The Peace Corps was established. In the Caribbean, Cuba, under the communist Castro regime, became a perceived threat to the United States; diplomatic relations were broken off, and an unsuccessful invasion of the Bay of Pigs embarrassed the new Kennedy administration. During the Cuban missile crisis in 1962, Russia eventually (after a six-day standoff) agreed to remove missiles installed on the island, and potential disaster was avoided. In Germany, the infamous Berlin Wall was erected. But the most traumatic events of the decade were the assassinations of President John F. Kennedy in 1963, Malcolm X in 1964, and Martin Luther King Jr. and Robert F. Kennedy in 1968. Riots followed in several cities, including Washington and Baltimore, and, during the Democratic Convention, in Chicago. As the war dragged on, increasing protests were mounted across the country, and at a protest at Kent State University in the spring of 1970, four students were killed by the National Guard. As the world grew in population to 3.1 billion, significant advances in medicine, including heart transplants and genetic analysis, were made; as a result of *Sputnik*, more emphasis was placed on science and mathematics education; and efforts to save the environment were also launched. John Glenn circled the earth, and in July 1969 Neil Armstrong stepped onto the moon's surface. It was also the age of long-haired hippies, peace signs, coffeehouses, the "free speech" movement, love beads, pot and LSD, flower children, Black Power, Woodstock, and the beginnings of more sexual freedom.

Western Maryland College celebrated its centennial in 1967 with the theme "The Liberal Arts College: Continuity and Change," and a Centennial Expansion Campaign was mounted. Enrollment caps were raised to meet the growing demand as the first of the "baby boom" generation were ready for college. Facilities were completed to accommodate a student body of 1,000, and the faculty was increased accordingly. Tuition and fees continued to escalate just to keep pace with inflation. In an era of protests and demand for more voice in decisions affecting them, the students were successful, in generally nonconfrontational ways, in forcing the college administration to stop acting in loco parentis in favor of individual responsibility; by the end of the decade, women no longer had curfews, enrollment in ROTC for men became voluntary, attendance at chapel and assemblies was no longer required, and dress codes were a thing of the past. Simultaneously, some students were looking beyond the confines of the campus for areas where they could be of service. More change in student life came to the college in the five years between 1965 and 1970 than in the previous 45.

FACULTY AND ADMINISTRATION

As the student body began to grow toward the planned maximum of 1,000 (raised from 850), the faculty grew to accommodate this 17% increase in student numbers. At the onset of the decade, there were about 60 full-time and 20 part-time faculty; of the full-time faculty 58% held doctorates. (The college ranked second only to Johns Hopkins among Maryland colleges in the percentage of doctorates on its faculty.) The decade also saw a record number of retirements (21, a third of the full-time faculty), as those hired during the 1920s and 1930s reached the magic age of 65, after which their employment was more uncertain, year by year, until 70, when mandatory retirement came into effect. Leaving the faculty as emeriti were Minnie M. Ward [1924–61], Hugh Elderdice [1929–61], Olive Ruth Russell [1949–62], Daisy W. Smith [1938–63], Marie Parker [1929–63], Margaret J. Snader [1930–63], Helen E. Gray [1938–64], Frank Hurt [1930–65], Roselda F. Todd [1930–65], Joseph

W. Hendren [1947–66], Samuel Schofield [1919–66], Joseph C. Willen [1933–66], Sara E. Smith [1926–67], Philip Royer [1930–67], Clyde A. Spicer [1929–68], Alfred deLong [1936–69], Kathryn B. Hildebran [1940–69], Evelyn Wingate Wenner [1931–69], Elizabeth Simkins [1946–70], Esther Smith [1926–70], and Ervin L. Szilagyi [1957–70]. For longevity on the faculty, Samuel Schofield still holds the record with 47 years (although he was on leave for several years in the 1930s). William G. Miller [1962–2007] is credited with 45 uninterrupted years, not counting sabbaticals, and Esther Smith is next with 44 (although she, too, was away for several years).

The college community bade sad farewells to three faculty members who died before reaching retirement. Mahlon F. Peck [1947–60], assistant professor of physics and mathematics, who had just completed his PhD at VPI after a leave of absence for part of 1959–60, died of a heart attack on September 12, 1960, at age 47. Rembrandt Dewees Summers [1942–64], professor of physics, died of pancreatic cancer on November 30, 1964, aged 65. In 1961, Summers was the first recipient of the Distinguished Teaching Award, an annual award established by the Baltimore Alumnae Chapter of Sigma Sigma Tau sorority. A year after his death, on November 18, 1965, Helen G. Howery [1946–65], associate professor of English and dean of women for 18 years, died at 51, following complications from an operation to remove an abdominal tumor. All were posthumously named emeriti professors by the trustees in 1998.[1] The campus community was additionally saddened to learn of the deaths of advisory football coach Richard C. Harlow in February 1962, and two emeriti faculty, Margaret Julia Snader in October 1964 and Dean W. Hendrickson in December 1969. In October 1967, word reached the campus that Lt. Col. James B. Moore '53, who served on the college's ROTC staff from 1963 to 1966, had died on October 10 of wounds received in action in Vietnam.

To fill vacant positions, as well as to expand many departments, about 30 additional faculty were hired over the ten-year period. Those who joined the full-time faculty and remained for a period of time included Julia T. Hitchcock [1960–85] in music, Theron B. Thompson [1961–73] in education, Fern R. Hitchcock '47 [1962–84] in physical education, Ronald F. Jones '55 [1962–81] in physical education, James E. Lightner '59 [1962–98] in mathematics, William G. Miller [1962–2007] in psychology, Keith N. Richwine [1962–94] in English, Cornelius P. Darcy [1963–98] in history, Jacques T. DeRasse [1963–76] in French, Donald E. Jones [1963–99] in chemistry, Raymond C. Phillips [1963–98] in English, Georgina Sabat-Guernica (Rivers) [1963–78] in Spanish, Joan R. Weyers [1963–99] in physical education, Ira G. Zepp '52 [1963–94] in religion, David R. Cross [1964–89] in chemistry, Mary Lee Younger Schmall '55 [1964–2007] in biology, William T. Achor [1965–94] in physics, F. Glendon Ashburn '53 [1965–95] in sociology, H. Samuel Case '63, '66M [1965–2004] in physical education, Edmund Makosky '62 [1965–84] in physics, Melvin D. Palmer [1965–94] in English, Nancy B. Palmer [1965–2002] in English, Donald R. Zauche '57 [1965–89] in German, David W. Herlocker [1966–2006] in chemistry, Alton D. Law [1966–2000] in economics, Donald Patrick [1966–79] in education, H. Ray Stevens '58 [1966–97] in English, Carl L. Dietrich [1967–91] in music, Carol Fritz '69M [1967–2007] in physical education, Wasyl Palijczuk [1967–2003] in art, Peter Yedinak [1967–93] in physics, Michael M. Brown [1968–] in biology, H. Peter Büttner [1968–98] in German, Lowell R. Duren [1968–77] in mathematics, Katherine L. Falconer '52 [1968–95] in the library, LeRoy L. Panek [1968–] in English, Ronald K. Tait [1968–98] in sociology, G. Samuel Alspach [1969–2006] in biology, Leonard Stanley Bowlsbey '52, '59M [1969–89] in education, J. Richard Carpenter '72M [1969–] in physical education, William Cipolla [1969–86] in French, Max W. Dixon [1969–86] in dramatic art, Mary Ellen Smith Elwell '50 [1969–86] in sociology, Linda R. Eshleman [1969–2005] in mathematics, Robert H. Hartman [1969–95] in philosophy and religion, Robert W. Lawler [1969–77] in English, Alexander G. Ober '63, '69M [1969–] in physical education, Ethan A. Seidel [1969–] in economics, McCay Vernon [1969–91] in education, and Robert J. Weber [1969–98] in political science.

By 1969–70 the faculty had grown to 88 full-time (about 50% holding doctorates) and 21 part-time teachers. The striking fact, which indicates the flexibility in the academic job market of the decade, is that about 125 people were hired in ten years to keep 85 or so full-time positions filled. Competition for new faculty was keen across the country, as many colleges and universities were expanding, and graduate schools could not keep up with the demand for advanced degrees from the baby boomers. Many newly hired instructors (chosen from limited pools of candidates) stayed only a year or two and then moved on, either because they found better-paying positions elsewhere, or because the college felt they did not meet its needs. President Ensor noted in his report to the trustees in April 1966 that it was becoming more difficult to insert young faculty "into the intangible spirit and atmosphere which for so long characterized [the college]." He went on to say, "I think we can expect, possibly, less institutional loyalty which comes only after many years of association with an institution" but also noted that the new folks brought a new vitality and enthusiasm to the college.[2] His conjecture about loyalty did not prove completely true, for the average tenure of those listed above is 29 years.

The faculty continued to bring honor to themselves and to the college. Biology professor H. P. Sturdivant was elected national president of Beta Beta

Beta, the biology honor society. Kathryn Hildebran was elected president of the National Federation of Modern Language Teachers. Isabel Royer was invited to teach biology at the University of Hanoi in Vietnam under the Smith-Mund Act in 1962. Ralph Price, William David, Earl Griswold, and Reuben Holthaus were tapped for special work in Asian history and cultures through grants from the Ford Foundation. Griswold was also selected by the Methodist Church to evaluate its mission movement in the Congo during part of 1960 and was invited to a White House conference on student volunteer programs in 1969. H. Ray Stevens was named book review editor for the international journal *Conradiana* in 1968. President Ensor was recognized with honorary doctor of laws degrees from the American University (in 1963) and the College of Notre Dame of Maryland (in 1968). In the former instance, he shared the stage with President John F. Kennedy, another honorary degree recipient, and he was hooded by Arts and Sciences dean Ralph C. John (who would succeed him as president of the college in 1972).

In the spring of 1968, in a move toward establishing a larger role for themselves in college governance, the faculty approved the formation of two new elected committees: the Advisory Committee on College Policy (ACCP) and the Faculty Affairs Committee (FAC). This brought to 23 the number of faculty committees.[3] The first members of the FAC were professors Richwine, David, Price, D. Jones, and Kerschner, and they soon presented new rules and guidelines for recruitment, promotion, and tenure. They also encouraged departments to expand their efforts to hire African-American faculty.

In 1960 Walter M. Baggs was hired as the first director of development. He would serve in that role for six years before retiring, to be succeeded by Alfred V. Clark [1966–73] (who had been part of the ROTC cadre on campus in the late 1950s). In 1962, because his services as chemistry professor were needed full-time, Dr. Schofield relinquished his position as dean of administration, a post he had held since 1939. The title was abolished, but his duties were assumed by Philip B. Schaeffer, who as treasurer and business manager acquired an assistant in Mary R. Shoemaker, cashier [1962–75]. To assist with management of the expanding campus, Eugene Willis '34 [1964–75], who had recently retired from an army career, joined the staff as the first director of the physical plant in 1964. The longtime superintendent of buildings and grounds, Edward M. Black [1934–64], retired after 30 years of service and was replaced by his nephew and assistant, Preston S. Yingling [1938–83]. In 1961 the bookstore lost its well-known, bow-tied manager, Charles Foutz, to the local Baltimore Federal Savings and Loan, and he was replaced by his assistant, Grace Z. Leroy [1958–66], who was replaced by Donald Guthrie [1966–68] and then William Rudrow [1968–74]. In 1963, the role of postmaster was taken over by B. Irene Young [1952–86], who had assisted in the bookstore for 9 years. In October 1966, longtime registrar Martha Manahan [1938–66] retired and was named registrar emerita, turning over the office to her assistant, Cora Virginia Perry [1938–77]. Marjorie Little Spangler '46 [1966–72] was then named assistant registrar. Margaret Shunk, the college's switchboard operator and receptionist, retired in 1966 after 19 years of service.

Long-time administrators: (L to R) P. Uhrig, C. Foutz, C.V. Perry, M. Manahan

William M. David relinquished the role of dean of men in 1963 and took on a full-time professorial role in political science. He was replaced by James E. Robinson [1963–69], who was named to the slightly expanded role of dean of students in 1967. When Robinson resigned in 1969, his successor was C. Wray Mowbray '58 [1963–83], who had returned to the Hill a few years earlier as an admissions counselor. Upon the death of Helen Howery in 1965, Dean Robinson, with help from the housemothers, handled all student-related affairs until Elizabeth Laidlaw [1966–82] was hired as the new dean of women the following year.

With the resignation in April 1965 of athletic director and football coach Robert Waldorf, Ronald F. Jones '55 was appointed head football coach and Richard A. Clower '50 was named athletic director. In 1968, Clower gave up basketball coaching and turned his team over to Ronald Sisk [1968–72], who also became an admissions counselor.

One of the more significant changes in the administration occurred in 1969, when John Makosky retired from the role of dean of faculty and returned to full-time English teaching. After a search by a faculty committee (Bailer, Holthaus, Price, Sturdivant, and Zauche), Harry L. Holloway Jr. [1969–71], formerly professor and chair of the Biology Department at Roanoke College, was hired; and he assumed the post in July. Eight months later, illness forced President Ensor to request an indefinite leave of absence to have a spleenectomy, an operation related to the blood condition from which he was suffering. The trustees turned to one of their own, Allan W. Mund, to step into the role of acting president.[4] Mund was a retired Baltimore industrial executive who as a trustee of Lebanon Valley College in Pennsylvania had acted as president there for 18 months several years before. He assumed the office but lived at home in

Allan W. Mund,
acting president, 1970

Towson and commuted daily to the college, taking no salary for the six-month stint. President Ensor recuperated during the summer and was well enough to return to his office in September as the new college year began.

During this decade about one-third (12) of the older trustees left the board, to be replaced by 15 new members, 9 of whom were alumni. Bishop Oxnam [1952–60], William Winslow [1950–62], Daniel W. Justice [1957–62], Miriam Baynes Matthews '98 [1939–64], and Roger J. Whiteford '06 [1934–65] resigned or took emeritus status. Death claimed Herbert P. Burdette [1950–62], Murray Benson [1936–63], T. W. Mather Jr. [1927–64], T. Newell Cox Sr. [1956–65], G. Frank Thomas [1951–65], William C. Scott [1922–66], and Charles Moylan [1948–69]. (Moylan was the first recipient of the Alumni Association's Alumnus of the Year Award in 1967.) Joining the board were Bishop John Wesley Lord [1960–72], Clarence L. Fossett [1960–83], Austin E. Penn [1961–76], Charles A. Stewart '26 [1961–80], Fred C. Malkus Jr. '34 [1962–85], William E. Firth [1962–75], Wilson K. Barnes '28 [1963–80], Scott S. Bair [1964–73], Arthur G. Broll '29 [1965–80], Robert D. Faw '41 [1966–89], Mary Brown Bryson '35 [1967–84], Richard W. Kiefer '34 [1967–85], Wilbur D. Preston Jr. '44 [1967–93], Clarence H. Bennett '28 [1967–80], and Clementine Peterson [1969–80].

Following the untimely death in June 1963 at age 67 of Murray Benson (LLD 1955), who had been a distinguished Baltimore attorney as well as board chairman for 14 years, Gen. Robert Gill, at age 74, was elected to the chair. He

Portrait of Brigadier General Robert Joshua Gill

served for 5 years before relinquishing it to Joshua W. Miles Jr. (LLD 1977) in 1968. In this decade, the board authorized formal portraits of General Gill and President Ensor.[5] These were completed by Furman J. Finck and unveiled in appropriate ceremonies. The Gill portrait hangs in the Gill Physical Education Learning Center, and the Ensor portrait is in McDaniel Lounge, with those of the third, fourth, and sixth presidents.

In the latter part of the decade, the board considered a number of recommendations by trustee Robert Faw for changes in its procedures and structure. He suggested that students, faculty, and alumni be given voting representation on the board; that the life tenure of members be eliminated in favor of limited terms; that committee assignments and chairmanships be rotated; that the board meet more than twice a year; and that trustees be given training and information about their responsibilities. After considerable discussion, the board determined that student representation would serve no purpose, that the current structure of committees and chairs was satisfactory, and that life tenure for board members was still appropriate.[6] The only change made, at the suggestion of President Ensor, was that the dean of the faculty would be invited to attend meetings without vote (and thus the faculty would have some representation). While the rest of the college was changing rapidly and radically, the board of trustees was apparently not yet ready, preferring the status quo at least for a few more years. However, the board did see the wisdom of forming two new permanent committees. The Development Committee was reconstituted in 1967, initially chaired by Joshua Miles and then by Allan Mund, to oversee the cultivation of potential donors and foundations, to establish a planned giving program with appropriate publications, and most important, to raise a half million dollars. The Long Range Planning Committee was appointed in 1969. It was a joint committee made up of trustees Mund, Mathias, and Preston; faculty members Price, Kerschner, Richwine, and Bowlsbey; administrators Holloway and Clark; and the presidents of the Student Government Association and the Argonauts; President Ensor and board chair Miles were ex officio. Both committees were significant "firsts" for the college.

As the college entered its second century, its relationship with the Methodist Church began to be discussed, in part because of the limited financial support and patronage from the church. A year later, in April 1968, the board unanimously deleted from the Fundamental Ordinances the requirement that one more than one-third of the members be Methodist ministers because it "serves no practical purpose."[7] The next decade would see a much more significant change in this relationship.

CURRICULUM

As the new decade began, with the faculty having turned down the proposed major curricular and calendar revision the previous spring, the curriculum was nevertheless amplified by courses in Russian and a two-course sequence in western civilization (the only part of the earlier package to be implemented, with a new faculty member hired to see to that). European history was broken into more units, courses were added in Russian and Asian history, and a course in the Civil War was offered. The program in home economics was phased out, ultimately closing in 1963 when its two faculty retired. A few students who were caught in the closure transferred to other institutions to complete their degrees. In economics, a reduced emphasis on business administration and a greater emphasis on theoretical economics took place. By 1966 new majors were being offered in Spanish, German, and dramatic art. The following year a new physical science course was offered to provide an alternative for students who wanted to meet the science distribution requirement with a more general course than the traditional biology. Introductory Psychology was no longer a distribution requirement, but the faculty did approve a required one-hour health education course for all students in 1961 (and rescinded the requirement in 1970). To make the learning of languages more efficient and effective, an electronic language laboratory was put in place in the basement of the new library. Students could go there to listen to tapes of the language they were studying. In the fall of 1968 the first French House was established on campus, six French students living with a director from France. In January 1969, bowing to increasing student pressure, the faculty voted to abolish required ROTC for men effective September 1969, making the program voluntary and requiring those not electing the military training to enroll in physical education.[8]

Dean Makosky spoke of academic change in an article in the April 1966 *WMC Magazine*, addressing the hypothetical question "Why not keep the college the way it always was?" His answer: "Today's environment leads to much greater sophistication at an earlier age among young people. Repeated national crises have led to a greater seriousness among those capable of facing realities. Vastly strengthened public schools lead to much improved competence among college-bound youth. You would not want your college to underrate, undervalue, or under-educate these young people. This is why the college cannot 'stay as it always was.'"[9] These were prophetic words, given the appearance on campus in the summer of 1966 of an IBM Model 1130 computer, purchased for use by faculty and students in research projects and by various administrative offices for record keeping and data processing. The small-scale scientific computer, located in the basement of Thompson Infirmary, was also going to be incorporated into a new course: Introduction to Computer Science and Data Processing, which would be taught by the new Computer Center director, Ray Albert '62. Some data-processing (card-sorting) equipment had been rented two years before, but this computer would allow the college to process and print the 1966 tax bills for the county (for a fee of $8,500).[10] Another technological innovation appeared in the library in the fall of 1966: a Xerox machine, which made seven copies per minute.

While there continued to be an active summer school, as well as a full summer conference program and the Baltimore Colts training camp, the campus was also busy with some special educational programs beginning in summer 1963. To meet the needs of teachers confronted with changes in science education, the college, under the auspices of the National Science Foundation, sponsored a number of summer institutes; H. P. Sturdivant was the director, and courses and laboratories were offered in biology and chemistry. A Latin workshop was coordinated by William R. Ridington, and a Workshop in Intergroup Relations was organized by the Education Department and directed by Eugene Nuss. In cooperation with five neighboring colleges and funded by the National Defense Education Act, an Asian Studies Institute in Chinese and Japanese history, directed by Reuben Holthaus, was held on campus for several summers beginning in 1966.

During the fall of 1963 the college underwent its periodic review by the Middle States Association and received reaccreditation. Because the college had prepared for this review by self-evaluation rather than the more traditional "checklist" approach, the college was asked if it would be willing to have the visiting team report read publicly at the commission meeting in Atlantic City in June 1964. President Ensor could hardly refuse. He later reported that, even though the college's accreditation was never in question, the experience was a difficult one, because he wanted to refute certain statements that he felt were inaccurate or misleading.[11]

Dean Makosky reported in 1961 that the total hours required for graduation had been lowered to 124, due in part to the reduction in credit

Ray Albert '62 (left) supervises installation of first campus computer in 1966.

allowed for military science. The other reason was the gradual strengthening and toughening of many courses, which put added pressure on students, so the average load per semester was reduced from 17 hours to about 15. In addition to tighter course requirements, students were now required to have a C average to enter the senior year, thus eliminating the possibility of students lagging behind in their progress toward the degree.[12] A pass-fail option for upper classmen became a reality in 1967, and the Graduate Record Examination, which had been used as a senior comprehensive examination, was replaced by the Undergraduate Record Examination in 1970.

To recognize honor students in their academic majors, three new national honor societies were chartered on campus. Pi Gamma Mu in the social sciences was formally installed on April 21, 1960; Kappa Mu Epsilon in mathematics was chartered on May 30, 1965; and a chapter of Omicron Delta Epsilon in economics was formed on May 3, 1968. In addition to these, the college's Chemistry Department affiliated with the Johns Hopkins chapter of Phi Lambda Upsilon, national chemistry honor society, and five Western Maryland students were inducted into that society on April 30, 1965.

An experimental January term was approved by the faculty to begin in January 1970; James Lightner was appointed director of the program. During the first two years of the experiment, half of the faculty (and even a few alumni) volunteered to teach courses, including study tours to France, Germany, Mexico, and Florida, as well as numerous special studies projects. The insertion of the three-week term necessitated a revision in the calendar.[13] Seventy percent of the student body elected to participate in the program, and formal evaluation by an ad hoc committee suggested that it was a popular and "most revolutionary change" to the regular curriculum.[14]

The change in the college calendar led to another change in the culture of the campus. In the traditional two-semester calendar, the college year began in mid-September, and students returned after the Christmas break to one or two weeks of classes followed by a reading period and then a week of three-hour examinations. This calendar, while creating some tension and anxiety for students during the Christmas vacation, did provide for a week or so of pre-holiday events, including the annual Christmas Dinner, dormitory and club parties, and dances. In the new calendar, the college year began earlier in September so that the entire first semester could be completed prior to the Christmas break. This forced a tightening of the pre-holiday schedule, a reduction in the reading period, and a steady, tense push toward examinations. The students could go home for the holidays free of the anxiety of examinations (but not of grades, which usually arrived between Christmas and New Year's) and return for a new educational experience in January.

Another innovation in the academic life of the college was introduced in the fall of 1963 when a Freshman Colloquium was held during the orientation period to set the stage for the academic activity of the years ahead. Incoming students were asked to read several books prior to their arrival on campus, and discussions were led by faculty members on topics related to the readings. Some themes during the decade were "The Individual and the State—The Eternal Dilemma," "Politics and Power," and "The Generation Gap." In 1969, a second-track or interdisciplinary colloquium was planned for a select group of freshmen (as an alternative to freshman English) with the theme "Man as Maker—Man's Attempt to Structure His World." This was the forerunner of the Honors Program.

A new graduate program was established in 1968 in conjunction with the Maryland School for the Deaf (MSD) in Frederick. As a result of the rubella epidemic during 1961–62, which left thousands of children deaf, teachers of the deaf were urgently needed. At the urging of David R. Denton, superintendent at MSD, and in consultation with Joseph Bailer, graduate studies director, a program was designed to meet this special need without any federal or state support (grants were later forthcoming, however). They soon were able to persuade McCay Vernon, an internationally known psychologist and expert in deafness, to join the college faculty and direct the program. Frank Bowe '69, a deaf graduate who went on to work in the field, commented, "In light of new and stimulating teacher training programs such as that at Western Maryland, enlightening and challenging new research, and experimental new programs in schools for the deaf, the future looks bright indeed."[15] Since its inception, the program has become recognized as one of the most successful training programs in the world for teachers of the deaf.

Students sign speech during a class in the deaf education program.

STUDENT LIFE

It would be an understatement to say that the 1960s were a "significant" decade in the changing social life of students at the college. Virtually everything related to student life changed: housing, dining, admissions, Greek life, class schedules, in loco parentis, participation in college governance, and more. One alumnus aptly noted that the college he attended in the early 1960s was not the same college his brother came to in the early 1970s.

Linda Sullivan Schulte '68 noted in an essay written in 1992,

We, the WMC classes of 1960 through 1969, were very much a nexus of that generation. Oddly enough, the class of 1960 and that of 1969 seemed removed by more than simply a span of years—a difference less of time and more of values and perspective. . . . The country went from Cold War to one that inflamed almost everyone on all sides. . . . The campus was a fertile field for:

Procrastination followed by despair.

Despair followed by action.

Action followed by a desire to learn more.

An attitude of, Don't let your classes get in the way of your education.

Rejections of things material. Existentialism defined.

The great unwashed became the great recognized.[16]

One significant (many would say long overdue) change was that African American students were now a part of the student body. Indeed, by mid-decade, they were being actively recruited. As early as 1962, a local African American young man, a transfer from Howard University, had been accepted as a day student (he planned to live with relatives in town), but he decided not to attend because of difficulties in arranging his courses and transfer credits. During the previous spring, the SGA surveyed the student body about potential integration on campus; 503 students out of 700 responded. They overwhelmingly (about 70%) felt that African American students should be admitted, although they were less enthusiastic about accepting an African American roommate. At the same time, there was discussion on campus about boycotting the segregated Carroll Theater.[17] In 1963, Rafael Mayamona '67 from the Congo and Charles Seabron, an African American transfer student from Morgan State College, enrolled, finally integrating the student body. (Seabron left after two semesters.) Two years later, Victor McTeer and Joseph Smothers, two academically talented young black men from Baltimore, were enrolled. Both were athletes, and that helped them to assimilate into the campus life, so that by the end of their freshman year, both were invited to join fraternities and did so. They both graduated in 1969.

McTeer wrote of his four-year experience on the Hill and its many frustrations and anxieties, but concluded, "When you've gotten as much out of it as I have, it's well worth it."[18] By the end of the decade, a few more black students had enrolled. In 1967 an exchange program with Clark University was arranged by Dean Ira Zepp, and six white WMC students spent a week on that predominantly black campus in March. After that successful

V. McTeer '69 and J. Smothers '69 meet with L. Scott '90.

endeavor, a semester-long exchange was discussed for the following year. The number of foreign students was also gradually increasing, further changing the nature of the campus.

With enrollment expanding through the decade faster than residence halls could be completed, students were sometimes crowded into the four dormitories, occupying every available space and often living in triple rooms. Rooms in houses near the campus were rented for women, who walked to and from campus for classes and meals. In 1963, 14 men were living in Forlines House, and in 1965–66, 5 young women even lived on the third floor of the President's House, with relatively little inconvenience to anyone. That year 14% of boarders were living in temporary quarters. Finally, in 1968, Whiteford and Rouzer halls were completed and opened, but not without some controversy. Some upperclassmen felt that the new halls were "too sterile"; also, the administration had decided that these halls would house incoming freshmen, and the upperclassmen, who were looking forward to living in the new facilities, were not at all pleased. However, that designation has maintained for a number of years.

Students were now clamoring for admission; the average number of applications received each year was about 1,000. As early as 1960, half the entering class stood in the top 10% of their high school class, and this trend generally continued throughout the decade with an average of 48% in the top 10%. The average IQ of an entering student was 121 (an average of 52% of each entering class having an IQ above 120). In 1962 the college began requiring the SATs for admission and joined the College Board. (Director of Admissions H. Kenneth Shook was appointed the college's voting member.) Over the decade, entering classes averaged 1131 on joint verbal and nonverbal scores, with a range from 1064 to 1200. The best class, statistically, was the one entering in the fall of 1965, whose 232 students (out of 1,100 applicants) presented an average SAT score of 1200 and an average IQ of 124, 60% standing in the top 10% of their high school class.[19] In 1964 almost 80% of those who were accepted enrolled, causing a bulge in the student body and putting great strain on facilities. By 1965, only one applicant in six was being admitted, and about 85% were enrolling. Clearly, such selectivity meant that those being admitted were quite able students. In his report to the board in April 1966, President Ensor noted, "As a result of our forced selectivity the intellectual caliber of students has been increasing and our students seem to be more aware of what's going on both on campus and in the world at large and want to be involved. 'Concern' and 'involvement' seem to be the two watchwords of the day."[20]

Rouzer Hall, a men's dormitory, was opened in 1968.

Family-style dining in Science Hall in 1964

The new dining hall (cafeteria) was not completed and opened until September 17, 1968, necessitating that lunches and dinners be served in two shifts in the Memorial Hall dining room for about three years to accommodate resident students. This inconvenience only aggravated the "rampant dissatisfaction" with the food, as reported on a survey of students in 1965. The average student missed seven meals a week and spent about $4 on supplemental nourishment. Least favorite foods were (not surprisingly—generations of students had indicated the same thing) chicken croquettes, shrimp creole, "mounds of joy," liver, ham hash, cold cuts, and "anything on toast." There were not enough greens, milk, or meat, and the food was too starchy. Many still felt there was simply not enough food served in the family-style service, although they liked that form of dining.[21] By the fall of 1966, the dissatisfaction had developed into unrest, and, perhaps in an effort to have a cause to protest, SGA president Ronald Kobernick '67 organized a dining hall walkout for October 19. Everyone arrived for the 6:00 p.m. meal, and then about 85% got up and walked out before the dinner was served, heading for the grille or local restaurants. The immediate result was expanded communication between the students and the dining steward, Mr. Rice (and his assistant, Helen Harbaugh), and some minor changes were made. The larger result was that the students gained participation in more

Cheerleaders and the Terror, mid-1960s

areas of campus governance, and by the end of the decade, there were student representatives chosen by the SGA on all the college committees except the Faculty Affairs Committee and the Administrative Advisory Council. It should be noted that after the new cafeteria was opened to generally positive reactions ("The hot food is now hot!"), food would soon again become an issue. In 1969 the students successfully petitioned for two main dishes at each evening meal. A planned cafeteria strike in March 1970 seems to have fizzled, since student-driven improvements were continuing to be made.

After considering it several times over the previous 100 years, the faculty rather quickly and painlessly made the decision in March 1967 to abolish Saturday classes, beginning in September 1967. This required a totally new class schedule to accommodate the three-hour classes that previously met on the Tuesday-Thursday-Saturday sequence. In an even more far-reaching action, the faculty in November 1968 voted to eliminate all attendance requirements at college events. With the new dining facility providing meals over an extended time period, the abolition of Saturday classes, and the lack of required attendance at events, a significant aspect of earlier student life was lost. No longer would the entire college community gather in one place at one time; no longer would announcements about campus events be made at meals. No longer would the Sunday midday dinner be a "dress up" affair, where men wore coats and ties and women wore dresses. No longer could a large audience

Pompon squad, mid-1960s

be guaranteed for an event, particularly on a Friday or Saturday evening; no longer would there be as much comradeship among diverse groups as had existed in the past as they shared meals together. The college, for better or worse, had made some irreversible decisions that changed student life forever.

Paralleling this new atmosphere on campus was the implementation during 1961–62 of the honor system, which had recently been accepted by students and faculty. The first Honor Court was selected in January 1962, with Joseph McDade '62 as chair. With the system in place, take-home examinations and unproctored tests and examinations became possible, reducing some of the pressure of test taking. Because of the newness of the system and the many values to be gained, few violations of the rules were recorded. In 1967 a pass-fail grading system was approved for one course each semester for upperclassmen; it was made permanent in 1969.

As the students were demanding more control over their lives, the college was providing more opportunities for good decision making by providing an excellent array of speakers, musical and artistic events, and dramatic presentations. During the decade such notable speakers as Henry Kissinger, Margaret Mead, Ashley Montague, John Ciardi, Stephen Spender, William Sloane Coffin, Bennett Cerf, Dick Gregory, Andrew Hatcher, Stanley Kauffmann, Sidney Hook, Sargent Shriver, William Stringfellow, Theodore McKeldin, Bruno Bettelheim, and John Brademas appeared in chapel or on the Alumni Hall stage as the result of an expanded budget for outside speakers. President Lyndon B. Johnson was invited to be the speaker at the 1968 Commencement concluding the centennial year, but he ultimately had to decline, and Milton S. Eisenhower, president emeritus of Johns Hopkins University, graciously filled in. Cultural opportunities were provided by such musicians as Anna Russell, the National Symphony, and Virgil Fox. The Alumni Hall stage was busy with such presentations by the College Players as *Inherit the Wind*; *J.B.*; *Take Her, She's Mine*; *The Threepenny Opera*; *The Matchmaker*; *The School for Scandal*; *The Cherry Orchard*; *Summer and Smoke*; and *Lysistrata*, as well as regular productions by the visiting National Players such as *School for Wives*, *Hamlet*, and *Six Characters in Search of an Author*. Wasyl Palijczuk had two one-man shows in the college gallery. And various student organizations sponsored such groups as the Four Freshmen, Buddy Morrow and His Orchestra, Flatt and Scruggs, the Drifters, Ian and Sylvia, and Martha Reeves and the Vandellas as fund-raisers or for homecoming and May Day.

In 1964, a delegation of Russian students visited the campus for several days to participate in small group discussions and observe American college life. During this coldest part of the Cold War, the visitors seemed almost like aliens from another world, but participants in the meetings reported that they came away realizing that the Russians were also human beings and not all that much different from themselves.[22]

New clubs during the decade included the Psychology Club, English Club, International Relations Club, Spanish Club, and a chapter of Circle K, sponsored by the local Kiwanis Club as another campus service organization. The College Choir continued its involvement with the Baltimore Symphony with a program of music by Rodgers and Hammerstein in the fall of 1960, but that ceased when the concerts were broadcast over the radio in Baltimore under the sponsorship of a local beer company. In 1960, the choir made a record entitled *High on the Hill*, which included sacred anthems and Christmas music and sold for $4.[23] Presentations of various oratorios continued to be a staple of the choir's activities throughout the decade. Alfred deLong's retirement came in 1969, when Oliver Spangler took over the choir for a few years.

The *Gold Bug* continued to be the major source of campus information for students (other than word of mouth), even though it was published only biweekly and ranged in size from 2 to 12 pages, depending on the budget. At various times it included short literary stories and poems (reminiscent of the earlier *WMC Monthly*), and for a time in 1964 it regularly published letters from Dean Helen Howery, who was spending her sabbatical in England to celebrate the 400th birthday of Shakespeare. (Florence Earp, wife of the sociology professor, filled in as acting dean of women.) A regular column throughout much of the decade was provided by Dean of the Chapel Ira Zepp, entitled "Somebody Up There?" in which he dealt with theological questions and campus religious life. He also reported on his trip to Selma, Alabama, where he marched with Martin Luther King Jr. Regular readers could find out about the latest coffeehouse, "happening," or "GIGIF"; the Greek Week "Hootenanny"; or the Miss WMC Contest, which was held in conjunction with the Miss Maryland Contest in the spring of 1968 at the suggestion of the 1967 Miss Maryland, Ingrid Larsen '67. (Beverly Ann Smith '66 had also been a Miss Maryland.)

Traditional events continued, although they began to be modified to fit the times. Regular dances were held, sponsored by the four fraternities in rotation, the homecoming and May Day dances usually being more formal. These were opportunities for students to invite their off-campus "steady" girlfriend or boyfriend to the campus, as well as for campus couples to enjoy a special evening. The Military Ball and other smaller-scale "hops" rounded out the year. The Christmas Dinner continued to be a special event, planned by the Trumpeters, to which everyone went in their best attire to enjoy a delicious dinner (usually roast beef with all the trimmings) and songs by the College Octet and the waiters; this was followed by a Christmas communion service in Baker Memorial Chapel with Dr. Ensor presiding. (By the end of the decade, the Trumpeters were having difficulty planning a dinner in the new cafeteria with students eating at various times.) The Junior Follies continued the pattern of spoofing college life and personalities, although on one occasion (1966) a well-known musical, *Bye Bye Birdie*, was performed instead. Homecoming events still followed the normal pattern, but May Day was slowly evolving. In 1964, there was still a May Pole Dance and crowning of the May Queen in the amphitheater in Harvey Stone Park, but by 1969, the students no longer chose a queen and court, and a carnival had replaced the older events. Freshman "rat rules" and initiation had been reduced to a single week by 1966, although beanies were still worn. By the end of the decade, all vestiges of this tradition had disappeared.

Freshmen in beanies scrub Carpe Diem gazebo.

In 1963, President Ensor invited Ira Zepp to become dean of the chapel and revitalize the Sunday evening chapel services; the president was becoming too busy to plan the services and preach regularly. Dean Zepp invited a number of well-known clergy and laymen to speak, and the students responded positively to the changes. However, several speakers invited to the pulpit provided some controversy, on campus and in the community. The Reverend Malcolm Boyd spoke to the chapel audience in February 1966 using language that many found offensive.[24] Since the chapel services were at that time broadcast over the local radio station, numerous Carroll Countians heard his comments and complained; the services ceased to be aired after the incident. Bishop James A. Pike appeared to a packed Baker Memorial Chapel in October 1967, addressing "Growth through Encounter." The well-known and well-publicized cleric (who also dabbled in the occult) challenged his listeners, even as they might have disagreed with him.

Probably the most significant cause célèbre during the decade erupted over the Student Government Association's invitation to George Lincoln Rockwell, head of the U.S. Nazi Party, to speak on campus in the fall of 1966. President Ensor strongly advised against issuing the invitation but, to his credit, permitted the students to go forward; Rockwell spoke in Alumni Hall on November 28. The appearance was met with picketing in front of the building by students and professors, including Dr. Theodore Whitfield,

Faculty—(L to R) R. Phillips, M. Crain, C. Crain, R. Price—and students protest George Lincoln Rockwell speech, 1966.

who was pictured determinedly carrying the American flag with a poster on his chest: "With Liberty and Justice for All." The faculty went on record as praising the administration for its "unqualified commitment to the principle of academic freedom."[25] But the Executive Committee of the board of trustees, in a disagreement (quite unusual) with Ensor, unanimously approved a resolution deploring Rockwell's appearance, saying it "tarnishes the image of the college in the eyes of the general public as well as its alumni and friends."[26] Ensor, probably with some justifiable pride, commented on the incident several months later in his report to the board:

> As you know, we did permit Rockwell to come, and as it turned out it was really a very salutary experience. I was proud of the mature manner in which the students listened without emotion or fanfare and completely rejected the hate propaganda that he stood for. My mail, of course, increased considerably for several weeks both pro and con. I am convinced that his presence served no good purpose and even the student leadership now agrees, but, after all, I think a good college standing for intellectual and academic freedom should be able to take a situation like this in its stride. The one lesson that the students learned is that they are not living in a world unto themselves and they can't have a man like Rockwell without causing reverberations that are far-reaching.[27]

The students found many things to complain about during this era and were much more vocally demonstrative than in earlier times. One issue was the absence of a railing along the sloping walk from the top of the hill down to the Winslow Student Center. Citing the danger of slipping and falling on ice or wet leaves, the students regularly petitioned, wrote articles in the *Gold Bug*, and generally kept the issue on the "front burner" from 1962 until a railing was installed in late 1967.[28] Concern for aesthetics seems to have deterred the administration from taking action earlier. The railing that was finally installed, made of two-by-fours and pipe, was hardly beautiful, but it did the job. It was later replaced by a more substantial metal railing matching others on campus. Another issue was the new method of taking attendance at chapel services. A self-reporting card system introduced when the services moved to Baker Memorial Chapel in 1958 had always had its problems, but the students began agitating to make this attendance reporting part of the honor system. This did not occur, but the issue was exacerbated in 1967 when a computer card was issued as the attendance device. The SGA president urged students to "dispose" of them (fold, spindle, or mutilate!) rather than turn them in, and that led to a campus-wide "communication assembly" with President Ensor, who quickly backed off from the new system, claiming it was an ill-advised experiment. By this time, attendance at chapel was not necessarily required, the students having many options to choose from for their "cultural requirement." The issue was the computer card, a symbol of dehumanizing actions being taken all over the country and the world. A year later, the need for attendance taking disappeared when all required attendance was abolished. Other issues concerned the lack of parking spaces (a perennial problem) and the newly installed speed bumps on the campus roads, a creation of the new director of the physical plant, Willis. The bumps were modified or removed after students threatened to take action if their cars were damaged.

When Mrs. Virgie Jefferson ("Mrs. J") '09 [1942–62], for 20 years the housemother in McDaniel Hall and "greatly loved by hundreds of students,"[29] retired in 1962, she was replaced for a few years by Mrs. Annie Bryan Mays [1962–65] and then by Mrs. Frances Frey. Mrs. Henrietta Scott supervised Blanche Ward Hall until 1967, when she retired and was succeeded by Mrs. Ruth Etter and Mrs. Dana George. By the end of the decade, thought was being given to replacing housemothers with married couples. The new dean of women was under considerable pressure from the students to liberalize women's curfew hours, and by 1968, keys had been made available to senior women so they could come and go as they pleased. Two years later, all women were afforded the same opportunity, and essentially curfews were abolished.[30] With a more open campus came security issues, and so a uniformed Pinkerton guard was hired to patrol the campus every night.

Dress codes were also gradually being relaxed for both women and men. By 1965, men were allowed to wear Bermuda shorts to the dining hall but not to class; coats and ties were still required at Sunday dinner. By 1966 women could wear slacks in some places on campus but not to classes or evening meals. Women students of the era have memories of Dean Howery going to the microphone at lunchtime on rare occasions to inform them that because of severe weather conditions, they would be allowed to wear slacks to afternoon classes, labs, the library, and the evening meal. Similarly, rules governing open houses in the men's dormitories and visitation by women students were relaxed by the end of the decade, at least on the weekends; however, room doors were not to be locked, and guests had to sign in to indicate their presence.

Possibly a factor encouraging changes in dress codes for women was the winter weather of the era. Harsh snowstorms made regular appearances, but classes were not cancelled. Students and professors were expected to be in their classrooms at the appointed times, and most were. The deep snow and bitter cold that almost forced the Kennedy inauguration inside in 1961 did not deter the academic activity at Western Maryland College. In February 1966 another especially heavy snowstorm blanketed the eastern seaboard, and a number of students were stranded at home, unable to return to campus for several days at the beginning of the second semester; but classes still began. Snows provided a relaxing opportunity for students to let off steam through snowball battles and "traying" (using the large dining hall serving trays) down the back hill behind the chapel straight to the football field.

The ROTC program continued to flourish and expand as enrollments grew, commissioning an average of 30 second lieutenants over the period. In January 1961, on a bitterly cold day, 34 cadets from the local unit joined cadets from neighboring schools to form a marching unit for the inaugural parade for John F. Kennedy. Men students of the era remember a grim evening meal in 1962 when the ROTC students wore their uniforms to dinner in anticipation of President Kennedy's televised speech regarding his response to the Cuban missile crisis.[31] When enrollment in the ROTC program became voluntary in September 1969, there was some concern that numbers would drop precipitously, but they did not. Of the 180 entering freshman men, 75 chose to enroll in the program. Over the decade, the military presence on campus changed dramatically. For decades, on Tuesdays, all ROTC enrollees sat down to lunch in uniform just prior to the drill period and attended classes and laboratories in the afternoon still in uniform (since there was no time to change). Military honor guards were also visible at homecoming and the Military Ball. By the end of the decade, however, 50 years after the ROTC unit had been established, uniforms were seen much less on campus.

Greek organizations continued to function more or less as they had for decades, the average size of a fraternity 48, and the average size of a sorority 52. Fraternities ranged in average size from 40 (Pi Alpha Alpha) to 55 (Alpha Gamma Tau), while sororities ranged from 32 (Iota Gamma Chi) to 64 (Phi Alpha Mu). However, as student enrollments grew, by about 40% over the decade, the groups remained roughly the same size, so that the percentage of eligible student participation dropped from 62% to 31%. A number of internal changes occurred within the groups, perhaps brought on by the changing student population. In the spring of 1963 the members of Iota Gamma Chi, in an effort to increase their membership (at a low of 6), revised their group entirely, changing colors (from red and black to green and white) and mascots (from worms to seahorses). A group of about 30 pledges redefined the group, and membership rose to a high of 69 in 1965–66, before dropping off again by the end of the decade to 19. This oldest women's group on campus (since 1894) would disappear in the next decade. Gamma Beta Chi fraternity temporarily affiliated with Tau Kappa Epsilon, a national group, in 1964 but never became a colony.[32] The college's aversion to having national fraternities was breaking down as the local fraternity system came under increasing scrutiny, especially the traditional hazing, including paddling, which had not diminished.

The new dean of men, James Robinson, saw the need for changes and called for a revitalization of the Interfraternity Council; new rush and pledge periods, whereby freshmen could rush in the spring, were implemented. The four end sections of Albert Norman Ward and MacLea halls were also designated as fraternity sections (a nod toward fraternity houses; members were paid to be the custodians of their sections as part of their financial aid).[33] While some things seemed to improve, dialogue and cooperation among the fraternities was still lacking, so Dean Robinson organized a workshop to address the problem in February 1966. Omicron Delta Kappa (the national men's leadership honor society, which had evolved from the Men's Leadership Society and was chartered on May 25, 1963) also sponsored a symposium, "The Fraternity System and the Individual." Then in late April, a group of 16 concerned campus leaders, students and faculty and mostly from within the Greek system, published a position paper calling for the abolition of fraternities on the campus; it was felt that the groups created barriers that inhibited personal and social interaction, fragmenting the campus community.[34] President Ensor immediately appointed a task force of six campus leaders and five faculty, chaired by Dr. Holthaus, to take a detailed and objective look at the fraternity system. Two years later the task force finally presented its report, which did not recommend abolition but also did not make any concrete suggestions for improvement. Its chairman called the results inconclusive and the committee a failure. It is interesting to note that, during the first year of committee deliberation, fraternity numbers dropped off by about 40%, but when the threat of abolition was no longer there, the numbers rose again. Nevertheless, the committee served a purpose. Jerry Hopple '71, in a *Gold Bug* editorial, noted that between 1965 and 1969, WMC students had "seen progress of tremendous proportions." He felt that the fraternity abolition movement of 1966 began it all as a "conscious effort to change this college. . . . WMC will never return to the days when civil rights, ghettos and the draft were problems only other people were concerned with." In the same issue of the *Gold Bug*, another student opined, "We grew, and Whimsee grew, and that's what it's all about."[35]

Some new organizations with service as their raison d'être appeared on campus during this decade. In the spring of 1962, the Student Opportunity Service (SOS) was formed, with Dr. Griswold as the adviser "to provide convenient opportunities to serve in areas of need around the world." By the summer of 1963, the group was planning to furnish a library for Luzon, Philippines, and began collecting $10,000 and 10,000 books. Seven students made the trip to deliver the books, the first of 27 such trips to areas including Puerto Rico, Bolivia, Belize, and Appalachia through 1971. In September

*Professor E. Griswold and Dr. Ensor bid farewell to
seven SOS students bound for the Philippines, 1963.*

1966, the mayor of Salinas, Puerto Rico, traveled to Westminster on a goodwill
mission to express his thanks for the library that had been established that
summer and present the key to his city to President Ensor. On the home front,
HINGE was formed in 1966 as a tutoring group primarily for black students
in neighboring elementary and middle schools, matching each young
student with a "big brother" or "big sister" on the campus in a one-on-one
relationship. A year later the group merged with SOS and continued its work
until 1984. Over the 20 or so years, about 275 students were involved in these
two programs. Their history is carefully documented in *The Journey Outward*,
edited by Ira Zepp and published by the college in 2003.

In sports, the college teams generally maintained a fairly equal number of
winning and losing seasons. The football team had winning seasons in 1960,
1961, and 1962 and was Mason-Dixon Champion in 1961 with an 8–1 season.

With the departure in 1965 of Coach Waldorf, who had directed the team to a record of 40 wins, 26 losses, and 4 ties during his eight seasons (1957–64), including six conference championships, a new era began in WMC football. The team saw a couple of losing seasons but picked up again under new coach Ronald Jones to garner two more winning seasons in the decade. In soccer, the decade opened with three winning seasons, including a 6–4–1 record in the 1960 season, during which All-American George Varga made 17 goals. When two-time All-American Dennis Harmon '57 turned over the team to another All-American, Homer Earll '50, in 1964, some of the powerhouse players were gone, but by the end of the decade the team posted two winning seasons. (A Junior Varsity team helped accommodate the increased interest in the game.) Assisting Earll with the coaching from 1968 to 1971 was German professor Peter Büttner, who received All-America honors at Grove City College (PA) in 1958 and 1959. During the 1969 season, Ronald Athey '72 was named to several honor teams, in part because of his performance in the 5–2 win over Mt. St. Mary's in which he scored three goals in five minutes, one with each foot and one with his head.

Dick Clower's basketball team had four winning seasons out of the eight he coached in the decade, the best one in 1961, when the record was 16–7. Even during the 1967 season, which ended 9–15, the team scored at least 100 points against their opponents three times. During the last two years of the decade, the team produced two 7–15 seasons under Ron Sisk. The wrestling team came on strong and was the most successful of the various college teams. Sam Case '63 was part of several winning teams and then coached briefly before leaving for Johns Hopkins. He was lured back, however, and his team soon was amassing wins. Two years running, in 1968 and 1969, it was Mason-Dixon Champion, and in the three years at the end of the decade, it gave up only one match. Many school records were broken by the wrestlers of this decade. The baseball team began to have winning seasons under new coach Fern Hitchcock '47, racking up three successive seasons with 12–4, 12–6, and 15–5 records. Other teams were more lackluster and did not attract as much student interest. In 1967 men's lacrosse made a reappearance as a club team after a 12-year hiatus and gradually improved its record by the end of the decade under Coach Case. The tennis team lost its venerable coach, Frank Hurt, to retirement in 1965; he was succeeded by one of his former players, Wray Mowbray, for four years, but the teams were not as successful as in earlier decades.

Named to All-America status for their individual efforts as athletes were Earl W. Dietrich '69, football, 1968; C. Victor McTeer '69, football, 1968; James F. Pusey '62, football, 1961; John K. Trainor '66, football, 1965; Richard N. Yobst '63, football, 1962; and Laszlo Zsebedics '63, soccer, 1961.

The rise in intercollegiate women's sports was a highlight of the decade, as field hockey, basketball, volleyball, and tennis teams began to attract more women; the teams began to play other colleges on a regular basis by the end of the decade. Women's sports had been almost exclusively at the intramural level, culminating in an intercollegiate sports day each spring, often with student player-coaches like Sherry Fischer '65 in field hockey. However, with the hiring of two women's coaches (Joan Weyers and Carol Fritz) and at least some commitment from the college to expand the program, women's varsity teams began playing neighboring colleges. The women students could now participate in a more organized way and at a higher level of activity than ever before.

In a decade full of political and social change and trauma, the assassination of President Kennedy certainly stands out as a watershed event. Alumni who were students at the time still remember where they were that Friday afternoon in November 1963 when they learned of the tragedy. Classes and labs were aborted, a uniformed ROTC student lowered the flag to half mast, and virtually everything came to a halt. On Friday evening a memorial service was held in Baker Memorial Chapel. The WMC–Johns Hopkins football game scheduled for Saturday was cancelled, for the first and only time in the 75-year history of the contest. Throughout the weekend, students were glued to the few television sets on campus; many saw the shooting of suspected assassin Lee Harvey Oswald on live television on Sunday. Many students traveled to Washington to walk past the bier in the Capitol rotunda. Classes were cancelled on Monday, the official day of national mourning, and everyone watched the daylong funeral proceedings. The campus eventually returned to relative normal after the Thanksgiving break later that week, but for many, the world and their lives would never be quite the same.

During the decade the campus also mourned the loss in Vietnam of five alumni in addition to Col. Moore: Homer C. McIntyre Jr. '57 in 1964, Ambrosio S. Grandea '53 and James C. Stephens '64 in 1967, and Arnold C. Hayward '54 and John DeMey '62 in 1969.

One cannot think of this decade without remembering the rising level of concern about the Vietnam War, which reached a climax with the Kent State protest. The country became weary of the war even as the majority of citizens continued to support it. On college and university campuses, various levels of support existed, although the vocal minority protesting it garnered the headlines. At Western Maryland College, war-related vigils, debates, and "teach-ins" occasionally were held from 1964 on, encouraged and participated in by some of the faculty. These were peaceful and accepted by the student body at large, even though many students refrained from getting involved. Indeed, as the decade moved on, *Gold Bug* editors regularly criticized their readers for being apathetic and having "negative attitudes" about various causes that were "hot buttons" on other campuses. The students, probably coming from more conservative backgrounds, seemed more interested in pursuing issues closer to home and of concern to them personally, such as dress codes, curfews, food, or Greek organizations. In a college referendum mirroring the political primaries in May 1968, the national collegiate results showed McCarthy to be a clear favorite for president, followed by Robert Kennedy and then Nixon, while at Western Maryland, Rockefeller took first place, followed by McCarthy and then Nixon.[36] A call for a nationwide moratorium on the war on October 15, 1969,

Students and faculty march in downtown Westminster
calling for a moratorium on the Vietnam War.

resulted locally in a quiet candlelit march downtown to the War Memorial and back. About 200 students and some faculty participated.[37] Even in the aftermath of Kent State in March 1970, while there was shock and sadness among the students, with subsequent memorial services attended by many, there were no debilitating riots, sit-ins, walkouts, or campus closings, perhaps in part because Acting President Mund appeared in the dining room the following morning to keep things calm. And even before that, in 1968–69, as students were seeking more involvement in their lives and the rules governing them, President Ensor cleared his calendar on Monday afternoons and opened his door to all comers to talk about issues of student concern. Unlike many other institutions, at Western Maryland College dissent was accepted, debate encouraged, and civility expected.

Ensor commented on this era in his 1967 report:

I can't help but compare in my own mind the situations that existed at the college in 1947, when my administration began, and those currently existent in 1967. Then we were facing the GI bulge with the return of great numbers of veterans clamoring for college admission but who brought with them a certain maturity and seriousness of purpose resulting from broad experience throughout the world. Many were married with families, and to them college was a most serious business and they were eager to take advantage of the unusual opportunities afforded them through the GI Bill. In contrast, today's students are younger, coming to college directly from high school, knowing little about the facts of life as they really exist in the world around them except as they have read and heard from the lips of others. There has developed, however, in the current student generation a growing dissatisfaction with the world they are inheriting, sometimes resulting from ignorance but frequently caused by a sincere idealism, sometimes misdirected but characterized by a desire to uncover sham and pretense wherever it exists in an effort to be completely honest. To be sure, there are some among them who are extremely vocal and make the newspaper headlines, but, for the most part, they are a sincere group earnestly endeavoring to find answers to many of the basic problems that are concerning the world. . . . I simply want to say that never in the 20 years of my administration has the college been faced with a greater challenge than that presented by today's youth. To say that I don't become concerned is far from the truth, but in my calmer moments of reflection I believe it is necessary to roll with the punch at times in the hope and confidence that their experiences at Western Maryland will help them develop into significant leaders of whom the college can be justifiably proud.[38]

BUILDINGS AND GROUNDS

President Ensor was becoming known as a "builder," almost rivaling his distinguished predecessor Thomas Hamilton Lewis. (By the end of Ensor's 25 years, he had overseen the building of 9 new structures; in 34 years Lewis planned and completed at least 13 buildings.) During the decade, the much needed library was built (with some construction delays) at a cost of $597,000 and opened in May 1962. The modern brick facility located on the brow of the hill next to Baker Memorial Chapel was the first building on campus to be air conditioned. It had a capacity for 100,000 volumes on its three upper floors, with space for 60,000 more volumes on its lowest floor (which would eventually also house the college archives).[39] On May 9, classes were cancelled for the day, and the students and faculty, under the general direction of Dr. James Earp, moved all the books (which were first vacuumed by Dean Howery) from the old library up the hill into the new one and placed them in their assigned spots. Earp had estimated that the job would require 6,600 trips by 600 students in about five hours; it actually took only about three hours, and the library was open for business the next day.[40] The old library building was then renovated and in 1963 became home to the Art Department, with a gallery on the first floor in the old periodical room. The publications and publicity offices were moved into Forlines House.

The next major structure to be built was the addition to Lewis Hall, to the south of the older building. It was designed to expand the laboratory

Students and faculty assist in moving all the books from the old library . . .

facilities of the Chemistry and Biology departments and to provide offices and classrooms for mathematics; the Physics Department would then take over the whole first floor of Lewis Hall. In preparation for this addition, the Dean's Cottage (1919), the home of the dean of women, was moved during the summer of 1963 to a foundation prepared near the stone gates, just beyond McDaniel House, facing on Main Street. The cottage was raised off its footings, turned around, and slid down the hill between the trees with all of Dean Howery's furniture, books, china, and pictures in place; only one teacup (left out on the kitchen drainboard) was broken. The basement and sub-basement for the Lewis addition were blasted out of the rock the following fall, and walls slowly began to rise. In an agreement with the Department of Agriculture, a below-ground sub-basement was prepared as a totally separate entity and rented to the DOA as a communication monitoring and document storage facility until 2000. The four upper floors contained offices, classrooms, and laboratories. The building was completed and occupied in the spring of 1966, after which the older facility was modernized. However, one chemistry classroom on the third floor retained its original form, with uncomfortable bench seats and small tablet arms, seating that had been transferred from the even earlier Yingling Science Hall in 1914. The addition was named Lewis Hall of Science, while the older building retained its 1914 name, Lewis Recitation Hall. In 1965 the astronomical observatory atop the older building was named the Rembrandt Dewees Summers Observatory in his memory.

To provide for the rapidly expanding student body, two new dormitories

. . . into the new library, which opened in 1962.

493

and a new dining hall were planned and constructed from 1965 to 1968. The new dining hall and kitchen were ready for occupancy and use in September 1968, the dining hall named for the Englar family, many of whom were alumni. During the planning phase for the new dormitories, a third floor was added to the men's facility to accommodate an additional 56 men and to balance the male-female housing options. Both dormitories were first occupied in September 1968, the men's named Rouzer Hall for trustee E. McClure Rouzer '07 (LLD '57), and the women's named Whiteford Hall for the late trustee Roger J. Whiteford '06 (LLD '43) and his wife.[41] The lounge area in the women's residence hall was named the Howery Lounge in memory of the former dean of women. Later in the fall of 1968, the pool beneath the dining room was completed and named in memory of Richard Harlow. Unfortunately, it had only five lanes, which often posed problems for swimming meets. No official reason can be located for this unusual arrangement, although it has been suggested that the athletic department was not consulted in the planning and that money was a factor.

To accommodate the heating needs for all the new buildings, which cost a total of $3,640,000, a new boiler plant was built on Union Street in 1965 and the campus heating system was renovated. After the new and larger dining facility was opened, the old dining room and basement kitchen area in Memorial Hall were renovated to create more classrooms and some offices. During 1964–65, the side porch of the President's House facing Main Street was enclosed to provide a large space for official entertainment.

Whiteford Hall, a women's dormitory, was opened in 1968.

During the decade several significant land purchases were made, and some property was sold. In 1961 some land beyond Carroll Hall was purchased from the Reifsnider family for $13,200, about 60 acres of the Beard farm beyond the golf course were added to the campus in 1965 for $71,000, and 2½ additional acres from the Geiman farm along Main Street were purchased in 1966 for $25,000.[42] Once the Beard property was in hand, the golf course was redesigned, holes relocated, and fairways expanded at a cost of $15,000, and 8.9 acres were sold to the State of Maryland for the construction of a new Route 31 (to New Windsor). Some haggling over the price occurred since the road would divide the college property (an under-road tunnel was even considered at one point), but finally the state and the college agreed on $17,500, and the road was constructed.[43]

Several properties abutting the campus on Pennsylvania Avenue were also purchased during the decade, including the Burall and Snyder garage, which was purchased for $20,000 and rented for a while. The second Reifsnider house and property along Main Street beyond the infirmary came on the market and were purchased in 1968 for $30,000. The house was remodeled and redecorated (at a cost of $20,000) and opened in May 1969 as the Harrison Alumni House, named in memory of T. K. Harrison (1882–1966), first alumni secretary. The second floor housed, for a time, the offices of the Alumni Association and a guest suite. In 1962 the Baltimore Chapter of the Alumni Association provided funds to create a pedestal containing the cornerstones of the buildings in the Old Main complex and topped by the Old Main bell. It was

The second Reifsnider house became the Harrison Alumni House in 1969.

The tower bell and the cornerstones from the Old Main complex were combined into a memorial.

situated between Baker Memorial Chapel and Lewis Hall.

The board of trustees also decided to divest itself of several pieces of property no longer needed. Vetville was sold to Messrs. Himler and Bollinger for $60,000 in 1962. (Married students and some faculty continued to rent apartments in the complex at modest rates. It is still in existence, with few changes.) The board also discussed disposing of some of the properties on Union Street, rather than renovating and improving them.[44] Selling the properties for a city-sponsored low-cost housing development was considered.[45] The college's ownership of these properties had been questioned in at least one student editorial, by Donald Elmes '69.[46] The properties would be transferred in the next decade.

In a spirit of ecumenicity, the college graciously invited St. John Catholic Church to use Baker Memorial Chapel for its services in 1968, after the downtown church had been struck by lightning and was ultimately condemned. The congregation worshiped on campus for at least a year until its new building could be built above the site of Vetville, northeast of the campus.

FINANCES

In a tuition-driven institution such as Western Maryland College, enrollments were always a concern. However, in this decade, the concern was not whether the college would be fully enrolled, but rather how many could be accommodated as more and more students sought admission. Rather than maintain a maximum enrollment of about 700, it was soon determined that it was in the best interests of the college and its total constituency if the enrollment were expanded, first to about 850, and then gradually to 1,000. Actually, it grew from 730 in 1960–61 to 820 in 1967–68, to 1,060 in 1969–70— a 45% increase. The average enrollment over the ten years was about 835, with women slightly outnumbering men, on average 430 to 405. The number of students in the entering classes fluctuated depending on available residence hall space but generally grew over the decade, from a low of about 180 in 1960 to 355 in 1969. The average freshman class was 260 (skewed upward by the classes entering in 1968 and 1969, which were larger by 100 because of the newly opened dormitories). Of course, as the numbers increased, so did the need for housing and dining facilities, which presented a whole new set of financial problems for the trustees.

Over the decade, annual tuition grew from $900 to $1,600, a 77% increase (mirroring previous decades), while room and board costs increased from about $750 to $950, about a 30% increase. In 1961, costs at the college were lower than those at nine of the colleges in the region (Goucher and Johns Hopkins were $500–$700 higher). By 1967, at a total cost of $2,600, Western Maryland was positioned at the midpoint in the list of regional colleges. As the number of students increased along with the tuition fees, the college was able to (and needed to) increase faculty salaries significantly. The top faculty ranks saw an increase of almost 90%, from a maximum of $8,000 to a maximum of about $15,000 in ten years. The minimum salary of the lowest rank (instructor) increased about 56%, from $4,800 in 1960–61 to about $7,500 in 1969–70. The deans' salaries rose over the same period from $10,500 to $19,000, a 45% increase. (The $19,000 salary for the new dean of faculty in 1969 was a full $2,000 more than the previous dean was earning after 20 years in the job.) The president's salary rose 47%, from $15,000 to $22,000 (from $20,000 to $22,000 in one fell swoop in 1969, when the new dean was hired). Relatively speaking, faculty salaries increased faster than administrators'; still, no one was being exorbitantly paid in comparison with the competition. President Ensor noted several times in his reports to the trustees that salaries would have to be increased significantly and quickly in order to attract and keep the faculty needed to teach the growing student body.

Also interesting was the issue of a pension for Ensor upon his retirement, planned for 1972. In discussing this with him, the trustees learned that he had not joined the TIAA program and was depending upon a small pension from the Methodist Conference (which he had served for 16 years as a pastor) and Social Security. The board voted an additional $400 a month for life ($200 a month for Mrs. Ensor if she survived him). He would thus be able to retire on an income of about half of his highest salary.[47]

In an attempt to improve the remuneration package for faculty, the board in 1961 approved a policy of providing educational grants to faculty children who would attend other colleges: 50% of the WMC tuition. The college was also a member of the Tuition Exchange Program, which permitted faculty children to attend other colleges in the program tuition free; this arrangement worked well until the number of outgoing students from WMC exceeded the number of incoming students from other member colleges. In 1963 President Ensor recommended and the board approved raising the college's contribution to TIAA for faculty and staff to 10% from 5% (while the faculty member still contributed 5%). Some additions to the major-medical program were also approved in 1965. A group term life insurance program for faculty and staff was approved in 1966, the premium to be paid equally by the college and the staff member.[48] In 1970 the board approved a pension plan for the 80 employees of the college not already covered by the TIAA plan. All of these fringe benefits were much appreciated by those concerned and at least partially made up for the lower basic salaries. A new policy of announcing to the faculty their salary and rank for the coming year by March 15 of each year was adopted in 1961 and was met with delight by the faculty, who, up to this point, as noted earlier, never knew what their salaries would be until after the opening of the new college year. The president noted that this policy, along with a new minimum wage law that affected student workers as well as staff, would create some problems in establishing the budget for the coming year, but the details would be worked out.

The decade saw the college endowment reach $2 million in 1961, $2.6 million in 1964, $2.8 million in 1965, $2.9 million in later 1965, and $3.1 million in 1968—a growth of over 50%. The draw from the endowment to support the college program (about 4%) also rose gradually, from about $85,000 to almost $100,000.

The Centennial Expansion Program to expand the college to 1,000 was announced in 1963, with a fund-raising goal of $1.5 million. It was noted that to achieve the expansion, about $3 million would be needed for facilities, the endowment should be doubled, and outside help would be needed.[49] Fund-raising consultants Ward, Dreshman and Reinhardt, Inc., from New York were

Trustees R. Gill, R. Kiefer, and Dr. Ensor plan centennial expansion.

hired to plan the campaign, which was to run through fall and winter of 1963–64. Originally, the several new buildings were projected to cost between $2.5 and $3 million, to be paid for from the donations of the campaign, a loan from the Federal College Housing Authority of $2.5 million, and a Maryland State capital grant of $750,000 (earmarked for the science addition). The last request was reduced by the legislature to $500,000 and was awarded to the college.

Soon thereafter, in September 1963, the Horace Mann League of Maryland filed suit to block the state grant and similar ones (for a total of $2.5 million) to Hood College in Frederick, the College of Notre Dame in Baltimore, and St. Joseph College in Emmitsburg on the basis that state money was being given to church-related institutions, a violation of the constitutional separation of church and state. The suit eventually went to court, where the grants were upheld; in 1966 the league appealed the ruling to the Maryland Court of Appeals, which reversed part of the original decision in a split vote, ruling that Hood College could be considered nonsectarian and therefore could receive the grant, but that Western Maryland and the two Catholic institutions were sufficiently sectarian to warrant denying the state funding. It was the opinion of many legal experts that the court picked out everything about Hood that would make it appear nonsectarian and everything about Western Maryland to characterize it as sectarian because it was unwilling to designate two Catholic colleges as sectarian and two Protestant colleges as nonsectarian, so one of the Protestant colleges had to be sacrificed. This ruling was appealed to the United States Supreme Court, which, in 1966, refused to hear the case. There the matter rested.[50] An emergency Urgent Needs Campaign for a half million dollars was launched to make up the difference, and its successful completion resulted in the total construction costs of $3,640,000 being met. Twice during the decade (1965–66 and 1967–68), the treasurer reported end-of-year budget deficits, but both were caused by construction bills coming due before pledges and grants had been paid. (Usually, there was about a 1% surplus as a carryover to the next year.) Ultimately, the Centennial Expansion was completed and paid for, and the college embarked on a new century of service relatively debt free except for the long-term federal loan.

As noted in chapter 10, the local J.C. Penney building had come to the college through a bequest from Mrs. Walter H. Davis and had been rented since 1954 (the annual rental income now being about $19,000). In 1961, when a lease was about to expire, the trustees considered selling the building but instead continued the lease (for another 14 years). The remainder of the Davis fund, valued at $256,500 when it was given, had appreciated by 75% to almost $450,000, and that money helped to build the new library in 1962.[51]

Additional funding for the library building was pledged in 1960 by the Methodist Church, $350,000 over a four-year period. President Ensor and others preached in many conference churches and the College Choir performed many concerts in this fund-raising endeavor, which concluded successfully. The church pledged an additional $500,000 in 1963 when the state grant appeared in jeopardy. By the end of the decade, however, payments were slow in coming, and the regular annual commitment was not being paid.

In a similar vein, the State of Maryland had for some years been lagging behind in its payments for state scholarships. As tuition increased, state funding remained the same. For instance, in 1964, scholarships totaled $126,600, but the state was paying only $100,000. The college was told that providing the total amount would take legislative action. The following year, the scholarship deficit was about $30,000. This particularly rankled the trustees, since the college had received only $250,000 from the state over the period 1952–62, while all the other independent colleges had received at least $500,000. And WMC was training the largest percentage of Maryland teachers of any college in the state.[52] In 1965, the legislature adopted a new scholarship program that would reimburse colleges at the actual rates being charged, but there is no record that the amounts in arrears were ever paid.

The college alumni continued to be generous to their alma mater, as evidenced by steady increases in the Annual Fund each year. Records show that contributions to the Alumni Fund grew during the decade from about $25,000 to over $80,000, a 220% increase, the number of donors also increasing.

During his seven months as acting president, Allan Mund scrupulously avoided making any changes in the college operation, preferring to "steer the ship" not "rock the boat." However, he did make one significant suggestion to the board, which it seemed to approve: that a detailed budget, with line items, be prepared for 1971–72, since the operating expenses of the college were now at about $3.5 million. He also suggested that a monthly balance sheet be prepared by the treasurer to keep abreast of the financial status of the college.[53] This was another step forward for the growing institution.

The new library was opened and dedicated in 1962.

MAJOR EVENTS

The first of a series of dedications and special celebrations during the decade was held on December 1, 1962, when the new library, which had been in use since the late spring, was formally dedicated in a ceremony in Alumni Hall. The academic procession included 54 representatives from colleges and universities in the Middle States Association, a number of librarians from Maryland schools and colleges, the district superintendents of the Baltimore Conference of the Methodist Church, and the faculty and trustees. The featured speaker for the occasion was the librarian of Congress, L. Quincy Mumford. In his address, entitled "A Princely Service," he discussed the value of books in one's life and the enrichment and enjoyment that can be obtained in a library. The College Choir sang four songs appropriate to the event from *From the Textbooks* by Charles Bryan. D. Carlysle MacLea, chairman of the trustee Committee on Buildings and Grounds, presented the keys to the building to librarian Elizabeth Simkins and John Blackburn '63, president of the SGA. Also participating in the dedicatory ceremony were Bishop Lord, who led the Act of Dedication and trustee John Bayley Jones '41, who gave the invocation. Following the ceremony everyone walked to the new library, where tea and refreshments were served and tours were conducted of the four-level structure.[54]

The National Symphony Orchestra had appeared on campus every year since 1936. In recognition of 30 years of continuous cultural entertainment, the college conferred the honorary doctor of fine arts degree on Howard Mitchell, who had become director in 1949, at the intermission of the annual concert on March 4, 1966. Rolled up in the diploma was a copy of a program

Lewis Hall of Science, an addition to the Lewis Recitation Hall,
was opened in 1966.

of the symphony's concert on campus in the 1940s in which Mitchell, then first cellist with the orchestra, had played a concerto. The program had been saved by Cora Virginia Perry (an admitted pack rat), who, as associate registrar, prepared the diploma for presentation.

The dedication of the Lewis Hall of Science, the addition to Lewis Recitation Hall, was held on October 15, 1966, during homecoming weekend. The dedicatory convocation held in Alumni Hall began with an academic procession of 40 delegates from neighboring colleges and several scientific societies, as well as the faculty and trustees of WMC. Dr. H. Bentley Glass, an internationally known geneticist formerly of Johns Hopkins University and now academic vice president at the State University of New York at Stony Brook, was the featured speaker; his topic was "Science and a Liberal Education." He indicated that science is a liberating and liberalizing force; therefore, it must be a central part of the liberal education: "It is crucial; the core within the apple, the skeleton within the human body; for it embodies the seeds of change and progress in civilization and it is the basis of support, giving form and shape to the social sciences, arts, and humanities of our time."[55] During the ceremony, an honorary doctor of science degree was conferred upon Glass. Also recognized with the ScD were Dr. L. Eugene Cronin '38, Dr. W. Edward Cushen '48, Dr. Frank E. Jaumot Jr. '47, and Dr. John F. Yost '43, alumni who had distinguished themselves in the fields of biology, mathematics, physics, and chemistry, respectively. Board chair Robert Gill formally presented the building to the college. Following the convocation, student guides were stationed in the building to explain its use. Of particular interest to many alumni was the new physical chemistry laboratory that had been named in honor of professor emeritus of chemistry Samuel Biggs Schofield, who had just retired. A buffet luncheon, as well as the homecoming parade, football game, and alumni reception, rounded out the afternoon. In the two weeks that preceded the formal dedication, the science departments had offered a series of lectures by outstanding individuals in the various disciplines, including the alumni honorary degree recipients.

The centennial year of the college was celebrated during 1967–68 using the theme "The Liberal Arts College—Continuity and Change." A number of special events were held during the year, including the Centennial Convocation held in Alumni Hall on October 21, 1967, another homecoming weekend. Trustee Wilson K. Barnes, chair of the Centennial Planning Committee, presided at the ceremony, which began with an academic procession of trustees, faculty, and 140 delegates from colleges and universities, including 19 institutional presidents, among them Lloyd Bertholf (Illinois Wesleyan University; former

Dignitaries process into Alumni Hall for the Centennial Convocation in 1967.

WMC professor and dean), Earle T. Hawkins '23 (Towson State College), and Wilbur Devilbiss '25 (Salisbury State College). Bishop Lord pronounced the invocation, and President Ensor welcomed the guests and introduced Dr. John A. Logan Jr., president of Hollins College, who addressed the centennial topic. "I firmly believe that the survival of the liberal arts depends on the survival of the smaller, private college. . . . I confidently predict that this college is on the threshold of another century of service to the state and to the nation," he said.[56] Greetings recognizing the college's 100-year commitment to higher education were brought by Dr. James A. Sensenbaugh, state superintendent of schools, representing the State of Maryland; Dr. A. Randle Elliott, president of Hood College, representing the academic community; Westminster mayor Joseph H. Hahn Jr., representing the local community; and Dr. Wilmer V. Bell '30, representing the alumni. After President Ensor conferred an honorary degree on President Logan, the delegates and faculty recessed to the accompaniment of the Alma Mater. A buffet luncheon for all attendees was held in the Blanche Ward gymnasium, and the delegates' luncheon was served in the college dining hall. These were followed by the traditional parade (with a centennial theme, of course); the football game before a record crowd, in which Western Maryland crushed Shepherd College 27–7; the alumni reception in McDaniel Lounge; and the homecoming dance in Gill Gymnasium. During the day, exhibits of artifacts from the college's history were on display in the Davis Room of the library, and an art exhibit was open in the Fine Arts Building.[57] A significant result of the centennial year was the establishment of the college archives in 1969, with Dr. Schofield as the first archivist. He persuaded his class (1919) to fund the creation of an archives room in the basement of the library as a 50th reunion gift to the college. A College History Committee, consisting of Eloise B. Ensor, Dorothy McDaniel Herr, Martha Manahan, Cora Virginia Perry, and Theodore Whitfield, with Schofield as chairman, was appointed in 1966. They undertook the task of pulling together the many artifacts and papers relating to the 100-year history and development of the college, and as archivist, Schofield put them into one central place, from which he began to draw information for *The Formative Years*, his history of the college 1867–1947, written in conjunction with Marjorie C. Crain and published by the college in 1982.

The evening before the convocation, a program of sight and sound, "A Hundred-Year Heritage," was presented in Alumni Hall. The script was by Miriam Royer Brickett '27, and the presentation was staged by Jerry Solomon of the Dramatic Art Department. The College Singers, under the direction of Oliver Spangler, provided appropriate music for each era in the presentation of the college's history. A Community-College Centennial Banquet was held in the college dining room on March 27. Over 500 Carroll County residents attended the event, at which Dr. and Mrs. Ensor were recognized for their 20 years at the college. The faculty and staff presented them with a citation and a large, etched Steuben vase. A collection of letters from the presidents of the 20 classes 1947–1967 was also presented to the president. In a departure from tradition, the senior investiture service was moved to May Day weekend and incorporated into an Honors and Investiture Convocation, where students receiving academic honors were recognized. The May 5 event included the traditional address by a member of the faculty, recognition of candidates for honors (general and departmental) and members of the Argonauts, presentation of a number of academic awards, and conferring of honorary degrees on Charles E. Bish '25 and Paul F. Maynard '45. A reception followed in McDaniel Lounge.

During the celebratory year a number of special speakers also appeared on campus, either in assembly or in chapel. The notables included Dr. Glenn A. Olds, Dr. J. Milton Yinger, Senator Gale W. Magee, and Father Philip Berrigan. Also scheduled to speak, on March 17, was Dr. Martin Luther King Jr., but he had to cancel two weeks before his appearance due to an urgent trip to Africa. (A month later he was assassinated.) Special events in drama included productions of Kafka's *The Trial* in the Understage Theater, Euripides's *The Bacchae*, and the premiere of *The Gamesman* by George A. Gipe '56, who had become a noted and award-winning Hollywood screenwriter. The College Choir, directed by Alfred deLong, also presented the complete Handel's *Messiah* in two parts during chapel services in December and April. The choir was expanded by voices from the Westminster Methodist Church Choir for those productions. Other special musical programs included Gerald Goodman, troubadour harpist, and a concert by the Bach Society of Baltimore.

The 100th Commencement of the college was held on June 7, 1970, with Acting President Allan Mund presiding. Joining members of the class of 1970 were surviving members of the class of 1920, who had received their degrees at the 50th Commencement, when the surviving members of the class of 1871 had been present. Special commemorative diplomas marking the occasion were presented by board chair Joshua Miles to those alumni celebrating their 50th reunion. The speaker for the occasion was U.S. Senator (Maryland) Charles McC. Mathias Jr. (Vice President Spiro T. Agnew, a former Maryland governor, had been invited but had declined.) In his address the senator reacted to the recent protests on many campuses by saying, "Because the [rebelling] youth of 1776 employed and regretted the use of violence, the system they created was designed to allow change without violence. . . . Young people today share the impatient idealism of the original Americans . . . and in most cases their demand is for fulfillment both domestically and internationally of the democratic ideals which they had been taught in school. . . . American political processes and institutions, though not as fully democratic and responsive as some wish, are far from inaccessible. The doors to legitimate political participation are wide open; they will be closed only if people blindly attempt to knock down the walls."[58] Bachelor's degrees were awarded to 187 graduates, master of education diplomas were presented to 32 teachers, and honorary degrees were conferred on Mathias (LLD), Merrill Drennan (DD), and Charles Engle '30 (DPhysEd), legendary football coach at Penn State and one of Richard Harlow's protégés.[59]

CONCLUSION

During this decade the college celebrated its one-hundred-year existence, and while no one was alive to make any comparisons between the fledgling college of 1867 and the successful and growing institution of 1967, it could be noted that Western Maryland College was formed during the chaos immediately following the Civil War, and had endured for a century, through several wars and especially during the chaos and upheaval surrounding the Vietnam War a hundred years later. Memories of the Lincoln assassination were still fresh in the founders' minds, and a century later, memories of the Kennedy assassination were etched in the psyches of students and faculty of the 1960s. The early college evolved amid technological advances such as railroads, electricity, and telegraphs and the industrial revolution of the late 19th century; a hundred years later, the college was poised to advance into an even more technological age with the advent of television, computers, and spacecraft. Great social changes such as the emancipation of slaves had occurred just prior to the college's founding, and in 1967, another age of social change was under way with the advent of integration, feminism, and student activism. Through it all, the institution persevered, grew, moved forward, and continued to achieve its mission.

Perhaps no decade thus far had seen more change in the college—socially, physically, financially, and academically—than the years between 1960 and 1970. Growing faster in student enrollments than the physical plant could accommodate, the institution moved forward to change the physical facilities and campus appearance, as well as to expand the faculty and administration. With new faculty came curricular changes to meet the new demands of society. The college could and would never be the same as it was in prior decades. As it moved into the next decade, it would experience even more substantive change.

CHAPTER 11 ENDNOTES

1. WMC board of trustees minutes, April 18, 1998.
2. Ensor, Report, April 29, 1966.
3. WMC faculty minutes, April 1, 1968.
4. WMC trustee Executive Committee minutes, March 5, 1970.
5. WMC board of trustees minutes, April 19, 1968.
6. Ibid., April 18, 1969.
7. Ibid., April 19, 1968.
8. WMC faculty minutes, January 8, 1969.
9. *WMC Magazine*, April 1966, 6.
10. Ensor, Report, October 15, 1965.
11. Ibid., September 18, 1964.
12. *WMC Magazine*, August 1961, 12.
13. WMC faculty minutes, December 4, 1968; January 29, 1969.
14. *Gold Bug*, December 12, 1969; February 2, 1970.
15. *The Hill*, April 1970, 7.
16. Ibid., May 1992, 15.
17. *Gold Bug*, March 9, 1962, 1.
18. Ibid., May 16, 1969, 6.
19. Admissions profiles, 1960–69, college archives.
20. Ensor, Report, April 29, 1966.
21. *Gold Bug*, November 19, 1965, 2.
22. Interview, Philip L. Meredith '66, 2005.
23. *Gold Bug*, December 9, 1960, 1.
24. Ibid., February 11, 1966, 1; March 11, 1966, 4.
25. WMC faculty minutes, November 7, 1966.
26. WMC trustee Executive Committee minutes, November 30, 1966.
27. Ensor, Report, April 21, 1967.
28. *Gold Bug*, November 3, 1967, 1.
29. Ensor, Report, April 27, 1962.
30. *Gold Bug*, November 22, 1968; February 3, 1970.
31. Interview, Meredith.
32. *Gold Bug*, February 28, 1964, 2.
33. Ibid., April 3, 1964, 3; October 23, 1964, 1.
34. Fraternity Position Paper, 1966, college archives.
35. *Gold Bug*, May 16, 1969, 2, 8.
36. Ibid., May 10, 1968, 2.
37. *Gold Bug*, October 24, 1969, 1.
38. Ensor, Report, April 21, 1967.
39. *WMC Catalogue*, 1963–64, 8.
40. *Gold Bug*, May 4, 1962, 1.
41. WMC trustee Executive Committee minutes, September 25, 1968.
42. Ibid., October 28, 1960; April 23, 1965; October 21, 1966.
43. Ibid., February 8, 1966; Ensor, Report, April 21, 1967.
44. WMC trustee Executive Committee minutes, March 7, 1968.
45. Buildings and Grounds minutes, May 10, 1968.
46. *Gold Bug*, September 27, 1968, 2.
47. WMC trustee Executive Committee minutes, September 17, 1969.
48. Ibid., March 11, 1966.
49. WMC trustee Executive Committee minutes, March 11, 1963.
50. Ensor, column, *WMC Magazine*, February 1967, 3–4.
51. Ensor, Report, April 28, 1961.
52. WMC trustee Executive Committee minutes, February 11, 1963.
53. Mund, Report, April 17, 1970.
54. *WMC Magazine*, February 1963, 9; Dedication Program, college archives.
55. *WMC Magazine*, December 1966, 9.
56. *The Hill*, December 1967, 17.
57. Program, Centennial Convocation, 1967.
58. *The Hill*, July 1970, 6.
59. Program, 100th Commencement.

MAJOR WORLD EVENTS

1961

Adolf Eichmann is found guilty of Nazi war crimes in Jerusalem trial.

Yuri Gagarin (USSR) orbits the earth in six-ton satellite.

U.S. breaks off diplomatic relations with Cuba.

Berlin wall is constructed.

Alan Shepard makes first U.S. space flight.

1962

Rachel Carson publishes *Silent Spring*.

World population tops 3.1 billion.

Edward Albee publishes *Who's Afraid of Virginia Woolf?*

Robert Bolt's *A Man for All Seasons* opens on Broadway.

Thalidomide causes children to be born with malformations.

How to Succeed in Business without Really Trying is Pulitzer Prize–winning drama.

John Steinbeck wins Nobel Prize for Literature.

U.S. spacemen Glenn, Carpenter, and Schirra orbit the earth separately.

1963

Nuclear testing ban is signed by U.S., USSR, and Great Britain.

Pope John XXIII dies; is succeeded by Pope Paul VI.

Dr. Michael De Bakey is first to use an artificial heart during surgery.

Popular songs include "Danke Schoen" and "Call Me Irresponsible."

Joan Baez and Bob Dylan are leading folk singers.

President John F. Kennedy is assassinated in Dallas; is succeeded by Lyndon Johnson.

Popular films include *Tom Jones*, *Irma La Douce*, *The Birds*, and *Dr. Strangelove*.

1964

Verrazano-Narrows Bridge, world's longest suspension bridge, opens in New York.

Warren Commission is appointed to investigate Kennedy assassination.

Poll tax is abolished by 24th Amendment.

Martin Luther King Jr. wins Nobel Prize for Peace.

Lyndon B. Johnson is elected U.S. president.

1965

750th anniversary of the Magna Carta is celebrated.

U.S. Medicare bill becomes law.

Picasso paints *Self Portrait*.

The first flight around the world over both poles is completed.

Citizens demonstrate in Washington against U.S. bombing of North Vietnam.

Out of 3.52 million, 2.63 million U.S. 17-year-olds are high school graduates.

Popular films are *Othello*, *Dr. Zhivago*, and *The Sound of Music*.

1966

oviet spacecraft *Luna 9* and U.S. spacecraft *Surveyor 1* both make successful soft landings on the moon.
Popular songs are "Born Free," "Eleanor Rigby," and "Strangers in the Night."
Man of LaMancha and *On a Clear Day You Can See Forever* open on Broadway.

1967

Dr. Christiaan Bernard performs world's first heart transplant in South Africa.
Popular films include *Bonnie and Clyde* and *Guess Who's Coming to Dinner*.
50,000 people demonstrate against Vietnam War at Lincoln Memorial.
100 million telephones are in service in the U.S.
3.6 million births are registered in the U.S.
Thurgood Marshall is appointed to Supreme Court.

1968

U.S. gross national product is at almost $861 billion.
Eero Saarinen's Gateway Arch in St. Louis is dedicated.
Martin Luther King Jr. is assassinated in Memphis hotel; riots erupt in major cities.
Democratic presidential primary candidate Senator Robert F. Kennedy is assassinated in Los Angeles.
Richard M. Nixon, promising to end the Vietnam War, is elected 37th U.S. president.
The United Brethren and Methodist Churches merge as the United Methodist Church.
Popular films include *The Thomas Crown Affair*, *The Odd Couple*, and *In Cold Blood*.

1969

Popular films include *Midnight Cowboy*, *Easy Rider*, *Isadora*, and *MASH*.
Woodstock Music and Art Fair attracts more than 300,000 participants.
Oh! Calcutta!, *Coco*, and *1776* are popular musicals on Broadway.
The Concorde supersonic aircraft makes first test flight.
***Apollo 11* lands lunar module on moon's surface; Neil Armstrong steps on moon.**
U.S. government takes steps to ban use of pesticide DDT.
Inflation becomes a worldwide problem.

1970

Israel and United Arab Republic agree to a 99-day truce along the Suez Canal.
U.S. strength in Vietnam is reduced to below 400,000 men.
Popular films are *Catch-22*, *Paint Your Wagon*, *True Grit*, and *Topaz*.
The Dow Jones Industrial Average drops to 631.
U.S. census shows smallest number of men (94.8) in ratio to women (100) in history.
U.S. has population of 205 million, 85 people per square mile (Japan has 1,083).
Nobel Prize for Literature goes to Soviet novelist Alexandr Solzhenitsyn.
First complete synthesis of a gene is announced by scientists at the University of Wisconsin.
dent protests against Vietnam War result in killing of four by the National Guard at Kent State University.

Elderdice Hall became the College Administration Building in 1959.

C H A P T E R

12

GROWING PAINS, CRISES, AND INDEPENDENCE

———◄ 1971–1980 ►———

As the United States prepared to celebrate the bicentennial of its independence, it endured the Watergate crisis, the resignation of President Richard Nixon, an inflationary spiral, and a major energy crisis with long gasoline lines. It also witnessed continued space exploration by NASA (and by the USSR), the establishment of the Amtrak rail system, the gradual opening of China to the West, the elimination of the military draft, and the ratification of the 26th Amendment to its Constitution, which extended the vote to 18-year-olds. After a year of bicentennial celebration, the country moved on, inaugurating Jimmy Carter as its new president, seeing its population grow to 216 million, learning of the election of Cardinal Karol Wojtyla as Pope John Paul II, being amazed at the birth of the first "test tube" baby in England, and being shocked and angry at the imprisonment of 66 American diplomats in Iran. Americans watched *All in the Family*, *Rocky*, and the "Battle of the Sexes" tennis match between Billie Jean King and Bobby Riggs; were alarmed by the emergence of legionnaire's disease; were surprised by the death of Elvis Presley at 42; and complained when the cost of a first-class stamp rose from 10¢ to 13¢. It was a time of crisis and jubilation, despair and wonder, anxiety and hope.

The college was not immune to the many pressures facing the country. The energy crisis caused fuel oil and gasoline costs to double, inflation pushed up food costs, and the federal government mandated minimum wage increases and increased payroll taxes; all of these forced tightly crafted budgets into deficits for several years. The college also faced several internal crises, including major changes in the administration and board of trustees, another lawsuit over state aid to church-related colleges, the dissolution of the 108-year fraternal and voluntary relationship with the Methodist Church, and a lack of satisfactory dialogue with the growing number of black students on campus. But it also moved forward, to build new and much needed student residences and a college center, as well as to renovate and modernize the venerable 80-year-old Alumni Hall. It happily welcomed establishment of a chapter of Phi Beta Kappa, underwent significant curricular and calendar revisions, and celebrated the bicentennial and a Year of the Humanities. And it wasn't too shocked when young males "streaked" across the campus wearing only their shoes or when women athletes began to make a name for themselves and the college on the courts and playing fields.

FACULTY AND ADMINISTRATION

The decade witnessed significant changes in the administration, governing body, and faculty, but certainly the most important change was in the executive office when President Ensor retired in 1972 after 25 years. This, coupled with changes in the chairmanship of the board of trustees and in the rules governing board membership, brought a new organizational structure to the college. In February 1971, Lowell Ensor announced his retirement, effective June 30, 1972. A presidential search committee was appointed, including trustees Fisher, Fossett, Gill, Jones, Meyls, Penn, Preston, and Mund. For the first time in the college's history, such a committee also included two faculty members, Earl Griswold and James Lightner.[1] The committee, chaired by Allan Mund, met often during the summer of 1971, screened many candidates, and interviewed three (all college administrators) in depth in consultation with representatives of the Alumni Association, faculty members on the Administrative Advisory Council, and the dean of faculty. It made its recommendation to the board of trustees at the board's October meeting, at which time Ralph Candler John was named president-elect. The Ensor years were concluded when Dr. and Mrs. Ensor moved from the President's House to their new home not far away, on Ridge Road in Westminster.

July 1, 1972, marked the beginning of a new era at WMC. Ralph C. John

Ralph Candler John,
sixth president

(1919–99) [1972–84], a native of Prince Frederick, Maryland, who was 53 when he took office, was the son of a Methodist minister. He had graduated from Berea College in Tennessee, obtained theological training (STB and STM) at Boston University, and received his PhD in public administration from the American University in 1950. He had been named distinguished alumnus of both Boston and American Universities. He had joined the American University faculty in 1949, becoming professor and chair of the Philosophy Department, while also serving as an associate minister at a Washington Methodist church. He was then named dean of students (1955–58) and dean of arts and sciences (1958–63) before becoming president of Simpson College in Indianola, Iowa, in 1963, a post he held for nine years before coming to WMC. During his time in Iowa he served as chair of the board of directors of the Central States College Association, and he received honorary doctorates from Iowa Wesleyan College and Simpson College. (WMC would also honor him with the doctor of humane letters degree in 1997.) Joining him in the President's House were his wife, Dorothy (née Prince), and teenage son, Randall. Two other sons, Byron and Douglas, were already in or through college and were rarely seen on campus.

Another significant administrative change occurred in the Dean of Faculty Office when Harry L. Holloway Jr. abruptly resigned in the summer of 1971 after only two years in the post. He had discovered that his administrative skills and personality were better suited to the challenges of chairing the Biology Department at the University of North Dakota in Grand Forks.[2] President Ensor prevailed upon John Makosky to return to the duties of dean, which he reluctantly agreed to do for two years with much appreciation from the faculty. In this way he overlapped the two presidents until President John could select his own dean. When Makosky retired from the deanship (again) and from the faculty in 1973, the Honors Convocation that May was dedicated to him, and he was awarded the honorary doctor of letters degree. His old friend and

John D. Makosky, dean of faculty

former student, now chair of the board of trustees, Wilbur D. Preston Jr. '44, presented him for the degree. Makosky was cited for being "an educational statesman, humanist and creative spirit [who encouraged] the pristine values of true liberal learning. A scholar who is both gentle and genteel, a warm human being, and one who has gathered the profound respect and lasting gratitude of this academic community."[3]

In July 1973, William McCormick Jr. assumed the offices of vice president–dean of academic affairs and professor of economics. Nominated by a committee composed of faculty, administration, and students, McCormick (1935–83) was a native of Indiana, a graduate of Indiana University (BS and MBA), and a recipient of the PhD from Case Western Reserve University. He had taught at Baldwin-Wallace College in Ohio and been a professor and associate dean in the College of Business Administration at the College of William and Mary for four years. He was also the son-in-law of Professor Reuben Holthaus.

Incoming President John requested the trustees to commission a careful study of the college and its organization by Dr. Earl J. McGrath, director of the Higher Education Center at Temple University. The McGrath Report (1973) suggested a number of administrative changes. It began with McGrath's impressions of the college and its administration:

> *Western Maryland College is in many respects an extraordinary institution. It has a long history of distinguished service. . . . It has had*

strong intellectual and spiritual leadership in its board of trustees, its administration, and in its faculty. Today the distinctiveness of Western Maryland College is equally arresting. Even to the outside observer this academic community conveys the impression of educational quality and financial soundness. . . . While hundreds of campuses have been riven by internal turmoil, . . . Western Maryland has dealt with the changing conditions of social life through the traditional procedures of a democratic society. . . . Compared to other colleges of similar size and complexity, this institution has an atypically small staff of administrative officers . . . and the percentage of the total current operating expenses incurred for administrative services is unusually small. President Ensor was obviously a highly competent administrator, but in his later years in office the burden of work exceeded what it was just to expect one person, however dedicated, to bear.[4]

In light of this report and his own experience, President John, with the approval of the trustees, restructured the administration on a corporate model and soon named four vice presidents to manage different areas of the daily operation: Philip Schaeffer '50 [1959–82], business affairs; William McCormick Jr. [1973–83], academic affairs; James F. Ridenour [1973–84], development; and C. Wray Mowbray [1963–82], student affairs.

The board of trustees also experienced considerable change, in personnel and structure. After hearing the McGrath Report, the board voted to restructure itself and to provide for more representation from constituent groups. Life tenure for board members was eliminated in favor of three-year terms with an age limit of 70, faculty visitors would attend board and committee meetings, and committee assignments would gradually be rotated.[5] Most of these were similar to the recommendations made by trustee Robert Faw in 1969, but, perhaps coming from a consultant and in line with the thinking of the new president, they were more easily acceptable. A later proposal by Faw to create alumni trustees, however, failed. But his proposal to allow three student visitors to attend trustee meetings without vote was approved.[6] The first student visitors, the following April, were David A. Reinecker '77, Michael Cunningham '78, and Carol L. James (Avery) '79. In April 1971, the leadership of the board again changed when Joshua Miles stepped down from the chairmanship after three years; his successor was Wilbur Preston, attorney and partner in the law firm Whiteford, Taylor and Preston in Baltimore.

The constituency of the board had an 80% turnover during this decade, brought on in part by the new structure. Trustees taking emeritus status included John A. Trader '20 [1955–71], John N. Link '25 [1929–71],

Portrait of President Lowell Skinner Ensor

E. McClure Rouzer [1952–72], Scott S. Bair [1964–73], Henry L. Darner '16 [1957–73], Robert Gill [1925–73], O. Bryan Langrall '21 [1953–73], D. Carlysle MacLea '22 [1949–75], Hilda Long Adkins '22 [1951–75], William E. Firth [1962–75], Joshua Miles [1959–76], and Austin E. Penn [1961–76]. Death claimed G. Russell Benson [1951–71], J. Earl Cummings '25 [1947–71], Miriam Baynes Matthews '98 [1938–73], John M. Clayton Jr. '21 [1953–73], Dorothy McDaniel Herr [1945–74], and James Straughn '99 [1915–74]. Bishop Straughn, who died at age 97, had worked with five of the six presidents, had been chairman of the board for 20 years [1929–49], was the longest-serving trustee in the history of the college, and was the last surviving clerical leader of the 1939 Methodist Union.

Trustee and President Emeritus Lowell Skinner Ensor (1907–75) [1945–75] continued in failing health because of the lingering blood disease, and on October 9, 1975, at the age of 68, he died at home. A Service of Commemoration was held in Baker Memorial Chapel on Sunday evening, October 12. It began with a procession of the College Choir and robed faculty and included tributes from Dr. William A. Keese for the church, Mr. F. Kale Mathias for the community, and former dean John Makosky for the college. Makosky described Ensor's feeling for the college as always "optimistic." He noted the former president's desire "to be in the center of things, to touch everything that was Western Maryland" and "his dedication to every minutia of college life." He commented on Ensor's responsiveness and approachability, due to his "warm open manner and a sincere desire to help" coupled with a "philosophy of moderation." He praised Ensor's ability to encourage and live with other points of view and his uncompromising protection of academic freedom. Makosky concluded by noting Ensor's total dedication to the college and its students and described him as "an excellent administrator and an excellent man," one who "gave the years of his prime to Western Maryland College."[7] Ensor's pastor, Rev. Julian A. Tavenner, presided at the service; President John, Bishop John Wesley Lord, and trustees Eugene C. Woodward and E. Cranston Riggin also participated. Burial was the next day in Louden Park Cemetery in west Baltimore.

During Lowell Ensor's 25-year presidency, the college had fluctuated in enrollment from 631 in 1952 to over 1,100 in 1972, with bulges due to the GI Bill in the late 1940s. The full-time faculty had increased by 50% from 60 to 90, and their academic credentials were much more impressive. The administrative staff had increased from 20 to 40. The combined tuition, room, and board fees had tripled, from less than $1,000 to over $3,000. Faculty salaries had quadrupled, as had the endowment, to almost $4 million. Nine new buildings, including three dormitories, a classroom and laboratory building, and a large chapel, had been erected, and many others had been remodeled. The campus was markedly different without the Old Main complex crowding the top of the hill and with the addition of the old seminary building and property. Ensor had worked with five board chairs and a large number of trustees, and when he died, he was second only to General Gill in seniority on the board. He had played a significant part in the development and improvement of Western Maryland College for more than 30 years as president and trustee; he had led it through some difficult times, including a major lawsuit, and had successfully guided it to the place of genuine respect it enjoyed in the state and region.

New trustees elected during the decade were W. Edward Cushen '48 [1971–75], Ralph G. Hoffman [1971–81], Arlie R. Mansberger Jr. '44 [1971–2002], Alleck A. Resnick '47 [1972–93], Samuel H. Hoover [1972–80], Richard H. Ellingsworth [1973–84], Bishop James K. Mathews [1973–82], Charles H. Schools [1973–88], Robert E. Bricker '42 [1974–91], Alfred L. Mathias [1974–80], Thaddeus W. Swank [1974–90], William Calormiris [1975–78], Albert C. Hall [1975–85], Richard F. Kline Jr. '57 [1975–90], Robert K. Mathias '48 [1975–95], Jonathan P. Myers '61 [1975–91], Jane Decker Asmis [1976–82], Frank W. Carman [1976–91], David M. Denton [1976–94], William B. Dulany '50 [1976–], Mary Todd Farson (Griffiths) '48 [1976–81], Rebecca Groves Smith '37 [1976–88], Charles H. Dorsey Jr. [1978–84], Charles C. Fenwick Sr. [1978–93], and Eloise Chipman Payne '38 [1978–88].

In April 1980, a class of trustees had to be reconstructed, as all the incumbents had reached the age limit of 70 and retired as emeritus: Wilson K. Barnes '28 [1963–80], Clarence H. Bennett '28 [1967–80], Arthur G. Broll '29 [1965–80], W. Lloyd Fisher [1946–80], Clarence L. Fossett [1960–80], Samuel H. Hoover [1972–80], John B. Jones '41 [1958–80], Alfred L. Mathias [1974–80], Allan W. Mund [1960–80], George A. Meyls Jr. '22 [1958–80], Clementine L. Peterson [1969–80], E. Cranston Riggin [1948–80], Charles A. Stewart '26 [1961–80], and Eugene C. Woodward '28 [1956–80]. As in earlier years, those elected to emeritus status were invited to all board meetings, and many continued to participate on committees; however, they no longer voted on motions during plenary sessions. Fourteen new trustees joined the board: Rodney A. Austin [1980–92], Clarence W. Blount [1980–95], Charles L. Hayes [1980–91], William A. Holmes [1980–85], William S. Keigler [1980–2003], Ann Burnside Love [1980–92], James O. Olfson [1980–95], M. Lee Rice '48 [1980–2006], Frank C. Robey Jr. '57 [1980–95], Robert W. Schaefer [1980–92], Dolores J. Snyder '63M [1980–], Mary Ruth Tereshinski '48 [1980–92], Lloyd B. Thomas [1980–97], and R. Peter Urquhart '57 [1980–85, 1992–94]. Following the removal of the "one more than one-third Methodist ministers" rule in 1968 and the severing of ties with the Methodist Church in 1975, there was only one minister among this new group of trustees. It is also evident that the board was now seeking younger individuals with broader backgrounds and closer ties to the metropolitan business communities.

A category of Honorary Trustee was created in 1974 to recognize individuals with a connection to the college or with whom the college wished to be connected. The first such individuals, elected in 1974, were Fannie Fox Decker, Caroline Wantz Taylor '26, and C. Harry Wahmann. Four years later Thomas Eaton '27, Wilma Johnston, and Victor Weybright were named to this distinction. In 1980 Bertha S. Adkins, Julia T. Burleigh, Clarence M. Mitchell Jr., and John H. Simms joined their ranks.

After acclimating President John to the office, his secretary, Helen Ohler [1925–73], a campus institution, retired in August 1973. Having worked closely with four presidents, one acting president, and six board chairmen, she was leaving the college after almost 50 years. Miss Ohler had been hired to assist A. N. Ward with a financial campaign in 1925, continued as secretary for Fred Holloway and Lowell Ensor, assisted Allan Mund, and finally turned over the office to her successor, Bernice T. Beard '74 [1962–89], two months into the John presidency. Earlier, in September 1971, Byron E. "Barney" Rice [1949–71] retired as director of food services. He delayed his retirement until after the Colts summer training camp, for which he had always handled the meals. He was succeeded by Arlene H. MacDonald, who had been his assistant for several years. In 1973 Director of Publications and Publicity Nancy Winkelman [1958–73] resigned to take a similar position at Goucher College and was replaced by R. Keith Moore [1973–77], who was replaced by Melady Klausmeier [1978–79] and then by Joyce D. Muller [1979–]. In the fall of 1975, H. Kenneth Shook '52 [1959–75] resigned as dean of admissions and financial aid to become director of the Maryland State Scholarship Board. His successor was L. Leslie Bennett [1976–83]. The first director of the physical plant (later administrative assistant for business affairs), Eugene "Stoney" Willis [1964–75], retired in 1975, as did Mary Shoemaker [1962–75], cashier in the Treasurer's Office for 13 years. The Registrar's Office experienced the retirement of another source of campus history and tradition, Cora Virginia Perry, who turned over the duties to her assistant, H. Hugh Dawkins '69, '71M [1970–89] in 1977. Perry had worked in that office since 1938. Her predecessor, Martha Manahan, commented of her friend, "Next to Dean Schofield, Cora Virginia has forgotten more about Western Maryland College than most of us know!"[8] In 1978, another longtime administrator, Philip E. Uhrig [1949–81], soccer coach for 9 years and director of alumni affairs for 29 years, relinquished the Alumni Office to Carol Armacost Preston

(Carter) '69 [1975–80]. Uhrig continued for 2 more years as a part-time associate director of development for planned giving. Perry and Uhrig were both named administrators emeriti. Two new administrators joined the staff during the decade. A new Office of Counseling and Career Services was opened with Jerald T. Wrubel [1974–77] as the first counselor in 1974. Joan M. Avey (Nixon) [1975–80] was named director of college activities in 1975, in preparation for the opening of the new college center.

The faculty continued to change, as older teachers retired and were replaced and new positions were created. Retiring during the decade were 16 individuals who had given years of service (an average of almost 30 years per professor) and were well known to generations of students: Joseph Bailer [1949–71] in education, Louise Shipley [1938–72] in art, Theodore Whitfield [1929–72] in history, James P. Earp [1938–73] in sociology, John Makosky [1935–73] in English, William Ridington [1938–73] in classics (and secretary of the faculty 1947–73), Oliver Spangler [1938–73] in music, Harwell P. Sturdivant [1948–73] in biology, Theron B. Thompson [1961–74] in education, Jacques T. DeRasse [1963–76] in French, Reuben Holthaus [1946–76] in philosophy, Ralph B. Price [1954–77] in economics, Edith Farr Ridington [1957–77] in classics, Charles E. Crain [1949–78] in religion, Isabel Royer [1942–79] in biology, and Jean Kerschner [1952–80] in biology. When the three biology professors (the strong and able "Bio Trio" for over 25 years, with 90 years of combined teaching) had all retired, many of their former students gathered for a special recognition dinner and honors colloquium on May 4, 1980, and established an endowed fund in their honor.[9] Upon John Makosky's retirement, his former English students accumulated funds to purchase books for the library. The college also bade farewell in 1979 to dramatic art professor William Tribby [1958–61, 1963–79], who resigned to become director (later dean) of general studies at the North Carolina School of the Arts in Winston-Salem.

The college community was saddened by the death of professor of chemistry J. Lloyd Straughn [1942–53, 1959–74] on March 5, 1974, at age 63 due to leukemia. It was also shocked by the suicide of Robert W. Lawler [1968–77], assistant professor of English, on May 1, 1977, at age 39. During the decade

"Bio Trio" I. Royer, H. Sturdivant, J. Kerschner

eight retired professors or administrators passed away: Hugh Elderdice Jr. [1929–61], assistant professor of chemistry emeritus, in October 1971; Joseph Bailer [1949–71], professor of education emeritus, in January 1974; Carl Schaeffer [1919–59], treasurer emeritus, in November 1974; Minnie M. Ward [1924–61], librarian emerita, in September 1975; Helen E. Gray [1938–64], associate professor of home economics emerita, in March 1976; Olive Ruth Russell [1949–62], professor of psychology emerita, in May 1979; Theron Thompson [1961–74], associate professor of education emeritus, in June 1979; and Sara E. Smith [1926–67], professor of education emerita, in March 1980. The 1974 Alumna of the Year, Dorothy Elderdice '11, well-known dramatist, costumer, teacher, and early suffragist and feminist, died on October 1, 1979. (Elderdice Hall had been named for her father, and the Elderdice Understage Theater in Alumni Hall would be named in her memory in July 1984.)

Joining the faculty during the decade and remaining for a significant period of time were George T. Bachmann Jr. [1970–93], librarian; Robert P. Boner [1970–2007], mathematics; Stephen W. Colyer [1970–99], psychology; Eleanor N. Richwine [1970–93], librarian; Samuel L. "Tim" Weinfeld [1970–96], dramatic art; F. Glendon Ashburn '53 [1971–95], sociology; Howard B. Orenstein [1971–2002], psychology; Harry L. Rosenzweig [1971–], mathematics; Robert W. Sapora [1971–2005], English; Richard H. Smith Jr. [1971–], chemistry; Ralph B. Levering [1972–81], history; Carol J. Quinn [1972–98], librarian; Daniel A. Williams [1972–2003], Spanish; Joan D. Coley [1973–], education; Theodore Evergates [1973–], history; Wilbur L. Long [1973–], biology; Donald R. Rabush '62, '70M [1973–95], education; Herbert C. Smith [1973–], political science; Charles Chapman Hermann Jr. [1974–94], sociology; Hugh T. Prickett Jr. [1974–93], education; Daniel K. Rees [1975–], sociology and social work; Francis M. "Skip" Fennell [1976–], education; Lawrence C. Wu [1976–2003], philosophy; Margaret W. Denman (West) [1977–96], education; Kathy S. Mangan [1977–], English; Julie O. Badiee [1978–2001], art history; Jack E. Clark [1978–2005], mathematics; Charles E. Neal [1978–], political science; Thomas G. Deveny [1978–], Spanish; and Esther M. Iglich [1979–], biology. These 30 faculty members have an average tenure of 28 years, but almost 60 faculty were hired during the decade; some stayed for only a short time for various reasons. However, the turnover was far less dramatic than in the previous decade because the job market was tighter, and there were fewer positions available nationwide. One example will suffice. In 1969 the number of applications for an open position in one of the departments was about 10; the following year, as the country suffered an economic downturn, 150 applications were received for a new position in the same department, and the top choice was hired.

Members of the faculty continued to bring honor to themselves and to the college. Earl Griswold was becoming known for his filmmaking; he produced two anthropological documentary films, *Tepotzlan* and *Tepotzlan in Transition* after visits to the remote Mexican town. In the summer of 1971 he produced a film on the life of Francis Asbury, Methodist missionary in the United States, for Asbury College in Kentucky. He cast a number of his colleagues, as well as some students, in various roles. William Tribby played the title role, and professors Case, Clower, Dixon, D. Jones, Lightner, Palmer, Panek, Weber, Weinfeld, and Zepp and President Ensor were seen bewigged and costumed by Dorothy Elderdice in this production filmed in the actual locations of Asbury's travels and preaching.[10] Griswold also produced films for several Maryland counties including Carroll, as well as *Africa 101*, which documented the January-term safari study tours he led four times during the decade. McCay Vernon was appointed national chair of the Psychology Commission of the World Congress of the Deaf in 1971. In 1972 he received the Distinguished Service Award of the National Association of the Deaf, and in 1975 he received an honorary LittD from Gallaudet College, both for outstanding service to deaf people.[11] William David received a Fulbright grant for a year's teaching and study in India in 1971–72. Samuel Case was elected to the American College of Sports Medicine in 1972. Ira Zepp was listed in the first edition of *Who's Who in Religion.* James Lightner was elected national president of Kappa Mu Epsilon, undergraduate mathematics honor society, in 1977; he had previously served as vice president for four years. Richard Clower was elected president of the United States Intercollegiate Lacrosse Association in 1979. Hugh Prickett was named to the college's first fully funded faculty chair, the Joseph D. Baker Inc. Chair in Deafness, in 1979.[12] It should also be noted that by the end of the decade, 70% of the faculty held a doctorate or other terminal degree, with six individuals close to completing dissertations. During this period, the rules for tenure and promotion were tightened considerably, and that encouraged faster completion of advanced degrees.

A chapter of Sigma Xi, a national scientific society, was established on campus in September 1970, its membership composed of old and new faculty from the biology, chemistry, physics, mathematics, and psychology departments.

As a result of the work of an Ad Hoc Committee on Committees (1971), a new governance system was approved by the faculty in 1972,[13] reducing the number of faculty committees while giving the faculty more involvement in governing the college. The Faculty Affairs Committee assumed some of the role of the former Administrative Advisory Council, and a new All-College Council consisting of six students, three faculty, and three administrators was established in 1974 to replace the former Student Life Council and bring all aspects of the college community together to discuss issues of mutual concern. However, this innovation proved to be redundant and was abolished a year later. A Faculty Council was established to represent the faculty and advise the administration on issues of concern to faculty. All members of these committees were to be elected by their respective constituencies.[14]

CURRICULUM

During his long tenure, Dean Makosky was often asked by student interviewers to describe how the college was different from the school he knew as a student or young professor. In one of his last interviews before he retired, he was asked what he felt was the biggest change in the college, and he replied that there had been a great academic improvement in the students. "It's not that today's good students are better than previous students, but the spectrum is narrower between the abilities of selected students. . . . Kids are much more aware of the necessity of a goal; the preparation is more specific."[15] At the beginning of the decade about 60% of the 1,000–1,100 applicants were accepted, and about 60% of those attended, creating entering classes of about 350.[16] By mid-decade, the college was bulging (in 1974 students were temporarily housed at Lee's Motel, in the infirmary, and in various college houses), and admissions standards were still high, with 80% of enrollees in the top 20% of their high school class.[17] In 1976 the profile had changed slightly, with about 90% of 1,000 applicants admitted and half of those enrolling; about 55% stood in the top 20% of their class. The verbal SAT median score was 504, while the median math score was 541. (The national averages were 445 verbal and 475 mathematics.) By 1979, the number of applications had risen to about 1,100 again, with 80% approved and half of those enrolled; 50% stood in the top 20% of their class, and SAT median scores had dropped slightly, to 498 verbal and 527 math. (The College Board reported that SAT scores had steadily declined between 1963 and 1977.) Toward the end of the decade, President John noted that the admissions process had become a "buyer's market" and the normal application flow was slowing. Demographic statistics also showed that in the next seven years there would be a 30% decrease in the college-age population.[18] The classes were still strong academically, but their profiles were not as impressive as during the mid-1960s, and the range of abilities had broadened.

As the college entered the decade, there was a groundswell of support for curricular revision. Innovations and experiments had been introduced with some hesitation, and most seemed to be successful. During the decade many would be permanently incorporated into the curriculum, other additions and revisions would take place, and a fresh look at the liberal arts requirements, stimulated by the Long Range Plan of 1972, would lead to further changes. The Long Range Plan included one statistic that pleased everyone and reflected well on past performance. The college produced the highest rate of doctorates per 1,000 male students, 15.794, of the 15 Maryland colleges and stood fifth highest, behind Swarthmore, Carleton, Oberlin, and Reed, in colleges of comparable size. Obviously, male students had been prepared well for graduate and professional schools; no data were available for women graduates.[19] Lest these data encourage complacency, the 1973 evaluation team from the Middle States Association of Colleges and Universities, which based its analysis of the college on the Long Range Plan, noted the excellent program but cautioned, "Build on your strengths, but don't rely on them."[20]

By 1975, the faculty had approved a number of changes in basic liberal arts requirements, creating five "distribution" groups covering the various areas, with 33 hours required overall. They also provided for students to "test out" via proficiency tests in English composition, foreign language, and physical education activity (or to take necessary courses for 0–12 hours credit). A 3-hour freshman seminar, Introduction to the Liberal Arts,[21] was established, and students were required to successfully complete two January terms.

The January term continued to provide versatility in the course offerings by providing special opportunities for experiences, travel, and in-depth study. By 1972 it had become an established part of the college program and calendar (which for a while used a 12-4-14-week pattern, with classes lengthened from 50 minutes to a full hour during the fall term). In 1973, for example, students remaining on campus took such courses as Classical Art and Archaeology, The Western in Story and Film, Children's Literature, The Works of William Faulkner, English Usage, History and Philosophy of Science. Environmental Chemistry, The Imperial Age of Venice, The American Involvement in Viet Nam, The Historical Novel, Photography, Intuitive Topology, Music Literature for the Recorder, Asian Studies Seminar, Classical Indian Literature, Outdoor Education, The Meaning of Death, and Social Welfare Agencies. They also had the opportunity to enroll in study tours to Mexico, the British Isles, France, Germany, western Europe, East Africa, and the Soviet Union. And they could intern in schools for the deaf, elementary school physical education, clinical psychology, and practical politics. Fourteen students interned in federal, state, and local governmental offices, including those in Annapolis during the legislative session. Five young men traveled across the continental United States, keeping journals of their experiences and conversations with other

Americans. Two other men studied winter camping and survival techniques by building a shelter and camping out for three weeks. Others interned and volunteered in science facilities to see firsthand the workings of those institutions and become immersed in potential vocational choices.[22] Almost 85% of the student body enrolled in the January term each year. It also provided an opportunity for faculty to try out new course ideas with an eye to incorporating them into the regular curriculum.

Three new majors were introduced in 1973. Comparative Literature and Classical Civilizations were created as alternatives to the traditional classics program, which was discontinued with the retirement of the Ridingtons. A program in criminal justice was also incorporated within sociology. The program in social work, directed by Mary Ellen Elwell, achieved accreditation by the Council of Social Work Education in 1972 (with reaccreditation in 1975 and 1978). In 1975, the chemistry program received official accreditation by the American Chemical Society. The Economics Department expanded its offerings and became the Department of Economics and Business Administration.[23] Three years later a Junior Achievement program was begun in which business majors served as advisors to companies formed by students in the several county high schools, an opportunity for the college students to put their theoretical knowledge into practice. Soon two new joint majors—economics and business administration, and psychology and biology—were approved, and the offerings in social work were expanded.[24] Another option was the self-designed major, for which a student, with an advisor, mapped out a major combining several disciplines, with approval by the Undergraduate Academic Policy and Curriculum Committee.[25] One of the more far-reaching additions to the curriculum was a program in elementary education, mirroring the long-standing minor in secondary education. For several years the college had negotiated with Hood College to train WMC students desiring to be elementary teachers, but in December 1975, the faculty voted to dissolve that relationship and provide its own program; Francis Fennell was hired in 1976 to organize the courses. The program became one of the strongest in Maryland, especially since it required an academic major in addition to the elementary education minor.[26]

In an effort to develop better teachers with a broader understanding of the ways students learn, the Education Department altered the traditional approach to student teaching in 1972. The old supervising teacher–student teacher model was replaced by a program that established two local public schools, Westminster East Middle School and Westminster High School, as student teaching centers. Senior education students spent their whole semester in one of those schools, working with the entire school faculty, observing and teaching in a variety of classes, and learning how the school operated. The education courses, particularly the subject-matter methods courses that were normally a part of the semester-long program, were taught on site in a center by the college faculty. As many as 25 students were assigned to a center, which had an education faculty member as coordinator. The new procedure gave the prospective teachers a more continuous period of professional laboratory experiences and more experience working directly with students. They also gained a broader understanding of the services and resources of the school system.[27]

Graduates of the college with a minor in education (and certified to teach) were always sought after in the Maryland school systems because of their sound preparation. This reception may also have been due to the fact that the superintendents of six Maryland counties were graduates of the program themselves: Homer O. Elseroad '40, Montgomery County; Charles W. Willis '30, Harford County; Jesse L. Starkey '48, Charles County; John L. Carnochan '40, '47M, Frederick County; Joseph L. Shilling '60, '65M, Dorchester County; and Richard L. Holler '58M, Kent County. In addition, Frederick J. Brown Jr. '47, '51M was associate state superintendent of schools, and Quentin L. Earhart '40, '50M was deputy state superintendent.[28]

After much discussion about the pressure of senior comprehensive examinations, as well as their long-term value and usefulness, the faculty voted in 1974 to eliminate them. In one form or another (Graduate Record Examination, Undergraduate Record Examination, or departmental examinations), all seniors had been required to pass this culminating activity since 1952. The vote was evenly divided, with the president casting the deciding vote in favor of abolition.[29] The faculty also eliminated the bachelor of science degree in 1975, so that all undergraduates received the bachelor of arts beginning in 1976. A change affecting all students was the move to a 4.0 system for grading, to be in concert with most other institutions, replacing the 3.0 system, which had been in use for decades.[30] By 1973, enrollment in ROTC was no longer limited to males. In that fall, five young women enrolled in the program, and there have been women cadets and commissioned officers ever since. During 1979–80 the college noted with pride the 60 years of ROTC on campus; WMC's program was one of the first to be formed on a college campus in the United States (1919).

The honor system received regular reviews of its philosophy and procedures as each generation of students interpreted it slightly differently and needed to be oriented to its value to them and to the college. Periodically, the regulations and procedures were adjusted to strengthen the way the system was implemented by faculty and students. Related to this was the introduction of self-scheduled examinations in May 1974. If a faculty member elected to employ this format, students could pick up an examination for the course at a central location, take it to some quiet location to complete, and return it for forwarding to the instructor. This put pressure on the students to operate within the Honor Code, but it also meant that the professor had to wait for the students to turn in their exams before he or she could determine class grades.[31] The procedure worked reasonably well for a few years, but it was ultimately abandoned because of procedural difficulties.

After 35 or so years of offering only the master of education graduate degree, the college petitioned the state and was granted approval to offer the master of liberal arts degree in 1976. The degree was designed to meet the needs of those graduate students who preferred a broader-based, cultural graduate experience. The degree required 30 credit hours of courses, including 12 in the area of "cultural heritage," 6 in "contemporary society," 3 in the "creative process," and 9 elective hours. An area of "humanities" was added a few years later. The program attracted a significant number of students and remains viable.

During 1978–79, the college concentrated on the humanities, and a sequence of two courses was especially designed for graduate credit to provide a broad humanities perspective to modern education through discussions and presentations. The courses met all day on alternate Saturdays throughout the year. A third course with the same theme was planned for the following summer session.

Richard M. Barnes '77 receives award from
President Gerald R. Ford in 1976.

Two more national honor societies came to the campus when a chapter of Psi Chi, psychology honor society, was formed in 1975, and Lambda Iota Tau, literary honor society, chartered a chapter in 1976. The most significant recognition of the college's increasingly high standards and reputation within the higher education community was the chartering of the Delta of Maryland Chapter of Phi Beta Kappa, the oldest and most prestigious of all the national honor societies, on May 1, 1980. With its formation, the Argonauts, the local honor society formed in 1935, became redundant and was disbanded.

In 1976 political science major Richard M. Barnes '77 was invited to the White House, along with his family and President and Mrs. John, to receive an award from President Gerald Ford because of his prize-winning essay on the political theory of John C. Calhoun, in a contest sponsored by the Military Order of the Loyal Legion. In 1979, German major Kathy Zepp '79 received a Fulbright fellowship for study in Zurich.

STUDENT LIFE

If the students of the late 1960s were activists for social change, the students who followed in the 1970s (at least some of them) were antagonists, constantly looking for issues on which to take stands (without debate) and to make demands. The curfew–open house issue bubbled over into the early 1970s, even as gradual changes had come about. When President John took office in 1972, he quickly abolished all curfews for women, and three years later, the dormitories were open for 24-hour visitation, not without some difficulties. Unlike President Ensor, who had started the discussion with the trustees in 1971, John was also able to convince the board in 1972 to allow the presence of alcohol on campus under strict guidelines requiring conformity to Maryland state law.[32] (In 1976, the state lowered the minimum drinking age to 18, making almost every student on campus eligible to drink beer and wine.) An intercampus telephone system had been installed in 1970, the much-needed career counseling office had been established in 1974, a women's clinic was available in the infirmary by 1975, and young houseparents (replacing older housemothers) were in place in all residence halls and complexes. Given that those issues had been resolved, the activist students looked elsewhere (while regularly complaining about the more apathetic student majority). As is probably typical of teenagers (but perhaps more so at this time), they were not very tactful, they wanted immediate results, and they wouldn't take no for an answer. During the decade they editorialized in the campus paper and petitioned for coeducational dormitories, changes in fraternity Hell Week, more adequate campus security, more convenient parking on campus, more social life on campus, more grade discrimination using pluses and minuses, and a grade review board to appeal student grades. They were against the administrative decision not to renew the contract of a young, conservative political science teacher (Terry Smith),[33] the drug "busts" occasionally orchestrated by the local police, the introduction of no-need or merit scholarships,[34] upward adjustment of requirements for graduation honors because of grade inflation,[35] the existing library hours, and the discipline procedures and methods employed by Associate Dean of Students Elizabeth Laidlaw.

One burning issue, which occupied several SGA meetings and much ink in 1976, was the placement of the newly planned student center connected to Elderdice Hall. The crowding of the center of the campus and the loss of trees (added to the fact that the complaining students had not been asked their opinion, although there had been input from student board visitors) were the main points of contention. Ironically, two years later, when the Decker College Center opened, newspaper editorials praised the placement because it was in the center of the campus and accessible to everyone. Presaging events 30 years later, in 1973 student editors took issue with the college's name, suggesting that it be changed so that "outsiders will finally know where the college is" and not think it is in Garrett County.[36] All of these causes célèbres were dealt with by the college administration, sometimes to the students' satisfaction but not always, and not without constant tension, heated discussions, and sometimes personal attacks. The average student was generally not involved in these "problems," so it was increasingly difficult to get students to sit on campus committees after their involvement was approved in 1974. Some were quite happy to attend parties, complain there was nothing to do on campus, wage water battles, and set fires in the men's quadrangle.

By 1975 there were 26 black students enrolled, and a Black Student Union was two years old. Black Weekend in 1974 focused on cultural pride. The Commodores, a well-known black R&B group, appeared on campus at the 1975 Homecoming. In October 1976, an "Evening in Black America" featured an appearance by Ossie Davis and Ruby Dee. During 1975–76, Herbert Watson '76, a black student, was elected president of the Student Government. The January term had often provided offerings in black literature, African-American history, and black and white relations. Even with more effort by the college to attract qualified minority applicants, black students continued to express their frustration at the lack of diversity in the student body and the faculty. They also were understandably upset by the occasional offensive graffiti scrawled on doors by a few of their fellow students.

Reacting to these pressures (as well as some ongoing faculty concerns),

President John admitted that more could have been done in the past to improve the diversity of races on campus; in 1977 he issued a "Statement and Plan for Minority Affairs,"[37] in which he proposed hiring a graduate assistant to work with minority students within the Student Affairs Office. He also indicated that the college would intensify efforts to recruit minority students, faculty, and staff. He recommended to the faculty that minority and black cultural issues be included in appropriate courses. Barbara Craig, a new staff member in Admissions, hired in 1976, and Henry Miller, the new assistant registrar hired a year later, were African American. However, the Black Student Union, led by Linda Thomas '78, reacted by saying this was not enough[38] and demanding that a full-time director of minority affairs be appointed and several minority faculty be hired immediately. In the fall the group charged the college with racism, calling it "an academic plantation,"[39] and filed a complaint with the NAACP. The BSU chose not to attend a workshop on minorities and women slated for a weekend in September 1977, feeling that the college's actions in not acceding to the BSU's demands had shown disrespect to the black students. In response to the escalating rhetoric, the college issued a long statement outlining past "positive steps toward racial diversification" and future plans to improve minority student recruitment and enrollment to 10% by 1982 and to hire black faculty as soon as possible.[40] After a positive meeting between the NAACP and the president and deans, the issue eventually died down as the

Diversity on campus had increased by 1975.

college proceeded with its plans (given budgetary constraints); an affirmative action program was put in place;[41] and an African American faculty member, Charles Neal, was hired in the Political Science Department (in 1978). The chairman of that department, William David, one of several faculty who had long felt that the college needed to move forward in race relations (and who had headed the Carroll County Human Relations Committee in the 1960s), commented during this difficult time, "[The black students] are not off base, they just have no perspective. . . . I don't think our record is that bad. I think a lot of the reason for this pressure is to tell us to keep it up. . . . We should all work harmoniously on this. . . . Conflict will only polarize us."[42] Further efforts continued on various fronts, including minority scholarships, and by the end of the decade the number of black enrollees had increased.

Interest in Greek organizations remained fairly constant during this decade, with an average membership per group of 47. In the fall of 1970 Iota Gamma Chi disbanded for lack of viable membership,[43] leaving three sororities that varied in average numbers from 40 (Sigma Sigma Tau) to 53 (Phi Alpha Mu). The four fraternities usually had membership numbers in the 50s, the smallest being Delta Pi Alpha, which averaged 33. In 1970 Pi Alpha Alpha became a colony of the first national fraternity on campus, Phi Delta Theta, which was formally chartered as the Maryland Beta chapter in April 1971. While college enrollment rose by about 23% over the decade, Greek involvement remained constant in numbers, averaging 335, and thus participation dropped from 34% to about 25%. In the fall of 1979, a new local sorority, Alpha Nu Omega, emerged on the scene with 24 charter members. The nature and style of initiations remained a perennial topic of concern, and related editorials, letters to the editor, and discussions in faculty meetings were fairly regular occurrences. The traditional activities continued, although there seemed to be a decline in the focus on humiliation. Later in the decade, however, the Preachers were sanctioned for some messy antics regarding animal parts. A survey of fraternity members conducted by the college newspaper soon thereafter, however, revealed that none of the fraternities was guilty of any hazing whatsoever!

Early in 1970 the Student Government's Cafeteria Committee made proposals for change: unlimited seconds of entrées, longer dinner hours, more balanced (i.e., less starchy) menus, a salad bar, and a sandwich bar. They noted, "The Army eats better than WMC students!"[44] A year later, when Mr. Rice retired and Mrs. MacDonald succeeded him, the students welcomed the change. A few years later, however, a petition was circulated, complaining about cold food, lack of balance in menus, greasy food, and discourteous servers; and some adjustments were made.[45] One alumna of 1974 remembered that there was little choice in the menu for a given meal: one entrée, several vegetable options, and a dessert. But, she said, "It was good, it was hot, and there was plenty of it." She recalled some innovations in food selection, including a salad bar, special "steak nights," and all-you-can-eat ice cream (where peanut butter ripple was the favorite flavor). Traditional fare continued with creamed chipped beef on toast for breakfast, homemade pies, and fried chicken and mashed potatoes for Sunday dinner. She also remembered that if you didn't like the dining hall food, you could head downtown to Harry's for a "loaded" hotdog or to Angelo's for great Italian food. To stave off the hunger pangs later in the evening, some enterprising gentlemen delivered hot steak submarine sandwiches to the dormitories about 10 P.M.[46] In March 1980, a food strike was called by the SGA Action Committee, but there is no mention of it in the following week's newspaper.

In response to the informality of the dining room, a special Wine and Dine etiquette program was begun during the 1974 January term and continued for several years.[47] Designed by Dean Laidlaw, Mrs. MacDonald, and Dr. Lightner, the program educated students in the finer points of dining etiquette during a predinner session, before they attended a "formal" (dress-up) reception and dinner in the president's dining room, where faculty couples served as table hosts and hostesses. The program was quite popular and continued for several months each year. A Second Spring program was sponsored by College Activities for the first time in 1976 and featured noncredit short courses taught by students and faculty. By 1972, the traditional May Day celebration had evolved into Spring Carnival, which was an outgrowth of the freshman interdisciplinary studies course, Man as Player, taught by William Tribby and Melvin Palmer; the class and the SGA cooperated in planning a variety of activities to interest people of all ages. Booths featured games (including a kissing booth) and sold all types of foods, and there were pony rides for children. The College Band gave a concert, acting classes offered poetry readings and presentations, and short films were shown throughout the day. The day concluded with a concert by several bands.[48]

Musical activities were a significant part of each college year. A Women's Glee Club was re-formed in 1971 under the direction of Evelyn Hering. The College Choir, now a concert group rather than a weekly chapel choir, performed several concerts each year. The group, under the direction of Oliver Spangler, occasionally sang off campus, twice at Temple Oheb Shalom in Pikesville in 1972 and 1973, performing the Hebrew music of the evening service, and in 1974 presenting a concert of sacred and contemporary music following the Friday evening service. When Spangler gave up the choir in 1976 (he had directed for eight years including three after he formally retired), Evelyn Hering took over for a year before Brent Hylton [1977–81] was hired. During his four years the choir was reduced in size and sang at various college

The College Choir, directed by Oliver Spangler,
presents a concert in the early 1970s.

functions. It also toured a number of southern cities during the spring break of 1979 and northern cities in February 1980. A Medieval Pageant, a liturgical drama with music by the choir, was produced on the steps of Baker Memorial Chapel at Easter 1974. A jazz band was also formed by interested students in 1972 and occasionally gave concerts on campus.

Publications continued to attract some students, although the decade saw significant problems in staffing the newspaper and yearbook. Indeed, by the fall of 1974, so few students were willing to volunteer to write for the *Gold Bug* that its editor, Cynthia O'Neal (Keefer) '76, was forced to disband the paper after the October 10 issue due to apathy. The paper was resurrected by other students, who redesigned it to provide more commentary (personal essays by students on all sorts of issues and topics) and to make it a weekly, more timely, publication. They renamed it *Scrimshaw*, and its first issue was February 12, 1975. The yearbook also experienced occasional difficulty getting staff. In the spirit of "change for the sake of change" abounding on college campuses everywhere, the name of the yearbook, which had been *Aloha* since its inception in 1893, was reinvented each year, beginning in 1970 with *Soft Fire and Eggshells.* Then it became *Traces; Mnemonic* (several times); *Crossroads; Landslide; Mortar, Stones and Memories*; and *Passages.* Other college traditions, including Lantern Chain and Rose Cup, also disappeared early in the 1970s.

The campus community was shocked and saddened by the deaths of two students in the fall of 1978. Patti Ann Stoner '80 was killed during a voluntary ROTC training activity in Bloomery, West Virginia, when she fell during a "slide for life" rope exercise.[49] A month later, James Herndon '81 died in his room in Rouzer Hall of an apparent heart attack.

During the decade an impressive list of speakers sponsored by various departments and campus organizations appeared on campus, usually to large and appreciative audiences: Alex Haley, P. Lal, Gloria Steinem, Philip Berrigan, Irving R. Levine, William Sloane Coffin, Kate Millett, Senator Joseph Tydings, Victor Weybright, Davíd Carrasco '67, William Kunstler, Benjamin Quarles, Willard Wirtz, Elizabeth Kübler-Ross, George Plimpton, Joni Eareckson, Carl Rowan, and Hans Morgenthau. Musical groups and personalities appearing on campus included Sha Na Na, the Commodores, Melba Moore, the Paul Winter Consort, and Tom Chapin.

Plays produced during the decade, under the direction of dramatic arts faculty or students, included *He Who Gets Slapped*; *Under Milkwood*; *Man of La Mancha*; *Twelfth Night*; *Blithe Spirit*; *Camino Real*; *Curse You, Jack Dalton*; *Cabaret*; *U.S.A.*; *West Side Story*; *And Miss Reardon Drinks a Little*; *Fiddler on the Roof*; *Bus Stop*; *The Imaginary Invalid*; *A Streetcar Named Desire*; *The House of Blue Leaves*; and *Dracula*. Once the Alumni Hall makeover was completed (see "Buildings and Grounds") and the building rededicated, the first play presented on the new stage was an old and famous one that had been presented several times before (and disallowed in 1888). The 19th-century melodrama *Ten Nights in a Bar Room* seemed to fit the old late-Victorian edifice while employing many of the new stage devices and lighting of the modern renovation. Off-campus companies also were invited to present productions of plays and operas, including *Oedipus Rex* and *La Boheme*. The junior class continued to produce the annual follies, still sometimes spoofing the campus with such titles as "Major Bones," "The Folly of Wmcical Isle," "One Pure Kiss," "No, No, Nanook," "Nothing's Funny Anymore," and "Don't Touch That Dial!" Gradually, the spoofs of personalities were downplayed, and different forms of entertainment were presented.

A student of the era, Dorothy Hitchcock (Keene) '74, remembered the life and times:

We came to campus in the early 1970s with fairly conservative wardrobes. Many girls wore skirts (of varying lengths . . .) and blouses or sweaters, while boys wore decent slacks and button down oxford cloth shirts. Over the years that changed substantially, as blue jeans became the newest fashion statement. . . . [Our rooms] had no air conditioning, phones were one per floor down the hall, and the rooms were not wired for computers or a lot of electronic devices. . . . Only a few of us had a [black and white] television set . . . our favorite show: MASH. And some of us had 8-track stereo systems and phonograph turntables. . . . The dorms were where we spent a lot of time and forged some special friendships. Our generation was used to having roommates, as we usually had a sibling or two and knew how to share space. . . . Boys and girls were allowed to visit each other in the dormitories; it was a thrill to be able to call out "man in the hall" and proudly announce that you had company. . . . Sports seemed to highlight the seasons on campus. As we flocked to football games, we admired the gorgeous fall foliage and crisp air. We enjoyed a real marching band at halftime, complete with baton twirlers and pom pon girls in addition to the cheerleaders (Rah rah ree, kick 'em in the knee; Rah rah rass, kick 'em in the other knee!). Lacrosse and field hockey had their own following and team spirit. Winter brought us skipping through the snow to Gill Gym to watch basketball (both girls and boys) and wrestling. Many of us did not play varsity sports but became stars of the intramurals games, most notably the 1973 standout volleyball team called Whiteford's Wild Women! And let us not forget sledding down the hills of the golf course (sometimes on "borrowed" cafeteria trays). . . . The college provided a safe and beautiful environment in which to learn, . . . challenging us to question and think on our own while building a sense of community spirit. . . . A person couldn't ask for a better experience. . . . [The college] did indeed change our lives.[50]

In 1972, the federally mandated Title IX amendment to the Civil Rights Act of 1964 was enacted to erase sex discrimination in educational institutions. Colleges across the country responded in various ways, especially as it affected their athletic programs. All college organizations were subject to the rules, as well, so Omicron Delta Kappa and the Trumpeters, previously single-sex honor societies, became coed in 1975. Given their similar nature and criteria for membership, the local society appeared to be redundant, but because of its history, it was retained and the groups' memberships each year had a large intersection of the same student leaders. One casualty of the ruling was Delta Omicron, the music honor society for women. Because of the rules governing the national organization, the local chapter could not induct men and so was forced to disband, having lost its college affiliation.

Not unexpectedly, with the advent of Title IX, women's sports at the college came into their own. A committee, chaired by Joan Coley, was formed in 1976 to investigate the college's compliance with the rules, and its report revealed some inequities between the men's and women's athletic programs. There were budgetary discrepancies, not always unavoidable; playing and dressing facilities were more of an issue, especially use of the gymnasium and training room. These were corrected by the director of athletics, Richard Clower, and efforts were made to expand the coaching staff and publicity for women's sports. By 1980, Coach Carol Fritz could state that Title IX had been an important breakthrough for women and women's sports. But, she said, "Time is needed for attitudes caused by fear and misunderstanding to disappear."[51]

As usual, intramurals drew lots of students to the playing fields and courts during the school year. In 1974, 55% of the student body participated in some way. The college, of course, also fielded intercollegiate sports teams. In men's sports, the football team completed five winning and five losing seasons during the decade. In 1977, Ronald Jones [1962–81] resigned as head coach after 12 years, to remain on the athletic staff and physical education faculty for 4 more years. He was replaced by James Hindman [1977–81], who named the 1976 team captain, David Dolch '77, as his assistant. Following both the 1978 and 1979 seasons, Ricci Bonaccorsy '80 was named to the NCAA Division III and Eastman Kodak Small College All-America first teams. The soccer team, celebrating 50 years at the college in 1976, unfortunately had a lackluster record of three winning and seven losing seasons. Following the 1978 season, Homer Earll [1964–78] retired after 15 years coaching soccer, to be replaced by his former player Steven Easterday '72 [1978–83]. The wrestling team turned in a four–six record for the decade, while the basketball and baseball teams both finished with three winning seasons and seven losing ones. Retiring as baseball coach because of heart problems in 1978 was Fern Hitchcock '47 [1962–84] after 15 seasons with a 161–110–3 record. He was replaced by his former player Peter Clark '77. Alex Ober '63, '69M [1969–] took over the basketball team in 1972. The cross-country and track teams turned in better, more winning records in this decade, as did the tennis and golf teams. The lacrosse team showed good progress, completing the decade with seven winning seasons, including the Middle Atlantic Conference championship in 1978. They were helped to their successes by the appointment of a new coach in 1976, William F. Thomas '39 [1976–81].

As women's sports grew and expanded, so did their successes. All the teams finished the decade with more winning seasons than losing. Basketball, field hockey, and tennis all attracted women with good skills. Volleyball made significant advances, and the team was regularly invited to regional tournaments, setting the stage for national exposure in the next decade. During the 1979 season, volleyball chalked up 36 wins against such schools as Princeton,

Coach Carol Fritz describes a basketball play to her team, which included Becky Martin '80, her successor.

The Sports Hall of Fame first class, in 1978; inductees and their representatives (L to R):
C. Havens, Mrs. Harlow, B. Shepherd, Mrs. Shepherd, C. Engle, Mrs. Twigg,
S. Fowble, P. Brannen (for C. Ortenzi), H. Kopp, R. Brannen, A. Sadusky

Yale, Navy, Hofstra, Catholic, and Syracuse and retained the Middle Atlantic Conference title for the fourth straight year, giving Coach Fritz a formidable record of 159 wins and 33 losses. A coed swimming team was building during this decade, although it won only two meets out of nine. While some would not consider it sport, a chess team was successfully fielded in 1974, and a number of young males obtained exercise by "streaking" the campus, outside (usually in cold weather!) and inside (running through the dining hall). The latter continued for several years; groups of fraternity pledges also were known to participate in a "nude run" past the women's residence halls during Hell Week.

The following athletes were named All-America for their individual records during the decade: Ronald F. Athey '72, lacrosse, 1972; Ricci G. Bonaccorsy '80, football, 1978, 1979; Knut Hjeltnes '77, track and field, 1973; Steve R. Wilson '75, track and field, 1974.

On October 6, 1978, the charter class of 11 distinguished former college athletes were inducted into the college's new Sports Hall of Fame. In this first class were Carl "Molly" Twigg '11, Charles A. "Rip" Engle '30, Carlo J. Ortenzi '48, Robert J. Gill '10, Charles W. Havens '30, Harold W. Kopp '33, William Shepherd x'35, Sterling "Sheriff" Fowble '36, George L. Ekaitis '31, Alfred H. Sadusky '34, and Richard C. Harlow, coach. Five were able to attend, and five were deceased. Each year since that time, five or six alumni athletes have been inducted; their pictures and sports biographies are mounted in the foyer of the Gill Center.[52]

BUILDINGS AND GROUNDS

Not really a part of the campus, the large, blue-green, 500,000-gallon water tower, erected in 1970 by the City of Westminster on an easement of college property behind Gill Gymnasium, certainly became a landmark. It was also a much-needed facility for the city and for the college, since it improved water pressure immeasurably for all living nearby. A perhaps apocryphal story is told that, prior to the building of the water tower, during the frequent major water battles held in the men's quadrangle, the water pressure in the nearby Pennsylvania Avenue homes would plummet to a trickle!

At his first meeting with the trustee Executive Committee, President John made two significant proposals. One was that a study of facilities be conducted; this was authorized and prepared by Christie, Niles and Andrews during the next six months.[53] The second was to create more student housing, so the college could accommodate 1,250 residents. His proposal was that garden apartments be constructed on Pennsylvania Avenue on the lower portion of the old seminary property. By the following fall, the planning had been done for three four-story buildings, each holding eight four-person apartments, for a total of 96 beds. The apartments cost about $625,000 to build and were ready for occupancy by upperclassmen the following fall (1974).

In 1975, the library was named the Samuel and Elsie Hoover Library in recognition of the Hoovers' continued and extensive support of the college.[54] The building was formally renamed in ceremonies following the April 18 board meeting with Dr. and Mrs. Hoover in attendance. On the same occasion, the Ensor Plaza in front of Baker Memorial Chapel, whose landscaping was partly funded by the faculty retirement gift to Dr. and Mrs. Ensor, was also dedicated. Dr. Ensor was able to attend but died six months later.

To provide more vehicular access to the new garden apartments and to create more parking, a new road was authorized and built in 1976 behind Levine Hall, the Fine Art Building, Blanche Ward Hall, and Whiteford Hall, extending from Main Street to Pennsylvania Avenue. In preparation for the new roadway, a two-story brick house, formerly the seminary's West Virginia Cottage and more recently a Spanish and German house, was picked up and moved not far away to a lot on Pennsylvania Avenue during the summer of 1976.[55] Late in 1974, the possibility of attaining Historic Landmark status for buildings in the "old" campus had been discussed; state funding could then be received for renovation and maintenance of those buildings. Included in early 1976 in the official listing in the National Register of Historic Places were the President's House (1889), Alumni Hall (1896), Baker Chapel (1895), Carroll Hall (1873), Levine Hall (1891), and Ward Memorial Arch (1898).[56]

The Garden Apartments were opened in 1974.

The 1972 Long Range Plan had recommended the building of three new facilities: a student center, a performing arts center, and a new gymnasium. After considerable discussion of those options and the funding for each, the trustees decided to build a new student center and gymnasium, but to remodel Alumni Hall for the performing arts.[57] Once the formal historic designation was obtained, the State of Maryland provided matching funds to renovate Alumni Hall (as well as Winslow Student Center). The Alumni Hall renovation, slated to cost over $1 million, began in early 1976 and took almost three years. The auditorium was outfitted with modern stage equipment and lighting, the raked stage was flattened and extended over an orchestra pit, and the seating was reconfigured and replaced. The building was air conditioned, a large elevator was installed in a tower added to the northeast corner of the building, the lower floor was redesigned to form a true experimental theater and a green room, and offices and classrooms were fitted into the remaining space on lower floors. During the renovation, a zealous worker tearing up the balcony floor to install air-conditioning ducts cut through the hundreds of wires and cables connecting the organ to the pipes in the chambers at the rear of the hall. The organ, which had played continuously in the space since 1935, could never be fully restored to its prior state.

After several years of discussion, a new student center was authorized in 1975, and planning went forward by Peter Christie of the Architectural

The Decker College Center opened in 1978.

Affiliation.[58] Fund-raising for the potential $2.5 million cost also moved forward and included a $100,000 anonymous gift in memory of Lowell Ensor and a matching grant of $150,000 from the Kresge Foundation. As the result of the gift of over $700,000 in Black and Decker stock from the Alonzo Decker family, the board named the new center Decker College Center and moved toward its completion in June 1978.[59] The construction encountered numerous difficulties and delays. Some of the most critical parts of the building were occupied at the beginning of the fall semester, 1978, and it was formally dedicated on October 7, 1978. The work continued in spurts and then essentially stopped; the roof leaked, and the mechanical systems needed more work. Early in 1979 the board decided to seek legal recourse against the Charles T. Frank Construction Corporation. By April liens had been put on the building by unpaid subcontractors as the Frank Corp. moved into bankruptcy. In May the contract with the Frank Corp. was terminated and the local Stuller Construction Company hired to complete the center, the additional work paid for by the bonding company.[60] Eventually, all the construction and repairs were completed, but the building has been plagued with roof leaks for 25 years. The contemporary, three-tiered structure was sited in front of and connected to Elderdice Hall and was conceived by the architect as a "nonbuilding," a link to the surrounding architecture, including Rouzer Hall (but not competing with it), pulling things together in the center of campus.[61]

Once the new student center was operational, the old Winslow Student Center could be renovated for other use. Christie again designed the plans,

Students gather in Ensor Lounge of the Decker College Center.

and the Operation Renovation Campaign was mounted to raise $1.5 million to pay for that and major renovation of the football stadium, to include regrading of the field, a new track, and new seating. The Winslow renovations began in January 1980, with plans to house the Psychology and Deaf Education departments there. That would release the lower floor of the library for stack expansion.[62]

Continuing with the campus plan and Long Range Plan, President John noted in April 1976 the need for an expanded physical education facility. Initial discussions about a new center were begun in 1977, with preliminary plans by William Gaudreau projecting a cost of over $5 million, including renovations to Gill Gymnasium and adjoining fields.[63] The building would not be begun until 1981 and not completed until May 1984.

In 1970 Operation HOPE was formed by concerned citizens to improve the housing on Union Street. A local minister and officer of HOPE soon called for the college to improve the 15 college-owned houses as part of this project. College officials responded that the residents of those houses held low-income jobs at the college, and so the rents were kept very low ($10–$25 per month), which would not pay for significant upgrading of the buildings.[64] After ongoing discussions throughout the decade, the board voted to sell the college-owned properties to HOPE for their assessed value; HOPE would then either renovate them or tear them down and build new townhouses in their place.[65] The final settlement and transfer of the Union Street properties was made on October 29, 1981.

FINANCES

The college began the decade with an enrollment of 1,082 and in each year but one (1973–74) saw a gradual increase until it reached 1,325 in 1979–80. This represented a 23% increase overall. In a tuition-driven institution, maintaining full enrollments is always the goal, so this growth was significant to meeting increasing expenses. Treasurer Philip Schaeffer reported to the trustees in 1971 that tuition and fees represented 83.5% of the budget. (The church was providing 1.8% of the income and the Alumni Fund 2.7%.)

Total fees for tuition, room, and board were $2,700 in 1970–71 but by the end of the decade had risen to $5,025, an 86% increase. During this ten-year period, the college budget grew from about $4 million to about $9.4 million, a 135% increase. (From 1967 to 1972, the last five years of the Ensor administration, the budget doubled, from $2.5 million to $5 million. In some years, particularly those in the middle of the decade, the budgets were very tight, reflecting rising prices of food and energy, especially during the "energy crisis.") President John noted that the budget for 1978–79 of $8.5 million reflected increases in Social Security taxes, an increased minimum wage, and a 25% increase in faculty and staff medical insurance premiums.[66] With the beginning of the John presidency, a formal budget process was put in place, in which all departments contributed projected needs and also dealt with budget freezes when spending or rising prices caused projected deficits. Strict controls and timely reporting by a controller using a new accounting structure, a new computer, and a central purchasing agent helped to keep budgets in focus.[67] Even with some of these constraints in place, the college ran deficits of as much as $157,000 during the early 1970s, depleting a reserve account but not requiring any borrowed funds. Soon, however, the situation improved, although constant vigilance was necessary to keep the growing annual budget in check. Indeed, in the spring of 1979 a freeze on all spending for the remainder of the year was put into effect to avoid a deficit, because costs of fuel and food were spiraling out of control.[68]

The major expense was always faculty and staff salaries, which had begun to rise during the previous decade and made major strides during the 1970s. Over the decade the average faculty salary rose 57%, from about $12,000 to $18,869, with salaries at all ranks rising proportionately. Effort especially was made to increase the salaries of full professors, the maximum of which increased from about $18,500 to $26,650, while keeping the other ranks competitive. For 1975–76, for example, salaries rose 10% on average just to keep up with inflation and to make up for earlier "lost ground." By 1979, President John was pleased to report that the college was ranked quite favorably with other colleges in the salary ratings published yearly by the American Association of University Professors. In 1973 the board had also approved a standard scale for part-time faculty: $700 to $1,000, depending on degree and rank of the instructor.[69] Faculty numbers held fairly constant in the mid-80s during the decade and resulted in a tenure rate approaching 80%. A 1978 change in federal law, raising the standard retirement age to 70 for all employees, further affected the planning and budget process.[70]

To support the growing budgets, the endowment saw a 100% growth over the decade, rising from about $2.9 million to $5.6 million, although the Long Range Plan had projected an endowment of $10 million by 1980. During the middle of the period, it had fluctuated somewhat, gaining and losing $500,000 over a two-year period, even reaching a high of $6.5 million at one point. The Alumni Fund also grew rapidly, from about $200,000 to $350,000, once a development program was firmly in place and fully staffed. President John was pleased to note in his report to the board in April 1979 that before 1972, average total gifts to the college averaged about $400,000, and in the years following, the average had been $1.34 million, an increase of over 200%. Of particular significance was a contribution from the estate of Mrs. Ella Frederick in 1977: $826,420, the largest bequest in college history to that time.[71]

The State of Maryland by 1972 had made a significant move to assist in the annual funding of private colleges in the state, awarding a grant of $500 per bachelor's degree recipient in each private college and university. This plan was immediately attacked by the ACLU in a suit filed in May 1972 against four Maryland Catholic colleges and Western Maryland, often called Roemer et al. Reminiscent of the suit a decade earlier, in which the college lost state funds for a capital project, this one attacked any state aid to church-related institutions. The trial to settle the suit began June 1, 1973, and continued for over a year. In April 1974, the Maryland legislature approved a new aid program on the recommendation of the Pear Commission (named for its chairman, Philip Pear, on whom the college would confer the honorary LLD degree in 1977), in which the state would pay an annual stipend of $243 per enrolled student (compared with $1,500 per student in state institutions). Once the suit was filed, the potential state funds were escrowed, about $125,000 in 1972 and 1973 and $417,000 in 1974.

In January 1974 the college was informed by leaders of the Baltimore Conference of the Methodist Church that no funds would be forthcoming from the church that year. For several years the college had been in a "fourth priority" category in the conference budget and had received only $25,000, but in 1974 even that would not be available. At its February 12 meeting, the trustee Executive Committee approved a resolution to be sent to the Baltimore

Conference requesting that the college no longer be included in future conference budgets or be considered for financial assistance.[72] By October 1974, the college had received a favorable decision in the Roemer et al. suit; both the majority and minority opinions of the three-judge panel had ruled in its favor. President John noted, "This verdict means a great deal to Western Maryland College, now and in the future."[73] The ACLU, however, appealed the decision to the United States Supreme Court, and the trustees sensed that, even if the appeal did not result in a reversal of the original decision (which ultimately was the case), there would be continued and ongoing pressure within the state not to fund church-related institutions. They concluded, "The college must change its posture" to avoid continual challenges to its eligibility for public funds. The trustees also felt that the college could not compete with other private colleges without state support.[74] Noting that the church was no longer providing any financial support (which had been very little in recent years) and realizing that the educational program of the college would be no different as an independent institution, a resolution that the college must become an independent liberal arts college with no church relationship was passed by the trustee Executive Committee with a vote of 8 affirmatives, no negatives, and 1 abstention. At a special meeting of the full board of trustees on March 11, 1975, the action was approved by a vote of 14 to 4, with Bishop Mathews abstaining. On April 7, 1975, after careful negotiations by Chairman Wilbur Preston, the college was formally dismissed from the Roemer et al. appeal case, bringing to an end all involvement and litigation over state aid to the college. The $417,000 escrowed funds were released with the proviso that the money be used for nonsectarian purposes.

President John noted in his annual report, "We recognize and are grateful for our heritage. With the relationship [with the Methodist Church] terminated, however, we move on confidently with the same educational philosophy goals and personnel and with no significant operational differences in the structure or program of the college."[75] Stipulations by the ACLU in dismissing the college from the suit included the agreement to eliminate a Baccalaureate Service (which had been dropped in 1973), to hire non-Methodist ministers (or nonclerics) for positions in the Philosophy and Religion Department as they arose through normal attrition, to remove the college funding from all religious-oriented organizations such as the Religious Life Council (which amounted to about $600), and to remove the crosses from Baker Memorial Chapel and Baker Chapel, to bring the buildings' architectural language into consistency with the official philosophical and educational objectives, which were nonsectarian (and since the buildings were now essentially nonsectarian classroom and office complexes).[76] It was only the last activity that caused any overt reaction, and for a few months after the crosses were removed in July, some alumni and mass media, including the Associated Press, called attention to the symbolic nature of the event. In his report to the board in October 1975, President John commented on the flood of letters, many quite mean-spirited (some from Methodist clergy), he had received as a result of the dissolution and cross removal. During the furor, the faculty sent a resolution to the board supporting the move and expressing its confidence in the president.[77] The United Methodist Church newspaper, the *Circuit Rider*, was full of denunciation from ministers decrying the demise of this "Christian college," but one essay in the October 3, 1975, issue, written by R. Bruce Poynter, chaplain at the American University, summarized the inherent dilemma:

> We have to try to see the fundamental difference in the task of the Church and Academy—a difference that exists even though both use words and ideas as their major tools. It is the task of the Church to preach the Gospel as The Truth. But it is the task of the Academy to pursue Truth with no a-priori assumptions whatever—including those of the Gospel. It is the task of the Church to teach Christian doctrine; but it is the task of the Academy to examine critically all doctrines, by whomever taught. It is the vocation of the Church to nurture faith; but it is that of the Academy to question all faiths.

The crisis eventually passed, and the college program went on as usual. Indeed, John noted two years later that there were more religious activities on campus then than in 1967. The Chapel Committee, Religious Life Council, and various denominational groups existed, without direct college support; the students appeared to him to be more "religious" than their parents and earlier generations.[78] A year later the *Circuit Rider*, in assessing whether ending the church relationship had made a difference at WMC, noted, "Religious life here is alive and well." The voluntary chapel services were now held at 11:00 A.M. on Sunday mornings and were reasonably well attended. Ira Zepp, who gave up the title of dean of the chapel in 1978, continued to speak occasionally, along with other clergy and laypeople. Other student religious groups also continued to function as usual.[79]

Twenty years later, in 1994, Zepp wrote an essay on the removal of the crosses and the disaffiliation with the church, noting,

> History should note that President Ralph John's rationale for disaffiliation was a very compelling one. It was not a matter of compromise, but one of integrity. Ralph wanted us to symbolize what we were—in reality, a private, independent college. . . . From the thirties on, we were probably not the Christian/Church college the public perceived us to be. I always worried about the distance between our institutional self-perception and

our public image. We were not aware how the cross unconsciously took care of that public image while hardly informing our day-to-day activity on campus. While we had the crosses on our chapels, we were dragging our feet with minority student enrollment and requiring ROTC. By the early seventies, required Chapel and one required religious studies course was eliminated from the [basic liberal arts requirements] and the Baltimore Annual Conference had placed us on the lowest rung of their priority list; this effectively meant that, for several years we received hardly any money, or none at all, from them. In a way the Church dropped us before we disaffiliated. Yet Church officials and many lay persons wanted to exact pounds of flesh from us out of all proportion to their current investment. This is not meant to sound ungrateful; quite the contrary, we should celebrate our Christian past in the form of the Methodist Protestants. But we should also celebrate the evolution of the college to a completely independent and private college which retains strong academic continuity with the past and continues to move ahead in ways the future demands.[80]

In 1973, a book entitled *The Politics of Lying: Government Deception, Secrecy, and Power* by David Wise was published and included a reference to a group called the Wartime Information Security Program (WISP), allegedly a group of eight men, some on the WMC staff, who would, in a war emergency, gather in their headquarters at the college (in the sub-basement of Lewis Hall of Science) to set up the machinery to censor American media. It did not take long for representatives of various media to descend on the campus to inquire into this "censorship center," about which few people on campus had any knowledge. President John held several news conferences and interviews, including an all-college meeting, at which he shared what he knew about the facility. Those purported to be part of WISP refused comment. President Emeritus Ensor, when asked about the facility, said, "Anything I know is highly classified."[81] The history of a federal facility occupying space on the campus went back to 1954, when officials of the Office of Defense Mobilization negotiated with the college to place a civil defense facility on campus, in the basement of Thompson Infirmary.[82] It remained there until the Lewis Hall of Science was built (1964–66), at which time the board agreed to build a sub-basement into which the civil defense group could move. The federal agency, by now renamed the Office of Emergency Preparedness (OEP), negotiated a ten-year renewable contract and paid about $100,000 in construction costs. While rent had been paid for the infirmary space, apparently the agency paid only about $50 per month for light and heat but no rent for the new space. When the federal facility came to light through the book, President

John commented in an article in the *Chronicle of Higher Education* that he did not know whether the space had been intended as a press censorship headquarters, although the OEP confirmed that censorship had been the purpose of the facility until a few months before that time. The article went on to say, "W.I.S.P.'s relationship to Western Maryland College was always on a standby planning basis, and the space was never activated or manned, either by military or civilian personnel. . . . Plans for use of this facility for the W.I.S.P. have been canceled. . . . The government is now using this facility for the storage of vital civil non-defense records."[83] Whatever the official (or unofficial) use, it was still classified, and the space was not open to the public or to the college. Over the years a small number of individuals were regularly observed coming and going from the facility. John promised that when the lease expired in 1976, the basement would revert to the college, because he felt that classified government operations "are not consistent with the focus of a liberals arts program." However, the lease was renewed by the trustees in 1976 with an annual rent, and the issue came up again in the spring of 1978; the student newspaper reported that "little is known about the use of the facility."[84] Reacting to the recurring issue, President John commented to the faculty that there was no danger attached to the classified activity. The space would continue to be leased until 2000, when the college finally reclaimed it, remodeling it for use as computer science laboratories.

The treasurer reported to the board in September 1975 that the J.C. Penney building on Main Street, which the college had received as a bequest in 1954, was now bringing in only about $5,000 in rent annually; he also reported that an organization was interested in buying the property, and the trustees approved the sale, which took place during the following year, netting the college $95,000.[85]

During the decade, several major fund-raising campaigns were launched, primarily for building projects. In 1972 the first Long Range Plan recommended a $10 million Capital and Endowment Campaign, but because of the economy, price controls, administrative changes at the college, budget deficits, and board restructuring, it took a while to launch. By October 1973, a $6 million goal was set, to be reached in three years, with another $5 million to be raised later.[86] With the planning for the new college center in place, capital funds began to increase. Two years later, with help from development consultants Marts & Lundy, Inc., a comprehensive capital campaign for $5 million was launched.[87] With the matching grant from the Kresge Foundation for $150,000, as well as the Decker gift, by October 1977, $8.5 million had been received or pledged. As plans developed for the renovation of Alumni Hall, the football stadium, and Winslow Hall, the Operation Renovation

Campaign with a goal of $1.5 million was under way by 1979. Included in this was $375,000 in capital bonds. The State of Maryland also made an appropriation of $643,000 toward the goal. To meet the second Long Range Plan goals, which included the new field house, the trustees strove to raise about $2 million a year from various sources.[88] As in past decades, fund-raising goals were continually reevaluated, revised, and readjusted as new projects and problems arose and priorities changed.

Major Events

As Lowell Ensor approached retirement after his 25-year tenure as president, it was deemed appropriate to honor him in several ways. At the board of trustees dinner held on May 5, 1972, the Ensors were surprised to see the entire faculty and representatives of the administration and alumni gathered with the trustees in Englar Dining Hall for a special tribute. Tables were decorated with candles and small gazebos (reminiscent of Carpe Diem), and after dinner a slide show, produced by Prof. Tribby and Dorothy Herr and narrated by Dean Makosky, highlighted the "Ensor Years." At the conclusion of the program, the Ensors were presented with a package containing the slides and tape of the presentation by Mrs. Herr. Master of Ceremonies Wilbur Preston then introduced Bryson Popham, the president of the SGA, who presented funds (the principal gift coming from the senior class) to establish a scholarship in the Ensors' honor, and Alfred V. Clark, president of the Faculty Club, announced that a garden would be created on the campus in their honor. Finally, a five-tiered decorated cake made especially for the occasion by Clarence Gale, the college baker, was wheeled in, cut, and shared with all.[89] Later on, as Commencement approached, a reception was held in McDaniel Lounge so that the Westminster community could express its good wishes and farewells. At the Commencement ceremonies, held for the first time in the large auditorium of the newly opened Westminster High School (Alumni Hall had become too small for the event), tributes were paid to Dr. Ensor by Dean Makosky for the faculty, Charles W. Sullivan '72 for the students, Wilbur Preston for the trustees, and Wilmer V. Bell '30 for the alumni. Dr. Bell, speaking to Dr. Ensor, said, "By your unflagging interest, enthusiasm, and zeal you have made more certain that 'college ties can ne'er be broken.' . . . You have well earned and justly merit the universal personal respect, esteem, and affection all alumni hereby proudly acknowledge."[90] The Commencement speaker was Nanette Fabray McDougal, who was awarded the honorary doctor of fine arts degree. She spoke of her life and her music and acting career and the difficulties because of her hearing impairment; she concluded her remarks by singing and signing "The Impossible Dream" from *The Man of La Mancha*, and there was not a dry eye in the house. Three years later, on April 18, 1975, the Ensor Plaza and garden were dedicated in front of Baker Memorial Chapel.

The formal inauguration of Ralph John as the sixth president of the college was held on May 1, 1973, as a climax to a variety of activities during the preceding week, including concerts, films, and poetry readings. On three successive evenings, symposia were held, focusing on "The Liberal Arts: A Sense of Community" led by Dr. Warren Bryan Martin, provost of the Old School, Sonoma State College, California. On each evening, Martin gave a short address that was followed by reactions from a panel of faculty, staff, students, and alumni.[91] Saturday dawned bright but blustery, but the events of May Day and the inauguration went off without a hitch. After a buffet luncheon, faculty, trustees, and the 163 invited delegates gathered in Gill Gymnasium to robe for the academic procession. (This was the first time that the trustees were robed for a special event; soon thereafter, appropriate regalia were purchased, and trustees have been robed for academic processions ever since.) Led by the marshals and to the music of the College Band, directed by Carl L. Dietrich, the procession wound its way down the hill and into a huge green and gold tent set up on the soccer field below the gymnasium. Greetings to the new president were extended by Isabel Royer representing the faculty; Robert E. Bricker '42, president of the Alumni Association; and Kendall R. Faulkner '73 for the students. The guest speaker for the occasion was Dr. Frederick Ness, president of the Association of American Colleges. Noting the inaugural theme, Ness commented on the value of the small college, and asked, "How can there be a sense of community at a university which mass produces 27,000 or more students at one fell swoop?" He went on to assert, "It is time for every liberal arts college to reassess its values and accomplishments" and develop "greater empathy and social consciousness, particularly among those who will be the [nation's] leaders."[92]

The new president was then formally inducted into office by Chairman of the Board Wilbur Preston and invested with the newly created sterling silver chain of office bearing the names of all former presidents, as well as the college seal. Earlier in the ceremony Alumni Association past president Wilmer Bell had presented this formal symbol of office to the college as a gift of the alumni. John accepted the presidential role and made his inaugural address, in which he reflected on the college's history and traditions and went on to say,

> *[The college] is ours today. Obversely, we belong to the college in this critical interval between yesterday and tomorrow. . . . [I have] faith in the future of Western Maryland College. In the company of its institutional*

peers, this college is in a strong position, with needs and problems to be sure, but without the brooding anxiety about survival capabilities that wear down the equanimity, and educational quality, of less fortunate places. It is an honor to have been elected this college's sixth president.[93]

Then, in a very personal ceremony, John conferred his first WMC degree, an honorary doctor of divinity, on his father, Byron W. John, who had been presented by President Emeritus Ensor. A reception followed in which the new president greeted the attendees. The following day, a chapel service, a concert, the Argonaut induction, and the Investiture and Honors Convocation dedicated to retiring dean John Makosky rounded out the special weekend.

The United States celebrated its bicentennial during 1976, and the college participated in the celebration in several ways during the year 1975–76. The year began with a Sigma Xi lecture by Dr. Melvin Kranzberg, a history film series, and a production by the College Choir of Menotti's *Amahl and the Night Visitors* in early December.[94] In a nod to our British heritage, performances of Gilbert and Sullivan's *H.M.S. Pinafore* were presented in Alumni Hall in late January. Directed by William Tribby with music under the direction of Carl Dietrich, the large cast included students, staff, and townspeople, including Kenneth Shook '52, Jean Beaver '76, Robin Cumberland '76, Edward Carll '77, Donald Smith, and even featured a cameo appearance by Queen Victoria (Tim Weinfeld in disguise). The production, which was well received, utilized the stage and main floor of Alumni Hall, from which the old wooden seats had been removed just before the building underwent major renovation.[95]

On February 8, 1976, a Bicentennial Celebration Convocation (the second of several Founders Day Convocations introduced in 1975) was held in Baker Memorial Chapel, honoring John Hanson, colonial patriot. Dr. Ralph Levering of the History Department had researched Hanson, one of Maryland's representatives to the Continental Congress and the first president of the United States in Congress Assembled, under the Articles of Confederation (1781). Levering's work was published by the college as a 32-page monograph, and its contents formed the basis of the centerpiece for the convocation: "The Experience of Freedom: A Reading for Three Voices." Participating in this presentation were Jane Davy, Derek Neal, and Paul Smith, directed by William Tribby. Interspersed throughout the readings were sections of "The Testament of Freedom" by Randall Thompson, sung by the College Choir under the direction of Oliver Spangler, with Evelyn Hering at the organ. Invited to the convocation and participating in the procession were the members of the Maryland General Assembly and the Maryland Bicentennial Commission. The Color Guard of the First Maryland Regiment, dressed in colonial uniforms, led the procession, which included the Student Senate, trustees, and faculty of the college. Following the musical and dramatic portion of the program, a posthumous honorary doctor of laws degree was conferred on John Hanson, through his descendant and namesake, John Hanson Briscoe, speaker of the Maryland House of Delegates. Governor Marvin Mandel presented Mr. Briscoe to President John and Chairman Preston for the degree.[96] The president said, in part,

> John Hanson Briscoe, distinguished descendant of a distinguished forebear..., we are proud to claim with you John Hanson, ... opponent of the oppressive measures of a proprietary government, representative of his fellow [citizens], ... organizer of personnel and resources for the successful execution of [the Revolutionary] War..., diligent public servant.... It is my pleasure to confer on John Hanson, posthumously and through you, a member of the family these generations removed, the honorary degree of Doctor of Laws.[97]

Decorating the auditorium for the occasion were national and state flags from 1776 to 1976 on loan from the Star-Spangled Banner Flag House in Baltimore. Guests attended a reception in the dining hall following the program and were invited to view the Bicentennial Mural in the conference room of Elderdice Hall; the mural was painted by Wasyl Palijczuk and students Rickey May '75, Margaret Powell '76, and Beverly Wilson '76 and had been dedicated at homecoming the previous November.[98]

In March a production of *A Streetcar Named Desire* was mounted by the Dramatic Art Department on the Alumni Hall stage. On April 4, a Bicentennial Festival Concert was presented by the College Brass Ensemble, Women's Glee Club, College Singers, and the Carroll County Orchestra. Alumni were invited to participate in special Bicentennial Continuous Studies on April 10, when presentations by faculty members compared and contrasted colonial with modern disciplines. A new sculpture was put in place on campus, near the Main Street entrance. Designed and constructed by Prof. Palijczuk, it was a welded steel structure that seemed to have outstretched arms welcoming all, while also pointing upward in a meditative mood. The year concluded with more concerts, art shows, and traditional ceremonies, including the Honors Convocation, at which Victor Weybright, author, publisher and Carroll County native, spoke, and the Commencement exercises, at which American novelist Joanne Greenberg addressed the class of 1976.

The academic year 1978–79 also had a special focus: "The Humanities and a Humane World" with a variety of activities and special programs, underwritten in part by a grant from the National Endowment for the Humanities. Invited lecturers included Alvin Poussaint, psychiatrist; Carl Rowan, journalist and lecturer; René Dubos, environmentalist; and Warren Bryan Martin, director of the Danforth Graduate Fellowship Foundation. A day-long seminar in December, "Perspectives on the Humanities," featured William J. Bennett and three Fellows from the National Humanities Center in North Carolina. A Workshop on Historic Preservation was held on the weekend April 6–7, with a number of Maryland historians and preservationists leading discussions during the day and English professor Keith Richwine sharing his research on early photojournalist Sadie Kneller Miller '85. A number of special concerts, exhibits, and plays rounded out the schedule. Throughout the year freshman students enrolled in interdisciplinary studies focused on "The Human Dimension of the Humanities" and studied Leonardo da Vinci, Elizabeth I, Thomas Jefferson, and Charles Darwin. During the January term a number of courses were also designed around the year-long theme.[99] Coordinating all these events was a campus-wide committee chaired by James Lightner, who had also coordinated the bicentennial year activities three years earlier.

At the center of the humanities celebration was the rededication of the 80-year-old Alumni Hall, after a major three-year renovation to convert it into a technically modern performing arts center. Originally scheduled for November, the rededication was postponed until February 10, 1979, because of construction delays. The day dawned very cold, but spirits were high as friends and alumni filled the newly outfitted and redecorated auditorium for the ceremony. The speaker was Dr. Walter Kaufmann, professor of philosophy at Princeton University, who addressed the topic "Humanity and the Humanities." Board chairman Wilbur Preston formally rededicated the space:

> From the stained glass windows that exquisitely celebrate the disciplines of liberal learning to the classical architectural features authentically associated with the period of its building, this edifice has served the artistic, intellectual and spiritual impulses of generations in this region and on this campus. . . . It is my honor to rededicate this edifice, Alumni Hall, and to commit it anew to the life and work of this college.[100]

The highpoint of the afternoon was the conferring of an honorary doctor of fine arts degree on Esther Smith, associate professor emerita of dramatic art. She was presented for the degree by her former student and colleague William Tribby '56, who reminded all her former students in attendance of the many moments when Miss Smith had touched them in some way. "Esther's real gift to us is that, by her example and her encouragement, she taught us to believe that we housed saints and poets within us—if we would only let them loose." President John conferred the degree and announced that Smith had been promoted to the rank of professor emerita. Miss Smith responded by thanking her predecessor, Nannie Lease; the three presidents with whom she had worked for 44 years; her late sister, Lillian Smith; and her many students and friends.[101] The honoree had come from her home in Clayton, Georgia, for the event and was the guest of honor at a reception following the ceremony.

As the decade proceeded, the college continued to grow, and the larger senior classes presented the problem of where to hold commencements. It has been noted that the 1972 ceremonies were held in the Westminster High School auditorium. In an attempt to keep the ceremonies on campus, the graduations for the classes of 1973–76 were planned for an outside site in a grove of trees down the hill from the Gill Gymnasium and Albert Norman Ward Hall. Unfortunately, rain moved the 1974 and 1975 exercises back to the high school. So beginning in 1977, a large green and gold tent, capable of holding 2,000 people, was erected behind Elderdice Hall, and Commencements were held there until 1984, when the new field house was opened. Three of those ceremonies are worthy of special mention. The 1977 Commencement speaker was Dr. Joseph E. McDade '62, scientific researcher at the Centers for Disease Control in Atlanta, who ultimately isolated the virus that caused legionnaire's disease. Dr. McDade, who was awarded the honorary doctor of science degree, spoke of the process that led to his discovery and urged the graduates to be persistent and not give up on their quests. In 1978, the speaker was Joseph Brown, professor of art and sculptor-in-residence at Princeton University, where he had also coached boxing for 25 years. His sculptures are displayed all over the United States. He was so pleased with the honorary doctor of fine arts degree the college gave him that he willed the college a collection of 25 of his sculptures, including one of Jesse Owens and a bust of Robert Frost, which arrived in 1997 and are now housed primarily in Hoover Library. Receiving an honorary bachelor of letters degree at the same ceremony was Joni Eareckson, who had been accepted for admission to the college in 1967 but was paralyzed in a swimming accident before she could enroll. She had gone on to write several inspirational books and star in a movie based on her life, encouraging young people to make the most of their abilities even if handicapped. At the 1979 Commencement, the speaker was Governor Harry Hughes, and honorary doctorates were awarded to several individuals including Dr. Samuel H. Hoover (doctor of science), a Baltimore dentist who joined the board of trustees in 1972 and became a major benefactor of the college. Receiving the doctor of humane letters was Dr. Sherry Fischer Manning '65, a leading voice in higher education and president of Colorado Women's College. Attending his 65th consecutive commencement was Dr. Samuel Schofield, who was awarded the doctor of laws degree and received a standing ovation in recognition and appreciation of his lifetime of devotion to the college. He and his wife, Corinne, moved from Westminster to Salisbury soon thereafter.

*Phi Beta Kappa Secretary K. Greene and Vice President C. Sims
present new charter to Professor C. Darcy and Dr. John.*

On May 1, 1980, the Delta of Maryland Chapter of Phi Beta Kappa
(PBK) was formally chartered at the college, making it only the fourth college
in Maryland to be so honored. (The others were Johns Hopkins University,
Goucher College, and the College of Arts and Sciences of the University of
Maryland–College Park.) After at least one earlier attempt to obtain a charter
had failed, the ten petitioning faculty members (already Phi Beta Kappa
members), led by Cornelius P. Darcy, who filed the detailed and lengthy
reports, learned in October 1979 that their application had received the
necessary positive votes at the PBK Council triennial meeting and a charter
would soon be granted. After a banquet held in the president's dining room,
the charter was formally presented by national vice president Catherine Sims
to the Charter Members: Mary Ann Ashcraft Alspach, William F. Cipolla,
Eulalia B. Cobb, Cornelius P. Darcy, Donna M. Evergates, David W. Herlocker,
Kathryn B. Hildebran, Esther M. Iglich, Ralph B. Levering, and Edith F.
Ridington. Joining them as Foundation Members were President John and
alumni faculty members Richard A. Clower '50, Mary Ellen Elwell '50, H.
Ray Stevens '58, James E. Lightner '59, and Paula J. Ottinger '71 (all of whom
had graduated with academic honors and were Argonaut Fellows). Following
the charter ceremony, 23 members of the class of 1980 were inducted as the
first members-in-course of the chapter. In the 27 years (1980–2007) since
the chapter was chartered, almost 800 graduating seniors have been initiated
into the society as members-in-course; 22 alumni members and 4 honorary

members have also been elected. The Argonaut Society was disbanded in 1980, but the name was retained for the highest academic honor bestowed by the college, the Argonaut Award, which is presented to the graduating senior with the highest grade point average for total academic work at the college. In 1990, the Delta of Maryland Chapter established the Edith Farr Ridington Phi Beta Kappa Writing Award to recognize the best honors paper written by a graduating senior. This award is named in memory of charter member and longtime chapter historian, Edith Ridington, senior lecturer emerita in classics [1957–77]. Both awards are presented each year during commencement.[102]

CONCLUSION

The decade was one of crisis and change for the college. There was significant turnover in the administration, board of trustees, and faculty, coupled with a growing student body that was slowly, though sometimes with tension, becoming more diversified. In the words of one alumna of the era, "We were largely conservative, largely white children of World War II veterans and stay-at-home moms. We came mostly from the mid-Atlantic states. We were too young to be Vietnam War soldiers or 1960s peace demonstrators, but old enough to be part of the 'baby boomers' group. We were good all-American kids."[103] Western Maryland College went through significant growing pains as it moved forward to implement the recommendations of two Long Range Plans, which included several new buildings, a revised curriculum, an improved endowment, and continued revisions in the life of the campus community. No longer tied, however loosely, to the Methodist Church and with many new and diverse faces on campus, the college was a much different place from that of ten years earlier, even with all the changes that had occurred in the 1960s. By the end of the decade it was being recognized as a private, independent liberal arts institution of considerable academic quality, one that was rising in the hierarchy of colleges in the region and becoming identified for its special programs, strong faculty and curriculum, and modern facilities. Even if the press coverage of various events had not always been totally positive, the college was nevertheless becoming better known and would remain known after the specific crises were forgotten.

Chapter 12 Endnotes

1. WMC board of trustees minutes, April 16, 1971.
2. Holloway, letter of resignation, July 1971.
3. *The Hill*, June 1973, 12.
4. McGrath Report, January 1973.
5. WMC board of trustees minutes, April 27, 1973.
6. WMC board of trustees minutes, October 16, 1976.
7. *The Hill*, December 1975, 1.
8. Ibid., May 1977.
9. Ibid., July/August 1980, 2–3.
10. *Gold Bug*, October 4, 1971, 3.
11. *The Hill*, October 1972, 12; July 1975, 4.
12. *The Hill*, September/October 1979, 3.
13. WMC faculty minutes, November 2, 1972.
14. *Gold Bug*, November 21, 1972, 2.
15. *Gold Bug*, January 24, 1972, 3.
16. Ensor, Report, October 1970.
17. John, Report, October 1974.
18. John, Report, April 1979; April 1980.
19. WMC faculty minutes, March 11, 1971.
20. Middle States Association, Report, November 11–14, 1973.
21. WMC faculty minutes, February 12, 1975.
22. *Gold Bug*, January 16, 1973, 1.
23. WMC faculty minutes, October 2, 1974.
24. Ibid., December 3, 1975.
25. Ibid., April 2, 1975.
26. Ibid., December 3, 1975.
27. *Gold Bug*, May 2, 1972, 4.
28. *The Hill*, May 1974, 5.
29. WMC faculty minutes, May 1, 1974.
30. Ibid., December 1, 1976.
31. *Gold Bug*, March 21, 1974, 5.
32. WMC trustee Executive Committee minutes, December 12, 1972.
33. *Gold Bug*, April 24, 1972, 6.
34. *Scrimshaw*, April 21, 1978, 1.
35. Ibid., May 3, 1979, 2; May 10, 1979, 1.
36. *Gold Bug*, December 11, 1973, 3.
37. *Scrimshaw*, April 8, 15, 1977, 1.
38. Ibid., May 20, 1977, 1.
39. Ibid., September 23, 1977, 1.
40. WMC faculty minutes, May 3, 1977.
41. WMC trustee Executive Committee minutes, October 21, 1977; WMC faculty minutes, November 1, 1977.
42. *The Hill*, November 1977, 2.
43. *Gold Bug*, November 16, 1970, 5.
44. Ibid., October 5, 1970, 1.
45. Ibid., March 7, 1974, 2.
46. Notes, Dorothy Hitchcock Keene '74, unpublished memoir, college archives.
47. *Gold Bug*, January 22, 1974, 3.
48. Ibid., May 2, 1972, 3.
49. *Scrimshaw*, October 12, 1978, 1.
50. Notes, D. H. Keene '74.
51. *Scrimshaw*, February 14, 1980, 6.
52. Ibid., October 5, 1978, 6.
53. WMC trustee Executive Committee minutes, September 13, 1972.
54. Ibid., February 11, 1975.
55. *The Hill*, July 1976, 1.
56. Ibid., May 1976, 1.
57. WMC trustee Executive Committee minutes, July 24, 1975.
58. Ibid., February 11, 1975.
59. Ibid., May 18, 1976.
60. WMC trustee Executive Committee minutes, February 21, 1979; May 21, 1979; July 24, 1979.
61. *The Hill*, September/October 1978, 1.
62. John, Report, April 1979.
63. WMC board of trustees minutes, April 21, 1978.
64. *Gold Bug*, October 19, 1970, 2; November 16, 1970, 1.
65. *Scrimshaw*, April 26, 1979, 1.
66. John, Report, April 1978.
67. Ibid., April 1974.
68. WMC trustee Executive Committee minutes, March 28, 1979.
69. Ibid., February 13, 1973.
70. Ibid., December 12, 1978.
71. John, Report, April 1977.
72. WMC trustee Executive Committee minutes, February 12, 1974.
73. *The Hill*, December 1974, 1.
74. WMC trustee Executive Committee minutes, December 3, 1974; January 14, 1975.
75. April 18, 1975.
76. *Scrimshaw*, September 17, 1975, 1; letter from President John to Friends of Western Maryland College, August 25, 1975, John Papers, college archives.
77. WMC faculty minutes, September 5, 1975.
78. John, Report, April 1977.
79. *The Hill*, July 1978, 1–2.
80. "Chapel Crosses Again: Some Reflections," April 1994, unpublished essay, college archives.
81. *Carroll County Times*, May 17, 1973, 1.
82. *Baltimore Evening Sun*, May 18, 1973, C4.
83. *Chronicle of Higher Education*, May 29, 1973, 3.
84. *Scrimshaw*, April 14, 28, 1978.
85. WMC trustee Executive Committee minutes, September 14, 1976.
86. WMC board of trustees minutes, October 19, 1973.

CHAPTER 12 ENDNOTES

87. WMC trustee Executive Committee minutes, July 1, 1975.
88. WMC board of trustees minutes, April 20, 1979.
89. *The Hill*, June 1972, 17–18; *Gold Bug*, May 16, 1972, 13.
90. *The Hill*, August 1972, 10.
91. Inaugural Week Program.
92. *The Hill*, June 1973, 10–11.
93. *The Hill*, June 1973, 5.
94. Program for Bicentennial Year.
95. *Gold Bug*, November 5, 1975, 3.
96. Program; *Scrimshaw*, February 12, 1976, 1.
97. *Scrimshaw*, February 12, 1976, 3.
98. Program of the event.
99. *The Hill*, September/October 1978, 1, 7.
100. Program of Rededication.
101. *The Hill*, March 1979, 1.
102. Program, 25th Anniversary of Delta of Maryland Chapter, Phi Beta Kappa, 2005.
103. Notes, D. H. Keene '74.

MAJOR WORLD EVENTS

1971

28th Amendment to U.S. Constitution lowers minimum voting age to 18.
The Kennedy Center for the Performing Arts opens in Washington, D.C.
An earthquake in Los Angeles kills 60 and causes $1 billion damage.
Violence worsens in Northern Ireland.
USSR soft-lands a space capsule on Mars.
Amtrak begins to operate U.S. passenger railroads.
"Pentagon Papers" controversy erupts.

1972

President Nixon visits China and Russia.
Apollo 16 astronauts spend 71 hours on the moon's surface.
Hurricane Agnes causes $1.7 billion damage to eastern U.S.
The Dow Jones Index for industrial stocks closes above 1,000 for the first time.
Leonard Bernstein's *Mass* premiers in Washington, D.C.
U.S. military draft is phased out; armed forces become all volunteer.
All in the Family is the leading television show in the U.S.
Life magazine ceases publication.

1973

U.S. vice president Spiro Agnew resigns; Gerald Ford succeeds him.
Kurt Vonnegut publishes *Breakfast of Champions*.
U.S. Supreme Court rules on *Roe v. Wade*, legalizing abortion.
A cease-fire is called in Vietnam.
Popular films include *Last Tango in Paris*.
Billie Jean King defeats Bobby Riggs in the tennis "Battle of the Sexes."

1974

"Streaking" becomes a fad in the U.S.
Following the Watergate investigation, Richard Nixon resigns the U.S. presidency.
Aleksandr Solzhenitsyn is stripped of his Soviet citizenship and exiled.
A USSR space probe lands on Mars.
The world's population reaches 3.782 billion.
Peter Benchley publishes *Jaws*.
Gerald Ford becomes 38th U.S. president.

1975

Peter Shaffer receives awards for his play *Equus*.
Generalissimo Francisco Franco of Spain dies; King Juan Carlos I is sworn in.
The cost of mailing a first-class letter in the U.S. increases from 10¢ to 13¢.
Six thousand life-sized pottery figures from the 3rd century B.C. are found in northwest China.
Popular films include *Jaws* and *The Sunshine Boys*.

1976

A mysterious illness, known as legionnaire's disease, kills 29, strikes 151 others.
North and South Vietnam are reunited as one country after 22 years of separation.
United States celebrates the bicentennial of the Declaration of Independence.
The Episcopal Church approves the ordination of women priests and bishops.
The world's first supersonic transport, the Concorde, is inaugurated.
U.S. Air Force Academy admits 155 women students.
Jimmy Carter is elected 39th U.S. president.

1977

Elvis Presley, the "king of rock and roll," dies at 42.
French is adopted as the official language of Quebec.
U.S. population reaches 216 million.
Oil begins to flow through 800-mile trans-Alaska pipeline.
President Carter warns that the energy crisis could bring on a "national catastrophe."
Scholastic Aptitude Test scores of college-bound students show steady decline 1963–77.
A massive blackout in New York City leaves 9 million people without electricity for a day.
The Apple II personal computer appears, selling for $1,298, with 4 kilobytes of memory.

1978

A "test-tube" baby is born in England, the first human baby conceived outside the womb.
United States ratifies new Panama Canal treaties.
The world's population is 4.4 billion, increasing by 200,000 per day.
Pope Paul VI dies; succeeded by Cardinal Karol Wojtyla as Pope John Paul II.
Camp David Accords are signed to bring East-West peace.
James A. Michener publishes *Chesapeake*.

1979

Rioting Iranians take 66 U.S. citizens hostage in Tehran; 52 are held for 444 days.
The Three Mile Island nuclear crisis occurs near Harrisburg, Pennsylvania.
The Shah of Iran is ousted after a 28-year rule; dies in 1980.
Margaret Thatcher is elected first female prime minister of England.
The Sony Walkman and Post-it notes are introduced.
Soaring inflation grips the U.S., worst since 1946.
The USSR invades Afghanistan.

1980

Mt. St. Helens erupts in Washington State.
Former Beatle John Lennon is assassinated.
U.S. armed forces academies graduate first women officers.
Designer jeans and the "preppy look" are popular with college students.
Lech Walesa leads a strike of shipyard workers in Gdansk, Poland.
ERA amendment fails to pass required number of state legislatures.

The Hoover Library addition was built in 1989–91.

CHAPTER

13

A Decade of Highs and Lows

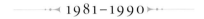

1981–1990

Life in the world of the 1980s could be characterized by euphoric highs and depressing lows. Inauguration Day 1981 brought with it the release of the 52 American hostages in Iran and ushered in the Ronald Reagan era. But soon the news of a worldwide AIDS epidemic and its cause (HIV) was attracting attention and concern. When the Vietnam Veterans Memorial was completed in Washington in 1982, the psychological wounds of that war began to heal. The television show *MASH* completed its long run, and everybody watched the final episode. On January 28, 1986, the *Challenger* space shuttle exploded 73 seconds after launch, and the nation grieved. A year later President Reagan and Russian leader Mikhail Gorbachev met in Reykjavik to lay the groundwork for an Intermediate-Range Nuclear Arms Treaty. In May 1989, the world was shocked by the brutality of the Chinese government as it killed about 3,000 students demonstrating for democracy in Beijing's Tiananmen Square. But in November of the same year the world was amazed to hear the good news that the Berlin Wall was coming down and East Germans were free to leave their isolation, and on February 11, 1990, Nelson Mandela was released from prison in South Africa after 27 years. It was a decade to be remembered.

In Westminster, R. Edward Shilling '63, '66M, was named Carroll County

Portrait of President Ralph Candler John

superintendent of schools, the *Carroll County Times* became a daily newspaper in 1980, the Davis Library moved into new facilities in the center of town, and the Cranberry Mall was under construction in 1986. Carroll County celebrated its 150th birthday with many events including a grand parade on May 30, 1986, with Roy Rogers as grand marshal. At the college, plans were under way to build a motel, conference center, and restaurant on property just west of the campus, to the general delight of the Westminster community. On the campus, ground was broken for two new buildings, and a new, young president was installed who promised to bring new vision to the old school. In the midst of an inflationary spiral and decreasing enrollments, the college tightened its belt and moved forward.

Faculty and Administration

The 1980s were years of significant change in leadership and administrative roles in every division of the college. The board of trustees and the faculty both experienced considerable infusion of new individuals with new ideas. A change of president and all four vice presidents sometimes produced anxiety among those who had been "holding down the fort" for a number of years. And in some administrative areas, a revolving door of directors resulted in a lack of stability that took its toll on morale and efficiency. By the end of the decade things had settled down a bit.

A major change in leadership occurred when Ralph John retired in 1984 after 12 years in the presidency, to be succeeded by Robert Hunter Chambers III. During his presidency, John saw the endowment triple; the annual budget double; tuition and fees almost triple; faculty salaries more than double (as the percent of those tenured rose from 66% to a high of 86%); enrollment fluctuate from about 1,100 to 1,320 and back to 1,175; the campus facilities expand by three major buildings (and several more renovated); and the expectations for the faculty broaden to include more academic research, publication, and service. As he retired, he commented in his report to the trustees that there had been a "measure of disquietude," a "pervading sense of insecurity, a psychological factor, that impacts on faculty morale" on campus that year.[1] This was perhaps a reaction to the president's occasionally mercurial temperament and some unpopular decisions. He had announced his intention to retire a full year before. A presidential selection committee chaired by Wilbur Preston was composed of appointed trustees Mary Bryson, William B. Dulany, Albert Hall, Robert Schaefer, and Dolores Snyder; elected faculty Mary Ellen Elwell, Francis Fennell, and Ethan Seidel; and student leader Elisabeth Siegenthaler '84. The committee

Robert Hunter Chambers III,
seventh president

functioned throughout the summer of 1983 to screen the 230 applications, interviewed 12 individuals, brought 2 to the campus for two-day open sessions with members of the college community, and ultimately recommended Chambers to the board, which formally elected him on January 10, 1984.

Robert H. Chambers (1939–) [1984–2000], a native of Winston-Salem, North Carolina, received his bachelor's degree in economics and business administration from Duke University in 1962. As a Rockefeller scholar, he attended Yale Divinity School, where he received a bachelor of divinity degree in literature and religion in 1965. Four years later he received a PhD in American civilization from Brown University. He returned to Yale to be an assistant professor of English and American studies and dean of Davenport College from 1969 to 1974, spending a funded leave at Clare College, Cambridge University, in 1972–73. Later he served as visiting lecturer and consultant in American studies at the University College at Buckingham, England. In 1975 he became dean of the College of Arts and Sciences at Bucknell University, a post he held for nine years before being elected WMC's seventh president. Chambers had published articles on the works of southern writer Robert Penn Warren, as well as contemporary educational policy. He was married to Alice L. Grant, and they had two children, daughter Lisa and son Grant.[2] The Chambers divorced in 1995.

Faculty members named emeriti during this decade included Gerald E.

Cole [1955–84], William David [1952–84], Fern Hitchcock '47 [1962–84], Earl Griswold [1956–85], Julia T. Hitchcock [1960–85], Stanley Bowlsbey '52, '59M [1969–89], David R. Cross [1964–89], Arleen Heggemeier [1950–89], and Donald R. Zauche '57 [1965–89]. These nine individuals had given a total of 245 years of service and had an average tenure of 27 years. William Cipolla [1969–86], Max Dixon [1969–86], and Mary Ellen Elwell '50 [1969–86] moved on to new positions elsewhere. New faculty faces on the campus included James D. Essig [1980–85] in history, John L. Olsh '67 [1980–] in economics, Louise A. Paquin [1980–] in biology, Helen B. Wolfe [1980–94] in education, William C. Chase [1981–2003] in history, Richard J. Claycombe [1981–] in economics, Richard W. Dillman [1981–2001] in computer science (later communications), Ira F. Domser [1981–] in dramatic art, D. Sue Singer [1983–2006] in business administration, Susan M. Milstein [1983–] in business administration, Christianna E. Nichols (Leahy) [1984–] in political science, Pamela L. Regis [1984–] in English, Susan R. Bloom [1986–] in art, Vasilis Pagonis [1986–] in physics, Gregory D. Alles [1987–] in philosophy and religion, Donna M. Evergates [1987–] in history and classics, Ronald R. Miller [1987–] in dramatic art, Herman E. Behling Jr. [1988–98] in education, Margaret A. Boudreaux [1989–] in music, Sherri Lind Hughes [1989–] in psychology, Martine Motard-Noar [1989–] in French, R. Patrick Reed [1989–2005] in history, Henry B. Reiff [1989–] in education, and Carol A. Rouzer '76 [1989–2000] in chemistry. As of 2007, this group of 24 had amassed a total of 471 years of service, with an average tenure of almost 20 years. Over the decade 39 people were hired to fill about 30 positions; while most remained, some went on to other positions after a short time, although the academic job market was not strong because enrollments nationwide were diminishing. In one unfortunate situation, unique in the college's history, a member of the tenured faculty was suspended for a semester in 1984 and two years later dismissed for improper and unacceptable conduct and insubordination.[3] While the total number of faculty (including military science officers) remained constant at about 95 over the decade, their academic preparation continued to rise, from 75% holding the PhD (or other terminal degree) in 1980 to 83% in 1990. (A terminal degree was now a prerequisite for tenure.) The administration and trustees raised concern over the rising number and percent of tenured faculty. About 77% of the faculty was tenured in 1980; the percentage rose to 86% by mid-decade and then dropped back to about 75% by 1990. (There was hope that it would recede to the national norm of about 60%.) Part-time faculty had been hired for years, and in 1987, those who had been faithful adjuncts for a number of years were appointed to a new faculty rank, senior lecturer; those individuals taught a half load and received a half salary and benefits. The first three were

Nancy B. Palmer [1965–2002], Donna M. Evergates [1976–], and Carol B. Sapora [1976–79, 1984–88]. Scholars-in-residence were first appointed in 1986, beginning with Bailey Young.

As the faculty continued to grow, so did the prestige of its members, as they brought increasing honor to themselves and to the college. English professor Keith Richwine prepared a traveling exhibit of his research on photojournalist Sadie Kneller Miller. Pianist David G. Kreider made his Carnegie Hall debut in 1986. LeRoy L. Panek of the English faculty continued his research and writing

Professor Ira Zepp was named CASE Maryland Professor of the Year in 1989.

on the detective story and published books that won him several Edgar Allan Poe Awards. Chemist Richard H. Smith Jr. garnered significant grants from the National Science Foundation for his ongoing research into the causes of cancer. He also was named a Senior Fellow of the National Institutes of Health in 1984. Ira Zepp was named Maryland Professor of the Year in 1989 by the Council for Advancement and Support of Education. James Lightner was named Outstanding Mathematics Educator by the Maryland Council of Teachers of Mathematics in 1986. Joan Coley was named Outstanding Teacher Educator by the Maryland Reading Association in 1989. McCay Vernon continued his research and writing in deafness and published a book on the psychology of deafness. He and his colleague Hugh T. Prickett Jr. also received national awards for their service to deaf-blind Americans in 1988. Samuel Case was named a Fellow of the American College of Sports Medicine; he also spent the fall of 1983 working in the sports medicine complex at the U.S. Olympic Training Center in Colorado Springs. Philosophy professor Robert Hartman was elected chair of the newly formed Potomac River Consortium of Colleges. Carol Fritz became the first woman elected to the presidency of the Middle Atlantic Athletic Conference. American College Testing and the National Academic Advising Association named Esther M. Iglich Outstanding Adviser for the region. French professor Eulalia B. Cobb was named an American Association of Colleges Fellow during 1985–86 and in 1988 left to become dean at Salem College in North Carolina. In 1989 Donald R. Rabush was named to the college's newly endowed Lawrence J. Adams Chair in Special Education. Donald E. Jones chaired the Scientific Council of the

Maryland Academy of Sciences and a committee of the American Chemical Society. Political scientist Christianna Nichols became active in Amnesty International. Skip Fennell was elected president of the Research Council for Diagnostic and Prescriptive Mathematics.

The college community was deeply saddened by the death of Dean of Academic Affairs William McCormick [1973–83] on May 20, 1983, at age 48 after a nine-month illness with a brain tumor. Two years later, on June 30, 1985, James D. Essig also succumbed to cancer, at age 33, after five years of service in the History Department. During the decade word reached the campus that ten well-known emeriti professors had died: Daisy W. Smith [1938–63] in December 1982, Joseph C. Willen [1933–66] in July 1983, James P. Earp [1938–73] in February 1984, Oliver Spangler [1938–73] in April 1984, Clyde Spicer [1929–68] in April 1984, Samuel Schofield [1919–66] in October 1984, Marie Parker [1929–63] in May 1986, John Makosky [1934–73] in October 1986, Evelyn Wingate Wenner [1931–67] in March 1989, and Isabel Royer [1942–79] in June 1990. Many also were sad to learn of the death of several former campus figures: Bruce Ferguson [1935–56] in October 1981; Virgie Jefferson [1942–62], at age 97 in May 1986; Winifred Holloway in January 1988 and her husband, Fred Holloway [1935–47], in June 1988 at age 90; and Helen Ohler [1925–73] in May 1990.

Changes in the administrative staff were numerous and significant over the decade. Because of Dean McCormick's illness, Stanley Bowlsbey, the associate dean for graduate studies, was appointed acting academic dean in November 1982; he served in that office until July 1983, when Melvin Delmar Palmer, professor of comparative literature, was appointed vice president and dean of academic affairs following nominations to the Faculty Affairs Committee. He served in the office until July 1990. To involve more women in the administration, Palmer named Joan Develin Coley and Esther M. Iglich as associate deans (part-time); after two years they were succeeded by Helen B. Wolfe [1985–88], Geraldine McVittie [1987–89], and LeRoy Panek [1989–90]. As the baby boomers got through high school, the pool of high school graduates dwindled and college enrollments began to ebb. In an effort to maintain WMC's share of entering freshmen, admissions directors were changed with regularity: L. Leslie Bennett [1976–83] turned the office over to Martha E. Gagnon [1983–85], who was replaced for one year by Prof. Coley, who was followed by Joseph S. Rigell [1986–89]. When he moved on, Caryl L. Connor '83 took over both admissions and financial aid. She was soon assisted by Martha O'Connell [1990–2006], who assumed responsibility for the office in September 1990 and gave stability to the admissions process for the next 16 years. The Registrar's Office also witnessed regular change when Hugh Dawkins

[1970–89] became director of special programs in development in 1984 and turned over the records to Pamela Roland [1982–84] for less than a year. She was succeeded by Arthur M. Cavanagh [1984–86], who passed on the office to Barbara Schaeffer Disharoon (Horneff) '84M [1976–2005] in 1986. The Alumni Affairs office welcomed a new director when Donna DuVall Sellman '45 [1980–2000] returned to her alma mater after a teaching and administrative career in the Carroll County public schools; she replaced Carol Armacost Preston '69 [1975–80], who moved into a career in university development in Pittsburgh. After 19 years in the role, Richard Clower [1957–98] turned over the position of director of athletics to J. Richard Carpenter Jr. '72M [1969–] in 1984. Mitchell Alexander '80, '86M [1989–] returned to the campus to become director of college activities. Bernice Beard [1962–89] retired as the president's executive assistant (and secretary of the college) in 1989 and was named emerita; she was replaced by Elizabeth Shevock [1989–92].

One of the more significant administrative changes occurred in 1982, when Philip Schaeffer [1959–82] retired as vice president for business affairs and treasurer, completing 23 years of service and bringing an end to the Schaeffer "dynasty" in that office, begun when his father, Carl, was named assistant treasurer (to Dr. McDaniel) about 1935. Like his father, Philip was named emeritus, received a board resolution of appreciation, and was feted at a dinner. He was succeeded by H. Thomas Kimball [1982–87]. When Kimball resigned in May 1987, the office was temporarily managed by trustee M. Lee Rice, with assistance from Prof. Ethan Seidel as business affairs manager, until December, when Jennie Mingolelli [1987–93] assumed the role of vice president for business affairs. Seidel was also named part-time assistant to the president. In 1988 Arthur Wisner [1988–] was named treasurer of the college as the College Finance Office was expanded and reorganized. Another significant change took place in the Student Affairs division when resignations were received from associate dean Elizabeth Laidlaw [1966–82] in spring 1982 and vice president and dean Wray Mowbray in December 1983. Laidlaw was replaced by Jeanne L. Higbee [1981–84], a recently hired career counselor, who was named acting dean of students upon Mowbray's departure mid-year. A national search resulted in Philip R. Sayre [1984–2006], previously dean of students at the University of Maine at Fort Kent, being named vice president and dean of student affairs. He named Charlene Cole [1985–89] associate dean. One more vice presidential change occurred in 1984 when James F. Ridenour, in Development, resigned to go to Berry College in Georgia. He was replaced for six months by Cynthia Gelhard before she, too, moved on, to be replaced by Walter Wahlen [1985–91] as vice president for college relations (a new name for the division). Thus, when Robert Chambers assumed the presidency, he had a cabinet of vice presidents new to their roles, at least at this college. Perhaps this was not unexpected, since a tradition was developing in higher education of presidents preferring to establish their own division leadership, and resignations prior to a new presidency were not uncommon.

The board of trustees continued to change by about 50%. Named emeritus during the decade were Mary Brown Bryson '35 [1967–84], Richard H. Ellingsworth [1973–84], Arlie R. Mansberger Jr. '44 [1971–84], Albert C. Hall [1975–85], Richard W. Kiefer '34 [1967–85], Frederick C. Malkus Jr. '34 [1962–85], F. Kale Mathias '35 [1958–84], Eloise Chipman Payne '38 [1978–88], Rebecca Groves Smith '37 [1976–88], and Robert Bricker '42 [1974–90].

Resigning from the board after a number of years of service were Mary Todd Griffiths '48 [1976–81], Bishop James K. Mathews [1973–82], Jane Decker Asmis [1976–82], Robert Faw '41 [1966–89], Jon M. Files [1984–90], Richard F. Kline Jr. '57 [1975–90], Frederick S. Nicholl '62 [1984–90], and Thaddeus W. Swank [1974–90]. Elected during the decade were S. Dennis Harmon '57 [1981–90], Nancy Caskey Voss '54 [1981–], Donald F. Clarke '50 [1982–94], Stanley E. Harrison [1982–94], Catherine Schumann Kiddoo '46 [1982–97], Jon M. Files [1984–90], Marjorie A. Lippy '77M [1984–96], Frederick S. Nicholl '62 [1984–90], Philip E. Hixon [1984–87], Linda M. Ryan [1984–85], Jerome P. Baroch '64 [1985–99], Frances D. Fergusson [1985–87], James L. D. Roser [1985–93], M. Lee Marston [1986–93], Kurt L. Schmoke LLD 1984 [1986–2000], Brantley P. Vitek '57 [1986–92], Lawrence J. Adams LHD 1993 [1989–92], Leslie M. Alperstein '63 [1989–92], Frank G. Bowe '69 [1989–92], Harold Donofrio [1989–90], Robert A. Howell [1989–2000], George F. Varga '61, HHD 1992 [1989–], Lawrence Blumberg '67 [1990–2000], Wayne K. Curry '72 [1990–], C. Dianne Briggs Martin '65 [1990–96], and Joseph D. Smothers '69 [1990–93].

Four new honorary trustees were also elected: Jane Decker Asmis [1982–97], Thomas F. Marshall [1982–91], Clarence M. Willis [1987–93], and Ann K. Walls McCool '38 [1988–]. The leadership of the board changed several times. Wilbur Preston turned over the chair in 1982 to Robert Bricker, who handed it to William S. Keigler in 1986.

The trustees also memorialized a number of their emeriti colleagues who died during the decade: E. McClure Rouzer '07 [1952–72], Fannie Fox Decker [honorary, 1974–81], O. Bryan Langrall '21 [1953–73], Eugene C. Woodward '28 [1956–80], Bertha S. Adkins [honorary, 1980–83], Robert Gill [1925–73], Clarence L. Fossett [1960–80], Clarence H. Bennett '28 [1967–80], William E. Firth [1962–75], Clarence M. Mitchell [honorary, 1980–84], E. Cranston Riggin [1948–80], Kale Mathias [1958–84], Joshua Miles [1959–76], George Meyls [1958–80], Charles A. Stewart '26 [1961–80], Lewis F. Ransom '35 [1957–81], Henry Darner [1957–73], D. Carlysle MacLea '22 [1949–75], Scott

Bair [1964–73], and John H. Simms '29 [honorary, 1980–90].

A final word about Robert Gill (1889–1983) is in order because of his significant presence and dedication to the college for 80 years, beginning with his enrollment at 14 in the preparatory school in 1903. (See his biography in chapter 5.) He died on June 22, 1983, on his 94th birthday. Burial was in the Yingling/Gill family plot in the Westminster Cemetery. Following his death, the major expansion of Gill Gymnasium was named the Robert Joshua Gill Physical Education Learning Center in 1986 in recognition of the bulk of his considerable estate being willed to the college.

CURRICULUM

As the college entered the new decade, the applicant pool continued to shrink, and admissions efforts were increased and improved. Over the ten-year period, the number of applications doubled from about 1,050 to 2,024, and correspondingly more students were accepted, usually about 70%–75% of the applicants, in order to maintain a freshman class of about 350. In spite of this, for about four years (1982–85), the number of new enrollees diminished each year, dropping to a low of 294 before rebounding to 330 in 1986 and continuing to increase to over 400 during the last three years (with a high of 425 in 1988). In the "lean years" academic profiles also slipped somewhat, with average total SAT scores dropping below 1000 for six years until 1987; the scores were still better than the national average, however. In all years, entering students showed better mathematical skills than verbal by about 50 points. Class standings and mean grade point averages showed a decline over the same period.

A college curriculum is a dynamic entity, constantly changing in small ways as courses and programs are discontinued, proposed, or altered with approval of the Curriculum Committee and faculty. A survey of the faculty minutes reveals such activity almost every month. Usually, the entire curriculum, especially the basic liberal arts requirements, is examined in detail about every decade, and comprehensive changes are made to reflect current trends and thinking. Such was the case in this decade when the objectives and goals of the college were reexamined as part of the Long Range Plan. The result of this process, spearheaded by professors Richwine and Palmer, was a new statement of college goals, entitled "First Principles," which was ultimately approved by the faculty and trustees in 1981[4] and has guided the college since (with only a few minor modifications):

Western Maryland College believes that liberally educated men and women think and act critically, creatively, and humanely. They take charge of their lives and develop their unique potentials with reason, imagination, and human concern. Western Maryland accepts the challenge to provide an academic and social environment that promotes liberal learning.

- *We place students at the center of a humane environment so that they may see and work toward their personal goals while respecting others and sharing responsibility for the common good.*
- *We provide a foundation of knowledge about the past and present so that students may be informed about the world.*
- *We provide various approaches to knowledge and personal achievement so that students can think critically about, respond creatively to, and form sensitive, intelligent decisions concerning the world and its future.*
- *We provide instruction in fundamental skills so that students can express themselves for their own satisfaction and to the larger community.*
- *We provide solid and respected professional programs for the committed student, and, more important, we provide a liberal arts education as an integral part of professional training so that students will be more flexible, more successful, and happier in the world of work.*

In the classrooms, in the dormitories, in the laboratories, on the playing fields, and in the lounges, Western Maryland College works to disseminate these First Principles.[5]

In his report to the board for 1981–82, President John described the previous year as one of "involvement and self-assessment at the college." Long-range planning continued with a special emphasis on better marketing of the institution. The relation of the liberal arts to career and vocational or professional objectives was under discussion. More offerings and improved scheduling of courses for nontraditional students were under way. And keeping the college fully enrolled when the college-age population was declining was an ever-present challenge.[6] By 1984, new liberal arts requirements reflecting the new goals were proposed and approved. They included a two-semester "heritage" sequence; course requirements in cross-cultural studies, fine arts, humanities, natural sciences, quantitative analysis, and social sciences; and proficiency requirements in writing and basic mathematics. Four years later a freshman seminar was proposed to give new students an introduction to the academic life of the college.[7] (Of course, this was not the first time for such an "innovation," it having been first introduced into the college program in 1922.) As part of the new curriculum a "Writing across the Curriculum" theme was adopted by the faculty in 1980, although the faculty did not approve a requirement of writing in each course. A few years later a staffed writing center was established in Memorial Hall, with Macintosh computers for student use.

In response to an editorial in the *Phoenix* (the college newspaper, renamed in May 1981) that discussed the recently changed college requirements, Dean M. D. Palmer commented about core requirements:

In the '60's when most schools disbanded core requirements, WMC held the line. In the mid-70's, when Harvard boasted of re-instituting core requirements, our own Dr. [Keith] Richwine wrote a piece for the Baltimore Sun *pointing out that WMC had never abandoned them. A curriculum is never static; but we change less than most schools do. . . . Whether this curricular conservatism is good or bad is another matter, but we have certainly not gone overboard in altering core requirements.*[8]

During the decade several new majors were approved and implemented, and modifications to others took place, in part to make the course offerings more appealing to prospective students. A major in business administration and a dual major in business and economics were approved by the faculty in 1981. Studies in communication was approved as a major in 1982; it was soon coupled with dramatic art for administrative purposes. At about the same time the Music Department, which had experienced a drop in majors, was combined with parts of dramatic art into a Performing Arts Department, and staff were hired to give some new direction.[9] However, that model did not prove very effective and was phased out in 1987. A year earlier the Music Department had been resuscitated with new courses and some joint major possibilities. By 1990, theater arts had again been revived as a full major, separated from communications, with new faculty hired to reestablish the traditional program. After a few years of upheaval and student discontent, the music and theater arts areas were stabilized, and with the addition of some new staff at the end of the decade, the campus would enjoy the results of their expanded programs in the years to come.

In 1988, a proposal for a new major leading to a bachelor's degree in nursing to be offered jointly by the college and Union Memorial Hospital School of Nursing was considered by the faculty. After much discussion between the principals, the details apparently could not be worked out, and the proposed program was terminated.[10] President Chambers also worked on a transfer program with Nagasaki Wesleyan Junior College to bring 10–20 junior students from Japan to the campus to complete their degrees. Once the program was under way and the students arrived for classes, it was quickly apparent that they did not have the English language skills necessary to

*International students visit Capitol Hill with
political science professors.*

handle college classes, and so the transfer relationship was soon dissolved.

During 1982–83, academic minors were established to provide more flexibility and breadth in student programs, and most disciplines outlined the requirements for a minor (usually 24 credit hours). Some new areas were introduced as minors, including biochemistry, commercial art, and sports medicine. In 1982 the language department revised its beginning language program, modeling it on Dartmouth College's "intensive language" approach. Only the language being taught was spoken in class, and students spent time listening to tapes and watching films and in laboratory experiences with teacher aides, as well. By the end of the decade this program was revised, retaining some of the intensive approach but returning to a more traditional course structure of 3 credits instead of 4. At the request of students, Greek was again offered on an alternating basis with Latin.[11]

For a number of years some of the faculty had felt that the college should provide an honors program for selected students. After much discussion in committees and faculty meetings over a two-year period, the Honors Program received formal faculty approval on October 10, 1985. Robert Boner was appointed the first director, and a committee worked the rest of the academic year to bring the first 20 students into the program in September 1986. Special "affinity" housing was provided in Daniel MacLea Hall. A program evaluation was held three years later and, while it made a few suggestions for change, found that the program had admirably achieved its purposes and should be continued. Over the subsequent years, the program continued to evolve, attracting excellent students while providing opportunities for special academic and social interaction. In an effort to encourage student independent research, a fund for student research and creativity grants was provided through the academic dean's office, mirroring the faculty research and creativity grant program.

The January term continued to be a popular curricular innovation, although the number of students enrolled each year began to diminish, due in part to changes in requirements, fees, credits, and administrative attention. The study tours abroad began to have more problems attracting students because costs of travel were going up; Ray Stevens, professor of English, reported that the first trip he led to England and Scotland in 1971 cost $476 per person for 22 days, but by 1981, a 15-day trip cost $1,500. Special programs and courses were still the highlight of the mini-term. For example, in 1983, a faculty lecture series entitled "Academic Potpourri" was mounted.

Opportunities for international study for a semester were formally established during the decade. Affiliation in 1980 with the Central College Consortium (of Iowa) allowed WMC students to study for a semester in England, Spain, France, Italy, Mexico, Wales, or Austria, and a number of students took advantage of those programs. In 1988, the college also affiliated with Harlaxton College in Grantham, England, and for several years students and one faculty member traveled there each fall to study and teach and to benefit from the experience of working with students from other countries.[12]

As an adjunct to the regular course offerings, departments were increasingly sponsoring guest lecturers related to their field. Students were encouraged (sometimes required) to attend, and the schedule of such events often was quite full. Three special endowed annual lectures were established during this decade. The Holloway Lecture series, named for former President Fred Holloway, was established in 1986 by Dr. and Mrs. Thomas F. Marshall, although they wished to remain anonymous until their deaths. (Thomas Marshall died in October 1991; Elizabeth Marshall died at 93 in December 2005.) On October 20, 1986, the first annual Holloway Lecture was given by Dr. Meyer Howard Abrams, from Cornell University, who had received an honorary doctor of letters from WMC at the 1985 Commencement. The second endowed lectureship was established in 1987 by Judge Elsbeth Bothe in memory of her stepson, B. Christopher Bothe '72 (1950–84), a poet and award-winning journalist and printer who died in 1984; the first Bothe Lecture, in April 1987, was given by John Wheatcroft, presidential professor of English at Bucknell University. The third lectureship was established by the will of Professor of English Emerita Evelyn Wingate Wenner in memory of her husband, C. Malcolm Wenner Jr., a railroad official, and her brother, W. Wilson Wingate, a noted Baltimore sportswriter. The annual Wenner-Wingate Memorial Lecture focuses on the history and literature of sport; the first was given on March 7, 1990, by Dr. Ronald A. Smith, a sports historian and professor at Pennsylvania State University.

In 1983 the college received from Winter Myers, via his will, a gift of 98 Egyptian pieces of art, mostly dating from the New Kingdom (c. 1570 B.C.E.), as well as some Greco-Roman pieces and a few pieces of Native American pottery. Mr. Myers was born in 1882 in a house next to Shadrack Simpson's on College Avenue, approximately where Blanche Ward Hall now stands; he also had several connections with President Ensor. Apparently, he had contemplated giving the collection to the college about 30 years earlier and established his legacy accordingly. The artifacts were stored in the library for a while (their sale was even contemplated for a time) before they were put on display on April 29, 1984, when Dr. Julie O. Badiee of the Art Department organized a program entitled "Images of Eternity" and gave an illustrated lecture about the pieces and how they fit into Egyptian religion and art. The pieces were then put on display in Hoover Library. Dr. Badiee said of the collection, "These artifacts make WMC unique among small colleges." Prior to their display, the artifacts had been restored by Professor of Art Wasyl Palijczuk, funded by a grant from the National Endowment for the Arts.[13]

Awarding honors to students who have excelled academically has always been part of the college program, and requirements for the awards have been discussed and debated in every era of the college's existence. By 1980, the number of graduating seniors receiving "Latin" honors (summa cum laude, magna cum laude, cum laude) had grown to such an extent, due primarily to nationwide grade inflation, that the faculty determined to raise the standards. Henceforth, minimum GPAs of 3.8, 3.6, and 3.4, respectively, would be required. These went into effect with the class of 1981—not without some grumbling from those who didn't make the new cuts. Two other opportunities for honor were provided when a chapter of Phi Alpha Theta, the national history honor society, was established on campus in 1981, and a chapter of Alpha Psi Omega in dramatic art was formed in fall 1983.

Nancy Weitzel '86 was one of about 550 American students that year to receive a Fulbright grant and the first at WMC since the 1950s. A German major with a secondary education minor, she spent a year studying the intellectual roots of the Revolution of 1848 at the University of Salzburg, where she had already spent her junior year.[14]

The graduate program continued to be recognized as a significant part of the college. In 1984, Stanley Bowlsbey was named dean of graduate studies, elevating his title and campus status (but not changing his duties) and putting the graduate program on a par with the undergraduate. In the same year, Hugh Prickett was named director of the Western Maryland College Center on Deafness, and the program to serve deaf-blind people received a $500,000 grant.[15] The board of trustees and the Maryland Higher Education Commission also approved offering the master of science degree rather than the master of education degree. The number of those seeking the MEd was decreasing because the number of teachers (and students) in the public schools was decreasing. The change provided a degree structure for noneducation-oriented programs, while encompassing most of the former MEd programs.[16]

While most of the editorials and letters in the college newspaper addressed some campus issue or gripe, toward the end of the decade two students commented favorably on the college and its academic program. Chris Rowley x'90 compared the college with a professional or technical school:

Western Maryland's liberal arts preparation offers you a broad range of interpersonal and communication skills that are applicable in any setting, both on and off the job. Courses off the track of study enrich one's knowledge and learning ability. . . . The WMC graduate enters the work setting ready to relate and with a balanced education and the ability to learn.[17]

Jason E. Plummer '90, reacting to a freshman who had written negatively about some of his first-semester experiences, commented,

To some people going to a small school is not a plus, but for those students who went to a small high school in the country then, yes, it is great. Here a person doesn't just become a number, like you do at College Park. Because Western Maryland College is so small, the . . . professors . . . are able to offer office hours and give personal help to every student in his/her class. The professors don't just end with office hours; they can schedule times that are convenient to both the students and themselves. Some . . . even go so far as to give students their telephone number at home. . . . It's time to grow up. . . . Stop blaming others for the things which are your own fault, not the college's![18]

STUDENT LIFE

If the students of the 1960s were activists and those of the 1970s antagonists, the students of the 1980s might be described as hedonists. Growing up in a generally affluent society, being sought after and wooed by colleges and universities as their numbers decreased, and enjoying legal alcohol consumption at age 18, many students of this generation looked at college as one more opportunity for personal pleasure. Sometimes called the "do nothing" generation, many students of this decade felt that they were owed a college education without much effort and a social life without restrictions. Realizing that this stereotype was not very positive or wholesome, one *Phoenix* editor tried to dispel it by pointing out that student activism did exist in the 1980s, although it was taking different forms. CROP walks for the hungry, anti-apartheid demonstrations, and fund-raisers for Save the Children and Food for Africa had been held on campus; and money had been collected and sent to Mexico to help build shelters for those left homeless following an earthquake. It was noted that there was a calmer tone and less anger to this activism, as students were using their advantages and education to help those less fortunate.[19] Of course, many students fit neither extreme and continued to benefit from the educational experiences provided by the college, but their academic efforts were sometimes hampered by the overall campus environment.

An impressive list of speakers appeared on campus during the decade and provided many divergent viewpoints. They included Senator Eugene McCarthy, Rev. Benjamin Chavis, Leon Stover '50, Isaac Asimov, John Barth,

Benjamin Hook, Ernest Thompson, Senator Bill Bradley, P. Lal, Margaret Zassenhaus, Speaker of the House Thomas "Tip" O'Neill, State Senator Gerald Weingrad '66, Helen Thomas, Joseph Spear '63, Arnold Newman, William Sloane Coffin, Paul Ehrlich, Senator Joseph Biden, Yolanda King, Roy Hoopes, Malcolm Miller, Kurt Schmoke, and Senator Barbara Mikulski. The regular complement of lectures sponsored by departments added to the fare, as did the annual Phi Beta Kappa visiting lecturer, who gave a public lecture and visited classes over a three-day period. One such lecturer was historian Gordon Wood from Brown University in February 1990.

Sen. "Tip" O'Neill speaks on campus.

Other college-sponsored cultural events included the North Carolina Dance Theatre; "An Evening with George Gershwin"; "Up With People"; the National Shakespeare Company's production of *As You Like It*; a concert by the Renaissance Ensemble of Baltimore; a foreign film series mounted by the Dramatic Art Department; and regular recitals, concerts, and art exhibits. The choir returned to its normal size in 1981, when Margaret Brengle assumed the directorship. She was followed in 1984 by Evelyn Smith Hering for a year, then by Beverly Gondolfo Chandler (Wells) '77 until 1989, when Margaret Boudreaux took over.

The Dramatic Art Department continued to produce numerous plays in various genres, employing casts drawn from department majors as well as from the general student body. Included in the extensive list of plays were *Trial by Jury*, *Tobacco Road*, *Waiting for Godot*, *The Boy Friend*, *A Doctor in Spite of Himself*, *Spoon River Anthology*, *Luv*, *Antigone*, *Agnes of God*, *Tartuffe*, *The Glass Menagerie*, *Major Barbara*, *A Midsummer Night's Dream*, *The Hairy Ape*, *American Buffalo*, *Dames at Sea*, *Zoo Story*, *Crimes of the Heart*, and *West Side Story*.

The Student Government Association and other student groups sponsored entertainment that included Crack the Sky, Sha Na Na, several "Mr. WMC" contests, a very successful talent show in 1989, and the annual Junior Follies (except in 1984, when apathy in the class of 1985 produced no writers or creative talent).

French horn section of the College Band in the 1980s

While the campus had experienced periodic outbreaks of illness, as enrollments increased, the potential for epidemics grew, even as combative medicines improved. Food (salmonella) poisoning caused distress for about 100 students in May 1984. Two outbreaks of highly contagious red measles occurred in 1984 and 1988, causing students and faculty to check their immunizations and get inoculations.[20] Strains of influenza also struck occasionally, especially in 1989. In an effort to focus on improved student health and illness prevention, in 1985 the college health service began holding an annual Wellness Week, which included a Wellness Fair at which various health agencies provided information to students on how to stay healthy. By this time the hazards of smoking were well known, and that health issue was part of these special foci, as well as the topic of an occasional editorial in the newspaper. Societal mores were changing, and so were those on campus. In previous decades, the sexual activity of students was somewhat ignored (or everyone pretended it did not occur). But in this decade the students (and the health service) openly discussed it; and articles dealing with herpes, chlamydia, and other sexually transmitted diseases regularly appeared in the *Phoenix*.[21] By the end of the decade, the health service was sponsoring Healthy Loving Week. Other health issues confronted the students, as well, including anorexia and bulimia, which were dealt with by the nurses, on-call doctor, and counselors. AIDS testing was also offered in the health center.[22]

Another health issue that spilled over into the general life of the campus was alcoholism. Until 1983, when the state law reverted to 21 (from 18) as the legal age for procuring and drinking alcoholic beverages, almost all students were legally able to drink on campus, and many did, some to excess. This led to many incidents of vandalism, theft, and violence. The trustee Student Affairs Committee discussed the growing problem regularly, and the Student Affairs office invoked many rules to govern alcohol consumption, often without much success. In many instances, the students involved in the inappropriate behavior (such as the vandalism of the Blanche Ward Hall lobby) acknowledged and apologized for their involvement but blamed it on being drunk and out of control.[23] Even the college newspaper took issue with the rising tide of vandalism and spoke out against it in editorials. The president of the Alumni Association, Eloise C. Payne '38, in a letter to the *Phoenix* raised a question that she said she'd "like to have answered by these students who are so destructive: How do you think we alumni feel about asking people to support the college knowing students are tearing up what we are trying to build?"[24] Some thefts of money, computers, and electronics were attributed to those needing money to purchase drugs, an increasing problem on campus and in society at large. Another aspect of the alcohol issue was that in 1986, the college gave up its license to sell beer and wine in the pub in the Decker Center because the liability insurance had become too expensive. Alcohol could still be served or given away at functions on campus, but nothing could be sold (except when day licenses were obtained). As expected, the students were unhappy, for this limited the opportunities for on-campus parties. The college was obligated to uphold the state law, and the campus policies reflected this, but as one *Phoenix* editor put it, "The new policy leaves very few options for the student who enjoys his alcohol. He may drink within the confines of his own room, join a Greek organization perhaps solely for the sake of imbibing, or withdraw from school. . . . [Perhaps] the trustees had no choice . . . [but] no one is obligated to like it."[25]

Three years later, the issue had not died down; campus rules on alcohol use were being enforced, and the students were feeling very "put upon." On September 21, 1989, about 120 students demonstrated on President Chambers's lawn at 1:30 A.M., protesting the "overzealous" campus safety officers who were enforcing the policies. Police were called, and the group was dispersed. A more reasoned voice editorialized in the *Phoenix* a few weeks later, noting that the administration, at least concerning alcohol, had been consistently fair:

> *If there had never been any abuses, would any of the privileges accorded to alcohol use have been eliminated? No. . . . As a result of alcohol abuse, sexual and other physical assaults and dormitory vandalism [have become] notoriously commonplace. We've been tried, convicted, and found guilty. Instead of being tossed into the prison of prohibition, . . . the administration has been lenient in only meting out a sentence of probation. . . . Yet we continue to violate probation. . . . The entire campus community has to take responsibility for alcohol: its privileges and its negative consequences. It's up to each individual to help win back the rights of alcohol consumption that were lost over the years. . . . Yes, as a society, we are all guilty, for we have created such an environment. How many people are going to demonstrate on President Chambers' lawn for the safety of our fellow students?*[26]

As suggested by the editorial, related to these problems was the occasional sexual assault on campus. Several women were assaulted in their dormitory rooms during the decade, sometimes by off-campus visitors who had gained access to the buildings through unlocked doors. Editorials preached that students had to assume responsibility for locking their doors to ensure safety and security. The sexual assault of a freshman in 1989 further disabused the students of the idea that "it can't happen here." A related issue was date rape, which was discussed quite candidly,[27] and self-defense techniques were offered by campus security. In 1981, sexual harassment policies were put in place by the faculty and trustees, but they did not always deter aggressors. By the end of the decade, safety was a big issue for women students, even though security had been increased and residence halls made more secure. President Chambers reported to the trustees in 1988 that "not everything was perfect in 'happy valley' all the time." Westminster was evolving from a quiet little town into a larger one with growing problems, he said, and the students were bringing more problems with them. During the previous months there had been two attempted suicides, as well as a baby born to a student whose parents had no idea she was pregnant.[28] At the beginning of the following semester, an editorial commented, "As idealistic and somewhat unrealistic as the goal of a non-racist, non-sexist, safe, and humane campus may seem, some people have organized and are looking for the very solutions to attain this goal."[29] The college was changing.

In the fraternities and sororities, membership numbers remained relatively constant, even as college enrollments fluctuated. An average of 366 students were members of Greek organizations during the decade, just slightly higher than the previous decade. The average fraternity membership ranged from 33 to 49, while the sorority average ranged from 40 to 55. Two local sororities affiliated with national organizations during the decade; Sigma Sigma Tau became Phi Sigma Sigma in 1980, and Delta Sigma Kappa rechartered as Phi Mu in 1989. Alpha Nu Omega considered colonizing with the national Alpha Omicron Pi but ultimately decided to remain local.[30] A new national fraternity appeared on campus when a chapter of Sigma Phi Epsilon was colonized and chartered in April 1983. This group served as a replacement for Delta Pi Alpha, which had its charter revoked by the college in February 1984. The Preachers had been under fire for several years, first for damaging their residence floor and then for a serious hazing violation. The Interfraternity Council commented, "The actions of the members of the Preachers were harmful and disruptive not only to themselves but also to the campus community as a whole." Noting the unfortunate national press attention the hazing incident received ("abusive brutalization of a 17-year-old freshman") and agreeing with the charter revocation, the *Phoenix* editor referred to the college's "First Principles" and urged the college to rebuke the "kind of thuggery and disregard for society that the Preachers as a collective group have come to proudly represent."[31] In subsequent years, the fraternity was unsuccessful in convincing the college administration to reinstate its charter, although a nucleus of the group continued to exist "underground" for years. Other fraternities and sororities also received sanctions, including probation and revocation of residence privileges, from time to time during the decade, usually for alcohol violations, destruction of property, or hazing. As more groups became nationally oriented, the theme of community service arose, and it was heartening to note that these groups began to participate more in the college and community at large in service projects of benefit to all. The local chapter of Phi Delta Theta proudly received three awards from the national fraternity in 1985, including one for community service.

Throughout this decade, many students expressed the feeling that the college administration was anti-Greek. This attitude was fostered, not surprisingly, by the college's increasing expectations for better behavior. In response to the Greeks, the Administrative Council (composed of the president, vice presidents, and deans) issued the following statement:

> The fraternities have asked that the college respect the fraternity tradition at Western Maryland College, especially the tradition of living together and having clubrooms. We do not object to recognizing this tradition, provided that . . . fraternities respect a much older and bigger tradition at WMC—the tradition of promoting adult behavior and academic, intellectual endeavors. . . . We believe that fraternities can contribute significantly to the total collegiate experience of schools like Western Maryland, but in our opinion, the fraternity system at [the college] is not a class act at all. . . . [The higher incidences of damage, vandalism, and disciplinary problems among fraternities] indicate poor behavior and fuel the perception that fraternities are anti-academic, anti-intellectual, anti-First Principles—in other words, that fraternities contradict the oldest traditions of this college. . . . In order for us to respect the fraternity tradition, we require a specific plan of action . . . guaranteeing support for the primary tradition of Western Maryland College.[32]

As it had for several decades, the college newspaper could be depended upon to raise issues of concern to students. Editorials each week (until the paper was forced by finances to become biweekly in April 1985) addressed such problems as fraternity hazing, limited library hours, parking, campus security, coed dormitories, raising the drinking age, the policy of no pets in the dormitories, various imposed disciplinary sanctions, problems in the dormitories, vandalism, anti-semitism, homophobia, and "the quad."

In the early 1980s, the men's quadrangle had become almost a "war zone," the residents of Albert Norman Ward Hall and Daniel MacLea Hall regularly doing battle not only in games, but also with noise and water and occasionally fire. One resident commented anonymously in a letter to the *Phoenix* editor, "Everybody who lives in the Quad is subject to verbal abuse and the fear of getting [water] bagged. This is a natural consequence of living in the Quad." Another rebutted, "It appears that some visitors do not have an understanding of the customs of the Quad. . . . We take pride in designing not a 'nightmare' but a pleasant homey environment." By 1984, the problems had escalated to the point that President John announced, "The college is interested in repossessing the quad and getting it back into the total residential program."[33] This was accomplished soon thereafter by the major renovation of both dormitories and relocating the fraternities, sororities, and independents so that both dormitories became coeducational (for the first time) by floor. Social clubrooms were reassigned, and the area between the dorms relandscaped. These actions resulted in a much better environment but did not meet with universal approval of the students at the time.

One of President Chambers's first actions was to appoint a Task Force on Student Life. It comprised trustees, faculty, students, and staff and studied all aspects of student life. After two years, it submitted its report, noting that its goal was "to promote a humane environment on campus." It dealt with the problems of alcohol and drug abuse and the inequities of resources for men and women, and it made recommendations in three areas. In residential life, dining hall improvements, a new freshman orientation program, and affinity housing options for upperclassmen were proposed. In Greek life, it recommended strengthening the Greek Council and the advising system, encouraging national affiliations, and permitting new member rush only after freshman year. To improve the social environment, the task force urged more enforcement of the alcohol regulations, the development of a student leadership program, more student-faculty interaction, and the enrollment of more black students. Some of the recommendations had already been implemented by the new dean of students, Philip Sayre, and almost all of the others were planned.[34] Indeed, the old Student Life Council, formed in the late 1950s, was resurrected in 1985 to provide for better communication about problems of campus life.

The SGA now had a Food Committee to meet regularly with dining hall management to make suggestions for better organization and menu choices. In 1984, the committee dealt with students' sometimes ridiculous requests: a deli bar at dinner, Oreo cookie ice cream at all times, microwaves, Pop-Tarts, less salt and pepper, alcohol at meals, and reservations for meals, for example. Overall, nine complaints and seven compliments were received. By 1990, students liked the soups, breads, cobblers, and the new microwaves but were asking for more variety of fruit and flavors of ice cream, more cheese, *sauerkraut*, and fewer fried items. The food service operation had always been handled in house, but in 1983, with the resignation of Arlene MacDonald, director of dining services for 12 years, the college hired the Marriott Corporation. Four years later, Marriott bowed out, and Seiler's Corporation took over.[35] In the fall of 1984, in response to the question "What is your opinion of the food and service in the Englar Dining facility?" in a small survey published by the *Phoenix*, several students responded rather negatively, prompting Nairy Ohanian '86 to comment,

I am sick and tired of students' complaints and derogatory attitudes towards the food we are daily served in the cafeteria. Yes—food—which we are served daily, 3 times. Over a fourth of the population in the world are lucky if they get one meal a day. . . . I am not suggesting we go sing praises to Englar. Yes—often the food is bland, not properly cooked, under seasoned and just not up to par with Mom's cooking, but . . . it is FOOD and it is EDIBLE and it fills the emptiness in our stomachs and quiets the hunger pangs. I have yet to see a student on campus whose rib-cage is sticking out or whose belly is bloated from improper nutrition.[36]

As in the previous decade, in the late 1980s the issue of racism on campus arose. Throughout the fall of 1988 a number of articles in the *Phoenix* dealt with black-white relations on campus, as the African American students again reminded the college of its unmet goals to increase the number of minority students (which stood at about 40) and faculty and staff and to broaden the curriculum. President Chambers addressed the issue head-on in an essay presented at a campus-wide meeting in November. In it he said,

Here at Western Maryland, we have much to answer for. This was a segregated institution until all-too-recently. It took us—like the nation as a whole—a long time to grow up. Various of our past brothers and sisters have struggled for our cause before we arrived, though, and they made this a far better place for us in the process. Now it is our task—and our opportunity—to build upon what they have given us. . . . I pledge to you my determination to do all that I can to erase racism from this campus. . . . Important steps are already being taken in that direction. . . .

The Black Student Union sponsored Black History Month.

Students living in the writers' suite helped produce The Phoenix.

The work of the Minority Task Force is [a significant] step. . . . [The admissions staff is working] to bring more minority students to the college and thereby enrich us all. . . . [And we are working] to bring more minority faculty to the campus next year. This we are determined to do. . . . [We want this institution to be] an exemplar of what a sophisticated multi-racial community can be.[37]

During Black History Month in 1989, the campus community supported racial harmony with a 100-participant candlelight march from Union Street to the Decker College Center. This was followed by an address by Rev. Herb Watson '76, who urged continued solidarity. In an article in the *Phoenix* looking back at campus race relations, Lynburg R. Scott '90, the president of the Black Student Union, commented, "Generally, most of the minorities who attend WMC find more ignorance than racism. I've found that most people are willing to learn." New courses in African American literature, history, and cultures were being developed. New black staff members were being sought. Increased financial aid was being provided for needy minority students, and Rodney Joyner '88 was hired as minority recruiter for the admissions office. The issue was still alive, but it was being discussed and addressed with less rancor and more civility. The alumni magazine also focused on "Blacks at Western Maryland" in the February 1990 issue, providing its readers with a better understanding of the problems faced by minority students at the college.

In 1987 an unsigned editorial in the *Phoenix* entitled "Credit/No Credit" took the student body to task when it said,

> *This college deserves some well-earned praise. . . . The administration and staff are constantly criticized for incidents that are most often the fault of the students. Blinded by the tuition fee, undergraduates create self-designated rights to protest regulations and procedures established to aid them. . . . The school deserves to be recognized for some of the positive accomplishments it has made, instead of constantly bombarded with complaints. In a world of higher education, couldn't someone thank a professor or faculty member once in awhile [sic]? Western Maryland College and its faculty and staff, though far from perfect, deserve more praise and admiration from the student body.*[38]

On the sports scene, the students were still very active in varsity and intramural activities. At least 20 varsity teams, some coed, attracted student involvement, and during the decade a women's soccer team and a men's ice hockey team were added. At mid-decade, the college left the Middle Atlantic Conference and helped create the new Centennial Conference (at first just for football, but eventually for all sports). The conference was composed of institutions not too far distant from one another and comparable to WMC: Dickinson, Franklin and Marshall, Gettysburg, Johns Hopkins, Muhlenberg, Swarthmore, and Ursinus. (When it expanded to include all sports, Haverford, Bryn Mawr, and Washington colleges joined.) At the same time, the first full-time football coach was hired.[39]

The football team began the decade under Coach James Hindman [1977–81], who was replaced by John Molesworth '52 [1981–86]. When the college decided to hire a full-time coach, Molesworth resigned, and Dale Sprague [1986–92] was hired from 100 applicants. Molesworth's team produced one winning and five losing seasons, and under Sprague three more losing seasons were chalked up. Indeed, in November 1987, the team ended a 29-game losing streak with a 14–3 win over Swarthmore. But things began to improve slowly from there.

Under men's soccer coach Steven Easterday, "Bunny's Brigade" turned in four winning seasons and got berths in the conference playoffs; Albert Mensah x'83 was named to the NCAA Division III All-America 3rd Team, the first time for such a nomination since 1950. Under Coach Michael Williams, who took over the team for three years in 1984, the Green Terrors had one winning season. Brian Blank coached for two years, and Matthew Robinson began a five-year stint in 1989, but both saw losing seasons for the last three years of the decade. Men's basketball, under Coach Alex Ober, turned in three winning seasons early in the decade and then began a slump of losing seasons that continued throughout the next decade. Ober retired in 1990 with a 185–207 record.

The wrestling team completed seven winning seasons and participated in some matches in Europe during the 1981 January term under Coach Sam Case, before he retired in 1990. Coach David Seibert '78, '81M [1981–] took over the baseball team in 1981, and by 1984, the Terrors were Middle Atlantic Conference champions. Most of the other seasons were not as successful. The men's lacrosse team was ranked 12th in NCAA Division III during the 1981 season and continued its winning ways through most of the decade. Coach Bill Thomas retired in 1981 after five years and was replaced by Michael Williams [1982–92], who led the team to four losing seasons followed by four straight winning seasons.

Women's sports teams continued to perform well, led by the championship volleyball teams, which turned in winning seasons and were conference champions every year, with six bids to the NCAA tournaments (in the nine years it had been held). During this time, Coach Carol Fritz tallied her 500th win. Field hockey began to come on strong, with winning seasons during the second half of the decade; it was ranked fourth in the nation at one time and was invited to the NCAA semifinals in 1988. The basketball team also started out slowly but by mid-decade gained momentum and completed five winning seasons under Coach Becky Martin '80, '81M [1985–]. Lacrosse showed a similar improvement, with five winning seasons. The record of the women's softball team was better than .500 for the decade, while the newly formed soccer team ended the decade with one winning and three losing seasons.

The coed teams for cross-country, swimming, track, and tennis generally turned in mixed results, depending on the talent available. In 1982, the women's swim team placed eighth in the NCAA Division III tournament at the University of Massachusetts in March. School records were broken, and individual efforts helped give the team its high ranking.[40] In 1990 the 100th anniversary of tennis at the college was celebrated with 100 hours of continuous playing May 9–11.

Selected to All-America teams were Michael H. Chavez '86, football, 1984; Laura C. Ciambruschini '88, lacrosse, 1987; K. Denise Frech '83, swimming, 1980, 1981, 1982, 1983; Anne H. Glaeser '83, swimming, 1981; William A. Hallett III '90, lacrosse, 1988, 1989; Richard C. Johnson '84, football, 1983; Rodney L. Joyner '88, football, 1987; Nancy B. Kammerer '88, lacrosse, 1987, 1988; Lisa K. Kleven '82, swimming, 1981, 1982; Susan Lapidus '83, swimming, 1981, 1982; Gregory A. Long '91, football, 1988; Marty T. Lurz '85, swimming, 1982; Joseph Menendez '81, football, 1980; Albert A. Mensah x'83, soccer, 1981; John B. Montanye '84, lacrosse, 1984; Charles E. Nolan '83, lacrosse, 1983; Harrison B. Peoples '80, football, 1980; Lynda L. Rennie '85, swimming, 1982; Cynthia L. Robey '87, lacrosse, 1987; Sharon Rowley '85, swimming, 1982; Eric C. Schwaab '82, lacrosse, 1982; Sandi L. Stevens '89, lacrosse, 1987, 1988, 1989; J. Jeffrey Weyer '85, baseball, 1985.

At the end of the decade, some major changes in the athletic program occurred when five faculty coaches turned over their teams to part-time staffers. The teaching load was being reduced for all faculty members, including physical education professors Case, Fritz, Carpenter, Ober, and Weyers, and they would no longer have time in their schedules for coaching. The next decade would see changes in the team programs.

The campus was saddened to learn of the deaths of Angel Pichardo, a recent addition to the admissions staff, on September 29, 1985, and Jean Alpaugh '90 on April 12, 1990, both in automobile accidents. Miss Alpaugh was awarded her BA degree posthumously that May and memorialized with an endowed award in interdisciplinary studies. As the result of another terrible automobile accident, which took the lives of Michael Beaver '79 and Pauline Grayson Beaver '79 in 1985, the Michael and Polly Beaver Award for Excellence in Education was established. Both awards are given annually. When Pan American flight 103 exploded over Lockerbie, Scotland, in 1988, the campus was shocked to learn that student Anne Lindsey Otenasek '90 and alumnus George Williams '86 were among the passengers.

BUILDINGS AND GROUNDS

As the decade opened, the renovations to Winslow Hall had been completed, and the building was in use. The renovations to the athletic stadium were slated to begin after the last home football game in November. A new all-weather track would be constructed, requiring the football field to be shifted slightly to the west to accommodate eight lanes. All of this work was slated to cost about $461,000. New metal seating (replacing the old, "comfy" concrete slabs) and a more adequate press box would also be constructed. A significant contribution to the project from trustee Scott Bair resulted in the stadium being named the Scott S. Bair Stadium, and a plaque was authorized to acknowledge the gift 60 years before from Arthur P. Hoffa, for whom the football field had originally been named. The new stadium was dedicated on October 3, 1981. A year

CSX caboose installed on campus, 1983

earlier, the improved tennis courts were named for Frank B. Hurt, professor and longtime tennis coach, who had made a substantial gift toward their renovation; Hurt attended the dedication on May 29, 1981.

Soon the stadium had a very visible reminder of the (probable) derivation of the college name, after the class of 1984 presented to the college a caboose bearing the "Western Maryland Railway" logo. The original plan was that the caboose would be turned into a refreshment stand for stadium events (but health department rules prohibited that venture). When the class officers, Ken Schaefer and Suzie Manning, approached the Chessie System (CSX) about acquiring the caboose, CSX readily agreed to donate one (appreciating the publicity such a gift would provide), and renovations were paid for jointly by the class and CSX. The gift arrived on campus the morning of July 29, 1983, thanks to the donated services of Thomas, Bennett, & Hunter, Inc. (local contractors whose president was trustee Lloyd B. Thomas), which picked up the car from the railroad crossing in the middle of town, transported it to the area above the football field, and installed and secured it on a section of railroad track. The caboose was then repainted and restenciled to include the year of the college's founding, 1867.

Further improvements to the college's athletic facilities, long overdue, continued with building of the $6 million Physical Education Learning Center, which had been in the planning stages for some time. It was originally conceived as a facility that could be built in two modules, but the college eventually decided to move forward with the whole building at a total cost of about $5 million.[41] Over a period of two years, many discussions were held about the interior design, and tensions arose when important decisions were

The Physical Education Learning Center was opened in 1984.

sometimes made without consulting the faculty and staff who would be using the facility. However, the building was completed just in time to hold the 1984 Commencement in it on May 26. It included a main playing floor, which held three basketball courts with movable baskets and seating for 2,000; a lower floor, which contained a padded wrestling room, a multipurpose room, a dance studio, locker rooms, and equipment storage; a one-story "hyphen," containing a box office, a memorabilia room, and rest rooms; and the older Gill Gymnasium, the locker rooms of which had been remodeled to provide offices for the Physical Education Department faculty and athletic staff.

During the decade, several large remodeling projects were undertaken. In the summer of 1984 Albert Norman Ward Hall was gutted, the four sections removed, and standard dormitory rooms and bathrooms on long halls installed. The administration felt that changing the internal structure of the building and making the dormitory coed by floor would eliminate some discipline problems.[42] The building was occupied early in the fall and was well received by the students. The following year Daniel MacLea Hall was also renovated completely, although the sectional configuration was retained. Suites of rooms were created on each floor and additional bathrooms installed. The suites were then offered to various coed affinity groups, including the students enrolled in the Honors Program. A smaller-scale remodeling project took place in Baker Memorial Chapel in 1981, when the chancel area was cleared of all furniture and railings, creating a large, open, multipurpose space. The altar, pulpit, and lectern were put on rollers so they could be rolled into place when they were needed for a religious service, but the old choir loft was eliminated. The basement area was partitioned into classrooms and offices, and the Foreign Language Department moved there in 1984. Once the Psychology Department had moved into Winslow Hall, the basement area of the library was remodeled to house 150,000 volumes. McDaniel Lounge also underwent a much-needed renovation during the decade. By the end of the decade, a new steam plant housing three boilers and an emergency steam boiler was approved to replace the former heating plant, which had become inadequate and inefficient. A new computer center was approved, to be put either in Lewis Hall or in another building; it would be financed from the revenue of the ten-year lease of the lower level of Lewis Hall to the Government Services Administration. The possibility of a new science laboratory facility was also being explored.[43]

Other remodeling and repair work was called for as a result of several fires on campus during the decade. A picnic fire got out of control and burned some of the roof of the Harvey Stone Pavilion in 1981; a room in Rouzer Hall was accidentally burned out in 1984. The most serious damage, however, was caused by a fire in Blanche Ward Hall in July 1988, one of a series of seven arson attempts on the campus that summer that included the caboose and a room in Rouzer Hall. The fire in Blanche Ward was confined to the first floor, but damage to the walls and wood floors was severe enough to require some major renewal that took several months. This necessitated 40 women students being housed in a motel until October 1, but insurance covered all the repair work, as well as the motel. A former campus security officer later admitted starting most of the fires, and he was incarcerated for a time.[44]

In 1984, the infirmary was closed, and a health room was created for basic medical services, a move that saved the college $60,000 a year. The Carroll County General Hospital was just across town, and its emergency room could handle the more difficult situations. Health services were moved first to the Decker College Center and then to Smith House (along with the Career and Counseling Office). Thompson Hall was eventually remodeled to provide offices for the Education Department and graduate program, which took over the facility in 1988. In turn, Carroll Hall, which had housed the Education Department for over 25 years, was soon remodeled to recapture its Victorian splendor and make it suitable for the Office of Admissions.

Properties contiguous to the campus (on Pennsylvania Avenue or Main Street) continued to be purchased as they became available. Of particular note was the procurement of the Geiman house at 245 W. Main Street, next door to Harrison Alumni House, which was purchased in 1987 for $150,000. For a number of years it has served as the home of the dean of students. In 1988, the Doyle property at the intersection of New Windsor Road and Uniontown Road, across the street from Carroll Hall, was purchased for $125,000. Other

In 1991, the addition to Hoover Library
doubled its size.

properties came to the college through bequests. One, known as the Grace Fox House, in Uniontown was received in 1984, and it was thought that it might serve as a college guesthouse. Some renovation of the property was achieved, and it saw some use as a staff residence; but the trustees eventually realized that it was too far from campus to be a useful addition to the facilities, and they determined to sell it. Some of the antique furnishings were given to the local historical society, where a Grace Fox Room was created; others were placed in Carroll Hall. In 1989 the house was sold for $228,000.[45]

In 1987 the college learned that it was the beneficiary of a portion of a property six miles south of Westminster through the will of Marthiel Mathews. The remaining two-thirds of the 68-acre property had been willed to Johns Hopkins University by Mrs. Mathews's brother, Charles S. Singleton, a Hopkins professor and internationally known Dante scholar to whom WMC had given an honorary LitD degree in 1965, when he was the commencement speaker. (Apparently, Singleton had planned to bequeath his share to WMC as well, but died before a new will could be drawn up.) The college was able to purchase that portion from Hopkins for $260,000 in October 1988, after which plans for development of the houses and grounds moved forward under the direction of George Grier x'39, an assistant to the president.[46] A number of uses, scientific and cultural, were suggested over the

*The Conference Center and Quality Inn
opened in 1986.*

years, and the several houses on the property were rented to staff members. Some of the acreage on a higher portion of the property was divided into eight building lots and sold, adding to the endowment. A third property came to the college through a gift of Claude Schaefer: 63 acres of land in Dundalk, in Baltimore County, worth about $1.2 million. Mr. Schaefer wanted to make the property into an early-childhood education center that the college would operate. However, much study of the property and the project suggested that selling it and placing the proceeds in the endowment would be best.

An interesting discussion was held in 1981 by college representatives with a New Windsor resident, Mrs. Clyfford Still, regarding the possibility of the college housing her husband's artworks. Clyfford Still was considered a major modern American artist, who had moved to rural Maryland to continue his painting some years before his death. Upon his death, his widow sought a place to house his many canvasses, some very large. However, the stipulations of his will were so restrictive (requiring a freestanding building devoted only to his work) that the college (and many other institutions) could not meet them, and the collection remained without a permanent home, even after her death 20 years later.

It is said that every 25 years a college library needs to be doubled in size to accommodate the materials and knowledge created during that time. Such was the case with Hoover Library, opened in 1962. It had been remodeled to incorporate all the lower-level space, but it needed more. Plans for an addition to the older building were begun in 1988, under the direction of David Neikirk [1987–2002], from the University of Delaware, who had been hired to be library director and to oversee the expansion project to completion. The Hillier Group of New Jersey was hired to be the architects, and in March 1988 a preliminary plan for a 34,000-square-foot addition, doubling the size of the building, was proposed at a projected cost of $8 million.[47] Construction was authorized in February 1989 and a groundbreaking held on July 10 with Governor William Donald Schaefer joining board chair William Keigler and President Chambers in turning the shovelfuls of earth. The trustees approved moving the stained-glass ceiling from the old 1908 library (now the fine arts building) to the new facility, where it was installed in the ceiling of the board room.[48]

Use of the 35 acres of land beyond Rt. 31 to the west of the campus had been under discussion for several years, its sale always a possibility. In 1980, the trustees authorized a land study and appraisal. In 1982, the sale of the land was postponed until a more favorable economic climate returned. But by 1983, discussions were under way with developers to build a motel, conference center, and restaurant complex on the property. In 1984, the Buildings and Grounds Committee reported to the trustee Executive Committee that such a complex was feasible and had long-term possibilities, and so approval was given to move ahead with a plan for a 100-room motel.[49] In its October 1985 meeting, the board directed that a private corporation be formed to manage the investment. The project moved forward quickly, the WMC Development Corporation—composed of trustee Dolores Snyder, President Chambers, and Vice President for Business Affairs Thomas Kimball—formed on December 9, 1985, to become an equal partner with the Harkins Group, a development company. The college trustees then sold the property to the corporation for $1.3 million. The project was to be funded through industrial revenue bonds through Carroll County; George Grier played a significant behind-the-scenes role in handling permitting and financing. Groundbreaking was held on March 11, with the motel projected to open in September 1986. In May the Marriott Corporation was hired to manage the new restaurant, which was slated to open in spring 1987 under the direction of a separate subcorporation composed of trustees Lloyd B. Thomas, Richard F. Kline Jr., and M. Lee Rice.

The Quality Inn motel complex opened in mid-October and immediately had a good occupancy rate; getting the restaurant up and running was more difficult. After much discussion, the Marriott Corporation bowed out and Seiler's Corporation entered into a contract to invest in and run the restaurant, as well as the college's food service operation.[50] The conference center opened for business on February 14 with a wedding reception, but the restaurant was behind schedule. In March it was agreed to name the restaurant McDaniel's and designate the lounge area as Billy Mac's. By April, the conference center was much in demand. The grand opening of the conference center complex, including the restaurant, was slated for June 26. The next several years were difficult for the Development Corporation as it struggled to keep management in place and deal with shortfalls in expected income, especially from the restaurant. There was even discussion of expanding the conference center to make it more profitable. A master plan for further development of the triangle of land bordered by State Routes 31, 32, and 140 was authorized.[51] This for-profit investment program would continue to have some financial and management problems for several years, but ultimately good planning prevailed and the college began to reap the benefits, as the corporation returned profits to the college endowment. More development of the property would occur during the next decade.

Chandler House, which stood at the bottom of the walk down the hill from Elderdice Hall, had been a seminary faculty house for a number of years (since c.1925) and was named for one of its longtime inhabitants, Dr. Douglas Chandler. The trustees decided that it should carry a name related to the history of the college, and in October 1982, it was formally renamed Smith House to pay tribute to John Smith, the first trustee board chair, who had loaned the bulk of the money to build the first college building. An earlier Smith Hall (1887) had been razed in 1959, and the name had been lost to the campus.

When he was a student, faculty member Jonathan Slade '88 [2000–], of the Communication Department, wrote a tongue-in-cheek article for the *Phoenix* in which he commented on the names of various campus buildings:

> *Those who named the various structures around WMC had a limited vocabulary. Yes, McDaniel and Daniel MacLea are two different dorms. And we've got both a Decker Auditorium and a Decker College Center, one for each side of the campus. There's also a Little Baker Chapel, a Big Baker Memorial, a Memorial Hall, a Ward Memorial Arch, and a Blanche Ward Hall. And what about A.N.W. (which is what the locals affectionately call the Albert Norman Ward dormitory)? A.N.W.? That's a root beer, isn't it? . . . It seems the trustees, then, have thrown six base words into a hat and, with every impending dedication ceremony, draw them out in a different order. (Incidentally, this fall the new Baker Decker Ward Memorial Conference Center opens.) Well, at least they got original when naming Hoover Library, even if it does suggest that WMC has a stake in the vacuum cleaner business.*[52]

FINANCES

P resident Chambers reported at his first faculty meeting in September 1984 that the pool of high school seniors was expected to continue to decrease until 1992 (by as much as 25% from 1979). The college experienced decreasing enrollments for five successive years, 1982–86, due in part to fairly high attrition—in 1983 almost 20%—between freshman and sophomore years.[53] Beginning the decade with about 1,300 students, the numbers gradually decreased to a low of 1,064 in 1986 before making a major jump back above 1,200 in 1987 (perhaps due to a better image and excellent admissions materials) and to a high of 1,261 in 1989. The average enrollment for the decade was 1,215, with a range from 1,064 to 1,320. For the years 1979–85, women outnumbered men in the entering classes, but beginning in 1986, men reversed the trend.

Costs were rising in every area due to inflation; the cost of heating oil increased 274% in five years, while overall operating costs increased 61%.[54] Consequently, tuition, room, and board fees saw annual increases averaging about 10%, the highest being 15% in 1986 (which may have been a factor in the decreasing enrollments). Total fees almost tripled, from $5,625 in 1980 to $14,530 in 1989. Even with these increases, the college was very competitive, its total costs below those of many institutions in the region. The annual budget rose from $10.3 million to $22.5 million, a 120% increase over the ten-year period. Even in tight budget years, however, the college usually ended with a slight surplus; in 1987 the surplus was $56,000, 0.3% of the year's budget of $19 million. Nevertheless, there was little extra for facility maintenance; only the most essential things were taken care of, which created larger problems for the future.[55] Because the entering classes of several years at mid-decade did not reach budget projections, the budgets had to be recreated in September to react to the loss of revenue.

In 1985 it was reported to the trustees by the vice president for finance that the college would be 74% dependent upon tuition and fees in 1985–86, while the national average for similar liberal arts colleges was 58% and for Maryland colleges, 61%. The need to reduce this dependency, to at most 62%, was very real in a time of declining enrollments. At first, any shortfalls could be covered by the reserve account, but in 1983, that fund had been depleted, and serious budgetary tightening was invoked to maintain equilibrium. (As of 1981, faculty were represented on the Budget Committee, which brought new perspectives to the process.) By 1985, President Chambers was pessimistic about maintaining balanced budgets, given the continuing enrollment declines, changing tax structures, soaring costs, and changing political scene in Maryland. He reported, however, that a budget director had been hired to keep a close eye on college finances, especially financial aid, to avoid shortfalls. Faculty and staff salaries made up the largest amount of the budget, about 60%, and over the ten-year span rose on average from about $20,000 to over $37,000—about 8% per year. The top professor's salary was $28,800 in 1980 and rose to $47,825 in ten years, almost a 70% increase; an average assistant professor's salary rose from about $18,000 to $30,670, again a 70% increase. Major efforts were made to more adequately compensate the highest professorial levels while remaining competitive at the lower levels. The highest salary paid in 1980 was the lowest amount paid in 1990. However, the increases, competitive and reasonable in light of national trends, had to be seen in light of the national economy. In 1983, economist Ethan Seidel, speaking for the Faculty Affairs Committee, noted that over the previous year the faculty had lost 20% in real income due to inflation, even though salaries had been raised 8%.[56]

Other significant financial factors that affected faculty and staff were that Medicare payments for retired employees over 65 were now covered,[57] and faculty committees were discussing the possibility of a six-course teaching load rather than a seven-course load, which had many budgetary implications.[58] By the end of the decade the latter had been approved, resulting in some curricular revision and more dependence on adjunct instructors.

In 1983, Ryland Homes made a gift of $100,000 to build a home in the Westminster area for people with developmental learning disabilities, to be staffed by students in the master's degree program in special education. This was the beginning of the TARGET program, designed by education professor Donald R. Rabush. An endowment fund was established in 1988 to provide scholarships for all graduate students in this special program and to pay for the director, who would be a member of the faculty in special education.[59] Trustee Lawrence J. Adams made a substantial contribution to the project, and the endowed chair was named for him.

One positive factor during these rather difficult times was that the endowment continued to grow. Over the decade, it almost tripled, from $6.1 million in 1980, to $10 million in 1985, to $16.8 million in 1990. There was some fluctuation during the late 1980s, but it rebounded. Aiding in its growth were several significant bequests, including $1 million from the estate of former trustee McClure Rouzer, a bequest of $216,000 from a nonalumnus whose father was in the class of 1886, $250,000 willed by Vivian Englar Barnes '21, and over $4 million from the Robert Gill estate.

During the decade, the trustees mounted three financial campaigns, two for capital improvements and one for general program support. The Operation Renovation Campaign of the previous decade wound down, having reached its goal of $1,375,000, and the next capital campaign, for the physical education center, was on the drawing boards, with help from Marts & Lundy, Inc. It was called the Physical Dimension, and the goal was $6 million.[60] The trustees pledged $1 million, and a $300,000 grant from Black & Decker laid the groundwork; $300,000 was allocated from the Gill bequest; and the State of Maryland contributed $1.325 million. The campaign continued for several years after the building was opened in 1984. A new campaign entitled Nurturing Quality was launched in 1986 to raise $750,000 for unrestricted support during mid-decade to help with many of the deferred projects.[61] Toward the end of the decade, the expansion of the library became the focus of a new capital campaign, for which the state provided $2 million (the largest state grant in the college's history). The college still had to raise millions toward the $10 million goal ($8 million to build the building and $2 to endow it). At this time, many institutions were moving toward large comprehensive campaigns seeking funds for capital improvements, endowments, and special projects, and the trustees began to consider this alternative to the specific fund-raising projects that had always been used in the past. Marts & Lundy was hired to do an audit of the college's fund-raising possibilities; it determined that more staff and time would be needed to build a giving base, attract potential donors, and mount a comprehensive campaign.[62]

James Ridenour, who was leaving his post of vice president for development, raised over $3 million, the best in the college's history, in his last year (1983–84). Indeed, the total decade of the 1980s produced $17,880,792 in contributions to the college, 80% from individuals and 20% from organizations and foundations. Nationally, 58% normally came from individuals and 42% from organizations and foundations. At WMC 48% of the total funding came from alumni, in part from the Annual Fund, which was rising every year, whereas nationally only 25% came from alumni. The trustees agreed that the college needed to cultivate new sources of revenue and not continue to depend on existing constituencies.[63]

As part of a long-range approach to fund-raising and improved admissions, a marketing study was approved by the trustees in 1984, and by 1985, efforts were being made to increase awareness of the college in the Washington, D.C., area. The market research report recommended an ad hoc market perceptions study committee, with an eye to changing the college name because it caused so many misperceptions among prospective students: "Western Maryland College is seen by its potential students as being a publicly supported institution in far-western Maryland, and the effect of its name is to diminish the perceived quality-level of the college."[64] In 1986, North Charles Street Design, a Baltimore public relations firm, submitted a proposal to help the college improve its image and be more competitive. The four-year program the firm proposed would cost about $35,000 per year, an expense that was approved because it seemed critical to the viability of the institution. It was paid for by funds borrowed from the endowment and paid back at 8% interest from future budgets. The marketing perceptions study report of 1988 revealed that the image of the college was good where it was known, but that the college needed to expand public awareness in new areas. To assist with this, North Charles Street Design produced a promotional video.

New admissions materials were also designed, incorporating Garry Trudeau's *Doonesbury* cartoons, of which the college had been given exclusive use by the creator, a former student of President Chambers at Yale and an honorary alumnus as of 1984. (Ironically, once this marketing tool was under way, Trudeau used marketing of a college as the theme of his cartoon for a while.) Merit (no-need) scholarships were also planned, and by spring 1986, 89 had been awarded to incoming students who had a 3.5 or higher high school GPA and a total of at least 1100 on the SAT. A few years later the college's Admissions Committee began to hold merit scholarship competitions each spring, in which eligible students were invited to campus for interviews and a judged essay writing experience. As a result of this, in the entering class in 1989, 22 received full-tuition scholarships, 36 were awarded half-tuition, and 66 received third-tuition merit scholarships. Maryland Distinguished Scholars were invited to the campus for a luncheon beginning in 1987; as a result, the college attracted a number of those fine students. The Carroll County Scholarship program was also established, providing $1,000 per year for any Carroll County resident attending the college. This was in part a reaction to the impending formation of the Carroll Community College. Another new program was designed for marginal students, who were admitted to summer school to prove themselves. In 1987, 82 were invited and enrolled in the summer courses, and 75% were deemed eligible for admission in the fall as a result.

Not only was the summer school busy with classes, primarily for graduate students by this time, the summer conference program continued to grow and provide additional funding. Longtime summer conference director (and emeritus music professor) Alfred deLong retired in 1983 after 47 years, and a new director of marketing and facilities management, Barry Bosley [1985–2003], was appointed. Beginning in 1981 the Maryland State Department of Education sponsored a series of programs for gifted and talented middle and high school students, one of which was held on the WMC campus. Classes were taught for several weeks by college faculty, and the students had an opportunity to see what it was like to live on a college campus (and get to know more about the college). In summer 1986 a biology institute drew 36 young scientists for research and study, several sports camps attracted 200 youngsters, 28 high schoolers attended a band camp, and 5 college chemistry students worked with Richard Smith on cancer research. It was announced in the fall of 1983 that the Baltimore Colts would be returning in summer 1984 after a 13-year hiatus.[65] Alas, this opportunity for prospective student visitation was not to be, for the Colts disappeared from Baltimore to new facilities in Indianapolis. An interesting financial fact was reported in an article by John Steadman, Baltimore sports columnist, about the Colts' days at the college. For the first camp in 1949, the team paid $4.25 per person per day for three meals. In the 1969 arrangement, they paid $8.00 per person per day for meals, plus a fee of $1,000 a week for use of the facilities. In 1971, the final year of camp, they paid $10,000 for rooms and the fields, plus $32,172.42 for meals, meaning that the Colts operated their six- or seven-week training camp for the economical sum of $42,172.42. John Unitas, Hall of Fame quarterback, commented of those days, "It's where it all began in 1956 for me. The set-up was perfect. Clean, spacious, good food, and friendly people."[66]

MAJOR EVENTS

On October 30, 1981, the undefeated 1951 football team held a reunion with its coach, Charlie Havens. Organized by Walter Hart '51, the team captain, along with Victor Makovitch '52, Ronald Jones '55, and Mitch Tullai '52, the event was held at Martin's Westminster with 25 players from the team in attendance, along with about 75 other friends. Players came from as far away as Florida and California, and many had not seen each other for 30 years. The guest speaker for the reunion was John Steadman, sports editor for the *Baltimore News American*. Remembering Coach Havens and the 1950s football era were the present WMC coaches, John Molesworth '52, Ira Zepp '52, and Walter Hart. They said of Havens, "He was a great coach. Everybody loved to play for him. It's hard to realize 30 years have gone by that quickly."[67] The group established the Charles W. Havens Award, to be given annually to a graduating athlete who shows the humanitarian traits evident in the life of Havens.

Theatre on the Hill (TOTH), a summer theater project sponsored by the college, began presenting plays in 1982 on the main stage and in the Elderdice Theatre in Alumni Hall. The project was designed by Ira Domser and Tim Weinfeld of the Theatre Arts Department and Del Palmer, administrator of the department and later dean of academic affairs. The first year, *Godspell* and *Man of La Mancha* were chosen because they were well known and "crowd pleasers." Following years saw such productions as

Professor I. Domser (left) produced
Theatre on the Hill beginning in 1982.

Oliver!, Charley's Aunt, Cabaret, Carousel, Jesus Christ Superstar, Once Upon a Mattress, Chicago, A Funny Thing Happened on the Way to the Forum, and *Camelot*, as well as more intimate musical revues like "Cole," "Side by Side by Sondheim," and "Berlin to Broadway"; comedies; and children's shows like *Peter Pan, The Hobbit*, and *Beauty and the Beast*. Except for two seasons when Alumni Hall was being renovated, TOTH produced quality entertainment for the community each summer.

The banner "Local Boy Makes Good" could have been stretched across the main entrance to the college on March 18, 1982, when Ernest "Dick" Thompson, son of late Associate Professor Emeritus Theron B. Thompson, visited the campus. Dick Thompson, who grew up in Westminster and graduated from Westminster High School in 1967 and the American University in 1971, was a successful actor and well-known author of the prize-winning play *On Golden Pond*. The play opened in 1978, made it to Broadway, and then went on tour, where it was a huge success. Thompson also wrote the screenplay for the film version of the play, which featured Katharine Hepburn, Henry Fonda, and Jane Fonda, and for which he won an Oscar in 1982; the film also won the Oscar for Best Picture. In February 1981 a local production of the play was mounted by the Carroll Arts Council, directed by Tim Weinfeld of the theater arts faculty and featuring English professor Ray Phillips in the role of Norman Thayer, a character based in part on the playwright's father. The 1982 return to Westminster was an opportunity for Thompson to visit the campus, spend time talking to the theater arts majors in Alumni Hall, and hold a press conference before a showing of the film version of the play at the Carroll Theatre. He said during those remarks, "When I walk across the campus, I feel [my father's] ghost follow me."

Oscar winner Ernest Thompson

That evening he returned to the Alumni Hall stage to give a lecture, at the close of which he presented the college with a gift of $5,000 in his father's name for use by the Education Department.[68] Thompson's next play, *The West Side Waltz*, also starred Katharine Hepburn on Broadway. He noted that the main character in that play, Margaret Mary Elderdice, was named for Dorothy Elderdice, whom he recalled as "a neighbor [on Green Street] and a force in his life."[69] Thompson returned to Westminster several more times during the decade. He was invited to give the address at the 1983 Commencement and to receive an honorary doctor of letters degree, for which he was presented by his justifiably proud former high school English teacher and mentor, William G. "Mike" Eaton '30. In 1987 he was the featured speaker at the Carroll County 150th birthday dinner attended by 1,000 people in the Physical Education Learning Center on January 19.

In June 1983, the college chapter of Phi Beta Kappa inducted an alumna into its ranks: Bessie Lee Gambrill of the class of 1902, the college's oldest alumna at that time. Dr. Gambrill had celebrated her 100th birthday on January 30 with a large party at the Whitney Center in Hampden, Connecticut, where she resided. She had graduated from WMC summa cum laude, earned her MA and PhD in psychology and education at Columbia University, and become the first female professor at Alfred University in New York. She had also taught for a time at Trenton (NJ) State Normal College (now the College of New Jersey) before being recruited by Yale. She was a pioneer in developing theories of child development. At Yale she was again the first woman faculty member, and as a member of the graduate faculty, the first woman to advise both male and female doctoral candidates. Speaking later about breaking the sex barrier, she said, "I didn't think about it. I was doing the job I was equipped for far better than anybody else." WMC awarded her an honorary doctor of letters degree in 1943. She was invited to go to Japan for four months after World War II to work with the American occupation helping Japanese leaders reestablish elementary schools and promote democracy. She retired from Yale in 1953 as associate professor emerita. Alumni director Donna D. Sellman and Phi Beta Kappa chapter secretary James Lightner traveled to Connecticut to confer the alumna membership and to hold a reception in her honor, also at the Whitney Center. Attending that reception were a number of Dr. Gambrill's former students, among them two former secretaries of the U.S. Office of Education. Later, she often mentioned her delight at being inducted into Phi Beta Kappa; it meant so much to her that she had postponed a bladder operation until after her induction, forthrightly telling her doctor that she did not want to take a chance on missing that.[70] Bessie Lee Gambrill died five years later at age 105.

As June 30, 1984, approached, appropriate activities to recognize the retirement of President John were planned. A faculty and trustee reception and dinner were held on May 19, followed by a slide presentation in Alumni Hall, "Right, Privileges, Honors, Headaches, and Accomplishments," highlighting the John years, with 300 in attendance. Serious and humorous events were recalled by friends and colleagues, including Hurst R. Anderson, president emeritus of The American University and John's early mentor; Bernice Beard for the president's office staff; Wilbur Preston for the trustees; Lisa H. McKinney '84 for the students; Eloise Payne for the Alumni Association; and Mike Eaton for the Westminster community. At the conclusion of the 90-minute tribute, Kale Mathias presented a gift, and President John expressed his thanks with the emotional response, "This is quite an evening for a country boy!" He also commented on his hobby of bee keeping: "Occasionally I am stung but it is not as painful as encounters I have with irate alumni and trustees." In addition to the lighthearted comments, the retiring president was praised for his leadership in fund-raising, for leaving the college in good financial shape, for governing the campus's growth, for encouraging students to do community service, and for strengthening a link between campus and community. At the 1984 Commencement a week later (the first event held in the new Physical Education Learning Center), John, at the request of the senior class, delivered the address "From the Threshold," and his retirement was again noted.[71]

Writing in the *Hill*, Dean Del Palmer noted several things about the John presidency that he felt were significant: He brought students into the work and development of the college, through committee assignments and as visitors to the board of trustees. He worked to have faculty visitors to the board of trustees, integrating this core group into the deliberations and planning for the institution. He emphasized development and involved the faculty with the wide network of the community, and especially with the alumni.[72] John, during an interview for the same publication, said he felt the most significant changes during his administration had been raising the level of collegiality among students, alumni, trustees, parents, and administrators; revamping the college's undergraduate curriculum and making the graduate program broader and more responsive to changing needs through two new degrees; establishing a Phi Beta Kappa chapter on campus; and building a new college center, athletic complex, and student apartments and renovating Alumni Hall, the athletic fields, Winslow Hall, and the library. He concluded, "I tend to be typed as a development president. This suits me fine, except that I [hope] other more fundamental things [will be] recognized."[73] Following his retirement, he received the Outstanding Civilian Service Medal for his support of the ROTC program on campus during his presidency. In July, Ralph and Dot John moved to their home in Ocean Pines, Maryland, but he returned to the campus occasionally to help with the ongoing Physical Dimension Campaign.

Homecoming 1984 was an especially happy day, for not only did the Terrors defeat Dickinson College 22–10, but the new Physical Education Learning Center (which would be named for Robert Gill in 1986) was formally dedicated in outdoor ceremonies in front of the building that morning. Taking part in the ribbon-cutting ceremony were board chair Robert Bricker; President Robert Chambers; and trustee William Keigler, national chair of the Physical Dimension Campaign. Keigler was delighted to announce that the college had received a $300,000 challenge grant from the Kresge Foundation toward the $6 million campaign goal. The challenge was that the college had to raise an additional $1 million by June 15, 1985, which was accomplished on schedule.

On July 1, 1984, the Chambers family moved into the President's House, which underwent some remodeling, including air conditioning and a new kitchen for entertaining. The trustees felt that a formal presidential inauguration should be held, and November 10 was chosen as the date. A weekend of special activities was planned by a committee of faculty, alumni, trustees, and students, cochaired by trustee Robert Mathias and Professor Lightner. The events began on Friday, November 9, with an inaugural lecture, "Unpopular Teaching," given by Dr. Dennis O'Brien, former president of

Bucknell University and the recently inducted president of the University of Rochester (NY). A reception followed in the President's House. The centerpiece of the weekend was the inaugural ceremony on Saturday at 10:30 A.M. in the Physical Education Learning Center. An impressive and colorful academic procession, including 150 delegates from colleges, universities, and academic societies, as well as the faculty and trustees, began the event, marching into the arena to music provided by the College Band. Presiding was Wilbur Preston, honorary chairman of the board of trustees. Greetings from the State of Maryland were extended by Comptroller Louis Goldstein, after which an address entitled "Great Heavens, We ARE Mad!" was given by Richard Warch, the president of Lawrence University (WI) and a friend of Dr. Chambers from their days on the Yale faculty. Warch explained that his theme was taken from the 1947 Peter Arno cartoon in *The New Yorker* when Western Maryland had played Harvard in football (see page 392). He stressed that the role of colleges like Western Maryland was to offer students learning experiences that increase potential and equip them with the tools to determine the meaning of work and life. And he expressed his feeling that the college had chosen the right man for its new president. The address was followed by the formal investiture of the chain of office by board chairman Robert Bricker, assisted by Dean of Academic Affairs Melvin Palmer, Alumni Association president Jerome P. Baroch '64, SGA president Peter Brooks '86, and President Emeritus John. In his inaugural response, President Chambers recalled the history of the college and praised the work of the small liberal arts college. He went on to say,

> I am happy to shoulder [the responsibilities of the presidency] because Western Maryland College is founded upon two academic pillars I hold most dear—liberal education and strong teaching. The purpose of this inauguration is to celebrate their embodiment in an institution standing at the very heart of the American academic enterprise. . . . Strong leadership has been here from the very beginning. . . . The fervent labors of [my predecessors] have steadily been joined with a growing faith among all constituents in what Western Maryland stands for. Thus over the years, our saga has evolved into the institution we see today. . . . My argument, then, is that the liberal arts college remains a strong and necessary ingredient of America's educational, cultural, and psychological well-being. It is, in fact, a national treasure and should be recognized as such.[74]

Honorary degrees were conferred on cartoonist Garry Trudeau; Kurt L. Schmoke, state's attorney and later mayor of the City of Baltimore; and James B. Tobin, Nobel laureate and Sterling Professor of Economics at Yale University.

(Schmoke, as well as Trudeau, was Chambers's former student and Tobin a faculty colleague at Yale.) Following the formal ceremony, a luncheon for all the delegates, faculty, and trustees was held in Gill Gymnasium. Servers for the event were members of campus fraternities and sororities. After lunch brief and sometimes humorous greetings were delivered by representatives of the faculty, student body, administration, alumni, and State of Maryland, as well as friends from Yale University, friends from Bucknell University, the "Colorado Four," and the honorary degree recipients. Western Maryland played Johns Hopkins in football in Baltimore that afternoon (losing 0–24), and an all-campus cocktail reception with a Broadway review and dancing was held that evening in Gill Gymnasium. On Sunday morning, a service in Baker Chapel featured a sermon by Rev. Dr. Stuart Henry of Duke University Divinity School. Henry had been a mentor to Dr. Chambers in his undergraduate days and inspired him to study literature and religions at Yale.[75] On Sunday afternoon, the Choral Arts Society of Carroll County presented a concert in Baker Memorial Chapel featuring Haydn's "Te Deum Laudamus" and Poulenc's "Gloria in Excelsis." During the second half of the program, the College Choir joined the society in performing several pieces, including Pinkham's "Christmas Cantata."

Every commencement is special for the graduates, but some have particular twists that make them stand out. Such was the case in 1986, when the graduating seniors and their families gathered for the Baccalaureate Service in Baker Memorial Chapel on May 24. After a 12-year hiatus, this ceremony had been resurrected the previous year. An equally old tradition, of having the speaker be a member of the faculty, whose identity would be revealed at the ceremony, was resurrected in 1986. (This tradition went back to the late 1890s and was part of the original investiture ceremony; it had been dropped when the investiture was combined with an honors convocation and an outside speaker was invited to give the address.) For this occasion the designated "secret" speaker was Professor James Lightner, who spoke on the nature of academic traditions, including academic freedom. Readings from the Judeo-Christian heritage were presented by senior representatives of various faiths, and benedictions were given by leaders of the faiths. Following the ceremony, a reception was held on the president's lawn, after which everyone moved to the Decker College Center for an all-campus party with students, parents, family, and faculty enjoying refreshments and dancing.

The following morning, the ROTC detachment commissioned the newest second lieutenants in a ceremony that featured an address by a visiting military officer. Seniors and their families enjoyed a buffet luncheon in the college dining room, and then the seniors lined up for the academic procession while their families took seats in the Physical Education Center for the 2 P.M. ceremony.

After the traditional procession of graduates and faculty into the arena to music provided by the College Brass Ensemble, the College Choir sang a musical setting of the Walt Whitman poem "Song of Democracy." President Chambers welcomed everyone to the event, and greetings were extended. Sharon K. Eimer, senior class president and recipient of the Mary Ward Lewis Prize, noted, "We've seen a lot of changes here on the Hill, but one of the things that remains constant is the friendship we've had with each other." Frederick W. Hubach '54, father of Karl S. Hubach '86, praised the class for its achievements, saying, "You have in some measure left an imprint on the college for those who will follow, and you can be proud of that." Speaking for the faculty who were sitting behind her on the dais, Eulalia Benejam Cobb, associate professor of foreign languages, commented that the graduates were more likely to remember their moments of passion than individual events that sparked their intellectual curiosity, but the cumulative effect of their learning experiences in college would remain: "The process that goes on during the acquisition of a liberal arts education is far more insidious, and far more indelible, than the transports of love. . . . We will be there, inside your brain, holding office hours in your head the rest of your life."[76] Cheryl Lynne Wheatley, a physics major with a 4.0 grade average, was presented with the Argonaut Award, and William J. Godwin Jr., a social studies teacher at Glenelg High School in Howard County, received the Distinguished High School Teacher Award.

Three honorary degrees were conferred by President Chambers. Thomas Howard Eaton '27, a retired engineer active in farming and conservation on the Maryland Eastern Shore, was presented for the doctor of humane letters degree by President Emeritus John. Eaton, a trustee of the college (and a later generous benefactor) encouraged the graduates to return to their alma mater often "to keep on learning." Professor McCay Vernon presented Roderick J. Macdonald for the doctor of humane letters. Macdonald, who was deaf and blind, was a computer scientist and president of the American Association for the Deaf-Blind. After the citation was read and signed into his hand by his interpreter, Macdonald praised the college for offering the only program in the country designed to train people specifically to work with the deaf-blind. The Brass Ensemble tooted the familiar jazz strains of "Minnie the Moocher" as Professor Ira Domser stepped forward to present Cabell ("Cab") Calloway for the doctor of fine arts degree. Illness prevented Calloway from attending the graduation, but his daughter Camay Calloway Murphy, chair of the Cab Calloway Jazz Institute at Coppin State University, accepted the degree for her father as her son, Peter Brooks '86, looked on proudly. Master's degrees were conferred on 131 individuals, and bachelor's degrees on 272 during the ceremony, after which everyone joined the reception in front of Hoover Library.

CONCLUSION

Just as the world witnessed many highs and lows during this decade, so did the college experience a roller coaster of activities and emotions. A number of major changes in leadership and faculty brought some adjustments to the college objectives, curriculum, and student life. New athletic facilities were completed, and construction was begun on an expanded library. Financial solvency had always been maintained, but budgets were tight at mid-decade as income at the tuition-driven college decreased due to slipping enrollments. The students' behaviors and attitudes at times were troubling, due in great measure to changing attitudes about alcohol and sexual activity on college campuses and in society at large. But the college moved on as usual: Classes were taught, meals were served, plays and concerts were performed, athletics were contested, parties were planned, tests and exams were given and (hopefully) passed, and ten more years in the college's development passed all too quickly.

Chapter 13 Endnotes

1. WMC board of trustees minutes, October 21, 1983; John, Report, 1983–84.
2. *The Hill*, Winter 1984, 8.
3. WMC trustee Executive Committee minutes, June 20, 1984; September 24, 1986.
4. WMC faculty minutes, April 7, 1981; WMC board of trustees minutes, April 24, 1981.
5. *WMC Catalogue*, 1983/1985, 11.
6. WMC board of trustees minutes, April 16, 1982.
7. WMC faculty minutes, March 1, 1988.
8. *Phoenix*, October 29, 1987, 4.
9. WMC faculty minutes, December 6, 1983.
10. Ibid., November 7, 1989.
11. *Phoenix*, April 25, 1985, 6.
12. Ibid., February 11, 1988, 1.
13. Ibid., April 19, 1984, 1.
14. Ibid., April 10, 1986, 2.
15. Ibid., May 10, 1984, 5.
16. WMC faculty minutes, November 3, 1981.
17. *Phoenix*, October 23, 1986, 8.
18. Ibid., February 11, 1988, 4.
19. Ibid., October 17, 1985, 6.
20. Ibid., May 10, 1984, 1; April 28, 1988, 1.
21. Ibid., November 11, 1982, 8; November 20, 1986, 8.
22. Ibid., February 12, 1987, 9; April 16, 1987.
23. *Phoenix*, November 5, 1981, 2.
24. Ibid., January 26, 1984, 3.
25. Ibid., September 6, 1986, 4.
26. Ibid., November 9, 1989, 4.
27. Ibid., February 25, 1988, 6.
28. WMC trustee Executive Committee minutes, November 15, 1988.
29. *Phoenix*, February 9, 1989, 4.
30. Ibid., February 12, 1987, 1.
31. Ibid., March 10, 1983, 1–2.
32. Ibid., March 22, 1984, 3.
33. Ibid., April 12, 1984, 1.
34. WMC board of trustees minutes, October 25, 1986.
35. WMC trustee Executive Committee minutes, January 28, 1987.
36. *Phoenix*, November 1, 1984, 5.
37. WMC trustee Executive Committee minutes, December 12, 1988.
38. *Phoenix*, November 12, 1987, 4.
39. WMC trustee Executive Committee minutes, October 19, 1985.
40. *Phoenix*, March 18, 1982, 1.
41. WMC trustee Executive Committee minutes, September 23, 1981; March 17, 1982; WMC board of trustees minutes, August 12, 1982.
42. WMC trustee Executive Committee minutes, January 25, 1984.
43. Ibid., March 28, 1990.
44. Ibid., September 14, 1988.
45. Ibid., September 20, 1989.
46. Ibid., May 18, 1988; *The Hill*, August 1989, 10–14.
47. WMC trustee Executive Committee minutes, March 16, 1988.
48. WMC board of trustees minutes, February 18, 1989.
49. WMC trustee Executive Committee minutes, November 21, 1984.
50. Ibid., January 28, 1987.
51. Ibid., December 21, 1988.
52. September 6, 1986, 5.
53. WMC faculty minutes, October 2, 1984.
54. *The Hill*, October/November 1980, 1.
55. Interview, M. Lee Rice, March 18, 2005.
56. WMC board of trustees minutes, October 21, 1983.
57. WMC trustee Executive Committee minutes, November 17, 1980.
58. Ibid., May 17, 1989.
59. Ibid., May 18, 1988.
60. WMC board of trustees minutes, August 12, 1982.
61. WMC trustee Executive Committee minutes, June 18, 1986.
62. Ibid., March 16, 1980.
63. WMC board of trustees minutes, April 20, 1990.
64. WMC trustee Executive Committee minutes, May 21, 1986.
65. WMC board of trustees minutes, October 21, 1983.
66. *The Hill*, November 1988, 47–49.
67. *Phoenix*, October 29, 1981, 4.
68. Ibid., April 2, 1982, 1.
69. *The Hill*, July 1982, 1.
70. Ibid., March 1983, 9; May 1986, 5–7.
71. *Carroll County Times*, May 23, 1984, C1.
72. *The Hill*, Winter 1985, 5.
73. Ibid., 5–6.
74. Ibid., 2–3.
75. Ibid., 1.
76. *Carroll County Times*, May 27, 1986, A5.

MAJOR WORLD EVENTS

1981
Columbia space shuttle is launched.
On Golden Pond wins Academy Award.
Sandra Day O'Connor becomes first female Supreme Court justice.
Poland government crushes the Solidarity movement.
Acquired Immune Deficiency Syndrome (AIDS) is discovered and named.
President Reagan is wounded in an assassination attempt.
Fifty-two American hostages are released in January after 14 months in captivity in Iran.
Lady Diana Spencer marries Charles, Prince of Wales; 700 million watch on TV.
Nintendo markets Pac-Man video game, which becomes an arcade craze.
The musical *Cats* opens on Broadway.

1982
Princess Grace of Monaco dies when her car hurtles over a cliff.
AT&T telephone company is broken up into 22 separate regional companies.
The Vietnam Veterans Memorial is erected in Washington, D.C.
The first artificial heart transplant takes place; the recipient lives 112 days.
Equal Rights Amendment to U.S. Constitution fails to be ratified.

1983
U.S. invades Grenada after coup on the island.
Sally Ride becomes first American woman in space.
Terrorists bomb the U.S. Embassy in Beirut, killing 40 people.
TV specials include *The Thorn Birds* and *Winds of War*.
Cajun cuisine, sushi bars, gourmet popcorn, and homemade pasta become eating trends.

1984
Apple Computer releases the Macintosh personal computer.
The first megabit chip is made at Bell Labs.
Trivial Pursuit is introduced.
Indira Gandhi is assassinated.

1985
Crack, smokable crystallized cocaine, starts to appear.
Earthquake in Mexico and volcano eruption in Colombia kill thousands.
Gorbachev becomes (the last) president of the Soviet Union.
Titanic wreckage is found and filmed by robotic camera in July.
Hole in the ozone layer, first detected in 1977, is now indisputable.
Baltimore novelist Anne Tyler publishes *The Accidental Tourist*.
Maryland novelist Tom Clancy publishes *The Hunt for Red October*.
Bruce Springsteen's *Born in the U.S.A.* is the top-selling album.

1986

Philippines president Ferdinand Marcos is deposed.
America celebrates national holiday Martin Luther King Jr. Day for the first time.
Worst nuclear disaster ever occurs in Chernobyl, USSR.
Statue of Liberty celebrates its 100th anniversary.
Space shuttle *Challenger* explodes after liftoff on January 28.
Holocaust survivor and author Elie Wiesel wins Nobel Peace Prize.

1987

U.S. budget reaches the trillion dollar mark.
World population reaches 5 billion.
The second-largest stock market drop in Wall Street history occurs on "Black Monday."
Van Gogh's *Irises* is bought for $53.9 million.
Andrew Wyeth's "Helga" pictures are exhibited in the National Gallery of Art.
Supreme Court rules that states may require all-male private clubs to admit women.
Earthquake measuring 6.1 hits Los Angeles; 6 killed, 100 injured.

1988

George H. W. Bush is elected 41st U.S. president.
CDs outsell vinyl for the first time.
Pan Am flight 103 explodes over Lockerbie, Scotland.
Prozac is introduced as an antidepressant.
Soviets begin to withdraw from Afghanistan.

1989

Students protest on Tiananmen Square, Beijing, China.
Sixty percent of American households have cable TV.
The Berlin Wall falls on November 9; the Cold War ends.
Vietnam withdraws from Cambodia, September 26, after almost 11 years of occupation.
U.S. invades Panama; Manuel Noriega surrenders and is tried for drug trafficking and racketeering.
Soviet Union begins fully withdrawing from Afghanistan after 10 years of fighting.
***Exxon Valdez* oil tanker spill of 11 million gallons in Alaska is largest in history.**

1990

Germany is reunified after 45 years.
Iraq's Saddam Hussein invades Kuwait.
Hubble space telescope is launched into orbit.
Americans With Disabilities Act is signed into law.
Smoking on domestic airplane flights is banned.
U.S. population reaches 248,709,873.

Eaton Hall (Science Laboratory Building) was opened in 1999.

CHAPTER

14

MORE FINANCIAL FLUCTUATIONS

—·◄ 1991–2000 ►·—

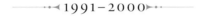

During this decade, as in the previous one, the world witnessed major changes, both positive and negative. Many Baltic nations became independent as the Soviet Union began to break up. In South Africa, apartheid was dismantled, and Nelson Mandela, long a political prisoner, was elected president and received the Nobel Peace Prize. An uneasy peace was achieved in Northern Ireland, the "Chunnel" between England and France was opened, and the U.S. women's soccer team won the World Cup. But politically and geologically, the world was also in upheaval. The Gulf War ended, but a civil war in Rwanda broke out, and there was turmoil in Bosnia. Al-Qaida's terrorism began to show itself when the U.S.S. *Cole* was attacked in Aden and the New York World Trade Center was bombed. The FBI attack on the Branch Davidians near Waco, Texas, followed by the bombing of the Oklahoma City Federal Building and the Columbine High School shootings kept Americans on edge. Mt. Pinatubo in the Philippines erupted, an earthquake in Turkey killed 13,000, Hurricane Andrew left 250,000 homeless in Florida, an ice storm paralyzed the northeast United States for weeks, and the Mississippi and Missouri rivers flooded much of the Midwest in mid-decade. It was a turbulent time. And reminiscent of a century before, there was also the occasional argument as to when the new century (and the new millennium) would begin, in 2000 or 2001.

The college also had its highs and lows. For three years early in the decade, enrollments steadily dropped, and revenues could not match expenses. Then there was a critical turnaround in enrollments, and that, coupled with the largest comprehensive fund-raising campaign in college history, put the institution on much firmer footing. Considerable change in faculty, trustee, and administrative personnel also contributed to a certain lack of stability. But the college built and opened several new buildings and remodeled others to prepare for the anticipated growth in the new century. The students, in addition to their normal studies and activities, followed closely the O. J. Simpson trial, the landing of *Pathfinder* on Mars, the development of the World Wide Web, the aftermath of Princess Diana's death, and the Bill Clinton scandal. It was a busy, sometimes tense, time for everyone.

FACULTY AND ADMINISTRATION

Just as the college witnessed many changes in the 1960s when 30 new faculty faces appeared, so 30 years later, as those individuals concluded their teaching careers, there were 30 retirements by faculty members whose average tenure was 28 years and whose total years of service numbered 837. The shortest span of tenure was 10 years and the longest was 42. Joining the emeriti ranks were Margaret Denman-West [1977–91], Carl L. Dietrich [1967–91], McCay Vernon [1969–91], George T. Bachmann Jr. [1971–93], Eleanor N. Richwine [1970–93], William T. Achor [1965–94], Charles "Chap" Herrman Jr. [1974–94], Melvin D. Palmer [1965–94], Keith N. Richwine [1962–94], Evelyn Smith Hering Winfrey [1951–55, 1966–94], Helen B. Wolfe [1980–94], Ira G. Zepp '52 [1963–94], F. Glendon Ashburn '53 [1971–95], Katherine Loose Falconer '52, '83M [1968–95], Robert H. Hartman [1969–95], Donald R. Rabush '62, '70M [1973–95], Samuel "Tim" Weinfeld [1970–96], H. Ray Stevens '58 [1966–97], Herman E. Behling [1988–98], Richard A. Clower '50 [1956–98], Cornelius P. Darcy [1963–98], James E. Lightner '59 [1962–98], Raymond C. Phillips Jr. [1963–98], Carol J. Quinn [1972–98], Ronald K. Tait [1968–98], Robert J. Weber [1969–98], Stephen W. Colyer [1970–99], Donald E. Jones [1963–99], Joan R. Weyers [1963–99], and Alton D. Law [1966–2000]. Carol Rouzer '76 [1989–2000] left the college to become a research professor at Vanderbilt University, and Hugh Prickett [1974–93] left to become superintendent of the Mississippi School for the Deaf.

To fill the shoes of this formidable group of individuals, 47 new faculty were hired, a dozen or so moving on after a short time, while the majority remained into the new century. In the latter group were Colette M. Henriette [1990–] in foreign languages, Michael L. Losch [1990–] in art history, Norberto Valdez [1990–95] in sociology, Terence A. Dalton [1990–] in English, Glenn G. Caldwell [1991–] in music, Linda L. Dudley (Parker) [1992–2007] in education, Judith Coryell [1994–2002] in education, Mohamed Esa [1994–] in foreign languages, Coleen Galambos [1994–99] in social work, David V. Guerra [1994–98] in physics, Ramona Kerby [1994–] in education, Debra C. Lemke [1994–] in sociology, Joel Macht [1994–2002] in education (TARGET), Jasna Meyer [1994–] in communication, Robin Armstrong [1995–] in music, Mary Bendel-Simso [1995–] in English, Rebecca Carpenter [1995–] in English, Julia L. Orza [1995–] in education, Kenneth W. Pool [1995–2006] in education, Brian D. Wladkowski '88 [1995–] in chemistry, Lauren Dundes [1996–] in sociology, Vera Jakoby [1996–] in philosophy, Robert Lemieux [1996–] in communication, Thomas J. Zirpoli [1996–] in education (TARGET), Mark A. Hadley [1997–2007] in religious studies, Ralene R. Mitschler [1997–] in biology, Simeon K. Schlossberg [1997–] in education, Robert M. Kachur [1998–] in English, Brian L. Lockard '69M [1998–2004] in education, Paul B. Miller [1998–] in history, Randall L. Morrison [1998–] in biology, Apollo Mian [1999–] in physics, and Jean Shin [1999–2006] in sociology.

The college community was saddened by the untimely deaths of Professor of Physics Peter D. Yedinak [1967–93] in May 1993, and Associate Professor of German Hans Peter F. Büttner [1968–93] in June 1993, both due to cancer, and adjunct dramatic art instructor and director Steven Miller [1982–94] in September 1994.

Word also reached the campus of the deaths of a number of emeriti faculty, one of whom, Maude Gesner [1917–55], who died in February 1993 (at age 103), had enjoyed 38 years of retirement after a 38-year college tenure. In addition to her death, the community was saddened to learn of the passing of William Ridington [1938–73] in December 1990, H. P. Sturdivant [1948– 73] in March 1991, Theodore Whitfield [1929–72] in March 1991, Kathryn B. Hildebran [1940–69] in July 1991, Edith F. Ridington [1957–77] in November 1991, Frank Hurt [1930–65] in February 1992, Earl Griswold [1956–85] in April 1992, Elizabeth Simkins [1946–70] in July 1992, Joseph W. Hendren [1947–66] in February 1993, Louise Shipley [1938–72] in April 1993, William David [1952–84] in December 1993, Ralph B. Price [1954–77] in February 1995, Esther Smith [1926–70] in January 1996, Joseph Willen [1933–66] in January 1996, Keith Richwine [1962–94] in April 1996, Alfred deLong [1936–69] in March 1997, Reuben Holthaus [1946–76] in April 1998, Evelyn Winfrey [1951–55, 1966–94] in July 1998, Katherine Falconer [1968–95] in

January 1999, Gerald E. Cole [1955–85] in June 1999, and Margaret Denman-West [1977–91] in October 1999.

Often at memorial services for deceased retired faculty, stories are told that bring a smile to those in attendance. One in particular was related by Ray Stevens at the funeral of Theodore Whitfield in 1991. As if addressing the memorable professor, Stevens noted,

> *You must know that you are a favorite for stories whenever alumni meet. Is there anyone who does not know about the day Sam Reed '57 arrived late for your class? The door opened slowly that day, a large Confederate flag preceded Sam into the room, and a voice almost as loud as [yours] boomed out: "Like Jeb Stuart at the Battle of Gettysburg, I am arriving late." Consensus has it that it was one of the few times you were at a loss for words.*[1]

The faculty and staff continued to bring credit to themselves and the college through their professional service and honors. Ethan Seidel was the recipient of the Teaching Excellence and Campus Leadership award from the Sears-Roebuck Foundation in 1990. Ira Zepp was named Alumnus of the Year by St. Mary's Seminary. The Council of the Advancement and Support Education named Vice President for Institutional Advancement Richard Seaman the District II Professional of the Year in 1997. Brian Lockard

Francis "Skip" Fennell receives CASE Maryland Professor of the Year award from Governor Glendening and Dr. Chambers in 1997.

received a Distinguished Alumni Achievement Award from Frostburg State University and the Golden Apple Award from the Maryland Parent Teacher Association. Richard Smith spoke at the 15th International Cancer Congress in Germany in 1990, was named the Maryland Chemist of the Year by the American Chemical Society in 1996, and received the Distinguished Alumnus Award from Washington College. Smith and biologist Wilbur Long also received significant grants from the National Science Foundation and the DuPont Company for continued scientific research. Carol Rouzer and Brian Wladkowski received several research grants from the National Science Foundation and the Research Corporation. Theodore Evergates was a Jesse Ball duPont Scholar at the National Humanities Center in North Carolina in 1995 and was offered the position of scholar-in-residence at the Institute for Advanced Studies at Princeton University for the second semester 1999–2000. Skip Fennell was named the Maryland Professor of the Year for 1997 by CASE, received a Leadership Award from the National Council of Supervisors of Mathematics, was honored as a Penn State University Alumni Fellow, received public television's version of an Emmy for his Number Sense project, and was elected to a three-year term as director of the National Council of Teachers of Mathematics. Ramona Kerby received an award from the State of Minnesota for her children's book *Thirty-Eight Weeks 'til Summer Vacation.*

Glenn Caldwell created musical arrangements for Stevie Wonder. Donald Rabush was named the Westminster Rotary Club's Outstanding Citizen of 1992 for his work with TARGET. Donald Jones was on loan to the National Science Foundation to be program director of chemistry teaching enhancements. Gregory Alles received an award from the National Endowment for the Humanities for college teachers in 1994 and was named associate editor of the *Encyclopedia of World Religions.* Carol Fritz was named the 1994 Administrator of the Year by the National Association of Collegiate Women's Athletic Administrators. The former volleyball coach, Fritz was remembered (and commended by the faculty) for her NCAA tournament appearances 1982–86 and 1990. She ended her volleyball coaching career with 575 wins, 134 losses, and 3 ties.[2] (She also had collected from alumnae and displayed a number of women's athletic costumes 1880–1970.) Rebecca Martin was selected as part of a Rotary Group Study Exchange team for six weeks in Australia in 1998. Kathy S. Mangan received her second Individual Artist's Award from the Maryland State Arts Council in 1997 for her poetry. Randall Morrison received the Pan American Society's Pigment Cell Research Young Investigator Award and a grant from the National Science Foundation. Linda Dudley was named Outstanding Teacher Educator for 1995 by the Maryland Association of Teacher Educators. David Guerra was named a NASA Summer Faculty Fellow in 1996. Christianna Nichols Leahy was named to the board of directors of Amnesty International. Charles Neal was elected chair of the board of the Pre-Law Advisers National Council in 1997. Samuel Case was named chair of the Maryland Governor's Physical Fitness Council in 1999. Joan Coley was named one of the Top 100 Women in Maryland for 2000.

Some administrative offices changed, as usual. Donna Duvall Sellman '45 [1980–2000] retired after 19 years and was named director of alumni affairs emerita. She was replaced by Robin Adams Brenton '86 [2000–]. When Barbara Schaeffer Disharoon became assistant academic dean in 1989, she nevertheless continued as registrar until 1992, when chemistry professor David Herlocker became acting registrar for a semester until Barbara Cain Shaffer '76 [1993–97] took over the office. She was succeeded by Elizabeth A. Pival for two years [1998–2000]. Disharoon (Horneff) concentrated her efforts on retention of students, especially from freshman to sophomore year, and established a peer mentoring program and revised the orientation program to better assist freshmen. In 1995 she was named dean of the first-year program to further emphasize this concern. Scott D. Kane [1994–2000] assumed the position of director of residence life in 1994 (he later was named assistant dean), and Christine J. Mathews [1995–] was hired as the new director of information services. The position of director of athletics was assumed by James M. Smith [1999–] when Richard Carpenter [1969–] gave up administrative duties after 15 years and returned to full-time teaching. The president's executive assistant (and secretary of the college) changed several times; Elizabeth Shevock (Scott-Keigler) [1989–92] resigned and was replaced by Theresa Bryant [1992–94], who was followed by Nancy Godwin [1982–2000], who turned the office over to Mary Ann Friday [1988–] in 2000. The community was saddened to learn of the deaths of former staff members Martha Manahan [1938–66], registrar emerita, in October 1993; Charles Havens [1934–57], former director of athletics, football coach, and 1982 Alumnus of the Year, in May 1996; Registrar Emerita Cora Virginia Perry [1938–77] in January 1997; William Allan MacDonald [1945–57], former art history professor and occasional adjunct instructor [1980–95], in February 1998; Daniel I. Welliver '50, LHD'98, college physician for 40 years and 1984 Alumnus of the Year, in December 1998; B. Irene Young [1952–86], bookstore assistant and postmaster for 21 years, in May 1999; and former cashier Mary Rohrer Shoemaker [1962–75] in July 1999.

The senior administration underwent change in every office except Student Affairs. In Academic Affairs, David B. Seligman was named vice president and dean in 1990 (he also held a professorship in philosophy), but three years later he had philosophical differences with President Chambers and soon moved on to be the academic dean at Ripon College (WI). He was replaced on an acting basis by Joan Coley, then dean of graduate affairs. During the following year, she received the permanent appointment and in 1994 was given the title of provost to suggest the importance of the faculty in administrative decisions and hierarchy. In 1995, Kenneth W. Pool [1995–2006] was appointed dean of graduate affairs. In the Office of Administration and Finance, Vice President Jennie Mingolelli [1987–93] resigned to take a similar position at Gettysburg College. She was replaced in 1994 by economics professor Ethan Seidel [1969–], who had been part-time presidential assistant and who continued to teach one course in economics and business administration for a while. In the area of development, Vice President Walter L. Wahlen [1985–91] retired in 1991 and was succeeded by Richard Seaman [1991–98] as vice president for institutional advancement. (The name of the division was changed from College Relations to Institutional Advancement with Seaman's appointment.) Upon Seaman's retirement seven years later, Richard G. Kief [1998–] assumed the office.

The most significant administrative change occurred at the end of the decade, when Robert Chambers resigned in the spring of 2000, 3 years into a 5-year contract, during a semester-long sabbatical awarded by the trustees after 15 years of service. He took the sabbatical "in order to pause and reflect upon the significance of the [15th anniversary] events and to pursue several personal and professional projects."[3] In his surprise resignation announcement, he said he felt that it was the right time to move on, both for himself and for the college, and he wished to pursue other interests. "I believe that Western Maryland College is now in the midst of a genuine 'lift-off' into the next century," he said. "It is time now for another person to pick up the torch and lead [the college] into a new century," said board chair James I. Melhorn. Chambers set out on a 500-mile journey across northern Spain in June and then became a consultant in higher education finance with Marts & Lundy, Inc. During his absence in the spring, Provost Coley had served as acting president. Upon receipt of the resignation in April, the trustees, confronted with the need to elect a new president, appointed Coley interim president; she in turn named Samuel Case, professor of exercise science and physical education, as acting provost. The trustees decided to employ consultative help to help them determine the direction of the college and its leadership needs in the new century. James L. Fisher, president emeritus of Towson University, and James C. Koch, president of Old Dominion University (VA), spent much of the summer interviewing faculty, staff, and trustees. They presented their report to the trustees at the end of the summer.

During the 16 years of his presidency, Chambers had seen the college change: The endowment had tripled, especially as the result of the first

Portrait of President Robert Hunter Chambers III

major comprehensive campaign the college had ever mounted. Enrollments had fluctuated from a low of 1,050 to a high of 1,550. The college budget had more than tripled, as had the total costs of attending the institution. Physically, the campus had been transformed with the addition of a library and a $13.4 million science laboratory building, as well as major renovations to the classroom buildings, dining hall, and residence halls. Chambers had presided at dedications or rededications of eight buildings and spaces and led the campus celebration of its 125th anniversary. A second campus had been established in Budapest. He had led the college through some difficult economic times, when enrollments dropped and belts were tightened. He also had kept a foot in the classroom, teaching one literature course each semester. Perhaps more than anything else, however, he was the consummate cheerleader for the institution, always presenting an optimistic and enthusiastic viewpoint about its future. He said at the end of 15 years in office, "My presidency at Western Maryland College was the best and most important period of my life, as well as the most productive." He also said, "I want it to be said when I leave here that everything I have had a hand in helped improve the place."[4] The general consensus of the college community was that he succeeded.

As in previous decades, the board of trustees experienced considerable turnover, as some individuals reached the retirement age of 70, others resigned, or as three-year classes were reconstituted. Taking emeritus status were Robert Bricker, Frank Carman, Alleck A. Resnick, Wilbur Preston, Robert Mathias, Clarence W. Blount, Catherine S. Kiddoo, and Lloyd Thomas. Over the ten-year span, the number of voting trustees fluctuated from 32 to 40. The maximum number of board members was raised to 48 in 1996,[5] and the revised age limit of 75 was abolished two years later.[6] Serving new terms during the decade were Eugene A. Arbaugh '60 [1992–97], Frank H. Menaker Jr. [1992–2007], Caryl Ensor Peterson '58 [1992–], R. Peter Urquhart '58 [1980–85, 1992–94], Susan Traylor Aldridge '78 [1993–96], Priscilla Caskey Carroll [1993–2003], Carol Armacost Carter '69 [1993–], Kevin F. Hanley '72 [1993–], Martin K. P. Hill [1993–], Carolyn Landis [1993–], James I. Melhorn [1993–], Charles E. Moore Jr. '71 [1993–], Eric Peacher [1993–97], Leon Kaplan [1994–97], Richard Klitzberg '63 [1994–2000], Diane Rehm DJourn'92 [1994–], R. Christine Royer '48 [1994–], Ferenc Somogyi [1994–], Michael E. Weinblatt '71 [1994–], Bruce Preston '75 [1995–], Peter Angelos [1996–2002], George R. Benson Jr. [1996–], Francis B. Burch Jr. [1996–2001], John A. Emens '66 [1996–2005], Sally Keck Gold '78 [1996–2004], G. Melvin Mills [1996–2003], Carolyn Seaman Scott '67, '76M [1996–], David M. Stout '76 [1996–2001], James L. Zucco Jr. '73 [1996–99], Richard D. Adams

[1997–], W. Walker Buckalew [1997–2000], Jerome H. Fader '56 [1997–], Steven D. Kesler [1997–], Albert J. Mezzanotte Jr. '78 [1997–], Carol S. Parham [1997–], Laura L. Lange [1998–2006], Dennis G. Sisco '68 [1999–2007], Constance M. Unseld [1999–], Leslie A. Wiley [1999–], and William H. Elliott III '70 [2000–]. Elected as honorary trustees were Catharine W. Eaton MHL'90 [1991–99], Lawrence J. Adams LHD'93 [1992–], Charles C. Fenwick [1978–93; honorary, 1993–], Elizabeth J. Marshall [1994–2005], and Margaret L. Tawes [1994–]. A conscious effort by the nominations committee was being made to bring a new generation onto the board.

During the decade, William Keigler concluded a five-year term as chair in 1991 and turned the leadership over to Lee Rice, who presided until 1996, when James Melhorn succeeded him.

The board minutes memorialized a number of emeriti and honorary trustees who died during the decade: Thomas F. Marshall [honorary, 1982–91], Albert C. Hall [1975–85], Alfred Mathias [1974–80], Clarence M. Willis [honorary, 1987–93], Richard H. Ellingsworth [1973–84], Ralph G. Hoffman [1971–81], Arthur G. Broll '29 [1965–80], W. Lloyd Fisher [1946–80], Thomas H. Eaton '27 [honorary, 1978–95], Clementine Peterson (at age 101) [1969–80], Jane Asmis [1976–82; honorary, 1982–97], Caroline Taylor '26 [honorary, 1974–97], Wilson K. Barnes '28 [1963–80], Eloise Payne '38 [1978–88], Austin E. Penn [1961–79], Catharine Eaton [honorary, 1991–99], and Fred Malkus '34 [1962–85].

In 1999, the campus community was saddened to learn of the death of President Emeritus Ralph John in Ocean Pines, Maryland, on November 25. A service was held at the Atlantic United Methodist Church in Ocean City on November 27, with Ira Zepp and Robert Chambers giving personal remarks. Burial was private. This was followed by a campus memorial service on April 2, 2000, in Baker Memorial Chapel. Zepp presided, and remembrances were provided by Acting President Coley, former faculty member William Tribby '56, and trustee Dolores Snyder '63M, LHD '89. During the ceremony, a prayer was given by John's former executive assistant, Bernice Beard '74, '81M, and a taped remembrance was played from President Chambers, who was traveling on his sabbatical and unable to attend in person. A reception for Mrs. John and her family followed in the President's House. In 1997, John had accepted an honorary doctor of humane letters degree from the college, which was conferred at an Eastern Shore alumni meeting held near his home, due to his failing health. Even though he was weak and using a cane, he rose to the occasion and, following the conferring of the degree by President Chambers, took the podium to make some personal comments of appreciation in an increasingly strong voice.

CURRICULUM

During the decade, the number of students fluctuated rather dramatically, as did the standards. Entering students in 1990 posted SAT scores of about 1000, but they rose to about 1150 by the end of the decade. Average high school GPAs also rose, from about 2.8 to about 3.3. The number of Maryland Distinguished Scholars more than doubled over the ten years. By the end of the decade, about 11% of new students were minorities.

The exchange program established with Harlaxton College, England, continued to attract students, who traveled there each fall with a faculty member to study and teach, respectively, and to enjoy the benefits of travel to neighboring Europe. This relationship continued through the fall of 1994, when the college focused on a new program.

In February 1993, another significant chapter in the college's history began with the exploration of a branch campus in Europe. At the annual meeting of the Association of Independent Colleges and Universities held in Washington, D.C., representatives of College International, a Budapest-based educational organization founded about ten years earlier, met with representatives of several American colleges and universities, seeking to establish a relationship whereby students could do their first two years of study in Hungary and complete their degrees at an American institution. These explorations had been initiated by Hungarian-born California congressman Thomas Lantos. During preliminary talks, President Chambers mentioned that a well-known Hungarian businessman, George Varga, CEO of Tungsram (GE's large economic venture behind the iron curtain), was a 1961 WMC graduate and trustee. Following these discussions, campus visits were soon made, Western Maryland was determined by College International to be the best school for this proposed relationship, and negotiations continued. In March 1993 President Chambers visited Budapest, continued the negotiations, and crafted a memorandum of understanding to establish a branch campus there. At its April meeting, the board of trustees formally approved the venture. In October, a small delegation from the Westminster campus went to Budapest for the official signing of the letter of intent in the presence of the American ambassador to Hungary, Charles Thomas, and about 50 Hungarian educational, business, and political leaders. In December, at a press conference at the U.S. Press Club in Washington attended by Tamas Vagi and Attila Horváth, representing College International, as well as the U.S. undersecretary of state for foreign affairs and the Hungarian state secretary, Ministry of Education, the relationship was formally announced and a similar signing ceremony took place. Never before had an accredited American undergraduate college established a branch in Hungary.[7]

First class of graduates from the Budapest program, 1998

In September 1994 the first classes—for 34 students from a half dozen central European countries—were begun with two majors offered: business and economics. Classes were held in rented facilities on a floor in the Open University and Conference Center on Villanyi Avenue in Buda. The building had housed the headquarters of the Education Ministry of the Communist Party before the USSR withdrawal and eventual collapse. Dr. Ferenc Somogyi was the first director, assisted by Dr. Gabor Drexler. The curriculum for the students in Budapest was the same as that offered to first- and second-year students on the Westminster campus with the exception of one additional course, Understanding Europe. Students applying to the program were required to demonstrate knowledge of English (since all classes were taught in English), submit recommendations and pass the same proficiency tests in writing and mathematics as entrants to the main campus, and be admitted by the college's Admissions Committee. Somogyi was soon called back into government diplomatic service, and Drexler was named director. Somogyi was invited to become chairman of the WMC Budapest board, which included Tamas Bacskai and Tamas Toth, both distinguished professors at the Hungarian University of Economics and teachers in the WMC program. Somogyi also joined the college's board of trustees that year. After the initial year of operation, Hungary formally gave official permission to operate the program, and, after a site visit in March by Dr. Gerald Patton of the Middle States Association of Colleges and Schools, the branch campus received full accreditation in June 1995. In 1996 the first class of 20 students arrived in

Westminster for their last two years of study, and in May 1998, 19 formally received their American degrees at Commencement, which was attended by a delegation of faculty from Budapest and the Hungarian ambassador to the United States, giving special attention to this unique program. In September 1996 foundation courses for two more majors (political science and communication) were added to the Budapest curriculum.

In September 1998, the first interchange of faculty and students occurred when Sue Singer, professor of business administration, and a group of a dozen students from the Westminster campus spent the fall semester in Budapest. During their time there, students and faculty had the opportunity to travel to Vienna and Prague, as well as to western Hungary for weekend tours. President Chambers reported to the board in October 1999 that two classes had graduated through the Budapest program and that at that moment there were 60 freshmen, 50 sophomores, 30 faculty, and some additional students in the preparatory program (created by College International to prepare the European students for college work where necessary). In addition, 13 students from the Westminster campus were studying in Budapest that fall, and Pamela L. Regis of the English Department was there teaching. About 45 foreign students were in Westminster in their junior or senior year of the program. This made a total of 165–170 students involved with the WMC Budapest program, greater than 10% of the college's undergraduate student body, Chambers pointed out.[8]

As the college was forced into some restructuring during a financial crisis in the early years of the decade, the elimination of several curricular programs was seriously considered. President Chambers commented, "For 125 years the college has had financial problems . . . but with good management and faith, we will get through."[9] In 1992 the place of the social work program in the liberal arts curriculum was questioned; after considering several alternatives, the faculty ultimately voted to retain it but agreed that its several open positions would be filled with three-year appointments.[10] The program's national accreditation was maintained. A year later the physics and German majors were considered for elimination, but after much discussion, they, too, were retained, and faculty positions were filled with three-year appointments.[11] The three-year appointments were turned into tenure positions after the financial crisis was over. In 1999, a women's studies minor was approved.

The college's military science (ROTC) program was also being reevaluated by the army during the first half of the decade because enrollments had dropped and the number of annual commissions was small. In 1991 there were 53 students in the program, compared with 130 in 1988. Scholarships had also dropped by $30,000. Efforts were made to keep the program viable, including a cooperative venture with Mt. St. Mary's College, and ultimately the program survived; in 1995, its 75th anniversary was celebrated. During the latter years of the decade, the numbers improved somewhat, and the program expanded its activities under the direction of Professor of Military Science Karen Helmeyer Doyle [1996–2000], the first female officer appointed to that post on the campus.

The names of three departments were changed during this time: Art became Art and Art History in 1990, and in 1995 Physical Education became Exercise Science and Physical Education and Political Science became Political Science and International Studies. In 1994, Sociology and Social Work were separated into distinct departments, responding to requirements from the Council on Social Work Education.[12] By mid-decade an academic skills center had been established and was meeting the special needs of about 10% of the student body. Indeed, the college was becoming known for its assistance of students with special needs.[13]

As in past decades, both the January term and the Honor System were periodically evaluated, debated, tinkered with, and ultimately maintained. The Honor System was the subject of considerable discussion among both students and faculty before it was revised and finally reaccepted by all parties in 1999. Both long-standing programs were generally popular with students but sometimes were met with less enthusiasm from the faculty.

Political internships were always available to students, especially during the January term, when there were opportunities to work with legislators during the Maryland General Assembly meeting. The college was well represented in the legislature by alumni who often welcomed students as interns. In 1992, the alumni legislators were Sen. Frederick Malkus '34, LLD'80, 1994 Alumnus of the Year (also Senate president pro tem); Sen. Gerald W. Winegrad '66; Sen. Clarence W. Blount LLD'81; Sen. Idamae Riley Garrott '36, LLD'76; Del. Ellen Richmond Sauerbrey '59, 1988 Alumna of the Year (also minority leader of the House of Delegates); Del. Richard N. Dixon LLD'88; Del. Peter G. Callas '49; Del. C. Ronald Frank x'63; and Del. A. Wade Kach '70.[14]

In February 1994, a recommendation came to the faculty from its Academic Policy and Curriculum Committee to totally revise the curriculum to make all courses carry four credits, with students enrolling in four courses and faculty teaching three each semester. This was presented as an opportunity to reduce student pressure by allowing them to focus on four rather than five courses. Students were expected to spend more time in classes, in the library, or in independent study. Reducing the semester teaching load to three courses had been a goal of the administration and faculty for several years. It was felt that such a major change would also force curricular revision and development of an exciting new program.[15] Over the next two years the details of this revision were gradually worked out, especially the basic liberal arts requirements. At the same time, each department was reorganizing its curriculum to create four-credit courses and offer them with the present staff. Scheduling became an issue, as the extra credit often required a fourth class hour. A flex period was created to accommodate this need, and a number of classes employed it for a while until it became cumbersome. The semester was also extended to 14 weeks. By 1997, many faculty were meeting their courses three hours per week as in the old system, requiring extra work of the students to justify the extra hour of credit, or simply offering the same course they had before the revision. Ultimately, the students were required to take fewer courses for the degree, and some within the college community felt that the breadth and depth of the degree had been compromised in order to reduce faculty and student course loads. The revised list of basic requirements included a freshman seminar (which included an introduction to the demands and processes of a college education); a Heritage Sequence (a two-semester overview of the development of western civilization through study of the history of a discipline); and a distribution of courses providing an introduction to the humanities, social sciences, natural sciences and mathematics, and global perspectives. Students were also required to show competence in English composition, exercise science and physical education, foreign languages, and mathematics. Added to the major requirements was a capstone or culminating experience for seniors. Considerable effort on the part of the faculty was spent in transitioning from old to new requirements, especially recasting the requirements for students in the middle of their degree programs. Consideration continued to be given throughout 1995 to requiring some attendance at campus cultural events, but ultimately this was not approved. Effort to implement Writing across the Curriculum also continued, and students and trustees continued to push for more training in the use of computers.[16]

By 1997, several more departmental honor societies had been formed on campus to recognize significant student achievement: Kappa Delta Pi in education, Lambda Pi Eta in communication, Society of College Journalists, Phi Alpha Delta in pre-law, Sigma Pi Sigma in physics, Phi Alpha in social work, and Epsilon Tau Epsilon in art history (the first chapter of what was hoped would become a national society). The Griswold-Zepp Award for Volunteerism was established in 1990 by the alumni of SOS/HINGE and students of professors Earl Griswold and Ira Zepp to support student volunteer projects benefiting the community. The college was honored when Kristine Holland '93 was selected to receive a Fulbright scholarship for study in India.

Of special significance to the faculty, and indirectly to the curriculum,

Physics students, directed by Professor V. Pagonis,
use computers for problem solving and research.

was the establishment in 1995 of two new awards, both endowed in honor of Professor Emeritus Ira Zepp by Charles E. '71 and Carol Hoerichs '70 Moore. One award was for outstanding teaching and the other for teaching enhancement, to be awarded in alternate years. These were in addition to the Distinguished Teaching Award established in 1961. Another significant faculty award was created in 1997 when James LHD'89 and Dixie Hindman created an endowed faculty chair in the humanities in honor of Ralph and Dorothy John. The endowment provided an annual salary supplement to pursue scholarly research and travel. The first faculty member named to the chair was Kathy Mangan.[17] The Chemistry Department received a grant from the Dreyfus Foundation in 1992 to fund a postdoctoral teaching fellow, Susan Ensel, who worked with the faculty. The Biology Department received two grants totaling $1.2 million from the Howard Hughes Medical Institute in 1993 and 1995, enabling it to expand and enrich programs and support student research.

Two new adjuncts to the curricular offerings were established in the decade. The Ridington Lecture Series, named in honor and memory of professors William and Edith Ridington and funded by the family and friends, was inaugurated on September 26, 1991, the first lecturer being the Ridingtons' son, Dr. Robin Ridington, professor of anthropology at the University of British Columbia and prize-winning author on the Indians of northeastern British Columbia.[18] In February 1995, Common Ground on the Hill, a nonprofit traditional music and arts center, was founded by Walter Michael '68,[19] who was named artist-in-residence in 1997. The group presented concerts, summer courses, and other opportunities to bring people together "on common ground."

The Honors Program continued to provide significant educational opportunities for selected students. In 1991 an Honors Committee was appointed to advise the director, and in 1992 Nancy Palmer assumed that role. She reported a year later that 30 students were enrolled in the program, which had been extended to transfer students and upperclassmen with average SAT scores of 1255. By 1996, the number had risen to 34, with 1335 average SAT scores and a 3.98 average high school GPA. The following year there were 37, with average SATs of 1394 and a 3.9 average GPA. Clearly, the program was appealing to excellent students, as the college's overall standards were rising. Each year more and more honors students were completing the program requirements and being named College Scholars. In light of the success of this program, President Chambers in 1993 appointed a Residential College Task Force to consider reorganizing the college into smaller residential units. However, the idea did not develop.

The college was not immune to grade inflation, a problem faced nation-wide by colleges of all types and sizes. In 1997, economics professor Richard Claycombe reported to the faculty that the college's overall GPA in the fall of 1987 had been 2.58. In the fall of 1992 it had risen to 2.76, and by the fall of 1996 it was 2.93. He noted that 100 students had achieved a 4.00 average in the fall of 1996. He went on to discuss the effect of plus and minus grades on overall GPAs, concluding that not many averages would change appreciably. However, after protracted discussion, the faculty approved a plus-minus system, which went into effect as soon as the computers handling grades were reprogrammed to handle the variations the new system created. A perfect A+ average would now be weighted 4.3.

The graduate program continued to grow, enrollments increasing by 50% in the period 1987–92. In 1991, 1,150 students were enrolled in at least one graduate course, 82% of them female. Two years later the number dipped slightly due to the reduction in reimbursements made by the counties for teacher enrollments. In 1995, graduate offerings were expanded to southern Maryland, and a year later new programs in human resources management and counseling of adults and the elderly were established. In 1997 a new program, Better Educators for the Students of Tomorrow (BEST), was established to prepare post–bachelor's degree students for certification.[20] By 1999 it was reported to the board that there were 13 graduate programs with 13 off-site centers and four collaborative programs.

As in every decade, the college was reevaluated by the Middle States Association of Colleges and Schools and received reaccreditation. In 1993 the college underwent the regular ten-year review, at a time when it was experiencing serious financial problems caused by enrollment deficits, reflecting the nationwide demographics of college-bound students. A number of recommendations had been made by the visiting evaluation team of college administrators and faculty, and five years later the college submitted a follow-up report reacting to those recommendations. The association's response in July 1998 was gratifying:

> In many respects, Western Maryland College demonstrates the regional accreditation process at its best. Having identified areas of concern in 1993, the college invested these past five years in serious evaluation and corresponding action to address these concerns. Major achievements have resulted. Now the college, having passed the years of addressing special concerns, can turn its attention to routine evaluation as a natural and central college function, even and especially when concerns are not as pressing. This puts Western Maryland College in the enviable position of having a planning and evaluation system [the five-year Strategic Plan] which will serve it well on a regular basis as it moves into the 21st century.[21]

STUDENT LIFE

The students of this decade continued to be concerned about issues but were a bit more tolerant of others' views. They adapted, relatively successfully and cheerfully, to fluctuating enrollments, which sometimes meant crowded residence halls and dining room and occasional crowded classrooms. They appreciated the special attention they received when their academic work did not meet minimum standards, and those with special needs received the assistance they needed to succeed. Megan Martin '01 wrote during her freshman year, "Over the last two months, I have seen WMC become my home away from home. This is a college where I can be myself and learn to think honestly and openly. There is a place here for everyone; I know I have found my niche."[22] Perhaps these are some of the reasons the college was included in Loren Pope's *Colleges That Change Lives* in 1996. Pope commented in the book,

The secret of these 40 colleges' magic is not in what they do, for they do many different things. It is how they do it, and that is where they have so much in common. These schools share two essential elements, a familial sense of communal enterprise that gets students heavily involved in cooperative rather than competitive learning, and a faculty of scholars devoted to helping young people develop their powers, mentors who become their valued friends.[23]

A multitude of campus organizations, clubs, and special interest groups continued to provide outlets for students to explore new areas and develop leadership potential. At one point, about 200 students were involved in five active religious groups on campus: Christian Fellowship, Catholic Campus Ministry, Jewish Student Union, Fellowship of Christian Athletes, and Baha'i Club.[24] As always, speakers from a variety of backgrounds and areas were invited to the campus to stimulate thinking. During the decade the list included Jeremy Rifkin, Julian Bond, Diane Rehm, Kurt Schmoke, Taylor Branch, Burns Weston, Bobby Seale, and Jackson Byer. The Theatre Arts Department continued to mount a diverse array of plays from various genres and eras, including *The Skin of Our Teeth, True West, Godspell, Hedda Gabler, Punch and Judy, Equus, Reckless, The Importance of Being Earnest, Damn Yankees, Dark of the Moon, Into the Woods, Dracula, Pippin, The Cherry Orchard, Tartuffe, Cabaret, Twelfth Night, Antigone, Scapin,* and *Marat Sade.* Presentations by the touring National Players also were well received.

The students enjoyed concerts by bands with such names as Angry Salad, Eve 6, and They Might Be Giants. They were also entertained by the irrepressible Carrot Top and a locally organized "Gong Show." Providing a more classical style of music was the series Sundays of Note, funded by the Yale Gordon Trust; a series of programs mounted by Chamber Music on the Hill, beginning in 1991; and a Monday Night Music series organized by and featuring members of the Music Department faculty. Of course, regular concerts by the College Choir, the College Band, the Madrigal Singers, the Gospel Choir (formed in 1997 under the direction of Eric Byrd '93), and various musical ensembles filled the yearly calendar. The first all-campus formal dance in five years was held in March 1993.

The number of students involved in sororities and fraternities fluctuated with the economy, especially as more of the groups became affiliated with national groups that had higher fees and insurance premiums. In 1990 the average membership in the four fraternities was 34, while the four sororities averaged 46. In the years 1996–99, numbers dropped by more than half, so that only about 13% of the student body was "Greek." By the end of the decade all organizations had seen some small growth, but the average membership was only about 20 for the fraternities and 28 for the sororities. As the student body began to grow in the latter part of the decade, three new national groups were colonized and chartered: Phi Kappa Sigma fraternity in 1998, Gamma Sigma Sigma (a service sorority) in 1999, and Alpha Phi Omega (a coed service group) in 1999. A colony of Delta Upsilon fraternity had also been formed in 1991 but was disbanded later in the decade primarily due to finances. In an effort to encourage leadership within these organizations, the Order of Omega, a Greek honor society, was formed in 1993. During the decade, however, there also occurred several instances of hazing, alcohol violations,

Students demonstrate for a cleaner environment.

and housing vandalism that brought sanctions, including temporary loss of bidding privileges and special housing, to the groups involved. In response to these problems nationwide, several Greek organizations had gone "alcohol free," including Phi Mu, Phi Sigma Sigma, Phi Delta Theta, and Phi Kappa Sigma. The local chapters were required to keep their living space and clubrooms alcohol free.[25] There was hope that this would bring about some positive changes in Greek life. One startling incident occurred in the wee hours of a December morning in 1997, when a drunk Preacher pledge (the fraternity had been underground for eight years) swerved off Main Street and into the porch of Dean of Student Affairs Philip Sayre. The teenager couldn't have picked a worse place to be stopped and soon found himself suspended. The incident did not improve the already tarnished reputation of the fraternity.[26] On a more positive note, at Homecoming in October 1998, the 75th anniversary of the founding of the Pi Alpha Alpha fraternity was celebrated with a luncheon, to which all former "Black and Whites" were invited. The event was planned and hosted by their successor group, the Maryland Beta Chapter of Phi Delta Theta. The oldest living member of the fraternity was Gerald E. Richter '26, who attended the reunion.

The *Phoenix* editors followed in their predecessors' footsteps, looking for campus issues to comment upon. Construction on campus caused noise and was disruptive at times, parking was a perennial problem, the fees were rising annually, the honor code was not working properly, and students were not consulted on every major change occurring on campus. ("Why did you do this, rather than that?" "Why wasn't money spent for this, rather than that?") All of these were discussed and sometimes debated in the biweekly newspaper. As in previous decades, the editors decried student apathy and called for more serious student response to local issues. Issues of a serious nature also came under scrutiny. Increasing campus-wide vandalism, burglaries and break-ins, drug busts, date rapes and sexual assaults, and occasional homophobic and racial incidents brought editorials, letters, and essays from all quarters. As the surrounding community became increasingly urbanized, more problems arose than in previous times. As the result of an incident of potential armed assault by noncollege, uninvited individuals in Blanche Ward Hall one Saturday evening in 1996, all residence halls were soon locked at all times, with residents having to admit guests, who telephoned in from the outside.[27] Security and safety trumped convenience.

In addition to the usual social and behavioral problems on campus, several specific incidents occurred that further suggested the changing mores of society and of the campus community. In May 1991, a number of students were charged with fraud for making false identification cards for other students so they could purchase alcohol illegally. In February 1996, 17 students (including 12 athletes) were suspended from the college after they admitted falsifying time sheets for work-study (part of their financial aid package). The total amount paid for nonwork (mostly refereeing in the intramural program) was $11,756. A year later a student was charged with stealing most of the copies of the April 24 issue of the *Phoenix*, because it contained a story about hazing that would raise problems with her national sorority, Phi Sigma Sigma. The newspaper was reprinted and distributed, and sanctions were placed on the student and the sorority. The following fall (1997), a student broke into the bookstore and stole $1,500 worth of computer software; he was apprehended and the software returned.

An omnipresent problem was use of alcohol by students. Throughout the decade there were regular incidents of alcohol poisoning, especially as a result of binge drinking, which was becoming a national fad. A sophomore woman was reportedly sent to the hospital after imbibing 24 shots of bourbon.[28] While the administration tried to enforce the rules governing underage drinking, students demanded the right to drink on campus and accused the administration of "forcing people off campus to drink and then to drive," to quote an underage junior.[29] An editorial in 1994 addressed alcohol and vandalism, attributing the problems to immaturity.[30] Another writer asked, "Why is it more important to get drunk and break two windows in one building than to learn how to properly spell the word 'amateur'? . . . If we can get our priorities straight, then maybe alcohol abuse would not be such a problem."[31] The Student Affairs Office regularly addressed the problem with educational programs, including On Campus Talking about Alcohol (OCTAA), which highlighted risks, options, and responsibility. The office also received a grant from the Maryland Alcohol and Drug Abuse Administration to assist campus groups in further education. Orientation of new students always confronted the problem and urged restraint, but peer pressures were strong, and many students felt they were entitled to drink and thought, "Nothing can happen to me." As the problems increased, President Chambers appointed a Commission on Community Behavior and Alcohol Abuse to address such questions as "Should alcohol be permitted on campus?" "Are we adequately educating students to the health issues involved with alcohol?" "How do we regulate alcohol use on campus?" and "How can we support students who do not abuse alcohol?"[32] In 1999 the *Phoenix* reported the results of a campus survey in which a high percentage of students admitted drinking excessive amounts; while 22% said they didn't drink at all, 38% reported drinking two or more times a week. Perhaps due to the increased emphasis on responsible drinking, the number of discipline cases involving alcohol over the last three years of the decade diminished each year.[33]

Drug use on campus was less of a problem, although it was a concern. A survey of entering freshmen in 1999 revealed that one-third had smoked marijuana and 15% had used another drug. Drug arrests rose from one to nine between 1991 and 1996 and then dropped off somewhat. An anonymous student drug dealer reported that he made $30,000 a year by selling nonaddictive drugs on campus but said he knew that some students were using cocaine, crystal meth, and heroin.[34] Concern about sexually transmitted diseases and HIV/AIDS continued, and ASAP (AIDS: Support, Awareness and Prevention) was formed to educate students about safe sex. The group conducted a survey in 1999 and found that 80% of students were sexually active and only 43% used condoms regularly. Many were active with more than one partner, and usually they were under the influence of alcohol.[35]

As this decade unfolded, minorities were better represented in the faculty and staff, as well as in the student body, as a result of aggressive recruitment, and the racial tensions of the previous three decades were largely diminished. However, in 1994, a spate of racial incidents occurred on campus, incited by off-campus agitators, and the campus was stunned. Racial epithets were painted on the tennis courts and golf course, and hate mail was sent to specific students. It was soon learned that other colleges and local high schools were experiencing the same things. The college community reacted by holding an open forum and a candlelight vigil to protest the incidents and support its minority colleagues. The administration issued a supporting statement. The local and regional media sensationalized the incidents, probably giving them more significance than they deserved. Two years later the *Phoenix* noted that racial equality and diversity were continuing to grow at the college as efforts were still being made to increase minority student and faculty applications.[36] In 1998, more racial epithets appeared on three doors in Rouzer Hall; however, the student involved was caught via video camera and suspended. Again, a candlelight vigil was held to show public solidarity and to set a tone of tolerance for the campus. The board of trustees issued a statement denouncing the incident. A student writing about it wisely noted, "Maybe the person who wrote the racist messages, whether he has been caught or not, will learn that there is no room in our society for messages of hate. We will learn, too, that hate and hate mongers are still out there, and we have a long way to go to reach complete harmony and respect."[37] A year later a national hate group, the World Church of the Creator, attempted to spread anti-black, anti-Jewish flyers on the campus and was escorted off the property, but not before another media frenzy of bad publicity.

Of course, dining services continued to receive criticism. However, an occasional kudo was expressed, as in 1993, when it was noted in the *Phoenix* that the bread, deli bar, and salad bar selections had been upgraded, and vegan entrées were now available, as well as pizza and hamburgers. Four years later, an editorial stated,

> Students find that GLAR [the nickname for Englar Dining Hall] food lacks taste and variety and that the cooking and cleanliness procedures are less than desirable. . . . On any given day during lunch, students will find grilled cheese sandwiches, french fries, salads, deli meats, hamburgers, pizza, and hot dogs. The problem is that the same food is served every lunch period, every single day.[38]

A month later that view was rebutted:

> GLAR is a cafeteria! The food they serve is mass produced. . . . It is not up to the standard of a fine restaurant or home made. . . . Most of the time GLAR serves good, basic meals. Usually nothing fancy, but we aren't paying for fancy. . . . GLAR will listen if students bother to speak. . . . Give GLAR a break. This ridiculous sport of GLAR-bashing has gone far enough.[39]

During this time, the new caterer, the Sodexho Corporation, merged with Marriott, but local management and staff remained the same.

An innovation in residence hall living was well under way by mid-decade: affinity housing. Since the beginning of the Honors Program, honors students

A student room in a residence hall, 1990s

636

had lived together in several suites in Daniel MacLea Hall. Now other suites were occupied by groups of like-minded students banded together for a specific purpose, such as a group interested in tutoring elementary students; majors in French, Spanish, or German; a group of elementary education minors who planned activities for third graders in the neighborhood; and students who regularly hosted prospective students, gave admissions tours, and generally promoted the college. A debate in 1997 over starting quiet hours at 9 P.M. in the residence halls produced the editorial comment, "Having quiet hours start as early as 9 P.M. is ridiculous. At 9 o'clock on most nights the evening is really just beginning." A coeditor rebutted, "What about those who occasionally would like to study? Isn't that one of the major reasons we are here?"[40]

The Trumpeters, the local leadership honor society, reorganized in 1998 "to better serve the college community"; the group decided to elect as many as 10% of both the junior and senior classes. At Homecoming 1997, the group also held a reunion of all former Trumpeters, and many returned to the Hill for a luncheon and recollection of earlier times.

In 1991, the name of the college was discussed again and debated in the *Phoenix*, but the editor thought there were more important issues to be dealt with. Early in 1993, the possibility of changing the name was discussed by the trustees within the context of market perceptions. The students were made aware of this through their representatives, and one editor commented that if the name were to be changed, it should be to a name of which everyone can be proud, not for money.[41]

In almost every decade after about 1950, student interest in ghosts on campus arose, and legends continued to abound. It was reported as fact that almost every building was haunted by the ghost of someone who had died therein. Purportedly, at least two women haunted Elderdice, although no women had ever lived (or died) in the old seminary building. Alumni Hall was certainly haunted by a man who had hanged himself from the balcony (although the only hanging on campus took place in Yingling Gymnasium, which was razed in 1956). And Carroll Hall was definitely haunted by a Civil War soldier who had been brought there (and died)* when the building was turned into a hospital following the Gettysburg campaign. The only problem was that that building had not been built until 1873, ten years after Gettysburg. The students could not be deterred with the truth because they heard weird sounds in the buildings, and stories continued to be promulgated about all manner of deaths occurring under bizarre circumstances in dormitories and classroom buildings. The curious thing is that these ghosts all seem to have manifested themselves in more recent times; earlier generations of students knew nothing about them (or just ignored them!).[42]

The campus was saddened to learn of the deaths of at least three students during the decade: John Earle '96 in July 1994; Douglas Combs '95 in January 1995; and Martin Oswiecimka '99 in December 1997.

In 1990 a trustee Commission on Athletics was appointed, with Jerome Baroch '64 as chair. Its report, issued a year later, revealed that 80% of the student body participated in intramural sports and suggested that the program needed more coordination. (A year later a new lacrosse coach was hired, whose duties were in part to provide that coordination.) Twenty-one varsity sports were being fielded, which was probably too ambitious for the size of the college; if future finances were to prove a problem, the recommendation was to cut certain programs rather than reduce the level of all programs. It noted the dependence on part-time coaches and recommended full-time coaches, especially in football and lacrosse for men and volleyball and basketball for women, sports that seemed to be the most viable and successful. Overall, it was felt that the college's athletic program received excellent bang for the buck.[43]

A major change in the athletic conference relationships occurred in 1992, when all of the college sports left the Middle Atlantic Conference to expand the Centennial Conference (previously only for football). At that time Washington College, Haverford, and Bryn Mawr also joined the conference. The team name was also changed from Terrors to Terror about 1993; the college Green Terror mascot was ranked 13th in the top 25 weirdest names and mascots by *U.S. News and World Report* in 1999.

The football team began the decade with some success, especially for Andrew Steckell, who was named Division III Player of the Week by *Sports Illustrated* in 1990, and Eric Frees, who was the all-time leading rusher in the NCAA at the end of his career in 1992 (5,281 yards). Steckell also broke the college record for pass reception yards (2,248) and touchdown receptions (24). In 1991, the college celebrated 100 years of football. In March 1992, the team garnered significant national publicity when it traveled to Russia to play a game with an all-star team of the Euro-Asian Football League in Moscow's Central Sports

Green Terror mascot and friend

*In 1997, Terror football players celebrate the first of three
undefeated seasons and conference titles.*

Club. Forty-seven players and 20 parents, coaches, and fans represented the
college and proudly celebrated the 47–4 victory. Following the fall 1992 season
Coach Dale Sprague [1986–92] left to take a similar position at Blackburn
College in Illinois. It was felt by many that he had gotten the team off to a good
start six years earlier but had not been able to keep the momentum going. His
replacement was Timothy Keating [1993–], formerly of Wesley College (DE).
(The announcement of Keating's selection as the college's 23rd football coach
was made at a press conference but not before the *Baltimore Sun* jumped
the gun to announce that someone else had been chosen.) During Keating's
second season, the team turned up its first winning season since 1990 (5–4) but

lost to Johns Hopkins 28–21 in the 100th meeting of that friendly rivalry. For the last three seasons in the decade, the team went undefeated (10–0) (the first time since 1951) and won the Centennial Conference title, which provided an automatic berth in the NCAA Division III playoffs. The team was now being recognized as one to be reckoned with. Keating was named Division III Coach of the Year in 1997, and in 1999 the first game of the NCAA playoffs was held in Bair Stadium, the Terror beating Catholic University 20–16. The following week Trinity College (TX) turned the tables and won by another 20–16 score, to quash hopes of a Division III championship as it had the previous year.

The soccer team played well early in the decade, although it lost games by close margins. After three winning seasons (1990–92) out of four, Coach Matt Robinson [1989–94] turned the team over to John Pleyvak [1994–2007], who led it to another winning season in 1999. Lacrosse began to improve when a full-time coach, Keith Reitenbach [1992–2002], was appointed. In 1997, the team turned in the best season ever (11–2) and narrowly missed a bid to the NCAA Division III playoffs. It had one more winning season in 2000, ending the decade with six winning and four losing seasons. The baseball team also turned in six winning seasons, especially in 1995 (19–8) and 1997 (18–12); in 1996, Coach David Seibert was named Coach of the Year by the Maryland State Association of Baseball Coaches. Men's basketball continued to have losing seasons during the decade; Head Coach Nick Zoulias retired from the team in 2000 after 11 seasons, with a 84–180 record. The team's best season was in 1990–91, when it went 12–12. The golf team regularly took the conference championship; it obtained national ranking (17th) in 1997 with 17 players and received the first of three consecutive NCAA tournament bids. In 2000, four WMC wrestlers were invited to the NCAA tournament, and Ukranian transfer Andrey Brener came home an All-America. The wrestlers posted five winning seasons in all. The tennis team and the men's swimming team each completed the decade with ten losing seasons.

In the women's arena, the basketball team, under Coach Rebecca Martin gradually strengthened its position in the conference with six winning seasons and in 1999 ended the season 17–8. Volleyball changed coaches in 1990 (to Jolene Jordan) and again in 1993, when Carole Templon Molloy '85, '87M [1993–] took over. Except during the period 1995–98, the team posted winning seasons, and in 1999 it was ranked sixth in the nation and ended as conference co-champion, the first since 1994. Women's tennis, under Coach Joan Weyers, turned in the best season in 23 years in 1998 with a 13–2 overall record and turned in six winning seasons overall. The softball team, coached by Jennifer Flynn Swanson [1990–97] and then by Scott Swanson [1998–2003], began to show its strength during the decade with ten winning seasons and an invitation to the NCAA playoffs in 1998. The lacrosse team also showed strength in eight winning seasons under longtime coach Kim Easterday [1977–99], while the women's swimming team chalked up only two winning seasons and the field hockey team produced four. In 1999 the women's cross-country team captured the first conference title in school history. Jill Krebs became the first college cross-country All-America by finishing 35th at the NCAA Division III championships.

As the college grew in enrollment, the sports program grew as well, and more students qualified for All-America status. In football, the All-America teams are usually chosen by sportswriters or directors; in soccer, lacrosse, and baseball, the teams are selected by the national coaches associations or governing bodies. In other sports, final standing in NCAA tournaments determines the award. In this decade a significant number of WMC's athletes were named All-America in their respective sports: Karen L. Alexander '96, swimming, 1993, 1994, 1995; Julie D. Backof '98, softball, 1997, 1998; Andrey L. Brener '01, wrestling, 1999; F. Dean Coccia '96, men's lacrosse, 1996; Charles C. Conaway '00, wrestling, 1999; Julie R. Cox '96, women's track, 1993, 1994, 1996; Marvin H. Deal '00, football, 1997, 1998; David P. Evans '01, men's track, 1999; Jamie L. Falcone '01, women's track, 2000; Eric C. Frees '92, football, 1989, 1990, 1991, 1992; Adam J. Gregori '95, football, 1991; Katie M. Haley '99, women's basketball, 1997, 1998; Stephen R. Hallowell '97, men's lacrosse, 1997; R. Ryan Hines '99, football, 1998; Matthew C. Hoppe '97, men's lacrosse, 1997; W. Robert Johns '03, wrestling, 1999; Jill M. Krebs '02, cross-country, 1999, 2000; Thomas J. Lapato '99, football, 1998; Kent L. Lightbourn '93, men's track, 1994; Mathew D. Mathias '99, football, 1998; Erin E. Murphey '97, women's basketball, 1996; Vincent J. Pedalino '02, wrestling, 1999, 2000, 2001; Thomas B. Selecky '00, football, 1997, 1998; John J. Torpy '97, men's lacrosse, 1997; Carl H. Von Tobel '97, men's track, 1994, 1995, 1996; Kerry B. Wilson '00, women's track, 1997, 1998; and Anthony D. Worm '99, golf, 1998.

BUILDINGS AND GROUNDS

As in every decade following World War II, the campus continued to evolve and change. Despite the temporary budgetary crisis of the early 1990s, capital improvements continued to be made, often funded by generous donations for specific purposes.

Early in the decade a new steam plant was built on Union Street to handle the planned campus expansion. Soon thereafter a new computer center was built, and it opened in January 1991 as an addition to the Decker College Center. It was funded, in part, from the rental fees paid by the Department of Agriculture for the storage space in the lower level of the Lewis Hall of Science.[44] The extensive $10 million addition to Hoover Library was completed and functional by February 1991, and the books were moved into it soon thereafter. It was formally dedicated the following October.

Reacting to internal needs and external pressures, the trustees authorized a number of renovations to provide for handicapped access into and inside Baker Memorial Chapel, Alumni Hall, McDaniel Lounge, Baker Chapel, and Memorial Hall. Doors were widened, ramps built, wheelchair lifts installed, and areas for wheelchair placement created. As other more extensive building renovations were planned, accessibility was provided.

The college had for many years owned and managed a bookstore, but in 1992 the board decided to lease the operation to an outside vendor, Barnes and Noble. The bookstore chain remodeled the space in the Decker Center, brought in its own management, and was soon ready for business. After a rapid turnover in managers over a two-year period, the company hired Kyle Meloche '94 [1994–], who gave stability to the new operation.

In 1993, the family of Caroline Foutz Benson '23 gave $25,000 to create a garden in the area just south of the Hoover Library. The focal point was an

Benson family dedicates Palijczuk sculpture fountain.

The Rice Gallery in Peterson Hall

eight-ton granite rock that was fashioned into a sculpture fountain by Professor of Art Wasyl Palijczuk. The artist said of his multisymbol work, "My idea of the fountain was to position it in a place of quietness and meditation such as you would find in the natural environment—in the woods. It expresses the inter-relatedness of the liberal arts and the human connectedness so central to living." The garden was dedicated October 1, 1993. Instrumental in making the gift were the honoree's son and trustee George R. Benson Jr., daughter Caroline Benson Schaeffer '49, and granddaughter Caroline R. Benson '85. They represented 14 family members who had attended the college over four generations.[45]

Beginning in the summer of 1994 and continuing throughout the next academic year, a number of renovation projects were undertaken, funded by special grants or by contributions to the beginning phases of the Defining Moment Campaign. The renovation of the 1908 fine art building, named Peterson Hall in appreciation for the $1 million gift from trustee emerita Clementine Peterson, was the first in the series. An elevator was added to the building; classrooms were equipped for technology, including computer graphics; and the basement area was refitted for drawing studios, offices, and a darkroom. The upper floor (the original library area and later the art studio) was redesigned to be an art gallery. The ceiling was refitted with translucent and stained glass, mirroring the original ceiling, which had been moved to the library board room a few years earlier to preserve it. The gallery was later named for Esther Prangley Rice, artist wife of trustee Lee Rice, who had made a $400,000 gift to the renovation projects. Other facilities for sculpture, oil painting, and crafts were also created or improved in the studios across Main Street in the old carriage house (former college shops) beyond Carroll Hall.

Simultaneously with the Peterson Hall renovations, Memorial Hall, a much larger facility, was undergoing major renovation that required the classroom and office building to be vacated for an entire academic year. Homes for the Humanities and Social Science departments housed there were found, classrooms were carved out of spaces in the library, and everyone soldiered on (without benefit of many books and files that were in temporary storage off-site). The four floors of the building were reconfigured to place the majority of the offices around the perimeter on the upper floors, with an inner core providing space for seminar rooms, as well as offices and storage for support staff. An elevator was added, and special circular, technologically "smart" classrooms were created on the first floor (the old college dining room), surrounding an open space. A small lecture hall was included, as well as a computerized writing laboratory. The basement area (or ground floor—the kitchens of an earlier era) was redesigned as a collection of small classrooms and offices. The project stayed fairly well on schedule, but a final coat of paint was being applied to the walls the morning of the dedication on October 13, 1995, and the ground-floor rooms were not finished until a few weeks later. The English, History, Political Science, and Sociology departments moved back in soon thereafter. At the dedication the building was renamed Hill Hall in recognition of the commitment and financial contributions of trustee Martin K. P. Hill.

In the open space between Hoover Library and Hill Hall, a brick plaza was created and landscaped, with circular grassy tiers formed by low granite walls. Into the top faces of the wall stones were etched the names of the 83 emeriti faculty and administrators who had spent their entire careers at the college. (The names of those longtime faculty who died in office were added a few years later, as were the names of those retiring as emeriti in subsequent years.) The area was named Memorial Plaza, not only as a memorial to those who had faithfully served the institution but also as a way of keeping the "Memorial" name, which had been appended to the old Science Hall to remember the several buildings in the Old Main complex. Moved from its earlier site and rebuilt in Memorial Plaza was the brick pedestal incorporating the cornerstones of the old buildings and topped by the Old Main bell, which is rung on ceremonial occasions. The Memorial Plaza project was made possible through an anonymous gift in honor of the faculty and especially Professor Emeritus William David Jr.

As a result of a special fund-raising effort, Baker Chapel was also renovated at this time. A new cedar-shingle roof was installed; a ramp and new doors provided easy access; and the inside was refurbished with new carpet, refinished pews, and a coat of paint on the walls. Because of a generous gift from Katherine R. Tillman '25, over the next two years the organ was rebuilt by Ken List, a member of the adjunct music staff, using parts of three older organs. The Alumni Hall organ had been silent since the renovation of that building in the late 1970s. The original Baker Chapel organ had been replaced in 1962 by one removed from the Towson Methodist Church

The Tillman Organ (1997) in Baker Chapel

chapel. Fortunately, all the pipes of all the organs had been saved and stored, and List was able to incorporate parts of them into the new instrument, which used the console of the second organ (on a movable platform) and the keyboards of the Alumni Hall organ. He expanded the capabilities of the organ to ten registers comprising 12 ranks with 791 pipes, added the chimes from Alumni Hall, and voiced it for the Baker Chapel space. Discovered in the chapel basement were the facade pipes of the original 1895 organ, which had survived well enough to be redecorated and put into place to resemble the organ of a century earlier (see page 223 for picture of original organ). List said of his work,

> It is my opinion that the re-use of materials in the form of available pipes from the older "Little" Baker Chapel and Alumni Hall organs represents, without musical compromise, an appropriate and realistic way in which the best of these organs, which played historic roles in the development of Western Maryland College's musical tradition, could be both preserved and functionally utilized. . . . The best of the past, conjoined with the best of today, has resulted in a fine and useful musical instrument for our time.[46]

While the college had endured several small fires through its history, amazingly, it had escaped a serious fire for almost 133 years, until sometime early on December 31, 1996, when a fire of unknown origin started in the basement of the old Gill Gymnasium. Discovered about 7 A.M., the blaze went to five alarms and was battled by 200 firemen from Maryland and Pennsylvania, pumping 1,000 gallons of water a minute throughout the foggy morning before they finally brought it under control about 1 P.M. It destroyed athletic equipment, many bulky items stored in the basement area, and much of the contents of the ROTC offices on the second floor. The adjacent physical education faculty offices, as well as the larger arena in the complex, suffered smoke and water damage. At first the old building was considered a total loss, and many feared it would have to be razed.[47] Richard Klitzberg '63, writing for the *Phoenix*, remembered the gymnasium:

> I am proud that, for four years, the gym was filled with excitement created by winning [basketball] teams. Victories over rivals such as Hopkins, Catholic U., Towson State, and Mt. St. Mary's made game-nights into memories I will never forget. Gill Gym had capacity for . . .

Fire seriously damaged Gill Gymnasium in 1996.

a thousand. The night we beat The Mount, I can still hear that tumult,
and the stillness of the building hours later. . . . For me it is the loss of a
place—I can no longer hear the friendly thumps of a dribble or the hiss
of a shot only catching net, or the shouts of voices from the past.[48]

After a national disaster response team cleaned up the charred rubble and
pumped out the water from the basement in preparation for an inspection by
the fire marshal's office, an assessment revealed that, although the windows
had been blown out, the roof badly damaged, and the wood floor destroyed,[49]
the walls were sound and the building could be repaired. By March rebuilding
was well under way, and the decision was made to replace the old floor with
a composition floor similar to that in the newer arena; simultaneously, a new
wood floor was laid in the newer building, providing a much more "forgiving"
playing surface for basketball and volleyball games.[50] By summer, the facility had
been repaired, the windows had been walled up, and the basement had been
deepened to make the area more useful; it now included a large classroom area,
as well as storage space. The gymnasium was again ready for physical education
classes and intramural use. Insurance covered the costs of rebuilding.

A much needed addition to Levine Music Hall, originally built in 1891,
was authorized in 1998 to provide facilities for ensemble and solo rehearsals,
instrument storage, and faculty teaching studios. Funded in part by significant
gifts from Evelyn Collison MacKenzie '31 and Edward J. Nygren '47, the $1.6
million facility was built and ready for occupancy in November 1999. Levine
Hall was then refurbished inside and out and the whole complex rededicated
in April 2002.

During the decade, a number of smaller projects were undertaken. Trustee
Larry Blumberg '67 provided a financial challenge to raise funds for a new

The addition to Levine Music Hall was opened in 1999.

physical fitness center in the lower level of the Gill Center, and in 1993 the Blumberg Fitness Center was opened for student use. The Carroll County Bank and Trust Company contributed funds in recognition of the 125th anniversary of the college; this led to naming the Joshua W. Hering Conference Room in the Administration and Finance offices in honor of the first treasurer of the college. A technology laboratory in Hoover Library was created in honor of Associate Professor Emerita Margaret Denman-West and dubbed the "Maggie Lab" in 1996. The Richwine Special Collections Room was dedicated in 1996 to house the collection of first editions of American writers donated by Eleanor Richwine in memory of her late husband, Professor of English Emeritus Keith Richwine. The baseball field was named in honor of trustee chairman emeritus Wilbur Preston in 1997, in recognition of a grant to the campaign from his Baltimore law firm.

For at least a decade the need for improved science laboratory facilities had been discussed. The most recent updating of laboratories had been in the mid-1960s with the addition to Lewis Hall, but the older facilities had not seen much improvement. The science faculty regularly brought their needs to the attention of the administration, and in 1996 the trustees approved the construction of a building,[51] with funding included in the Defining Moment Campaign. Fund-raising and architectural planning committees were appointed, many drafts of the interior design were considered and modified, and estimated costs rose by 25%, but ground was broken in April 1997 for the center, which would connect to the Lewis Hall of Science and sit on the ridge above Winslow Hall. Construction was under way by October, and the unnamed science center, designed primarily to be a laboratory building for biology and chemistry, opened for classes in August 1999. The first floor housed laboratories for freshman courses in both fields. The second floor was devoted to biology and comprised faculty offices, small research laboratories, and larger well-equipped laboratories where classes could also be held. The third floor was dedicated to chemistry and had a number of faculty offices and small research facilities, as well as larger laboratories. Joint student-faculty research had long been encouraged, and now special facilities were provided for it. The $13 million facility had a large air-filtering system in its basement, as well as an air-conditioning system capable of cooling the air for all the neighboring buildings, including Baker Memorial Chapel. The building was formally dedicated on October 16, 1999. Soon thereafter, plans for the renovation of Lewis Hall and Lewis Hall of Science were under way, at a cost of $6.5–$7 million. As of December 31, 1999, the federal government vacated the lower level of Lewis Hall of Science after 33 years, and that space was incorporated into the renovations.

FINANCES

This is a time of trial and a time of testing. In some respects, the current events of the year have been trying. The enrollment is smaller than usual. Collections have been slower than I have ever known them. The State seems to pay its appropriations after October." These words might well have been expressed by President Chambers in 1992 as the college faced a serious enrollment and budgetary shortfall and potential deficits for the immediate future. The words, however, are those of T. H. Lewis, in 1915. Just as the college had endured some hard times throughout its history, especially 77 years earlier for similar reasons, so it faced some difficult times during the early part of the 1990s.

In 1990, President Chambers wrote a position paper on the future of the college in the 21st century. He speculated on what the students, curriculum, student life, and faculty would be like in 2010. He estimated that the college budget could rise as high as $160 million, but more probably to $82 million, in 20 years. Over the same period, based on previous trends, he predicted tuition to rise to $71,000 per year. He hoped that the endowment would grow to about $60 million. He concluded by saying that a comprehensive capital campaign to raise $30–$35 million needed to be mounted by the mid-1990s and still might not be enough to keep the college from continuing to be financially strapped. (These speculations were made shortly before the critical downturn.) He also raised questions about how to improve the quality and diversity of the institution, how to make the college distinctive, and how to overcome the increasing problems and misperceptions caused by the college's name.[52]

Due to a smaller freshman class and upperclass attrition, the 1990 enrollment was 1,172 (about 80 below the previous year); the numbers dropped almost to 1,000 by 1993, then gradually grew again, to a maximum of about 1,550 by 1999 (a 50% increase overall). Freshman classes began at about 333, dropped below 300 in the early 1990s, then grew again to exceed 500 (the largest in the college's history) by the end of the decade. Such fluctuations played havoc with budgets, which were still largely tuition driven.

The tuition rose regularly, from $11,590 in 1990–91 to $18,650 in 1999–2000. Room and board fees increased less than $1,000 over the decade. After 1993, the trustees capped total fee increases at 4% or less, so that total student expenses saw only a 50% increase, from $15,980 to $24,000, from 1990 to 1999. Total costs remained in the mid-range of comparable colleges.[53]

To keep pace with rising expenses, the college budget almost doubled, growing from about $25 million to about $48 million over the decade. Even as it grew, receipts could not keep pace with expenses. As early as 1990, because of a shortfall of 50 in enrollment (below the number on which the budget was built), an original deficit of $95,000 had to be met by some deep budget pruning and judicious management. The following year, an enrollment deficit of 53 forced cuts totaling $863,000. For 1992–93, in anticipation of an even smaller enrollment, no salary increases were budgeted (but no layoffs or salary reductions were planned), building improvements were kept to a minimum, and a larger draw from the endowment was included. The trustees worried that deferred maintenance could cause serious problems in the future.[54] With no guaranteed improvement on the horizon, and with the Maryland appropriation simultaneously reduced by $150,000, a restructuring committee was appointed to examine how to make the college more efficient and keep costs to a minimum. Through faculty retirements and the elimination of 11 administrative positions, the task force created considerable savings. The faculty (now almost 80% tenured) was not truly accepting of or willing to accommodate to the financial difficulties facing the college, and unavoidable tensions arose. The teaching load, just reduced to three courses each semester, was raised to seven courses over the year for 1991–92, and some faculty were unhappy.[55] The trustees, grappling with the deficits, noted that the faculty had to understand that some programs might have to be cut or scaled back if the college was to remain viable.[56]

Usually the optimist, even President Chambers quoted from *Time* magazine, "The small liberal arts school with a meager endowment and largely local reputation is an endangered species."[57] The 1993–94 budget was still very tight, although the money borrowed from the endowment to balance the 1992–93 budget was immediately replaced. Enrollment growth and retention were still significant issues, and the Enrollment Management Committee, first appointed in 1990, worked diligently to assist the admissions office. By the spring of 1994, the admissions picture was much better, and enrollments produced an additional $1 million revenue; salary improvements were approved, and the corner had been turned. During the remainder of the decade, the budget was balanced without significant adjustments, enrollments and retention improved, and faculty and staff morale returned to its usual positive status. The endowment tripled, from about $14 million to about $42 million, during the decade, especially as a result of the capital campaign and the receipt of several large bequests, including over $3 million from the McClure Rouzer estate. Annual support from various sources, including the Annual Fund, was also growing yearly.

Faculty and staff salaries over the decade grew about 40%, from an average of $38,000 to $52,000. At the beginning of the decade the salaries of the top

*The Defining Moment Campaign goal is announced
by Trustee Chair J. Melhorn in 1996.*

professorial ranks compared well with national averages. After they were held constant for two years, they were increased by 5%–6% yearly to catch up, but it would take more to bring them into parity with other institutions. An early-retirement program with the rather ominous name Terminal Sabbatical was instituted in 1993; faculty members prior to age 62 who chose to retire under this plan would be paid for an additional "sabbatical" year at full salary. Seven faculty immediately opted for the program in 1994. A phased retirement program was also created, and a few faculty elected that option. Simultaneously, the health care program for retirees was modified; after 1994, retiring faculty would not remain in the college health plan but would be given a monthly stipend to purchase a supplemental plan to Medicare. For faculty hired after January 1, 1994, health benefits would cease at retirement.

After several years of planning and considerable quiet fund-raising, the board of trustees in 1996 set a goal of $40 million for the comprehensive capital campaign called the Defining Moment Campaign. It was formally launched the following September and concluded December 31, 1999. Trustee Martin Hill served as campaign chair and spearheaded the trustee contributions by pledging $1.5 million at the outset, insisting, "You can't lead where you're not willing to go." Ultimately, almost half of the total amount raised, $41,118,138, came from the trustees.

Theatre on the Hill was still active in the summer, performing such plays as *The Secret Garden, Greater Tuna, My Fair Lady, Noises Off, Ruthless*, and *Blood Brothers*; but two seasons were canceled due to renovations in Alumni Hall, losing money for the college.

In 1996, the Baltimore Ravens football team signed a contract to hold a training camp on the campus, beginning that summer. That first year, the team rented the campus facilities for $25,000 and paid $45 per night per room in the college motel (turned over to the team exclusively for the duration of camp). They also paid $38 per day per person for food service provided by the Sodexho Corporation and served in the adjacent conference center.[58] The summer conference program continued to make a major contribution to the budget. In 1997, for example, the college hosted "Common Ground on the Hill"; Maryland Boys' State; a science institute; band and cheerleading camps; the Art Monk Football Camp; and sports camps for lacrosse, volleyball, soccer, basketball, and wrestling. Other adult groups also met on campus for various periods of time. The Gill Center, the largest space in the area, became the scene of graduations for all the Carroll County high schools, as well as several schools from Baltimore County and Carroll Community College. Once the arena was set up with a large dais and chairs on the floor for the college's commencement in late May 2000, the space could be rented to other schools without much change. This also served to introduce hundreds of high school students and their families to the college.

The WMC Development Corporation was still grappling with how to make the motel and restaurant complex profitable. Plans for selling all or part of the property were put on hold in 1991, and several management adjustments were made. The motel was downgraded to a Comfort Inn (to attract more business at lower fees), and McDaniel's restaurant was reconfigured to become a less formal dining operation renamed Reunions. Soon a 35% increase in revenues was realized. Appraised at $2.29 million, the complex was at last considered a valid investment by the college auditors. By 1994, the restaurant was again in financial and management trouble, however, so it was closed and a new management company was hired for the motel and conference center. The following year, the officers of the corporation reported to the trustees that losses were reduced and no further cash input from the college was needed. In late 1997, the corporation leased ten acres of the unused property at $230,000 per year for 31 years to Black Rock Associates to build a shopping center and install a road through the property from Route 140 to Main Street (naming it WMC Drive). Ground for the College Square Shopping Center was broken on October 21, 1998, and the Safeway anchor store opened the following summer. By April 2000, a branch of the New Windsor State Bank and a Burger King had been approved.

After several delays caused by county regulations and building moratoria, seven lots on the upper part of the Singleton property were offered for sale, first to members of the college community, to raise a total of $350,000–$400,000.

As the decade concluded, word was received that Catharine Welker Eaton '90M (honorary) had died on July 12, 1999; her husband, Thomas H. Eaton '27, LHD'86, had died May 15, 1995. The Eatons, who had no children in their 64-year marriage, had been generous to the college in several ways, including an endowed fund for campus enhancement. In March 2000, the trustees learned that the bulk of their estate would come to the college for the endowment: $8 million, the largest single gift from any source in its history.[59]

MAJOR EVENTS

It was a decade of dedications and rededications, beginning with dedication of the newly expanded Hoover Library on October 13, 1991. The ceremony was held in the plaza in front of the library on a pleasant fall Sunday afternoon and featured an address by Lillian Moore Bradshaw '37, LitD'87, former president of the American Library Association and longtime head of the Dallas Public Library System. The building was presented by board chair Lee Rice and formally accepted by H. David Neikirk, director of the library. An honorary doctor of humane letters was conferred upon board chair emeritus William Keigler. A special tribute was paid to Dr. and Mrs. Hoover for their continued support of the college and especially the library. (Governor William Schaefer was scheduled to be present and receive an honorary degree, but two days before the event, fearing picketers because of an unpopular financial decision, he declined.) After the ribbon cutting, the faculty, trustees, and guests moved into the library for a reception and tours. Inside they were able to view the colorful acrylic mural *Weavings*, painted by Ellen Von Dehsen Elmes '69, depicting aspects of the college's history in the context of American and world happenings. They also observed, above the steps near the rotunda, the visually striking set of seven modern stained-glass panels created by Tim Hirneisen of Art Glass Crafters; they depicted the seven liberal arts, incorporating etched symbols relating to each area in a colorful flowing spectrum.[60] The college was now possibly unique in having two sets of liberal arts stained-glass windows (the other in the understage of Alumni Hall).

The following year, the college celebrated its 125th anniversary throughout the academic year. An informal celebration was held on September 4 around the Old Main cornerstone to remember the first classes held in that building.

125th anniversary celebration at the Old Main cornerstone; (L to R):
W. Dulany, C. Scott, R. Chambers, H. Smith Humbert, J. Lightner, D. Sellman

A bronze bas-relief of the Old Main complex, created by Sue Maseth Lucy '83 and mounted on top of the cornerstone, was unveiled. Relatives of John Smith were invited as special guests. A Founder's Convocation was held on October 3, 1992, coinciding with Parents' Weekend. During the event guests were welcomed by SGA president Kourtnay Sweeney '93 and entertained by the College Choir. The speaker was Louis Rukeyser, the financial analyst and author. He gave "Some Thoughts for the Class of 1993" and was presented with the honorary doctor of humane letters. The John Smith Memorial Medallion Award was presented to Alonzo Decker Jr., a generous benefactor of the college. The award had been created in April 1981 in honor of one of the founders of the college and was presented to nonalumni who showed a significant commitment to the college. (The first recipient was Frank Baker Jr.) Following the convocation, Decker unveiled a picture of his late father, trustee Alonzo Decker Sr., in the Ensor Lounge of the Decker College Center.

On April 25, 1995, the renovated fine art building (and first free-standing college library) was dedicated and named Peterson Hall. The ceremony was held in Alumni Hall at 4 P.M. and focused on the arts with an address by Gary Vikan, director of the Walters Art Gallery in Baltimore: "Art in Our World, Art in Our Lives: The Aesthetic Trace Element." The building was presented by board chair Rice and accepted by Susan R. Bloom, chair of the Art and Art History Department. Remarks on the significance of the building were made by Provost Coley; art major J. Patrick Barry '96; and alumna Kimberly Jones '87, assistant curator of 19th-century art at the National Gallery of Art. President Chambers paid special tribute to trustee emerita Clementine Peterson DHum'75, whose $1 million gift had made possible the renovation of the building and the college's expansion of facilities for the fine arts. Mrs. Peterson, whose health prevented her from attending, was represented by Clarisse Mechanic DPS'91, Baltimore community leader and patron of the arts. A videotape of the dedication ceremony was afterward presented to Mrs. Peterson, who died 18 months later. A ribbon-cutting ceremony and reception followed in Peterson Hall. During the board's weekend of meetings the following year, the Esther Prangley Rice Gallery on the second floor of Peterson Hall was dedicated on April 20, 1996, a gift of retiring board chair Rice in honor of his artist wife.

Almost precisely 100 years after it was first dedicated, the renovated Baker Chapel was rededicated on May 7, 1995. Paralleling the original service in part, the participants processed to the strains of "A Mighty Fortress," and the Gospel Choir and the Madrigal Singers each performed a selection. The speaker for the occasion was William E. Smith '45, DD'65. President Emeritus John and Wesley Seminary president Douglass Lewis each brought greetings. Susan Fritz, grandniece of William G. Baker Jr., commented on the original gift of the Baker family, after which President Chambers rededicated the chapel. Other participants included Joan Coley, Velva A. Cooper, Mark Lancaster, and Rosemary M. Maxey. A reception followed in McDaniel Lounge. Two years later, on April 26, 1997, the Baker Chapel organ was rededicated. As part of the refurbishing of the chapel, a generous gift from Katherine R. Tillman '25 provided for a new organ for the space in which she had been married in 1927. During the ceremony, Margaret Boudreaux, David Kreider, Ira Zepp, and organ builder Ken List each spoke of the significance of the instrument to the chapel and to the music program of the college. On June 1, the dedicatory recital was presented by Victoria Sirota, vicar of the Church of the Holy Nativity in Baltimore and an accomplished organist. She played a variety of pieces to demonstrate the versatility of the instrument and concluded with a festival prelude on "Now Thank We All Our God" written by her husband, Robert Sirota, director of the Peabody Institute.

After significant renovations, Memorial Hall (previously Science Hall) was renamed Martin K. P. Hill Hall in ceremonies on October 13, 1995. Hill had given the largest gift ever made to the college by a single individual up to that time and was chairing the capital campaign, which had provided some of the $4.5 million for the renovation. In recognition of the $1.9 million grant from the State of Maryland toward the project, Governor Parris Glendening made remarks. Alumni and students in the disciplines of English, sociology, social work, and political science spoke of the importance of the building to the college program. Participating were Mary Ellen Elwell '50, C. Victor McTeer '69, Timothy J. Collins '96, and Holly A. Roback '96. Board chair Rice presented the building, Provost Coley accepted it on behalf of the faculty and students, and special recognition of Mr. Hill was made by President Chambers. Hill responded that he was proud that his daughter Jennifer had graduated from the college, in 1993, the same year he joined the board of trustees, and commented, "Where else in my life would I have more of a positive influence on the lives of so many people than through [this college]?"[61] A week later, on October 21, Memorial Plaza, between Hoover Library and Hill Hall, was dedicated.

On October 28, 1995, ScienceFest was held as the kickoff for the Science Center fund-raising campaign (part of the Defining Moment Campaign), drawing a crowd of interested alumni and townspeople to hear lectures about the history of science at the college; faculty perspectives on science teaching; and updates on biology and chemistry research and application from a number of alumni, faculty, and students. Via a videotape, biology professor emerita Jean Kerschner, the honorary chair of the Science Center Committee, brought greetings from her home in North Carolina. The luncheon speaker was Dr. Theodore E. Woodward ScD'50, professor emeritus at the University of Maryland School of Medicine, who talked about "Health, the Physician, and Society," and the dinner speaker was Dr. Benjamin Carson ScD'94, director of pediatric neurosurgery at Johns Hopkins Hospital, who talked about "Thinking Big."

The Defining Moment Campaign was formally launched and the target goal announced at festivities entitled "A Day of Illumination" on September 28, 1996. Guests were invited to hear a keynote address, "Defining Lessons," by Bob Keeshan (a.k.a. Captain Kangaroo) LHD'96, and attend a variety of educational programs on technology and education presented by faculty and students. These included "What Harmony Sounds Like," "What Poetry Sounds Like," "Back to the Future," "Art Is a Verb," "A Dramatic Collection," "Creating a Masterpiece," "Saving the Planet," and "Stargazing" and attracted hundreds of visitors to a number of the academic buildings. After a buffet dinner in the forum of the Decker Center, the extravaganza continued in the Gill Center, where illusionist Scott Grocki '95 entertained and mystified the crowd of 3,000 prior to a spectacular indoor laser, light, and sound production that capped off the evening. In the course of the festivities, the campaign goal of $40 million was announced, and materials outlining the needs were distributed. Anticipated uses for the funds were "Ensuring Continuity," $7,000,000 (from the Annual Fund); "Building the Learning Environment," $19,300,000 (for a new science laboratory building and renovations to six other facilities); "Enhancing Teaching and Learning," $7,300,000 (for the endowment, faculty development, library, and technology); "Affirming Community," $1,950,000 (primarily for residence hall renovations); "Creating Access," $3,950,000 (for scholarships); and "Seizing Opportunities," $500,000 (for discretionary and venture funds).

Four years later, the largest comprehensive campaign in the institution's 133-year history concluded successfully. To celebrate, a gala dinner for trustees, faculty, and special guests was held on April 14, 2000, in the Englar Dining Hall. Board chair James Melhorn welcomed the group, Acting President Joan Coley told those in attendance why this was the defining moment in the college's history, and campaign chair Martin Hill described how the goal was reached and thanked everyone for their support. "The success of this campaign prepares us to move forward and set our sights higher as we look to the future," he said. Members of the head table then led the group out of the dining room and into Memorial Plaza, where the trustees each rang the Old Main bell; everyone then proceeded along the new brick walkway lit with luminaria, viewing the campus buildings specially illuminated for the evening. At several spots along the way, small musical groups played. The procession ended at the illuminated Ward Memorial Arch, where a brief celebratory program followed, during which Melhorn and Coley surprised Hill by presenting him with the John Smith Medal in recognition of his significant leadership of the campaign and his strong commitment to the college.

On October 16, 1999, the dedication of the new Science Center (named Eaton Hall in October 2001) was held in Baker Memorial Chapel at 2:00 P.M. Following a procession of faculty and trustees to music provided by the College Brass Ensemble, board vice chair Dolores Snyder gave the invocation, guests were welcomed by President Chambers, and Maryland secretary of state John T. Willis brought greetings from the governor and the state. The Madrigal Singers performed two selections, after which the honorary doctor of science degree was conferred on Paul A. J. Janssen, chairman of the Janssen Research Foundation. (This was his first American honorary degree, although he had received 19 from foreign universities.) Dr.

Janssen spoke briefly on the importance of science in the modern world. The significance of the new laboratory building to the college's science program was highlighted by alumni Dr. Philip L. Meredith '66, DuPont Company chemist, and Dr. George Thomas '59, Kennedy-Kreiger Institute geneticist; biochemistry major Diane E. Grove '00; Dr. Louise Paquin, professor of biology; and Dr. Richard H. Smith, professor of chemistry. The building was formally presented by board chair Melhorn and accepted by Provost Coley. After concluding remarks by President Chambers, the guests moved to the new building for a ribbon cutting, reception, and tours of the building by members of the scientific honor societies.

CONCLUSION

It was another decade of highs and lows. Early in the decade enrollments had dropped to late 1960 levels, creating havoc with the college budget and forcing a freeze on faculty and staff salaries (and some staff layoffs) for the first time since the Great Depression. But by the end of the decade the college had to accommodate the largest enrollment in its history. Three new buildings or additions were built, and most other academic facilities tastefully renovated, including the fire-damaged Gill Gymnasium. All this caused campus upheaval, noise, and dust for a number of years. The college also mounted and successfully completed the largest and most comprehensive fund-raising campaign in its history. There were significant administrative changes, as well, as the board of trustees expanded and changed leadership and when a popular and optimistic president resigned unexpectedly, requiring a rethinking of the direction for the future. The faculty also saw many of its stalwarts retire and be replaced with a new generation of academics possessing varied backgrounds, new ideas, and strong disciplinary allegiances. Through it all, the college strove to maintain and improve its standards and prepared itself to meet the unknown demands of the 21st century.

Chapter 14 Endnotes

1. *The Hill*, August 1991, 28.
2. WMC faculty minutes, September 2, 1992; sports information brochure, college sports information files.
3. *Phoenix*, December 9, 1999, 1.
4. *The Hill*, Spring 2000, 3; *Phoenix*, November 4, 1999, 2.
5. WMC board of trustees minutes, April 20, 1996.
6. Ibid., April 18, 1998.
7. Interviews, Ferenc Somogyi, Gabor Drexler, Tamas Vagi, Attila Horvath, Laszlo Frenyo, and Janos Szirmai, September 2001.
8. WMC board of trustees minutes, October 16, 1999.
9. Ibid., October 24, 1992.
10. WMC faculty minutes, December 10, 1992.
11. Ibid., December 7, 1993.
12. WMC faculty minutes, December 6, 1994.
13. WMC board of trustees minutes, September 28, 1996.
14. *The Hill*, November 1992, 4–13.
15. WMC board of trustees minutes, April 16, 1994.
16. WMC trustee Executive Committee minutes, October 16, 1996.
17. *The Hill*, Spring 1999, 4.
18. Ibid., August 1991, 17.
19. Ibid., February 1995, 2–3.
20. WMC board of trustees minutes, April 19, 1997.
21. *Middle States Evaluation Report*, July 1998, 5.
22. *Phoenix*, October 23, 1997, 4.
23. Page 3.
24. *Phoenix*, May 8, 1997, 13.
25. Ibid., October 21, 1999, 3.
26. Ibid., December 11, 1997.
27. Ibid., February 29, 1996, 1.
28. Ibid., December 10, 1998, 1.
29. Ibid., April 24, 1992, 5.
30. Ibid., October 22, 1998, 6.
31. Ibid., November 3, 1994, 2.
32. Ibid., December 5, 1995, 1.
33. Ibid., October 21, 1999, 3.
34. Ibid., May 6, 1991, 1.
35. Ibid., May 6, 1999, 8.
36. Ibid., October 3, 1996, 5.
37. Ibid., November 5, 1998, 1.
38. Ibid., October 23, 1997, 3.
39. Ibid., November 20, 1997, 2.
40. Ibid., May 8, 1997, 4.
41. Ibid., January 22, 1993, 4.
42. Ibid., October 31, 1996, 12.
43. WMC board of trustees minutes, October 19, 1991.
44. Ibid., October 20, 1990.
45. *The Hill*, November 1993, 40.
46. K. List, program for the organ dedication.
47. *Carroll Express*, January 4, 1997, 1–2.
48. *Phoenix*, February 20, 1997, 3.
49. *Carroll County Times*, January 2, 1997, 1, 4.
50. WMC trustee Executive Committee minutes, March 19, 1997.
51. Ibid., July 17, 1996.
52. Chambers, "Into the Twenty-first Century: A Working Paper," 12–14, Chambers Papers, college archives.
53. WMC trustee Executive Committee minutes, September 16, 1992.
54. WMC board of trustees minutes, February 29, 1991.
55. WMC trustee Executive Committee minutes, February 13, 1991.
56. Ibid., December 16, 1992; January 20, 1993.
57. WMC board of trustees minutes, April 25, 1992.
58. WMC trustee Executive Committee minutes, May 15, 1996.
59. WMC trustee Executive Committee minutes, March 22, 2000; June 4, 2000; *The Hill*, Summer 2001, 19–20.
60. *Carroll County Times* supplement, "WMC 125 Years," October 1991, 12–13.
61. *The Hill*, Fall 1995, 17.

Major World Events

1991

Per capita income in the U.S. lags behind inflation for the first time since 1982.

Soviet Union breaks up as republics declare independence; Gorbachev resigns presidency.

The Civil Rights Act of 1991, dealing with job discrimination, is signed into law.

Thurgood Marshall retires from the Supreme Court; Clarence Thomas is appointed.

Operation Desert Storm gets under way to repel Iraq's takeover of Kuwait and its oil.

Postal rate for first-class mail rises to 29¢.

The Dow Jones average ends year at 3,168.83.

1992

The U.S. national debt is $4.003 trillion.

Twelve million people worldwide have died from AIDS.

Arkansas governor Bill Clinton is elected 42nd U.S. president.

Johnny Carson retires from the *The Tonight Show*, is replaced by Jay Leno.

Massive riots in Los Angeles occur as a result of police brutality on black motorist.

Hurricane Andrew hits south Florida and Louisiana, leaving 250,000 homeless.

U.S. Marines are sent to relieve famine in Somalia under Operation Restore Hope.

Environmental Protection Agency declares secondhand smoke a known carcinogen.

1993

Strategic Arms Reduction Treaty is signed by presidents Bush and Yeltsin.

Federal agents storm a Waco, Texas, religious cult compound; 84 are killed.

Holocaust Memorial Museum is opened in Washington, honoring 6 million Jews.

Pope John Paul II visits U.S. for World Youth Day; reaffirms Church ban on birth control.

Thousands of gay people march in Washington for equal rights.

Israel and the PLO sign peace accords at the White House.

Explosion rocks the World Trade Center in New York City.

1994

Civil war breaks out in Rwanda; 500,000 people killed.

Ice storm paralyzes the northeast U.S.

Earthquake in Los Angeles, measuring 6.7, kills 67, does $20 billion damage.

First fully free elections in post-apartheid South Africa bring Nelson Mandela to power.

U.S. major league baseball players go on strike; World Series is canceled.

Hubble telescope provides evidence of black holes in the universe.

1995

Japan suffers large earthquake.

Ebola virus kills 244 Africans.

DVD media format is announced.

Million Man March is held in Washington, led by Louis Farrakhan, Nation of Islam leader.

Federal Building in Oklahoma City is bombed in April; Timothy McVeigh is later convicted.

1996

Osama Bin Laden issues a "Declaration of Jihad", a call for a holy war against the U.S.
President Clinton is reelected.
U.S. troops are sent to Bosnia.
Eastern United States is hit by one of worst blizzards in history.
Unabomber Theodore Kaczynski is arrested; later convicted and sentenced.
Musical *Rent* opens on Broadway.

1997

Mother Teresa dies.
Hong Kong is handed over to China by Great Britain.
Mars Pathfinder lands on Mars and takes pictures and samples of the surface.
The F.W. Woolworth Company closes its doors after 117 years of business.
Princess Diana is killed in an automobile accident in Paris.
First of the Harry Potter book series by J. K. Rowling is published.
Comet Hale-Bopp is spotted.
A sheep, Dolly, is cloned in Scotland.
Avian flu virus is found in China.

1998

America and Britain carry on air strikes in Iraq.
Historic peace accords signed in Northern Ireland on Good Friday.
Apple Computer unveils the iMac.
Google is founded.
President Clinton undergoes impeachment hearings over Lewinsky affair; is acquitted of perjury.
U.S. embassies in Africa are bombed; attributed to Osama Bin Laden.
Microsoft Corporation is broken up in antitrust suit.

1999

Two students go on a shooting rampage at Columbine High School (CO), killing 13.
The Y-2K scare grips the country as everyone prepares for the coming of 2000.
The Euro is created to replace currencies in countries in the European Union.
NATO launches strikes in Yugoslavia; U.S. intervenes in Kosovo.
Pokemon fever grips the U.S. as children clamor for the toys, cards, etc.
Turkey suffers earthquake which kills 13,000 people.
Dow Jones average closes above 11,000 for first time.
The 6 billionth person is born into the world (in Sarajevo).

2000

George W. Bush is elected U.S. president in a contested election.
U.S.S. *Cole* is attacked by al-Queda terrorists while refueling in Yemen.
The Concorde crashes just after takeoff in Paris; the supersonic transport is soon grounded.
Millennium events held, although new millennium does not really begin until January 1, 2001.

In 2002, the college was renamed for William Roberts McDaniel.

CHAPTER

A NEW NAME AND NEW LEADERSHIP

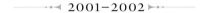

The two-year period 2000–2002 saw more disruption of normal life in the world than any decade since the 1940s. The horrific terrorist attack by al-Qaida on the New York World Trade Center and the Pentagon in Washington on September 11, 2001, changed the world, and especially the United States, forever. Religious and cultural intolerance wreaked some havoc on contemporary society as personal liberties were curtailed in the name of security, and retaliations, first in Afghanistan and then in Iraq, fanned the flames of discord. Anthrax attacks and the scandal surrounding the bankruptcy of the Enron Corporation added to the disquietude. On a more positive note, the world admired the longevity and constancy of the monarchy in Great Britain when Queen Elizabeth II celebrated her Golden Jubilee, the second-longest reign in the thousand-year history of that nation.

The college underwent significant changes both physically and in leadership. Old buildings were renovated, and new ones were planned under the direction of a new president, the first faculty member to rise to the position and the first woman to be selected. She and the board of trustees set some lofty goals, including raising the endowment significantly and enhancing the image of the college. To accomplish the latter, the college in 2002 took the bold step of changing its name to McDaniel College, the most significant action since dissolution of the filial relationship with the Methodist Church 30 years before. The years were challenging ones for everyone.

FACULTY AND ADMINISTRATION

The consultants hired by the trustees to examine the needs of the college examined the institution in some detail and made (for them) the unprecedented recommendation to the Transition Committee that the acting president should be installed permanently. The trustees agreed and in October 2000 formally elected Joan Develin Coley as the eighth president of the college, with a public announcement on October 24.[1] Coley was born in Philadelphia and attended Albright College, from which she graduated with honors as an English major. She enrolled in the University of Maryland graduate school, attaining the degrees of master of education and doctor of philosophy, with a specialization in reading disabilities. She spent several years as a reading specialist for the Prince George's County public schools. After arriving on the WMC campus in the fall of 1973 to direct the graduate program in reading and teach undergraduate education courses, she rose through the professorial ranks and accepted administrative assignments including associate academic dean, director of admissions, chair of the Education Department, dean of the graduate program, and provost. In the latter role, she also served as acting or interim president for eight months during the sabbatical and after the resignation of Robert Chambers. During her career she published extensively, writing articles and reviews for national journals and authoring or coauthoring several books. Coley and her former husband, Robert Coley, had one son, David. (In August 2006, she would marry trustee emeritus M. Lee Rice.)

The faculty continued to change regularly. The campus was especially saddened to learn of the death of colleague Julie O. Badiee [1978–2000] of a brain tumor at age 54 on May 20, 2001. News also reached the campus that assistant professor of art history emeritus Ervin L. Szilagyi [1957–70] died in October 2000, and associate professor of sociology emeritus Charles E. "Chap" Herrman [1974–94] died in April 2002. Retiring as emeriti during this two-year period were Richard W. Dillman [1981–2001], H. David Neikirk [1987–2002], Howard B. Orenstein [1971–2002], and Nancy B. Palmer [1965–2002]. Also retiring was Joel Macht [1994–2002]. Joining the faculty were Sharon Craig [2000–] in education, Roxanna E. Harlow [2000–] in sociology, Eddy F. Laird [2000–] in education, Jeffrey D. Marx [2000–] in physics,

Joan Develin Coley,
eighth president

Margaret McDevitt [2000–] in psychology, Kevin McIntyre [2000–] in economics, Janet Medina [2000–] in education, Catherine Orzolek-Kronner '86 [2000–] in social work, Marcia T. Virts [2000–7] in education, Stephanie Madsen [2001–] in psychology, Paul Mazeroff '67 [2001–] in psychology, Stephen D. McCole [2001–] in exercise science and physical education, Gretchen K. McKay [2001–] in art history, Mary Ann Reichelt [2001–] in education, and Susan C. Scott [2001–] in art and art history. The college also welcomed Psyche Williams-Forson in English in 2000 and Debora Johnson-Ross in political science in 2001; both were Jesse Ball duPont scholars funded through a grant shared with Goucher and Washington colleges establishing a three-year pilot program for African American educators. Both received a permanent tenure-track appointment following their special assignment.

The faculty continued to receive professional honors. Mohamed Esa received a certificate of merit for outstanding German teaching from the American Association of Teachers of German and the German American Friendship Award from the Ambassador of the Federated German Republic. Theodore Evergates was selected as visiting scholar at Oxford University. Samuel Case was inducted into the National Wrestling Hall of Fame. Joan Coley was named an outstanding educational leader by the University of Maryland and selected for the Greater Baltimore Leadership Class for 2002. Ira Zepp published a book of his prayers and *A Muslim Primer* during 2000. Thomas Deveny presented his research on Spanish film at an international symposium held at Ohio State University.

Lawrence Blumberg '67 [1990–2000], Robert A. Howell [1989–2000], Richard Klitzberg '63 [1994–2000], Kurt L. Schmoke [1986–2000], Francis B. Burch Jr. [1996–2001], David M. Stout '76 [1996–2001], and Peter G. Angelos [1996–2002] resigned from the board of trustees, and William H. Elliott III '70 [2000–], Kenneth R. Gill '61 [2002–], and William J. Westervelt Jr. '71 [2002–] were elected. Dorothy P. John, widow of the sixth president, was elected an honorary trustee in 2002. Memorialized were emeriti trustees Samuel H. Hoover [1972–80], who died at age 97 in October 2000, and Frank W. Carman [1976–91], who died in April 2001. As the college moved forward into the new century, the trustees set forth four priorities: increase the endowment, enhance the college image, improve the quality of the institution, and expand orientation for new trustees. In 2001, the bylaws of the charter were amended again, to remove any age limit for trustee service and to require 15 years of service for emeritus trustee status.[2] The committee structure was also examined and streamlined.

The campus was also saddened to hear of the death of Eloise Ensor Parker, widow of fifth president Lowell Ensor, on September 8, 2001. (In 1983 she had married Robert H. Parker DD'53, president emeritus of Wesley College in Delaware.) A memorial service was held in Baker Chapel on September 13, during which her many contributions to the college during President Ensor's 25-year tenure were remembered. A month later, the death of Charles Tucker, a steam room technician, in the steam room on Union Street from a heart attack shocked the campus community.[3]

In the administration, Samuel Case was named acting provost and then provost in March 2001, when Joan Coley became president. Early in 2001 Elizabeth S. Towle was appointed assistant dean of student affairs, and Jan A. Kiphart was appointed registrar. The new position of director of instructional technology was filled by Steve A. Kerby.

CURRICULUM

The large (450) entering class of 2000 was chosen from over 2,000 applicants and presented an average SAT score of 1131 and high school GPA of 3.4. In the class were 84 Maryland Distinguished Scholars, representatives from 20 states, and 14% minorities. That same year the 38 Honors Program enrollees had an average 1380 SAT and 3.92 GPA. There were now 120 students enrolled in the program at various levels. In 2001, the college joined a growing number of institutions that made the SAT tests optional for entering students with a 3.5 or better GPA in high school or from the top 10% of their graduating class. As standards continued to slowly rise, the college was pleased to be included in *Peterson's Guide to Competitive Colleges* in 2000.[4]

There were no major changes in the curriculum over these two years, although a dual major in political science and social work was approved in 2000. The faculty again considered requiring student attendance at some cultural events during the academic year but did not make a decision, although the SGA did not oppose the idea. A computer science major was under discussion by the faculty, but the need for qualified teaching staff and financial support for equipment posed problems.[5] The Middle States reevaluation process was under way again, and the strategic plan was being updated. To encourage academic performance in the freshman year, a new honor society for first-year students, Alpha Lambda Delta, was formed in November 2001.[6] The January term continued to be an integral and popular part of the curriculum; however, in reaction to the 9/11 tragedy and subsequent concern for travel safety, the study tours for January 2002 were cancelled.[7]

In February 2001, Provost Case reported to the board that there were 60 freshmen and 55 sophomores enrolled in WMC Budapest, and 71 junior

Building on Bethlen Gabor Square housing the Budapest program

and senior Budapest students enrolled on the Westminster campus. In September 2001, because the WMC program had outgrown its rented space in Budapest, College International leased and totally renovated a building on Bethlen Gabor Square in Pest to provide much larger and more comfortable classrooms, library space, and lounges for the 350 students enrolled in College International programs, most of whom were with WMC Budapest. The students were housed in double rooms in a hotel in the Buda hills and traveled to the school by public transportation. Dr. Gabor Drexler became director of administrative affairs, and supervision of faculty and curriculum was provided on site by Dean Laszlo V. Frenyo, appointed by the WMC provost. The WMC president, provost, and some trustees and faculty members visited the branch campus twice a year.

The college's venture into international education with its campus in Budapest seemed to be an educational and financial success. The young European students were satisfied with the rigor and challenge of the WMC academic program and made the transition to the Westminster campus with minimal problems. They brought a new level of sophistication and excitement to the Maryland campus and fitted in well with the campus culture. They gave a good account of themselves academically, several each year being inducted into Phi Beta Kappa and several student-athletes making All-Centennial Conference teams.

The only change in the graduate program was a revamping of some of the requirements for the master of liberal arts degree to make it more responsive to personal and professional interests. Two courses were now required in cultural heritage, two in contemporary society, and one in the creative process, and a significant final project was a capstone to the degree. The number of credit hours required was raised to 36.[8] The program in deaf studies, aided by a $1.5 million grant from the U.S. Department of Education in 2000, expanded to include an immersion laboratory in American Sign Language, as well as a Gallaudet semester. An undergraduate minor also was designed.[9]

STUDENT LIFE

The college continued to experience growing pains as enrollments overfilled housing at times; the fall of 2000 found a number of freshmen crowded into triples for a few weeks and some upperclassmen temporarily housed at the Best Western Motel until renovations to some residences were completed. The students were pleased to learn that more student housing was planned; indeed, ground was broken in the area beyond the water tower near Pennsylvania Avenue in May 2002 for the new North Village complex of apartments.[10]

Even as the pub, or grille, added more options to its menu and Sodexho tried to meet student desires for changes in the dining room offerings, dissatisfaction with the food service continued. Complaining letters to the editor of the *Phoenix* abated for a while after French House director Emmanuelle Bednarak took the writers to task in a letter praising the dining hall, especially the number of choices and quantity of food. She was appalled at the amount of food wasted by the "spoiled students" and mentioned the relatively poor food service she had experienced in Paris.[11] When complaints started again, they were rebutted by an editorial that appealed to students to stop complaining and start thinking and being concerned about the real problems confronting society and the world.[12] Some of the dissatisfaction was eliminated when several new meal plan options were announced, allowing 90, 175, and 210 meals per semester, depending on where students lived.

Cecelia Bowens [1966–], longtime dining hall staff member remembered by generations of students, was interviewed for the *Hill* and commented on many things:[13]

"I don't care who you are, I will call you sweetheart or baby."

"A man last year came up and said, Cecelia, you're still here! [His daughter and her brother] went to school here, too. I said, boy, I'm getting old."

"I think the food these days is better than it used to be. We got a lot of new things."

"The black students used to sit in their own little groups. And I used to ask them, why y'all sit in your own little groups like that? . . . I said, y'all gotta communicate with one another. I noticed that during the years gone by they started talkin' with one another. Now you see 'em spread out, sittin' with each other. The campus is better for it."

The program of special lectures in 2001–2 included journalist Robert Faw, Israeli Moshe Fox, Green Party candidate Ralph Nader, and Harvard professor Davíd Carrasco '67. A series of concerts by campus organizations and Music Department faculty added to the cultural offerings as always. Chamber Music on the Hill presented a gala tenth anniversary concert that featured the College Choir. The Theater Arts Department mounted productions of *Lysistrata*, *The Crucible*, *Little Shop of Horrors*, and *Children of Eden*, and the National Players brought *A Comedy of Errors* and *Les Liaisons Dangereuses* to the campus.

Interested students formed several new clubs, to pursue photography, ultimate frisbee, and power lifting. Heroes Helping Hopkins was created to assist with the children's center at Johns Hopkins Hospital.[14] Another fraternity, Alpha Sigma Phi, was formed in 2001. The SGA continued to sponsor performances from such bands as Georgia Avenue, Nuance, Pharcyde, and Dropkick.

The newspaper writers continued to highlight what they perceived to be campus issues: parking for commuters, lighting in certain areas, safety screens in Albert Norman Ward Hall, and the increase in room burglaries. In an interesting reversal from the usual negativity, one student wrote an open letter of apology to the Residence Life staff, thanking them for fixing the problems he had complained about the previous year in the now improved Rouzer Hall.[15]

The campus continued to be plagued by burglaries and break-ins to offices and dormitory rooms (although some students continued to leave their rooms unlocked); drug-related arrests also occurred occasionally, and, of course, the two issues may have been related. Alcohol continued to be the drug of choice for most students, and its abuse continued to be a problem. Editorials and letters in the *Phoenix* decried the vandalism in the residence halls caused by drunken students (for which all residents were billed). As one letter preached, "Get a clue, and be a little responsible!"[16]

Equally disturbing in the fall of 2000 was another spate of graffiti targeting homosexual individuals and groups. Again, this behavior was met with candlelight vigils and "Rallies for Unity," as well as resolutions and newspaper articles and letters. One student writing in the *Phoenix* appealed to the students for civility and acceptance of diversity, suggesting adherence to the Golden Rule.[17]

The Student Government mounted an appeal for a Student Bill of Rights that was first presented in the fall of 2000. It would continue to be discussed and evaluated. In an effort to get students more involved with and connected to the college, the Alumni Association established a Student Alumni Council.[18]

The college community was shocked and saddened by the tragedy of the terrorist attacks on September 11, 2001. As events unfolded throughout the morning of that fateful Tuesday, students, faculty, and staff were glued to television sets in residences and lounges, watching the ongoing horror and confusion. Memorial services were soon held to remember those killed in the attacks and to provide some solace. An increased spirit of patriotism swept the campus, even as uncertainty about safety grew.

In September 2000, the college joined the Eastern College Athletic Conference (ECAC), the nation's largest conference, with 308 institutions providing championship tournaments in many sports. At about the same time, Swarthmore College dropped football, which presented some scheduling problems within the Centennial Conference. This did not stop the Terror football team from finishing 9–1 in 2000 and 2001. In each case they took the conference championship and went on to the NCAA Division III tournament (six consecutive times for each honor). In 2000 they beat Emory and Henry 38–14 but lost to their nemesis, Trinity College, 32–10 in the second round. The next year they lost to Washington and Jefferson College 24–21 in the first round. The soccer team produced two winning seasons, ending the 2001 season with a 14–6 record, the most wins in college history. The basketball team under new coaches Darrell Brooks [2000–1] and Jay Dull [2001–5] continued its losing streak, but the lacrosse team chalked up two winning seasons, 11–4 and 12–2, and won the ECAC Southwest championship in 2001. Unfortunately, an off-campus celebration party in 2002 led to the coach being arrested, and he resigned soon after. The baseball (16–14–1 and 16–17), golf, and track teams acquitted themselves well.

A women's golf team was added in 2000, bringing the number of men's and women's sports into parity. In 2002, led by Kelly Cramp '05, the team captured the conference championship. Field hockey continued to have success, especially in 2001, when the team posted 13–5, the best season in 53 years, and won a bid to the ECAC tournament. The soccer team had one winning (17–5) and one losing (8–10) season under coach Scott Swanson [1998–2003], as did the volleyball team, which finished 17–16 and 15–16. The softball team, under longtime coach George Dix [1989–2004], continued its strong winning streak with 28–6 and 23–6 seasons, missing the conference championship in 2001 but taking it in 2002 and winning a bid to the NCAA Division III playoffs. Women's

*Standout athlete Kelly Cramp '05 celebrates first-ever
Centennial Conference basketball championship in 2002.*

track took first place in the conference for the fourth year. The basketball team posted two winning seasons and in 2002 went on to the NCAA playoffs, losing to Scranton 71–61 in the first round. Women's lacrosse, under new coach Mindy McCord [2000–3], split two seasons, 5–10 and 10–6.

Ten athletes were named All-America for their individual efforts: Nick Alevrogiannis '03, football, 2001; Ifeanyi Ani '03, indoor and outdoor track and field, 2002; Aaron Bartolain '01, football, 2000; April Brown '03, outdoor track, 2002; Thomas Brown '02, lacrosse, 2001, 2002; Joseph Ellis '03, lacrosse, 2001, 2002; Christopher McNally '02, wrestling, 2002; Vincent Pedalino '02, wrestling, 2001; Brett Sweeney '01, lacrosse, 2001; Jason Winegeart '02, football, 2000, 2001.

An anonymous senior student perhaps summed up the college experience for many of his or her peers in a letter to the *Phoenix* at the conclusion of four years:

> For me, WMC is a place that has changed my life, making me the person I am today; a better one than four years ago. The college is an extraordinary place with many great elements; it is a place that changes lives. . . . WMC [is] a unique community coming together to solve problems and improve itself.[19]

BUILDINGS AND GROUNDS

The renovations to the Lewis Recitation Hall and Lewis Hall of Science continued throughout 2000–1, as both buildings were refitted to remove the old laboratories and create new office suites and classrooms. In the older building, while the original oak paneling, glazed wall tiling, and tin ceilings were maintained, new lighting, flooring, and office and room configurations upgraded the academic facilities while maintaining the historic nature of the 1914 building. In a nod to this history, the old student benches in the chemistry lecture room on the third floor were maintained, though the seating space between the writing arms had to be widened to accommodate 21st-century posteriors. These benches had been created for Yingling Science Hall (1904) and reinstalled in Lewis Hall, which replaced it. In the 1966 building, a new elevator was installed to reach all five floors of the facility (since the sub-basement, previously leased to the government, was incorporated into the renovations to house computer laboratories). The remaining floors were reconfigured to house more computer laboratories, departmental office suites, seminar rooms, and classrooms, as well as specialized laboratories on the top floor for physics, which had moved from the older building. The other residents of the "new" complex were the departments of sociology, economics and business administration, communication, and mathematics (several of which were returning "home" after 40 years in the "wilderness" of Memorial Hall).

Renovated Lewis Complex, Eaton Hall, and courtyard, 2000–1

673

While the renovations to various academic facilities were going on, some changes were completed in the President's House, as well. A ramp to the front porch was added, a two-car enclosed garage replaced the open carport, and a second, handicapped-accessible bathroom was added to the first floor. All three floors were redecorated, and the top two were reserved as private quarters for the new president.

North Village apartment complex

The fate of Winslow Hall was still under consideration early in this period; at first, it was thought best to raze the structure because of interior problems, but eventually the building was renovated for other uses. The faculty of the departments housed there, as well as the Education Department and graduate offices located in Thompson Hall, were excited to learn in the spring of 2002 that a new facility would be planned for them, to be sited in the parking lot between Hoover Library and Albert Norman Ward Hall. (This building was opened in 2005 and called Academic Hall.) This was made possible in part by the availability of state funds awarded to the private institutions on a regular cycle.

To provide more living space for students, ground was broken for the North Village apartment complex in 2002 during Reunion Weekend (which had been moved to the first weekend in May in 2000 and now incorporated all quinquennial class reunions).

In the spring of 2002, the ground floor of Baker Memorial Chapel was again renovated to provide offices and a laboratory for the Foreign Language Department, space for the Philosophy and Religious Studies Department, restrooms in the lobby on the main floor, and air conditioning. The steeple was also relighted in 2001 through a gift of the family of John Manspeaker '36.

674

FINANCES

As the student body continued to grow (to almost 1,700 by fall 2002), so did the annual fee structure. The total tuition, room, and board fees for 2000–1 were about $24,000, and they rose by about $1,500 each year into 2002–3. The college budget rose a bit faster, from about $52 million, to $55.5 million, to almost $59 million for 2002–3. The endowment saw steady growth as the college successfully concluded the Defining Moment Campaign. As the college entered the new decade, the endowment stood at about $55 million; it would grow to $58 million as some significant bequests, including $2.9 million from the Hoover estate, were received.[20] The State of Maryland appropriation was now about $2,855,000 and was an important part of the budget each year.

MAJOR EVENTS

While the college had hosted many special events during its long history, including the launch and later celebration of the Defining Moment Campaign in the previous decade, nothing could quite match the long-standing academic tradition of a college presidential inauguration. On April 21, 2001, the college held its fifth formal inauguration in its 134-year history when it installed Joan Coley. The event was a chance to gather old and new friends to celebrate a fresh beginning for the college, and it was a golden opportunity for enhanced visibility and expanded public relations. The night before the event, the trustees hosted the faculty at a gala pre-inaugural dinner in the Englar Dining Room, the first of several joint gatherings in subsequent years. Toasts to the new president were given by William B. Dulany for the trustees and Francis Fennell for the faculty. Maryland secretary of state John Willis brought greetings from the governor and State of Maryland. The following morning, the board of trustees held its plenary session, while the invited delegates from colleges, universities, and learned societies began to be welcomed to the college. A luncheon for the 125 delegates and the trustees followed at noon in the dining room, after which everyone moved to their specific robing areas for the academic procession, which formed in Baker Memorial Chapel. At about 2:15 P.M. with flags of the foreign countries represented in the student body separating the various groups, the colorful procession of 300 delegates, faculty, and trustees marched out of the chapel, past the Old Main bell, which was rung with gusto, and on to the Gill Center for the formal ceremony.

Entering to martial music played by the College Brass Ensemble under the direction of Donald Horneff, the delegates and trustees were seated in front of the platform, while the faculty sat on the raised area behind the rostrum. After the preliminaries, expressions of welcome to the new president were given from the State of Maryland by state treasurer Richard N. Dixon LLD'88 and from the alumni by Kimberly Andrews O'Connor '90, '95M. Douglas W. Foard, secretary of Phi Beta Kappa, was scheduled to speak on behalf of the delegates but had been taken ill and was unable to attend. His remarks were read by Chief Marshal and Inaugural Committee chair James Lightner. Bringing greetings from the students was SGA vice president Amanda J. Cline '01; Barbara A. Ward, residence life secretary, brought greetings from the staff; and trustee George Varga '61, HHD'92, represented the faculty and students at WMC Budapest.

Biology professor Wilbur L. Long, who had joined the faculty with Coley in 1973, spoke on behalf of his colleagues. He announced that the president was "anatomically complete": She had feet planted firmly in reality, a heart hard enough to resist the easy path and soft enough to embrace the needs of others, a strong backbone to carry the college into the new millennium, and a brain endowed with intelligence to analyze large quantities of data and wisdom to "separate the wheat from the chaff." He pronounced the eighth president a fine specimen whom the college should prize and support.[21]

The ceremony of installation was performed by board chair James Melhorn, assisted by vice chair Dolores Snyder, provost Samuel Case, Alumni Association president Philip G. Enstice '71, and SGA president Steven D. Sharkey '01. After being invested with the silver chain of office and acknowledging the accolade from the audience, President Coley delivered her inaugural address. In it she recalled several books that had played a significant part in her life, remembered her first days as a young assistant professor of education at the college, and pledged to make the college even better. "We are deservedly proud of who we are. We are excellent at what we do, and we will become superior. . . . We [need to be recognized] for our excellence." She went on to outline four areas of her vision for the college: improved residence halls and a continued commitment to diversity as the college focused on the student living and learning community; encouragement and support of excellence among the faculty; tripling the endowment by 2010; and attention to the many people who make individual commitments to the ongoing life of the college. She concluded with these words: "We surely do change lives [at this college]. . . . Here on this Hill we work actively to build a dynamic and inclusive community. Here on this Hill individuals are inspired every day to strive for their own personal excellence. We must now work collectively to reach our communal vision of excellence. It is a worthy challenge. Join me—I dare you."[22]

Perhaps not a unique event but surely a first for this college, a poem, "The Light-Gatherers," had been written especially for the occasion by professor of English Kathy Mangan, who read her creation:

Il faut cultiver notre jardin.
—Voltaire, *Candide.*

Let us affix our lens on the evening skies,
and sift from the funneling darkness star-
glitter, so our telescope clarifies,
pierces the deeper realms spiraling far

beyond us, where vast clouds of natal dust
swirl in nebulae. This moment, a mote
in astral time—already these words rush
outward, scatter toward heaven to float

in the bright river of our Milky Way.
There constant Cassiopeia reigns. Queen,
she perches on her royal chair, arrays
a five-star, studded W between

her King and daughter. Each myth—of hero,
goddess, fabled beast—spins a human tale
as it wheels above us: pride, courage, woe,
betrayal, love. As mortals, we prevail

by gleaning truth from shadow; we await
the glint of answers racing through the night.
Now our *Story unfurls. Let us navigate*
by the beam of its clear, outlasting light.[23]

President Coley then conferred honorary doctor of literature degrees on novelist Alice E. McDermott, author of *That Night* and *Charming Billy*, and journalist Loren B. Pope, author of *Colleges That Change Lives*. Each recipient spoke briefly in response and appreciation. After the singing of the Alma Mater, the recessional led everyone to a reception in front of the Gill Center in honor of the newly installed president.

That evening, after a special green and gold fireworks display over the

Alice McDermott, President Coley, Trustee Chair James Melhorn,
and Loren Pope prior to inauguration, 2001

soccer field at 9 P.M., an all-campus party in Gill Gymnasium got under way featuring student jazz and rock musicians. The following day, a Gala Inaugural Concert included the premier performance by the College Choir and Madrigal Singers of a piece commissioned by the college for the occasion: *A New Song for Psalms* by Baltimore composer Lorraine Whittlesey. Also performing during the concert were organist Ted Dix; pianists David Kreider, Donald Horneff, and Eric Byrd; the College Flute Choir under the direction of Linda Kirkpatrick; the College Gospel Choir; and the combined choirs (including alumni who were in attendance), which sang the "Hallelujah Chorus" from Handel's *Messiah* under the direction of Margaret Boudreaux. A reception in the Science Center Plaza hosted by the Woman's Club of Westminster followed the concert.[24]

As renovations were completed, the buildings were rededicated with appropriate ceremony and celebration. On October 26, 2001, the completely renovated Lewis Recitation Hall and the adjoining Lewis Hall of Science were officially opened. Professor of mathematics Robert P. Boner spoke of the significance of the buildings to the college, its programs, and its students; and representatives of all the departments housed in the complex (physics, mathematics and computer science, economics and business administration, sociology, and communication) helped cut the ribbons. The brick walkway stretching from the Decker College Center to Main Street and defining the pedestrian-friendly campus was then formally named in honor of board of trustees chair James Melhorn and his wife, Lora, whose generous gift funded the project. A plaque in front of the Lewis complex, denoting the name and gift, was unveiled. At the trustee-faculty dinner following the reception held in the Science Center Plaza, it was officially announced that the science laboratory building would be named Eaton Hall in recognition of the generosity of the late Thomas H. '27 and Catharine Welker Eaton, of Royal Oak, Maryland. A plaque in Eaton Hall lobby, containing a bronze bas-relief picture of the Eatons, was unveiled later that evening.

On April 19, 2002, the addition to the Levine Music Hall, as well as the renovations to the older building, was dedicated in ceremonies held at the entrance to the addition under threatening skies. After the traditional presentation and acceptance ceremony, Music Department chair Margaret Boudreaux spoke on the significance of the building to the music program and the life of the college. Several music students joined President Coley, Chairman Melhorn, Provost Case, and Dr. Boudreaux in officially cutting the ribbons and inviting everyone inside for a reception in the recital hall and tours of the improved facility. Student musicians performed at various spots throughout the building. The program for the event highlighted in words and pictures the history of the music program at the college and the special gifts from alumni and friends that made the project possible.

As previous chapters of this history attest, the issue of the institutional name had arisen from time to time for at least four decades. Four presidents—Ensor, John, Chambers, and Coley (and perhaps Holloway before them)—had

A brick pedestrian walkway stretches across the top of the Hill.

confronted the problems inherent in a name that suggested that the college's location was in western Maryland (where there was already a state college, in Frostburg) and that, like most other geographically named colleges in the United States, it was affiliated with the Maryland state system of higher education. Decades of experience and two quantitative research studies had demonstrated that the name "Western Maryland College" caused confusion and misperceptions among prospective students and donors, who did not associate the name with a private liberal arts college in the resource-rich Baltimore–D.C. metropolis. Everyone agreed that the name had served the college well at the beginning, associating the institution with a successful and growing commercial Carroll County enterprise. The college had made great strides, but the question was whether it could continue and move forward into a robust future with a name that was increasingly becoming a liability. There had always been reluctance to make a change because of tradition, concerns over the costs involved, and the anticipated negative alumni reaction. Board chairs and presidents had recognized the problem but had not been able to convince enough board members of the necessity. Indeed, President Chambers suggested a name change several times in the 1990s and was backed by marketing studies, but some older and influential board members were not yet willing, preferring to keep the issue on the back burner. By 2001, however, increasing competition for students in a market with potentially diminishing demographics and concerns for the future financial health of the institution propelled the issue to the forefront again, and the trustees, reacting to research studies in September 2000 that reaffirmed the earlier results, finally took the bold step at its October 2001 meeting, unanimously voting to change the college's name.[25] (During the previous three years over 300 colleges had changed their names in some way.) On January 11, 2002, board chair Melhorn and President Coley announced to an all-college assembly the trustee decision; it was met with surprise, joy, sadness, agreement, and anger. But President Coley set the tone for the future when she closed her remarks with words written by Professor Emeritus Ira Zepp:

> *Secure in our identity*
> *Confident in our mission,*
> *Resolute in our purpose,*
> *Loving the liberal arts,*
> *Operating from unprecedented strength,*
> *Honoring our past,*
> *Welcoming the future . . .*
> *Anchored, centered, grateful, with vulnerability and pride,*
> *We move forward.*

The next phase of the project, in partnership with consulting firm Lipman Hearne of Chicago, was devoted to gathering further perceptions about the college; holding focus groups and information sessions with students, alumni, and friends about the name-change process; and explaining the necessity of the change and the plans for the future. It was expected that the most strenuous objection would come from alumni who could not understand the problems caused by the old name. In a world rife with change, especially soon after the 9/11 tragedy, losing the tradition and constancy of the name of one's college was difficult for some to accept. Some reactions expressed to individuals on campus, especially the president, were emotional and sometimes mean spirited. It would take time for logic, reason, and facts to overcome visceral reactions. A 32-member Naming Committee, chaired by Provost Case and Joyce D. Muller, associate vice president for communications and marketing, was appointed by the trustees and included representatives of every constituency of the college: faculty, emeriti faculty, students, trustees, alumni, and parents. This group solicited suggestions from the alumni for a new name and received 2,100, which yielded 418 names. Each was considered and discussed in committee sessions during February, March, and April. From the outset it was decided that the name was not "for sale"; whatever name was chosen would not depend upon a financial contribution to the college. The criteria were (1) Did

the proposed name suggest the private liberal arts nature of the college? and (2) Did it relate directly to the institution (its history, location, philosophy, etc.)? Of secondary importance was the placement of the name in an alphabetical listing of institutions; "Western Maryland" always placed the college at the end of such listings, especially in college admissions events, a perceived disadvantage in recruiting students.

Some names had to be eliminated because they were already in use or would cause further confusion. Ultimately, a short list was agreed upon by the committee and presented to the board for consideration. At its April 20, 2002, meeting, the board unanimously adopted the name McDaniel College, honoring William Roberts McDaniel, a legendary

College namesake William R. McDaniel

figure in the college's history, whose life embodied the mission of the college and who had died exactly 60 years earlier. He had been a student, alumnus, professor, parent, vice president, treasurer, acting president, and trustee over a 65-year period, 1877–42.[26]

As the trustees had wisely prophesized in April 1942,

Somehow or other, one feels that the life of William R. McDaniel will be interwoven into the destiny of Western Maryland College, as his life has been into every decade of its history. For while William R. McDaniel, the mortal, is gone; William R. McDaniel, the spirit, lives—and motivates the lives of others. It will continue to do so 'til time and eternity meet.

Three weeks later, on May 10, a ceremony was held in Memorial Plaza at 8:30 P.M., and in a brief presentation involving members of the Naming Committee, the name was gradually revealed through discussion of McDaniel's significant role in the college's history. This was immediately followed by a short video of photographs of McDaniel and the new logo for the college, the distribution of commemorative T-shirts to all attendees, and colorful fireworks. An estimated 3,000 people gathered in the plaza to hear the announcement, some even holding cell phones high to relay the name to others elsewhere. Newspapers and television joined in the excitement, quickly reporting the new name for immediate publication and announcement. Alumni and friends not in Westminster logged on to the college website or dialed the college telephone system to be informed of the name.

New McDaniel name and logo are displayed.
Courtesy of the Baltimore Sun Company, Inc. All Rights Reserved

On July 1, when the new name officially took effect, town-gown activities were held to link the name to Westminster. Staff ambassadors in teams of two delivered McDaniel coffee mugs and information booklets to more than 100 Main Street merchants. The name was launched, and the college embarked on a new era.

The Main Street entrance to McDaniel College; the wall was added in 2004.

CONCLUSION

The opening years of the new century were quite significant and challenging ones for the college, for it officially welcomed a new president with a new vision, renovated and opened several classroom facilities, saw an increase in the endowment, and changed its name, honoring one of its most illustrious forebears. The institution was poised to move forward in many ways in the years to come.

CHAPTER **15** NOTES

1. WMC board of trustees minutes, October 22, 2000.
2. Ibid., April 21, 2001.
3. *Phoenix*, October 21, 2001, 1.
4. WMC faculty minutes, October 3, 2000.
5. *Phoenix*, April 26, 2001, 5.
6. Ibid., November 14, 2001, 2.
7. Ibid., October 31, 2001, 1.
8. WMC faculty minutes, April 2002.
9. *The Hill*, Summer 2001, 2; *Phoenix*, March 15, 2001, 4.
10. *Phoenix*, February 13, 2002, 1.
11. Ibid., December 7, 2000, 5.
12. Ibid., October 31, 2001, 5.
13. Spring 2002, 1.
14. *Phoenix*, April 12, 2001, 2.
15. Ibid., September 21, 2000, 6.
16. Ibid., April 12, 2001, 6.
17. Ibid., December 7, 2000, 5.
18. Ibid., November 16, 2000, 2.
19. Ibid., May 10, 2001, 8.
20. WMC faculty minutes, October 2, 2001.
21. *The Hill*, May 2001, 17; inaugural program.
22. *The Hill*, May 2001, 15–18; inaugural program.
23. K. Mangan, *Inaugural Poem*, college archives.
24. Concert program.
25. WMC board of trustees minutes, October 27, 2001.
26. Ibid., April 20, 2002.

Major World Events

2001

New millennium begins January 1.

El Salvador and India suffer severe earthquakes.

Baltimore Ravens win Super Bowl XXXV, defeating New York Giants 34–7.

Timothy McVeigh is executed for the Oklahoma City bombing.

Google is awarded a patent for the PageRank algorithm in its search engine.

Anthrax attacks begin.

Apple Computer releases iPod; Microsoft releases Windows XP.

Enron Corporation files for bankruptcy.

The People's Republic of China resumes normal trade status with the U.S.

Gladiator wins Academy Award; its star, Russell Crowe, is deemed Best Actor.

Almost 3,000 are killed on September 11 in terrorist attacks on the World Trade Center in New York, the Pentagon in Virginia, and in rural Shanksville, Penn.

U.S. Office of Homeland Security is formed.

U.S. invades Afghanistan; war on terrorism is launched.

2002

Euro becomes the only legal tender in European Union countries.

Britain's Queen Elizabeth II celebrates 50 years on the throne.

Queen Elizabeth, the queen mother, dies at 100 in Britain.

Iraq rejects UN weapons inspections.

Telecommunications giant WorldCom files for bankruptcy.

Switzerland, known for its neutrality, joins the United Nations.

Weapons inspections finally begin in Iraq.

Reality shows dominate U.S. television.

Washington beltway is terrorized by two snipers for weeks before they are arrested.

Former President Jimmy Carter visits Castro in Cuba, is first president to visit Cuba since 1959.

Rubens's painting *The Massacre of the Innocents* is sold at auction for $76.2 million.

K-Mart corporation becomes largest retailer in U.S. history to file for bankruptcy.

NASA's *Mars Odyssey* begins mapping the surface of Mars.

Epilogue

We have come to the end of this journey, reporting and interpreting the history of Western Maryland College from its inception in 1866 until 2002, when it was renamed McDaniel College. It is left to someone else to interpret the significance of this bold move, as well as to report the history of future decades.

Over the 136 years since Fayette R. Buell conceived the idea of building a college in Westminster and enlisted the help of such pioneers as J. T. Ward, John Smith of Wakefield, and Joshua Hering, the institution and its leadership have confronted many crises. These have always been met fearlessly and boldly, with optimism. In each case the college confronted the crisis, dealt with it, and moved on, always mindful of its basic educational mission and philosophy.

No doubt McDaniel College will continue, well into the 22nd century, thoughtfully and carefully planning for the future as best it can, with all the uncertainties surrounding our society, and higher education in particular. It will rationally and boldly deal with unexpected crises as they arise.

May the college, as the motto on its seal declares, continue to call its students "from darkness unto light" as it has so successfully during all the years of its existence. There is no more lofty mission.

Bibliography

Aloha, Western Maryland College annual yearbook. 1883, 1899–1904, 1910, 1916, 1922–1970. McDaniel College archives.

Beakes, K. Douglas. *The Legacies of Western Maryland College*. Baltimore: Gateway Press, 2003.

Callcott, George H. *A History of the University of Maryland*. Baltimore: Maryland Historical Society, 1966.

Chandler, Douglas R. *Pilgrimage of Faith: A Centennial History of Wesley Theological Seminary 1882–1982*. Washington, DC: Seven Locks Press, 1984.

Drinkhouse, Edward J. *History of Methodist Reform and the Methodist Protestant Church*, vol. 2. Norwood, MA: Norwood Press; Board of Publications of the Methodist Protestant Church, 1899.

Ensor, Lowell S. Papers. McDaniel College archives.

The Gold Bug, Western Maryland College student newspaper. 1924–75. McDaniel College archives.

Hering, Joshua W. *Recollections of My Life*, vol. 2, chapter 47. Baltimore: Maryland Historical Society.

The Hill, Western Maryland College alumni magazine. 1967–present. McDaniel College archives.

Irving Literary Gazette, 1881–87. McDaniel College archives.

Kiefer, Richard W. *The Life and Times of Richard W. Kiefer, Catonsville, Maryland: An Autobiography*. Self-published manuscript, 2002. Trustee files, President's Office, McDaniel College.

Lewis, Thomas Hamilton. Papers. McDaniel College archives.

Makosky, John D. *Western Maryland College in the Nineteenth Century*. Westminster, MD: Western Maryland College Alumni Association, 1940. McDaniel College archives.

Maryland Annual Conference of the Methodist Protestant Church, minutes. 1866–1938. McDaniel College archives.

McDaniel, William Roberts. Papers. McDaniel College archives.

McDaniel, William Roberts. Scrapbooks of events (collected annually), 1885–1935. McDaniel College archives.

The Methodist Protestant, publication of the Maryland Conference of the Methodist Protestant Church, Baltimore, MD. McDaniel College archives; Methodist Protestant Church archives, Baltimore.

Myers, Philip. *Fiftieth Reunion Memoir: Fearless and Bold*. Unpublished manuscript, 1966. McDaniel College archives.

The Phoenix, Western Maryland College student newspaper. 1981–2002. McDaniel College archives.

Pick, Robert. "A Brief History of Campus Planning at Western Maryland College." Unpublished honors paper, 1993. McDaniel College archives.

Pollitt, L. Irving. *Biographies of the Trustees*. Unpublished manuscript, c.1952. McDaniel College archives.

Reese, James. *History of Western Maryland College*. Unpublished manuscript, c.1898. McDaniel College archives.

Schofield, Samuel B. Notes. McDaniel College archives.

Schofield, Samuel B., and Marjorie C. Crain. *The Formative Years, 1866–1947*. Westminster, MD: Western Maryland College, 1982.

Scrimshaw, Western Maryland College student newspaper. 1975–81. McDaniel College archives.

Stegman, Carolyn B. *Women of Achievement in Maryland History*. Forestville, MD: Anaconda Press, 2002.

Ward, James T. *A Brief History of My Connection with the College Enterprize at Westminster*. Unpublished manuscript, May 1868. McDaniel College archives.

Ward, James T. Diaries, 1866–86. McDaniel College archives.

Ward, James T. *Outline of the History of Western Maryland College*. Unpublished manuscript, 1874. McDaniel College archives.

Ward, James T. Papers. McDaniel College archives.

Ward, James T. Scrapbooks. McDaniel College archives.

Warner, Nancy M. *Carroll County, Maryland: A History 1837–1976*. Bloomsburg, PA: Haddon Craftsmen, 1976.

Wells, David A. *Recent Economic Changes, and Their Effect on the Production and Distribution of Wealth and the Well-Being of Society*. New York: D. Appleton, 1889.

Western Maryland College annual catalogs, 1868–2002. McDaniel College archives.

Western Maryland College board of trustees meeting minutes, 1867–2002. McDaniel College archives.

Western Maryland College Bulletin, 1921–61. McDaniel College archives.

Western Maryland College faculty meeting minutes, 1867–2002. McDaniel College archives.

Western Maryland College *First Annual Circular*, 1867. McDaniel College archives.

Western Maryland College Magazine, alumni magazine. 1961–67. McDaniel College archives.

Western Maryland College Monthly, 1887–1926. McDaniel College archives.

Wills, George S. *History of Western Maryland College*, vol. 1 (1866–86), May 30, 1949; vol. 2 (1886–1951), May 30, 1952. Westminster, MD: Historical Society of Carroll County.

Wright, C. Milton. *Memoir*. Unpublished manuscript. McDaniel College archives.

INDEX

This index is primarily an organized list of the people, buildings, and organizations of the college; it is not intended to be comprehensive. Page numbers for illustrations are in bold type.

Biggs, John, 21
Billingslea, C. C., 230
Billingslea, Charles, 27, 117, 204, 242
Billingslea, James Levine, 117
Bio Trio, 520, **520**
Bish, Charles E., 278, 505
Black, Edward M., 395, 465
Black, William, 116, 120, 123, 136, 141, 158, 159
Black and White, 270, 278, 279
Black and White Club, 276, 277, 278, 282. *See also* Pi Alpha Alpha
Black Student Union, 529, 530, **584**
Blackburn, John, 501
Blanche Ward Hall, 338, **339**, 591
Blanchette, Roland Raymond, 377, 380
Blank, Brian, 587
Bloom, Susan R., 565, 655
Blount, Clarence W., 518, 621, 626
Blumberg, Lawrence, 569, 647, 666
Blumberg Fitness Center, 648
Bohn, Donald Chant, 380
Bonaccorsy, Ricci G., 536, 537
Boner, Robert P., 521, 574, 678
Bonnotte, Ferdinand, 116, 126, 158, 190, 202, 223, 262, **278**, 310
Bosley, Barry, 599
Bothe, B. Christopher, 575
Bothe, Elsbeth, 575
Boudreaux, Margaret A., 565, 578, 655, 678, 679
Bowden, Caleb H., 139
Bowe, Frank G., 473, 569
Bowens, Cecelia, 669–70
Bowers, Daniel, 13
Bowers, John H., 21
Bowlsbey, Blanche Ford, 272, 275
Bowlsbey, Leonard Stanley, 431, 464, 469, 565, 567, 576
Boyer, James, 437–38
Bradshaw, Lillian Moore, 653
Brainard, Helen, 388
Brener, Andrey L., 640, 641
Brengle, Margaret, 578
Brenneman, Richard F., 435
Brenton, Robin Adams, 618
Bricker, Robert E., 391, 518, 549, 569, 604, 605, 621
Brickett, Miriam Royer, 504
Brockett, Robert L., 51, 54, 57, 62, 73
Broll, Arthur G., 467, 518, 622
Brooks, Darrell, 671
Brooks, Harriet, 298

Brooks, Peter, 605, 607
Brooks, Robert Milton, 380
Brown, April, 672
Brown, Frederick J., Jr., 526
Brown, Joseph, 553
Brown, Michael M., 464
Brown, Thomas, 672
Browning Literary Society, 34, 55, 60, 97, 230, 327. *See also* literary societies
Browning-Philomathean Society, 327. *See also* Browning Literary Society; Philomathean Society
Bruno, Charles, 428
Bryant, Theresa, 618
Bryson, Brady O., 338, 451
Bryson, Mary Brown, 467, 563, 569
Buckalew, W. Walker, 622
Budapest program, 623–25, **624**, 667–68, **668**
Buell, Fayette Rufus, **3**, **27**; died, 204; early life, 3; and founding, 5–9, 11–16, 21, 28; positions, 7, 16; and sale, 24, 25–28; schools, 3–4, 5, 11, **12**, 27, 398
Buell, Mrs. F. R., 18
Buell house, **12**
Burch, Francis B., Jr., 621, 666
Burdette, Herbert P., 467
Burdette, Hubert, 413
Burgee, Amon, 148, 159
Burgee, Fred P., 437
Burleigh, Julia T., 519
Butler, J. B., 20
Butler, Robert W., 437
Büttner, Hans Peter F., 464, 488, 615
Byerly, Louise, 322
Byham, Leroy, 391
Byrd, Eric, 631, 678
Byrd, Harry C., **174**, 345, 350–51

C

Caldwell, Glenn G., 615, 617
Callas, Peter G., 626
Calormiris, William, 518
Campbell, Leroy, 349
Campus Capers, 428
Cantwell, Benjamin Ellsworth, 380
Carll, Edward, 550
Carman, Frank W., 518, 621, 666
Carmichael, Katherine K., 367, 385
Carnes, Mrs. A. J., 100, 103
Carnochan, John L., 526
Carpe Diem, 154, **481**

College historian James E. Lightner, professor emeritus of mathematics, is a member of the class of 1959. He holds a master's degree from Northwestern University and a PhD from The Ohio State University. He was only 25 years old when he was invited back in 1962 to join the faculty of his undergraduate alma mater, and during his 36-year tenure he became known as a teacher who was at once demanding of and intensely devoted to his students. He brought honor to the college when he was national president of Kappa Mu Epsilon, undergraduate mathematics honor society, and when he was elected a senator of the Phi Beta Kappa Society. Dr. Lightner's organizational abilities, meticulousness, and talent for telling stories are well known. He has given freely of these skills in service to McDaniel College in myriad ways, including the 7 years he spent researching and writing *Fearless and Bold*.

Design by
Lisa Cadieux, Liquid Studio, Burlington, Vermont

Copyediting and indexing by
Jill Mason, Winooski, Vermont

Cover photo by
C. Kurt Holter

Printing by
Villanti & Sons, Printers, Inc., Milton, Vermont

Project management by
Joyce Muller, McDaniel Communications and Marketing